高等院校英语专业
翻译实践与鉴赏教程

A Comparative Study of Literary Translation

文学翻译佳作对比赏析

主编 崔永禄

编著 （按姓氏笔画排列）

王 雪　　叶家莉　　李 晶

张 怡　　陆 林　　周蓉娟

柳绪燕　　崔永禄

南开大学出版社

图书在版编目(CIP)数据

文学翻译佳作对比赏析 / 崔永禄主编. —天津：南开大学出版社，2001.6(2021.12 重印)
高等院校英语专业翻译实践与鉴赏教程
ISBN 978-7-310-01484-7

Ⅰ.文… Ⅱ.崔… Ⅲ.文学－英语－翻译－高等学校－教材 Ⅳ.H315.9

中国版本图书馆 CIP 数据核字(2001)第 53684 号

版权所有　侵权必究

文学翻译佳作对比赏析
WENXUE FANYI JIAZUO DUIBI SHANGXI

南开大学出版社出版发行
出版人:陈　敬
地址:天津市南开区卫津路 94 号　邮政编码:300071
营销部电话:(022)23508339　营销部传真:(022)23508542
https://nkup.nankai.edu.cn

河北文曲印刷有限公司印刷　全国各地新华书店经销
2001 年 6 月第 1 版　2021 年 12 月第 8 次印刷
880×1230 毫米　32 开本　16.5 印张　2 插页　472 千字
定价:35.00 元

如遇图书印装质量问题,请与本社营销部联系调换,电话:(022)23508339

PREFACE 前言(代序)

前　言(代序)

这本书起名为《文学翻译佳作对比赏析》。

记得鲁迅先生曾经说过,他从不相信什么"小说作法"之类。他劝有志于文艺创作的青年朋友,多去看一些写得好的文学作品,看看作家们是怎么写的,从中学习他们的创作方法。

其实翻译又何尝不是如此。我们学习翻译,除了要具有扎实的外语基本功外,就提高翻译技巧而论,还应多读一些有影响的译作。在对译作的阅读研究中,可以看看翻译家们是如何翻译的,看看他们如何做到形与神的统一,如何处理文化理解与语言表达上的困惑;处处难点,他们从何种角度加以剖析,种种关系,他们又是以何种开拓精神进行探讨。他们的胸襟,他们的立意,他们的理论,他们的技巧,无不体现在他们的译著之中。要了解严复的信达雅,就要读他翻译的《天演论》,要了解傅雷的神似,就要读他的译作《高老头》,要深刻理解奈达的动态对等,最好读一读他翻译的《圣经》,至于金隄和萧乾,就更有必要读一读他们各自所译的《尤利西斯》了。每一部成功的译作都是一座翻译知识的宝库,一本现成的翻译教科书。

我们强调阅读译著,丝毫也不意味着忽视对翻译理论的学习研究,恰恰相反,阅读正是翻译理论研究必不可少的。掌握一定的翻译理论,可以更有利于统观全局,更好地指导翻译实践;但缺乏翻译实践,缺乏对译著的研究,只会背诵几句干巴巴的理论条条,没有感性经验为支柱,理论也就成了空中楼阁。

收入本书的有九种世界文学名篇的译著,其中五种汉译英,四种英译汉,每种著作一般选了两个译本,有的选了三个。由于翻译事业的发

PREFACE 前言(代序)

展,一种名著经常有两个甚或两个以上的译本,这使我们的对比分析有了可能。编选两种或两种以上的译著,主要目的是为了进行比较。我们的眼力有限,需要借助于比较。有比较才有鉴别。现在的译著评论,正面褒奖者多,这我们是赞成的,因为这有利于发扬成绩。但有些译著,明明质量一般,有的甚至误译之处颇多,但某些评论却仍然誉之谓"妙笔生花","上乘之作",这不仅背离了评论的宗旨,而且不利于我国翻译事业的发展。

自然,我们把两种译文放在一起进行比较,其主要目的不在于分清哪个更好一些,哪个更差一些。而是要学习研究不同译者的经验,如有不足就要总结其中的教训,以使后来的翻译工作做得更好。

造成译文差别的原因有许多。奈达在他的《语言、文化和翻译》一书中指出,任何一个译本都是一定历史时期的产物。不同的历史时期就会对翻译提出不同的要求,施加不同的影响。《钦定本英文圣经》和奈达所译的《圣经》的差别,很多就打着时代的烙印。民族间和文化间交流的情况也会影响到翻译。赛珍珠翻译《水浒》时搞出了一些不可思议的译句,随着中外文化交流的发展,这种情况大概再也不会出现了。另外,译者对原作社会意义理解的不同以及翻译目的的不同,都会导致译文产生很大的差别,本书所选的《论语》的两种译本,就是极好的例证。因此进行比较就应该考虑到各种因素,尽量使结论客观。我们所进行的对比翻译研究,便是沿此方向进行的一些探讨,可算引玉之砖。

我国的翻译事业,随着改革开放进程的加快而迅速发展,历史已经证明,一个伟大的时代,文化交流总是兴旺的,翻译事业也总是发达的。汇入这个伟大时代的潮流,尽我们的绵薄之力,就是我们编写本书的宗旨。

编　者
2000 年 10 月

CONTENTS 目录

目 录

前言(代序)

第一篇 从语言功能看《尤利西斯》的两种译本(崔永禄) / 1
　　附:*Ulysses* 原文节选及金隄和萧乾、文洁若的两种译文 / 11

第二篇 《哈克贝利·费恩历险记》两种中译本比较(周蓉娟) / 75
　　附:*The Adventure of Huckleberry Finn* 原文节选及张万里和成时的两种译文 / 86

第三篇 《苔丝》两个译本的比较(叶家莉) / 114
　　附:*Tess of The D'Urbervilles* 原文节选及张谷若和吴笛的两种译文 / 122

第四篇 直译·意译 形似·神似 / 183
　　——《汤姆叔叔的小屋》(第三十八章"胜利")两种译文比较评析(李 晶)
　　附:*Uncle Tom's Cabin* 原文节选及黄继忠和张培均的两种译文 / 196

第五篇 理解的困惑与作者的意图 / 231
　　——《论语》两种译文的对比分析(崔永禄)
　　附:《论语》原文节选及 Thomas Cleary 和 Arthur Waley 的两种译文 / 240

第六篇 《红楼梦》两种译文之比较赏析(王 雪) / 248
　　附:《红楼梦》原文节选及 David Hawkes 和 Yang Hsien-yi and Gladys Yang 的两种译文 / 264

第七篇 《水浒传》三种英译本之比较鉴赏(张 怡) / 326

CONTENTS 目录

附:《水浒传》原文节选及 Sidney Shapiro,J. H. Jackson 和 Pearl S. Buck 的三种译文 / 341

第八篇 《聊斋志异》三个英译本的比较(柳绪燕) / 408

附:《聊斋志异》原文选篇及 Herbert A. Giles,Yang Hsien-yi and Gladys Yang 和 C. Denis 的三种译文 / 421

第九篇 诗歌翻译别是一家(陆 林) / 498

——《枫桥夜泊》等唐诗的两种译文比较

附:唐诗选及许渊冲和王守义与约翰·诺弗尔的两种译文 / 507

第一篇　从语言功能看《尤利西斯》的两种译本

崔永禄

爱尔兰作家詹姆斯·乔伊斯的小说《尤利西斯》于1922年全书问世,至今已经历70多个春秋。西方文艺界对这部小说的认识虽经历了大起大落,但现在多数评论家和读者都把它视为西方文学的一部奇书,有口皆碑的传世名著,"登峰造极的小说"。以研究此书为宗旨的"尤学"已出现在欧洲和美国,艰巨而日益深入的研究工作方兴未艾。

我国第一个翻译此书的是金隄先生。他选译的《尤利西斯》于1987年由天津百花文艺出版社出版。到1994年萧乾先生和文洁若女士全文译出《尤利西斯》并由译林出版社推出,才使中国读者见到了这部书的全貌。

本文仅就该书第二章中一个片断的翻译进行分析,研究吸收他们的经验,以供翻译工作者借鉴。

一、直译加注的翻译法

无论是金隄的译本(下称金译本)还是萧乾和文洁若的译本(下称萧译本)非常显著的特征之一就是数量众多的注释。金译本的五章中,少的一章也有数十条注释,多的一章更达150多条。萧译本因是全书,有的一章注释竟达近千条。这和中国文学名著如《红楼梦》等的英译本注释之少形成鲜明对照。

《尤利西斯》一书旁征博引,典故成语比比皆是,有的部分对原文读者都晦涩难懂,对译文读者则更加困难。而且该书自首次出版至今,几经修订,1984年6月16日的"布卢姆日"的新版本,重新修订竟达5000多处。因此,译者在翻译过程中加注说明,自是体现了为读者着想的一片苦心。

第一篇 《尤利西斯》Ulysses

从翻译理论角度来看,《尤利西斯》这本优秀的西方文学名著,处处闪烁着典型西方文化的光辉,而一定时期的文化又是以往历史传统的积淀。这在《尤利西斯》一书中表现得尤其清楚。要把这些传译到典型的东方文化中来,而且使对西方文化只有一般性了解或知之甚少的中国读者读得懂,需要做出艰巨的努力。对这类问题,译者通常采用的方法大致有三:

一是所谓"文化翻译"法,即为了取得等同效果,为了方便译文读者理解,译者在译文中用译入语文化现象代替原文文化现象。这种作法的结果虽使译文易懂,但最大的问题是译文中模糊或抹煞了原文的文化特征,因而带来不可估量的损失。如果说在特殊情况下翻译个别文化现象或许有时可用,但以这种办法翻译《尤利西斯》这样的著作却是不可取的。

二是增益法,即在译文中对难点和不易理解的文化现象作说明性的扩展补充。这种方法偶可采用,但对《尤利西斯》的翻译许多地方难以做到,而且考虑到需加扩展补充之处数量之巨,译者只能望而却步。

三是直译加注释的方法。这一方法许多翻译理论家都赞成使用。如Hatim 和 Mason 就指出,直译加注的方法有利于保存原文的文化特征,而且利于译文读者的理解。金译本和萧译本采用的就是这种方法,这是应该加以肯定的。

综观两种译本的注释,大致可分三种情况:一是得体而且必要的;二是似乎不太必要的;三是注释有不当之处。

第一种情况为绝大多数,主要涉及历史事件、人名地名及引语等,如第二章斯蒂芬历史课上涉及到的阿斯库伦战役、皮洛士将军、海恩斯的小册子、皮洛士死于阿尔戈斯老妪手下、凯撒的被刺、织风的人及布莱克过分的翅膀等,两种译本都有很好的注释。没有这些注释,一般译文读者就会有很大的困难。另一种注释涉及英语中的 play on words,译文只能传达部分内容,却一般很难译出基于英语语言特征的巧妙双关表达方式。如斯蒂芬问学生关于 Pyrrhus 时,学生不知道,就说那是栈桥。皮洛士何以成为栈桥,那是因为英语中的皮洛士(pyrrhus)和栈桥(pier)谐音,而这一点不懂英语的中文读者是不容易弄明白的。金译本和萧译本都加了很好的注释。

第二种是似乎不太必要的注释。如学生把皮洛士说成是栈桥之后教师大发感慨说:"Yes, a disappointed bridge."金译本的译文为:"是的,一座失望的桥梁。"未加注,只是在前面的注释中谈到学生糊涂的回答引起老师对历史的感慨。萧译本的译文为:"是啊,一座失望之桥。"并加注如下:

> [12]皮勒斯那场以惨重的伤亡换得的胜利,使斯蒂芬联想到栈桥,栈桥不能通到彼岸,所以是一座失望之桥。

这段注释前半部分只提出一个关于惨重伤亡之胜利的事实,但这一事实前面正文中已有交代,"Another victory like that and we are done for."因此这里没必要再次重复。

注释的后半部分是译者对历史教师所以发出这种感慨进行的一种推测。权且不说这种推测正确与否,这种推测本身就是一种代替读者思考或者说是剥夺读者思考权利的作法。译者在翻译过程中,总会按照自己的理解去进行,所以以诠释学的观点来看,译文中很难摆脱译者对原文的认识。但是如另在注释中说明自己对某句话理解的推测,则是把自己的可能不属于原作者的观点强加给了读者,这种作法是不妥当的,至少是不必要的。应该相信读者有他们自己的理解和判断能力。

第三种是不太恰当的注释,虽数量不多,但应尽力避免。如历史教师看到学生在课上偷偷摸摸吃蛋糕又回答不上问题,脑子中引起了联想:

> With envy he watched their faces: Edith, Ethel, Gerty, Lily.

金译:他怀着妒羡的心情注视着一张张脸庞:伊迪丝、爱瑟尔、歌蒂、莉莉。[1]

注[1]伊迪丝等全是女孩子的名字,而这里却是一座男校。所以她们不是他课堂上的学生,而是与他们类似的富裕家庭中的姑娘。

萧译:他怀着妒意注视着一张张的脸:伊迪丝、艾塞尔、格蒂、莉莉。[11]

第一篇 《尤利西斯》Ulysses

注[11]斯蒂芬教的是男校,他从班上男生的脸联想到可能与他们相好的女孩子的名字。

这里金译本的注释较为合乎情理,而萧译本则有些欠妥,因为这条注释包含着一个前提假设,即斯蒂芬意识中这些男孩子有女朋友,而且还可进一步推想斯蒂芬知道这些男孩子的女朋友的名字。这似乎不近情理,因而可能误导读者。

综上所述,两译本绝大多数注释对读者有益,因而是必要的。但也有一些并不必要,不妨不注,留待读者自己思考答案。还有一些不太恰当的注释则应极力避免。一本译著有数千条注释,足见译者用心良苦。但从另一方面来看,注释会打断读者的思路,因此最好精简压缩,只保留那些必不可少的条目。

二、功能的传译

好的译文应尽可能传达原语的所有功能。按照以韩礼德(Halliday)为代表的功能语言学派的观点,语言有三种基本功能:一是概念功能(Ideational function);二是人际功能(Interpersonal function);三是篇章组织功能(Textual function)。下面我们试从这三种功能的传译对两种译文的一些句子和片断进行比较分析。

1. 历史教师问一个学生战役发生地点时,
 The boy's blank face asked the blank window.
金译:孩子的茫茫然的脸转过去问白茫茫的窗户。
萧译:孩子把茫然的脸掉过去问那扇茫然的窗户。

原文用两个 blank 加深了学生不能回答问题时无助的气氛。金译本把第二个 blank 译成了"白茫茫",丢掉了原文的拟人手法,因而失去了部分信息功能。也许用"茫然"修饰"窗户"有人会认为搭配不正常,但正如卡特福德在《翻译的语言学理论》一书中所指出的,"当原语文本本身在搭配上就不正常时,译语文本中等值的搭配异常只能是'佳译'的标志。"

2. —Asculum, Stephen said, glancing at the name and date in the gorescarred book.
金译:"阿斯库伦,"斯蒂汾说着,朝血污斑驳的书上的名字和年代看了一眼。

萧译:"阿斯库拉姆,"斯蒂芬朝着载满血腥事迹的书上那地名和年代望了一眼。

这里主要涉及 gorescarred 一词的译法。原文使用的是移就(transferred epithet)修辞法,名为说教科书,实指战斗的血腥。金译本力图传达这一修辞意义,用了"血污斑驳的书上"的译法,但我们觉得却似乎未达目的,因为它传给人的意思是书上有"血污",而且"斑驳"。原因在于使用移就修辞格时应使人感到"移就",即修饰语与被修饰语之间不自然的搭配,表明修饰语另有所指,如英语的"the indefatigable bell"和汉语的"怒发冲冠"等。"血污斑驳"与"书"之间很难说有这样的关系,因而不能激发读者进行移就思考。倒是萧译本的方法,把修辞意思直接表达出来,更符合原文的意旨,当然也属不得已而为之。

3. From a hill above a corpsestrewn plain a general speaking to his officers, leaned upon his spear. Any general to any officer. They lend ear.

金译:陈尸遍野的平原,将军站在小山上,手扶长矛,向部属讲话。任何将军对任何部属。他们都洗耳恭听。

萧译:尸骸累累的平原,将军站在小山岗上,拄着长矛,正对幕僚训话。任何将军对任何幕僚训话,他们都洗耳恭听。

两译文大同小异,只是"任何将军对任何部属(幕僚)(训话)"一句,金译本遵从原文,后面用了句号,而萧译本则改成了逗号。坚持"他们都洗耳恭听"自成一句,可回指上述,表明的是一个个的事实,一个个的真实场面。萧译本改成逗号后,使后面半句的译文变成了对前半句的一种解释说明,事实没有了。改动一个标点,就改变了原文的组织结构,丢掉了一层意思。

4. The words troubled their gaze.

金译:凝视的目光中现出了困惑的神色。

萧译:凝视的目光中现出一片迷茫。

应该说,"迷茫"和"困惑"还是有区别的。迷茫是表示脑中空白,对事情无知,迷离恍惚,而困惑则表示疑难,往往是对事情本有看法,却遇到了更为明确的不同认识,于是困惑不解。这里学生不明白老师何以把栈桥说成是一种桥梁,于是就有接着的发问:"How, sir? Comyn asked. A bridge is across a river."所以上面句子中用"困惑"更能准确表达原意。

5. A swarthy boy opened a book and propped it nimbly under the breastwork of his satchel. He recited jerks of verse with odd glances at the text.

金译:一个脸色黝黑的学生打开书,敏捷地把书支在自己的书包盖底下。他一楷突,一楷突地朗诵起来,眼睛偶尔瞅一下书本。

萧译:一个面色黧黑的少年打开书本,麻利地将它支在用书包充当的胸墙后面。他不时地瞥着课文,急促地背诵着诗句。

Swarthy 是指 dark complexion, 而黧黑则指黑而且黄,增加了原文中未有的意思,似乎欠妥,这里用"黝黑"则更好一些。

Breastwork 原指战士在战壕前面用土砸实的托枪和抵挡敌人子弹的土脊,常译成"胸墙"。作者用此词表明学生对教师的提防,把书包立起放在课桌前面以阻挡教师的视线,搞点小动作不易被教师发觉。萧译本较好地传达出了原文的内容,把"胸墙"加注效果会更好。金译本的"支在书包盖下面"缺少了一层意思,师生间的人际关系未能表示出来。

最后两个子句的处理,萧译本把"瞥着课文"放在前面突出地位,使之成了两个动作中的主要动作或至少是与"背诵着诗句"并列的动作,这似乎有背原文用句子带分词结构所表达的主次关系。金译本把分词结构译成子句放在后面,使之起补充作用,主次分明,较好地传达了原文的结构意义。作者选用一定结构,是为了表达特定的功能,译者应利用译文中合适的结构传达原作的意图。

6. —What was the end of Pyrrhus?

—End of Pyrrhus, sir?

……

—Do you know anything about Pyrrhus?

……

—Pyrrhus, sir? Pyrrhus, a pier.

第一篇 《尤利西斯》Ulysses

金译:"…皮洛士到头来怎么样?"
"皮洛士到头吗,老师?"
……
"…你知道皮洛士是怎么一回事吗?"
……
"皮洛士吗,老师?皮洛士就是栈桥。"
萧译:"皮勒斯的结局怎么样?"
"皮勒斯的结局呢,老师?"
……
"…关于皮勒斯,你知道点什么吗?"
……
"皮勒斯吗,老师?皮勒斯就是栈桥。"

这段中英语的 end 一词,可理解为事情的结局,又可是事物的端点。正因为如此,学生不知道 Pyrrhus,把其说成是栈桥时,end 就成了桥的端点。萧译本使用的"结局"一词,只能指人或一件事,和下文的"栈桥"就无法连接。相形之下,金译本则处理较好,用了"到头来怎样",既可指人,又可指物,为学生后面错误的回答打下了伏笔,文章前后连贯,读者不感突兀。学生不论多蠢,听到"结局"一词之后,怎么也不会说出"栈桥"来。加注可以说明一部分问题。金译本则找到一个较好的解决办法。

7. A sweetened boy's breath.

金译:他的呼吸中带有甜丝丝的儿童的气息。
萧译:少年的呼吸发出一股甜味儿。

两译本差别在于金译本的"甜丝丝的儿童的气息"中的"儿童"是泛指,指一类人,而萧译本的"少年的呼吸"则是定指,指上文回答问题的 Armstrong。回头看原文,意思也是泛指。金译本更好地传达了原文的意图。泛指的优点在于可以唤起人人都可能有的类似的经历,因而更能激发读者的思考。

三、发挥译文的优势

翻译中常谈的一个问题是发挥译文的优势的问题。发挥译文的优势不应该理解为严复的用秦汉以前的文字,也不应该只是追求文字的漂亮。文学翻译自然应该具有文采,尤其是名著,但这种文采应该说是原文文采的再现,就是说用译文特有的表达手段,准确而深刻地传达原文的各种功能。只追求文字的华丽应该说是翻译的一个误区。

1. That phrase the world had remembered.

金译:这话人们记住了。

萧译:世人记住了此语。

这句话中的 That phrase 指前面的一个警句,Another victory like that and we are done for。原文作者为了加强警句效果采用了宾语前置的形式。金译本保留了原句的形式,也用宾语前置,但译文读起来却似乎起不到加强效果的作用。究其原因,英语中宾语前置属于很特殊的结构,一旦使用则非常突兀,令人耳目一新,效果明显。而汉语中则宾语前置的句子太普通,太一般,如"这篇论文评委们都很称赞","这话谁都不喜欢听"等等,因而产生不了英语宾语前置所起到加强效果的作用。

萧译本没有宾语前置,只是用提高词的品位的办法,用"世人"译 the world,用"此语"译 that phrase,结果是精辟醒目,和上面的警句相呼应,与英语可以说是异曲同工,精确地传达了原文句子的功能。

2. I hear the ruin of all space, shattered glass and toppling masonry, and time one livid final flame.

金译:我听到整个空间的毁灭,玻璃稀里哗啦地粉碎,砖瓦成片地倒塌,而时间则成了惨淡无光的最后一道光焰。

萧译:我听到整个空间的毁灭,玻璃碎成碴儿,砖石建筑坍塌下来,时光化为终极的一缕死灰色的火焰。

应该说,金译本的"玻璃稀里哗啦地粉碎"和"砖瓦成片地倒塌"是很好的译法,传达出了"空间毁灭"时动的一面,比萧译本强调结果的"玻璃碎成碴儿"更为传神。但最后一句的译法则略显平淡,尤其是以"惨淡无光的""光焰"来译 livid flame,搭配也不甚理想。倒是萧译本的用"终极"译 final,用"死灰色"来译 livid,更显得深刻隽永,揭示出原文更为深刻的含义。

3. ... and in my mind's darkness a sloth of the underworld, re-

luctant, shy of brightness, shifting her dragon's scaly folds. Thought is the thought of thought. Tranquil brightness. The soul is in a manner all there is: the soul is the form of all forms. Tranquility sudden, vast, candescent: form of all forms.

金译:而在我头脑中的暗处,却是一条底层世界的懒虫,它不愿动弹,怕亮光,慢慢地挪动着龙一般带鳞的躯体。思想是关于思想的思想。宁静的明亮。灵魂在某种意义上说来就是全部存在:灵魂是形式的形式。突如其来的、巨大的、白炽的宁静:形式的形式。

萧译:在我心灵的幽暗处,却是下层世界的一个懒货,畏首畏尾,惧怕光明,蠕动着那像龙鳞般的褶皱。思维乃是有关思维的思维。静穆的光明。就某种意义而言,灵魂是全部存在。灵魂乃是形态的形态。突兀、浩瀚、炽烈的静穆:形态的形态。

比较起来,两种译本都传达出了原文的基本思想,但萧译本的译文却使读者感到译出了深刻的哲理,更给人以美的享受,文章光彩照人,读之如品尝芬芳浓郁的美酒。"蠕动"比"挪动"更为生动形象;"思维的思维"比"思想的思想"更深刻地揭示了过程而不是结果;"形态"比"形式"具有更高层次的抽象与概括涵盖力,因而也更加贴切;至于不说"突如其来"而说"突兀",不用"巨大"而用"浩瀚",不说"白炽的宁静"而说"炽烈的静穆",则更把译文优势发挥得淋漓尽致。这种优势来源于对原文深刻的洞察理解,结果于译文的深刻的精确表达,显示出作为作家的翻译家之深厚底蕴和艺术造诣,堪称优秀译文。

参 考 文 献

1. Hatim, B. and Mason, I., *Discouse and the Translator*, London and New York: Longman, 1990
2. Halliday, M. A. K., "Language structure and language function," in J. Lyons (ed.) *New Horizon in Linguistics*, Harmondsworth: Penguin, 1970
3. Leech, G. and Short, M., *Style in Fiction—A Linguistic Introduction to Eng-*

lish Fictional Prose, London and New York: Longman, 1981
4. Nida, E. A. and Taber, C. R., *The Theory and Practice of Translation*, Leiden: E. J. Brill, 1969
5. Steiner, G., *After Babel*, London Oxford New York: Oxford University Press, 1975
6. 余立三:《英汉修辞比较与翻译》,商务印书馆,1985年。

附：

Ulysses (Excerpts)

James Joyce

[2]

* —You, Cochrane, what city sent for him?
—Tarentum, sir.
—Very good. Well?
—There was a battle, sir.
—Very good. Where?

The boy's blank face asked the blank window.

Fabled by the daughters of memory. And yet it was in some way if not as memory fabled it. A phrase, then, of impatience, thud of Blake's wings of excess. I hear the ruin of all space, shattered glass and toppling masonry, and time one livid final flame. What's left us then?

—I forget the place, sir. 279 B.C.

— Asculum, Stephen said, glancing at the name and date in the gorescarred book.

—Yes, sir. And he said: *Another victory like that and we are done for.*

That phrase the world had remembered. A dull ease of the mind. From a hill above a corpsestrewn plain a general speaking to his officers, leaned upon his spear. Any general to any officers. They lend ear.

—You, Armstrong, Stephen said. What was the end of Pyrrhus?
—End of Pyrrhus, sir?
—I know, sir. Ask me, sir, Comyn said.
—Wait. You, Armstrong. Do you know anything about Pyrrhus?

A bag of figrolls lay snugly in Armstrong's satchel. He curled them between his palms at whiles and swallowed them softly. Crumbs adhered to the tissue of his lips. A sweetened boy's breath. Welloff people, proud that their eldest son was in the navy. Vico road, Dalkey.

—Pyrrhus, sir? Pyrrhus, a pier.

All laughed. Mirthless high malicious laughter. Armstrong looked round at his classmates, silly glee in profile. In a moment they will laugh more loudly, aware of my lack of rule and of the fees their papas pay.

—Tell me now, Stephen said, poking the boy's shoulder with the book, what is a pier.

—A pier, sir, Armstrong said. A thing out in the water. A kind of a bridge. Kingstown pier, sir.

Some laughed again: mirthless but with meaning. Two in the back bench whispered. Yes. They knew: had never learned nor ever been innocent. All. With envy he watched their faces: Edith, Ethel, Gerty, Lily. Their likes: their breaths, too, sweetened with tea and jam, their bracelets tittering in the struggle.

—Kingstown pier, Stephen said. Yes, a disappointed bridge.

The words troubled their gaze.

—How, sir? Comyn asked. A bridge is across a river.

For Haines's chapbook. No-one here to hear. Tonight deftly amid wild drink and talk, to pierce the polished mail of his mind. What then? A jester at the court of his master, indulged and disesteemed, winning a clement master's praise. Why had they chosen all that part? Not wholly for the smooth caress. For them too history was a tale like any other too often heard, their land a pawnshop.

　　Had Pyrrhus not fallen by a beldam's hand in Argos or Julius Caesar not been knifed to death. They are not to be thought away. Time has branded them and fettered they are lodged in the room of the infinite possibilities they have ousted. But can those have been possible seeing that they never were? Or was that only possible which came to pass? Weave, weaver of the wind.

—Tell us a story, sir.
—O, do, sir. A ghoststory.
—Where do you begin in this? Stephen asked, opening another book.
—*Weep no more*, Comyn said.
—Go on then, Talbot.
—And the story, sir?
—After, Stephen said. Go on, Talbot.

　　A swarthy boy opened a book and propped it nimbly under the breastwork of his satchel. He recited jerks of verse with odd glances at the text:

*Weep no more, woful shepherds, weep no more
For Lyoidas, your sorrow, is not dead.
Sunk though he be beneath the watery floor* ...

　　It must be a movement then, an actuality of the possible as possible. Aristotle's phrase formed itself within the gabbled verses and floated out into the studious silence of the library of Saint Genevieve, where he had read, sheltered from the sin of Paris, night by night. By his elbow a delicate Siamese conned a handbook of strategy. Fed and feeding brains about me: under glowlamps, impaled, with faintly beating feelers: and in my mind's darkness a sloth of the underworld, reluctant, shy of brightness, shifting her dragon scaly folds. Thought is the thought of thought. Tranquil brightness. The soul is in a manner all that is: the soul is the form of forms. Tranquility sudden, vast, candescent: form of forms.

Talbot repeated:
—*Through the dear might of Him that walked the waves.*
Through the dear might ...
—Turn over, Stephen said quietly. I don't see anything.
—What, sir? Talbot asked simply, bending forward.

His hand turned the page over. He leaned back and went on again, having just remembered. Of him that walked the waves. Here also over these craven hearts his shadow lies and on the scoffer's heart and lips and on mine. It lies upon their eager faces who offered him a coin *of the tribute*. To Caesar what is Caesar's, to God what is God's. A long look from dark eyes, a riddling sentence to be woven and woven on the church's looms. Ay.

Riddle me, riddle me, randy ro.
My father gave me seeds to sow.

Talbot slid his closed book into his satchel.
—Have I heard all? Stephen asked.
—Yes, sir. Hockey at ten, sir.
—Half day, sir. Thursday.
—Who can answer a riddle? Stephen asked.

They bundled their books away, pencils clacking, pages rustling. Crowding together they strapped and buckled their satchels, all gabbling gaily:
—A riddle, sir? Ask me, sir.
—O, ask me, sir.
—A hard one, sir.
—This is the riddle, Stephen said:

第一篇 《尤利西斯》Ulysses

The cock crew,
The sky was blue:
The bells in heaven
Were striking eleven.
' Tis time for this poor soul
To go to heaven.

—What is that?
—What, sir?
—Again, sir. We didn't hear.

　　Their eyes grew bigger as the lines were repeated. After a silence Cochrane said:
—What is it, sir? We give it up.

　　Stephen, his throat itching, answered:
—The fox burying his grandmother under a hollybush.

　　He stood up and gave a shout of nervous laughter to which their cries echoed dismay.

　　A stick struck the door and a voice in the corridor called:
—Hockey!

　　They broke asunder, sidling out of their benches, leaping them. Quickly they were gone and from the lumberroom came the rattle of sticks and clamour of their boots and tongues.

　　Sargent who alone had lingered came forward slowly, showing an open copybook. His thick hair and scraggy neck gave witness of unreadiness and through his misty glasses weak eyes looked up pleading. On his cheek, dull and bloodless, a soft stain of ink lay, dateshaped, recent and damp as a snail's bed.

　　He held out his copybook. The word *Sums* was written on the headline. Beneath were sloping figures and at the foot a crooked signature with blind loops and a blot. Cyril Sargent: his name and seal.
—Mr Deasy told me to write them out all again, he said, and show

them to you, sir.

Stephen touched the edges of the book. Futility.

—Do you understand how to do them now? he asked.

—Numbers eleven to fifteen, Sargent answered. Mr Deasy said I was to copy them off the board, sir.

—Can you do them yourself? Stephen asked.

—No, sir.

Ugly and futile: lean neck and thick hair and a stain of ink, a snail's bed. Yet someone had loved him, borne him in her arms and in her heart. But for her the race of the world would have trampled him underfoot, a squashed boneless snail. She had loved his weak watery blood drained from her own. Was that then real? The only true thing in life? His mother's prostrate body the fiery Columbanus in holy zeal bestrode. She was no more: the trembling skeleton of a twig burnt in the fire, an odour of rosewood and wetted ashes. She had saved him from being trampled underfoot and had gone, scarcely having been. A poor soul gone to heaven: and on a heath beneath winking stars a fox, red reek of rapine in his fur, with merciless bright eyes scraped in the earth, listened, scraped up the earth, listened, scraped and scraped.

Sitting at his side Stephen solved out the problem. He proves by algebra that Shakespeare's ghost is Hamlet's grandfather. Sargent peered askance through his slanted glasses. Hockeysticks rattled in the lumberroom: the hollow knock of a ball and calls from the field.

Across the page the symbols moved in grave morrice, in the mummery of their letters, wearing quaint caps of squares and cubes. Give hands, traverse, bow to partner: so: imps of fancy of the Moors. Gone too from the world, Averroes and Moses Maimonides, dark men in mien and movement, flashing in their mocking mirrors the obscure soul of the world, a darkness shining in brightness which brightness could not comprehend.

—Do you understand now? Can you work the second for yourself?

—Yes, sir.

In long shaky strokes Sargent copied the data. Waiting always for a word of help his hand moved faithfully the unsteady symbols, a faint hue of shame flickering behind his dull skin. *Amor matris*: subjective and objective genitive. With her weak blood and wheysour milk she had fed him and hid from sight of others his swaddlingbands.

Like him was I, these sloping shoulders, this gracelessness. My childhood bends beside me. Too far for me to lay a hand there once or lightly. Mine is far and his secret as our eyes. Secrets, silent, stony sit in the dark palaces of both our hearts: secrets weary of their tyranny: tyrants, willing to be dethroned.

The sum was done.

—It is very simple, Stephen said as he stood up.

—Yes, sir. Thanks. Sargent answered.

He dried the page with a sheet of thin blottingpaper and carried his copybook back to his bench.

—You had better get your stick and go out to the others, Stephen said as he followed towards the door the boy's graceless form.

—Yes, sir.

In the corridor his name was heard, called from the playfield.

—Sargent!

—Run on, Stephen said. Mr Deasy is calling you.

He stood in the porch and watched the laggard hurry towards the scrappy field where sharp voices were in strife. They were sorted in teams and Mr Deasy came away stepping over wisps of grass with gaitered feet. When he had reached the schoolhouse voices again contending called to him. He turned his angry white moustache.

—What is it now? He cried continually without listening.
—Cochrane and Halliday are on the same side, sir, Stephen said.
—Will you wait in my study for a moment, Mr Deasy said, till I restore order here.

And as he stepped fussily back across the field his old man's voice cried sternly:
—What is the matter? What is it now?

Their sharp voices cried about him on all sides: their many forms closed round him, the garish sunshine bleaching the honey of his illdyed head.

Stale smoky air hung in the study with the smell of drab abraded leather of its chairs. As on the first day he bargained with me here. As it was in the beginning, is now. On the sideboard the tray of Stuart coins, base treasure of a bog: and ever shall be. And snug in their spooncase of purple plush, faded, the twelve apostles having preached to all the gentiles: world without end.

A hasty step over the stone porch and in the corridor. Blowing out his rare moustache Mr Deasy halted at the table.
—First, our little financial settlement, he said.

He brought out of his coat a pocketbook bound by a leather thong. It slapped open and he took from it two notes, one of joined halves, and laid them carefully on the table.
—Two, he said, strapping and stowing his pocketbook away.

And now his strongroom for the gold. Stephen's embarrassed hand moved over the shells heaped in the cold stone mortar: whelks and money cowries and leopard shells: and this, whorled as an emir's turban, and this, the scallop of saint James. An old pilgrim's hoard, dead treasure, hollow shells.

A sovereign fell, bright and new, on the soft pile of the tablecloth.

第一篇 《尤利西斯》Ulysses

—Three, Mr Deasy said, turning his little savingsbox about in his hand. These are handy things to have. See. This is for sovereigns. This is for shillings. Sixpences, halfcrowns. And here crowns. See.

He shot from it two crowns and two shillings.

—Three twelve, he said. I think you'll find that's right.

—Thank you, sir, Stephen said, gathering the money together with shy haste and putting it all in a pocket of his trousers.

—No thanks at all, Mr Deasy said. You have earned it.

Stephen's hand, free again, went back to the hollow shells. Symbols too of beauty and of power. A lump in my pocket: symbols soiled by greed and misery.

—Don't carry it like that, Mr Deasy said. You'll pull it out somewhere and lose it. You just buy one of these machines. You'll find them very handy.

Answer something.

—Mine would be often empty, Stephen said.

The same room and hour, the same wisdom: and I the same. Three times now. Three nooses round me here. Well? I can break them in this instant if I will.

—Because you don't save, Mr Deasy said, pointing his finger. You don't know yet what money is. Money is power. When you have lived as long as I have. I know, I know. *If youth but knew.* But what does Shakespeare say? *Put but money in thy purse.*

—Iago, Stephen murmured.

He lifted his gaze from the idle shells to the old man's stare.

—He knew what money was, Mr Deasy said. He made money. A poet, yes, but an Englishman too. Do you know what is the pride of the English? Do you know what is the proudest word you will ever hear from an Englishman's mouth?

The seas' ruler. His seacold eyes looked on the empty bay: it seems history is to blame: on me and on my words, unhating.

—That on his empire, Stephen said, the sun never sets.

—Ba! Mr Deasy cried. That's not English. A French Celt said that.

He tapped his savingsbox against his thumbnail.

—I will tell you, he said solemnly, what is his proudest boast. *I paid my way.*

Good man, good man.

—*I paid my way. I never borrowed a shilling in my life.* Can you feel that? *I owe nothing.* Can you?

Mulligan, nine pounds, three pairs of socks, one pair brogues, ties. Curran, ten guineas. MeCann, one guinea. Fred Ryan, two shillings Temple, two lunches. Russell, one guinea, Cousins, ten shillings, Bob Reynolds, half a guinea, Koehler, three guineas, Mrs MacKernan, five weeks' board. The lump I have is useless.

—For the moment, no, Stephen answered.

Mr Deasy laughed with rich delight, putting back his savingsbox.

—I knew you couldn't, he said joyously. But one day you must feel it. We are a generous people but we must also be just.

—I fear those big words, Stephen said, which make us so unhappy.

Mr Deasy stared sternly for some moments over the mantelpiece at the shapely bulk of a man in tartan filibegs: Albert Edward, prince of Wales.

—You think me an old fogey and an old tory, his thoughtful voice said. I saw three generations since O'Connell's time. I remember the famine in '46. Do you know that the orange lodges agitated for repeal of the union twenty years before O'Connell did or before the prelates of your communion denounced him as a demagogue? You fenians forget some things.

Glorious, pious and immortal memory. The lodge of Diamond in

Armagh the splendid behung with corpses of papishes. Hoarse, masked and armed, the planters' covenant. The black north and true blue bible. Croppies lie down.

Stephen sketched a brief gesture.

—I have rebel blood in me too, Mr Deasy said. On the spindle side. But I am descended from sir John Blackwood who voted for the union. We are all Irish, all kings' sons.

—Alas, Stephen said.

—*Per vias rectas*, Mr Deasy said firmly, was his motto. He voted for it and put on his topboots to ride to Dublin from the Ards of Down to do so.

> *Lal the ral the ra*
> *The rocky road to Dublin.*

A gruff squire on horseback with shiny topboots. Soft day, sir John! Soft day, your honour! ... Day! ... Day! ... Two topboots jog dangling on to Dublin. Lal the ral the ra. Lal the ral the raddy.

—That reminds me, Mr Deasy said. You can do me a favour, Mr Dedalus, with some of your literary friends. I have a letter here for the press. Sit down a moment. I have just to copy the end.

He went to the desk near the window, pulled in his chair twice and read off some words from the sheet on the drum of his typewriter.

—Sit down. Excuse me, he said over his shoulder, *the dictates of common sense.* Just a moment.

He peered from under his shaggy brows at the manuscript by his elbow and, muttering, began to prod the stiff buttons of the keyboard slowly, sometimes blowing as he screwed up the drum to erase an error.

Stephen seated himself noiselessly before the princely presence.

Framed around the walls images of vanished horses stood in homage, their meek heads poised in air: lord Hastings' *Repulse*, the duke of Westminster's *Shotover*, the duke of Beaufort's *Ceylon*, *prix de Paris*, 1866. Elfin riders sat them, watchful of a sign. He saw their speeds, backing king's colours, and shouted with the shouts of vanished crowds.

—Full stop, Mr Deasy bade his keys. *But prompt ventilation of this allimportant question ...*

Where Cranly led me to get rich quick, hunting his winners among the mudsplashed brakes, amid the bawls of bookies on their pitches and reek of the canteen, over the motley slush. *Fair Rebel! Fair Rebel!* Even money the favourite: ten to one the field. Dicers and thimbleriggers we hurried by after the hoofs, the vying caps and jackets and past the meatfaced woman, a butcher's dame, nuzzling thirstily her clove of orange.

Shouts rang shrill from the boys' playfield and a whirring whistle.

Again: a goal. I am among them, among their battling bodies in a medley, the joust of life. You mean that knockkneed mother's darling who seems to be slightly crawsick? Jousts. Time shocked rebounds, shock by shock. Jousts, slush and uproar of battles, the frozen deathspew of the slain, a shout of spearspikes baited with men's bloodied guts.

—Now then, Mr Deasy said, rising.

He came to the table, pinning together his sheets. Stephen stood up.

—I have put the matter into a nutshell, Mr Deasy said. It's about the foot and mouth disease. Just look through it. There can be no two opinions on the matter.

May I trespass on your valuable space. That doctrine of *laissez*

第一篇 《尤利西斯》Ulysses

faire which so often in our history. Our cattle trade. The way of all our old industries. Liverpool ring which jockeyed the Galway harbour scheme. European conflagration. Grain supplies through the narrow waters of the channel. The pluterperfect imperturbability of the department of agriculture. Pardoned a classical allusion. Cassandra. By a woman who was no better than she should be. To come to the point at issue.

—I don't mince words, do I? Mr Deasy asked as Stephen read on.

Foot and mouth disease. Known as Koch's preparation. Serum and virus. Percentage of salted horses. Rinderpest. Emperor's horses at Mürzsteg, lower Austria. Veterinary surgeons. Mr Henry Blackwood Price. Courteous offer a fair trial. Dictates of common sense. Allimportant question. In every sense of the word take the bull by the horns. Thanking you for the hospitality of your columns.

—I want that to be printed and read, Mr Deasy said. You will see at the next outbreak they will put an embargo on Irish cattle. And it can be cured. It is cured. My cousin, Blackwood Price, writes to me it is regularly treated and cured in Austria by cattledoctors there. They offer to come over here. I am trying to work up influence with the department. Now I'm going to try publicity. I am surrounded by difficulties, by ... intrigues by ... backstairs influence by ...

He raised his forefinger and beat the air oldly before his voice spoke.

—Mark my words, Mr Dedalus, he said. England is in the hands of the jews. In all the highest places: her finance, her press. And they are the signs of a nation's decay. Wherever they gather they eat up the nation's vital strength. I have seen it coming these years. As sure as we are standing here the jew merchants are already at their work of destruction. Old England is dying.

He stepped swiftly off, his eyes coming to blue life as they

passed a broad sunbeam. He faced about and back again.
—Dying, he said again, if not dead by now.

> The harlot's cry from street to street
> Shall weave old England's windingsheet.

His eyes open wide in vision stared sternly across the sunbeam in which he halted.
—A merchant, Stephen said, is one who buys cheap and sells dear, jew or gentile, is he not?
—They sinned against the light, Mr Deasy said gravely. And you can see the darkness in their eyes. And that is why they are wanderers on the earth to this day.

On the steps of the Paris stock exchange the goldskinned men quoting prices on their gemmed fingers. Gabble of geese. They swarmed loud, uncouth, about the temple, their heads thickplotting under maladroit silk hats. Not theirs: these clothes, this speech, these gestures. Their full slow eyes belied the words, the gestures eager and unoffending, but knew the rancours massed about them and knew their zeal was vain. Vain patience to heap and hoard. Time surely would scatter all. A hoard heaped by the roadside: plundered and passing on. Their eyes knew their years of wandering and, patient, knew the dishonours of their flesh.

—Who has not? Stephen said.
—What do you mean? Mr Deasy asked.

He came forward a pace and stood by the table. His underjaw fell sideways open uncertainly. Is this old wisdom? He waits to hear from me.

—History, Stephen said, is a nightmare from which I am trying to awake.

From the playfield the boys raised a shout. A whirring whistle:

goal. What if that nightmare gave you a back kick?

—The ways of the Creator are not our ways, Mr Deasy said. All human history moves towards one great goal, the manifestation of God.

Stephen jerked his thumb towards the window, saying:

—That is God.

Hooray! Ay! Whrrwhee!

—What? Mr Deasy asked.

—A shout in the street, Stephen answered, shrugging his shoulders.

Mr Deasy looked down and held for awhile the wings of his nose tweaked between his fingers. Looking up again he set them free.

—I am happier than you are, he said. We have committed many errors and many sins. A woman brought sin into the world. For a woman who was no better than she should be, Helen, the runaway wife of Menelaus, ten years the Greeks made war on Troy. A faithless wife first brought the strangers to our shore here, MacMurrough's wife and her leman, O'Rourke, prince of Breffni. A woman too brought Parnell low. Many errors, many failures but not the one sin. I am a struggler now at the end of my days. But I will fight for the right till the end.

For Ulster will fight
And Ulster will be right.

Stephen raised the sheets in his hand.

—Well, sir, he began ...

—I foresee, Mr Deasy said, that you will not remain here very long at this work. You were not born to be a teacher, I think. Perhaps I am wrong.

—A learner rather, Stephen said.

And here what will you learn more?

Mr Deasy shook his head.

—Who knows? he said. To learn one must be humble. But life is the great teacher.

Stephen rustled the sheets again.

—As regards these, he began ...

—Yes, Mr Deasy said. You have two copies there. If you can have them published at once.

Telegraph. Irish Homestead.

—I will try. Stephen said, and let you know tomorrow. I know two editors slightly.

—That will do, Mr Deasy said briskly. I wrote last night to Mr Field, M. P. There is a meeting of the cattletraders' association today at the City Arms hotel. I asked him to lay my letter before the meeting. You see if you can get it into your two papers. What are they?

—The *Evening Telegraph* ...

—That will do, Mr Deasy said. There is no time to lose. Now I have to answer that letter from my cousin.

—Good morning, sir, Stephen said, putting the sheets in his pocket. Thank you.

—Not at all, Mr Deasy said as he searched the papers on his desk. I like to break a lance with you, old as I am.

—Good morning, sir, Stephen said again, bowing to his bent back.

He went out by the open porch and down the gravel path under the trees, hearing the cries of voices and crack of sticks from the playfield. The lions couchant on the pillars as he passed out through the gate: toothless terrors. Still I will help him in his fight. Mulligan will dub me a new name: the bullockbefriending bard.

—Mr Dedalus!

Running after me. No more letters, I hope.

—Just one moment.

—Yes, sir, Stephen said, turning back at the gate.

Mr Deasy halted, breathing hard and swallowing his breath.

—I just wanted to say, he said. Ireland, they say, has the honour of being the only country which never persecuted the jews. Do you know that? No. And do you know why?

He frowned sternly on the bright air.

—Why, sir? Stephen asked, beginning to smile.

—Because she never let them in, Mr Deasy said solemnly.

A coughball of laughter leaped from his throat dragging after it a rattling chain of phlegm. He turned back quickly, coughing, laughing, his lifted arms waving to the air.

—She never let them in, he cried again through his laughter as he stamped on gaitered feet over the gravel of the path. That's why.

On his wise shoulders through the checkerwork of leaves the sun flung spangles, dancing coins.

《尤利西斯》(节选)

金 隄 译

涅斯托耳[①]

"你说,科克兰,什么城市请他[②]?"
"塔林敦[③],老师。"
"很好。后来呢?"
"有一个战役,老师。"
"很好。在什么地方?"
孩子的茫茫然的脸转过去问白茫茫的窗户。

---

① 这是小说第二章,描写斯蒂汾在都柏林郊区学校教书的情况。在古希腊荷马史诗所描述的特洛伊战役中,涅斯托耳是希腊军中年事最高的将领,以深谙世故、知识渊博著称;战后尤利西斯十年未归,其子寻找父亲时曾去向他探听消息,他热心地提供了许多情况,但是其中并没有尤利西斯儿子所需要的消息。
② 斯蒂汾在进行历史课提问,所涉及的"他",是希腊北部伊庇鲁斯的国王皮洛士(公元前 319—272)。
③ 塔林敦即今意大利南部城市塔兰。公元前三世纪初罗马军队进逼时,塔林敦向皮洛士求援。

第一篇 《尤利西斯》Ulysses

是记忆的女儿们编造的寓言①。然而,即使不和记忆编造的寓言一样,也还是有一定的事实的。那么,是一句不耐烦的话了,是布莱克那过分的翅膀②的一阵扑击。我听到整个空间的毁灭,玻璃稀里哗啦地粉碎,砖瓦成片地倒塌,而时间则成了惨淡无光的最后一道火焰。那样的话,我们还剩下了什么呢?

"我忘了地点,老师。公元前279年。"

"阿斯库伦③,"斯蒂汾说着,朝血污斑驳的书上的名字和年代瞥了一眼。

"是的,老师。他还说:'再打这么一个胜仗,我们也就完了。'④"

这话人们记住了。头脑处于一种迟钝的轻松状态。陈尸遍野的平原,将军站在小山头上,手扶长矛,向部属讲话。任何将军对任何部属。他们都洗耳恭听。

"你,阿姆斯特朗,"斯蒂汾说,"皮洛士到头来怎么样?"

"皮洛士到头吗,老师?"

"我知道,老师。问我吧,老师,"科明说。

"等一下。你说,阿姆斯特朗。你知道皮洛士是怎么一回事吗?"

阿姆斯特朗的书包里藏着一袋无花果冻夹心蛋糕。他不时把蛋糕放在掌心里,合掌搓成小卷儿,悄悄地塞进嘴里。嘴唇上还沾着蛋糕屑呢。他的呼吸中带有甜丝丝的儿童气息。富裕家庭,大儿子当上了海军,

---

① "记忆的女儿们"典故来自英国诗人布莱克(1757—1827)的《最后审判的景象》:"寓言或讽喻是由记忆的女儿们编造的。想象是受灵感的女儿们包围的……"按照希腊神话,九位掌握各种文艺(包括历史、诗歌等等)的女神,都是大神宙斯和记忆女神所生的女儿。

② 布莱克主张听任自己的想象力自由驰骋,主张以过分的行动去抵消另一种过分,他说:"鸟飞不愁高,只要它用的是自己的翅膀。"

③ 阿斯库伦在今意大利南部,皮洛士战胜罗马军队的两个战役之一在此进行。

④ 这是皮洛士在阿斯库伦之役的胜利之后说的话,因为他在这一战役中损失了大批精兵良将。由此人们把得不偿失的胜利称为"皮洛士的胜利"。

一家人都很得意。道尔盖① 的维柯路。

"皮洛士吗,老师？皮洛士就是栈桥②。"

哄堂大笑。并不欢乐的尖声怪笑。阿姆斯特朗环顾同学,露出一个傻笑的侧影。呆一会儿,他们体会到我管教不严,想到他们的爸爸缴的学费,笑声还会更大些。

"现在你说说,"斯蒂汾用书捅捅孩子的肩膀说,"栈桥是什么？"

"栈桥啊,老师,"阿姆斯特朗说,"是伸到水里的东西。一种桥呗。金斯敦码头③,老师。"

又有几个人笑了:不欢乐,但有含意。后排有两个人在交头接耳。是的。他们是知道的:从没有学习过,可也从来不是外行。全都如此。他怀着妒羡的心情注视着一张张脸庞:伊迪丝、爱瑟尔、歌蒂、莉莉④。同一个类型的人:呼吸中也带着红茶和果酱的甜香味,手臂上的镯子在挣扎中发出吃吃的笑声。

"金斯敦码头吗,"斯蒂汾说。"是的,一座失望的桥梁。"

这话使他们凝视的目光中现出了困惑的神色。

"怎么呢,老师？"科明问,"桥不是架在河上的吗？"

可以收进海恩斯的小册子⑤。这里可没有人听。今天晚上放怀痛

---

① 道尔盖是都柏林的一个滨海郊区,即学校所在地。
② "皮洛士"(Pyrrhus)读音似英语的 Pier (栈桥,或凸码头)后续拉丁字尾 us,再加上刚才听老师问"皮洛士到头",更促使这个糊涂学生张冠李戴,以为是谈海边的栈桥。但是他的糊涂联想,倒恰好引起了下文斯蒂汾对历史的感慨("失望的桥梁")。
③ 金斯敦是都柏林的一个海港区,现已改名丹莱里,有东西两大码头伸入海中,形成一个人造的港湾,离学校所在地道尔盖不远。
④ 伊迪丝等全是女孩子的名字,而这里却是一个男校,所以她们不是课堂中的学生,而是与他们类似的富裕家庭中的姑娘。
⑤ 海恩斯是本书第一章中出现的一位英国人。跟本段有关的情节有二:(一)海恩斯说他要收集斯蒂汾的警句,编成集子。(二)斯蒂汾对海恩斯说,自己是一个仆人侍候着两个主人,即英帝国和罗马天主教廷。海恩斯说,这似乎要怪历史。

饮、神聊,妙语如剑,可以刺透他罩在思想外面的锃亮的甲胄。那又怎么样呢?无非是一个在主子的宫廷上逗人发笑的小丑,受了宽容也遭到鄙视,在宽宏大量的主子跟前赢得一声夸奖而已。为什么他们都愿意扮演这样一个角色?不完全是为了那和蔼的抚摩。对于他们也是一样,历史成了老生常谈,他们的国土成了当铺。

假定皮洛士没有倒在阿尔戈斯老妪手下①,或是朱利叶斯·凯撒没有被人刺死②呢?事实是无法按主观愿望抹掉的。时间已经给它们打上烙印,它们已经被拴住了,占据着被他们排挤出去的那些无穷无尽的可能性的地盘③。但是,那些可能性既然从未实现,还说得上可能吗?还是只有成为事实的才是可能的呢?织风的人④,织吧。

"给我们讲一个故事吧,老师。"

"讲吧,老师。讲个鬼故事。"

"这该从什么地方开始?"斯蒂汾打开另一本书问。

"'别再哭泣',"科明说。

"那么你念下去,塔尔博特。"

"故事呢,老师?"

"呆会儿,"斯蒂汾说。"念吧,塔尔博特。"

一个脸色黝黑的学生打开书,敏捷地把书支在自己的书包盖底下。他一楫柮,一楫柮地朗诵起来,眼睛偶尔瞅一瞅书本。

---

① 皮洛士死于公元前272年阿尔戈斯巷战中,当时有一个老妇人从屋顶上扔下一片瓦来,把他从马背上砸下,他才被人杀死。

② 罗马帝国的独裁者凯撒于公元前44年被罗马贵族杀死。许多历史学家认为此事是罗马长期动乱的起因。

③ 指古希腊哲学家亚里士多德关于可能性的理论:事情发生之前,具有各样的可能性,而在其中的一个可能性变成了现实之后,其它的可能性就全被排除了。

④ 织风典故有几种不同的说法,其中可能性较大的是布莱克在《耶路撒冷》中的诗句:"阿尔宾的女儿们,将世世代代的事情编织成网。"其中"阿尔宾的女儿们",即前面所说的:"记忆的女儿们。"

第一篇 《尤利西斯》Ulysses

别再哭泣,悲伤的牧羊人,别再哭泣,
你们哀悼的莱西达斯并没有死去,
尽管他已经沉到了水面底下……①

那么,一定是一种运动了,可能性因为有可能而成为现实②。在急促而含糊的朗诵声中,亚里士多德的论断形成了,飘出教室,飘进圣日内维也符图书馆③内的勤奋、肃静的空气中。他曾经一夜又一夜地躲在这里阅读,这里不受巴黎的罪恶的侵袭。在紧挨着他的座位上,有一个文弱的暹逻人④在钻研一本战略手册。为我周围的头脑提供了并继续提供着养料:头顶上是一些用小铁栅围起来的放电灯,伸出微微扑动着的触须;而在我头脑中的暗处,却是一条底层世界的懒虫,它不愿动弹,怕亮光,慢慢地挪动着龙一般的带鳞的躯体⑤。思想是关于思想的思想⑥。宁静的明亮。灵魂在某种意义说来就是全部存在:灵魂是形式的形式⑦。突如其来的、巨大的、白炽的宁静:形式的形式。

塔尔博特一遍又一遍地背诵着:

凭借履波如夷的他⑧ 的亲切法力

---

① 此系出自英国诗人弥尔顿为溺死的同窗所写的悼念诗《莱西达斯》(1638)。
② 亚里士多德曾多次论述,潜在的可能性变为现实的过程就是运动。
③ 圣日内维也符图书馆在巴黎,晚上在此读书的几乎全是学生。乔伊斯本人在巴黎时也常在此研读。
④ 暹逻即今泰国。
⑤ 布莱克在《天堂与地狱的结合》中说,知识传播过程是在地狱里一个印刷所中进行的,其中共有六个洞窟,第一窟中有一些龙样的人和龙在清理垃圾和掏土挖洞。
⑥ 亚里士多德在《形而上学》中提出,关于思想的思维是基本的推动力。
⑦ 亚里士多德在《论灵魂》中说:"正如手是工具的工具,头脑(灵魂)是形式的形式……"意思是说一切事物都只有通过头脑的活动才能认识。
⑧ 指耶稣。据《圣经·新约》记载,耶稣曾在风浪中踏着水面走到离岸很远的船上。

第一篇 《尤利西斯》Ulysses

凭借履波如夷的他……

"翻过去吧,"斯蒂汾静静地说。"我看这儿没有了。"

"您说什么,老师?"塔尔博特向前倾着身体,单纯地问。

他的手翻过一页书。他想起来了,于是又坐直身子继续朗诵。履波如夷的他。他的影子也投射到这里,笼罩在这些怯懦的心灵上,在嘲笑者的心灵上和嘴唇上,在我的心灵上和嘴唇上。笼罩在把一枚纳贡的金币献给他的那些人的热切面容上。将属于凯撒的交给凯撒,将属于上帝的交给上帝①。一道从深色的眼睛中射出来的长久的目光,一句谜语般的句子,供教会的纺织机织了又织。可不是吗。

  猜一猜,猜一猜,朗的罗,
  我爸爸给我种子让我播②。

塔尔博特把书合上,滑进书包。

"都朗诵完了吗?"斯蒂汾问。

"完了,老师。十点钟打曲棍球,老师。"

"半天儿,老师。是星期四哪。"

"谁会猜谜语?"斯蒂汾问。

孩子们收书的收书,装笔的装笔,铅笔嗒嗒作响,纸张窸窸窣窣。他们一边绑着、扣着书包,一边挤成一团,兴高采烈、七嘴八舌地说:

"老师,猜谜语吗? 老师,我猜!"

"我猜,我猜,老师。"

"来个难的,老师。"

---

① 据《新约》记载,在耶稣宣讲必须敬重上帝的教义时,有人问他向罗马政府交纳税金是否违背这一教义,耶稣不直接回答,而指出金币上铸的是凯撒头像,说"将属于凯撒的交给凯撒,将属于上帝的交给上帝"。斯帝汾认为这是"谜语般的句子",下文的两个谜语也由此而引起。

② 这是一个谜语的头两句。后两句是:
  种子是黑的,地儿是白的
  你猜到这个谜语,我就给你喝的。 (谜底:写信。)

"这个谜语是这样的,"斯蒂汾说:

> 公鸡打鸣儿
> 天空见蓝色儿
> 天上有钟儿
> 敲响了十一点儿
> 可怜的灵魂儿
> 到时候了,该归天儿了。

"是什么?"
"老师,怎么说的来着?"
"再说一遍,老师。我们没听清。"
谜语重说了一遍,孩子们的眼睛睁得更大了。沉默了一会儿之后,科克兰说:
"老师,是什么?我们猜不着。"
斯蒂汾回答的时候,嗓子里有些发痒:
"是狐狸在冬青树下埋葬自己的奶奶[①]。"
他站起身来,发出一阵神经质的大笑,而孩子们的回音是一片扫兴的嚷嚷声。
门外有人用棍子敲门,同时在走廊里喊:
"曲棍球!"
孩子们立即散开,纷纷穿过桌椅,有侧着身子挤过去的,有从上边跳过去的。很快人都走光了,从贮藏室传来棍棒的撞击声、乱哄哄的脚步声和说话声。
只有萨金特没有走,他捧着一本打开的抄本,慢慢地走上前来。厚厚的头发,瘦骨嶙峋的脖子,都证明他的迟钝;模糊的镜片后面是两只无神的眼睛,仰望着,乞求着。他的脸灰暗而无血色,面颊上有一块新抹

[①] 这是爱尔兰的一个取笑谜语的谜语,意思是说有些谜语是无法猜的,但一般把谜底说成狐狸埋葬自己的妈妈,斯蒂汾改为奶奶显然与当时的思想状态有关。

第一篇 《尤利西斯》Ulysses

上去的墨水,枣子形,还湿漉漉的呢,象蜗牛的窝儿似的。

他捧上抄本,页头标着"算术"二字。字下面是斜斜的数目字,最底下是一个曲里拐弯的签名,带圈的笔划都是实心的;另外还有一团墨水渍。西里尔·萨金特:名字加图记。

"老师,戴汐先生叫我全部再抄一遍,"他说,"还要交给您看。"

斯蒂汾摸着抄本的边。徒劳无功。

"你现在会做了吗?"他问。

"十一题到十五题,"萨金特回答说。"戴汐先生叫我照着黑板上抄的,老师。"

"你自己会做吗?"斯蒂汾问。

"不会,老师。"

又丑,又没出息:细脖子,厚头发,一抹墨水,蜗牛的窝儿。然而也曾经有人爱过他,在怀里抱过他,在心中疼过他。要不是有她,他早就被你争我夺的社会踩在脚下,变成一摊稀烂的蜗牛泥了。她疼爱从自己身上流到他身上去的孱弱稀薄的血液。那么那是真实的了?生活中唯一靠得住的东西①?他母亲平卧的身子上,跨着圣情高涨的烈性子高隆班②。她已经不复存在:一根在火中烧化了的小树枝,只留下颤巍巍的残骸,花梨木和沾湿了的灰烬的气味③。她保护了他,使他免受践踏,自己却

---

① 斯蒂汾的朋友克兰利曾规劝他对母亲要体贴,并说:"在这个臭粪堆似的世界上,不管别的东西怎么靠不住,母亲的爱总是靠得住的。……"见乔伊斯的另一部小说《艺术家青年时期写照》最后一章。

② 高隆班(约543—615)是爱尔兰著名僧侣和圣人,以学问高深和布道热心著称。他不顾其母反对外出传道。"高隆"在拉丁文和爱尔兰语中是"鸽子"的意思,而根据《圣经·新约》(《约翰福音》),圣灵曾化为鸽子降落在耶稣身上,因此斯蒂汾有可能借此影射圣灵。按《新约》记载,圣母玛利亚是由圣灵受孕而生耶稣的。

③ 花梨木和沾湿的灰烬等都是小说第一章中提到的。斯蒂汾的母亲临死时要求他跪下为她祈祷,他没有照办。此后与他同住的马利根据姑母的谴责,说他害死了母亲,他也经常感到良心受谴责。他梦见母亲时,闻到她身上有蜡和花梨木的气息,嘴里有沾湿的灰烬味。

还没有怎么生活就与世长辞了。一个可怜的灵魂升了天;而在闪烁不已的繁星底下,在一块荒地上,一只皮毛带着劫掠者的红色腥臭的狐狸,眼中放射出残忍的凶光,用爪子刨着地,听着,刨起了泥土,刨了又听,听了又刨。

斯蒂汾坐在孩子旁边解题。他用代数证明莎士比亚的阴魂是哈姆雷特的祖父①。萨金特歪戴着眼镜,斜眼瞅着他。贮藏室里有球棍的磕碰声,球场上传来了发闷的击球声和喊叫声。

抄本页面上的代数符号在演出一场字母的哑剧,它们头上戴着平方形、立方形的古怪帽子,来回地跳着庄严的摩利斯舞②。拉手,交换位置,相对鞠躬。就是这样:摩尔人的幻想的产物。阿威罗伊、摩西·迈蒙尼德③也都已经不在人间,这些在容貌举止上都是深沉的人,用他们的嘲弄的明镜对准世界,照出它那隐蔽的灵魂。这是一种在明亮之中闪光而又不为明亮所理解的深沉。

"现在懂了吗?第二道自己会做了吧?"

"会了,老师。"

萨金特用长大而颤巍巍的笔划抄录着数字。他一面不断地期待着老师开口指点,一面忠实地临摹那些多变的符号,他那灰暗的皮肤下隐隐地闪烁着羞愧的色调。**母亲之爱**:主生格和宾生格④。她用自己的孱弱的血液和清淡发酸的奶汁喂养了他,并且把他的褴褛布藏在人们看

---

① 斯蒂汾有一套关于莎士比亚的理论,在小说第九章中,他向一些朋友发表他的观点,其中涉及莎士比亚和哈姆雷特及其父亲的阴魂之间究竟是什么关系。在第一章中,马利根讽刺他是用代数证明这些关系的。

② 摩利斯舞是一种禳灾祈福的舞蹈。"摩利斯"一词来自"摩尔人";摩尔人是非洲西北部柏柏尔人与阿拉伯人混合的一个民族,在公元八世纪入侵西班牙,代数也是经摩尔人传入欧洲的。

③ 阿威罗伊是十二世纪的阿拉伯哲学家、医学家,摩西·迈蒙尼德是十二至十三世纪的犹太哲学家、医学家,二人对亚里士多德哲学思想有深入研究,对中世纪西方思想界产生了重大的影响。

④ "母亲之爱",原文为拉西文,按主生格讲是"母爱",按宾生格讲是"对母亲的爱"。

不见的地方。

　　有些象他,我这个人;也是这么瘦削的肩膀,也是这么叫人看不上眼。在我旁边弯着腰的就是我的童年。太遥远了,想用手摸一下或是轻轻碰一下都够不着。我的是远了,而他的呢,象我们的眼睛一样深奥莫测。我们两人心灵深处的黑殿里,都盘踞着沉默不语、纹丝不动的秘密,这些秘密已经倦于自己的专横统治,是情愿被人赶下台去的暴君。
　　题做好了。
　　"很简单,"斯蒂汾说,同时站起身来。
　　"是的,老师,谢谢您,"萨金特回答说。
　　他用一张薄薄的吸墨纸把本上的墨水吸干,拿着抄本走回自己的座位。
　　"快去拿上球棍,出去找同学们吧,"斯蒂汾一边说,一边跟着孩子的笨头笨脑的背影向门口走去。
　　"是,老师。"
　　在走廊里,听到了球场那边喊他名字的声音。
　　"萨金特!"
　　"快跑,"斯蒂汾说。"戴汐先生在喊你了。"
　　他站在门廊里,望着笨学生急急忙忙奔向争夺场,场上这时只听见一片尖着嗓子吵闹的声音。孩子们分好了拨儿,戴汐先生迈着戴鞋罩的脚,跨过一簇簇的草丛走过来。他刚走到房前,吵吵嚷嚷的声音又在喊他了。他扭回了怒气冲冲的白色八字胡。
　　"又怎么啦?"他反复地大声喊着,也不听人家究竟在说什么。
　　"先生,科克兰和哈利戴分在一边了,"斯蒂汾提高嗓门说。
　　"请你在我书房里等一下,"戴汐先生说,"我把这里的秩序整顿好就来。"
　　于是,他又大惊小怪地回头向球场走去,一面扯着苍老的嗓子厉声喊道:
　　"怎么回事?又是怎么回事了?"
　　孩子们的尖嗓子从四面八方冲着他叫嚷:他们蜂拥而上,把他团团围住,他那没有染好的蜜色头发,被耀眼的阳光漂成了白色。

书房里空气陈浊,烟雾腾腾,室内摆着的那些黄褐色皮椅,发出一种磨损了的皮革的气味。第一天他在这里和我讨价还价时,就是这个样子。起始如此,现在仍是如此。墙边柜子上摆着那盘斯图亚特钱币,泥沼里的等外宝物①:永将如此。在褪了色的紫红丝绒的餐匙盒里,舒舒服服地卧着曾向一切非犹太人布道的十二使徒②:无究无尽③。

门外传来一阵急促的脚步声,走过门廊的石板地,进了走廊。戴汐先生吹着稀疏的八字胡子,走到大桌子边才站住。

"首先,咱们小小的财务结算,"他说。

他从上衣口袋里,掏出一个用细皮条扎住的皮夹,啪的一声打开,取出两张钞票,其中一张还是由两个半张拼接起来的,小心翼翼地摊在桌子上。

"两镑,"他说着,又把皮夹扎好,收了起来。

现在他该动他的金库了。斯蒂汾的不好意思的手,轻抚着堆在冷冷的石钵里的各式各样贝壳:峨螺、子安贝、花豹贝:这个旋涡形的象埃米尔的头巾,这个扇形的是圣詹姆斯扇贝④。老朝圣者的宝藏,死的珍宝,空壳。

在台面呢的柔软绒面上,落下一枚崭新的金镑,亮晶晶的。

"三镑,"戴汐先生转动着手里的小小储蓄盒说。"这种东西,有一个真方便。瞧,这是放金镑的,这是放先令的。放六便士的,放半克朗的。

---

① 斯图亚特是英国王室,1603—1714年间统治英国。其中的詹姆斯二世于1688年后在英国被黜后逃到爱尔兰,次年用劣金属铸币,使爱尔兰币大为贬值,但是这些不值钱的硬币后来成为稀有物品,有人加以收藏。

② 十二使徒指匙柄上的人像。据《新约》说,耶稣原来要求他的使徒们只向犹太人传教,但后来使徒们根据彼得直接从上帝获得的启示,决定也向非犹太人展开传教活动。

③ "起始如此……无究无尽,"这些散在本段各处的词句出于天主教礼拜仪式中诵唱的《小荣耀颂》:"荣耀归于圣父、圣子、圣灵;起始如此,现在仍是如此,永将如此,无究无尽。"

④ 圣詹姆斯神祠在西班牙,是中世纪欧洲朝圣胜地之一。该祠采用扇贝作为标志,朝圣者佩戴以为纪念。另外,贝壳也象征金钱。

第一篇 《尤利西斯》Ulysses

这里是放克朗①的。瞧。"

他从盒子里倒出两个克朗,两个先令。

"三镑十二先令,"他说。"你看一看,我想没有错。"

"谢谢您,先生,"斯蒂汾说着,腼腆地急忙把钱敛成一堆,一古脑儿塞进了裤子袋里。

"根本不要谢,"戴汐先生说。"这是你应得的报酬。"

斯蒂汾的手又自由了,又去摸那些空壳。也是美的象征和权力的象征。我口袋里有了一小把:被贪婪和苦难玷污了的象征。

"钱不能这样装,"戴汐先生说。"不定在哪儿掏东西带出来,就丢了。你买上这样一个机器好。你会觉得非常方便的。"

得回答点什么。

"我要是有一个,那也常常是空的,"斯蒂汾说。

同一间房间,同一个时辰,同样的智慧:我也还是我。已经三次了。我身上已经在这里套上了三道箍,怎么样?我可以立刻把它们挣断,如果我愿意的话。

"这是因为你不存钱,"戴汐先生伸手指着他说。"你还不懂得金钱的意义。钱就是权。将来你活到我这个年龄就明白了。我是懂的,我是懂的。少壮不晓事嘛。但是,莎士比亚是怎么说来着?'只消荷包里放着钱。'"②

"伊阿古③,"斯蒂汾自言自语地说。

他把视线从静止不动的贝壳上,移向老人那双盯着他的眼睛。

"他懂得金钱的意义④,"戴汐先生说。'他会赚钱。不错,是一个诗

---

① 克朗、先令都是英国当时通用的钱币,按当时英国币制,一镑合二十先令,一先令合十二便士。克朗是一种值五先令的银币。
② "少壮不晓事"是一个谚语的开端,谚语劝人从早积攒,以免老来匮乏。
③ 伊阿古是莎士比亚悲剧《奥赛罗》中的反面人物。"只消荷包里放着钱"是他教唆别人干坏事时说的,见该剧第一幕第三场。戴汐引用这话,显然文不对题。
④ "他"指莎士比亚。

人,可也是一个英国人。你知道什么是英国人的骄傲吗?你知道你能从英国人嘴里听到的最自豪的话是什么话吗?"

海洋的统治者。他那冷如海水的眼睛眺望着空荡荡的海湾:似乎要怪历史;也用同样的目光看待我和我说的话,倒是心平气和的。①

"认为自己的帝国有永远不落的太阳,"斯蒂汾说。

"才不是呢!"戴汐先生大声嚷道。"那不是英国人的话:是一个法国的凯尔特人说的。"②

他用储蓄盒轻轻地敲打着大拇指的指甲盖。

"我来告诉你他们最爱吹嘘什么吧,"他庄严地说,"'我不该不欠。'"

好人,好人。

"'我不该不欠。我一辈子没有借过一个先令的债。'你能有这样的感觉吗?'无债一身轻'。你能吗?"

马利根,九镑,三双短袜,一双粗皮鞋,几根领带。柯伦,十个几尼③。麦卡恩,一个几尼。弗雷德·赖恩,两先令。坦普尔,两顿午饭。拉塞尔,一个几尼;卡曾士,十先令;波勃·雷诺兹,半个几尼;凯勒,三个几尼;麦克南太太,五个星期的饭钱。我这一小把不顶事。

"眼下还不能,"斯蒂汾回答说。

戴汐先生笑了,流露出富足快乐的心情。他把储蓄盒放了回去。

"我知道你不能,"他兴高采烈地说。"但是将来你必须有这种感觉才行。我们是一个慷慨的民族,但我们也必须公正。"

"我怕这些堂皇的字眼,"斯蒂汾说,"这些话给我们造成了那么多的不幸。"

---

① 斯蒂汾想到了早上与英国人海恩斯谈话的情景。

② "日不没国"是一种夸耀帝国幅员的说法,从纪元前五世纪的波斯帝国以来的各大帝国时期都有,说法大同小异,但是据考证没有一个说法是"法国的凯尔特人"提出来的。戴汐先生喜欢引经据典,但往往不符历史事实。

③ 几尼是英国旧金币,一几尼合二十一先令。

第一篇 《尤利西斯》Ulysses

戴汐先生有好一会儿神情严肃地瞪着壁炉上方，看着墙上那位穿苏格兰花格短裙、身材魁伟、气宇轩昂的男人：威尔士亲王艾伯特·爱德华①。

"你认为我是一个老顽固，老保守党，"他的若有所思的声音说。"从奥康内尔②时期以来，我亲眼目睹了三代人的历史。我记得四六年的大饥荒③。你知道吗，奥伦治协会④早就鼓动废除联合议会了，比奥康内尔的鼓动，比你们教派的高级教士们把他斥为政客⑤还早二十年呢！你们芬尼亚分子⑥对有些事情是记不住的。"

---

① 艾伯特·爱德华(1841—1910)在维多利亚女王时期是威尔士亲王，英国王储，在小说涉及的1904年，他已经成为英王爱德华七世。

② 奥康内尔(1775—1847)是著名的爱尔兰民族运动领袖，因发动信奉天主教的广大人民群众争取爱尔兰天主教合法地位而被爱尔兰人称为"救星"（除北爱尔兰情况特殊外，绝大多数爱尔兰人信奉天主教）。政治上他主张废除英、爱联合议会，建立独立的爱尔兰议会。

③ 从1845年起，爱尔兰的土豆生产连年遭灾，而土豆是当时爱尔兰劳动人民的主食，因此造成1846—1847年的大饥荒，饿殍遍野，瘟疫流行。这是爱尔兰历史上一次极大的灾难，人口因而锐减。

④ 奥伦治协会是十八世纪末年由英国殖民者在爱尔兰北部建立的宗教、政治团体，主要宗旨是维护在北爱尔兰占优势的新教的利益，反对天主教势力，并反对脱离英国。据考证，该协会在最初成立时，确曾反对将爱尔兰议会并入英国议会。但是当时的爱尔兰议会完全由信仰新教的英国殖民者把持，所以他们那时反对联合议会，和后来爱尔兰人民废除联合议会的要求（即作为一种争取民族解放的民权运动）显然意义完全不同，戴汐先生把两事相提并论，反映了他自己性格上的特点。

⑤ 爱尔兰的天主教主教都支持奥康内尔，虽有少数对他的方法有意见，但并没有人把他"斥为政客"。

⑥ "芬尼亚运动"是一个爱尔兰民族主义组织，主张通过武装暴动脱离英国。该组织成立于1858年，最活跃的时期是十九世纪六十年代，至七十年代后逐渐消亡。斯蒂汾当然不可能是这一组织的成员。

第一篇 《尤利西斯》Ulysses

光荣的、虔诚的、不朽的纪念①。光辉的阿尔马郡的钻石会厅里,悬挂着天主教徒的尸体②。嘶哑着嗓子、戴着假面具、拿着武器,殖民者的誓约③。黑色的北方,真正地道的《圣经》④。推平头的倒下去⑤。

斯蒂汾做了一个简短概括的手势。

"我身上也有反叛者的血液,"戴汐先生说。"母系的。但是我的祖先是投票赞成联合议会⑥的约翰·布莱克伍德爵士。我们全是爱尔兰人,全是国王的后代。"

"够呛,"斯蒂汾说。

"走直路⑦,"戴汐先生神情坚决地说,"这就是他的格言。他投的是

---

① 引自奥伦治协会纪念英王威廉三世的祝酒辞:"纪念伟大光荣、虔诚、不朽的好国王威廉三世,他拯救了我们……"该协会以威廉三世为号召,因为英帝国征服爱尔兰的殖民事业是在他任英国国王期间(1689—1702)完成的。此人在继承英国王位之前是奥伦治亲王,被称为"奥伦治的威廉"。
② 阿尔马郡在爱尔兰北部,这一带的英国殖民者曾在十八世纪大举迫害天主教徒,企图把他们全部逐出该郡。最严重的一项事件是1795年的"钻石之战",他们屠杀了拒绝外迁的天主教徒二三十人,奥伦治协会即在这一事件之后建立。
③ 从十七世纪初开始,英国将爱尔兰北部大批土地没收,赐给英国殖民者,接受者必须宣誓忠于英王。
④ 新教牧师布道时均穿黑袍。新教强调《圣经》本身的重要性,这是和强调仪式的天主教的主要区别之一。
⑤ "推平头的"指爱尔兰民族主义者,他们在1798年起义时曾推平头以示向往法国革命。"推平头的倒下去"是奥伦治派反对爱尔兰独立的歌曲词句。
⑥ 指1800年5月爱尔兰议会表决是否并入英国议会一事。当时即便在由英国殖民者把持的议会中,反对联合的力量也是十分强大的,英国用了公开贿买和封官许愿的手段才使议案通过。戴汐所说的爵士在历史上确有其人,是联合以前的爱尔兰议员,但是事实上他坚决反对联合,见下页注①。
⑦ 原文系拉丁文。

赞成票,并且特地穿上他的长统马靴,从当郡的阿兹骑马到都柏林来投票的①。"

　　啦尔—德—啦尔—德—啦
　　崎岖的道路通向都柏林哪。

一个脾气暴躁的绅士,骑着马,穿着贼亮的长统马靴。有点小雨啊,约翰爵士。有点小雨,阁下……小雨!……小雨!……两只长统靴颠呀颠的,一直颠到都柏林。啦尔—德—啦尔—德—啦,啦尔—德—啦尔—德—啦底。

"这倒提醒了我,"戴汐先生说。"有一件事可以请你帮帮忙,代达勒斯先生。请你找几个你在文学界的朋友。我这里有一封给报界的信。你坐一下。我把结尾的一段打完就行了。"

他走到窗边的书桌前,把椅子往前拖了两下,望着打字机滚筒上的信纸念了几个字。

"坐下吧。对不起,"他转过头来说,"'事属常识,无可非议。'一会儿就完。"

他挑起两道粗眉,盯着放在肘边的原稿,一面嘟嘟囔囔地念着,一面开始慢慢地戳打字机上的僵硬的钢键,有时又转动滚筒,用橡皮擦掉打错的字,吹两口气。

斯蒂汾面对着仪表堂堂的亲王像,无声无息地坐了下来。四周墙上的画框里,恭恭敬敬地站着如今已经不复存在的骏马的形象,马头全都顺从地扬在空中:黑斯廷斯勋爵的"御敌"、威斯敏斯特公爵的"飞越"、

---

① 阿兹是爱尔兰北部当郡地区的一个半岛,当郡是英国在爱尔兰的殖民中心之一,历史上的约翰·布莱克伍德是该郡的议员之一,在酝酿联合议会时英国许他晋升爵位,要他投票赞成联合,但他拒不接受。他家的一个后代曾在致乔伊斯的信中提到此事说:"请记住,约翰·布莱克伍德是在正要穿上他的长统马靴到都伯林去投反对票时死去的。"

博福特公爵的"锡兰",1866年巴黎大奖①。骏马上骑着小精灵似的骑手,静候着信号。他看到了他们为国王的旗号赛跑的速度,随着不复存在的观众的欢呼声而欢呼。

"句号,"戴汐先生吩咐他的字键说。"'然而,及时公开讨论这一极其重要的问题……'"

克兰利带我去找发财捷径,在溅满泥水的赛马车之间钻来钻去,寻找可能获胜的号码;赌注经纪人各占一方地盘,大声地招揽主顾;五颜六色的泥浆地上,一股强烈的食堂气味。"美叛逆!""美叛逆!"大热门,一赔一;冷门票,一赔十②。我们追随着马蹄和色彩缤纷的骑装、骑帽,匆匆路过骰子摊、扣碗摊③,还路过一个脸上肉嘟嘟的妇女,一个肉店老板娘,她正渴不及待地把嘴凑到一块橙子上去啃。

从孩子们的球场那边,传来了尖尖的喊叫声和一阵滚动的哨子声。

又进了一球。我就在他们中间,在他们挤成一团、混战一场的身体中间。这就是生活的拼搏。你是说那个妈妈的宝贝疙瘩,那个外罗圈腿的,似乎有点丝虫病的孩子吗?拼搏。时间受了惊吓,弹跳起来,一回又一回,疆场上的拼搏、泥泞和酣战声,战死者临终的呕吐物冻成了冰块,长矛矛尖勾出血淋淋的肚肠时的狂叫声。

"好了,"戴汐先生站起来说。

他一面用大头针把纸别在一起,一面向桌子边走来。斯蒂汾站了起来。

---

① "御敌"、"飞越"、"锡兰"都是曾在重要赛马中得大奖的名马。"巴黎大奖"是法国最盛大的赛马活动,每年一次,1866年的大奖即由"锡兰"获得。希腊史诗中的涅斯托耳也以爱马著称。

② "美叛逆"是一匹马的名字。该马1992年在都柏林附近的一次赛马中获胜。斯蒂汾回忆的下赌注办法正是那一次的实际情况。

③ "扣碗"是类似押宝的赌博。三个小碗倒扣在地上,猜哪一个扣着小球或豆子。

第一篇 《尤利西斯》Ulysses

"我写得很简明扼要,"戴汐先生说。"谈的是口蹄疫问题。你看一看吧。关于这个问题,人们是不可能有两种意见的。"

拟借贵报一角宝贵篇幅。自由放任原则在我国历史上曾多次。我国牧牛业。我国各项老工业之道路。利物浦集团操纵戈尔韦① 建港计划。欧洲大火。粮食运输通过海峡狭窄水道②。农业部门绝对彻底的麻木不仁。恕我引经据典。卡珊德拉③。一个不过尔尔的女流之辈④。言归正传。

"我够干脆的,是吧?"戴汐先生在斯蒂汾看信时插嘴问他。

口蹄疫。人称科克配方。血清与病毒。免疫马匹百分比。牛瘟。下奥地利慕尔斯代戈御用马群。兽医外科。亨利·布莱克伍德·普赖斯先生。自献良方颇可一试。事属常识,无可非议。极其重要的问题。确系抓住要害。承蒙慷慨提供贵报版面,谨致谢意。

"我要这封信见报,让人们都看到,"戴汐先生说。"你等着瞧吧,下次再闹牛瘟,他们就要对爱尔兰牛实行禁运了。然而这种病是可以治好的。人家实际上就治好了。我的表弟布莱克伍德·普赖斯来信说,奥地利的牛瘟,就都是由当地的牛医治疗的,并且治好了。他们主动表示愿意到这里来。我正在部里想办法。现在我要试试公开宣传。我是困难重重呵,周围尽是……阴谋诡计,尽是……后门势力,尽是……"

---

① 戈尔韦是爱尔兰西部一个大港,在十九世纪五十年代中曾有人企图把它发展成为一个国际航运中心,但开办航线后连遭事故,于六十年代以失败而告终。但据考证,此事并无"利物浦集团"插手。
② "欧洲大火"指欧洲大战,戴汐的意思大概是,如果戈尔韦建港计划没有被破坏,那么万一欧洲发生大战,粮食运输就可以不必通过爱尔兰东部易受战火威胁的海峡,而可以用直达大西洋的戈尔韦港。
③ 卡珊德拉是希腊神话中特洛伊国王的女儿,她能预言凶祸却无人听信,因此不能阻止凶祸发生。
④ "不过尔尔的女流之辈"是英国谚语用词,指水性杨花的女人。这里戴汐指的是希腊神话中的著名美女海伦,特洛伊战争由她引起。

他伸出食指,老气横秋地敲击着空气,为下边的话作准备。

"注意我的话,代达勒斯先生,"他说,"英国是落在犹太人手里了。进了所有的最高级的地方:财政界、新闻界。一个国家有了他们,准是衰败无疑。不论什么地方,只要犹太人成了群,他们就能把国家的元气吞掉。这些年来,我一直在注意,问题越来越严重。情况再明白不过了,犹太商人已经在下毒手了。古老的英国快完了。"

他快步向一边走去;在经过一束宽阔的阳光时,他的眼睛活了起来,呈现出蓝色的生命。接着他又转身走了回来。

"快完了,"他说,"如果不是已经完了的话。"

> 婊子的满街招呼
> 将织下英格兰的裹尸布①。

他走到那道阳光中间站住了,两只眼睛若有所见似的在阳光里瞪得滚圆,神色严厉。

"凡是商人,"斯蒂汾说,"不管是不是犹太人都要贱买贵卖,难道不是吗?"

"他们不光明,"戴汐先生严肃地说。"你看吧,连他们的眼睛里面都是黑的。正是因为这个缘故,他们直到今天还在地球上四处流浪。"

在巴黎证券交易所的台阶上,金色皮肤的人们伸出戴宝石戒指的手指报着行情。鹅群的嘎嘎乱叫声。他们成群结队地在圣殿里转悠②,声音嘈杂,模样古怪,脑袋上戴的是不得体的大礼帽,里面装的是密密匝匝的计谋。全不是他们的:这些衣着,这种言谈,这些手势。他们的圆圆的、迟缓的眼睛否定了这些话,这些热烈而不冒犯人的手势。他们知道周围聚集着敌意,知道自己的热忱全是白费力。白白地耐心积蓄、贮存。时间肯定会把一切都冲散。路边堆积的财货:一经劫掠,全都易手

---

① 这两行诗引自布莱克的《清白的征兆》,原诗有关段落抨击英国当时允许公开卖淫和嫖娼的制度。

② 据《圣经·新约》,耶路撒冷的圣殿里原来有许多人在做买卖和兑换银钱,后来都被耶稣赶走。

了。他们的眼睛懂得流浪的岁月;含辛茹苦的眼睛,懂得自己的骨肉所受的凌辱。

"谁不是这样的呢?斯蒂汾说。

"你是什么意思?"戴汐先生问。

他朝前跨了一步,站在桌子旁边。他的下颌歪向一边,疑惑不定地张着嘴巴。这是老年人的智慧吧?他等着听我的。

"历史,"斯蒂汾说,"是一场恶梦。我正在设法从梦里醒过来。"

球场上又传来孩子们的一阵叫喊声。滚动的哨子声:进球了。要是恶梦象劣马似的① 尥蹶子,踢你一脚呢?

"造物主的规律可由不得我们,"戴汐先生说。"人类的全部历史,都向着一个大目标走:体现上帝。"

斯蒂汾翘起大拇指,指向窗户说:

"那就是上帝。"

呼啦!啊哎!呜噜哝噫!

"什么?"戴汐先生问。

"街上的喊叫声,"斯蒂汾耸耸肩膀回答。

戴汐先生用手指捏着鼻翼,低头往下面看了一忽儿,等他再抬起头来的时候才把鼻子放开。

"我比你幸福,"他说。"我们犯过许多错误,有过许多罪孽。一个女人把罪恶带到了人间②。为了一个不过尔尔的女流之辈,就是墨涅拉俄斯的那个跟人私奔的老婆海伦,希腊人同特洛伊打了十年的仗③。一个不忠实的妻子把外人带进了我们这个岛国,那就是麦克默罗的老婆和

---

① 英语的"恶梦"(nightmare)是一个复合词。其中第二个部分(mare)与"母马"(mare)同形。

② 指《圣经·旧约》所述夏娃偷吃"善恶知识树"的禁果,导致亚当、夏娃被上帝逐出乐园,开始过劳碌辛苦的人间生活。

③ 指希腊史诗《伊利亚特》所述特洛伊王子帕里斯拐走希腊斯巴达国王墨涅拉俄斯的夫人海伦,从而引起特洛伊战争。

她的情夫,布雷夫尼的王爷奥鲁厄克①。帕内尔也是因为一个女人才倒了霉②。许多错误,许多失败,但是唯独没有那一种罪孽。我现在已经是风烛残年的人了。但是,我还要为正义而战斗到底。"

  因为厄尔斯特③ 将要战斗,
  为正义而战决不会错。

斯蒂汾举起了手里拿着的信。
"这个,先生……"他开始说。
"我可以预见,"戴汐先生说,"你在这里干不长。你天生不是当教师的材料,我觉得。也许我错了。"
"倒是当学生的,"斯蒂汾说。
那么在这里你还能学到什么呢?
戴汐先生摇摇头。
"谁知道呢?"他说。"要学,就得虚心。而生活就是伟大的教师。"
斯蒂汾又把手里的几张纸抖了抖。
"关于这封信……"他开始说。
"对,"戴汐先生说。"你手里拿的是两份。看你能不能设法让它们马上见报。"
《电讯报》,《爱尔兰家园报》。
"我去试试,"斯蒂汾说,"明天给您回音。我跟两位主编有一面之

---

① 戴汐这里所说涉及爱尔兰十二世纪的历史,但是颠倒了人物。历史事实是,爱尔兰的一个小国伦斯特的国王麦克默罗拐走另一个小国布雷夫尼的国王奥普厄克的妻子,从而引起争端。麦克默罗被逐出爱尔兰后引来英国军队,这就是英国入侵爱尔兰的开始。
② 帕内尔(1846—1891)是爱尔兰自治运动的领袖,他是新教徒,但是能得到整个民族的拥护,被称为"爱尔兰的无冕之王"。他在1889年因男女关系丑闻而失去领袖地位,爱尔兰民族运动也因此受到重大挫折。
③ 厄尔斯特即爱尔兰北部六郡的总称,这两句话出自十九世纪的一个英国政治家之口,他在竞选时煽动厄尔斯特反对爱尔兰自治的情绪说了这些话,后来成为爱尔兰北部反对爱尔兰自治、反对天主教的战斗口号。

第一篇 《尤利西斯》Ulysses

交。"

"那就行了,"戴汐先生兴致勃勃地说。"昨天晚上我已经给国会议员菲尔德先生写了信。牧牛业贸易协会今天在城标饭店开会。我请他把我的信提交给会议。你想想办法。看能不能把它弄到你那两种报纸上去。是什么报纸?"

"《电讯晚报》……"

"那就行了,"戴汐先生说。"时间要紧。现在我得给我表弟写回信了。"

"早安,先生,"斯蒂汾说着把信放进了口袋。"谢谢您。"

"不谢,"戴汐先生一面翻着书桌上的文件找东西,一面说。"我年纪虽然大了,倒还是喜欢跟你交交锋的。"

"早安,先生,"斯蒂汾又说,并对他弯着腰的背影鞠了一个躬。

他出了敞着的门廊,走上用碎石铺的林阴小路,这时又听到操场上学生们的喊叫声和球棍的噼啪声。他走出大门,门柱顶端高踞着狮子:没有牙齿而仍张牙舞爪的东西。可是我还是愿意助他一臂之力。马利根准会给我起一个新的外号:阉牛之友派诗人。

"代达勒斯先生!"

追上来了。不至于又有什么信吧,我希望。

"等一下。"

"我等着,先生,"斯蒂汾说着,在大门口转回了身。

戴汐先生站住了,大口大口地喘着气。

"我就说一句话,"他说。"爱尔兰,人们说她很光荣,是唯一的从来没有迫害过犹太人的国家。你知道吗?不知道。你知道这是为什么吗?"

他冲着明亮的空气,威严地皱着眉头。

"为什么呢,先生?"斯蒂汾问着,开始有些忍俊不禁了。

"因为爱尔兰从来没有放他们进来过①,"戴汐先生严肃地说。

---

① 事实上爱尔兰从很早的时期起就有犹太人,十三世纪也驱逐过他们,从十七世纪起又来了不少,十八十九世纪期间还有明确的立法行动帮助犹太人归化。

一团笑咳从他喉咙里蹦出来,后面喀啦啦地带着一长串痰。他迅速转过身去,咳着,笑着,同时抬起两只手在空中摇晃着。

"她从来就没有放他们进来过,"他夹着笑声,又提高嗓门重复一遍,同时还用两只戴鞋罩的脚使劲地跺着碎石路面。"就是这么一回事!"

在他富于智慧的肩膀上,太阳光透过星罗棋布的树叶,投下了许多亮晶晶的圆片,跳动着的金币。

《尤利西斯》(节选)

萧 乾 文洁若 译

二

"你说说,科克伦,是哪个城市请他① 去的?"
"塔兰图姆②,老师。"
"好极了。后来呢?"
"打了一仗,老师。"
"好极了。在哪儿?"
孩子把茫然的脸掉过去问那扇茫然的窗户。

记忆的女儿们③ 所编的寓言。然而,即便同记忆所编的寓言有出入,总有些相仿佛吧。那么,就是一句出自焦躁心情的话,是布莱克那过分之翅膀的扑扇④。我听到整个空间的毁灭,玻璃碎成碴儿,砖石建筑

---

① 指皮勒斯(公元前319—公元前272),希腊西北部伊庇鲁斯的国王。
② 塔兰图姆乃今意大利东南部城市塔兰托的旧称。公元前八世纪沦为希腊殖民地。公元前三世纪罗马军队进逼时,塔兰图姆向伊庇鲁斯求救兵。
③ "记忆的女儿们"指希腊神话里主神宙斯与摩涅莫绪涅(记忆女神)之间所生的九位缪斯(司文艺、音乐、天文等的女神)。语出英国诗人威廉·布莱克(1757—1827)的名句:"寓言或讽喻系记忆的女儿们所编。想像被灵感的女儿们所包围……"见《最后审判的景象》(1810)。
④ 这是把布莱克的《天堂与地狱的婚姻》(约1790)中的两句箴言合并而成:"过分之路导向智慧之宫"和"只要凭自己的翼,不愁鸟儿飞不高"。

坍塌下来,时光化为终极的一缕死灰色火焰。① 那样,还留给我们什么呢?

"老师,地点我忘记啦。是公元前二七九年。"

"阿斯库拉姆②,"斯蒂芬朝着载满了血腥事迹的书上那地名和年代望了一眼,说。

"是的,老师。接着他又说:'再打赢这么一场仗,我们就同归于尽啦。'③"

世人记住了此语。心灵处于麻木而宽松的境况。尸骸累累的平原,一位将军站在小山岗上,挂着矛枪,正对幕僚们训话。任何将军对任何幕僚训话,他们都洗耳恭听。

"你,阿姆斯特朗,"斯蒂芬说,"皮勒斯的结局怎么样?"

"皮勒斯的结局吗,老师?"

"我晓得,老师。问我吧,老师,"科敏说。

"等一等。阿姆斯特朗,你说说,关于皮勒斯,你知道点什么吗?"

阿姆斯特朗的书包里藏着一袋无花果夹心面包卷。他不时地把面包揉在掌心里,搓成小团儿,悄悄地咽下去。面包渣子还沾在他的嘴唇上呢。少年的呼吸发出一股甜味儿。这些阔人以长子进了海军而自豪。多基④ 的韦克街。

"皮勒斯吗,老师? 皮勒斯是栈桥⑤。"

---

① 在第三章中,描述炸监狱的场面时,也用了"玻璃碎成碴儿,砖石建筑坍塌下来"之句。见该章注[130]及有关正文。"终极的一缕死灰色火焰"出自《天堂与地狱的婚姻》。

② 阿斯库拉姆是阿斯科利·萨特里亚诺的古称,在今意大利南部。公元前二七八年,皮勒斯在此击败罗马军队。

③ 皮勒斯是在伤亡惨重的情况下,于阿斯科利·萨特里亚诺之役中取得胜利的。

④ 多基是斯蒂芬执教的学校所在地,位于都柏林郡海滨区,属旅游胜地,到处是富人的住宅及别墅。

⑤ 皮勒斯(Pyrrhus)与栈桥(pier)二字发音近似。这里,阿姆斯特朗搞错了。

第一篇 《尤利西斯》Ulysses

大家都笑了,并不快活的尖声嗤笑。阿姆斯特朗四下里打量着同学们,露出傻笑的侧影。过一会儿,他们将发觉我管教无方,也想到他们的爸爸所缴的学费,会越发放开嗓门大笑起来。

"现在告诉我,"斯蒂芬用书戳戳少年的肩头,"栈桥是什么?"

"老师,"阿姆斯特朗说,"栈桥就是伸到水里——像一座桥梁。国王镇① 栈桥,老师。"

有些人又笑了:笑得不畅快,却别有用意。坐在后排凳子上的两个在小声讲着什么。是的。他们晓得:从未学习过,一向也不是无知的。全都是这样。他怀着妒意注视着一张张的脸:伊迪丝、艾塞尔、格蒂、莉莉②。她们跟他们是一路货:呼吸也给红茶、果酱弄得甜丝丝的;扭动时,腕上的镯子也在窃笑着。

"国王镇码头,"斯蒂芬说,"是啊,一座失望之桥③。"

这句话使他们凝视着的眼神露出一片迷茫。

"老师,怎么会呢?"科敏问,"桥总是架在河上的啊。"

这可以收入海恩斯的小册子④。这里却没有一个人听得懂。今晚在豪饮和畅叙中,如簧的巧舌将刺穿罩在他思想外面的那副锃亮的铠甲。然后呢?左不过是主人邸第里的一名弄臣,既被纵容又受到轻视,博得宽厚的主人一声赞许而已。他们为什么都要扮演这一角色呢?图的并不完全是温存的爱抚。对他们来说,历史也像听腻了的故事,而他们的

---

① 国王镇(见第一章注[15])与学校所在地多基相距不远。东码头长达一英里,夏季常有乐队在此举行露天音乐会。
② 斯蒂芬教的是男校,他从班上男生的脸联想到可能与他们相好的四个女孩子的名字。
③ 皮勒斯那场以惨重伤亡换得的胜利,使斯蒂芬联想到栈桥。栈桥不能通到彼岸,所以是一座失望之桥。
④ 当天早晨即将离开圆塔时,海恩斯曾对斯蒂芬说,他想把斯蒂芬的名言警句搜集成册。见第一章。

国土是一片当铺①。

倘若皮勒斯并未在阿尔戈斯丧命于一个老太婆手下②,或是尤利乌斯·恺撒不曾被短剑刺死③呢?这些事是抹煞不了的。岁月已给它们打上了烙印,把它们束缚住,关在被它们排挤出去的无限的可能性的领域里④。但是,那些可能性既然从未实现,难道还说得上什么可能吗?抑或惟有发生了的才是可能的呢?织吧,织风者⑤。

"老师,给我们讲个故事吧。"

"老师,请讲吧。讲个鬼故事。"

"这一本从哪儿开始?"斯蒂芬打开另一本书,问道。

"莫再哭泣,"科敏说。

"那么,接着背下去,塔尔博特。"

"老师,故事呢?"

"呆会儿,"斯蒂芬说,"背下去,塔尔博特。"

一个面色黧黑的少年打开书本,麻利地将它支在用书包充当的胸墙后面。他不时地瞥着课文,急促地背诵着诗句:

　　莫再哭泣,悲痛的牧羊者,莫再哭泣,
　　你们哀悼的利西达斯不曾死去,

---

① 此语令人联想到莎士比亚的历史剧《约翰王》第3幕第4场中康斯丹丝的一句台词:"人生犹如一段重复叙述的故事那样可厌,扰乱一个倦怠者的懒洋洋的耳朵……"

② 公元前二七二年,在阿尔戈斯巷战中,皮勒斯正要杀一个敌人时,其老母从屋顶上对准骑着马的他抛下一片瓦,致使他坠马丧命。

③ 古罗马统帅尤利乌斯·恺撒(公元前100—前44)集执政官、保民官、独裁官等大权于一身,被以布鲁图和卡西乌为首的共和派贵族阴谋刺死。

④ 古希腊哲学家亚理斯多德(公元前384—前322)在《形而上学》中提出,事情发生之前,有多种可能性;一旦其中一种成为事实之后,其他可能性便统统被排除掉了。

⑤ 织风者,参看第一章注[118]。

第一篇 《尤利西斯》Ulysses

虽然他已沉入水里……①

说来那肯定是一种运动了,可能性由于有可能而变为现实②。在急促而咬字不清的朗诵声中,亚理斯多德的名字浮现出来,飘进圣热内维艾芙图书馆那恬然幽静、孜孜不倦的气氛中;他曾一夜一夜地隐退在此研读③,从而躲开了巴黎的诱惑。邻座上,一位纤弱的暹罗人正在那里展卷精读一部兵法手册。我周围的那些头脑已经塞满了,还在继续填塞着。头顶上是小铁栅围起的白炽灯,触须般的灯丝微微颤动着。在我心灵的幽暗处,却是下层世界的一个懒货,畏首畏尾,惧怕光明,蠕动着那像龙鳞般的褶皱④。思维乃是有关思维的思维⑤。静穆的光明。就某种意义上而言,灵魂是全部存在:灵魂乃是形态的形态⑥。突兀、浩瀚、炽烈的静穆:形态的形态。

塔尔博特反复背诵着同一诗句:

借着在海浪上行走的主那亲切法力,⑦
借着在海浪上……

"翻过去吧。"斯蒂芬沉静地说,"我什么也没看着。"

---

① 出自英国诗人弥尔顿(1608—1674)为悼念一六三七年八月十日溺死于爱尔兰海的友人爱德华·金而作的《利西达斯》(1638)一诗。
② 亚理斯多德在《物理学》中指出,潜在可能性变为现实的过程即是运动。
③ 圣热内维艾芙(约422—约500)是巴黎的女主保圣人。这座图书馆即以她的名字命名。乔伊斯本人在巴黎时常来此阅读。下文中的暹罗是泰国旧称。
④ 布莱克在《天堂与地狱的婚姻》中写道:"我在地狱的一家印刷厂里看见知识怎样一代代地传播。第一车间有个龙人在清除洞口的垃圾;里面,一批龙在挖洞。"
⑤ 亚理斯多德在《形而上学》中提出了"主导力是有关思维本身的思维"的论断。
⑥ 参看亚理斯多德的《论灵魂》:"正如手是工具的工具,头脑乃是形态的形态。"头脑即指灵魂。意思是:一切事物都须通过头脑的活动来认识。
⑦ 见《马太福音》第14章第25节:"耶稣在海面上走,往门徒那里去。"

第一篇 《尤利西斯》Ulysses

"老师,您说什么?"塔尔博特向前探探身子,直爽地问道。

他用手翻了一页,想起来了。于是,他挺直了身子背诵下去。关于"在海浪上行走的主"。他的影子也投射到这些怯懦的心灵上,在嘲笑者和心坎和嘴唇上,也在我的心坎和嘴唇上。还投射到拿一枚上税的钱币给他看的那些人殷切的面容上。"属于恺撒的归给恺撒,属于天主的归给天主。"① 深色的眸子长久地凝视着,一个谜语般的句子,在教会的织布机上不停地织了下去。就是这样。

  让我猜,让我猜,嗨哟嗨。
  我爸爸,给种籽,叫我播。②

塔尔博特阖上书,悄悄地把它塞进书包。
"都背完了吗?"斯蒂芬问。
"老师,背完了。老师,十点钟该打曲棍球啦。"
"老师,这是星期四。只上半天儿课。"
"谁会破谜语?"斯蒂芬问。

他们把铅笔弄得咯吱咯吱响,纸页窸窸窣窣,将书胡乱塞进书包。你拥我挤,勒上书包的皮带,扣紧了,一起欢天喜地地吵吵嚷嚷起来:
"破谜语吗,老师?让我破吧,老师!"
"噢,让我破吧,老师。"
"出个难的,老师。"
是这么个谜儿,"斯蒂芬说。

  公鸡叫,
  天色蓝。
  天堂钟声响,

---

① 据《马太福音》第 22 章第 15 至 21 节,法利赛人想用耶稣的话陷害耶稣,便问他可否纳税给恺撒。耶稣问:上税的钱币上的像和号是谁的?人们答以是恺撒的。耶稣便说了这句话。

② 这是一个谜语的前半段,后半段是:"黑黑的籽儿,白白的地儿。/这谜语,你能破,我就给你喝。"(谜底:写信。)

第一篇 《尤利西斯》Ulysses

> 整整十一点。
> 可怜的灵魂,
> 该升天堂啦。①

"你们猜猜看。"
"您说什么来着,老师?"
"再说一遍,老师,我们没听清楚。"
重复这些词句时,他们的眼睛越睁越大了。沉默半晌后,科克伦说:
"是什么呀,老师?我们猜不着。"
斯蒂芬回答时,嗓子直发痒:
"是狐狸在冬青树下埋葬它的奶奶②。"

他站起来,神经质地大笑了一声,而学生们的反响则是一片扫兴的喊叫。

有人用棍子在门上敲了敲,并在走廊里嚷着:
"打曲棍球去!"

他们忽啦一下散开来,有的侧身从凳子前挤出去,有的从桌面上一跃而过,很快就消失了踪影。接着,从堆房传来棍子的碰击声、皮靴的橐橐声和叽叽呱呱的交谈。

萨金特独自留了下来。他慢慢腾腾地走过来,拿出一本摊开的练习本。他那浓密的头发和瘦削的脖颈都说明他的笨拙。透过模糊不清的镜片,他翻起一双迟钝的眼睛,央求着。他那灰暗而毫无血色的脸蛋儿上,沾了块淡淡的枣子形墨水渍。刚刚抹上去,还湿润得像蜗牛窝似的。

他递过练习本来。头一行标着"算术"字样。下面是歪歪拧拧的数字,末尾是弯弯曲曲的签名。带圈儿的笔划填得满满当当,另外还涂了些墨水渍。西里尔·萨金特:姓名和印记。

---

① ② 这个谜语见 P.W. 乔伊斯著《我们今日在爱尔兰所说的英语》一书。斯蒂芬把词句改得简练了,而且因对其亡母有着负疚感,故把原谜底中的"母亲"改为"奶奶"。原来的谜语和谜底是:"我猜谜,猜个准儿:/昨晚我看见了啥?/风儿刮,/公鸡叫。/天堂钟声响,/整整十一点。/我可怜的灵魂,/该升天堂啦。"(谜底:狐狸在冬青树下埋葬它的母亲。)

"老师,迪希先生叫我整个儿重写一遍,"他说,"还要拿给您看。"斯蒂芬摸了一下本子的边儿。感到真是徒然。

"你现在会做了吗?"他问。

"十一题到十五题,"萨金特回答说。"老师,迪希先生要我从黑板上抄下来的。"

"你自己会做了吗?"斯蒂芬问。

"老师,不会。"

长得丑,而且没出息:细细的脖颈,密密匝匝的头发,一抹墨水渍,蜗牛窝。但是,居然还有人疼爱过他,搂在怀里,疼在心上。倘非有她,在这谁也不让谁的世间,他早就被脚踩得烂成一摊无骨的蜗牛浆了。她爱的是从她自己身上流进去的他那虚弱稀薄的血液。那么,那是真实的喽?是人生唯一靠得住的喽?①暴躁的高隆班②凭着一股神圣的激情,曾迈过他母亲那横卧的身躯。如今她已经不在人间了:一根在火中燃烧过的小树枝留下的颤巍巍的残骸,散发着黄檀和湿灰气味。她拯救了他,使他免于被践踏在脚下,而她自己却没活多久就溘然长逝了。一副可怜的灵魂升了天堂:星光闪烁下,在石楠丛生的荒野上,一只皮毛上还沾着猎物那血红腥臭的狐狸,一双残酷的眼睛贼亮贼亮的,用爪子刨地,听了听,且刨且听,刨啊,刨啊。

斯蒂芬挨着他坐下来解题。他用代数运算出莎士比亚的亡灵是哈

---

① 在《一个艺术家年轻时的写照》第5章的末尾,克兰利曾对斯蒂芬说:"在这个臭狗屎堆的世界上,你可以说任何东西都靠不住,但母亲的爱可是个例外。……她的感觉至少是真实的。"

② 高隆班(约543—615),爱尔兰人,凯尔特族基督教传教士。他不畏迫害,辗转在欧洲各地传教。他生性暴躁,在瑞士传教时曾放火焚烧过异教的教堂。死后被教皇封为圣徒。为了阻止他外出传教,他母亲曾横卧在家门口。

姆莱特的祖父①。萨金特透过歪戴着的眼镜斜睨着他。堆房里有球棍的碰撞声;操场上传来了钝重的击球声和喊叫声。

这些符号戴着平方形、立方形的奇妙帽子在纸页上表演着字母的哑剧,来回跳着庄重的摩利斯舞②。手牵手,旋转,向舞伴鞠躬。就是这样;都是出自摩尔人的离奇幻想。阿威罗伊和摩西·迈蒙尼德③也都离开了人世。这些在外表和行踪上都诡秘莫测的人,用他们那嘲讽的镜子④照着朦朦胧胧的世界之灵⑤。黑暗在光中照耀,而光却不能理解它。⑥

"这会子你明白了吧?第二道自己会做了吗?"

① 在第一章中,勃克·穆利根曾对海恩斯说,斯蒂芬用代数运算出了莎士比亚与哈姆莱特及其父王亡灵的关系。现在斯蒂芬想起了穆利根这番话,然而这里的词句与前文略有出入。
② 摩里斯一词源于摩里斯科,意为"摩尔人的"。摩尔人是在非洲西北部定居下来的西班牙、阿拉伯及柏柏尔人的混血后代。
③ 中世纪西欧人将阿拉伯哲学家伊本·路西德(1126—1198)的名字拉丁化了,称他为阿威罗伊。他属于摩尔族,是出生在伊斯兰教徒统治下的西班牙哲学家。他提出"双重真理"一说,对西欧中世纪和十六至十七世纪哲学和科学摆脱宗教束缚而获得发展,有过一定的影响。摩西·迈蒙尼德(1135—1204),出生于伊斯兰教徒统治下的西班牙的犹太族哲学家。他企图调和亚理斯多德哲学与犹太主义。主要著作有用阿拉伯文写成的《迷途指津》。十三世纪传入西欧译为拉丁文后,对经院哲学家如托马斯·阿奎那等影响甚大。
④ 阿威罗伊和迈蒙尼德被控用"巫镜"(水晶球或盛满了水、表面发光的容器)进行占卜。
⑤ "世界之灵"是意大利哲学家、数学家、天文学家乔达诺·布鲁诺(1548—1600)在《关于原因、原则和一》(1584)中使用过的词。他将亚理斯多德的二元论演绎成一元论。
⑥ 参看《约翰福音》第1章第5节:"光在黑暗中照耀,而黑暗却不能理解它。"光指耶稣(见《约翰福音》第8章第12节:"我是世界的光,跟从我的会得着生命的光……"),黑暗指世人。这里,作者把原话颠倒过来了。

"会做啦,老师。"

萨金特用长长的、颤悠悠的笔划抄写着数字。他一边不断地期待着得到指点,一边忠实地描摹着那些不规则的符号。在他那灰暗的皮肤下面,是一抹淡淡的羞愧之色,忽隐忽现。母亲之爱[①]:主生格与宾生格。她用自己那虚弱的血液和稀溜发酸的奶汁喂养他,藏起他的尿布,不让人看到。

以前我就像他:肩膀也这么瘦削,也这么不起眼。正在我旁边弯着腰的就是童年的我。离得太遥远了,已无从用手去摸一下,即使是轻轻地。我的童年相距太遥远了,而他的呢,就像我们的眼睛那样深邃。我们两人心灵的黑暗宫殿里,盘踞着缄默不语的一桩桩秘密:这些秘密对自己的专横已感到厌倦,是情愿被废黜的暴君。

题已经算出来了。

"这简单得很,"斯蒂芬边说边站起来。

"是的,老师。谢谢您啦,"萨金特回答说。

他用一张薄吸墨纸把那一页吸干,将练习本捧回到自己的座位上。

"还不如拿上你的球棍,到外面找同学去呢,"斯蒂芬边说边跟在少年粗俗的背影后走向门口。

"是的,老师。"

在走廊里就听见操场上喊着他名字的声音:

"萨金特!"

"快跑,"斯蒂芬说,"迪希先生在叫你哪。"

他站在门廊里,望着这个落伍者匆匆忙忙地奔向那正在进行着角逐的操场:场上是一片尖声呐喊。他们分好了组。迪希先生迈着戴鞋罩的脚,踏过一簇簇的草丛踱来。他刚一走到校舍前,一片嗓音就争先恐后地喊起他来了。他把怒气冲冲的白色口髭转过去。

"这回又怎么啦?"他一遍接一遍地嚷着,并不去听大家说的话。

"先生,科克伦和哈利戴分到同一组里去啦,"斯蒂芬大声说。

"请你在我的办公室等一会儿好不好,"迪希先生说,"我把这里的

---

① 原文为拉丁文。按主生格讲是"母爱",按宾生格讲是"爱母"。

秩序整顿一下就来。"

他煞有介事地折回操场，扯着苍老的嗓子严厉地嚷着：

"什么事呀？这回又怎么啦？"

学生们的尖嗓门从四面八方朝他喊来，高矮胖瘦不一的身姿把他团团包围住，刺目的阳光将他那染得不匀的淡黄色头发晒得发白了。

办公室里空气浑浊，烟雾弥漫，同几把椅子那磨损成淡褐色的皮革气味混在一起。跟第一天他和我在这里讨价还价时完全一个样。厥初如何，今兹亦然。①靠墙的餐具柜上摆着一盘斯图亚特②硬币。从泥塘里挖出来的劣等收藏品。以迄永远。③在褪了色的紫红丝绒羹匙匣里，舒适地躺着十二使徒④，他们曾向一切外邦人宣过教⑤：及世之世⑥。

沿着门廊的石板地和走廊传来一阵急促的脚步声。迪希先生吹着他那稀疏的口髭，在桌前站住了。

"头一桩，把咱们那一小笔帐结了吧，"他说。

他从上衣兜里掏出一个用皮条扎起来的皮夹子，啪的一声打开，从里面取出两张钞票。其中一张还是由两个半截儿拼接起来的，小心翼翼地摊在桌子上。

"两镑，"他说着，又把皮夹子扎上，收了起来。

现在该开保险库取金币了。斯蒂芬那双尴尬的手抚摩着堆在冰冷的石钵里的贝壳：油螺、子安贝、豹贝。这个有螺纹的像是酋长的头巾。

---

① 这里，作者把天主教《圣三光荣颂》的下半段拆开来引用了。全文是："天主父，天主子，天主圣神，我愿其获光荣。厥初如何，今兹亦然，以迄永远，及世之世，啊们。"

②③ 斯图亚特家族自一三七一年起为苏格兰王室，一六○三年起为英格兰王室。一六八五年詹姆斯二世继位，一六八八年被黜，逃到爱尔兰，次年用贱金属铸币，后成为罕见的收藏品。

④ 指刻在羹匙柄上的十二使徒的像。

⑤⑥ 据《新约·使徒行传》第 15 章第 7 节："彼得就起来，说：'诸位弟兄，你们知道：神早已在你们中间拣选了我，要我把福音的信息传给外邦人，好使他们听见而相信。'"从此，使徒们不但向犹太人，也向外邦人（即非犹太人）传教。

还有这个圣詹姆斯的扇贝①。都是昔日香客的收藏品,死去了的珍宝,空洞的贝壳。

一枚崭新的金镑,亮光闪闪,落在厚实柔软的桌布上。

"三镑,"迪希先生手里摆弄着他那只小小的攒钱盒,说,"有这么个玩艺儿可便当啦。瞧,这儿放金镑。这儿放先令。六便士的,半克朗的。这儿放克朗,瞧啊。"

他从里面倒出两克朗和两先令。

"三镑十二先令,"他说,"你点点,我想没错儿吧。"

"谢谢您啦,先生,"斯蒂芬说,他难为情地连忙把钱拢在一起,统统塞进裤兜里。

"完全不用客气,"迪希先生说,"这是你挣的嘛。"

斯蒂芬的手空下来了,又回到空洞的贝壳上去。这也是美与权力的象征。我兜里有一小簇:被贪婪和贫困所玷污了的象征。

"不要那样随身带着钱,"迪希先生说,"不定在哪儿就会掉丢了。买上这样一个机器,你会觉得方便极啦。"

回答一下吧。

"我要是有上一个,经常也只能是空着,"斯蒂芬说。

同一间房,同一时刻,同样的才智:我也是同一个我。这是第三次②了。我的脖子上套着三道绞索。唔,只要我愿意,马上就可以把它们挣断。

"因为你不攒钱,"迪希先生指着他说,"你还不懂得金钱意味着什么。金钱是权。当你活到我这把岁数的时候就懂得啦。我懂得。我懂得。倘若年轻人有经验……然而莎士比亚怎么说来着?只要把银钱放

---

① 圣詹姆斯(或圣雅各)的圣祠坐落在西班牙的康波斯贴拉。中世纪的香客到此朝圣回去时,在附近拾一枚扇贝佩带在帽子上作纪念。贝壳又是金钱的象征。

② 故事发生在这一天是六月十六日。这所私立学校每半个月发一次薪。这是斯蒂芬第三次领薪水,说明他是从五月初开始执教的。

在你的钱袋里。①

"伊阿古,"斯蒂芬喃喃地说。

他把视线从纹丝不动的贝壳移向老人那凝视着他的目光。

"他懂得金钱的价值,"迪希先生说,"他赚下了钱。是个诗人,可不,然而又是个英国人。你知道英国人以什么为自豪吗?你知道能从英国人嘴里听到的他最得意的话是什么吗?"

海洋的统治者。他那双像海水一样冰冷的眼睛眺望着空荡荡的海湾:看来这要怪历史。对我和我所说的话也投以那样的目光,倒没有厌恶的意思。

"说什么在他的帝国中,"斯蒂芬说,"太阳是永远不落的。"

"不对!"迪希先生大声说,"那不是英国人说的,而是一个法国的凯尔特族② 人说的。"

他用攒钱盒轻轻敲着大拇指的指甲。

"我告诉你吧,"他一本正经地说,"他最爱自夸的话是:我没欠过债。"

好人哪,好人。

"我没欠过债。我一辈子没该过谁一先令。你能有这种感觉吗?我什么也不欠。你能吗?"

穆利根:九镑,三双袜子,一双粗革厚底皮鞋,几条领带。柯伦:十基

---

① "倘若年轻人有经验"是意大利一句谚语的前一半。被省略的后一半是:"而老人有精力,则世上无难事。""只要把钱放在你的钱袋里"是莎士比亚的悲剧《奥瑟罗》中的坏蛋伊阿古挑唆威尼斯绅士罗德利哥为非作歹时所说的话,见第1幕第3场。迪希只是从字面上来理解此语。

② 凯尔特族是公元前一千年左右居住在欧洲莱茵、塞纳等河流域的一个部落。其后裔今散布在法国北境、爱尔兰岛、苏格兰高原、威尔士等地。凯尔特族分布的地区虽广,但从未形成一个帝国,所以也不会这样夸口。"太阳是永远不落的"一语,最早是古希腊历史学家希罗多德(约公元前484—前430/前420)说的,他指的是波斯帝国。到了近代,英帝国也曾这样自诩过。参看第十二章注[138]。

尼。麦卡恩：一基尼。弗雷德·瑞安：两先令。坦普尔：两顿午饭。拉塞尔：一基尼。卡曾斯：十先令。鲍勃·雷诺兹：半基尼。凯勒：三基尼。麦克南太太，① 五个星期的饭费。我这一小把钱可不顶用。

"现在还不能，"斯蒂芬回答说。

迪希先生把攒钱盒收了回去，畅快地笑了。

"我晓得你不能，"他开心地说，"然而有朝一日你一定体会得到。我们是个慷慨的民族，但我们也必须做到公正。"

"我怕这种冠冕堂皇的字眼儿，"斯蒂芬说，"这使我们遭到如此之不幸。"

迪希先生神情肃然地朝着壁炉上端的肖像凝视了好半晌。那是一位穿着苏格兰花格呢短裙、身材匀称魁悟的男子：威尔士亲王艾伯特·爱德华②。

"你认为我是个老古板，老保守党，"他以若有所思的嗓音说，"从打

---

① 康斯坦丁·P·柯伦和詹姆斯·H·卡曾斯分别为乔伊斯在都柏林的朋友和熟人（均见艾尔曼所著《詹姆斯·乔伊斯》第151页）。麦卡恩和坦普尔均为《一个艺术家年轻时的写照》第5章中的人物。费雷德·瑞安，参看第九章注[179]。T.G.凯勒是乔伊斯在都柏林的一个文友（同上书第164页、200页）。乔伊斯曾于一九〇四年做过麦克南太太的房客（同上书第151页）。

② 艾伯特·爱德华(1841—1910)，维多利亚女王的长子，出生一个月即被其母封为威尔士亲王。女王于一九〇一年去世后，他成为大不列颠和爱尔兰国王，即爱德华七世。

第一篇 《尤利西斯》Ulysses

奥康内尔①时期以来,我看到了三代人。我记得一八四六年的大饥荒②。你晓得吗,橙带党③分支鼓动废除联合议会要比奥康内尔这样做,以及你们教派的主教、教长们把他斥为煽动者,还早二十年呢?你们这些芬尼社社员④ 有时候是健忘的。"

---

① 丹尼尔·奥康内尔(1775—1847),十九世纪英国下院中第一位爱尔兰民族独立领袖,毕生为爱尔兰人信仰天主教的自由和废除英、爱联合议会,建立独立的爱尔兰议会而奋斗,他曾成功地在爱尔兰境内各地组织一系列群众集会,因而于一八四四年以阴谋煽动叛乱罪被捕,监禁三个月。这里,迪希却将英政府当局把他斥为"煽动者"一事说成是天主教的主教、教长们所为。

② 自一八四五年起,爱尔兰人民的主食土豆便歉收,一八四六、一八四七年间很多人死于大饥荒。

③ 橙带党(原名奥伦治党)是爱尔兰新教教徒组成的一个政治集团,旨在维护新教及其王位继承权。一七九五年,该党在爱尔兰和英国各地秘密组成分支,加强抵制爱尔兰自治法案,坚决反对地方自治。橙带党初成立时,曾反对将爱尔兰议会并入英国议会。然而那时的爱尔兰议会反正是操纵在信仰新教的英国殖民者手里的,所以他们反对联合议会,与爱尔兰人民开展的主张废除联合议会的民族主义运动,其意义迥然不同。

④ 芬尼是爱尔兰古部落名。芬尼社是由爱尔兰革命家詹姆斯·斯蒂芬斯(1825—1901)所领导的小资产阶级秘密革命组织,主张推翻英国统治,废除大地主所有制,建立共和国。该组织是一八五七年在美国成立的,不久即在爱尔兰本土展开反英活动。一八六六年十一月斯蒂芬斯因内奸告密被捕,关在都柏林的里奇蒙监狱里。不出几天,芬尼社成员就在看守女儿的协助下,把他救了出去。次年二月,偷渡到美国,被选为在美国的芬尼社领袖。美国的芬尼社社员于一八六六、一八七〇年和一八七一年三次越境至加拿大举行起义,均告流产。爱尔兰的芬尼社亦称爱尔兰共和兄弟会。这里,迪希是把芬尼社社员一词作为激进的共和党人的俗称来用的。

第一篇 《尤利西斯》Ulysses

光荣、虔诚、不朽的纪念①。在光辉的阿马镇钻石分支的会堂里,悬挂着天主教徒的尸首②,作为点缀。戴面罩、手执武器的殖民者们沙哑着嗓子宣誓③。险恶的北部,确实正统的《圣经》。打倒推平头的④。

斯蒂芬随随便便打了个简短的手势。

"我身上也有造反者的血液,"迪希先生说,"在我母亲这边。然而我又是投联合议会赞成票的约翰·布莱克伍德爵士的后裔。我们都是爱尔兰人,都是国王的子嗣⑤。"

"哎呀!"斯蒂芬说。

"他的座右铭就是走正路⑥,"迪希先生坚定地说,"他投了赞成票,

---

① 此语出自橙带党纪念英国国王威廉三世(1650—1702)的祝酒辞:"纪念伟大的好国王威廉三世,他光荣、虔诚、不朽,拯救了我们,免于受教皇制度……"威廉生在海牙,原为奥伦治亲王。一六八九年英国议会宣布信天主教的詹姆斯二世退位,威廉加冕为英格兰和苏格兰国王,并于一六九一年征服了爱尔兰。

② 钻石分支是由新教长老派信徒组成的,属于橙带党。一七九五年九月,他们在北爱尔兰阿马郡首府阿马镇,与信天主教的农民发生冲突,农民惨败,二十余人遭杀害。

③ 自十七世纪初起,英政府便没收了爱尔兰北部大批土地,凡是迁移到那里的英国殖民者,只要宣誓效忠于英王,并承认信新教的英王为宗教领袖,就能领到土地。从此,信天主教的爱尔兰当地农民便沦为佃农。

④ "打倒推平头的"一语出自橙带党反对爱尔兰独立运动的一首歌。"推平头的"指爱尔兰民族主义者。一七九八年,那些主张在爱尔兰实行共和制者,曾效仿法兰西革命者,也推成平头,故名。

⑤ 约翰·布莱克伍德(1722—1799)是爱尔兰议员。英国曾以晋升爵位为钓饵,要他投联合议会的赞成票,但他坚决抵制。后却在前往都柏林去投反对票的途中,遽然去世。其子约翰·G·布莱克伍德倒确实投了联合议会的赞成票,从而被封为达弗林爵士。这里,迪希把儿子的事写在父亲身上了。"所有的爱尔兰人都是国王的子嗣"是一句成语。

⑥ 原文是拉丁文,出自《旧约·诗篇》第25篇第8节。全句为"耶和华是善良正直的,所以他必指示罪人走正路。"

是穿上长统马靴,从当郡的阿兹①骑马到都柏林去投的。"

  吁——萧萧,吁——得得,
  一路险巇,赴都柏林。②

一个粗暴的绅士,足登锃亮的高统马靴,跨在马背上。雨天儿,约翰爵士。雨天儿,阁下!……天儿!……天儿!……一双高统马靴荡悠着,一路荡到都柏林。吁——萧萧,吁——得得。吁——萧萧,吁——得得。

"这下子我想起来啦,"迪希先生说,"你可以帮我点儿忙,迪达勒斯先生,麻烦你去找几位文友。我这里有一封信想投给报纸。请稍坐一会儿。我只要把末尾誊清一下就行了。"

他走到窗旁的写字台那儿,把椅子往前拖了两下,读了读卷在打字机滚筒上那张纸上的几个字。

"坐吧。对不起,"他转脸说,"按照常识行事。一会儿就好。"

他扬起浓眉,斜望着肘边的手稿,一面咕哝着,一面慢腾腾地去戳键盘上那僵硬的字键。时而边吹着气,边转动滚筒,擦掉错字。

斯蒂芬一声不响地坐在亲王那幅仪表堂堂的肖像前面。周围墙上的那些镜框里,毕恭毕敬地站着而今早已消逝了的一匹匹骏马的留影。它们都温顺地昂起了头:黑斯廷斯勋爵的"挫败",威斯敏斯特公爵的"跨越",波弗特公爵的"锡兰",一八六六年获巴黎奖③。小精灵般的骑手跨在马上,机警地等待着。他看到了这些佩带着英王旗色的马的速度,并随着早已消逝了的观众的欢呼而欢呼。

"句号,"迪希先生向打字机键盘发号施令,"但是,立即公开讨论这

---

① 当郡是北爱尔兰东部一郡。十七世纪有大量移民涌入。阿兹是北爱尔兰的一个区,当时即属当郡。
② 《一路险峻,赴都柏林》是一首爱尔兰歌谣,写一个穷苦的农村少年行路时受尽侮辱、遭到抢劫的经历。
③ "挫败"在英国新集市一年一度的赛马会中获一千基尼奖金(1866)。小母马"跨越"在新集市的赛马中获二千基尼奖金(1822)。"锡兰"在法国最著名的巴黎赛马中获大奖(1866)。

个最为重要的问题……"

为了及早发上一笔财,克兰利曾把我领到这里来。我们在溅满泥点子的大型四轮游览马车之间,在各据一方的赛马赌博经纪人那大声吆唤和饮食摊的强烈气味中,在色彩斑驳的烂泥上穿来穿去,寻找可能获胜的马匹。"美反叛①!""美反叛!"它是大热门,一对一;其他冷门马是十对一。② 我们跟在马蹄以及戴竞赛帽穿运动衫的骑手后边,从掷骰摊和玩杯艺③摊跟前匆匆走过,还遇上一个大胖脸的女人——肉铺的老板娘。她正饥渴地连皮啃着一掰两半的桔子,连鼻孔都扎进去了。

操场上传来少年们一片尖叫声和打嘟噜的哨子声。

又进了一球。我也是他们当中的一员,夹在那些你争我夺、混战着的身躯当中,一场生活的拼搏。你指的是那个妈妈的宠儿"外罗圈腿"吧?他好像宿酒未醒似的。拼搏啊。时间被冲撞得弹了回来,冲撞又冲撞。战场上的拼搏、泥泞和喊声。阵亡者弥留之际的呕吐物结成了冰,长矛挑起鲜血淋漓的内脏时那尖叫声。

"行啦,"迪希先生站起来说。

他踱到桌前,用大头针把打好了的信别在一起。斯蒂芬站了起来。

"我写得简单明了,"迪希先生说,"是关于口蹄疫问题。你看一下吧。大家一定都会同意的。"

可否借用贵报一点宝贵的篇幅。自由放任主义的原则在我国历史上屡见不鲜。我国的牲畜贸易。我国各项旧有工业的方针。利物浦集团巧妙地操纵了戈尔韦建港计划④。欧洲战火。粮食就可以通过海峡狭

---

① "美反叛"是一匹名马,曾在位于都柏林西南六英里的豹镇一年一度的赛马中获胜(1902)。
② 参看第十五章注[753]。
③ 杯艺是一种赌博,有三个扣着的顶针状小杯,叫观众猜测哪一只底下藏着豆子。
④ 戈尔韦是爱尔兰戈尔韦郡港市。十九世纪五十年代,一度计划把它开辟为国际航运中心,后未能实现。但这里所说此事是被利物浦集团巧妙地操纵,与史实相悖。前文中的"自由放任主义",原文为法语。

第一篇 《尤利西斯》Ulysses

窄的水路运输①。农业部完全无动于衷。恕我借用一个典故。卡桑德拉。由于一个不地道的女人的关系。② 现在言归正题。

"我够单刀直入了吧?"斯蒂芬往下读时,迪希先生问道。

口蹄疫。通称科克配方③。血清与病毒。免疫马的百分比。牛瘟。下奥地利慕尔斯泰格的御用马群。兽医外科。亨利·布莱克伍德·普赖斯④ 先生,献上处方,恭请一试。只能按照常识行事。无比重要的问题。名副其实地敢抓公牛角。⑤ 感谢贵报慨然提供的篇幅。

"我要把这封信登在报上,让大家都读到,"迪希先生说,"你看吧,下次再突然闹瘟疫,他们就会对爱尔兰牛下禁运令了。可是这病是能治好的。已经有治好的了。我的表弟布莱克伍德·普赖斯给我来信说,在奥地利,那里的兽医挂牌医治牛瘟,并且都治好了。他们表示愿意到这里来。我正在想办法对部里的人施加点影响。现在我先从宣传方面着手。困难重重啊。……各种阴谋诡计……幕后操纵,还有……"

他举起食指,老谋深算地在空中摆了几下才说下去。

"记住我的话,迪达勒斯先生,"他说,"英国已经掌握在犹太人手里了。所有高层的位置,金融界、报界都由他们把持住。这是一个国家衰

---

① 按日俄战争已于这一年(1904年)的二月八日爆发。这里指万一战争蔓延到欧洲,横渡大西洋的船只就只好不取道爱尔兰与威尔士之间的圣乔治海峡或爱尔兰与苏格兰之间的北海峡,而径直驶入戈尔韦湾了。

② 卡桑德拉是希腊神话中特洛伊最后一个国王普里阿摩斯的女儿,为阿波罗神所爱,被赐予卜吉凶的本领。但因不肯委身于阿波罗,受其诅咒,致使她的预言没人相信,因而无法避免灾祸。"不地道的女人"指的是海伦。她已嫁给斯巴达国王墨涅拉俄斯,却和普里阿摩斯王的儿子帕里斯一道私奔到特洛伊,从而引起了持续十年之久的特洛伊战争。

③ 这是德国医生、细菌学家罗勃特·科克(1843—1910)研究出来的预防炭疽病(不是口蹄疫)的配方。

④ 亨利·布莱克伍德·普赖斯是乔伊斯的朋友。关于医治在爱尔兰流行的口蹄疫问题,他曾于一九一二年和乔伊斯通过信。参看理查德·艾尔曼所著《詹姆斯·乔伊斯》(第325页)。

⑤ "敢抓公牛角"是英国谚语,意思是敢于处理棘手之事。

败的兆头。不论他们凑到哪儿,他们就把国家的元气吞掉。近年来,我一直看着事态的这种发展。犹太商人们已干起破坏勾当了,这就跟咱们站在这里一样地确凿。古老的英国快要灭亡啦。"

他疾步向一旁走去。跨过一束宽宽的日光时,两眼又恢复了生气勃勃的蓝色。他四下里打量了一下,又朝这边走来。

快要完蛋了,"他又说,"如果不是已经完蛋了的话。"

   妓女走街串巷到处高呼,
   为老英格兰织起裹尸布。①

他在那束光里停下脚步,恍惚间见到了什么似的睁大了眼睛,严峻地逼视着。

"商人嘛,"斯蒂芬说,"左不过是贱买贵卖。犹太人也罢,非犹太人也罢,都一个样儿,不是吗?"

"他们对光② 犯下了罪,"迪希先生严肃地说,"你可以从他们眼睛里看到黑暗。正因为如此,他们至今还在地球上流离失所。"

在巴黎证券交易所的台阶上,金色皮肤的人们正伸出宝石累累的手指,报着行情。嘎嘎乱叫的鹅群。他们成群结队地围着神殿③转,高声喧噪,粗鲁俗气,戴着不三不四的大礼帽,脑袋里装满了阴谋诡计。不是他们的:这些衣服,这种谈吐,这些手势。他们那睁得圆圆的滞钝的眼睛,与这些言谈,这些殷切、不冲撞人的举止相左;然而他们晓得自己周围积怨甚深,明白一腔热忱是徒然的。耐心地积累和贮藏也是白搭。时光必然使一切都一散而光。堆积在路旁的财宝:一旦遭到掠夺,就落入人家手里。他们的眼神表露出流浪的岁月;他们是如此地坚忍,了解自

---

① 出自布莱克的《清白的征兆》。原诗抨击了当时英国准许娼赌的政策。
② 这里的光即指耶稣。参看 59 页注⑥。
③ 巴黎证券交易所的建筑,是十九世纪初叶仿造罗马的韦斯巴芗神殿盖起来的。斯蒂芬所回忆的这个场面,使人联想到《马太福音》第 21 章第 12 节:"耶稣进了神殿,赶出殿里一切做买卖的人,推倒兑换银钱之人的桌子,和卖鸽子之人的凳子……"

己的肉体所遭受的凌辱。

"谁不是这样的呢?"斯蒂芬说。

"你指的是什么?"迪希先生问道。

他向前迈了一步,站在桌旁。他的下巴颏歪向一边,犹豫不定地咧着嘴。这就是老人的智慧吗? 他等着听我的呢。

"历史,"斯蒂芬说,"是我正努力从中醒过来的一场恶梦。"①

操场上,传来一片孩子们的喊叫声。一阵打嘟噜的哨子声:进球了。倘若那场恶梦像母马② 似的尥蹶子,踢你一脚呢?

"造物主的做法跟咱们不一样,"迪希先生说,"整个人类的历史都是朝着一个伟大的目标前进:神的体现。"

斯蒂芬冲着窗口翘了一下大拇指,说:

"那就是神。"

好哇! 哎呀! 呜噜噜噜!

"什么?"迪希先生问。

"街上的喊叫③,"斯蒂芬耸了耸肩头回答说。

迪希先生朝下面望去,用手指捏了捏鼻翅。他重新抬起头来,并撒开了手。

"我比你幸福,"他说,"我们曾犯过许多错误,罪孽深重。一个女人④把罪恶带到了人世间。为了一个不地道的女人——海伦,就是墨涅拉俄斯那个跟人私奔了的妻子,希腊人同特洛伊打了十年仗。一个不贞的老婆首先把陌生人带到咱们这海岸上来了——就是麦克默罗的老婆

---

① 这里套用法国印象派诗人朱尔斯·拉弗格(1860—1887)的遗作《杂记》(1903)中的书信里的句子:"历史是一场古老而变化多端的恶梦……"
② 英语中,恶梦(nightmare)由夜晚(night)和母马(mare)二词组成。当天晚上斯蒂芬借用了迪希在下面所说的"朝着一个伟大的目标前进"一语。见第十五章注[705]。
③ 这里套用《箴言》第1章第20节的"听吧,智慧在街市上呼唤,……在热闹街头喊叫"。
④ 一个女人指夏娃。

和她的姘夫布雷夫尼大公奥鲁尔克①。巴涅尔②也是由于一个女人的缘故才栽的跟头。很多错误，很多失败，然而惟独没有犯那种罪过。我已经进入暮年，却还从事着斗争。我要为正义而战斗到最后。"

　　因为阿尔斯特要战斗，
　　阿尔斯特在正义这一头。③

斯蒂芬举起手里那几页信。
"喏，先生，"他说。
"我估计，你在这里干不长，"迪希先生说，"依我看，你生来就不是当老师的材料。兴许我估计错了。"

---

① 这里，迪希把事件中的人物关系颠倒了。史实是：一一五二年，爱尔兰的小国伦斯特的麦克默罗王把另一小国布雷夫尼的大公奥鲁尔克之妻拐走（另有一种说法是二人一道私奔的），从而引起战争。麦克默罗向英国的亨利二世求援。这便是英国人侵爱尔兰的开始。

② 查理·斯图尔特·巴涅尔（1846—1891），十九世纪末爱尔兰自治运动和民族主义领袖。一八七九年任爱尔兰农民争取土地改革的土地同盟主席。土地同盟遭到镇压后，各地不断发生恐怖事件。巴涅尔很快就使民族主义运动受到严格纪律的约束。一八八二年五月，英国政治家、爱尔兰事务大臣卡文迪和次官伯克在都柏林西郊的凤凰公园散步时，被民族主义秘密团体"常胜军"成员刺杀。一八八七年四月十八日《泰晤士报》发表"巴涅尔信件"的影印图片，指控巴涅尔包庇凤凰公园暗杀案的凶手。巴涅尔立即指出这是纯属捏造的。约两年后，伪造信件者畏罪自杀，巴涅尔在英国自由党人的眼中成为英雄。这时期是他一生的顶峰。一八八九年他因与有夫之妇姘居，被其丈夫奥谢上尉控告。天主教的主教们指责他道德败坏，不宜担任领导职务。次年与奥谢夫人结婚，舆论哗然，他的事业遂前功尽弃。

③ 阿尔斯特是爱尔兰古代省份之一。一五九四至一六〇一年，这里曾发生反对伊丽莎白女王的叛乱。一六〇七年以后数千名苏格兰人移居此地。这两句话是英国政治家伦道夫·斯潘塞·丘吉尔（1849—1895）在竞选时为了煽动本地人反对爱尔兰自治而说的。后即成为爱尔兰北部反对爱尔兰自治、反对天主教的口号。

第一篇 《尤利西斯》Ulysses

"不如说是来当学生的,"斯蒂芬说。

那么,你在这儿还能学到什么呢?

迪希先生摇了摇头。

"谁知道呢?"他说,"要学习嘛,就得虚心。然而人生就是一位伟大的老师。"

斯蒂芬又沙沙地抖动着那几页信。

"至于这封信……"他开口说。

"对,"迪希先生说,"这是一式两份。你要是能马上把它们登出来就好了。"

《电讯报》,《爱尔兰家园报》①。

"我去试试看,"斯蒂芬说,"明天给您回话。我认识两位编辑,可并无深交。"

"那就好,"迪希先生爽快地说,"昨天晚上我给议会议员菲尔德先生写了封信。牲畜商协会今天在市徽饭店开会②。我托他把我的信交到会上。你看看能不能把它发表在那两家报纸上?是什么报来着?"

"《电讯晚报》……"

"那就好,"迪希先生说,"可得抓紧。现在我得回我表弟那封信了。"

"再会,先生,"斯蒂芬边说边把那几页信放进兜里,"谢谢您。"

"不客气,"迪希先生翻找着写字台上的文件,说,"我尽管上了岁数,却还爱跟你争论一番哩。"

"再会,先生,"斯蒂芬又说一遍,并朝他的驼背鞠个躬。

踱出敞开着的门廊,他沿着砂砾铺成的林荫小径走去。听到操场上的喊叫声和球棍的击打声。迈出大门的时候,雕在门柱上端的是一对蹲着的狮子:没了牙齿却还在那里耍威风。尽管如此,我还是要在斗争中

---

① 《电讯报》,即都柏林的《电讯晚报》,创刊于一七六三年。《爱尔兰家园报》是都柏林的一份周报。
② 牲畜商协会每星期四在市徽饭店开一次会。

帮他一把。穆利根会给我起个新外号：阉牛之友派"大诗人"①。

"迪达勒斯先生！"

从我背后追来了。但愿不至于又有什么信。

"等一会儿。"

"好的，先生，"斯蒂芬在大门口回过身来说。

迪希先生停下脚步。他喘得很厉害，倒吸着气。

"我只是要告诉你，"他说，"人家说，爱尔兰很光荣，是唯一从未迫害过犹太人的国家。你晓得吗？不晓得。那么，你知道是为什么吗？"

他朝着明亮的空气，神色严峻地皱起眉头。

"为什么呢，先生？"斯蒂芬说，脸上开始漾出笑容。

"因为她从来没让他们入过境②，"迪希先生郑重地说。

他的笑声中含着一团咳嗽，拖着一长串咕噜咕噜响的粘痰从他嘴里喷出来。他赶快转过身去，咳啊，笑啊，在空中挥着双臂。

"爱尔兰从来没让他们入过境，"他一边笑着一边高声叫喊，同时两只鞋上戴罩的脚踏着砂砾小径，"就是由于这个缘故。"

阳光透过棋盘格子般的叶隙，从他那睿智的肩头，撒下亮晶晶的圆片，宛如跳动着的金币。

---

① 阉牛之友派"大诗人"暗指荷马，因为在他笔下，《奥德修纪》卷12中，凡是宰食了太阳神的牛者，全都送了命。

② 这种说法与史实不符。其实早在十三世纪爱尔兰就驱逐过犹太人，十八、十九世纪还通过立法，迫使犹太人归化。

第二篇 《哈克贝利·费恩历险记》
两种中译本比较

周蓉娟

作为 19 世纪美国现实主义文学的主要奠基人之一,马克·吐温提倡而且在实践中把目光对准社会,对准人民的生活,运用大众的语言来刻画人物形象,展示社会风貌。美国文学史上,真正开始走出欧洲文学的影子,独立创始美国文学则首推马克·吐温。不仅如此,马克·吐温在语言风格方面也为美国文学的发展作出了卓越的贡献。他推崇生动活泼的人民语言,开创了美国小说口语化的先河,第一次使不规范的语言登上了大雅之堂,并对后世作家产生了巨大的影响[1]。

马克·吐温的传世之作《哈克贝利·费恩历险记》是一部用生动、地道的口语和方言描绘真实的美国的作品。它以 19 世纪中期内战前的美国南方为背景,讲述了白人小孩哈克(Huckberry Finn 的昵称)为躲避酒鬼父亲和一成不变的刻板生活而决心远离他生活的偏僻山村。黑奴吉姆(Jim)听说女主人要将他卖掉,便逃往北部去寻求自由,两人不期而遇,结伴乘木筏顺密西西比河而下,并结下了真挚、深厚的友谊。小说以两人的旅程为线索,描述了他们途中所见所闻和种种奇遇。

《哈克贝利·费恩历险记》最大的特色是语言的口语化。作者熟练、老道地驾驭美国口语和方言,栩栩如生地勾画了人物的心理和性格,塑造出了美国文学史上经久不衰的人物形象。第一人称的采用,保存了巧

---

[1] 语言学中并未有明确的"不规范英语"这一概念的界说。"不规范"只是一个相对的概念,并无地位高低之分。所谓的不规范是指其与核心英语相对,在语法、用词方面出现了变异。它往往与说话者的背景,说话场景有关,多出现于日常生活和作品中的人物对话中。

第二篇 《哈克贝利·费恩历险记》The Adventure of Huckberry Finn

妙而生动的口语特点。这一技巧的运用使该小说获得了空前的成功①。马克·吐温利用第一人称让读者通过哈克来观察美国社会。一切的人和事,心理和感情的变化都是通过孩子的一双眼睛来观察,用孩子的口吻来讲述的。哈克对自己的所见所闻发出感叹和评论,作者的幽默和嘲讽便巧妙地隐藏其后。

马克·吐温能在《哈克贝利·费恩历险记》中通篇运用好几种方言和口语,这在美国文学史上还是第一人。正如他在小说说明中提到的一样"这些不同色彩的方言不是杂乱无章,或全凭臆测写下来的,而是殚精竭力,煞费苦心的。"作家为反映社会生活,塑造人物形象,必须使用社会各阶层所使用的语言。语言风格必须和他要表达的思想相适应,与所塑造的人物相适应,以生动逼真地反映人物的个性。全文没有一句不符合哈克或吉姆身份的话。活生生的方言和土话使文中人物的形象、性格以及主人公内心细致而微妙的思想感情变化得到淋漓尽致的刻画。通篇文笔清新,文字生动活泼,给人以情趣盎然的感觉。

《哈克贝利·费恩历险记》这部文学名著目前已出了三个中文译本:张友松、张振先合译的《哈克贝利·费恩历险记》(1983),张万里译的《哈克贝利·芬历险记》(1984)和成时译的《赫克尔贝利·费恩历险记》(1989)。文学的艺术性质决定了文学作品的翻译应传神,传达原文的精神实质与风格韵味。钱钟书的"化"实际上是风格韵味传神的定义。《哈克贝利·费恩历险记》中口语化的语言,形象化的人物,风趣幽默的格调构成了该小说的主要艺术特色。再现典型环境中的典型人物是文艺创作中一个十分重要的问题。作者根据自己的创作意图,赋予人物一定的身份、背景以及相关语言特色,从而形成人物特有的个性和言语风格。汉译这样一部作品,能否保持原作的神韵、意境和人物形象,关键便在于其风格主体——语言风格的传译:如何才能传神,传达原文的形象

---

① 在文学作品中,作者会采用不同的叙事人称,恰当地变换叙述角度(point of view)。采用第一称,作者以一个主要或次要人物出现,这样可以缩短作者和读者之间的距离,容易引起共鸣,且能使笔调轻松活泼,语言生动。

第二篇 《哈克贝利·费恩历险记》The Adventure of Huckberry Finn

化、艺术化和个性化语言,再现书中人物的音容笑貌。本文拟从语言风格的角度,通过比较张万里的译本(以下简称张译)和成时的译本(以下简称成译)对某些段落和句子的处理及其效果,来领略原作的美妙之处并探讨语言风格的再现问题。

人物语言的运用贵在得体。不同年龄、性格、地位和背景的人说话不可能是一样的。语如其人,人物形象才能生动、丰满。说话人的身份、地位、年龄等个人因素以及交际背景会对语言运用产生极大的制约作用,从而产生"语言变体",这种变体可反映在词汇、语法、语音等方面[①]。作者正是通过各种变体来刻画人物形象,形成独特风格的。语言变体具体表现为不同的语言形式,而它们正是风格形成的物质要素。语言形式不是创作的目的而是手段,它反映和体现了人物形象与社会现实。傅雷说过,"翻译所求的不在形似而在神似","要得其精而忘其粗,在其内而忘其外"(罗新璋,1984:558—559)[②]。艺术真实在原作中是以一定的语言形式固定下来的。译者应"从原作艺术意境出发,考虑原作语言形式,在译文语言中重新找到完美的语言形式,所得到的则是原文的韵味和精神——这就是神似"(张今,1998:42)[③]。因此,在传达原作人物语言风格时,译者应通过风格的载体——语言形式领略到原语言风格及其所要刻画的人物形象和体现的艺术意境。以原作的艺术意境为出发点,力求在译语中找到可以再现这种意境的最好形式,而不受原文词语或结构形式的束缚。忠实于原作者用原语言形式所创造的形象为限度,充分发挥译语优势,以做到"神似",便是再现马克·吐温这部名著语言风格的关键。

《哈克贝利·费恩历险记》是以一个小孩的口吻来叙述的。哈克的年龄、生活环境以及所受教育程度使得他的语言出现了不规范的口语,所用的词汇及句式简单、朴素。全书语言风格便具有非正式性和随意

[①] 语言在运用中,由于各种社会因素而产生变异,形成各种变体,可在语音、词汇、语法及修辞等方面体现出来。

[②] 转引自罗新璋《翻译论集》,1984年,第558—559页。

[③] 见张今:《文学翻译原理》,1987年,第42页。

性,译者应在整体把握语言风格的基础上,利用汉语的优势,灵活、充分地传达出原文的语体风格,尽量使译文与原文"雅俗如之,深浅如之,口气如之,文体如之"(王佐良,1987)[①]。张译和成译都能较好地抓住哈克语言的特色,在译文中尽量再现原文的口语化特点。两译本各有其译得精妙传神之处,但总的来说,张译倾向于忠实于原文的结构,而成译则根据汉语重意和的特点,抓住原文句子的精神,灵活变化语序,并充分利用汉语丰富的词汇,尤其是语气助词和副词,补足语气,力求全文口语化,且符合一个天真小孩的口吻。

原文语言的另一特点是黑人语言的运用。黑人语言是一种特殊的社会方言,在美国语言系统和社会系统中有其特殊的地位。黑人语言在语法和发音上都具有不规范性,这种不规范性在文学作品中通过拼写的不规范反映出来,成为黑人语言的一种形式标志。而在汉语中并不存在相对应的一种社会方言或带有社会阶层性的语言变体,这便给翻译带来了很大的困难。张译采用普通话来译黑人语言,译文流畅,但另一方面却抹杀了吉姆所操的黑人语言的特色,进而影响了人物形象的再现。成译则意识到这一点,采用了汉语中的近音词来代替原词,以标识吉姆发音的不标准。这是对方言翻译的可喜的尝试,取得了一定的效果。但成译并非无缺憾之处,用近音词或别字来译原文以标记不规范语言,影响了译文的可读性,并可能产生原文所不具有的某种特别效果。

本文选用原作第十六章中的某些片段作为译例,详细比较两译本的翻译手法及效果。在这一章中,哈克与吉姆在途中因不识路而错过了目的地开罗,哈克又机智而巧妙地骗走了两个追寻黑奴的白人。在对待吉姆的态度上哈克内心的矛盾冲突得到了生动、细致的刻画。

哈克讨厌一成不变、刻板僵死的生活,因而逃离偏僻、狭隘的小镇。对一个只有十来岁的孩子来说,外面的世界新奇、有趣、自由自在。马克·吐温让哈克自己来讲述这个故事,其用词、语气及表达的情感真真切切地符合哈克的身份。译者在译成相应的汉语时,应力求保持其真实面目。

---

① 见杨自俭、刘学云,《翻译新论》,1994年,第287页。

第二篇 《哈克贝利·费恩历险记》The Adventure of Huckberry Finn

1. ... a little ways behind a monstrous long raft that was as long going by as a procession. She had four long sweeps at each end, ... She had five big wigwams abroad, wide apart, and an open camp fire in the middle, and a tall flag-pole at each end. There was a power of style about her. It *amounted* to something being a raftsman on such a craft as that.

张译：……有一排很长很长的木筏……它每一头有四根长桨……筏子上搭着五个大窝棚，彼此离得很远，木筏当中还生着一个露天大火堆，每一头还有一根大旗杆。它的气派实在是大极了。在这样的筏子上当个伙计，那才真够神气的哪。

成译：……有一列长得出奇的木排……那木排前后各有四支长桨……它上面有五座木棚，彼此相隔挺远，中间生着一个露天的大篝火，两头各有一根高高的旗杆。整个木排看起来好不威风。在这样的船上当个木排夫，那才够意思。

这一段描写的是哈克在河上看到一排大木筏时的情景和想法。原文句子结构简单，用词朴素，简简单单的几个形容词就勾画出哈克眼中的木筏：monstrous，big，wide，tall。而最后两句更是活脱脱地描绘出哈克惊奇、羡慕的口吻和神态。原文词句中所含有的情感必须在译文中得到同样的体现，才能使译文保留原文形象及韵味，达到"神似"，张译充分利用汉语的优势，利用富有儿童气息的词语，再现了哈克的心理。张译把 big，tall 二个形容词一律译为大（窝棚）大（火堆）大（旗杆）以及后文的（气派）大极了，一连四个"大"字，似乎脱离了原文，搭配也不合适。可这正是译者的匠心所在。四个"大"字表面上与原文不符，实际却丝毫不偏离，其神韵比字面忠实有过之而无不及。四个"大"字连用，读起来给人一种层层递进的感觉，隐含着哈克的羡慕之情越来越强，另一方面也反映了教育程度不高的哈克词汇不丰富。成译则忠实地译出了原词，在味上稍逊一筹，而且句子结构、选词严谨，与哈克的身份不符。两译本在最后两句描写哈克心理的翻译都比较成功，译出了哈克的羡慕向往之情。张译抓住原句的精神，灵活加入了副词和语气词"实在是大极了"，"那才真够神气哪"（着重号为笔者所加）。这些词的运用，恰如画龙点睛,整个译文变得生动活泼起来,哈克的神态、语气跃然纸上,栩栩如生。就这一段而言,张译更好地传达了原文韵味,译文形象生动,琅琅上口。

2. 'I will, sir, I will, honest—but don't leave us, please. It's the—the—gentlemen, if you'll only pull ahead, and let me heave you the head-line, you won't have to come a-near the raft—please do.'

张译:"我一定说,先生,我一定老老实实地说——可是千万别离开我们。那种病是——是——诸位先生,只要你们把船划过去,等我把筏子头上的绳子交给你们。你们根本不必到木筏跟前去——千万帮个忙吧。"

成译:"我说,先生,我说老实话——可请你们千万别丢下我们不管。他得的是——是——先生,你们只要往前划,我把缆绳扔给你们,你们用不着靠近木排——我求求你们。"

吉姆想到自己快自由了,便兴奋不已,憧憬着未来的生活,哈克却内心倍受良心的谴责,于是他准备划到岸边去告发吉姆,却正好碰到两个白人在追捕出逃的黑奴。哈克急中生智,谎称他爸爸身染病躺在船上。这是一段他与两白人的对话。哈克"欲纵故擒",故意吞吞吐吐,避而不谈他爸爸的病,以吓跑他们。哈克绘声绘色,装得像模像样。原文句子简短,充分体现了哈克假扮出来的焦急、担心、恳切的神态,读原文如听原话,其机敏、慧黠历历在耳。张译比较忠实地译出了原文中的词和句子意思,如"千万别离开我们"、"那种病是——"、"等我把……交给你们"、"不必"、"千万帮个忙吧"。对照原文,张译并无大的错误。可整段读起来,句子太长而且拗口,更主要的是译文中的那种神情、韵味已不见了,出现在读者面前的是一个咬文嚼字的成人,哈克的聪明可爱已不见了。成译却能跳出原文字句的束缚,灵活地转换角度,用汉语中的口语词汇和短句来再现哈克的语气神态。如"千万别丢下我们不管"、"他得的是——"、"用不着"、"我求求你们"等。成译用地道的汉语口语,十分生动、逼真地为读者再现了一个"撒谎不脸红"的小孩的形象,真正地忠实于原文,达到了"神似"。

第二篇 《哈克贝利·费恩历险记》The Adventure of Huckberry Finn

3. (They went off, and I got abroad the raft), feeling bad and know, because I knowed very well I had done wrong, and I see it warn't no use for me to try to learn to do right; a body that don't get started right when he's little, ain't got no show- when the pinch comes there ain't nothing to back him up and keep him to his work, and so he gets beat.

张译:……无精打采,非常难过,因为我知道明明是做了一件错事,我知道我就是想学好也办不到了;一个人从小时候就不好,后来也决不会有好的机会——到他遇见了难办的事,就没有一股力量支持着他,让他继续干下去,结果他就败下阵来了。

成译:……心里怪难受,提不起劲儿来,因为我知道我做了错事,最后也明白:我就是想学走正道也学不了啦;一个人从小一开头就不走正道,就不会有出息——遇上急难的时候,背后没有东西支撑他,让他守自己的本分,最后只有垮台了事。

哈克与吉姆在漂流之中结下了深厚的友谊,但最开始哈克却有一种矛盾的心理,看到吉姆就快自由了,良心不安,想去告发吉姆;吉姆面临危险时又毫不犹豫地救了吉姆;救了他之后,内心又很难过。哈克对吉姆的感情和态度便是在一次次的矛盾冲突中逐渐得到升华而走向成熟。这一段便是骗走两个白人后哈克内心矛盾、不安的一部分。19世纪的美国仍留有蓄奴制,等级观念、种族差别在人们心目中根深蒂固。哈克虽然善良、富有同情心,但他毕竟还是个读书不多的孩子,不能理智地分析自己。哈克救了吉姆后,又一次面临自己的感情和白人社会的道德观念之间的冲突。原文用了两个极简单的词 right 和 wrong 来代表哈克内心中的正确的道德标准。哈克的分析是不成熟的。作者通过短短的几句话便勾勒出一位年少、处于迷惘之中而又试图用自己单纯的思想去分析事物的人物形象。那么在译文中应如何传达出这一暗含意义呢?两译本都比较好地把握了字里行间的精神,再现了哈克的心理活动。成译一方面保留了口语体风格,运用了"怪,啦"等口语词汇及儿化音,同时还有意识地用了一些较规范、相对而言的大词,如"不走正道……不会有出息","遇上急难……守自己的本分",从而突出了两种力量、两种标准的对比，较好地反映出哈克思想逐渐走向成熟的一个阶段。张译在某些地方的处理不如成译自如，影响了整段译文的连贯性：从小时候就不好……不会有好的机会……遇见了难办的事……继续干下去。这些加点的译文显得含糊不清，什么是好的机会，继续干下去是干什么——做对事还是错事？张译在准确表达哈克内心动态方面略逊一筹。

4. We didn't say a word for a good while. There warn't anything to say. We both knowed well enough it was some more work of the rattle-snake skin; so what was the use to talk about it? It would only look like we was finding fault, and that would be bound to fetch more bad luck—and keep on fetching it, too, till we knowed enough to keep still.

张译：我们呆了半天没出声。根本也没什么可说的了。我们两个明明知道这又是那条蛇皮在作祟；那还谈它干什么？那仿佛是我们还在抱怨，结果一定还会碰上倒霉的事——照这样一直碰下去，最后受够了教训，只好不声不响。

成译：有好一阵子，我们作不得声。没有什么好说的。我们俩心里都透亮：又是那响尾蛇在作怪；有什么可议论的；那只会使我们像是在批判抱怨，准保会招来更多的倒霉事儿——而且会不断地招来倒霉事儿，一直到我们明白过来，一声不吭才完。

哈克和吉姆发现他们所藏好的划子不见了，两人便知道是那条响尾蛇在作怪。这只是一种迷信的说法，他们却深信不疑，心中又是沮丧又是害怕。首句"we didn't say a word for a good while"便很好地反映出他们当时的心情。成译利用汉语句式，突出"good"一词，又抓住 not say a word 的真正原因，巧妙而又生动地译成"有好一阵子，我们作不得声"，无论形式、精神，还是语气上都接近原文。张译的这句译文则略显平淡。成译的"没什么好说的"比"根本也没什么可说的"更能传达出他们的无可奈何，无话可说。全段最后一句"bound to fetch"和"keep on fetching"十分成功地描绘出了哈克的担心。张译译成了"会碰上倒霉事——照这样一直碰下去"，原文的力度便减弱了许多，而且"照这样一直

第二篇 《哈克贝利·费恩历险记》The Adventure of Huckberry Finn

碰下去"显得生硬、拗口。成译则灵活运用汉语词汇,交换结构,补足语气:准保会招来更多的倒霉事儿——而且会不断地招来倒霉事儿。"招"字很传神地译出了哈克的心思,"准保""不断"以及儿化音使译文通顺、流畅而又口语化。译文最后加上一句"一声不吭才完"更使得整段译文语气、风格与原文丝丝入扣。

从以上几例可以看出,要传达这部小说中自然清新的口语体语言风格,再现栩栩如生的人物形象,必须从原作形式传达的内容信息和风格信息出发,通过加词,角度转换等多种手法,以求用最佳译语形式来表现原作,真正做到"神似"。过分囿于原文形式只会造成原作神韵上的损失。

黑人吉姆是马克·吐温在这部小说中塑造的另一个主要人物形象。在作者笔下,吉姆被刻画成一个有思想,有感情,追求自由的真正的人。除了他所经历的一系列事情外,吉姆的语言也有助于他形象的刻画。

黑人英语是一种不规范语言,长期以来已在语音、词汇、语法等方面形成系统的"变体",如发音时常吞掉词的某个音节或音素,并用省略号"'"表示:po = poor 'spected = suspected。黑人语言的形成与其社会地位以及所受教育程度是分不开的。文学作品中黑人所说的不规范英语都拼写出来了,成为塑造黑人形象不可缺少的一部分。真实的语言才能展示真实的人物形象。这种特殊的社会语言变体是否应在译文中反映出来呢？回答是肯定的。但英汉语属于不同语系,有着太多的不同,要反映出语言变体有很大的困难,译者应"尽能译的范围去翻译原作中的形容发音不正确的俗体字……翻译粗人口里的粗字"(茅盾语)[①]。

5. 'Pooty soon I'll be a-shout'n for joy, en I'll say, it's all on accounts o'Huck; I's a free man en I couldn't ever ben free ef it hadn' ben for Huck; Huck done it. Jim won't ever forgit you, Huck; you's de bes' fren'. Jim's ever had; en you's de only fren' ole Jim's got now.'

---

① 引自陈福康《中国译学理论史稿》,1992年,第246页。

张译:"再等会儿,我就要高兴得使劲儿喊了,我就说,这都是哈克的功劳;我成了自由人了,要是没有哈克,我永远也得不着自由,这都是哈克做的好事。我吉姆一辈子也忘不了你的好处,哈克;你是我顶好的朋友;你也是我老吉木独一无二的朋友"。

成译:"布(不)用陀久(多久),我就会快活得叫起来,我约(要)说:这陀跪(多亏)赫克。我史过(是个)自由人啦,要布史有赫克,我这一攀(辈)子也布想自由;赫克帮了我的忙,杰姆我永世忘布了你赫克;你史我杰姆顶好的奔(朋)友;我劳(老)杰姆此刻只有你这奔友。

哈克准备划船上岸去告发吉姆,吉姆却以为哈克是为他去看看开罗到了没有,于是吉姆深情感激地说出这一段真挚的话。小说对话中的语法或语音变异是为了刻画人物形象,这种不规范语很难如实加以传达。在英译汉中尤其如此。英语作为拼音文字,词的书写形式直接表示所指对象。英语中可采用 pooty 代表 pretty,forgit 代表 forget,再加上一些带有省略音符的词,把笔下人物的不规范发音拼写得丝毫不差而不会产生歧义。汉语却不行。张译通篇用普通话译出,译文流畅。可是原人物的语言特征以及相关的个人背景情况却被抹杀掉了,不可避免地影响了译文的效果,失去了原文所有的韵味。成译则力图再现原文所塑造的人物腔调,用读音相近的字来代替原字,让读者知道其发音不准,这就是汉语中语音飞白。它和英语的语音变异一样,是为表现人物发音不准而故意违反语言常规的一种表现手法。用汉语飞白译英语语音变异在一定程度上可以反映出说话者的不规范语言,但句子念起来磕磕绊绊,令读者已无暇去领略译者的苦心了。有时替代字本身的词汇意义和联想意义可能会干扰译文语意的表达。

原文中的不规范语难译,甚至是不可译,为了保证原文色彩尽可能多地传译,译者应充分利用汉语自身的特点,尽量保存原作风貌而又不影响译文的可读性。英汉语之间的差异使译者不可能亦步亦趋地仿效原文每处变异,译者可根据英语重形合,汉语重意合的特点,在保证译文传达原文总体效果的前提下,把原文的语音变异转为汉语中较易体现的语法或搭配变异①。

　　文学翻译的最高境界是要"神似"，入"化"境。译者应从整体上把握原作的或人物的语言风格与个性，并根据此充分发挥译语优势来处理各细节，以保证原作的主要精神、意境气氛、风格特征很好地再现，尽量达到"神似"和"等效"。这便是翻译的艺术创作性所在。马克·吐温的这部名著语言口语化，生动活泼，人物形象逼真，刻画细腻，熔谐趣、讽刺、幽默于一炉。张译和成译在语言风格上的传译均显示出两人不凡的功力，能较好地体现原著的精神。张译有不少妙笔，极为传神。但就总体而言，成译更能充分利用汉语的特点，灵活地变化句式，采用多种手段，成功地再现原文风貌，并"力求全文口语化，且要符合一个略识之乎的孩子的口吻"。（成译本序言）

　　《哈克贝利·费恩历险记》不仅是美国文学也是世界文学中一颗璀璨的明珠，它的中译本也为中国文学添上不同凡响的一笔。

参　考　文　献

1. 陈福康：《中国译学理论史稿》，上海外语教育出版社，1992年。
2. 成时：《赫克尔贝利·费恩历险记》，人民出版社，1988年。
3. 侯维瑞：《英语语体》，上海外语教育出版社，1988年。
4. 李宜燮、常耀信：《美国文学选读》，南开大学出版社，1991年。
5. 罗新璋：《翻译论集》，商务印书馆，1984年。
6. Twain, Mark. *The Adventure of Huckberry Finn*. Beijing: Foreign Language Press, 1994.
7. 杨自俭、刘学云：《翻译新论》，湖北教育出版社，1994年。
8. 张今：《文学翻译原理》，河南大学出版社，1987年。
9. 张万里：《哈克贝利·芬历险记》，上海文学出版社，1984年。

---

① 关于文学作品中不规范/标准英语的翻译（方言、黑人语言为主），译界有过不少争论。除文中提到的三种译法外，还有人用汉语中某方言来译原文的方言，以传达原文人物语言特色，如张谷若先生在《德伯家的苔丝》中便采用陕北方言中的"俺""昨个晌午"等词以标记人物语言的地方性。

第二篇 《哈克贝利·费恩历险记》The Adventure of Huckberry Finn

附:

The Adventure of Huckberry Finn
(Excerpts)

Mark Twain

CHAPTER 16

We slept most all day, and started out at night, a little ways behind a monstrous long raft that was as long going by as a procession. She had four long sweeps* at each end, so we judged she carried as many as thirty men, likely. She had five big wigwams aboard, wide apart, and an open camp fire in the middle, and a tall falg-pole at each end. There was a power of style about her. It *amounted* to something being a raftsman on such a craft as that.

We went drifting down into a big bend, and the night clouded up and got hot. The river was very wide, and was walled with solid timber on both sides; you couldn't see a break in it hardly ever, or a light. We talked about Cairo, and wondered whether we would know it when we got to it. I said likely we wouldn't, because I had heard say there warn't but about a dozen houses there, and if they didn't happen to have them lit up, how was we going to know we was passing a town? Jim said if the two big rivers joined together there, that would show. But I said maybe we might think we was passing the foot of an island and coming into the same old river again. That disturbed Jim—and me too. So the question was, what to do? I said, paddle ashore the first time a light

---

* Especially long oars.

showed, and tell them pap was behind, coming along with a trading-scow, and was a green hand at the business, and wanted to know how far it was to Cairo. Jim thought it was a good idea, so we took a smoke on it and waited.

There warn't nothing to do, now, but to look out sharp for the town, and not pass it without seeing it. He said he'd be mighty sure to see it, because he'd be a free man the minute he seen it, but if he missed it he'd be in the slave country again and no more show for freedom. Every little while he jumps up and says:

'Dah she is!'

But it warn't. It was Jack-o-lanterns, or lightning-bugs; so he set down again, and went to watching, same as before. Jim said it made him all over trembly and feverish to be so close to freedom. Well, I can tell you it made me all over trembly and feverish, too, to hear him, because I begun to get it through my head that he *was* most free—and who was to blame for it? Why, *me*. I couldn't get that out of my conscience, no how nor no way. It got to troubling me so I couldn't rest; I couldn't stay still in one place. It hadn't ever come home to me before, what this thing was that I was doing. But now it did; and it staid with me, and scorched me more and more. I tried to make out to myself that *I* warn't to blame, because *I* didn't run Jim off from his rightful owner; but it warn't no use, conscience up and says, every time, 'But you knowed he was running for his freedom, and you could a paddled ashore and told somebody.' That was so—I coudn't get around that, noway. That was where it pinched. Conscience says to me, 'What had poor Miss Watson done to you, that you could see her nigger go off right under your eyes and never say one single word? What did that poor old woman do to you, that you could treat her so mean? Why, she tried to learn you your book, she tried to learn you your manners, she tried to be good to you every way she knowed how.

第二篇 《哈克贝利·费恩历险记》The Adventure of Huckberry Finn

That's what she done.'

I got to feeling so mean and so miserable I most wished I was dead. I fidgeted up and down the raft, abusing myself to myself, and Jim was fidgeting up and down past me. We neither of us could keep still. Every time he danced around and says, 'Dah's Cairo!' it went through me like a shot, and I thought if it *was* Cairo I reckoned I would die of miserableness.

Jim talked out loud all the time while I was talking to myself. He was saying how the first thing he would do when he got to a free State he would go to saving up money and never spend a single cent, and when he got enough he would buy his wife, which was owned on a farm close to where Miss Watson lived; and then they would both work to buy the two children, and if their master wouldn't sell them, they'd get an Ab'litionist to go and steal them.

It most froze me to hear such talk. He wouldn't ever dared to talk such talk in his life before. Just see what a difference it made in him the minute he judged he was about free. It was according to the old saying, 'give a nigger an inch and he'll take an ell.' Thinks I, this is what comes of my not thinking. Here was this nigger which I had as good as helped to run away, coming right out flat-footed and saying he would steal his children—children that belonged to a man I didn't even know; a man that hadn't ever done me no harm.

I was sorry to hear Jim say that, it was such a lowering of him. My conscience got to stirring me up hotter than ever, until at last I says to it, 'Let up on me—it ain't too late, yet—I'll paddle ashore at the first light, and tell.' I felt easy, and happy, and light as a feather, right off. All my troubles was gone. I went to looking out sharp for a light, and sort of singing to myself. By-and-by one showed. Jim sings out:

'We's safe, Huck, we's safe! Jump up and crack yo' heels, dat's de good ole Cairo at las', I jis knows it!'

第二篇 《哈克贝利·费恩历险记》The Adventure of Huckberry Finn

I says:

'I'll take the canoe and go see, Jim. It mightn't be, you know.'

He jumped and got the canoe ready, and put his old coat in the bottom for me to set on, and give me the paddle; and as I shoved off, he says:

'Pooty soon I'll be a-shout'n for joy, en I'll say, it's all on accounts o' Huck; I's a free man, en I couldn't ever ben free ef it hadn' ben for Huck; Huck done it. Jim won't ever forgit you, Huck; you's de bes' fren' Jim's ever had; en you's de *only* fren' ole Jime's got now.'

I was paddling off, all in a sweat to tell on him; but when he says this, it seemed to kind of take the tuck all out of me. I went along slow then, and I warn't right down certain whether I was glad I started or whether I warn't. When I was fifty yards off, Jim says:

'Dah you goes, de ole true Huck; de on'y white genlman dat ever kep' his promise to ole Jim.'

Well, I just felt sick. But I says, I *got* to do it—I can't get *out* of it. Right then, along comes a skiff with two men in it, with guns, and they stopped and I stopped. One of them says:

'What's that, yonder?'

'A piece of a raft,' I says.

'Do you belong on it?'

'Yes, sir.'

'Any men on it?'

'Only one, sir.'

'Well, there's five niggers run off tonight, up yonder above the head of the bend. Is your man white or black?'

I didn't answer up prompt. I tried to, but the words wouldn't come. I tried, for a second or two, to brace up and out with it, but I warn't man enough—hadn't the spunk of a rabbit. I see I was weakening; so I just give up trying, and up and says—

'He's white.'

'I reckon we'll go and see for ourselves.'

'I wish you would,' says I, 'because it's pap that's there, and maybe you'd help me tow the raft ashore where the light is. He's sick—and so is mam and Mary Ann.'

'Oh, the devil! we're in a hurry, boy. But I s'pose we've got to. Come—buckle to your paddle, and let's get along.'

I buckled to my paddle and they laid to their oars. When we had made a stroke or two, I says:

'Pap'll be mighty much obleeged to you, I can tell you. Everybody goes away when I want them to help me tow the raft ashore, and I can't do it by myself.'

'Well, that's infernal mean. Odd, too. Say, boy, what's the matter with your father?'

'It's the—a—the—well, it ain't anything, much.'

They stopped pulling. It warn't but a mighty little ways to the raft, now. One says:

'Boy, that's a lie. What *is* the matter with your pap? Answer up square, now, and it'll be the better for you.'

'I will, sir, I will, honest—but don't leave us, please. It's the—the —gentlemen, if you'll only pull ahead, and let me heave you the head-line, you won't have to come a-near the raft—please do.'

'Set her back, John, set her back!' says one. They backed water. 'Keep away, boy—keep to looard. Confound it, I just expect the wind has blowed it to us. Your pap's got the smallpox, and you know it precious well. Why didn't you come out and say so? Do you want to spread it all over?'

'Well,' says I, a-blubbering, 'I've told everybody before, and then they just went away and left us.'

'Poor devil, there's something in that. We are right down sorry for you, but we—well, hang it, we don't want the smallpox, you see.

第二篇 《哈克贝利·费恩历险记》The Adventure of Huckberry Finn

Look here, I'll tell you what to do. Don't you try to land by yourself, or you'll smash everything to pieces. You float along down about twenty miles and you'll come to a town on the left-hand side of the river. It will be long after sun-up, then, and when you ask for help, you tell them your folks are all down with chills and fever. Don't be a fool again, and let people guess what is the matter. Now we're trying to do you a kindness; so you just put twenty miles between us, that's a good boy. It wouldn't do any good to land yonder where the light is — it's only a wood-yard. Say — I reckon your father's poor, and I'm bound to say he's in pretty hard luck. Here — I'll put a twenty dollar gold piece on this board, and you get it when it floats by. I feel mighty mean to leave you, but my kingdom! It won't do to fool with small-pox, don't you see?'

'Hold on, Parker,' says the other man, 'here's a twenty to put on the board for me. Good-bye, boy, you do as Mr Parker told you, and you'll be all right.'

'That's so, my boy — good-bye, good-bye. If you see any runaway niggers, you get help and nab them, and you can make some money by it.'

'Good-bye, sir,' says I, 'I won't let no runaway niggers get by me if I can help it.'

They went off, and I got aboard the raft, feeling bad and low, because I knowed very well I had done wrong, and I see it warn't no use for me to try to learn to do right; a body that don't get *started* right when he's little, ain't got no show — when the pinch comes there ain't nothing to back him up and keep him to his work, and so he gets beat. Then I thought a minute, and says to myself, hold on, — s'pose you'd a done right and give Jim up; would you felt better than what you do now? No, says I, I'd feel bad — I'd feel just the same way I do now. Well, then, says I, what's the use you learning to do right, when it's troublesome to do right and ain't no trouble to do wrong, and the wages is just the same? I was stuck. I couldn't answer that. So I reckoned I wouldn't bother no more about it, but after this always do whichever come handiest at the time.

I went into the wigwam; Jim warn't there. I looked all around; he warn't anywhere. I says:

'Jim!'

'Here I is, Huck. Is dey out o' sight yit? Don't talk loud. '

He was in the river, under the stern oar, with just his nose out. I told him they was out of sight, so he come aboard. He says:

'I was a-listenin' to all de talk, en I slips into de river en was gwyne to shove for sho' if dey come aboard. Den I was gwyne to swim to de raf' again when dey was gone. But lawsy, how you did fool 'em, Huck! Dat *wuz* de smartes' dodge! I tell you, chile, I 'speck it save' ole Jim—ole Jim ain't gwyne to forgit you for dat, honey. '

Then we talked about the money. It was a pretty good raise, twenty dollars apiece. Jim said we could take deck passage on a steamboat now, and the money would last us as far as we wanted to go in the free States. He said twenty mile more warn't far for the raft to go, but he wished we was already there.

Towards daybreak we tied up, and Jim was mighty particular about hiding the raft good. Then he worked all day fixing things in bundles, and getting all ready to quit rafting.

That night about ten we hove in sight of the lights of a town away down in a left-hand bend.

I went off in the canoe, to ask about it. Pretty soon I found a man out in the river with skiff, setting a trot-line. I ranged up and says:

'Mister, is that town Cairo?'

'Cairo? No. You must be a blame' fool. '

'What town is it, mister?'

'If you want to know, go and find out. If you stay here bothering' around me for about a half a minute longer, you'll get something you won't want.'

I paddled to the raft. Jim was awful disappointed, but I said never mind, Cairo would be the next place, I reckoned.

We passed another town before daylight, and I was going out again; but it was high ground, so I didn't go. No high ground about Cairo, Jim said. I had forgot it. We laid up for the day, on a tow-head tolerable close to the left-hand bank. I begun to suspicion something. So did Jim. I says:

'Maybe we went by Cairo in the fog that night.'

He says:

'Doan' less' talk about it, Huck. Po' niggers can't have no luck. I awluz 'spected dat rattle-snake skin warn't done wid its work.'

'I wish I'd never seen that snake-skin, Jim—I do wish I'd never laid eyes on it.'

'It ain't yo' fault, Huck; you didn't know. Don't you blame yo'self 'bout it.'

When it was daylight, here was the clear Ohio water in shore, sure enough, and outside was the old regular Muddy! So it was all up with Cairo.

We talked it all over. It wouldn't do to take to the shore; we couldn't take the raft up the stream, of course. There warn't no way but to wait for dark, and start back in the canoe and take the chances. So we slept all day amongst the cotton-wood thicket, so as to be fresh for the work, and when we went back to the raft about dark the canoe was gone!

We didn't say a word for a good while. There warn't anything to say. We both knowed well enough it was some more work of the rattle-snake skin; so what was the use to talk about it? It would only look like we was finding fault, and that would be bound to fetch more bad luck— and keep on fetching it, too, till we knowed enough to keep still.

第二篇 《哈克贝利·费恩历险记》The Adventure of Huckberry Finn

By-and-by we talked about what we better do, and found there warn't no way but just to go along down with the raft till we got a chance to buy a canoe to go back in. We warn't going to borrow it when there warn't anybody around, the way pap would do, for that might set people after us.

So we shoved out, after dark, on the raft.

Anybody that don't believe yet, that it's foolishness to handle a snake-skin, after all that that snake-skin done for us, will believe it now, if they read on and see what more it done for us.

The place to buy canoes is off of rafts laying up at shore. But we didn't see no rafts laying up; so we went along during three hours and more. Well, the night got gray, and ruther thick, which is the next meanest thing to fog. You can't tell the shape of the river, and you can't see no distance. It got to be very late and still, and then along comes a steamboat up the river. We lit the lantern, and judged she would see it. Upstream boats didn't generly come close to us; they go out and follow the bars and hunt for easy water under the reefs; but nights like this they bull right up the channel against the whole river.

We could hear her pounding along, but we didn't see her good till she was close. She aimed right for us. Often they do that and try to see how close they can come without touching; sometimes the wheel bites off a sweep, and then the pilot sticks his head out and laughs, and thinks he's mighty smart. Well, here she comes, and we said she was going to try to shave us; but she didn't seem to be sheering off a bit. She was a big one, and she was coming in a hurry, too, looking like a black cloud with rows of glow-worms around it; but all of a sudden she bulged out, big and scary, with a long row of wide-open furnace doors shining like red-hot teeth, and her monstrous bows and guards hanging right over us. There was a yell at us, and a jingling of bells to stop the engines, a pow-wow of cussing, and whistling of steam—and as Jim went overboard on one side and I on the other, she come smashing straight through the raft.

   I dived—and I aimed to find the bottom, too, for a thirty-foot wheel had got to go over me, and I wanted it to have plenty of room. I could always stay under water a minute; this time I reckon I staid under water a minute and a half. Then I bounced for the top in a hurry, for I was nearly busting. I popped out to my arm-pits and blowed the water out of my nose, and puffed a bit. Of course there was a booming current; and of course that boat started her engines again ten seconds after she stopped them, for they never cared much for raftsmen; so now she was churning along up the river, out of sight in the thick weather, though I could hear her.

   I sung out for Jim about a dozen times, but I didn't get any answer; so I grabbed a plank that touched me while I was 'treading water,' and struck out for shore, shoving it ahead of me. But I made out to see that the drift of the current was towards the left-hand shore, which meant that I was in a crossing; so I changed off and went that way.

   It was one of these long, slanting, two-mile crossings; so I was a good long time in getting over. I made a safe landing, and clum up the bank. I couldn't see but a little ways, but I went poking along over rough ground for a quarter of a mile or more, and then I run across a big old-fashioned double log house before I noticed it. I was going to rush by and get away, but a lot of dogs jumped out and went to howling and barking at me, and I knowed better than to move another peg.

第二篇 《哈克贝利·费恩历险记》The Adventure of Huckberry Finn

《哈克贝利·芬历险记》(节选)

张万里 译

第十六章 蛇皮再惹祸

我们几乎睡了一整天,到了夜里才动身走,有一排很长很长的木筏,好像一大队游行的人马似的,在我们的前面漂着。它每一头有四根长桨,我们猜想那上面恐怕至少载着三十个人。筏子上搭着五个大窝棚,彼此离得很远,木筏当中还生着一个露天的大火堆,每一头还有一根大旗杆。它的气派实在是大极了。在这样的筏子上当个伙计,那才真够神气的哪。

我们顺水漂到一个大河湾里,这时候,黑夜的天空,被云彩遮住,闷热得很。这一段河面很宽,有长得很密的大树林子,像城墙似的立在两岸;你难得看见树林子上有什么缺口,也瞧不出一点儿光来。我们谈到开罗,可是不知道到了那儿能不能认识那个地方。我说我们恐怕不认识,因为我听说那儿只有十几户人家,假如他们恰巧没有点灯,那我们怎么会知道是路过一个镇呢?吉木说,那两条大河在那儿汇合,一定看得出来。可是我说,也许我们会以为那是路过一个岛尾,仍然又回到原来的大河里来。这件事弄得吉木非常着急——我也是一样。所以问题就出来了:究竟该怎么办呢?我说,只要看见有灯光,立刻划到岸上去,就对人家说爸爸在后面坐着商船马上过来,他做生意还是个生手,想要打听一下到开罗去还有多远。吉木觉得这是个好主意,于是我们就一边抽着烟想,一边走着瞧。

现在我们只好聚精会神地看着,千万可别没看见那个镇就走过去

第二篇 《哈克贝利·费恩历险记》The Adventure of Huckberry Finn

了。吉木说他保险一定看得见，因为他一看见那个镇，他就成了自由人，可是他如果错过了，他就又到了贩卖奴隶的地方，再也没有自由的机会了。每隔一小会儿，他就跳起来说：

"在那儿哪！"

但是那并不是。那不过是些鬼火，或是萤火虫罢了；于是他又坐下来，照旧眼巴巴地望着。吉木说他离自由越来越近了，弄得他浑身上下又发抖、又发烧。老实说，我听见他这样说，也弄得我浑身上下又发抖、又发烧，因为我脑子里也渐渐想起他已经差不多要自由了——这究竟怨谁呢？当然是怨我。我无论怎样也不能叫我的良心不责备我。这件事弄得我心里七上八下，坐立不安，简直没法好好地在一个地方呆着。我从来没想到我干的究竟是件什么事。可是现在我想起来了；这个想法老在我心里盘旋，让我越来越觉得心焦。我想尽方法对我自己解释，说这并不是我的错处，因为我并没有叫吉木由他那合法的主人那儿逃走；可是这都是白费。我的良心每回都对我说："可是你明明知道他是为找自由而逃跑呀，你本来可以划到岸上去对人说呀。"事情就是这样——我怎么也推脱不开。难处也就在这儿。良心还对我说："可怜的瓦岑小姐怎么虐待了你，叫你亲眼看着她的黑奴逃跑，连一句话都不说？那个可怜的老太婆有哪点儿对不起你，叫你用这么坏的手段去对付她？她尽力教你念书，她尽力教你做人，她想尽种种办法对你好。她就是那样对待你的呀。"

我渐渐觉得我实在是太没良心、太不要脸了，真是恨不得死掉才好。我在筏子上不耐烦地走来走去，心里暗暗地骂我自己，吉木也在我的旁边不耐烦地走去走来。我们两个谁也沉不住气。每逢他手舞足蹈地喊着说："那不就是开罗吗！"我一听这话，就觉得好像挨了一枪似的，我想假如那真是开罗的话，我大概会难受得死过去。

吉木一直在那儿大声说话，可是我老是在暗自盘算。他说的是到了自由州以后，他要做的第一件事，就是拚命地存钱，一分钱也不花，等到存够了的时候，他打算到瓦岑小姐家附近的那个庄子上去，把他的老婆赎回来；然后他们夫妻两个做工挣钱，再把那两个孩子也赎回来；假如他们的主人不肯卖的话，他们就找个反对奴隶制度的人去把他们偷回来。

他这一套话弄得我几乎凉了半截。他以前从来也不敢说这种话。你看他刚一认为他快要自由了,就跟以前大不相同了。有句老话说得好:"黑奴不知足,得寸就进尺。"我心里想:这都是我做事不用脑筋惹出来的。眼前摆着这个黑人,他差不多要算是我帮着逃出来的,现在他理直气壮地说要去把他的孩子偷回来——那些孩子的主人,我根本就不认识,人家从来也没得罪过我。

我听见吉木说的这些话,心里也替他很难受,他这样说,实在是叫人看不起。我的良心又把我鼓动起来,叫我觉得忍无可忍,后来我就对我的良心说:"请你饶了我吧——现在还不算晚呀——等我一看见灯光,我就划到岸上去告他。"这么一来,我立刻觉得又安心,又高兴,心里轻快得像根鹅毛似的。我的烦恼都没有了。我仔细望着岸上,看看有没有灯光,心里像是在唱歌似的。不久就有一个灯光露出来。吉木高兴地喊着说:

"咱们可有救了,哈克,咱们可有救了!快跳起来立个正、行个礼吧!咱们可来到老开罗这个好地方了,我准知道!"

我说:

"等我先坐着小船过去看看,吉木。你要知道,那也许还不是哪。"

他跳过去把船准备妥当,拿他的旧大衣垫在底下,让我坐在上面,然后把桨交给我;我刚撑开船的时候,他说:

"再等一会儿,我就要高兴得使劲喊了,我就说,这都是哈克的功劳;我成了自由人了,要是没有哈克,我永远也得不着自由;这都是哈克做的好事。我吉木一辈子也忘不了你的好处,哈克;你是我吉木顶好的朋友;你也是我老吉木独一无二的朋友。"

我刚把船划开,急着想去告发他;可是一听他说的这些话,我那股冲劲就不知道哪儿去了。我就慢慢地往前划,并不十分清楚我是高兴还是不高兴。等我离开了五十码的时候,吉木说:

"你走啦,你这忠实的老哈克;在白人里头,只有你对我老吉木讲信用。"

我简直难受得要命。可是我说非把这件事办了不可——我没有法

子避免。正在这时候,打那边过来了一只小船,上面坐着两个拿枪的人,他们停下了,我也停下了。其中有一个人说:

"嘿,那边是什么?"

"是一节木筏,"我说。

"你是那个筏子上的人吗?"

"是啊,先生。"

"那上面还有人吗?"

"只有一个,先生。"

"今天晚上,上头那边河湾口上跑了五个黑奴。你那个人是白人,还是黑人?"

我没有立刻回答。我本打算回答,可是话总是说不出口。我迟疑了一两秒钟,想要一鼓作气地说出来,可是我没有那么大的勇气——我连一只兔子的勇气都没有。我知道我已经泄气了;我就放弃了原来的想头,直截了当地说:

"他是白人。"

"我看咱们得亲自过去看看。"

"我也希望你们能过去看看,"我说,"因为那边是我的爸爸,也许你们能够帮个忙,把木筏拖到那边有灯光的地方去。他病了——妈妈跟玛莉·安也都病了。"

"啊,真他妈的!我们忙得很,你这孩子。可是我看我们还是得走一趟。走啊——用点儿力气摇你的桨,咱们一块儿过去看。"

我就用力摇我的桨,他们也使劲儿地划他们的船。我们才划了一两下,我就说:

"我敢说爸爸会从心里感激你们。我每回求人家帮我把筏子拖到岸上去,不管是谁都赶快走开,我自己一个人又拖不动。"

"那可真他妈的太狠心了。也太奇怪了啊。我问你这孩子,你爸爸得的是什么病呀?"

"他得的是——那个——嗐,并没有什么了不得的病。"

他们就停下不划了。这时候离木筏已经不远了。有一个人说:

"孩子,你说的都是瞎话。你爸爸到底得了什么病啦?现在你给我乖乖地说出来,那样对你也会有好处。"

"我一定说,先生,我一定老老实实地说——可是千万别离开我们。那种病是——是——诸位先生,只要你们把船划过去,等我把筏子头上的绳子交给你们,你们根本不必划到木筏跟前去——千万帮个忙吧。"

"把船退回去,约翰,把船退回去!"一个人说。他们立刻往后退。"快躲开点儿,孩子——快躲到下风去。他妈的,我算计着那阵风已经把它刮到我们身上来了。你爸爸得的是天花,你知道得比谁都清楚。可是你为什么不痛痛快快说呢?难道你打算让大家都传染上吗?"

"哼,"我哭哭啼啼地说,"我以前见着谁就对谁说实话,可是他们马上就走开,不管我们了。"

"你这可怜的小鬼头,原来你也有苦衷。我们也替你难过,可是我们——对了,他妈的,我们决不想得天花,你明白啦。你听着,我来给你想个办法。你一个人可千万别靠岸,否则你可就坏了事。你往下游再漂上二十几英里,你就会走到大河左边岸上的一个镇。到那时候,太阳早已出来了,你再求人家帮你的忙,对他们说你家里的人都在发疟子。别再那么不知好歹,让人家猜着是怎么回事。我们这是想帮你的忙,所以你一定要离开我们二十英里,那才是个好孩子哪。你要是在有灯的那边上岸,根本也没有什么好处——那不过是个木厂子。嘻,我想你爸爸一定很穷,我准知道他的运气也一定够坏的。你看——我把这块值二十块钱的金圆,放在这块板子上,等它漂过去的时候,你把它捡起来。我觉得把你丢开不管,实在是太不像话,可是,我的天!传染上天花可不是闹着玩儿的,你明白不明白?"

"先别撒手,巴可,"另一个人说,"替我把这二十块钱也放在板子上,是我给的。再见吧,孩子,你就照着巴可先生对你说的话去做,什么问题都解决了。"

"对啦,我的好孩子——再见,再见。假如你看见有跑掉的黑奴,你就找人帮你把他们抓住,你还可以挣点儿钱哪。"

"再见,先生,"我说,"只要我办得到,我决不会放走一个逃跑的黑奴。"

他们走开了,我也回到木筏上来,无精打采,非常难过,因为我知道

第二篇 《哈克贝利·费恩历险记》The Adventure of Huckberry Finn

明明是做了一件错事,我知道我就是想学好也办不到;一个人从小时候起就不好,后来也决不会有好的机会——等到他遇见了难办的事,就没有一股力量支持着他,让他继续干下去,结果他就败下阵来了。然后我又想了一分钟,心里这样地盘算着:先别忙,假若你做对了,把吉木一下子交给人家,那么你会比现在觉得好受些吗?我说,不会的,我也会觉得难过,我会觉得跟现在一样的难过。我说,那么,好了,做对的事反而要惹麻烦,做错的事根本就不费劲儿,而且代价都是一样,那么你又何必要学着做对的事情呢?我可让它给难住了。我没法回答这个问题,所以我想我再也不为它操心了;从此以后干脆就看当时的情形,怎么方便就怎么做吧。

我钻到窝棚里去;吉木并没在那儿。我各处找了一遍;哪儿也找不着他。我就喊了一声:

"吉木!"

"我在这儿哪,哈克。他们已经走远了吗?可别大声说话呀。"

他原来是泡在河里面,躲在筏尾的桨底下,只把鼻子露在外面。我告诉他说,他们已经走远了,于是他就爬上来了。他说:

"我听见你们说的话,我就溜到河里去,假如他们走上来,我打算游到岸上去。等他们走了以后,我再回到筏子上来。可是,我的天,你可把他们骗苦了,哈克!你这一手耍得真叫漂亮啊!我告诉你,好孩子,我想这就救了我老吉木了——老吉木决忘不了你的恩典,老弟。"

然后我们就谈到那些钱。这下子可真捞了不少——每人二十块钱。吉木说我们现在能够到轮船上去打统舱票,这些钱足够我们在那些自由州里到处走,爱跑多远就跑多远。他说乘着筏子再走二十英里,并不算太远,可是他恨不得我们已经到了那边。

天快亮的时候,我们就拢了岸,吉木特别小心地把筏子藏得好好的。然后他忙了整整一天,把东西都打起捆来,一切都准备好了,只等离开木筏。

那天晚上十点钟左右,我们在下游靠左手的河湾一带,看见一座灯光点点的小镇。

我把小船摇过去,想要打听一下。不大一会儿,我在河里遇见一个

人坐着小船,正在下一条拦河钩绳。我划过去问他:

"先生,那个镇是开罗吗?"

"开罗?不是。你他妈的一定是个大傻子。"

"那是个什么镇啊,先生?"

"你要是打算知道,滚过去自己看看。你假如在我这儿再打搅我半分钟的话,我就要对你不客气啦。"

我又划到木筏上来。吉木觉得大失所望,可是我说不要紧,我看下一个地方就要到开罗了。

我们在天亮以前,经过了另一个镇,我本想再过去看看;但是因为那一带是高地,所以我没有去。吉木说,开罗附近没有高地。我起初把它忘了。我们在离左边河岸很近的一个沙洲上,躲着混过这一天。我渐渐疑惑起来。吉木也是一样。我说:

"也许咱们在下雾的那天夜里,把开罗走过去了吧。"

他说:

"别再说了,哈克。可怜的黑人是交不了好运的。我一直疑惑那条蛇皮给我带来的晦气,还没有完呢。"

"吉木,我要是根本没遇见那条蛇皮,有多么好——我真希望我根本就没看见它。"

"哈克,那并不是你的错;你事前根本不知道。你千万别怪你自己。"

天光大亮的时候,岸这边果然是俄亥俄河湛清的河水,靠外面那一边还照旧是那条黄澄澄的老浑河①!原来开罗确实是过去了。

我们把事情从头到尾谈了一遍。由岸上走是办不到的;我们当然也没法把木筏划到上游去。唯一的办法是等到天黑,再坐小船回去撞撞运气。所以我们在白杨丛里睡了一整天,为的是干起活来有精神,可是天快黑的时候,我们回到木筏这里一看,那只小船不见了!

我们呆了半天没出声。根本也没什么可说的了。我们两个明明知道这又是那条蛇皮在作祟;那还谈它干什么呢?那仿佛是我们还在抱怨,结果一定还会碰上倒楣的事——照这样一直碰下去,最后受够了教

---

① 密西西比河。

第二篇 《哈克贝利·费恩历险记》The Adventure of Huckberry Finn

训,只好不声不响。

随后我们又商量究竟怎么办才好,我们觉得没有别的办法,只有坐着木筏往下漂,等有机会买一只小船往回走。我们虽然偶尔看见周围没有人,可是并不打算去借一只,象爸爸常常干的那样,因为那样干就会有人追。

所以,天黑了以后,我们就坐着木筏走开了。

玩弄蛇皮是一桩蠢事;如果有人知道了那条蛇皮给我们带来这么些背运以后,仍然不肯相信的话,那么就请他继续往下看,看看它又让我们遇见了什么,他就会相信了。

由停泊在岸边的木筏上,经常可以买到独木船。可是我们并没看见有木筏停在岸边,所以我们就一直往前走了三个多钟头。这时候,晚上变得黑暗而阴沉,这种天气跟下雾差不多是一样的讨厌。你既说不清河上的情形,也看不出距离的远近。大约到了夜深的时候,忽然有一条轮船由下游开过来。我们马上点起灯笼,以为它一定能够看见。上水船通常不靠近我们;它们总是闪到一旁,沿着沙洲,挑选暗礁脚下的静水走,可是在这样的黑夜里,它们就来到大河的当中,不顾一切地向上拱,好象是跟整条大河作对似的。

我们听得见它砰砰地开过来,可是一直等它走到跟前才看清楚。它对准了我们冲过来。有时候,他们这样走,是想看看能不能由我们旁边擦过,而不把我们撞翻;有时候,汽船的轮子把一根长桨切掉了。于是那个领港就探出头来哈哈大笑,自以为这一手耍得很漂亮。现在,它朝着我们开过来了,我们还说它又想要"刮我们的胡子"了;但是它并没有往旁边转舵。它是一条大船,又来势汹汹,看上去好象是一朵乌云,周围有一排一排象萤火虫似的亮光;但是,它突然现了原形,大得叫人害怕,一排敞开的锅炉门发出火光,仿佛是烧红了的牙齿似的,它那大得要命的船头和保险栏,已经伸到我们的头顶上了。船上有人对我们喊了一声,跟着丁丁当当地一阵铃响,是打算把机器停住,又听见一片乱喊乱骂和放汽的声音——这时候,吉木从那一边,我从这一边刚跳下水去,它就一下子把木筏从正当中撞了个粉碎。

我扎了一个猛子——想要摸着河底,因为船上有一个三十英尺的大轮子要由我头上转过去,所以我打算躲它远一点儿。我平常在水里能呆一分钟;这回我算计着我在水里呆了一分半钟。然后我急忙窜到水面,因为我简直快要憋死了。我一下子伸出头来,水齐着我的胳肢窝那儿,一边由嘴里往外喷水,一边由鼻子里往外擤水。当然,这一带的河水流得很急;这只船停了十秒钟之后,就又开动机器,照样前进,因为那些人对于筏夫从来不关心。现在它正向上游冲过去,虽然我还能听见它的声音,可是它已经在阴暗的夜里消失了。

我大声喊了吉木十几次,可是一声回答也听不见;正当我"踩水"的时候,有一块木板碰了我一下,我就推着这块板子往岸上游。但是我发现这一带河水是向左边岸上流的,这就是说,我来到一条横水道里;所以我就改变了方向,对着那面凫过去。

那是一条足有两英里长的斜斜的横水道;所以我费了很大的工夫才凫过去。我找了个妥当的地方爬上岸来。我没法看得很远,只好在那坑坑洼洼的地上摸索着往前走了四五百码,然后无意之中来到一所二合一的旧式大木房子跟前。我本打算赶快走过去,躲开这里,可是有好几条狗由门里跳出来,对我汪汪乱叫,所以我认为还是站住不动为妙。

第二篇 《哈克贝利·费恩历险记》The Adventure of Huckberry Finn

《赫克尔贝利·费恩历险记》(节选)

成 时 译

第十六章

  我们差不多睡了一整天,晚上动身。有一列长得出奇的木排,象一支游行队伍,过了好长时间,我们就在它后面不远跟着。那木排前后各有四支长桨,因此我们断定它大概载着三十个人。它上面有五座木棚,彼此相隔挺远,中间生着一个露天大篝火,两头各有一根高高的旗杆。整个木排看来好不威风。在这样的船上当个木排伕,那才叫够意思。

  我们一路下去,进了个大河湾,夜里云层密布,天气变得热了。河面很宽,两岸各有一堵树木的墙夹着它,连一道墙缝、一盏灯火也难得看见。我们谈着凯劳,说是我们到了那地方,也不知能不能认出它来。我说怕认不出,因为听人说,那儿不过有十几户人家,万一那些人家没有点灯,我们又怎么能知道正路过一个镇子呢?杰姆说,如果那两条大河真在那儿汇合,那就能看出来。可是我说,兴许我们还以为正经过一个岛尾,回到了同一条大河里。这么一说,杰姆不放心啦——我也不放心。现在的问题是怎么办?我说:一见有个灯火,我就划到岸边去,告诉人家我爹在我后头,在一条运货驳船上,他干这营生还是个生手,想打听一下凯劳离这儿有多远。杰姆觉着这主意不错。于是我一边抽烟盘算这事儿,一边等。①

---

① 以下有写木排伕一节,约一万字,出版时作者应出版人之请从原稿中抽去。现作为附录译出。

第二篇 《哈克贝利·费恩历险记》The Adventure of Huckberry Finn

这时,除了留神察看,别错过那个镇子以外,我们无事可做。杰姆说,只要经过那镇子,他准能认出它来,因为一见了它,他就是个自由人啦;万一错过了它呢,那他又回到蓄奴地区,再也不用想自由啦。每隔一会儿,他就跳起来说:

"瞧,灯火!"

其实那不是灯火,是磷火或是萤火虫。于是他又坐下来照旧张望。杰姆说,想起离自由这么近啦,他不由得浑身哆嗦、发烧。好,我告诉你们:听他这么说,我也是浑身哆嗦、发烧,因为我开始明白过来,他眼见得要自由啦——这事儿怨谁呢?还不是我。我的良心死活也安不下来。它闹得我坐也不是,立也不是;想静静地待一会,可哪儿也待不住。我以前一直没有想到:我眼下干的就是这事儿。现在我明白啦,不由得死死想着它,心里越想越焦躁。我想跟自己解释:这不怨我,因为我并没有叫杰姆逃离他的合法的主人;然而这不管用,每回良心就出来说:"可你知道他是逃出来投奔自由的,你尽可以划到岸边去告发他。"说得对——这一点我怎么也躲不过去。这正是我的心病。良心对我说,"可怜的华珍小姐哪一点亏待你啦,你竟然看着她的黑奴在你眼皮子底下跑了,一声也不吭?这可怜的老婆子哪一点亏待你啦,你竟然做这样对不起她的事?她尽心教你念书,尽心教你做人的规矩,她千方百计地照管你。她就是这样对待你。"

我越想心里越难受,越觉得自己不是个东西,真恨不得死了才好。我在木排上来回折腾,心里自己骂自己。杰姆也在我面前来回折腾。我们俩谁也安静不下来。每回他蹦蹦跳跳地说,"凯劳掏(到)啦!"我的心就象给人捅了一下,我心里想:那要真是凯劳,我多半会难受死。

我暗自思量的时候,杰姆一直在大声嚷嚷。他说,他到一个废奴州,头一件要做的事就是攒钱,一分钱也不花,攒够了钱,就给华珍小姐住处一户农庄上为奴的他的老婆赎身,然后夫妻两人干活挣钱再给两个孩子赎身,要是孩子的主人不让赎,他们就找个废奴主义者去把他们盗走。

听他这样说,我全身发凉。以前他怎么也不敢说这种话。你瞧,一到他认定快要自由了的时候,他的变化有多大。正如老话说的:"你给一个黑奴一吋,他就问你要一呎①。"我心想:这就是不动脑筋的结果。眼前这个黑奴,等于是我帮他逃出来的,现在居然直截了当地说出要盗走他的孩子的话来——那两个孩子的主人,我连认识也不认识,更谈不上有什么冤仇。

我听杰姆说出这种话来,这样自己作践自己,心里很难过。我的良心煽得我的火从来没有这么旺过,我终于对它说,"饶了我吧——现下还不晚——我见了第一个灯火就划到岸边去告发。"我马上觉得轻松快活,身子象要飞起来似的。所有我的苦恼都烟消云散。我过去留神察看灯火,心里象要唱起歌来。过了一会,一个灯火出现了。杰姆高兴得叫起来:

"我们并(平)安无事啦,赫克,我们并安无事啦!挺起身子行礼吧,这就史(是)我们日夜念叨的凯劳,我一看就知道!"

我说:

"我坐上划子去看看,杰姆。你要知道,它兴许不是凯劳。"

他跳过去把划子准备好,把他的旧上衣铺在舱底让我坐,把桨交给我;我划开去的当儿,他说:

"布(不)用陀旧(多久),我就会快活得叫起来,我约(要)说:这陀跪(多亏)赫克。我史过(是个)自由人啦,要布史有赫克,我这一攀(辈)子也布用想自由;赫克帮了我的忙,杰姆我永世忘布了你赫克;你史我杰姆顶好的奔(朋)友;我劳(老)杰姆此刻只有你这过奔友。"

我本来划着桨,心急火燎地要去告发他,可是他一说这番话,我的气似乎泄了个精光。我的桨放慢了,自己也拿不定这次上岸去,我是高兴还是不高兴。我离开木排五十码光景,杰姆说:

"你去啦,我的好赫克;白人先商(生)里头,只有你对劳(老)杰姆说话酸(算)话。"

我听了难受极了。可是我想:我只能这么做——这事我躲不过去。正在这当儿,来了一条平底船,船上有两个带枪的人,他们停了船,我也停下了。其中一人问:

---

① 指古尺,合 45 英寸。

"那边是什么?"

"一截木排,"我说。

"你是木排上的?"

"是的,先生。"

"那上面有人吗?"

"只有一个人,先生。"

"哦,今夜河湾上头跑了五个黑奴。你那个人是白人还是黑人?"

一时间我没有回话。我想回话,可就是说不出来。我又使了一下劲,想一鼓气说出来,可是我够不上一个男子汉——胆量还不如一只兔子。我知道我越来越泄气,索性不干了,便脱口而出:

"他是个白人。"

"我想咱们还是亲眼去看看。"

"我巴不得你们去,"我说,"因为是我爹在那儿,你们兴许肯帮我把木排拖到岸边那有灯火的地方。他病啦——我娘和曼丽·安也病啦。"

"嘿,活见鬼!我们有急事,孩子。不过我想咱们总得去看看。来——使劲划你的桨,咱们一块儿去。"

我使劲划起桨来,他们扳他们的。我们刚划了一两下,我就说:

"我可以告诉你们,爹准会对你们千恩万谢。我求人帮我把木排拖到岸边,个个听了都走得远远的,我一个人又干不了。"

"这心太狠啦。事儿也有点儿怪。喂,孩子,你爸爸到底得了什么病?"

"是那——呃——那——嗯,不是什么大毛病。"

他们停了桨。这时离木排只有一丁点儿路了。一个人说:

"孩子,你是在撒谎。你爹到底害的什么病?这回要老老实实回话,这对你有好处。"

"我说,先生,我说老实话——可请你们千万别丢下我们不管。他得的是——是——先生,你们只要往前划,我把缆绳扔给你们,你们用不着靠近木排——我求求你们。"

"退回去,约翰,退回去!"一个说。他们倒着划了。"离开,孩子——到下风头去。该死的风,我正担心风把它吹给我们。你爹得的是天花,你心里明白得很。你为什么不痛痛快快说出来？你要让它散布得到处都是吗？"

"嗳，"我呜呜哭着说，"我以前告诉了每一个人，他们一听掉头就走，不管我们。"

"可怜的小东西，说的也有道理。我们为你十分难过，可是我们——好，去它的，我们不愿意染上天花，你明白吗？听着，我告诉你怎样办。你一个人别上岸去，要不，你会闯大祸。你往下游漂约莫二十哩，就到了河的左手边一个镇子。那时候，太阳早就出来啦，你求人帮忙的时候，就说你一家人全得了寒热病。别再犯傻，让人家猜出是什么病来。我们这是在帮你的忙；你只要离开我们二十哩，你就是个好孩子。你在那边有灯火的地方上岸，不会有好处——那只是个木材场。喂，你爸爸大概挺穷，我不能不说，他够倒楣的。喏——我把这二十块钱的金币放在这木板上，它漂过来，你就拿了。我撇下你不管，心里真不是滋味儿，可是老天爷！跟天花打交道不是闹着玩的，你明白吗？"

"等一等，派克，"那一个说。"这是二十块钱的一个金币，替我放在木板上。再见，孩子，你照派克先生说的办，会平安无事的。"

"是这样，我的孩子——再见，再见。你要遇上逃跑的黑奴，就找人帮你拿住他们，那样你还能得些钱。"

"再见，先生们，"我说，"只要我办得到，我不会让逃跑的黑奴在我身边溜掉的。"

他们划走了，我上了木排，心里怪难受，提不起劲儿来，因为我知道我做了错事，我也明白：我就是想学走正道也学不了啦；一个人从小一开头就不走正道，就不会有出息——遇上急难的时候，背后没有东西支撑他，让他守自己的本分，最后只有垮台了事。接着转念一想，我跟自己说：且慢——就算你做得对，告发了杰姆；你会比现在好过吗？不会，我会觉得难受——就跟我现在一样。既然如此，既然走正道麻烦，做错事并不费事，得的工资又是一般多，学走正道又有什么用？我给难住了。我解答不了这问题。于是我打算再也不去操这份心啦，以后有事，就看当时怎么方便怎么办。

我走进木棚；杰姆不在那儿。我四下里张望，哪儿也不见他。我叫道：

"杰姆！"

"我在这耳(儿)，赫克。他们走得不见真(踪)影了吗？说话小声点。"

原来他在河里，躲在后梢桨底下，只露出个鼻子。我告诉他：那两人已经走得不见踪影啦，他才上了木排。他说：

"我一直听着你们说话，我滑掏(到)河里，正打酸(算)他们上木坯(排)的话，我就优(泅)掏岸边去。灯(等)他们走后，再优回木坯。赫克，你真能，叫他们上了当！这真史(是)顶顶机伦(灵)的一招！跟你说吧，孩子，我就痴方(指望)这一招救我劳(老)杰姆啦——乖乖，劳杰姆忘布(不)了这救命之哼(恩)。"

随后我们谈起钱来。这回添了真不少，一人二十块大洋。杰姆说我们现在可以买票搭轮船走啦，有了这些钱，我们可以到解放黑奴各州里我们想去的地方。他说木排走二十哩不算远，可是他巴不得我们已经到了那儿。

将近天亮的时候，我们靠岸。杰姆为了藏好木排，挑拣了半天地方。然后他花了一整天收拾东西打成包裹，一切准备停当，单等丢了木排上岸。

那天晚上十点钟光景，我们看到前面左手边河湾里一个镇子的灯火。

我上了划子划出去打听。不多久我发现一个人在河上一条平底船里放钓鱼的滚钓线。我靠过去问：

"先生，这是凯劳镇吗？"

"凯劳？不是。你准是个大笨蛋。"

"这镇叫什么，先生？"

"你想知道，就自己去打听。你要待在这儿再打扰我一时半刻，别怪我对你不客气。"

我划回木排。杰姆大为失望，可是我说这没有什么，下一个码头大概就是凯劳。

天亮之前，我们又到了一个镇子，我正想再去；但是那是块高地，所以没有去。杰姆说过，凯劳周围没有高地。我把这忘了。我们就在靠左

第二篇 《哈克贝利·费恩历险记》The Adventure of Huckberry Finn

边河岸挺近的一个滩头上度过白天。我开始心里犯疑。杰姆也一样。我说：

"兴许那天晚上我们在雾里就过了凯劳啦。"

他说：

"我们布（不）谈这过（个），赫克。科（可）怜的黑奴走布了好运。我醒（心）里一直犯嘀咕：那响尾蛇皮的事还没有韩（完）。"

"我要没发现那蛇皮就好啦，杰姆——我真懊悔当初不该朝那儿看了一眼。"

"这布（不）怨你，赫克；你布知道这忌讳。别为这事耳（儿）商（生）自个耳（儿）的气。"

天亮以后。果然不错，岸边是俄亥俄河清清的河水，外面是那条地道的泥汤河！看来凯劳是过去啦①。

我们细细商量了一番。丢了木排走陆路不成；坐木排上水去自然办不到。想来想去，只有等到天黑，坐划子往回走，试试运气。于是我们在杨树丛里睡了一整天，恢复了精神好干活，天擦黑的时候，我们回到木排上，发现划子不见了。

有好一阵，我们作不得声。没有什么好说的。我们俩心里都透亮：又是那响尾蛇皮在作怪；有什么可议论的？那只会使我们象是在挑刺抱怨，准保会招来更多的倒楣事儿——而且会不断地招来倒楣事儿，一直到我们明白过来，一声不吭才完。

过了一会，我们讨论起下一步怎么走才好，结果是没有别的法子，

---

① 凯劳位于比较清澈的俄亥俄河流入含泥量很高的密西西比河入口处。现在在一条河中看到清浊两种水，说明赫克和杰姆已经过了凯劳。作者原来计划让杰姆溯俄亥俄河而上，进入废奴各州而获得自由。然而离开密西西比河，作者在创作中便失去了感情和观察体验上的依托，因此作了使主人公错过凯劳、延长他们的逃亡的选择。但延长逃亡实际上使逃亡成功的希望越来越渺茫。作者落入了一种两难境地，一时不知如何处理。于是在以后几段中结束了这个主题，并搁笔三年。——部分据诺顿版注。

只有坐着木排往下走,一有机会就买只划子再回头。爹遇上这种情形会趁四下里没有人的当儿,借一只划子,可是我们不能这么干,因为这兴许会招人来追我们。

于是天黑以后,我们坐上木排朝前走。

有人看到这里,看了那响尾蛇皮叫我们吃了多少苦头,还不信响尾蛇皮是碰不得的,那末他往后看下去,看它叫我们吃更多的苦头,那时候他自会信的。

买小划子的地方应该离靠岸木排不远。可是我们看不见靠岸的木排;因此我又走了三个多钟头。那一夜夜色灰蒙蒙、昏沉沉的,除了起雾,就数这样的夜色顶讨厌。你看不清河的形状,看不出距离的远近。夜一定很深了,一片寂静。随后来了一条上水的轮船。我们点亮了灯,心想它一定会看见。上水船通常不会驶近我们;它们顺着沙洲,挑那礁脉底下水势平缓的地方上;可是在这样的夜里,它们只得顶着整条河的水势,硬是走航道。

我们听得见它轰轰开来,可是在靠近之前,我们看不清它。它正对着我们驶来。这些轮船常来这一手,看看它能挨得多近而又不碰小船;有时它们的明轮撞断小船上一支长桨,然后引水的伸出脑袋来嘿嘿地笑,自鸣得意。这一回,它来啦,我们以为它想来刮我们的胡子;可是看来它毫无闪开一点的意思。这是条大轮船,开得又急,活象一块乌云,四周围缀着一排排萤火虫;突然间,它暴涨了许多,大得吓人,一长列大开着炉火通红的炉门好似血红的牙齿,那怪物似的船头还有那些防护装置向我们头顶压来。有人冲我们叫了一声,响起一串铃声通知机房关机,哇啦哇啦的咒骂,汽笛呜呜的叫——它直冲过来,从木排上压过去,杰姆从木排一边,我从木排另一边,双双落水。①。

我一头扎进水里——而且存心扎到河底,因为那直径三十呎的轮子要在我头上滚过去,再加我希望离轮子尽量远些。平时我可以伏在水

---

① 马克·吐温于1876年夏写作本书,写了四百页原稿,大致在此处搁笔。三年以后开始续写,在1879年秋至1883年之间写出第十七至二十章和二十一章的部分。全书于1884年夏完成,1885年初出版。——诺顿版注。

下一分钟;这一回我想我伏在水下有一分半钟。然后我腾一下蹿到水面上,因为人快要炸啦。我蹿出来一直到胳肢窝,打鼻孔里喷出了水,吸了几口气。河水不用说流得哗哗的,轮船不用说在引擎关了十秒钟以后又开动了,因为木排伕的死活他们是不大在心的;这里它正喘嘘嘘地往上水开,在浓重的夜色中消失了,虽然我听得见它的声音。

我叫了杰姆十来声,可是听不到任何回应;正好在我"踩水"的当儿,一块木板漂到我身边,我抓住了它,推着它在我前头,朝岸边泅去。我看清了水流的势头偏向左手岸边,这说明我正在一处横渡中;于是我转向那一路泅去。

密西西比河上有些横渡,船得斜着走两哩,我碰上的正是这样一个横渡口;所以费了好长时间才过了河。我平平安安地登陆,爬上了河岸。我朝前看只能看一小截路,但是我摸索着走了四分之一哩多高低不平的地面;不等我看清,我已来到了一所双幢老式的大木头房子跟前。我正想快步走过去,哪知道有好多狗跳出来,冲着我汪汪狂叫,我知道这时最好是一步不动。

第三篇 《苔丝》两个译本的比较

叶家莉

《苔丝》是19世纪末英国杰出批判现实主义作家哈代的代表著作。小说通过苔丝在爱情和婚姻上的悲剧揭示了资产阶级道德伪善,反映出农民的悲惨命运,对当时社会的黑暗进行了抨击。故事情节紧凑,结构严谨,语言质朴,景物描写与情节的发展水乳交融,几乎达到了完美的境地。

这部小说早在30年代就被我国著名翻译家张谷若译成中文,深受广大中国读者喜爱。张谷若先生致力于研究、翻译哈代的作品,以多部优秀译著享誉译坛。虽然六十多年已经过去,他所译的《苔丝》仍拥有大量的读者。在近几年中,《苔丝》又有了好几个译本,这里笔者选了1991年浙江文艺出版社出版的吴笛的译作。以下将从几个方面对两个译本进行比较。

一、意义的准确性

翻译是一项用一种文字将另一种文字表达的思想内容转达出来的活动。对于原文意义的"信"在文字翻译上是至关重要的。泰特勒的翻译三原则将"翻译应是原著思想内容的完整再现"放在第一位。因此译文不可脱离原文,任意发挥。

1. The most impressed of them said:

"Be you really going to christen him, Tess?"

The girl-mother replied in a grave affirmative.

张译:其中有一个受感动最深的问:

"姐姐,你真要给他行洗礼吗?"

那个年纪轻轻的母亲郑重地答应了一个"是"字。

第三篇 《苔丝》Tess of the D'urbervilles

吴译：其中有一个问题给人印象最深：
"苔丝，你真的给他施洗礼吗？"
年幼的母亲庄严地作出了肯定的回答。

张与吴对于"The most impressed of them"有着不同的理解。张认为这是指人，将其译为"其中有一个受感动最深的"，在上文中曾提到苔丝的弟弟妹妹跪在她四周，等着她做洗礼。这里的"them"就是回指她的弟妹们，因此理解是正确的。吴则认为这是指给人印象最深的一个问题。单看中文译文似乎也解释得通，但对照原文，就会发现"them"如做"问题"，在前文中找不到所指，而且"impressed"指"受感触深的"，一般是修饰人的。

最后一句两个译文内容基本一致。但张将"replied"译作"答应"，似乎意义稍违原文。"答应"可表示同意做某事或应声要做某事，而这两种意思都不符合苔丝当时的情况，因而译成"回答"更为贴切。

2. Her mother knew Tess's feeling on this point so well, though no words had passed between them on the subject, that she never alluded to the knightly ancestry now.

张译：虽然她们是母女，并没提及这一节。她母亲却很知道，苔丝对于这一方面，有什么样的感情，所以现在再也不说武士世家的话了。

吴译：虽然她们母女俩没有谈到这方面的问题，可做母亲的非常清楚女儿的情感，所以她一次没有提及武士世家之类的话。

两段译文最大差异在于"that"引导的从句的翻译，原文中的"now"是不可忽略的，这表明苔丝母亲在以前和现在对于"德伯"这个远房亲戚的想法是根本不同的。前文中她曾大力主张苔丝去与之攀亲，以此炫耀，而现在却再不提及了，张译本较好地反映了原意，突出了苔丝母亲的转变。吴译本似乎强调从未谈起过，没有领会她从希望到失望的极大转折。

二、译文语言的表达力

翻译本身具有交际功能，这就需要译文有很强的可读性，译者要时

第三篇 《苔丝》Tess of the D'urbervilles

刻想着读者，使其作品通顺严谨，让读者感觉不到语言的隔阂。彼特·纽马克在提到翻译是艺术时，曾指出，译者要顺利地把理解到的东西表达出来，表达时可能需要再创作。可见译文的表达力是十分必要的。

英语和汉语属于不同语系，两者各方面差异很大，例如在句法上，"英语忌松散，主谓宾没有形式标定，主谓关系松散，宾语无定格，无定位，主句的超句承接功能强。"（刘宓庆）在英语汉译时一定要符合汉语的语言规律，否则就失去了表达力，也就无法保证译文的准确性，成为严复所说的"顾信矣不达，虽译犹不译也"。下面从《苔丝》中一些句子的翻译来比较一下译文的表达力。

1. When the infant had taken its fill the mother sat it upright in her lap, and looking into the far distance, dandled it with a gloomy indifference that was almost dislike; then all of a sudden she fell to violently kissing it some dozens of times, as if she could never leave off, the child crying at the vehemence of an onset which strangely combined passionateness with contempt.

张译：小孩吃足了奶以后，那位年轻的母亲就把他放在腿上，叫他坐直了，逗弄他，眼睛却瞧着远处，脸上是一种阴郁沉闷的冷淡神情，几乎好像是嫌憎的样子。于是忽然又不顾轻重，往他脸上亲了十几下，好像老也亲不够似的；孩子叫那一阵又痛爱，又奇怪地夹杂着鄙夷的猛烈动作，吓得哭了起来。

吴译：当婴孩吃足奶之后，年轻的母亲让婴孩坐直在自己的腿上，自己的眼睛望着远方，带着一种几乎算成憎恨的阴郁的冷漠，播弄着婴孩；接着，她突然不顾轻重地把婴孩亲吻了几十遍，仿佛永远亲不够似的，孩子经不住由痛爱和鄙夷奇特结合起来的猛烈进攻，哇地哭了起来。

这段文字突出表现了苔丝爱恨交加的心情，我们这里着重讨论原文分号以前的部分。原文是一句较长的复合句，体现出英语逻辑性强的特点，两个主要动作是"sat it upright"和"dandled"，关于目光的描述是

第三篇 《苔丝》Tess of the D'urbervilles

伴随性的。理清这一关系后,翻译中就应注意句子的安排,以便使读者无理解困难。张译本重新调整了词句顺序,按照汉语习惯译成了几个分句,先描写苔丝对待孩子的充满母爱的动作,再写她冷漠的目光和神情,强烈的反差一目了然,译文读起来颇为流畅自然。吴译本则基本遵照原文词句顺序,将眼睛和手的动作混在一起写,这样的汉语显得有些杂乱无章。特别是在刚提到眼睛的冷漠后,又突然写到"播弄着婴孩"。使读者心理上一时难以接受。

另外一些词句上吴的选择也略有欠缺,如"让婴孩坐直在自己的腿上","带着一种几乎算作憎恨的阴郁的冷漠"。这些译文翻译腔过浓,生硬拗口。相比之下,张译本的"把他放在腿上,叫他坐直了"。"脸上是一种阴郁沉闷的冷漠表情,几乎好像是嫌憎的样子",则更加自然,更加符合汉语的表达方式。

2. The marble hardness left her face, she moved with something of her old bounding step, and flushed in all her young beauty.

张译:她脸上不像先前跟大理石一般那么硬了,她的举动也带出了一些她往日轻快活泼的样子来了,她那焕发的容光,更显出她青春的美丽。

吴译:大理石一般生硬的神气也从她脸上消失了,她的脚步也变得轻快自如,无拘无束了,她周身洋溢着青春的美丽。

原文中的暗喻生动形象,把人物刻画得栩栩如生。译者必须既保留原文的生动性,又保证译文的可接受性。张译本保留了原文的本体和喻体——"跟大理石一般那么硬"。这里用"硬"来修饰脸似嫌达意不够,让人不知所云,不但表达力与原文相差甚远,而且原文的意义也随之丢失。吴译本将"marble hardness"引申为"大理石一般生硬的神气",甚是巧妙。这一必要的增补使得译文贴切地道,并保存了生动之感,原意传达比较成功。

3. But it had not been in Tess's power—nor is it in anybody's power—to feel the whole truth of golden opinions while it is possible to profit by them.

张译:但是世界上的人总是等到这种金石之言,不再能于他们有益的时候,才能完全懂得其中的道理,想要早点儿懂得,是苔丝办不到的,也是无论谁都办不到的。

吴译:但是,无论是苔丝,还是任何别的人,都只有在那些金玉良言不再有益于他们的时候,才会领会它们的全部道理。

原文用了强调句式,把两个否定形式的介词短语放在句首处,语气较强。张注意到这点特征,试图保存原来的否定形式,译为"……是苔丝办不到的,也是无论谁都办不到的。"这一努力虽好,但前半句话冗长拗口。吴译本没有把重点放在否定上,而是用了汉语有强调口气的条件句"只有……才"表示出原文的意思,清晰通顺,也较易于读者理解。

4. Symbols of reflectiveness passed into her face, and a note of tragedy at times into her voice.

张译:她脸上带出来沉思深念的象征,语言里也有时露出凄楚伤感的腔调。

吴译:她脸上映出了沉思的符号,她声音中也时常出现了悲剧的音调。

两个译本的直译色彩都过重,如将"Symbol"分别译为"象征"和"符号"。在句中的搭配尽力保持了原文的表达方式,结果却是不合汉语习惯,没有表达力。与其这样,笔者认为还不如采用中国人习惯的词语,译作"她脸上带出来沉思的神情,声音中也常有悲凉的音调。"

三、原文意境的再现

好的文学作品往往都是意境表现的上乘之作。我国著名美学家朱光潜曾在文章中这样谈到:"要读者深刻地感觉到某人在某境中哀如何哀,乐如何乐,就必须把它所伴的具体情境烘托出来。因此,言情常须假于叙事状物。美学家谈表现,以为情感须与意象融合,就因为这个道理。"文学翻译十分重视原文意境的再现。也就是说,翻译文学作品要意合神合,入情入味。原文的内涵、神韵都要通过译文的字里行间体现出来,使得原著中活生生的人物形象,真切动人的生活场景,能逼真地再现于译文读者的面前。正像茅盾所说的,"文学翻译是用一种语言把原

第三篇 《苔丝》Tess of the D'urbervilles

作的艺术意境传达出来,供读者在读译文的时候能像读原作时一样得到启发,感动和美的感受。"

哈代尤其注意意境的表现,他被称为文学画家,他用画家的眼光看待要反映的事物,用画家的手法描写周围变化的环境。然而,在他的作品中,很少是为了描绘而描绘,而是把描写的物质环境纳入故事情节的轨道,烘托人物悲剧命运,从而大大加强了小说描写的感染力。《苔丝》一书就体现了这一特征。译者能否再现原文的意境,直接影响到译文的整体效果。

1. On these lonely hills and dales her quiescent glide was of a piece with the elment she moved in.

   张译:在这些旷山之上和空谷之中,她那悄悄冥冥的凌虚细步和她所活动于其中的大气,成为一体。

   吴译:在这些寂静的山林和溪谷中,她那轻轻的脚步与她周围的环境极其融合。

这里作者并非只是单纯描述某件事情或某种行为,而更多的是为了烘托出一种气氛来激起读者对自然的特殊感受,从而理解苔丝那种要"躲开人类"的心理反映。吴译本只停留在描述一层上,略显平淡,读过之后很难引起读者共鸣,如"Lonely"被译作"寂静",没有充分表现出作者给山林和谷地赋予的超然感觉;"quiescent glide"被译作"轻轻的脚步",令人很难体会出原文中苔丝步态轻盈,飘然如仙的美感。张译本将这两处分别译作"旷山之上和空谷之中"和"悄悄冥冥的凌虚细步",用词之妙,值得称道。原文的色彩、氛围得到成功的再现,一种空灵飘渺之感在译文中油然而生。

2. As the hour of eleven drew near a person watching her might have noticed that every now and then Tess's glance flitted wistfully to the brow of the hill, though she did not pause in her sheafing.

   张译:快到十一点钟的时候,如果有人瞅着苔丝,他一定能看见她带着欲有所求的神气,往山头那儿时瞥时瞟,不过她却始终没停止工作。

第三篇 《苔丝》Tess of the D'urbervilles

> 吴译:快到十一点钟的时候,如果有人观察一下苔丝,就会发现,尽管她没有停住捆麦的活儿,但她的目光却不时焦虑地投向远方的山坡。

这段描述通过苔丝焦急期盼孩子被送来,为之喂奶,又不愿让人家察觉出心理的神情、动作,表现其内心矛盾的心情。关键词句在于"every now and then Tess's glance flitted wistfully to the brow of the hill."

张、吴两个译本都力图把苔丝的焦虑表达出来。细读起来,可以发现吴译本未能把苔丝快速向远方瞥一眼,又转过目光,以掩示内心感情的生动细节全部转达出来。"目光却不时焦虑地投向远方的山坡"给人的感觉是动作较慢,持续时间长。张译本注意到了这一点,将 wistfully 提出,转为动词词组"带着欲有所求的神气",又用了"时瞥时瞟",力求再现原文内在神韵,可谓略胜一筹。然而在具体的遣词上稍显文采不足。笔者试将此处译为"他一定能看到苔丝会不时若有所盼地向着山头那边瞥上一眼。"

3. In the blue of the morning that fragile soldier and servant breathed his last, and when the other children awoke they cried bitterly, and begged Sissy to have another pretty baby.

> 张译:在晨光熹微中,那位脆弱的兵士和仆人就喘了他最后一口气,别的孩子们醒过之后,一个个哭得伤心极了,他们恳求苔丝姐姐再给他们生一个漂亮的娃娃。

> 吴译:在清幽幽的晨光中,这名脆弱的战士和奴仆喘出了他们最后一口气,别的孩子们醒过之后,一个个哭得伤心极了,他们恳求苔丝姐姐再给他们生一个漂亮的娃娃。

两个译文大同小异,主要区别在于对"blue"一词的处理。"blue"突出感情色彩的关键,集中体现出这段文字的意境。张译本用"晨光熹微",有些含糊,更重要的是,无法表现出原文中悲伤凄凉的意境。吴译本用了"清幽幽",情节顿然富于色彩,效果基本等同于原文。

可见要使译文和原文神合,收到同样的表达效果,译者就必须通读原著,充分理解上下文,挖掘深层内涵。就如何把原文情感的佳妙处译

第三篇 《苔丝》Tess of the D'urbervilles

出时,朱光潜的看法是:"第一步须设身处在作者的地位,透入作者的心窍,和他同样感,同样想,同样地努力使所感所想凝定于语文。"这段话或许可以成为我们再现意境的指导思想。

参考文献

1. 刘宓庆:"思维方式,表现法和翻译问题",《中国当代翻译百论》,杜承南、文军主编,重庆大学出版社,1994年。
2. 刘重德:《翻译漫谈》,陕西人民出版社,1984年。
3. Newmark, P., Approaches To translation. Prentice Hall International (UK) Ltd., 1988.
4. 张世君:《〈德伯家的苔丝〉鉴赏》,重庆出版社,1986年。
5. 朱光潜:"具体与抽象",《谈文学》,安徽教育出版社,1997年。
6. 朱光潜:"谈翻译",《谈文学》,安徽教育出版社,1997年。
7. 朱琳:《英国文学简史》,海南出版社,1993年。

附：

Tess of the D'urbervilles (Excerpt)
Thomas Hardy

XIII

The event of Tess Durbeyfield's return from the manor of her bogus kinsfolk was rumoured abroad, if rumour be not too large a word for a space of a square mile. In the afternoon several young girls of Marlott, former schoolfellows and acquaintances of Tess, called to see her, arriving dressed in their best starched and ironed, as became visitors to a person who had made a transcendent conquest (as they supposed), and sat round the room looking at her with great curiosity. For the fact that it was this said thirty-first cousin, Mr d'Urberville, who had fallen in love with her, a gentleman not altogether local, whose reputation as a reckless gallant and heart-breaker was beginning to spread beyond the immediate boundaries of Trantridge, lent Tess's supposed position, by its fearsomeness, a far higher fascination than it would have exercised if unhazardous.

Their interest was so deep that the younger ones whispered when her back was turned—

'How pretty she is; and how that best frock do set her off! I believe it cost an immense deal, and that it was a gift from him.'

Tess, who was reaching up to get the tea-things from the corner-cupboard, did not hear these commentaries. If she had heard them, she might soon have set her friends right on the matter. But her mother heard, and Joan's simple vanity, having been denied the hope of a dashing marriage, fed itself as well as it could upon the sensation of a dashing flirtation. Upon the whole she felt gratified, even though such a limited and evanescent triumph should involve her daughter's reputation; it might end in marriage yet, and in the warmth of her responsiveness to their admiration she invited her visitors to stay to tea.

Their chatter, their laughter, their good-humoured innuendoes, above all, their flashes and flickerings of envy, revived Tess's spirits also; and, as the evening wore on, she caught the infection of their excitement, and grew almost gay. The marble hardness left her face, she moved with something of her old bounding step, and flushed in all her young beauty.

At moments, in spite of thought, she would reply to their inquiries with a manner of superiority, as if recognizing that her experiences in the field of courtship had, indeed, been slightly enviable. But so far was she from being, in the words of Robert South, 'in love with her own ruin,' that the illusion was transient as lightning; cold reason came back to mock her spasmodic weakness; the ghastliness of her momentary pride would convict her, and recall her to reserved listlessness again.

And the despondency of the next morning's dawn, when it was no longer Sunday, but Monday; and no best clothes; and the laughing visitors were gone, and she awoke alone in her old bed, the innocent younger children breathing softly around her. In place of the excitement of her return, and the interest it had inspired, she saw before her a long and stony highway which she had to tread, without aid, and with little sympathy. Her depression was then terrible, and she could have hidden herself in a tomb.

In the course of a few weeks Tess revived sufficiently to show herself so far as was necessary to get to church one Sunday morning. She liked to hear the chanting—such as it was—and the old Psalms, and to join in the Morning Hymn. That innate love of melody, which she had inherited from her balladsinging mother, gave the simplest music a power over her which could well-nigh drag her heart out of her bosom at times.

To be as much out of observation as possible for reasons of her own, and to escape the gallantries of the young men, she set out before the chiming began, and took a back seat under the gallery, close to the lumber, where only old men and women came, and where the bier stood on end among the churchyard tools.

Parishioners dropped in by twos and threes, deposited themselves in rows before her, rested three-quarters of a minute on their foreheads as if they were praying, though they were not; then sat up, and looked around. When the chants came on one of her favourites happened to be chosen among the rest — the old double chant 'Langdon'—but she did not know what it was called, though she would much have liked to know. She thought, without exactly wording the thought, how strange and godlike was a composer's power, who from the grave could lead through sequences of emotion, which he alone had felt at first, a girl like her who had never heard of his name, and never would have a clue to his personality.

The people who had turned their heads turned them again as the service proceeded; and at last observing her they whispered to each other. She knew what their whispers were about, grew sick at heart, and felt that she could come to church no more.

The bedroom which she shared with some of the children formed her retreat more continually than ever. Here, under her few square yards of thatch, she watched winds, and snows, and rains, gorgeous sunsets, and successive moons at their full. So close kept she that at length almost everybody thought she had gone away.

　The only exercise that Tess took at this time was after dark; and it was then, when out in the woods, that she seemed least solitary. She knew how to hit to a hair's-breadth that moment of evening when the light and the darkness are so evenly balanced that the constraint of day and the suspense of night neutralize each other, leaving absolute mental liberty. It is then that the plight of being alive becomes attenuated to its least possible dimensions. She had no fear of the shadows; her sole idea seemed to be to shun mankind—or rather that cold accretion called the world, which, so terrible in the mass, is so unformidable, even pitiable, in its units.

　On these lonely hills and dales her quiescent glide was of a piece with the element she moved in. Her flexuous and stealthy figure became an integral part of the scene. At times her whimsical fancy would intensify natural processes around her till they seemed a part of her own story. Rather they became a part of it; for the world is only a psychological phenomenon, and what they seemed they were. The midnight airs and gusts, moaning amongst the tightly-wrapped buds and bark of the winter twigs, were formulae of bitter reproach. A wet day was the expression of irremediable grief at her weakness in the mind of some vague ethical being whom she could not class definitely as the God of her childhood, and could not comprehend as any other.

　But this encompassment of her own characterization, based on shreds of convention, peopled by phantoms and voices antipathetic to her, was a sorry and mistaken creation of Tess's fancy—a cloud of moral hobgoblins by which she was terrified without reason. It was they that were out of harmony with the actual world, not she. Walking among the sleeping birds in the hedges, watching the skipping rabbits on a moonlit warren, or standing under a pheasant-laden bough, she looked upon herself as a figure of Guilt intruding into the haunts of Innocence. But all the while she was making a distinction where there was no difference. Feeling herself in antagonism she was quite in accord. She had been made to break an accepted social law, but no law known to the environment in which she fancied herself such an anomaly.

XIV

It was a hazy sunrise in August. The denser nocturnal vapours, attacked by the warm beams, were dividing and shrinking into isolated fleeces within hollows and coverts, where they waited till they should be dried away to nothing.

The sun, on account of the mist, had a curious sentient, personal look, demanding the masculine pronoun for its adequate expression. His present aspect, coupled with the lack of all human forms in the scene, explained the old-time heliolatries in a moment. One could feel that a saner religion had never prevailed under the sky. The luminary was a golden-haired, beaming, mild-eyed, God-like creature, gazing down in the vigour and intentness of youth upon an earth that was brimming with interest for him.

His light, a little later, broke through chinks of cottage shutters, throwing stripes like red-hot pokers upon cupboards, chests of drawers, and other furniture within; and awakening harvesters who were not already astir.

But of all ruddy things that morning the brightest were two broad arms of painted wood, which rose from the margin of a yellow cornfield hard by Marlott village. They, with two others below,

第三篇 《苔丝》Tess of the D'urbervilles

formed the revolving Maltese cross of the reaping-machine, which had been brought to the field on the previous evening to be ready for operations this day. The paint with which they were smeared, intensified in hue by the sunlight, imparted to them a look of having been dipped in liquid fire.

The field had already been 'opened'; that is to say, a lane a few feet wide had been hand-cut through the wheat along the whole circumference of the field, for the first passage of the horses and machine.

Two groups, one of men and lads, the other of women, had come down the lane just at the hour when the shadows of the eastern hedge-top struck the west hedge midway, so that the heads of the groups were enjoying sunrise while their feet were still in the dawn. They disappeared from the lane between the two stone posts which flanked the nearest field-gate.

Presently there arose from within a ticking like the lovemaking of the grasshopper. The machine had begun, and a moving concatenation of three horses and the aforesaid long rickety machine was visible over the gate, a driver sitting upon one of the hauling horses, and an attendant on the seat of the implement. Along one side of the field the whole wain went, the arms of the mechanical reaper revolving slowly, till it passed down the hill quite out of sight. In a minute it came up on the other side of the field at the same equable pace; the glistening brass star in the forehead of the fore horse first catching the eye as it rose into view over the stubble, then the bright arms, and then the whole machine.

The narrow lane of stubble encompassing the field grew wider with each circuit, and the standing corn was reduced to smaller area as the morning wore on. Rabbits, hares, snakes, rats, mice, retreated inwards as into a fastness, unaware of the ephemeral nature of their refuge, and of the doom that awaited them later in the day when, their covert shrinking to a more and more horrible narrowness, they were huddled together, friends and foes, till the last few yards of upright wheat fell also under the teeth of the unerring reaper, and they were every one put to death by the sticks and stones of the harvesters.

The reaping-machine left the fallen corn behind it in little heaps, each heap being of the quantity for a sheaf; and upon these the active binders in the rear laid their hands — mainly women, but some of them men in print shirts, and trousers supported round their waists by leather straps, rendering useless the two buttons behind, which twinkled and bristled with sunbeams at every movement of each wearer, as if they were a pair of eyes in the small of his back.

But those of the other sex were the most interesting of this company of binders, by reason of the charm which is acquired by woman when she becomes part and parcel of outdoor nature, and is not merely an object set down therein as at ordinary times. A field-man is a personality afield; a field-woman is a portion of the field; she has somehow lost her own margin, imbibed the essence of her surrounding, and assimilated herself with it.

The women—or rather girls, for they were mostly young—wore drawn cotton bonnets with great flapping curtains to keep off the sun, and gloves to prevent their hands being wounded by the stubble. There was one wearing a pale pink jacket, another in a cream-coloured tight-sleeved gown, another in a petticoat as red as the arms of the reaping-machine; and others, older, in the brown-rough 'wropper' or over-all—the old-established and most appropriate dress of the field-woman, which the young ones were abandoning. This morning the eye returns involuntarily to the girl in the pink cotton jacket, she being the most flexuous and finely-drawn figure of them all. But her bonnet is pulled so far over her brow that none of her face is disclosed while she binds, though her complexions may be guessed from a stray twine or two of dark brown hair which extends below the curtain of her bonnet. Perhaps one reason why she seduces casual attention is that she never courts it, though the other women often gaze around them.

Her binding proceeds with clock-like monotony. From the sheaf last finished she draws a handful of ears, patting their tips with her left palm to bring them even. Then stooping low she moves forward, gathering the corn with both hands against her knees, and pushing her left gloved hand under the bundle to meet the right on the other side, holding the corn in an embrace like that of a lover. She brings the ends of the bond together, and kneels on the sheaf while she ties it, beating back her skirts now and then when lifted by the breeze. A bit of her naked arm is visible between the buff leather of the gauntlet and the sleeve of her gown; and as the day wears on its feminine smoothness becomes scarified by the stubble, and bleeds.

At intervals she stands up to rest, and to retie her disarranged apron, or to pull her bonnet straight. Then one can see the oval face of a handsome young woman with deep dark eyes and long heavy clinging tresses, which seem to clasp in a beseeching way anything they fall against. The cheeks are paler, the teeth more regular, the red lips thinner than is usual in a country-bred girl.

It is Tess Durbeyfield, otherwise d'Urberville, somewhat changed—the same, but not the same; at the present stage of her existence living as a stranger and an alien here, though it was no strange land that she was in. After a long seclusion she had come to a resolve to undertake outdoor work in her native village, the busiest season of the year in the agricultural world having arrived, and nothing that she could do within the house being so remunerative for the time as harvesting in the fields.

The movements of the other women were more or less similar to Tess's, the whole bevy of them drawing together like dancers in a quadrille at the completion of a sheaf by each, every one placing her sheaf on end against those of the rest, till a shock, or 'stitch' as it was here called, of ten or a dozen was formed.

They went to breakfast, and came again, and the work proceeded as before. As the hour of eleven drew near a person watching her might have noticed that every now and then Tess's glance flitted wistfully to the brow of the hill, though she did not pause in her sheafing. On the verge of the hour the heads of a group of children, of ages ranging from six to fourteen, rose above the stubbly convexity of the hill.

The face of Tess flushed slightly, but still she did not pause.

The eldest of the comers, a girl who wore a triangular shawl, its corner draggling on the stubble, carried in her arms what at first sight seemed to be a doll, but proved to be an infant in long clothes. Another brought some lunch. The harvesters ceased working, took their provisions, and sat down against one of the shocks. Here they fell to, the men plying a stone jar freely, and passing round a cup.

Tess Durbeyfield had been one of the last to suspend her labours. She sat down at the end of the shock, her face turned somewhat away from her companions. When she had deposited herself a man in a rabbit-skin cap and with a red handkerchief tucked into his belt, held the cup of ale over the top of the shock for her to drink. But she did not accept his offer. As soon as her lunch was spread she called up the big girl her sister, and took the baby off her, who, glad to be relieved of the burden, went away to the next shock and joined the other children playing there. Tess, with a curiously stealthy yet courageous movement, and with a still rising colour, unfastened her frock and began suckling the child.

The men who sat nearest considerately turned their faces towards the other end of the field, some of them beginning to smoke; one, with absent-minded fondness, regretfully stroking the jar that would no longer yield a stream. All the women but Tess fell into animated talk, and adjusted the disarranged knots of their hair.

When the infant had taken its fill the young mother sat it upright in her lap, and looking into the far distance dandled it with a gloomy indifference that was almost dislike; then all of a sudden she fell to violently kissing it some dozens of times as if she could never leave off, the child crying at the vehemence of an onset which strangely combined passionateness with contempt.

'She's fond of that there child, though she mid pretend to hate en, and say she wishes the baby and her too were in the churchyard,' observed the woman in the red petticoat.

'She'll soon leave off saying that,' replied the one in buff. 'Lord, 'tis wonderful what a body can get used to o' that sort in time!'

'A little more than persuading had to do wi' the coming o't, I reckon. There were they that heard a sobbing one night last year in The Chase; and it mid ha' gone hard wi' a certain party if folks had come along.'

'Well, a little more, or a little less, 'twas a thousand pities that it should have happened to she, of all others. But 'tis always the comeliest! The plain ones be as safe as churches—hey, Jenny?' The speaker turned to one of the group who certainly was not ill-defined as plain.

It was a thousand pities, indeed; it was impossible for even an enemy to feel otherwise on looking at Tess as she sat there, with her flower-like mouth and large tender eyes, neither black nor blue nor gray nor violet; rather all those shades together, and a hundred others, which could be seen if one looked into their irises—shade behind shade—tint beyond tint—around pupils that had no bottom; an almost standard woman, but for the slight incautiousness of character inherited from her race.

A resolution which had surprised herself had brought her into the fields this week for the first time during many months. After wearing and wasting her palpitating heart with every engine of regret that lonely inexperience could devise, commonsense had illumined her. She felt that she would do well to be useful again—to taste anew sweet independence at any price. The past was past; whatever it had been it was no more at hand. Whatever it consequences, time would close over them; they would all in a few years be as if they had never been, and she herself grassed down and forgotten. Meanwhile the trees were just as green as before; the birds sang and the sun shone as clearly now as ever. The familiar surroundings had not darkened because of her grief, nor sickened because of her pain.

She might have been that what had bowed her head so profoundly—the thought of the world's concern at her situation—was founded on an illusion. She was not an existence, an experience, a passion, a structure of sensations, to anybody but herself. To all humankind besides Tess was only a passing thought. Even to friends she was no more than a frequently passing thought. If she made herself miserable the livelong night and day it was only this much to them—'Ah, she makes herself unhappy.' If she tried to be cheerful, to dismiss all care, to take pleasure in the daylight, the flowers, the baby, she could only be this idea to them—'Ah, she bears it very well.' Moreover, alone in a desert island would she have been wretched at what had happened to her? Not greatly. If she could have been but just created, to discover herself as a spouseless mother, with no experience of life except as the parent of a nameless child, would the position have caused her to despair? No, she would have taken it calmly, and found pleasures therein. Most of the misery had been generated by her conventional aspect, and not by her innate sensations.

Whatever Tess's reasoning, some spirit had induced her to dress herself up neatly as she had formerly done, and come out into the fields, harvest-hands being greatly in demand just then. This was why she had borne herself with dignity, and had looked people calmly in the face at times, even when holding the baby in her arms.

The harvest-men rose from the shock of corn, and stretched their limbs, and extinguished their pipes. The horses, which had been unharnessed and fed, were again attached to the scarlet machine. Tess, having quickly eaten her own meal, beckoned to her eldest sister to come and take away the baby, fastened her dress, put on the buff gloves again, and stooped anew to draw a bond from the last completed sheaf for the tying of the next.

In the afternoon and evening the proceedings of the morning were continued, Tess staying on till dusk with the body of harvesters. Then they all rode home in one of the largest wagons, in the company of a broad tarnished moon that had risen from the ground to the eastwards, its face resembling the outworn gold-leaf halo of some worm-eaten Tuscan saint. Tess's female companions sang songs, and showed themselves very sympathetic and glad at her reappearance out of doors, though they could not refrain from mischievously throwing in a few verses of the ballad about the maid who went to the merry green wood and came back a changed state. There are counterpoises and compensations in life; and the event which had made of her a social warning had also for the moment made her the most interesting personage in the village to many. Their friendliness won her still farther away from herself, their lively spirits were contagious, and she became almost gay.

But now that her moral sorrows were passing away a fresh one arose on the natural side of her which knew no social law. When she reached home it was to learn to her grief that the baby had been suddenly taken ill since the afternoon. Some such collapse had been probable, so tender and puny was its frame; but the event came as a shock nevertheless.

The baby's offence against society in coming into the world was forgotten by the girl-mother; her soul's desire was to continue that offence by preserving the life of the child. However, it soon grew clear that the hour of emancipation for that little prisoner of the flesh was to arrive earlier than her worst misgivings had conjectured. And when she had discovered this she was plunged into a misery which transcended that of the child's simple loss. Her baby had not been baptized.

Tess had drifted into a frame of mind which accepted passively the consideration that if she should have to burn for what she had done, burn she must, and there was an end of it. Like all village girls she was well grounded in the Holy Scriptures, and had dutifully studied the histories of Aholah and Aholiban, and knew the inferences to be drawn therefrom. But when the same question arose with regard to the baby, it had a very different colour. Her darling was about to die, and no salvation.

It was nearly bedtime, but she rushed downstairs and asked if she might send for the parson. The moment happened to be one at which her father's sense of the antique nobility of his family was highest, and his sensitiveness to the smudge which Tess had set upon that nobility most pronounced, for he had just returned from his weekly booze at Rolliver's Inn. No parson should come inside his door, he declared, prying into his affairs, just then, when, by her

第三篇 《苔丝》Tess of the D'urbervilles

shame, it had become more necessary than ever to hide them. He locked the door and put the key in his pocket.

The household went to bed, and, distressed beyond measure, Tess retired also. She was continually waking as she lay, and in the middle of the night found that the baby was still worse. It was obviously dying—quietly and painlessly, but none the less surely.

In her misery she rocked herself upon the bed. The clock struck the solemn hour of one, that hour when fancy stalks outside reason, and malignant possibilities stand rock-firm as facts. She thought of the child consigned to the nethermost corner of hell, as its double doom for lack of baptism and lack of legitimacy; saw the arch-fiend tossing it with his threepronged fork, like the one they used for heating the oven on baking days; to which picutre she added many other quaint and curious details of torment sometimes taught the young in this Christian country. The lurid presentment so powerfully affected her imagination in the silence of the sleeping house that her nightgown became damp with perspiration, and the bedstead shook with each throb of her heart.

The infant's breathing grew more difficult, and the mother's mental tension increased. It was useless to devour the little thing with kisses; she could stay in bed no longer, and walked feverishly about the room.

'O merciful God, have pity; have pity upon my poor baby!' she cried. 'Heap as much anger as you want to upon me, and welcome; but pity the child!'

She leant against the chest of drawers, and murmured incoherent supplications for a long while, till she suddenly started up.

'Ah! perhaps baby can be saved! Perhaps it will be just the same!'

She spoke so brightly that it seemed as though her face might have shone in the gloom surrounding her.

　　She lit a candle, and went to a second and a third bed under the wall, where she awoke her young sisters and brothers, all of whom occupied the same room. Pulling out the washingstand so that she could get behind it, she poured some water from a jug, and made them kneel around, putting their hands together with fingers exactly vertical. While the children, scarcely awake, awe-stricken at her manner, their eyes growing larger and larger, remained in this position, she took the baby from her bed—a child's child—so immature as scarce to seem a sufficient personality to endow its producer with the maternal title. Tess then stood erect with the infant on her arm beside the basin, the next sister held the Prayer-Book open before her, as the clerk at church held it before the parson; and thus the girl set about baptizing her child.

　　Her figure looked singularly tall and imposing as she stood in her long white nightgown, a thick cable of twisted dark hair hanging straight down her back to her waist. The kindly dimness of the weak candle abstracted from her form and features the little blemishes which sunlight might have revealed—the stubble scratches upon her wrists, and the weariness of her eyes—her high enthusiasm having a transfiguring effect upon the face which had been her undoing, showing it as a thing of immaculate beauty, with a touch of dignity which was almost regal. The little ones kneeling round, their sleepy eyes blinking and red, awaited her preparations full of a suspended wonder which their physical heaviness at that hour would not allow to become active.

　　The most impressed of them said:

　　'Be you really going to christen him, Tess?'

　　The girl-mother replied in a grave affirmative.

　　'What's his name going to be?'

第三篇 《苔丝》Tess of the D'urbervilles

She had not thought of that, but a name suggested by a phrase in the book of Genesis came into her head as she proceeded with the baptismal service, and now she pronounced it:

'Sorrow, I baptize thee in the name of the Father, and of the Son, and of the Holy Ghost.'

She sprinkled the water, and there was silence.

'Say "Amen", children.'

The tiny voices piped in obedient response 'Amen!'

Tess went on:

'We receive this child' — and so forth — 'and do sign him with the sign of the Cross.'

Here she dipped her hand into the basin, and fervently drew an immense cross upon the baby with her forefinger, continuing with the customary sentences as to his manfully fighting against sin, the world, and the devil, and being a faithful soldier and servant unto his life's end. She duly went on with the Lord's Prayer, the children lisping it after her in a thin gnatlike wail, till, at the conclusion, raising their voices to clerk's pitch, they again piped into the silence, 'Amen!'

Then their sister, with much augmented confidence in the efficacy of this sacrament, poured forth from the bottom of her heart the thanksgiving that follows, uttering it boldly and triumphantly in the stopt-diapason note which her voice acquired when her heart was in her speech, and which will never be forgotten by those who knew her. The ecstasy of faith almost apotheosized her; it set upon her face a glowing irradiation, and brought a red spot into the middle of each cheek; while the miniature candle-flame inverted in her eye-pupils shone like a diamond. The children gazed up at her with more and more reverence, and no longer had a will for questioning. She did not look like Sissy to them now, but as a being large, towering, and awful—a divine personage with whom they had nothing in common.

Poor Sorrow's campaign against sin, the world, and the devil was doomed to be of limited brilliancy—luckily perhaps for himself, considering his beginnings. In the blue of the morning that fragile soldier and servant breathed his last, and when the other children awoke they cried bitterly, and begged Sissy to have another pretty baby.

The calmness which had possessed Tess since the christening remained with her in the infant's loss. In the daylight, indeed, she felt her terrors about his soul to have been somewhat exaggerated; whether well founded or not she had no uneasiness now, reasoning that if Providence would not ratify such an act of approximation she, for one, did not value the kind of heaven lost by the irregularity—either for herself or for her child.

So passed away Sorrow the Undesired—that intrusive creature, that bastard gift of shameless Nature who respects not the social law; a waif to whom eternal Time had been a matter of days merely, who knew not that such things as years and centuries ever were; to whom the cottage interior was the universe, the week's weather climate, new-born babyhood human existence, and the instinct to suck human knowledge.

Tess, who mused on the christening a good deal, wondered if it were doctrinally sufficient to secure a Christian burial for the child. Nobody could tell this but the parson of the parish, and he was a new-comer, and did not know her. She went to his house after dusk, and stood by the gate, but could not summon courage to go in. The enterprise would have been abandoned if she had not by accident met him coming homeward as she turned away. In the gloom she did not mind speaking freely.

'I should like to ask you something, sir.'

He expressed his willingness to listen, and she told the story of the baby's illness and the extemporized ordinance.

'And now, sir,' she added earnestly, 'can you tell me this — will it be just the same for him as if you had baptized him?'

Having the natural feelings of a tradesman at finding that a job he should have been called in for had been unskilfully botched by this customers among themselves, he was disposed to say no. Yet the dignity of the girl, the strange tenderness in her voice, combined to affect his nobler impulses—or rather those that he had left in him after ten years of endeavour to graft technical belief on actual scepticism. The man and the ecclesiastic fought within him, and the victory fell to the man.

'My dear girl,' he said, 'it will be just the same.'

'Then will you give him a Christian burial?' she asked quickly.

The Vicar felt himself cornered. Hearing of the baby's illness, he had conscientiously gone to the house after nightfall to perform the rite, and, unaware that the refusal to admit him had come from Tess's father and not from Tess, he could not allow the plea of necessity for its irregular administration.

'Ah—that's another matter,' he said.

'Another matter—why?' asked Tess, rather warmly.

'Well—I would willingly do so if only we two were concerned. But I must not—for certain reasons.'

'Just for once, sir!'

'Really I must not.'

'O sir!' She seized his hand as she spoke.

He withdrew it, shaking his head.

'Then I don't like you!' she burst out, 'and I'll never come to your church no more!'

'Don't talk so rashly.'

'Perhaps it will be just the same to him if you don't?... Will it be just the same? Don't for God's sake speak as saint to sinner, but as you yourself to me myself—poor me!'

How the Vicar reconciled his answer with the strict notions he supposed himself to hold on these subjects it is beyond a layman's power to tell, though not to excuse. Somewhat moved, he said in this case also—

'It will be just the same.'

So the baby was carried in a small deal box, under an ancient woman's shawl, to the churchyard that night, and buried by lantern-light, at the cost of a shilling and a pint of beer to the sexton, in that shabby corner of God's allotment where He lets the nettles grow, and where all unbaptized infants, notorious drunkards, suicides, and others of the conjecturally damned are laid. In spite of the untoward surroundings, however, Tess bravely made a little cross of two laths and a piece of string, and having bound it with flowers, she stuck it up at the head of the grave one evening when she could enter the churchyard without being seen, putting at the foot also a bunch of the same flowers in a little jar of water to keep them alive. What matter was it that on the outside of the jar the eye of mere observation noted the words 'Keelwell's Marmalade'? The eye of maternal affection did not see them in its vision of higher things.

XV

'By experience,' says Roger Ascham, 'we find out a short way by a long wandering.' Not seldom that long wandering unfits us for further travel, and of what use is our experience to us then? Tess Durbeyfield's experience was of this incapacitating kind. At last she had learned what to do; but who would now accept her doing?

If before going to the d'Urbervilles' she had vigorously moved under the guidance of sundry gnomic texts and phrases known to her and to the world in general, no doubt she would never have been imposed on. But it had not been in Tess's power—nor is it in anybody's power—to feel the whole truth of golden opinions while it is possible to profit by them. She—and how many more—might have ironically said to God with Saint Augustine: 'Thou hast counselled a better course than Thou hast permitted.'

She remained in her father's house during the winter months, plucking fowls, or cramming turkeys and geese, or making clothes for her sisters and brothers out of some finery which d'Urberville had given her, and she had put by with contempt. Apply to him she would not. But she would often clasp her hands behind her head and muse when she was supposed to be working hard.

She philosophically noted dates as they came past in the revolution of the year; the disastrous night of her undoing at Trantridge with its dark background of The Chase; also the dates of the baby's birth and death; also her own birthday; and every other day individualized by incidents in which she had taken some share. She suddenly thought one afternoon, when looking in the glass at her fairness, that there was yet another date, of greater importance to her than those; that of her own death, when all these charms would have disappeared; a day which lay sly and unseen among all the other days of the year, giving no sign or sound when she annually passed over it; but not the less surely there. When was it? Why did she not feel the chill of each yearly encounter with such a cold relation? She had Jeremy Taylor's thought that some time in the future those who had known her would say: 'It is the—th, the day that poor Tess Durbeyfield died'; and there would be nothing singular to their minds in the statement. Of that day, doomed to be her terminus in time through all the ages, she did not know the place in month, week, season, or year.

Almost at a leap Tess thus changed from simple girl to complex woman. Symbols of reflectiveness passed into her face, and a note of tragedy at times into her voice. Her eyes grew larger and more eloquent. She became what would have been called a fine creature; her aspect was fair and arresting; her soul that of a woman whom the turbulent experiences of the last year or two had quite failed to demoralize. But for the world's opinion those experiences would have been simply a liberal education.

She had held so aloof of late that her trouble, never generally known, was nearly fogotten in Marlott. But it became evident to her that she could never be really comfortable again in a place which had seen the collapse of her family's attempt to 'claim kin' — and, through her, even closer union—with the rich d'Urbervilles. At least she could not be comfortable there till long years should have obliterated her keen consciousness of it. Yet even now Tess felt the pulse of hopeful life still warm within her; she might be happy in some nook which had no memories. To escape the past and all that appertained thereto was to annihilate it, and to do that she would have to get away.

Was once lost always lost really true of chastity? she would ask herself. She might prove it false if she could veil bygones. The recuperative power which pervaded organic nature was surely not denied to maidenhood alone.

She waited a long time without finding opportunity for a new departure. A particularly fine spring came round, and the stir of germination was almost audible in the buds; it moved her, as it moved the wild animals, and made her passionate to go. At last, one day in early May, a letter reached her from a former friend of her mother's, to

第三篇 《苔丝》Tess of the D'urbervilles

whom she had addressed inquiries long before — a person whom she had never seen — that a skilful milkmaid was required at a dairy-house many miles to the southward, and that the dairyman would be glad to have her for the summer months.

It was not quite so far off as could have been wished; but it was probably far enough, her radius of movement and repute having been so small. To persons of limited spheres, miles are as geographical degress, parishes as counties, counties as provinces and kingdoms.

On one point she was resolved: there should be no more d'Urberville air-castles in the dreams and deeds of her new life. She would be the dairymaid Tess, and nothing more. Her mother knew Tess's feeling on this point so well, though no words had passed between them on the subject, that she never alluded to the knightly ancestry now.

Yet such is human inconsistency that one of the interests of the new place to her was the accidental virtue of its lying near her forefathers' country (for they were not Blakemore men, though her mother was Blakemore to the bone). The dairy called Talbothays, for which she was bound, stood not remotely from some of the former estates of the d'Urbervilles, near the great family vaults of her granddames and their powerful husbands. She would be able to look at them, and think not only that d'Urberville, like Babylon, had fallen, but that the individual innocence of a humble descendant could lapse as silently. All the while she wondered if any strange good thing might come to her being in her ancestral land; and some spirit within her rose automatically as the sap in the twigs. It was unexpended youth, surging up anew after its temporary check, and bringing with it hope, and the invincible instinct towards self-delight.

《德伯家的苔丝》(节选)

张谷若 译

13

苔丝·德北从那位冒牌本家的府上回来了这件事，到处传说开了，如果在方圆一英里的地面上，到处传说这种字眼，不算夸大其词的话。下午的时候，马勒村有好几个年轻的女孩子，都是苔丝的老同学和老朋友，来拜访她，她们是把她们顶好的衣服浆洗烫平了穿着来的，为的是她们这些客人，好更配得上那位作了超凡绝尘的征服而胜利归来的主人；（象她们所认为的那样）同时她们坐在屋里，以极感稀罕奇异的神情瞧着她。因为和她发生恋爱的，是她那位隔着八十层远的族兄德伯先生，一位并不完全仅仅属于一区一隅的乡曲之士，并且他那种不择手段、拈花惹草、全无心肝、厌旧喜新的狼藉名声，正开始传布到纯瑞脊本地以外；她们认为，苔丝所处的地位，是含有这种令人担心的情况的，这比起无险可冒的场合，增加了更大的魔力。

她们既是对她非常羡慕，所以她刚一回身的时候，那几个年纪较小的女孩子就低声说：

"她怎么长得那么好看！配上那件连衣裙，更好看了！那不定花了多少钱买的哪，还准是他送的。"

苔丝正伸手往碗橱里去拿茶具，没听见这几句评语。她要是听见了，那她会把她的朋友在这方面的误会一会儿就纠正过来的。但是她母亲却听见了，于是昭安单纯的虚荣心，既然抓不到大结其婚的希望，就借着德伯和她女儿大调其情这一点，尽力地过了一回瘾；大体上说起

第三篇 《苔丝》Tess of the D'urbervilles

来,她是觉得得到满足的,虽然这种区区有限、转眼即逝的胜利,关系到她女儿的名声;因为她女儿也许终究还是有嫁给他那一天呢;她见了她们对苔丝那样羡慕,欣喜之余,一阵热情,就把她们都留下了吃茶点。

她们的闲谈,她们的笑声,她们旁敲侧击的趣话,更加上她们闪闪烁烁的艳美,使苔丝的兴致也复活了;晚上的时间渐渐过去,她也渐渐受了她们那种兴奋的感染,差不多也嬉笑起来了。她脸上不象先前跟大理石一般那样硬了,她的举动也带出了一些她往日轻快活泼的样子来了,她那焕发的容光,更显出了她青春的美丽。

虽然她有心事,但是有的时候,她回答起她们的问题来,却往往带出身份优越的神气,好象自己承认,她在情场中的经验,真有点足以叫人羡慕的地方。不过她绝不象拉贝特·骚司①说的那样,"跟自己的毁灭恋爱,"所以她的幻想,只象闪电那样,一瞬就过去了。冷静的理智恢复了,对她乍阴乍阳出现的欠缺,加以嘲弄讥笑;她那一阵骄傲里可怕的情况又谴责她,使她恢复了以前那种没精打采、不说不笑的状态。

第二天早晨,已经不是礼拜日,而是礼拜一了,顶好的衣服也收起来了;嬉笑欢乐的客人们也早就走了,只有自己在旧日的床上醒来了,周围是那些天真烂漫的小孩儿,安安静静地在睡眠中呼吸;那时候,她多么沉闷抑郁啊!她回到家来那股新鲜劲儿和因新鲜而引起的意趣,全都不见了,她只见到,她前面是一条崎岖的绵绵远道,得自己单人独行,颠颠跛涉,没人同情,更没人帮助。她想到这儿,她的抑郁就达到了可怕的程度,恨不得眼前有一座坟,她好钻到里面去。

过了几个礼拜的工夫,苔丝才慢慢地恢复了足够的生意——能不怕人家笑话,敢在一个礼拜天早晨到教堂里去了。她喜欢听作礼拜的歌咏——虽然只不过是那样的歌咏——和那些古老的圣诗,喜欢跟着他们唱《晨间颂》②。她母亲既是爱唱民歌,她也由她母亲那儿继承了生来

---

① 拉贝特·骚司(1634—1716),英国神学家兼作者。所引见他的《讲道辞》。哈代在他的短篇小说《贵妇一组·贵妇第三》里,也引了骚司一句话,并说他的讲道辞,应有多人读。
② 《晨间颂》为主教肯思(1637—1711)所作。

第三篇 《苔丝》Tess of the D'urbervilles

就好歌曲的天性，所以有的时候，最简单的音乐，对她都有一种力量，有时几乎能把她那颗心，从她的腔子里揪出来。

一来因为自己的特殊原因，她尽力躲避别人注意，二来因为对青年的殷勤，要一概摆脱，所以她老是趁着教堂的钟还没响的时候，就起身往教堂里去，并且在楼下后排、靠着存放东西的地方，找坐位落座；那儿除了老头儿和老太婆以外，别的人就没有去的；在那儿，棺材架子竖着立在掘圹刨坟的家伙中间。

作礼拜的人，三三两两地进了教堂，在她前面一排一排地坐好，先把前额低下去一分钟的四分之三那么大的工夫，好象祈祷似的①（其实并没那回事），然后再坐直了，往四面瞧。歌咏的时候，恰巧选了一个她爱听的调子，选了那个叫"浪敦"的老双节歌咏②，不过她却不知道它叫什么，虽然她很希望能够知道。她只感觉到——却不能精确地把这种感觉用语言表达出来——这个作曲谱的人，一定有非常奇异、赛过上帝的力量，所以他才能躺在坟里，还把他独自首先经验过的感情，叫一个象她这样向来没听见过他的姓名、并且永远一点也不会知道他是怎么一个人的女孩子，又一次跟着他一步一步地经验一番。

先前回头瞧的那些人，在礼拜进行之中，又回头瞧；后来瞧出来是她坐在那儿，就互相低声谈论起来。她知道他们低声谈的是什么，心里难过起来，觉得再也不能到教堂里来了。

从此以后，她和几个弟妹一块儿占用的那个寝室，更成了她成天价离不开的地方了。就在那几方码的草房顶下面，她看着风风雨雨，霜晨雪夜、灿烂的夕阳，和由缺而圆的满月。她销声匿迹，丝毫不露踪影，所以到后来，差不多人人都以为她已经离家出走了。

在这个时期里，苔丝唯一的活动，就是天黑了以后作的那一种；就

---

① 英美人习惯，进了教堂入座之时，把帽子摘下，端在面前，作为祈祷的样子。
② 叫作"浪敦"的歌咏有单节、双节、四节之分，看那一个调子唱几节而定。歌咏多为短调，平淡简单，故前面有"只不过是那样的歌咏"之语。浪敦即理查·浪敦（1735—1803），英国风琴家，尝为爱司忒大教堂等风琴师，著有《颂神乐谱》，为圣诗及《赞美诗》乐谱。

第三篇 《苔丝》Tess of the D'urbervilles

是那一会儿,跑到树林子里面去,她才好象最不孤独。原来黄昏时候,有那么一刻的工夫,亮光和黑暗,强弱均匀,恰恰平衡,把昼间的蹋天踏地和夜间的意牵心悬,互相抵消,给人在心灵上留下绝对的自由;她知道怎样就能丝毫不爽,把这一刹那的时候恰好抓住。就在这种时候,在世为人这种窘迫,才减少到最低的可能限度。她对于昏夜,并不害怕;她唯一的心思,好象就是要躲开人类,或者说是躲开那个叫作世界的冷酷集体;这个集体,从整个看来,非常可怕,但是从每一个单位看来,却又不足畏,甚至还可怜。

在这些旷山之上和空谷之中,她那悄悄冥冥的凌虚细步,和她所活动于其中的大气,成为一片。她那袅袅婷婷、潜潜等等的娇软腰肢,也和那片景物融为一体。有的时候,她那想入非非的绮思深念,使她周围自然界的消息盈虚,深深含上感情,一直到它变得好象是她个人身世的一部分。或者不如说,她周围自然界的消息盈虚,就是她那身世的一部分;因为世界只是心理的现象,自然的消息盈虚,看起来怎么样,也就是怎么样。半夜的暴风和寒气,在苞芽紧裹的枯林枝干中间呜噎哽咽,就是一篇诰诫,对她苦苦责问。淋漓的雨天,就是一个模糊飘渺的道德神灵,对她那无可挽救的百年长恨痛痛哀悼。不过这个模糊飘渺的道德神灵;她不能确确实实把他划归她童年信仰的上帝之中,而却又想象不出来他是任何另外的一类。

苔丝根据了破旧褴褛的余风遗俗,安插了与己忤违的魅形妖影、鬼哭神嚎,硬造出来这样一些幻象虚境,把自己包围,这都不过是她自己想象模拟出来的一些怪诞荒谬、不值一笑的东西,没有道理、恫吓自己的一群象征道德的精灵妖怪。和实际世界格格不入的,本是这些东西,不是苔丝自己。她在鸟宿枝头的树篱中间走动的时候,或者在月光之下山兔蹦跳的兔窝旁边瞧看的时候,或者在山鸡群栖的树枝下面站立的时候,都把自己看作是一个罪恶的化身,侵入了清白流连的地域。不过在所有这种时间里,苔丝全是在本无自然异同之处,强要区分人为异同。她觉得和一切矛盾,而实在却和一切和谐。她不由自己所破坏了的,只是人类所接受的社会法律,而不是她四围的环境所认识的自然法律;她在她四围的环境中,也不是自己所想象的那样不伦不类。

第三篇 《苔丝》Tess of the D'urbervilles

14

那是八月里的一天,太阳刚出来,烟雾迷腾腾的。夜里更浓的雾气,现在叫温暖的光线一照临,就分散、收缩,变得一堆一簇,藏在低洼的山谷和浓密的树林子里,等着叫太阳晒得无影无踪才罢。

太阳因为有雾气的关系,显得不同寻常,好象一个人,有五官,能感觉;想要把他表现得恰当,总得用阳性代名词才成①。他现在的面目既是那样,再加上一片大地上,连一个人影儿都没有,这就立刻叫我们明白了古代崇拜太阳的原故。我们自然而然地要觉得,通行天地间的宗教,没有比这一种再近情合理的了。这个光芒四射的物体,简直就是一个活东西,有金黄的头发,有和蔼的目光,神采焕发,仿佛上帝,正在年富力强的时期,看着下面包罗万象的世界,觉得那儿满是富有趣味的事物。

过了一会儿,他的光线就透过了农舍的百叶窗缝儿,一直射到屋子里面,把碗橱、抽屉柜和别的家具,都映上了一条一条的红线,好象烧红了的通条一般;把躺在床上还没起来那些收拾庄稼的工人,也都晒醒。

不过那天早晨,在所有红彤彤的东西里,顶鲜明的还得数那两根涂着颜色的宽木条,正耸立在马勒村外一片金黄色的麦地边儿上。原来昨天,地边儿上运来一架收割机,预备今天用,机器上有一个转动的马尔他式十字架②,就是这两根木条和下面另外两根互相交错而作成的。那个十字架,本来涂的就是红色,现在叫太阳一映射,红色显得更加浓重,好象是在液体的火星蘸过似的。

那片麦地已经"开割"了;所谓"开割"了的意思,就是说,已经用手把四周围的麦子整个地割去了一溜,开辟出来大约有几英尺宽的一条小路,好叫马匹和机器头一次走得过去。

---

① 太阳不是活东西,普通用中性代名词表示。现在哈代认为它是活东西,所以要用阳性代名词表示。

② 马尔他式十字架:欧美的十字架有各式各样,如拉丁式＋,希腊式＋,等。马尔他式十字架形状为玉。

第三篇 《苔丝》Tess of the D'urbervilles

　　篱路上已经来了两班工人,一班是男人和男孩,一班是女人,他们来的时候,正好是东边树篱顶儿的影子落到西边树篱的中腰上,因此他们的头在朝阳里,他们的脚仍旧在黎明里。他们离开篱路,走进最靠跟前那块地地边上的栅栏门,在门两旁的石头柱子中间消失。
　　一会儿的工夫,地里发出来一种象蚂蚱求爱所作的格哒格哒之声。机器开始活动起来了;只见三匹马套在一块儿,拉着刚才提过的那辆摇摇晃晃的长身机器,在栅栏门那一面往前挪动;拉机器那三匹马里面,有一匹驮着一个赶马的,机器上有个座儿,坐着一个管机器的。机器全部先顺着地的一边往前一直地走,机器上的十字架慢慢地转动,后来下了山坡,叫山挡住,就完全看不见了。待了一会儿,它又象刚才一样,不紧不慢地在地的那一边儿出现,最先看得见的,是前面那匹马马额上发亮的铜星儿,在割剩下来的麦秆上面升起,跟着看得见的,是颜色鲜明的十字架,最后看得见的,才是全副的机器。
　　机器绕着地走了一个圈儿,地四周割剩下来的麦秆也加宽一层;早晨的时光慢慢过去,地里还长着麦子的面积也慢慢缩小。大兔子、小兔子、大耗子、小耗子,还有长虫,都一齐往地的内部退却,好象那就是最后的防地一般;却不知道,它们庇身之所,是不会持久的,它们命中注定的死亡,是无法逃避的;因为等到午后,它们避难的地方,更令人可怕地越缩越小了,它们无论从前是朋友还是仇敌,更越挤越紧了,最后那直立地上的麦子,只占几码地了,也都叫那架毫不通融的机器割断了,于是那些收拾庄稼的工人们,就拿起棍子和石头,把它们一个一个都打死完事。
　　收割机把割下来的麦子,都一堆一堆撂在机器后面,每一堆刚好够扎成一抱;跟在机器后面的是些手灵脚快的工人,就把这些麦子动手捆扎。这些工人里,还是女的占大多数;但是也有几个男的,他们都是上身只穿着印花布衬衣,下身用皮带把裤子系在腰上,因此腰后那两个钮子就用不着了,他们一动,钮子就在日光下,又象独星闪烁,又象繁星闪耀,好象他们腰眼上长了两个眼睛似的。
　　但是那些捆麦子的工人里,还是那些女的顶有意思,因为女人一旦成了户外自然界的重要部分,不象平素只是一件普通物品放在那儿,她们就生出一种令人着迷动情的神情。地里的男工,只是一个男人在地里就是了;地里的女工,却是田地的一部分,她们仿佛失去了自身的轮廓,吸收了四周景物的要素,和它融化而形成一体。

那些女人——或者勿宁说女孩子,因为她们差不多都很年轻——头戴簇摺儿的布帽,帽上帽檐下垂,遮挡太阳,手戴皮手套,保护双手,免得叫麦秆划破。她们里面,有一个身穿粉红裌子,有一个身穿米色窄袖长袍,有一个腰系红裙,红得和机器上的十字架一样;其余那些年纪大一点儿的,都穿着棕色粗布"连根倒",也就是外罩;这原是地里的女工们古式的服装,也是顶适当的服装,不过年轻的人却都慢慢地不大穿它了。这天早晨,大家的眼睛都不由自主地往那穿粉红布裌的女孩子那儿瞧,因为在这一群人里面,论起身段的袅娜苗条,她得算是第一。但是她的帽子,却很低地扣在前额上,所以她捆麦子的时候,一点儿也看不见她的脸,不过她的肤色,却可以从直垂帽檐下面一两绺松散开来的深棕色头发上,猜出一二。①那时候,别的女人时常四面了望,她却一心作活,从不求人注意,也许就是因为这样,所以才反倒惹得人家偶尔看她一两眼吧。

她捆麦子的动作,进行得象钟表一样地单调。她从刚捆好了的一抱麦子里,抽出一把麦穗儿来,用左手的手掌,把麦穗头儿拍齐了;再弯腰往前,双手把一抱麦子拢到膝盖,把戴着手套的左手插到那一抱麦子底下,和那一抱麦子那一面的右手合拢,象情人一般,把一抱麦子整个抱住,再把绳子的两头拉到一块儿,跪在那一抱麦子上把它系好;有时微风把裙子吹了起来,还得用手把它送回去。她的胳膊,在暗黄色的皮手套和衣袖之间,露出了一块,工作久了,胳膊上柔嫩的皮肤,都叫麦秆划破了,往外流血。

过一会儿,她就把身子站直了,休息一下,把松了的围裙系紧了,或者把歪了的帽子戴正了。在那时候,就可以看出来,她是一个眉清目秀的青年女子,脸是鸭蛋形的,眼睛深而黑,头发长而厚,一绺一绺,伏伏贴贴,好象无论落到什么东西上头,都要紧紧箍住,毫不放松似的。以一个平常生长在乡间的女孩子而论,她的面颊更灰白,牙齿更整齐,两片红嘴唇也更薄。

---

① 人种学依人的肤色,把高加索人种分成两类。一类叫作 blond,皮肤色淡,发淡棕、淡黄、或红棕,眼睛蓝或灰。一类叫 brunet,肤色深,眼和头发,棕或黑。故由头发的颜色可推知皮肤的颜色。

第三篇 《苔丝》Tess of the D'urbervilles

那个女人正是苔丝·德北（或者说是德伯），多少改变了一点儿——是那个人，却又不是那个人；她现在住在这儿，仿佛住在异乡外国一样，其实她住的地方，完全是她的故乡。她在家里躲了许多天了，后来才拿定主意，在本村作点儿户外工作，因为那时正是庄稼地里顶忙的时候，她在屋里所能作的事儿，比不上收拾庄稼挣的钱那么多。

其他女人的动作，也差不多和苔丝的一样。每次束好了一抱，大家都象跳四面舞那样，四面聚拢来，每人把自己捆的一抱，和别人的竖着靠在一起，一直等到十抱或十二抱聚拢成一个麦捆（或者照着本地的说法，一个麦"簇"①）才罢。

他们吃了早饭，又都回来，照旧工作起来。快到十一点钟的时候，如果有人瞅着苔丝，他一定能看见她带着欲有所求的神气，往山头那儿时瞥时瞭，不过她却始终没停止工作。在那个钟点马上就来到的时候，有一群小孩儿，年龄由六岁到十四岁，从一块有麦茬竖立的凸起山田后面，露出脑袋来。

苔丝见了，脸上微微一红，不过她还是没停止工作。

那一群孩子往前走来，里面年龄最大的是个女孩儿，身上披着一个三角形的大围巾，一直拖到麦茬上，怀里抱着一样东西，刚一看好象是一个泥娃娃，仔细一看，却原来是一个裹在襁褓里的小婴孩。又有一些孩子拿着些食物。收麦子的工人都停了工，各人拿起各人吃的东西来，靠着一个麦捆坐下。大家就在那儿吃起饭来，男工还把一个砂罐儿随意地倒，把一个杯子大家轮流着传。

苔丝·德北是最后歇工的一个。她靠着麦捆的一头坐下，把脸掉过去一点儿，背着她的伙伴。她坐好了，有一个头上戴着兔皮帽子、腰带上塞着一块红手绢的男工，把麦酒杯举到麦捆顶上，递过去叫她喝。不过她没接受这种殷勤。她的饭刚摆出来，她就把那个大女孩儿——她妹妹——叫了过来，从她手里把婴孩接过去；她妹妹正乐得解去负担，走到另一个麦捆跟前，和另几个在那儿玩儿的孩子，跑到一块儿去了。苔丝脸上

---

① 多塞特郡本地习惯，一英亩所产之麦都以麦捆或"麦簇"(stitch)为单位计算。一捆一般为十抱或十二抱。但有时有的地区，稍有不同。

越来越红,又有点儿怕人,又有点儿大胆,把褂子解开,给小孩奶吃。

坐得靠她顶近的那几个男工,都不好意思,把脸往地的那一头掉过去,还有几个抽起烟来;其中有一个尽自出神儿,想他的爱好,把那倒不出酒来的罐子怅惘地直摸。除了苔丝,别的女人都开始生动地谈起话来,并且整理她们乱了的发髻。

小孩吃足了奶以后,那位年轻的母亲就把他放在腿上,叫他坐直了,逗弄他,眼睛却瞧着远处,脸上是一种阴郁沉闷的冷淡神情,几乎好象是嫌憎的样子。于是忽然又不顾轻重,往他脸上亲了十几下,好象老也亲不够似的;孩子叫那一阵又痛爱、又奇怪地夹杂着鄙夷的猛烈动作,吓得哭了起来。

"她只管外面装着恨他,只管嘴里说不及她和孩子都死了好,其实她心里还是照样地疼他哪,"那个系红裙子的女人说。

"她过不了几天,就不再说那样话了,"那个穿黄的说。"老天爷呀!日子多了,一个人对这类事儿,不管怎么都能习惯,真了不得!"

"俺想,这种事情当初总要费点事儿,不能只是劝说劝说就行了吧!去年有一天晚上,有人从围场过,听见里面有人哭,要是人们上前去看,就一定要有人吃大亏了!"

"不管怎么说,反正这样事儿,叫她遇上了,真是万分可怜。不过话又说回来啦,这样事儿,总是顶漂亮的人儿,才遇得上。丑的俺管保一点儿危险也没有,对不对,捷内?"说话那个人转身向人群里一个女人问,那个女人,要是说她丑,不能算说错了。

这话一点儿不错,委实是万分可怜。那时候苔丝坐在那儿的样子,就是她的仇人见了,也不能说不可怜;因为她的嘴唇儿象花朵一般;一双柔媚的大眼睛,说它黑也不是,说它蓝也不是,说它灰,说它紫,都不是,不如说这些深浅不一的颜色,样样都有,还夹着一百样别的;你只要一直瞅着她的虹彩,就能看出一层一层深浅不同的颜色,一道一道浓淡各异的明暗,围在瞳人四周,瞳人自己却又深又远,看不见底;假使她的家族没遗传给她那种稍微不懂小心谨慎的毛病,她简直就是女性中的完人了。

她好几个月以来,老躲在家里,这个礼拜,居然会走到地里去工作,就连她自己也没想到,她会有这么大的决心。她那样一个没有阅历的人,独居

第三篇 《苔丝》Tess of the D'urbervilles

孤处，想出种种自悔自恨的方法，折磨、消耗她那颗搏动跳跃的心，这样以后，通常情理又使她心里豁亮起来。她觉得，她还很可以再作点儿有用的事情，再尝一尝独立的甜味，无论出什么代价。过去究竟是过去；无论它从前怎么样，反正眼前它不存在了。无论它有什么结果，时光总会把它都掩盖了。在若干年之内，它就都要和并没发生过的一样，她自己也要叫青草掩埋，没人记得了。同时树木仍旧要象以前一样地青绿，鸟声仍旧要象以前一样地清脆，太阳仍旧要象以前一样地辉煌。所有天天看见的景物，并没有因为她的忧伤而变成憔悴，也没有因为她的痛苦而变得惨淡。

她老觉得全世界都正注意她的情况，不敢抬头见人；其实她早应该明白，这种想法，完全是建立在幻想之上的。除了她自己以外，别人没有把她的生存、她的感情、她的遭遇、她的感觉，放心上的。所有的人，对于苔丝，只是有时想起她来，转眼又把她忘了就是了。即使她的朋友，也不过是想起她的时候多几次罢了。假使她整天整夜，自怨自悔，在他们看来，不过是觉得她自寻苦恼罢了。假使她尽力找痛快，把一切麻烦都不放在心上，从阳光、花儿和婴孩身上觅取快乐，在他们看来，也不过是觉得她有涵养，能忍受罢了。而且比方，她一个人，住在一个荒岛上，她会对于自己的遭遇觉得难过吗？不会很难过吧。再比方说，她是刚被上帝创造出来的，一出世就没有配偶而生下一个孩子来，除了知道这个不知道该姓什么的孩子是她生的以外，别的世事人情一点儿也不知道，那样的话，她会感到绝望吗？不会吧，不但不会，她一定还要恬然处之，还要觉得其中有乐趣呢。所以她的苦恼，大半都是由于她有了世俗的谬见而来，不是由于她天生本有的感觉[1]而起。

不管苔丝怎么个想法，反正有一种力量诱导她，使她穿戴得和从前

---

[1] 哈代有一首诗叫作《有生以前和以后》，大意说，从前有过一个时期，人类还没有"意识"这种东西，那时候人类没有由于死亡、疾病、恋爱而受罪。那时候，人类不知道什么是悔恨、绝望、烧心。有什么不生存了，没人放悲声。光明变暗，黑暗弥漫，没人感到不快。但是后来有了感情、意识，种种病痛就因之而生，有了"是"的概念，就有了"非"的概念。是非都是由于有意识感觉而生。无识无知的懵懂，何时能再回来呢？这种思想，和此处表达的一样。

一样地干净整齐,出了门儿,去到地里;因为那时正需要收拾庄稼的人手。就是因为这样,所以她才能够大大方方地去到外面,即使怀里抱着孩子,有时也敢抬头见人,毫不羞怯。

收拾庄稼的工人们从麦捆旁边站起来,伸胳膊伸腿,弄灭了烟袋。刚才卸下来的马也都喂饱了,又套到红彤彤的机器上。苔丝已经急忙吃完了饭,把她大妹妹叫过来,接走了小孩,自己把衣服系紧了,又戴上了黄皮手套,重新弯下腰去,走到刚才束好的那一抱麦子跟前,抽出作绳子用的麦穗,去捆另一抱麦子。

午前的工作,继续到下午,继续到傍晚。苔丝和那些工人都待到昏黑的时候。那时大家才都坐在一辆顶大的大车上,一齐动身回家。一轮昏黄失泽的大月亮,正从东面的地上升起,照着他们,月亮的圆盘好象蛀虫咬坏了那些特司肯圣人① 头上的金叶光轮一般。苔丝的女伴唱起歌儿来,极力表示,见了她出门工作,非常高兴,非常同情;但是,她们却又忍不住要淘气,因此就唱起几段曲子来,曲子里说的是一个大姑娘跑到快活逍遥的绿树林子里,回来就变了样儿。② 人生的事情往往祸福相抵;同是一件事,既使苔丝成了大家警戒的榜样,又使她在许多人眼里成了村中最稀罕的人物。她们那种亲热的劲儿使她把自己的往事更撂开一些,她们那种活泼的精神把苔丝也感染了,所以她也几乎快活起来了。

现在她在道德方面的悲哀渐渐消失了,而在她那不懂得社会法律的天性方面,却又发生了一段新的悲哀。原来她到了家,知道她的小孩下午忽然得病,心里感到极为悲痛。小孩的体格本来就又小又嫩,得病得灾本是意料中的事;但是在作妈的看来,仍旧觉得是意外的飞灾。

---

① 特司肯圣人:特司肯为意大利画家之一派,所作多为圣像,涂于金底,画于木版上,多存于英国伦敦立名画馆。英国十九世纪诗人布朗宁的诗《一副脸》里说过,"画在淡金底子上,象特司肯初期艺术家喜欢画的那样"。
② 英国民歌《国王幼女珍妮公主》,言公主到一逍遥快活的绿树林子里游玩,遇一青年,横加奸污,后知此青年为其多年外出,已不相识之亲兄。公主遂以刀自刎,二人相抱而死。歌载查勒得的《英格兰、苏格兰流行民歌集》,其中第五十二首即此歌,应为此处所指。

第三篇 《苔丝》Tess of the D'urbervilles

　　这孩子来到世上,本是一件触犯社会的罪恶,但是那个年纪轻轻的母亲,却早把这种情况忘了;她一心一意只想要孩子活下去,使这件罪恶继续。但是不久就清楚了,这个拘在肉体之内的小小囚徒①得到解脱的时间,眼看就要来到了,她虽然知道他早晚必不中用,却没想到会这么快。她看出这一点来,就异常地难过起来,比只为小孩死去难过还要厉害。因为她的小宝宝还没受洗礼②呢。

　　苔丝对于自己,完全变成一副老实忍受的态度:她觉得要是自己犯的罪应该下地狱、叫火烧,那么下地狱、叫火烧就完了,没有什么别的可说的。她和所有的乡下女孩子一样,把一本《圣经》记得烂熟③;她曾细心研究过阿荷拉和阿荷利巴的事迹④,知道从那个故事里可以得到什么结论。但是同样的问题发生到她的小婴孩身上,她的看法可就不同了。她的小宝贝儿要死了,还没免罪就要死了,这可怎么好呢?

　　那会儿差不多是睡觉的时候了,但是她却急忙跑到楼下,问是否可以去请牧师。她父亲刚从露力芬一星期一次的醺醉中归来,心里对于他是古老贵族人家这件事正感觉得最强烈,对于他女儿给他在古老贵族家世上抹的这块黑也正感觉得最强烈。所以他就说,这件事遮盖还恐怕遮盖不过去,哪儿还能在这时候,找一个牧师来家,对自己的家丑横加刺探。不能请牧师。他把门锁了起来,把钥匙放在自己的口袋儿里。

---

① 拘在肉体之内的小小囚徒,原文 prisoner of the flesh,比较《旧约·耶利米哀歌》第三章第三十四节,prisoners of the earth。
② 受洗礼:基督教观念,人一生下来就带有罪恶,因此必须受洗,一方面为洗去罪恶之标志,一方面为允许进教会的表示。小孩不及受洗就死了的,不能上天堂,永远在地狱里,或在地狱边上另一处叫做林苞的地方受苦。
③ 这里根据事实而写。哈代青年时,曾在故乡当过主日学校教员,校中即有女生能背诵《圣经》全章。本书里的玛琳,即以此校中女生之一为底本。
④ 阿荷拉和阿荷利巴的事迹,见《旧约·以西结书》第二十三章。耶和华说,有两个女子,一母所生,在埃及行邪淫。姐姐叫阿荷拉,妹妹叫阿荷利巴,必有义人,审判她们,因为她们是淫妇。我必使多人来攻击她们,使她们抛来抛去,被人抢夺;这些人必用石头打死她们,用刀剑杀害她们,又杀戮她们的儿女,用火焚烧她们的房屋,好叫一切妇人都受警戒。

一家人都上床睡下了,苔丝虽然痛苦万分,但是没有法子,只得也跟着睡下。她躺在床上,老不断地醒来;到了半夜一看,那娃娃的情况更坏了。他分明是只有出气,没有入气了,看样子倒是安安静静,无甚痛苦,其实却是毫无疑问,正慢慢死去。

她疼得无法可想,只在床上来回翻腾。钟声刚敲了一点那个庄严的时刻。就在这种时候,毫无根据的想象,才越出理智的范围,心头种种恶毒的揣测,才变成牢不可破的实事。她就想到,那个孩子,既是私生,又没受洗,两罪俱罚,① 于是就打到了地狱最下层的角落上;她看见那个大魔鬼,拿着一把三刀叉,象他们烤面包的时候热烤炉用的那样,把这孩子叉来叉去;在这种想象里,她又添了许多另外奇奇怪怪的惨酷刑罚,这都是她平素听人讲的,因为在这一个信基督教的国家里,有时给小孩讲道,就这么个讲法。在人们都睡着了的屋子里,静悄悄的,她越琢磨,那种森然阴惨的情况,就越活现,她的睡衣都叫冷汗湿透了,她的心跳一下,她的床也跟着动一下。

婴孩喘气越来越费劲,妈妈难过着急也越来越厉害。即使象狼吞虎咽一样老拿嘴亲那个小东西,也一点都不顶事。她在床上躺不住了,下了床在地上疯了一样来回转磨。

"哎呀,慈悲的上帝呀!你慈悲慈悲吧!慈悲慈悲我这个可怜的孩子吧!"她喊着说。"所有你想加的罪过,你都加到我身上好啦,我情愿受罚,但是你对这孩子却慈悲慈悲吧!"

她靠在抽屉柜上,夹七夹八地嘟囔着哀告了许久,于是她心里一下亮堂起来。

"哦,也许这孩子还有救星!也许那么一办,也是一样!"

她说这话的时候,精神那样焕发,仿佛她的脸都在四围的昏暗中发出亮光。

她点起一支蜡烛,走到靠墙放着的第二张和第三张床前面,把睡在床上的弟弟妹妹们全都叫醒(他们全睡在一个屋子里)。她又把洗脸台拉出一点儿来,自己站在台后面,又从水盂② 里倒出一些清水;叫那些孩子围在那前面跪着,每人两手伸得笔直,对合起来,那时候那些孩子

---

① 基督教的说法,通奸所生之婴儿,死后要下地狱。

② 水盂:盛洗脸水的用具,相当大,和脸盆配成一套,非饮水或漱口用的水盂。

还没有完全醒过来，看着那种样子，觉得庄严可怕，眼睛越睁越大；就在这种情况下，她从床上抱起那个小小的婴孩——那个孩子的孩子——因为他那样不成熟，简直地难以说生他那个人有资格称为母亲。苔丝把婴孩擎在胳膊上，自己笔直地站在脸盆旁边，她大妹妹象教堂的助手①对牧师那样，给她把《祈祷书》②展在前面端着；一切都布置好了，那女孩子就给她的小婴孩行起洗礼来了。

她穿着白色的长睡衣站在那儿，显得特别高大，特别威严，黑头发编成一条锚缆一样的粗辫子，从脑后一直垂到腰下。微弱的烛光，黝黝阴翳，蔼蔼慈祥，把她身上和脸上在日光下要显出来的小毛病——胳膊上叫麦茬划破了的道子，眼睛里露出来的惺忪倦容——全都勾抹掉了。心里的精诚表现到脸上，使得她的面目变得和平常不一样，使得那副害了她的面孔显得纯洁无瑕地美丽，并且带出一些差不多和王后一样地尊严。那些孩子们跪在四周，蒙眬的眼睛还带红意，一眨一眨地看着她作洗礼的准备，把满怀的诧异暂时挂起，因为睡魔使他们头脑昏沉，所以他们的好奇心不能活动。

其中有一个受感动最深的问：

"姐姐，你真要给他行洗礼吗？"

那个年纪轻轻的母亲郑重地答应了一个"是"字。

"那么你打算给他起个什么名儿哪？"

她还没想到这一节哪，但是她继续作着洗礼的仪式，可就想起《创世记》里有一句话③来了，所以念道：

---

① 助手，俗人而执行教堂中不重要的宗教事项者，所司为作礼拜时领导回答或辅助礼拜之进行等。

② 《祈祷书》即《公祷书》，是英国教堂举行礼拜、祈祷时所用，内载举行礼拜、婚礼、丧礼、洗礼、圣餐礼等等仪式的规程。一五四九年第一次刊行，后数经修改。唯无大变动，至今沿用。

③ 指"上帝说……我要大大地增加你的苦恼，……你生小孩要有很大的苦恼。……你一生吃饭，都要在苦恼中"等处而言。见《旧约·创世记》第三章第十六节及第十节。

第三篇 《苔丝》Tess of the D'urbervilles

"苦恼,我现在以圣父、圣子及圣灵的名义,给你行洗礼。①"

念到这儿,她洒起水来,一时都静悄悄的。

"孩子们,你们都说'阿门'。"

细小的声音,听了吩咐,都异口同音,应声说道"阿门"。

苔丝又接着念:

"我们纳受这婴孩"——等等——"我们给他划一个十字作记号。"

念到这儿,她把手在水盆里蘸了一蘸,用食指照着小孩热热烈烈地划了一个很大的十字。接着又把普通行洗礼念的那些话——象说他要奋勇地和世俗、罪恶、魔鬼交战,要自始至终作上帝忠实的仆人和兵士等等——一直念到末了。于是又按着规矩往下念《主祷文》,孩子们也都象蚊子似的、咿咿呀呀跟着她念,念完最后一句,他们都和教堂的助手一样,又提高了嗓门,在静悄悄的屋子里,齐声尖喊"阿门!"

那时他们的姐姐,越来越相信这场圣礼的效力很大,接着就从心灵的最深处,倾吐出随后而来的感谢上帝祷文,念的时候,神采奕奕,意气扬扬,声音渊渊而琅琅,仿佛闭管的风琴②,每逢她心诚神聚的时候,她的声音就是这样,也是听见她的人永远忘不了的。因虔诚而生出来的魂飞魄扬之至乐,使她差不多变成了天神;叫她脸上光辉四射,腮上生出红晕,眼睛里倒映出的两个小烛光,也象两颗钻石一样地闪耀。孩子们越看她越觉得起敬,再也无心发问了。她现在不象他们的姐姐了,而是一个伟大、威严、令人敬畏的人物了——而是一位天神了,和他们一点儿相同的地方都没有了。

可怜的苦恼,对于世俗、魔鬼、罪恶的奋斗,却命中早就注定了,只能有有限度的光辉——这于他倒也很好,因为他刚一起始,就不象是前途光明的样子。在晨光熹微中,那位脆弱的兵士和仆人,就喘了他最后的一口气了,别的孩子们醒来的时候,都痛哭起来,并且要姐姐再给他们一个可爱的小婴孩。

---

① 婴孩洗礼有两种,一种是在教堂里当着会众举行的,一种是在婴儿家中举行的。现在这里所用的仪式是第二种。

② 闭管的风琴,与开管相对。闭管为木管,声如笛,清脆。开管为金属管,声雄厚而沉重。

第三篇 《苔丝》Tess of the D'urbervilles

苔丝自从行洗礼的时候,就心平气静,一直等到小孩死了,还是那样。天亮了以后,她觉得夜间对于小孩死后的灵魂作那样可怕的揣测,未免有点太过。无论她所想的有没有根据,反正如今她心里是安定了的了。她的理由是,要是上帝不承认这种以权为经的行动,因为还不合正式的规定,就不准小孩进天堂,那这种天堂,无论为自己,无论为小孩,就都不稀罕了。

苦恼这个小讨厌鬼儿,就这样与世长辞了。他只是一个不请而来的人,他只是那不顾社会理法、没有羞耻之心的"自然"当礼物白送来的一件杂种贱货。他这个弃儿,不知道曾有过什么叫一年,什么叫一世纪;对于他永恒的时间只是几天的事情;对于他,一所小草房儿就是整个的宇宙;一礼拜的阴晴风雨就是一年的寒暑温凉;婴孩的时代就是一生的寿命;吃奶的本能就是人类的知识。①

苔丝对于这场洗礼,心里已经琢磨了好久,现在又琢磨起来,不知道在理论上,能不能按照教会的仪式把孩子埋葬。② 除了区上的牧师,没有别人能给她解决这个问题,但是这个牧师是新来的,不认识她。她趁着黄昏以后,跑到牧师住宅的栅栏门口,但是怎么也鼓不起勇气来,进门里面去。她刚要前功尽弃,动身回去,碰巧牧师从外面回来了,和她走了个对面。在昏暗的夜色里,她就不顾一切,把心事对他和盘托出。

"我有点儿事情,想要请教请教你,先生。"

他表示了愿意听一听她有什么事儿,她就告诉他,说她的小孩怎么病来着,她又怎么自己暂行职权,给他行洗礼来着。

"现在,先生,"她很诚恳地又添了一句说,"请你告诉我,这种办法,是不是和你给他行洗礼是一样的?"

他刚一听这些话,心里只觉得,本来应该请自己作的一样差事,却叫主顾们胡来乱闹,苟且了事,这种买卖人的心理,本来使他想要回答说不一样。但是他再一看那女孩子那种大方的态度,一听她那种异样柔

---

① 哈代一八六五年十二月的日记:"这十二个月,对于昆虫便是一个时代,对于树叶便是一生,对于啁啾的鸟便是一世,对于人却只是一年。"
② 教会规矩,没正式受洗,就不能算正式基督教,所以就不能按着基督徒的仪式埋葬。

第三篇 《苔丝》Tess of the D'urbervilles

和的语气,他的良心(或者不如说,他这十年以来,虽然从事传教,硬要叫怀疑的人信仰规定好了的上帝,却还没昧尽了良心)不觉发现。人和教士在他心中交战,结果战胜了的是人。

"我这亲爱的女孩子,"他说,"那完全是一样的。"

"那么你可以按着教会的仪式,把他埋葬了吧?"她急忙跟着问。

牧师觉得自己叫她挤到墙角里去了。原来他听说小孩得病,曾经良心发现,天黑以后,要到她家给他行礼来着;他并不知道,不许他进门的,是苔丝的父亲,并不是苔丝自己,所以现在他不许苔丝以有私人行礼的必要这种话来作辩护。

"啊,那又是另一回事了,"他说。

"另一回事?为什么?"苔丝未免有点火辣辣地问。

"啊,这件事,要是只关系到咱们两个,我很愿意那么办。不过因为还有别的原因,所以我就不能那么办了。"

"不过我只求你办这一次啊,先生。"

"我真不能那么办。"

"哦,先生!"她说的时候,抓住了他的手。

他把手缩回去,一面摇头。

"那么我不喜欢你了!"她忽然发作起来说,"我永远再也不上你的教堂里去了。"

"说话别这么冒失。"

"比方你不给他行礼,对他是不是也是一样?……是不是一样?请你看着上帝,不要象圣人对罪人那样来对我说话。请你象平常人对平常人那样说好啦,唉!"

这位牧师,对于这种事情既然有绝不通融的看法,那他遇到这类事情,要怎么回答,才能和他的看法不相背谬呢?简直不是我们俗人所能说得出来的,虽然并不是我们俗人不能原谅的。他因为有点受了她的感动,所以也象刚才那样回答她说:

"那也正是一样。"

于是那天夜间,把那个小小的婴孩,装在一个小小的松木匣子里,盖上一块女人用过的旧围巾,送到教堂的坟地,花了一个先令和一品特

第三篇 《苔丝》Tess of the D'urbervilles

啤酒，雇了教堂的司事①，点着灯笼，在上帝分配的那小小一块长着荨麻的荒芜地边上②，把他和那些著名的酒鬼、自尽的懦夫、没受洗礼的婴孩③以及其他所谓不能上天堂的人，埋在一块儿。苔丝也不顾那块坟地象不象样子，也一样地大胆无畏，用一根小绳儿，把两块柳木捆成一个十字架，扎上鲜花，趁着一天黄昏前后人看不见的时候，跑到坟地，把它树在坟的上首；又找了一个小瓶子，也插上同样的鲜花，灌上清水养着，放在坟的下首。虽然瓶子外面，冷眼一看，还写着"奇勒维④橘酱"字样，但是那又有什么关系？一个慈爱的母亲，在眼睛里，只看见高尚的事物，看不见这类平常的东西。

15

洛节·爱铿⑤说："只凭经验，我们得经过遥遥辽远的汗漫之游，才能得到便利直捷之径。"那种遥遥辽远的汗漫之游，把我们弄得旅程难继的时候，并不在少数，那么有了那种经验，又有什么用处？苔丝·德北的经验正是这种没有用处的。她到底学会了该作什么了，但是现在她所作的，有谁认为有可取之处呢？

假如她还没上德伯家去以前，她一举一动，都严厉不苟，按照她自己和一般人都知道的各种格言圣训，实践履行，那她自然就永远也不会

---

① 司事，教堂的小职员，司保管教堂衣物、打钟等，兼司掘坟。
② 赫门·里在《哈代的维塞司》里说："现在的教堂坟地，都修拾整齐，但直到前一世纪后半的初年，许多乡村教堂坟地，实有那种地边，给所谓不能上天堂的人预备。"
③ 著名的酒鬼、自尽的懦夫、没受洗礼的婴孩，这都是基督教认为不能上天堂的人。自尽在基督教中也认为是一种罪恶。这般人只能埋葬在教堂坟地的北面未经奉献圣化的地方。
④ 奇勒维，英国糖果公司名，在伦敦。
⑤ 洛节·爱铿（1515—1568），英国文人，尝为女王玛利的秘书，及女王依丽莎白的第一师傅，所著最有名者为《塾师》。此处所引，即见此书第一卷，此处所引的下一句为，"学问在一年之所教给我们的，胜于经验二十年"。

吃亏上当的了。但是世界上的人，总是等到这种金石之言，不再能于他们有益的时候，才能完全懂得其中的道理，想要早点儿懂得，是苔丝办不到的——也是无论谁都办不到的。她——还有许许多多别的人——很可以学一学圣奥格斯丁①的口气，讥诮上帝道："你所订的规章，超过了你准许人依之而行的程度！"

她冬天的那几个月，都待在她父亲家里，拔鸡毛、填鹅和火鸡，再不就把德伯送她的华丽服装，她自己不屑穿而扔在一边的，给她的弟妹们改成了衣裳。写信求他，她是不肯的。不过别人以为她正在那儿努力做活儿的时候，她却常常用两手抱着后脑出神儿。

她拿哲学家冷静清醒的眼光，注意那些岁月循环中去而复来的日子，有她自己在纯瑞脊以林深月黑的围场为背景，留下终身遗恨那个惨痛的一夜；有她的婴孩下生的那一天和死去的那一天；有她自己下生的那一天；还有其它因为发生过于她有关的事情，而成了不同寻常的日子。有一天下午，她正照镜子，看自己的美貌，忽然想起来，还有一个日子，对于她比哪一天都重要，而她从前却没想到，那就是她死的日子，她的容貌都要消逝了的那一天；那一天，蔫不唧地没人看见，藏在三百六十五日里面，年年岁岁，她都要过那一天，但那一天却又总是不声不响，一点儿表示都没有，然而却又不能说，一年里头，没有那一天。这个日子，到底是哪一天呢？为什么她每年遇到这样一个冷酷无情的日子，从来没觉得冷气袭人呢？她和捷露·太雷②，有同样的想法，她想到，认识她的那些人，将来到了某一天，就该说啦："今天是几儿几儿，可怜的苔丝·德北就是这天死的。"她还想到，他们说这句话的时候，心里一定不会觉得有什么特别的地方。可是她自己对于那一天，那个她自己一朝死

---

① 圣奥格斯丁（354—430），尝为希波主教，著作甚多，最著名者为《上帝之城》及《忏悔录》。此处所引，见《忏悔录》第十卷第四十一节。

② 捷露·太雷（1613—1667），英国主教兼作家。著作最著名者为《神圣的生》和《神圣的死》。此处所指，见后书。那里面说，"我们不论活多久，但是结局，总是一死完事。人们也只有一阵谈起我们……有一样事，总归要发生一次，那就是，在街坊邻居中间，要有人说，某人死了。这是关系到我们每一个人的。"

第三篇 《苔丝》Tess of the D'urbervilles

去永无生期的那一天,却不知道是在哪一月,哪一星期,哪一季,哪一年。

苔丝就这样,差不多由头脑简单的女孩子,一跃而变为思想复杂的妇人了。她脸上带出来沉思深念的象征,语言里也有时露出来凄楚伤感的腔调。她的眼睛长得越发大起来,越发有动人的力量。她长成了一个早已应该叫作是所谓的"尤物"了;她的外表,漂亮标致,惹人注目;她的灵魂,是一个纯洁贞坚的妇人的,虽然有过近一两年来那样纷扰骚乱的经验,而却完全没腐化堕落。如果不是由于世俗的成见,那番经验简直就是一种高等教育。①

她近来一点儿也不和外人交接,所以她的遭际,本来就不是尽人皆知,现在在马勒村里,差不多都没人记得了。但是她看得很明白,她在那儿,就老得难受;因为那个地方,亲眼看到她们企图和有钱的德伯"连宗",再通过她作更进一步的结合,亲眼看到那种企图塌了台。最低的限度,总得过许多年,到她对于深刻印在心里这件事完全涂抹掉了的时候,她才能不再感到难过。然而即使现在,她都老觉出来,富有希望的生命,仍旧在她心里热烈地搏动;也许在一个对于她的旧事一概无知的一隅之地,她还可以快活。不错,逃开已往以及跟已往一切有关的事物,就是把已往一扫而光;而想要作到这一点,她就非离开老家不可。

她时常自问,女人的贞节,真是一次失去了,就永远失去了吗?要是她能把过去掩盖起来,或许就可以证明这句话并不足信了。一切有机体都有逐渐恢复本原的能力,为什么单单处女的贞节,就该不许有这种能力呢?

她等了许久,始终没遇到再创新路的机会。转眼又是一番特别明媚的春光,草木的嫩芽幼蕾里,滋长发育的活动差不多都可以听得出声音来。这种情况感动了苔丝,也和感动了野兽一样,使她急欲离家远去。结果等到五月初,她母亲一个老朋友(她从来没见过面,不过她很久以前,曾写信托过她),给了她一封信,说往南去好些英里,有一个牛奶厂,想用一个手头灵巧的女工,厂主很愿意雇苔丝一夏天。

---

① 本书第一次在《图画周刊》上发表的时候,本书第一期的标题为,"在学费昂贵的学校里所受的教育"。

第三篇 《苔丝》Tess of the D'urbervilles

　　这个地方，还不到她希望的那样远；不过也许够远的了；因为她活动的范围，她闻名的区域，本来就小得很。对于一个活动范围有限的人，平常一英里就好象地球一度，一区就好象一郡，一郡就好象一省，好象一国。

　　有一方面，她是打定了主意了的：从此以后，在她的新生命里，不论在梦想方面，也不论在实际方面，都不许再有空中楼阁的德伯氏存在。她只想作一个挤牛奶的女工苔丝就完了，不想作别的。虽然她们母女，并没提到这一节，她母亲却很知道，苔丝对于这一方面，有什么样的感情，所以现在再也不说武士世家的话了。

　　但是人却往往自相矛盾。这个新地方所以使苔丝发生兴趣的原因之一，就是那个地方，离她祖宗的故土很近这种意外的好处（因为虽然她母亲是一个地地道道的布蕾谷人，他们却都不是）。她所要去的那个牛奶厂，叫作塔布篱，离德伯家从前有的几处宅第不远，就在她祖宗奶奶和她们那些声势烜赫的丈夫们一门埋葬的大坟穴附近。她也许能够看一看这些坟穴，可以想一想，不但是德伯家，象巴比伦一样①，一去不回，就是一个卑下微贱的后裔所有的清白操守，也会同样无声无息，就成了落花流水。在这个时期里，她老纳闷儿，不知道会不会因为她在祖宗的故土上，有什么新鲜的奇事、新鲜的好事出现、发生；同时心里老有一种精神，自动地涌现，好象树枝里的汁液一般。这就是尚未消耗的青春，经过暂时的压制，又重新涌出涨起，并且还带来了希望和无法制止、寻找快乐的本能。

---

① 象巴比伦一样，见《旧约·以赛亚书》第二十一章第九节："巴比伦倾倒了。"《新约·启示录》第十八章第二节："巴比伦大城倾倒了。"

第三篇 《苔丝》Tess of the D'urbervilles

《苔丝》(节选)

吴笛译

第十三章

　　苔丝·德贝菲尔离开冒牌的贵族,回到家乡这件事,很快就传开了,弄得满城风雨,不过,在不到方圆一英里的小地方,用"满城风雨"这个词未免太夸大了。下午时分,马洛特的几个年轻的姑娘,前来拜访她。这几个姑娘都是苔丝的老同学、老相识,拜访苔丝的时候,也都是把自己最好的衣裳浆洗、熨平之后,才穿着来的,好让自己算得上是苔丝的客人,配得上这位卓越的征服者(她们是这么认为的)。她们坐在屋子里,带着极大的好奇心看着苔丝。因为和她闹上恋爱的,是她那个与她八代不连宗的堂兄,一个并非土生土长的上等人,而且他作为玩世不恭、令人心碎的好色之徒,坏名声正开始远扬到特兰岭的范围之外。由于这种令人担忧的情形,使得苔丝这一被人设想的处境,比无险可冒的情形,具有了更大的魅力。

　　她们对苔丝极其羡慕,所以,当她刚转过身子的时候,年纪稍小的姑娘们便悄悄地议论开来了:

　　"瞧她是多么好看呀!那件衣服多合身呀!那衣服一定花了不少钱,没准是他送的礼物呢。"

　　苔丝这时正在从拐角的碗橱里拿茶具,所以没听到这些议论。如果她听到了,她也许会把朋友们的误会矫正过来。不过她母亲却是听到了,可她有着单纯的虚荣心,觉得,既然未能阔阔气气地结婚,那么,漂漂亮亮地调情,也算是挺过瘾的了。总的来说,虽然这有限的、转瞬即逝的胜利会关系到她女儿的名声,可她还是觉得比较满足,或许,女儿终究还会嫁给他呢。所以,见了这几个姑娘对苔丝羡慕不已,她就一阵兴奋,热情地留她们喝茶。

她们的闲谈,她们的笑话,她们那并无恶意的旁敲侧击,以及她们那闪烁不定、忽隐忽现的妒忌,也使苔丝的情绪振奋起来了,随着夜晚的时光渐渐流逝,她也慢慢受到她们那种兴奋的感染,几乎变得愉快活泼了。大理石一般生硬的神气也从她脸上消失了,她的脚步也变得轻快自如、无拘无束了,她周身洋溢着青春的美丽。

有的时候,尽管她心事重重,可她也能带着高人一等的神气回答她们的提问,仿佛供认不讳:她在情场上的经验真的有点令人嫉妒了。但是,她绝不像罗伯特·索斯① 所说的那样,是"爱上了自己的堕落",所以,她的幻想如同闪电一般,倏忽即逝了。冷静的理智恢复了,嘲笑她一时的糊涂认识,她也会认识到方才那一阵骄傲是极其可怕的,于是,她又恢复了沉默寡言、无精打采的状态。

到了第二天凌晨,已经不再是礼拜天,而是礼拜一,漂亮的衣裳收起来了,欢笑的客人也都走了,只有她一个人在她过去床上醒了过来,周围是熟睡的小弟弟小妹妹,他们在轻轻地呼吸,这时,她是多么失望、多么沮丧啊!她返回家园的兴奋,以及她回家所引起的兴趣,全都荡然无存了,她所看到的,是一条她必须跋涉的漫长而坎坷的道路,没人帮助,绝少同情。想到这里,她的沮丧到了令人可怕的地步,她恨不得一下子钻到坟墓里去,远远地躲开人间。

过了好几个礼拜,苔丝才恢复过来,敢于在一个礼拜天的早晨抛头露面,上了教堂。她喜欢听别人歌唱(仅是歌唱而已),喜欢听古老的赞美诗,喜欢跟别人一起唱晨祷圣歌。这种对乐曲的天生的爱好,是她从爱唱民歌的母亲那儿继承的,就连最简单的音乐,有时都能对她产生一种回肠荡气、沁人肺腑的力量。

一方面,由于自身的原因,她想竭力避人耳目,另一方面,她想躲开年轻人对她献殷勤,所以她趁教堂的钟还没敲响的时候,就动身上了教

---

① 罗伯特·索斯(1634—1716),英国神学家。

堂,并在楼下后排靠近存放杂物的地方找了一个座位,那个地方,除了老头子老太婆,是没人去的,而且,在挖坑刨坟的工具之中,还竖着棺材架子。

教区居民三三两两地走进教堂,在她前面的座位上一排一排地坐了下来,坐定之后,把额头下垂了近一分钟的时间,好像在祷告似的(其实并没有),然后坐直身子,四下张望。圣歌开始唱起来了,所选的恰好是她最爱听的,是一首由兰敦①谱曲的古老的双节圣歌,但她却不知道这首圣歌叫什么,虽然她很想知道。她觉得(她这种感觉很难用确切的文字表述出来),这位谱曲者的力量无比奇异,不亚于上帝,不然的话,他这会儿在坟墓里躺着的时候,怎么能引导着像她这样的一个姑娘跟着他一步一步地重新体验他首先独自体验过的情感呢?而且她还从来没有听过他的名字,也永远不会知道他的为人。

做礼拜的时候,先前那些四下张望的人,又掉过头来张望,后来他们看到她坐在那里,就开始相互间低声议论起来。她知道他们会议论些什么,心中不免难过起来,觉得自己以后再也不会上教堂了。

从此以后,她与几个弟弟妹妹共同居住的那个房间,便成了她离不开的避难所了。她就在几个平方的茅顶下面,观望着风雨、白雪、灿烂的落日、以及有着阴晴圆缺的月亮。她如此深居简出,到后来几乎人人都以为她已经走了。

在这段时间里,苔丝唯一的活动是天黑以后,这时,她跑到树林里,好像觉得自己最不孤单了。傍晚时分,光明和黑暗恰好是分布均匀,白昼的压抑和黑夜的不安相互抵消,只剩下了一种绝对的心灵自由。她总是善于纤毫不让地捕捉这样的时刻。只有在这种时刻,活在世上的痛苦才能减少到最低可能的限度。她并不害怕昏暗的夜晚,她唯一的念头似乎就是躲开人类,或是说躲开那个叫做世界的冷酷的集合体。从整体来看,它非常可怕,但是从个体来看,却又并不可畏,甚至还很可怜呢。

在这些寂静的山林和溪谷中,她那轻轻的脚步与她周围的环境极其融洽。她那晃荡去、飘忽不定的身姿,也构成了整个景物的一部分。

---

① 兰敦(1730—1803),英国风琴家和作曲家。

有的时候，她那怪诞的幻想，也会增加她周围自然程序的内涵，好像自然程序也是她个人经历的一部分，因为世界只不过是一种心理的现象，好像心里觉得是什么样子，事实上也就是什么样子了。午夜的寒气和冷风，在冬枝的紧裹着的包芽和茎皮之间悲鸣，成了苦苦责问的公式。阴雨绵绵的天气，就是一个模糊的道德神灵在对她无可弥补的过失表示哀伤，不过，她不能准确无误地把这一神灵划归为她童年时代的上帝，也不能把它理解为任何别的一类。

苔丝的身上由于有着传统习俗的残余，所以，她总是以为周围满是与她毫不相容的形体和声音，其实，这不过是她想象的产物，一种可悲的错误的想象，一堆她毫无理由害怕的道德上的怪物。本来，与实际世界不相协调的，就是这些东西，而不是苔丝。当她走在有着鸟儿熟睡的树篱中间的时候，或者望着兔子在沐浴着月光的围地里蹦跳的时候，或者站在栖满山鸡的树枝之下的时候，她总是把自己看成是一个罪恶的形象，闯入了天真清白的领地。不过，她在这种时候，只是在毫无区别的地方划分区别。她觉得跟一切都发生矛盾，实际上却与一切和谐。别人迫使她违背的，只是一条为人类所接受的社会法律，并不是周围环境所认识的自然法则，而且，她与周围的环境，也并不是像她所想象的那样格格不入。

第十四章

这是八月里的雾气蒙蒙的日出时分。夜间那格外浓密的雾气，现在被暖烘烘的太阳一照，纷纷瓦解，缩成一团一团，躲进低谷和密林深处，在那儿等着被阳光晒得无踪无影。

由于雾气的缘故，太阳有了一种奇特的情绪以及和人类一样的目光，要想把它充分表达出来，得用男性代名词才行。他现在这副面貌，加上景色中没有一个人影，所以立刻清楚地向我们解释了古代人所以崇拜太阳的原因。我们会感觉到，普天之下再没有别的宗教更为合情合理了。这个发光的物体有着金色的头发，温柔的目光，神采奕奕，犹如上帝，他朝气蓬勃、目光热切地凝望着趣味横生的大地。

过了一会儿,他的光线穿过农舍百叶窗的隙缝,渗入屋内,一条条光带,犹如烧红了的火钳,被他投射到碗橱、五斗橱、以及别的家具上,并且唤醒了还没有起床的收割者。

但是这天早上,在所有红色的东西里面,最艳的要算是两根漆过的粗大木头了,它们耸立在马洛特村外,耸立在一片金黄色的麦田里。它们和下面的另外两根木头一起,构成了收割机上旋动的马耳他式十字木架。这台收割机是昨天傍晚运到地里的,是为今天预备的。交错的木头上所漆的颜色,在阳光下显得浓艳,看起来好像是在液体的火焰中浸过似的。

麦地早就"开镰"了,也就是说,用人工把麦地周围割出了一条数英尺宽的通道,好让马儿和机器第一趟就能开得过去。

大路上走来了两帮人,一帮是男的,一帮是女的,这个时候,东面树篱的荫影正好落至西面树篱的中部,所以,这些男工女工的头部已在朝阳的照晒之下,而脚部却仍在黎明的阴影之中。他们离开大路,经过两旁有石柱的最近的栅栏门,走进地里。

紧接着,从田地里发出了像蚱蜢做爱一般的格达格达的声音。机器开动了,从门边望去,可见三匹马套在一起,拖动着前面所说的摇摇晃晃的大机器,其中一匹马上坐着一位赶马的,后面收割机的座位上还坐着一位助手。整部收割机顺着麦田的一边走,十字形木架慢慢地旋动,然后走下山去,从视野里消失了。一两分钟之后,它们以同样的速度,从麦地的那一面出现了,首先映入眼帘的是前面一匹马额上的发亮的铜星,仿佛是从麦茬上升起来的,然后是红艳的十字形木架,接着才是整部机器。

收割机每绕一圈,周围的麦茬地就更宽一层,随着早晨时光的流逝,未割的麦地也越来越少。野兔、蛇、耗子等等越来越紧地退向麦地的深处,它们不知道自己的避难所是极其短暂的,在这一天的晚些时候,它们注定的命运是无法逃脱的,那时,它们的避难的场所将越缩越小,窄到可怕的地步,它们不管是朋友还是敌人,全都挤作一团,最后,直立的麦子只会剩下一两分地,但是,也要被收割机那没有偏差的牙齿啃得精光,于是收割的人们便用石头和棍棒把它们全都打死,一个也不剩。

第三篇 《苔丝》Tess of the D'urbervilles

　　收割机把割下的麦子一小堆一小堆地搁在后面,每一堆正好够捆成一捆。跟在收割机后面捆麦捆的多半是妇女,也有少数几个男的,上身穿着印花布衬衫,下身的长裤被皮带系在腰上,因而,腰后那两颗钮扣就没有用途了,每当他们动弹一下,钮扣就在阳光下一闪,仿佛他们身后长了一双眼睛似的。
　　然而,在捆麦子的人群里面,最有趣的还是女性,因为一旦女人成了户外自然的一个组成部分,就获取了一种魅力,不再像平常那样只是一件放在室内的物品了。地里的男人只不过是地里的一个人体,而地里的女人则是田地的一个部分,她们不知怎地失去了自身的界限,吸收了周围景物的精华,与这些景物融为一体了。
　　妇女们(或者是姑娘们,因为她们多半都很年轻)头上戴着抽花的布帽,很大的帽边拉下来遮挡太阳,手上还戴着手套,以防手指被麦茬划破。她们当中,有一个穿着粉红色的上衣,另一个穿着乳白色的紧袖长衫,还有一个穿着像收割机十字臂一样鲜红的裙子,其他一些年长的妇女穿着褐色的罩衫,——这种服装式样古老,但最适合田地里干活的妇女穿,但是,它现在却已经渐渐地被年轻姑娘淘汰了。这天早晨,人们的目光不由自主地投向穿粉红色布衣的姑娘,因为她是其中最显眼的身段苗条、曲线优美的女性。但是,她的帽子差不多拉到了眉头上,因此,她低头捆麦子的时候,她的面部特征一点也看不见,不过,从她那帽檐下露出来的一两绺深褐色的头发上,也可以猜出她的脸部肤色。也许,她之所以引人注目,是因为她一心干活,不求惹人注目,而别的女人却总是四下张望。
　　她捆麦子的过程,像钟表摆动一样单调。她从刚捆好的麦捆里抽出一把麦秸,用左手掌把头儿拍齐,绞成草索。接着,她弯腰向前,用双手把麦子拢到膝盖,把戴着手套的左手伸到麦捆底下,去接应从另一边伸去的右手,然后像情人一样把麦子整个儿抱在怀里。接着她抓住草索的两头,用膝盖狠劲一压,然后把它系好。她时而还用手把被微风吹起来的裙子弄下来。在浅黄色皮革防护手套和上衣的袖口之间,她的胳膊常露出一截,时间长了,女性的光洁的皮肤被麦茬多次划破,流出血来。
　　她有时也歇一会儿,直起腰来,系紧弄松了的围裙,或者把帽子扶

第三篇 《苔丝》Tess of the D'urbervilles

正。这时，人们可以看见，这是一个容貌美丽的年轻女子，有着圆圆的脸蛋、深邃的目光，满头厚密的秀发显得服服贴贴的，好像不管落在哪里，都能够紧紧地粘在上面似的。就通常的乡村姑娘而言，她的脸更白皙、牙齿更整齐，两片红红的嘴唇也显得更薄。

这是苔丝·德贝菲尔，或德伯维尔，多少有点变了——是那同一个人，可又不是同一个人，在目前的状况下，她生活在这儿好像是异国他乡的陌生人，尽管这是生她养她的故土。过了长久的隐居生活之后，她决定在本村做点户外的活计，一年中的农忙季节来临了，在这个时候，就得到的报酬而言，不管在家里做什么活，都不如在地里收庄稼。

别的女人捆麦子的动作或多或少跟苔丝差不多，捆完一捆之后，她们大家就像跳四对舞一样，聚拢到一起，每个人都把自己的麦捆竖着靠在别人的旁边，一直靠到十个或十二个，形成一堆，或按当地的说法，形成一垛。

他们去吃了早饭，然后又回来了，活儿照以前一样进行着。快到十一点的时候，如果有人观察一下苔丝，就会发现，尽管她没有停住捆麦的活儿，但她的目光却不时焦虑地投向远处的山坡。在十一点即将到来的时候，一群孩子，大约从六岁到十四岁，从布满麦茬的山地后面，露出了脑袋。

苔丝的脸色微微一红，但她还是没有停下手中的活儿。

来的这群孩子中，最大的是个女孩，她披着一条三角形大围巾，有一个角一直拖到麦茬上，她怀里抱了一样东西，乍一看，好像是个洋娃娃，仔细一看，才发现原来是裹在襁褓里的婴孩。另外一个孩子带来了午饭。收割的人停下活儿，各自拿出各自的食物，靠着麦垛坐了下来。他们在这儿吃饭时，男人们还随意地倒着一个砂罐，传着一个杯子。

苔丝·德贝菲尔是最末一个歇工的。她坐在麦垛的一角，脸掉了过去，背对同伴们。她刚坐好，有一个男的头上戴着兔皮帽，腰带上缠着红手绢，把一杯淡色啤酒递过麦垛，叫她喝。但她谢绝了。她的午饭刚摆出来，她就把大女孩子——她的妹妹——叫了过来，从她手里接过婴孩，她妹妹乐得轻松，跑到邻近的麦垛，和别的孩子一起去玩了。苔丝脸色越来越红，带着一种奇特的羞怯和大胆，解开上衣，开始给小孩喂奶。

第三篇 《苔丝》Tess of the D'urbervilles

坐得离她最近的几个男人不好意思地扭过脸,对着田地的另一边,有些人开始抽烟,还有一个满怀痴情、怅然若失地抚摸着不再淌出酒来的砂罐。所有的女人,除了苔丝,都参与热烈的交谈,并且理着弄乱的发结。

当婴孩吃足奶之后,年轻的母亲让婴孩坐直在自己的腿上,自己的眼睛望着远方,带着一种几乎算作憎恨的阴郁的冷漠,播弄着婴孩;接着,她突然不顾轻重地把婴孩亲吻了几十遍,仿佛永远亲不够似的,孩子经不住由疼爱和鄙夷奇特结合起来的猛然进攻,哇地哭了起来。

"她可疼那孩子啦,虽然她装作憎恨的样子,嘴上还说她恨不得让孩子和她自己都死掉算了。"穿红裙子的女人说道。

"她过不了多久就不会那么说了。"一个穿浅黄色衣服的人接过话茬。"谢天谢地,反正日子长了,一个人对什么样的事情也都适应了。"

"俺猜,当初呀,也不是那么随随便便讲几句好听的话,事情就干了起来吧。去年有一天晚上,人们打狩猎林经过,就听见林子里面有人呜呜地哭呢。若是那个人走过去一看,那可就倒了八辈子的霉喽。"

"唉,不管事情是怎么发生的,反正叫她遇上了,真是万分可惜呀。不过,话也说回来,这种事,通常只是长得最标致的才能轮得上哩。相貌不好看的人哪,俺敢说没有丝毫危险,对不对,詹妮?"说这番话的果真是个相貌不好看的人。

的确,真是万分可惜,即使是苔丝的仇人,看到她眼下这种情形,也会觉得可惜;她坐在那儿,一张嘴像一朵鲜花,一双眼睛又大又温柔,既不黑,也不蓝,既不灰,也不紫,而是把这些色泽集于一身,此外还有许许多多别的色调,只要你仔细看一看这些彩虹般的色调,就能发现,在深不见底的瞳孔的四周,围着一层又一层色彩,一道又一道阴影,若是没有从她家族继承下来的一点点漫不经心的神色,她简直就是标准的女人了。

这个礼拜,是她第一次跨出家门,走进田地。她这个决定连她自己也感到震惊。好多个月来,她用一个阅历不深的人所能想得出来的种种悔恨,消耗、折磨着她那颗悸动的心,现在,她却已经想通了。她觉得,她可以再次成为有用的人,再一次尝一尝独立自主的甜蜜滋味,不管付出

第三篇 《苔丝》Tess of the D'urbervilles

什么样的代价。过去的已经过去了,无论过去怎样,反正眼前已不存在了。无论过去导致了什么后果,反正时光会淹没一切的,过不了几年,发生过的事情就好像什么也没发生似的,就连她自己,也将埋没在青草之下,被人遗忘。与此同时,树林还照样是青枝绿叶,鸟儿照样鸣啭,太阳照样光辉灿烂。周围那些熟悉的景物不会因她的悲伤而阴沉,也不会因她的痛苦而憔悴。

她以为全世界都在注意她的情形,所以总是把头垂得低低的,其实这种想法,完全是建立在幻想基础之上的。她的存在、她的经历、她的激情、她的感觉,除了她自己,不属于任何人。对所有的人来说,苔丝不过是一个转瞬即逝的念头。即使对她的朋友们来说,也不过是多几次关于她的念头罢了。假若她没日没夜地自悲自怜,他们也不过是说一句:"唉,她真是自作受啊。"假若她力求欢快,排遣烦恼,从阳光、鲜花和孩子身上获取乐趣,他们也不过是念头一转:"嗨,她真能挺得住啊。"况且,若是一个人呆在荒岛上,她会悲叹自己的遭遇吗?恐怕不会吧。还有,她若是一被上帝创造出来就发现自己是个未婚的母亲,没有任何生活经历,只是一个无名的孩子的母亲,那么,这种状况会使她陷入绝望吗?不,她只会心神恬然地对待一切,并且从中获得无穷的乐趣。由此可见,她的痛苦多半出于世俗的偏见,而不是出于自己生来固有的感觉。

不管苔丝是怎么推理的,反正有一种精神,促使她像从前一样,把自己打扮得干净整齐、下地干活了,这时恰逢农忙季节,需要人手。正因为这样,她开始自尊自信了,有的时候,即使是手里抱着孩子,她也能大大方方地看着别人了。

收割的人们从麦垛上站了起来,伸了伸腰,并熄了烟管。卸下来喂食的马儿再次被套到了红通通的机器上。苔丝快速吃完自己的午饭,招呼大妹妹走到身边,抱走婴孩,接着她系紧裙子,又戴上浅黄色皮革手套,弯下腰,又从先前捆好的麦捆中抽出麦秸,做成草索,去捆另外一捆了。

下午和傍晚,重复着上午的劳动程序,苔丝和大家一直干到黄昏时分。然后,他们都坐在一辆最大的马车上,动身回家。一轮硕大的没有光彩的月亮,刚刚从东方的地面上升起,伴送着他们,月亮的脸庞很像被虫蛀的托斯兰纳圣像头上的金叶光环。苔丝的女伴们唱着歌曲,表示她们对苔丝出门干活感到高兴,感到同情。但是,她们又忍不住恶作剧地哼几句谣曲,说是有一个姑娘,走进了一片可爱的绿林,出来的时候完全变了样儿。生活中,事情往往是祸福两抵的,苔丝身上发生的同一件事情,既让人们觉得应当引以为戒,又使苔丝成了村里面许多人心目中的最稀罕的人物。同伴们的这种友善举动使苔丝得到了更多的排遣,活泼的情绪是具有感染力的,苔丝几乎变得快活起来了。

但是,道德上的烦恼渐渐消逝以后,一个新的痛苦又升腾在她那不懂社会法律的天性里面。她下工回到家时,很难过地得知,婴孩在午后突然得病了。这孩子的身体又娇嫩又弱小,生灾害病是很可能的事,但是她仍旧感到出乎意料的震惊。

婴孩来到世上,是一种触犯社会的行为,但年少的母亲已经忘记了这一点,她心灵的渴望就是好好地保护孩子的生命,使这种触犯继续进行下去。然而,很快她就明白,这个肉体小囚徒得以解脱的时刻将会降临,这比她所估计到的灾难来得还早。她发现这一点后,陷入了极度的痛苦,因为她所难过的不仅仅是孩子的死亡,而是孩子还没受洗礼呢。

对于自己,苔丝是采取听天由命的态度,她心想,她所犯的罪,如果下地狱必遭火烧,那就烧个够吧。像所有的乡村姑娘一样,她对《圣经》念得很熟,并且按照要求读了有关阿荷拉和阿荷利巴的故事①,知道从这个故事中会得出什么样的结论。但是,同样的问题涉及到她孩子的时候,她的看法就完全不同了。她的小宝贝就要死了,可灵魂还未获拯救呢。

差不多是睡觉的时间了,但她却冲到楼下,询问父亲是否可以去请牧师。这个时刻,恰逢她父亲对于古老高贵的家族感受最为强烈的时刻,对于苔丝玷污了高贵的荣耀也体会得最为敏感,因为他是从罗利弗酒店刚刚回来,在那儿经历了每个礼拜一次的畅饮。所以他声称,哪个牧师也不准进入他的家门,干涉他的事情,特别是在这个时候,更没有

---

① 阿荷拉和阿荷利巴是《圣经·旧约·以西结书》第二十三章中所描述的淫妇,受到了石击和刀剑杀害的惩罚。

必要让家丑外扬了。他把门锁了起来,钥匙装进了自己的口袋。

全家人都上床睡觉了,苔丝尽管极度痛苦,也只好睡下。她躺在床上,不断地醒来,到了午夜时分,她发现孩子的病情加重了,分明是奄奄一息了,看上去好像平平静静,没有痛苦,而实际上,无疑是正在死亡。

她心里难受极了,在床上翻来覆去、辗转不安。钟敲了庄严的一点,在这个时刻,幻想跳出理性的桎梏,险恶的猜测变成坚如磐石的事实。她想,这孩子既然没受洗礼,又是非法的私生子,两罪俱在,一定会被打到地狱最底层的一个角落。她看见魔王手里抓着三刃叉,就像他们烤面包时用来热炉子的一样,把这孩子叉来叉去;在这个想象的画面里,她还增添了许许多多别的离奇古怪的惩罚,具体都是这个信基督教的国家平时给年轻人布道时所讲过的那些惩罚。她越想越可怕,觉得这些耸人听闻的情形活灵活现地显出在这幢寂静、沉睡的屋子里,她吓了一身冷汗,睡衣都湿透了,她的心脏每跳动一下,床也跟着晃动一下。

婴孩的呼吸越来越艰难,母亲精神上的紧张也越来越加强。她即使吻遍这个小东西,也已无济无事了,她在床上再也躺不住了,因而在房间里心急如焚地走来走去。

"啊,大慈大悲的上帝呀,可怜可怜我的孩子吧!"她喊着说。"你有多少怒火,全都发泄到我身上来吧,我心甘情愿地受罚,可是,可怜可怜这个孩子吧!"

她靠在五斗橱上,语无伦次地祈求了好长时间,直到后来她猛然跳了起来。

"哦!也许宝贝儿还能拯救!也许这样办也行!"

她说话的时候,显得那么快活,仿佛她的脸都在周围的昏暗中发出了光芒。

她点燃一支蜡烛,走到靠墙而放的第二张和第三张床前,唤醒了也睡在这间屋子里的弟弟妹妹。她把洗脸台往外拉了一点,自己站在台子后面,又从大水壶里倒出了一些水,叫弟弟妹妹们合着手掌,跪在她的前面。这些孩子们还没有完全醒过来,看到姐姐的举动,一双双眼睛便越睁越大,但仍旧保持着下跪的姿势。苔丝从自己的床上抱起婴儿,一个孩子的孩子,因为这婴儿如此弱小,生他的人简直没有资格被称为母亲。然后,苔丝抱着婴儿,笔直地站在脸盆旁边,她的大妹妹翻开祈祷书,放在苔丝面前,就像教堂执事对待牧师那样,于是,姑娘预备为自己的婴孩行洗礼。

她身穿白色的长睡衣站在那儿,因而显得特别高大、庄严,一条又黑又粗的发辫在背后一直垂到腰部。微弱的烛光,和蔼暗淡,遮掩了她身上和面部那些在阳光下会暴露出来的瑕疵:手腕上被麦茬划破的痕迹,以及她眼中的倦容。高度的精诚,起了一种美化的效果,使那张曾经坑害过她的面孔,显示出纯洁无瑕的美丽,并且带有差不多与皇后一般的尊严。弟弟妹妹们跪在四周,他们那睡意蒙眬的眼睛显得发红,一眨一眨地等着姐姐做洗礼的准备,他们在这个时刻,因为昏沉欲睡,所以提不起精神,对眼前的事也不太感到好奇了。

其中有一个问题给人印象最深:

"苔丝,你真的给他施洗礼吗?"

年幼的母亲庄严地作出了肯定的回答。

"那么你给他取什么名字?"

她以前没想过这一点,但是,当她继续施洗礼的时候,《创世纪》中的一个词语① 出现在她的脑中,于是她现在念道:

"哀愁,我现在以圣父、圣子和圣灵的名义,给你施洗礼。"

她洒起水来,顿时一片静穆。

"孩子们,你们说'阿门'。"

细小的声音恭顺地说出了"阿门!"

苔丝继续说:

"我们接受这孩子。"——如此等等——"我们给他画一个十字。"

这时,她把手在水盆里蘸了蘸,用食指对着孩子热烈地画了一个很大的十字,接着又念了一些行洗礼时惯用的句子,如说他要英勇地反抗罪孽、世俗和恶魔,并且自始至终做上帝忠诚的奴仆和战士。她接着规规矩矩地念了主祷文,孩子们像蚊子似的含含糊糊地跟着她念,念到最

---

① 在《创世纪》中,雅各的妻子拉结在分娩中死亡之前,把孩子取名"便俄尼"(Ben—oni),希伯莱语的意思是"我的哀愁之子"。见《圣经·旧约·创世纪》第三十五章第十八节。

第三篇 《苔丝》Tess of the D'urbervilles

后一句时,他们把嗓门提高到教堂执事的程度,对着一片寂静,齐声喊出了"阿门!"

这时,他们的姐姐越发坚信这一圣事的功效,便从心灵深处倾倒出接在后面的感恩祷文,她念得大方,念得狂热,声音像调整了音调的风琴,每当她心口如一的时候,总是会有这种声音,而且,不管是谁听见了,总是永远难忘的。虔诚的狂喜几乎使她羽化登仙,她的脸上仿佛光辉四射,腮帮上也生出了两朵红晕,甚至连映在那眼中的小小的烛光,也像钻石一样闪烁。孩子们越来越恭敬地看着她了,不再有心思向她提问了。在他们看来,她现在不像是大姐姐了,而是一位高高屹立的威严的巨人,一位天神,与他们毫无相同之处。

那个可怜的哀愁反抗罪孽、世俗和恶魔的斗争,注定只能得到有限的荣耀,考虑到他不幸的诞生,这对于他或许还是一件幸运的事。在清幽幽的晨光中,这名脆弱的战士和奴仆喘出了他的最后一口气,别的孩子们醒过之后,一个个哭得伤心极了,他们恳求苔丝姐姐再给他们生一个漂亮的娃娃。

自从施过洗礼之后,苔丝的心情就安稳了,一直保持到婴儿断气。天亮之后,她觉得自己在夜间对于小孩灵魂的恐怖猜测,的确有点过分,不管有没有根据,她反正现在已经恢复平静了,因为她觉得,如果上帝对这种非正式的洗礼仪式不予认可,不准孩子的灵魂升入天堂,那么,无论是对于她还是对于她的孩子,这种天堂都是不值一提的了。

这个不请自来的哀愁就这样离开人间了,他是个贸然闯入的人物,是不尊重社会法则的、伤风败俗的"自然"送来的一件劣质礼物。这个弃儿,还不知什么是一年,什么是一个世纪,对他来说,永恒的时光只不过是几天的事,一间农舍就是一个宇宙,一个礼拜的天候就是四季的气象,短暂的婴孩生活就是整个人生的体验,吸奶的本能就是人类的知识。

苔丝对于施洗礼的事已经考虑得够多了,现在又得考虑孩子在教义上能否按基督教徒埋葬。这一点,除了教区牧师,谁也说不准,可他是个新来的,不认识苔丝。黄昏之后,她来到他家,站在门口,但没有勇气进去。她正准备放弃这一打算,转身返回,恰好遇上牧师从外面回家。因此,在幽暗的夜色中,她把自己的心事一古脑儿说了出来。

"先生,我有件事,想要请教你。"

他表示他愿意听一听,于是她跟他说了婴孩生病的事以及她怎么临时给他施了洗礼。

"先生,"她诚恳地补充说,"现在请你告诉我,我这样做,对于他,是不是和你施洗礼是一样的?"

他自然而然地想到,自己就像一个生意人,本来应该叫他去做的事,却被顾客自己笨手笨脚地做了,所以他想说不一样。然而,姑娘的尊严以及她的声音中的奇特的温情合在一起,影响了他,使他作出了高尚的举动,或者可以说,尽管十年以来,他竭力要让怀疑宗教的人们机械地信仰上帝的存在,可他的良心却没有完全泯没。人性和教士在他体内展开搏斗,结果,获胜的是人性。

"好姑娘,"他说,"效果完全一样。"

"那么,你能按基督徒来安葬他喽?"她快速问道。

牧师觉得自己被逼到了进退两难的境地。听说婴孩病情很重,他在夜幕降落之后,诚心诚意地到过她家,想给孩子行洗礼仪式,他不知道拒绝他进入家门的是苔丝的父亲,而不是苔丝本人,因而他不准许这一请求,认为这是不合常规的。

"啊——那是另外一回事了。"他说。

"另外一回事?为什么?"苔丝相当激动地问道。

"唉,如果这只是我俩之间的事,我一定会愿意的。可是,由于宗教方面的特别的原因,我怎么也不能。"

"就这一回,先生!"

"我真的不能!"

"哦,先生!"她边说边抓住他的手。

他抽出手,摇了摇头。

"那么我就不喜欢你了!"她忽然发起怒来,"我永远也不再上你们的教堂去了!"

"说话别这么莽撞嘛。"

"如果你不愿意,对他来说是不是也一样?……是不是也行?看在上帝的份上,跟我说话的时候,不要拿圣人对待罪人的态度,请你像平常的人对待平常的人那样,唉!"

牧师怎样把自己的回答与自己在对待这类事情上的严格观念调和起来,这是我们常人所不能理解的,当然我们可以原谅。他多少有些感动,因而又像方才那样回答说:

"效果完全一样。"

于是在那个晚上,婴孩装在一个小小的松木箱子里,上面搭了一条用旧了的女人披巾,被带到教堂墓地,点了灯笼,花了一个先令和一品特啤酒雇了教堂司事,把婴儿葬在墓地的一角。在这个寒酸破乱的角落里,上帝允许荆棘生长,允许用来埋葬未受洗礼的婴孩、劣迹昭彰的酒鬼、自尽的懦夫、以及别的可以想得出的该被打入地狱的人。然而,苔丝也顾不得这块地方是否适宜,她在一个傍晚时分,趁人不备的时候,溜进了墓地,大着胆子用一根绳子把两片板条绑成了一个十字架,扎上鲜花,竖在婴孩的坟头,在坟脚也放上了一束鲜花,并且插在能把花儿养活的小水罐里。尽管罐子外面,略微一看,就可以发现写着"基维尔果酱"的字样。可是,这又有什么关系呢? 一个慈爱的母性处于高远的幻觉之中时,她的眼睛是不会注意到这类东西的。

第十五章

罗杰·阿斯堪①说:"根据经验,我们得经过长久的游荡,才能发现一条捷径。"然而,通常的情况是,这种长久的游荡把我们弄得不适宜继续前行。那么,我们的经验对于我们又有什么用处? 苔丝·德贝菲尔的经验也正是这种无能为力的了。她最终学会该怎么做人,可是,她现在学会了,又有什么用呢?

假若是在上德伯维尔家之前,她的一言一行都受到她和大众所知的各种格言圣训的强有力的引导,那么,毫无疑问,她是决不会上当受骗的。但是,无论是苔丝,还是任何别的人,都只有在那些金玉良言不再

---

① 阿斯堪(1515—1568),英国学者及作家。

第三篇 《苔丝》Tess of the D'urbervilles

有益于他们的时候,才会领会它们的全部道理。她,还有好多别的人,会学着奥古斯丁的口气,讥讽地对上帝说:"你制定出的章程,超出了你准许人照办的程度。"①

在冬季的那几个月里,她一直呆在父亲的家中,拔拔鸡毛,喂喂火鸡,养养鹅鸭,要么就把她轻蔑地丢弃一旁的衣服找出来,改给弟弟妹妹穿。这些都是原先德伯维尔送给她的华丽服装。现在写信求他嘛,她可不愿意。但是,人们以为她在一个劲儿干活的时候,她却常常双手抱在脑后出神。

她以哲学家的眼光来观察岁月循环中的日子:在特兰岭的那个夜晚,以狩猎林作为黑暗的背景,留下了她遗憾终身的灾难,还有那婴孩出生和去世的日子,还有她自己出生的日子,还有别的发生了与她有关的事件而显得特别的日子。有一天下午,当她对着镜子欣赏自己美貌的时候,她突然想到,还有另外一个日子,比她的任何一个日子都更为重要,那就是她死亡的日子,到时候,全部美颜将会丧失殆尽,这一天将悄然藏进一年中的其他日子之中,每当她年复一年地经过这个日子时,它也不发出一点声息,可是这个日子确确实实地存在着。这个日子到底是哪一天呢?为什么她每年遇到这个冷酷的日子时,一点也不觉得寒气袭人?她只是有着和杰里米·泰勒② 一样的想法,觉得在将来的某一天,熟悉她的人会说:"今儿——是可怜的苔丝去世的日子。"说这句话时,他们心里头不会产生什么特别的东西。可是,这个弃世归天、完结生命的日子,她还不知道是哪年哪月,哪个星期,哪个季节呢。

苔丝就这样差不多一下子由单纯的姑娘变成了复杂的妇人。她脸上映出了沉思的符号,她声音中也时常出现了悲剧的音调。她的双眼变得更大,也更富有表情。她变得这么标致,应当称之为完美的创造物了。她的外貌楚楚动人,引人注目,她那颗女性的灵魂也没有沉沦,尽管经历了过去一两年的繁乱可怕的遭遇,可她没被压垮。假若不是世俗的偏见,她的那番经历倒真的是一次难得的教育呢。

① 引自奥古斯丁(354—430)《忏悔录》第十卷第二十九章。
② 杰里米·泰勒(1613—1667),英国神学家。

第三篇 《苔丝》Tess of the D'urbervilles

她由于离群索居,加上她的遭遇本来就不是人人皆知,所以现在马洛特村里几乎没人记得那些事了。但是,她心里也很明白,在这块地方,她是永远不会真正好过的,因为这儿的人亲眼见过她家企图与有钱的德伯维尔一家"连宗"。而且还企图通过她,来实现更亲密的结合,亲眼见过这种企图最后归于失败。至少,得待到多年以后,待到她完全忘却这件事情之后,她在这儿才会感到轻松。然而,即使现在,苔丝也感觉到,充满希望的生命仍旧在心里热烈地搏动,在一个不知道她往事的僻静的角落里,她一定可以喜气洋洋。逃避过去,逃避一切与过去有关的事物,那就是把过去化为虚无,而要做到这一点,她就必须离开此地。

她不禁自问:女人的贞操真的是一次失去就永远失去了吗?她若是能够把过去的事情遮掩起来,那么她就会证明这句话是不足信的。一切有机体都有复原的能力,这一规律为什么偏偏不适用于处女的贞操呢?

她等了好长时间,始终没有找到重新离开的机会。眼前又将是一番春光明媚的景象了。几乎听得见万物萌芽、蠢蠢欲动的声音了,这一情形感动了她,正如也感动了野兽一样,使她急于远走高飞了。结果,在五月初的一天,她母亲的一个老朋友给她寄来了一封回信(苔丝从未见过她,不过很久之前,曾写信向她询问过),说是往南好些英里的地方,有一个牛奶场需要一个手脚灵巧的挤奶女工,场主很乐意雇用苔丝一个夏天。

这地方还没有她所企盼的那么遥远,不过,大概也够远的了,因为她的活动范围实在很小,知道她的人实在有限。对活动范围有限的人来说,一英里就好像地球一度,一区就好像一郡,一郡就好像一省、一国。

有一个方面,她态度是很坚决的:以后在她的新生活里,不管是在梦幻还是在现实中,都不能再受德伯维尔这个空中楼阁般的姓氏纠缠了。她这个苔丝只想做一个挤奶女工,不想做任何别的。虽然她们母女俩没有谈到这方面的问题,可做母亲的非常清楚女儿的情感,所以她一次也没提及武士世家之类的话。

然而,人的思想常常是自相矛盾的,这个新地方之所以对苔丝发生兴趣,原因之一就是它恰好在她祖辈故土的附近(因为尽管她母亲是个地地道道的布莱克摩人,可他们却不是)。她要去的那个牛奶场叫做塔尔勃塞,离德伯维尔家族从前的几处宅第不远,就靠近她一些有钱有势的老祖宗的坟地。她或许可以去看一看,想一想,不仅是德伯维尔家族像巴比伦一般倾倒了,而且连一个卑微的后裔也无声无息地失去了个人的清白。她老是在想,会不会由于她在祖辈的领地上,因而可以遇到什么新奇的好事?她体内有种精神自动地升腾起来,就像嫩枝里的液汁一样。这是没有耗尽的青春,经过暂时的压抑之后,又重新激荡起来,并且还带来了希望,以及寻求欢乐的不可抑制的本能。

第四篇　直译·意译　形似·神似
——《汤姆叔叔的小屋》两种译文比较评析

李　晶

美国长篇小说《汤姆叔叔的小屋》对于黑奴所遭受的深重苦难作了十分真实、详细的描绘。以主人公汤姆为代表的黑奴形象被刻画得栩栩如生；以雷格里为代表的奴隶主骇人听闻的残暴形象也被刻画得淋漓尽致。小说植根生活，情节感人，一直拥有众多读者，被列为"改变世界历史"的十六部名著之一。

关于小说的中文译本，最早曾有林纾翻译的《黑奴吁天录》(商务印书馆1981)，由于它用古文译成，虽文字古雅优美，但现代读者难以接受。后来又有了张培均的白话文译本《黑奴吁天录》(漓江出版社1982)和黄继忠译的《汤姆大伯的小屋或贱民生涯》(上海译文出版社1982)。

翻译这种实践活动需要以一定的翻译理论和模式作为依据。本文旨在以中国的主要翻译理论为依据，通过对小说第三十八章"胜利"的两种译文(简称"张译"和"黄译")的比较评析，探讨翻译理论在翻译实践中当中的运用。

首先要有必要对本文所依据的翻译理论和模式作一简要说明。

早在19世纪末，我国著名翻译家严复就提出了"信、达、雅"的翻译标准。"信"强调忠实原文；"达"讲的是要使译文能够准确、通顺地转达原文的意思，即"达旨"；"雅"可以理解为"文雅和优美"，为翻译的更高层次的要求。"信"和"达"都要求忠实原文，力求准确，两者的关系是辩证的。正如严复所说："为达即所以为信也"，两者的重要关系可见一斑。关于严复"信、达、雅"的理论，后人的理论和解释大同小异，以茅盾的概括最为精辟："信即忠于原文，达即译文能使别人看懂，雅即译文要有风采。"《茅盾译文选集序》。严复之后的中国翻译理论，包括鲁迅的"宁信而不顺"；傅雷的"形似与神似"以及钱钟书的"化境"等都严复"信、达、雅"的翻版或在此基础上的发挥和提高。

根据"信、达、雅"的标准所采取的翻译方法大致可以概括为两种，即"直译"和"意译"。因此在评析两译文之前，我们有必要对"直译"和"意译"做一些简要概述。

刘重德在《爱玛》重译版自序中提出了他关于"直译"与"意译"的理解："在读者读了能懂而且读起来通顺的条件下，应在尽量保持原文意义的同时，也设法保全其语法基本结构和修辞比喻形象，即采用所谓直译法。遇有直译不通的情况，就必须根据有关两种语言的特点，将原文的精神实质融会贯通，改用相应的适当的表达法来译，即采用所谓意译法。"由此可见，"直译"指翻译要尽量保持原作的语言形式，包括用词、句子结构、比喻手段等，同时又要求语言通顺易懂。"意译"则要求将原文的大意表达出来，不一定采用原作的表达形式，译文自然流畅即可。但"意译"并不意味着可以将原文内容随意删改或添枝加叶。"直译"注重对原作的忠实，"意译"强调译文应符合译语的习惯。但二者又不是截然分开的。译者的最高原则应是最大限度地忠实于原著，再现原著。为了达到这一目的，应兼取"直译"和"意译"之长，二者相辅相成，互为补充。

本文将根据"信、达、雅"等中国翻译理论和模式，就两译文"直译"与"意译"两种翻译方法在一些具体内容上的运用以及由此产生的不同效果方面进行一些比较评析。

小说的第三十八章"胜利"讲述了主人公汤姆在惨遭毒打和辛苦劳作，经历了肉体上的创痛和疲惫以及精神上的屈辱和绝望之后，从每日苦读《圣经》的过程中，似乎感到了与上帝心灵上的沟通，从而逐渐产生了一种超脱的感觉，似乎从自己恐怖的厄运中找到了莫大的鼓舞和安慰，感觉自己经历了生死关头的考验，正在一步步迈向天堂，见到上帝。"生命的旅程已经缩短，天国的幸福就在眼前"。汤姆因此获得了精神上的"胜利"。

作者斯陀夫人在本章中运用了大量的篇幅将汤姆的心理历程刻画得入木三分，一个虔诚、仁慈而又顺从的人物形象活灵活现地展现在读者面前。

第四篇 《汤姆叔叔的小屋》Uncle Tom's Cabin

从总体上看，两译文在忠实地传递原文内容，表达原文风格以及汉语的表达上均可称为成功之作，从中可见两译者深厚的文学和翻译功底。从"直译"和"意译"的角度来总体判断两译文，张译基本属于"直译"，黄译基本属于"意译"，但有时两种方法也交替使用。现就一些具体例句进行比较。

能直译就尽量直译：

1. Have not many of us, in the weary way of life, felt in some hours, how far easier it were to die than to live?

   张译：我们中间有许多人，在人生厌倦的道路上，不是有时候会感觉到，一死了之远比生活下去容易得多吗？

   黄译：我们有许多人在令人厌倦的人生旅途中，不是有时感到生不如死吗？

2. "What the devil's got into Tom?" Legree said to Sambo. "A while ago he was all down in the mouth, and now he's peart as a cricket."

   张译："到底有什么东西钻进汤姆的肚子里去了呢？"雷格利问桑波。"一会儿以前他还是愁容满面，而现在却像蟋蟀一样愉快活泼。"

   黄译："真见鬼，汤姆是怎么了？"雷格里问山宝道。"前两天还是垂头丧气的，现在却这么精神勃勃。"

在以上两个例句中，张译追求直译，保留原句的语言结构，将每一个字都译了出来，因而更加忠实于原文，达到与原文近似的语言效果，且意思清楚，译文的可接受性强。黄译注重"意译"。例1中"生不如死"比"一死了之远比生活下去容易得多"更加简洁、概括。例2中的"前两天还是垂头丧气的，现在却这么精神勃勃"也将原句的大意译了出来。然而，我们应该看到，大凡一种语言表达一种思想，常常采用比喻等修辞手法，使语言生动并富有感染力。黄译的两个例句虽然忠实于原文的内容，但原文中生动形象的比喻却没有了，效果不免逊色许多。正如鲁迅所言："凡是翻译，必须兼顾着两面，一当然力求其易解，一则保存着原作的丰姿。"要保存原作的丰姿，则应在忠实于原文，而又符合译语

第四篇 《汤姆叔叔的小屋》Uncle Tom's Cabin

表达习惯的前提下,能直译尽量直译。因此,以上两个例句的翻译,张译好于黄译。

当直译不能体现原文的风格和神韵时,应求意译:

傅雷曾说:"以效果而论,翻译应当像临画一样,所求的不在形似而在神似"。这里的"神"指的是原作的精神。好的文学作品具有丰富的感情,深邃的意境,强烈的感染力和艺术效果。"神似"也叫"传神",就是除了传达意义外,还要尽力保存原作的风格和神韵。请看下面几个例句:

1. But to live, — to wear on, day after day, of mean, bitter, low, harassing servitude, every nerve dampened and depressed, every power of feeling gradually smothered, — this long and wasting heart—martyrdom, this slow, daily bleeding away of the inward life, drop by drop, hour after hour, — this is the true searching test of what there may be in man or woman.

张译:但是,活下去吧,——一天一天的时间过去,在卑贱、辛苦、低微、折磨的奴役之中,每一根神经都感到挫折与抑郁,每一种感觉的能力都被遏制,——这长期损耗在心上的痛苦牺牲,这缓慢的、一天天血在流去的内心生活,一滴复一滴,一小时又一小时,——这是对于男男女女的彻底考验,看他们到底是何等样人。

黄译:可是要活下去,在卑微、痛苦、下贱、恼人的奴役下,一天一天消沉、颓唐、麻木不仁地捱下去,这种精神上的长期损耗和折磨,这种内在生命一点一滴、一个时辰一个时辰、一天一天的消蚀,这才是对人的本质最彻底的考验呢。

张译过于直,甚至逐字地翻译,将原文的标点符号也完全保留下来,似乎绝对忠实于原文,但却过分拘泥于原文的形式,与汉语表达方式相悖,译文显得累赘,有时令人费解。如"一天一天的时间捱过去……";"这是对男男女女的彻底考验,看他们到底是何等样人"(后半句属于赘述)。"男男女女"过于直白、通俗。黄译打破了原文的语言形式,

第四篇 《汤姆叔叔的小屋》Uncle Tom's Cabin

按照汉语的习惯表达方式翻译，全句既忠实地表达了原句的意思，语言又简洁、通顺，同时也再现了原句的风格和神韵，合乎"信达雅"的标准。

2. Long before his wounds were healed, Legree insisted that he should be put to the regular field-work;

张译：远在他的创伤治愈之前，雷格利就坚持安排他做正常的田间工作；

黄译：汤姆的伤还远远没有复原时，雷格里就逼他照常下地去干活；

张译将"insisted"照字面翻译，虽然准确，但不及黄译的发挥："逼"字把雷格里残忍狠毒的个性贴切地表达了出来，因此就更加传神。

3. In the height of the season, Legree did not hesitate to press all his hands through, Sundays and weekdays alike.

张译：在这大忙紧张季节，雷格利毫不犹豫，胁迫全体工人工作，礼拜天和非礼拜天一样。

黄译：在农忙高潮时，雷格里索性逼着黑奴们连轴转，连礼拜天也不例外。

张译采取直译，保留原文的句子结构。意思虽然准确，但原文的风格和神韵却没有了，黄译摆脱原文句式的束缚，用词颇具匠心，尤其是"索性逼着"；"连轴转"；"连……也……"，既达旨又传神，形神兼似，不失为妙笔。

4. "Come, Tom, don't you think you'd better be reasonable！— heave that ar old pack of trash in the fire, and join my church!"

张译："来，托姆，你不觉得明白道理比较好些吗？——把这本尽是废话的老书丢在火里，来参加我的教会！"

黄译："得啦，汤姆，我看你还是放聪明点儿！把那本破书扔进火里去，改信我的教吧！"

这是汤姆的主人雷格里对汤姆说的话，原句的特点是非常口语化。因此，从"忠实"的角度讲，译文应尽量保留原句的口语化风格。张译完全照字面翻译，甚至完全保留了原句的标点。虽然从语言形式上完全忠实于原句,但结果只达到了形似,而原句的风格却破坏,感情色彩也没有译出,即没有译出原句的神韵,没有达到神似。而黄译译得非常漂亮,译者根据说话人的身份和性格特点,将原句译"活"了。"得啦!""你还是放聪明点儿!""那本破书"将雷格里对黑奴的专横跋扈、粗野无理的特征活灵活现地展现在读者面前。

5. It was a superb moonlight night, and the shadows of the graceful China-trees lay minutely penciled on the turf below,...

张译:这是一个美丽的月夜,优雅的楝树的树影,密致地洒落在下面的草坪上,如铅笔画的一般;

黄译:那天夜晚月色皎洁,两行亭亭玉立的楝树清晰如绘地倒影在草地上。

张译将"penciled"译为"铅笔画的",只考虑到了该句的表层意义,而它的深层意义应为"描绘",在整个句子中,"minutely penciled"应译出它的深层意义,即黄译的"清晰如绘"。原句的如诗如画般的意境和神韵被黄译准确地表现了出来。

6. "No, ye poor, lost soul, that ye mustn't do"

张译:"不行,你这个可怜的、失魂落魄的家伙,决不可以这样做。"

黄译:"不,你这迷途的羔羊啊!千万不能这样做。"

女黑奴凯茜来找汤姆,她想趁机逃跑,并企图说服汤姆与她一起走。这是汤姆极力劝阻她时说的话。张译"可怜的、失魂落魄的家伙"只忠实于原句的表层意义。汤姆笃信基督,熟谙《圣经》,从上下文可以看出,他企图用《圣经》的教义劝慰凯茜,因此借用《圣经》中"迷途的羔羊"一说非常贴切传神,既符合讲话人的人物特点,又与上下文语义贯通,表现了原文的内涵和神韵。

7. And this, oh, Africa! Latest called of nations, —called to the crown of thorns, the scourge, the bloody sweat, the cross of agony, —this is to be thy victory, by this shalt thou reign with Christ when his kingdom shall come on earth.

第四篇 《汤姆叔叔的小屋》Uncle Tom's Cabin

张译:啊!非洲!你这最近才称之为民族的,——召唤到耶酥的荆棘冠冕面前来,这灾难、这血汗、这苦痛磨难,——这就是你们将来的胜利;就是为此,你们将和基督一同统治国家,当基督的国来到地上的时候。

黄译:而这将是(哦,非洲啊,你最后受召唤的民族!上帝召唤你去戴荆棘之冠,受鞭挞、流血汗,背起苦难的十字架)——这将是你的胜利。当上帝的国降临人间时,你将因此和基督一同为王。

　　这是概括本章中心思想的一句话。它的翻译是非常重要的,既要准确地表达出原句的思想内容,又要尽量忠实地表现原句的艺术风格。从这两方面判断,黄译大大优于张译,原因有三:一、张译拘泥原句结构(保留两处破折号),与汉语习惯不符,句子混乱不通;黄译打破原句结构,改用一个括弧(汉语中括弧当中的内容可为补充说明),符合汉语习惯,句子结构通顺、意思明确。二、张译将 latest called of nations 中的 called 理解为"称之为",从整个句子判断,这里的 called 应与后面的 called to the crown of thorns... 中的 called 意义一致,应为"召唤"。因此黄译理解准确。三、张译将 the cross of agony 译为"这苦痛磨难",只达旨不传神,读来平淡无味;黄译"苦难的十字架"将 cross 的神韵表达了出来(cross 有十字架之意),既达旨又传神。原句中有三个名词短语 the scourge, the bloody sweat, the cross of anony,张译保留原来的形式,译成三个名词短语,忠实通顺。然而黄译将它们转译为三个动宾结构:"受鞭挞,流血汗,背起苦难的十字架"可谓形神兼似,妙不可言。

　　从以上几个例句可以看出,就文学作品的翻译而言,"意译"往往更能传达原文的风格和神韵,因为所谓"信"或"忠实"在文学翻译中不仅应体现在内容上,还应体现在风格上。钱钟书说得好:"翻译的最高标准是'化',把作品从一国文字转变成另一国文字,既不能因语文习惯的差异而露出生硬牵强的痕迹,又能完全保存原有的风味,那就算得入于'化境'"。可见"化境"即"形神兼似"。从这个意义上说,黄译对很多内容的"意译"处理方法,其效果要好于张译的过分直译的方法。

　　郭沫若非常推崇严复的"信达雅"标准,他曾说:"不信就是乱译、错

第四篇 《汤姆叔叔的小屋》Uncle Tom's Cabin

译,不达就是死译、硬译,不雅就是走到极端的不成话。"

两译文中也存在着一些属"误译"和"死译"的地方。举例如下:

误译现象:

1. "...I never have prayed since my children were sold!"

张译:"从孩童时候卖出来以后,我从来没有祷告过!"

黄译:"自从我的儿女被卖掉以后,我就再也不做祷告了。"

这是女黑奴凯茜对汤姆说的话。不知张译为何将 since my children were sold 这个意思非常简单的从句误译为"从孩童时候卖出来以后",或许是疏忽大意所致吧!

2. "... Lord, help us to follow His steps, and love our enemies."

张译:"主啊!帮助我们追随你,亦步亦趋,爱我们的敌人。"

黄译:"上帝啊,帮助我们以他为榜样,爱我们的敌人。"

原句中 His 大写,指 Lord,因此张译准确;而黄译"他"似指别人,照字面翻译,属误译。或许是没有注意到 His 的大写形式。

3. A coarse laugh roused him; he looked up, —Legree was standing opposite to him.

张译:一个粗鲁的笑声惊醒了他;他抬头一看,——雷格利站在他对面。

黄译:一阵粗野的笑声惊动了他。他抬头一看,面前站的是雷格里。

这句话中有三个地方张译属误译:首先,coarse 形容"笑声",应译为"粗野",有"粗鲁"一般指行为举止。其次 a laugh 中的 a 根据汉语的表达习惯,应译为"一阵"(笑声),而不是"一个"(笑声)。以上两点属词不搭配。再次,roused 应译为"惊醒",还是"惊动",这要取决于上下文。此时汤姆正坐在柴火旁读《圣经》,而不是在睡觉,因此应为"惊动"。这些都属于不求甚解的误译,下面的例子也属同样情况:

4. and if it wore out a few more hands, he could buy better ones.

张译:若是再有几个工人做死了,就再买几个好的。

第四篇 《汤姆叔叔的小屋》Uncle Tom's Cabin

黄译：如果多累死了几个农奴，他可以再买几个体格更结实的。

"做死了"显然是用词不当，令人费解。另外，张译在本章中有时将为种植园主干活的黑人称为"工人"，也是不妥当的，他们不是"工人"，而是"农奴"。

死译现象：

直译并非字对字的翻译，因为两种语言结构和表达习惯的不同，字对字的翻译是不可能的。这种过分的直译可能导致"死译"，请看以下几例：

1. Tom sat, like one stunned, at the fire.

    张译：托姆坐在火跟前像个发呆的人。

    黄译：汤姆正坐在柴火旁边出神。

张译将 like one stunned 的形式完全照搬到汉语中，但它并不符合汉语表达习惯。我们说"某人在发呆"，而不说"某人像个发呆的人"。因此，张译属死译。

2. The psychologist tells us of a state, in which the affections and images of the mind become so dominant and overpowering, that they press into their service the outward senses, and make them give tangible shape, to the inward imagining.

    张译：心理学家告诉我们，在这种情况下，心之所钟与心上的形象，变得占据优势而压倒一切，以至迫使外面的官能为其服务，为内在的想象赋予捉摸得到的形状。

    黄译：心理学家谈到过这种现象：当一个人的感情和幻想激动得难以控制时，它们会强制外部的感官为它们服务，迫使他们将内心的幻象转变为具体形象。

这是张译过分直译乃至死译的一个典型例子。它完全从原句的表层结构出发，从字面翻译。其中...tells us of a state, in which...张译的翻译与原句意思出入很大。译文完全拘泥于原文形式，不符合汉语表达方式，尤其是"心之所钟与心上的形象"晦涩难懂。相比之下，黄译打破原文句式，按汉语习惯表达，行文简洁流畅，意思明确。下面一例属同一种情况：

第四篇 《汤姆叔叔的小屋》Uncle Tom's Cabin

3. The principle of reliance and unquestioning faith, which is its foundation, is more a native element in this race than any other; and it is often been found among them, that a stray seed of truth, borne on some breeze of accident into hearts of the most ignorant, has sprung up into fruit, whose abundance has shamed that of higher and more skillful culture.

张译：信赖的真谛,和赖以为基础的盲目信仰,在这个种族里,和其它种族比较起来,<u>更是本地原有土生的成分</u>；在他们中间往往发现这样的事情；真理的一粒飘荡的种子,乘着<u>某一事件的微风,吹进最愚蠢的心里就发芽、成长,其果实之丰盛</u>,叫文化较高较精深的地方的收获,感到惭愧。

黄译：它的基础是推心置腹的信仰和依赖这一基本道理。非洲人的这一天性,其他民族是<u>望尘莫及</u>的。黑人中时常见到这种情况：<u>一颗随风飘扬的真理种子</u>,偶尔落到<u>一些最愚昧的心田中,后来开花结果,茂盛无比</u>,往往使一些具有高尚修养的文明人羞愧无地。

张译死死拘泥于原文的语言结构,译文语言晦涩,意义含混,不知所云。特别是划线部分,属死译、硬译；黄译的"意译"处理法,既忠实于内容,又通顺流畅,尤其是划线部分,语气连贯自然,一气呵成。但最后一句"具有高尚修养的文明人"似乎与原文出入太大,这里应指出与非洲文化相对的更高更精深的民族文化。

4. Nay, he found the placid, sunny temper, which had been the habitute of his life, broken in on, and solely strained, by the inroads of the same thing.

张译：而他要保持一生习惯的温和愉快,也很是勉强,他也被同样的坏脾气闯进来了。

黄译：不但如此,他发现连自己往常那种温和、乐观的脾气,在苦难的不断侵袭下,也被打乱了阵脚,已经成为强弩之末,难以维持下去了。

相比之下,黄译译文有些啰嗦,但句子通顺,意义明确；张译则过分直译,属于死译。什么叫"被同样的坏脾气闯进来了"呢?实在令人费解。可见,"死译"是由于过分拘泥于原文表达方式所致,结果往往令读者感到莫名其妙。

对于一部名著而言,误译、死译之处颇令人遗憾。中国的各种翻译理论都将"信"或"忠实"放在首位,而要达到这种标准,则要求译者多从译语和译文读者的习惯和接受能力考虑,尽力杜绝或减少失误,做到先"信"而后至"达"、"雅"。

关于两译文的比较评析,最后还有一点需要提及,即翻译中"文化冲突"问题的处理。

语言不仅是信息的载体,也是文化的载体。汉英两种语言之间存在着很大的文化差异。这种差异涉及风土人情、历史传统、民族心理以及宗教信仰等等。英国语言学家约翰·莱昂斯说:"……翻译不仅是语言的转换过程,同时也是文化的移植过程。译者为这个过程的主体,不仅应该精通原语和译语这两种语言,而且通晓这两种语言所反映的文化。"因此,译者既要使译文在意义和风格上忠实于原著,又要照顾原语和译语的不同文化特点,注意解决好翻译中的"文化冲突"问题。

本章多处涉及《圣经》方面的内容,虽然原作者没有加注解,但《圣经》是英美的必读书,《圣经》故事人人皆知。因此原文无加注的必要。而译成汉语就应从汉语读者的接受心理考虑,在有确切出处的地方,都应加注解,以帮助译文读者了解原著的思想内容和作者的创作意图。关于这一点,两译文在很多地方都各自加了注解,但也都有疏漏的地方。本章中涉及文化内容的地方还有以下两例:

1. From this time, an inviolable sphere of peace encompassed the lowly heart of the oppressed one, — an everpresent Saviour hallowed it as a temple.

    张译:从这时候起,有个不可侵犯的和平区域围绕着这个被压迫者的谦恭的心,——永存的救世主基督称之为一所庙。

    黄译:从此以后,这个被压迫者的谦卑的心灵就形成了一个不可侵犯的平安区,无所不在的救世主使它变成了一座圣殿。

    temple 一词意为"神殿";"庙宇";"寺院",而"庙"在汉语中只能指道教、佛教的殿堂。张译将"庙"与"基督"放在一起,虽是从译文读者的文化背景考虑,但这种译法本身就存在着"文化冲突"现象,令人啼笑皆非;而黄译将 temple 模糊地译为"圣殿"既达意又优雅。

2. "Mas'r, let me 'lone for dat," said Sambo. "I'll tree de coon. Ho, ho, ho!"

  张译:"主人,让我一个人干就是了,"桑波道,"我叫这只狐狸精弄得上不得上,下不得下。哈!哈!哈!"

  黄译:"老爷,这事包在我身上,"山宝说,"我有办法对付这只老狐狸"。

根据上下文得知,山宝与雷格里正在谈论如何对付汤姆。"狐狸精"在汉语文化中有它特殊的意义,一般用来指"以美色勾引男人的女人"。显然,张译用"狐狸精"比喻汤姆是个失误。而黄译"老狐狸"则生动贴切,意指"狡猾的人"。

从以上对两译文的比较评析,可以这样概括:张译和黄译都是以"信"为最高原则。总的来说,两译文都忠实地再现了原作的内容,语言表达也算通顺。但两译者采用了两种不同的翻译方法,张译基本属"直译",译文中有些误译和死译现象;而黄译基本属"意译",译文不乏"神似"妙笔,较张译为更加成功之作。

通过对两译文的比较评析可以得出这样的结论:"信达雅"的翻译标准中当以"信"为首。"信"即忠实于原文,而"忠实"应体现在忠实于原文的思想内容和艺术风格两个方面。在尽量贴近原语的表达方式的同时,又不破坏译语的语言规范。在这一标准的前提下,应兼取"直译"和"意译"之长,二者相辅相成,相得益彰。

参考文献

Stowe, Harriet. Beecher *Uncle Tom's Cabin*. New York: Airmont Publishing Company, INC., 1967.

《翻译研究论文集》(1949-1983),外语教学与研究出版社。

《中国翻译》,1998 年第 1、2、3 期(总第 127,128,129 期)。

范仲英:《实用翻译教程》,外语教学与研究出版社,1994 年。

第四篇 《汤姆叔叔的小屋》Uncle Tom's Cabin

黄继忠译:《汤姆大伯的小屋或贱民生涯》上海译文出版社,1982年。
刘重德:《文学翻译十讲》,中国对外翻译出版公司,1991年。
喻云根:《英美名著翻译比较》,湖北教育出版社,1996年。
张培均译:《黑奴吁天录》,漓江出版社,1982年。

第四篇 《汤姆叔叔的小屋》Uncle Tom's Cabin

附：

Uncle Tom's Cabin (Excerpt)

H. P. Stone

38 The Victory

"Thanks be unto God, who giveth us the victory."

Have not many of us, in the weary way of life, felt, in some hours, how far easier it were to die than to live?

The martyr, when faced even by a death of bodily anguish and horror, finds in the very terror of his doom a strong stimulant and tonic. There is a vivid excitement, a thrill and fervor, which may carry through any crisis of suffering that is the birth-hour of eternal glory and rest.

But to live, — to wear on, day after day, of mean, bitter, low, harassing servitude, every nerve dampened and depressed, every power of feeling gradually smothered, — this long and wasting heart-martyrdom, this slow, daily bleeding away of the inward life, drop by drop, hour after hour, — this is the true searching test of what there may be in man or woman.

When Tom stood face to face with his persecutor, and heard his threats, and thought in his very soul that his hour was come, his heart swelled bravely in him, and he thought he could bear torture and fire, bear anything, with the vision of Jesus and heaven but just a step beyond; but, when he was gone, and the present excitement

第四篇 《汤姆叔叔的小屋》Uncle Tom's Cabin

passed off, came back the pain of his bruised and weary limbs, — came back the sense of his utterly degraded, hopeless, forlorn estate; and the day passed wearily enough.

Long before his wounds were healed, Legree insisted that he should be put to the regular field-work; and then came day after day of pain and weariness, aggravated by every kind of injustice and indignity that the ill-will of a mean and malicious mind could devise. Whoever, in *our* circumstances, has made trial of pain, even with all the alleviations which, for us, usually attend it, must know the irritation that comes with it. Tom no longer wondered at the habitual surliness of his associates; nay, he found the placid, sunny temper, which had been the habitude of his life, broken in on, and sorely strained, by the inroads of the same thing. He had flattered himself on leisure to read his Bible; but there was no such thing as leisure there. In the height of the season, Legree did not hesitate to press all his hands through, Sundays and week-days alike. Why shouldn't he? —he made more cotton by it, and gained his wager; and if it wore out a few more hands, he could buy better ones. At first, Tom used to read a verse or two of his Bible, by the flicker of the fire, after he had returned from his daily toil; but, after the cruel treatment he received, he used to come home so exhausted, that his head swam and his eyes failed when he tried to read; and he was fain to stretch himself down, with the others, in utter exhaustion.

Is it strange that the religious peace and trust, which had upborne him hitherto, should give way to tossings of soul and despondent darkness? The gloomiest problem of this mysterious life was constantly before his eyes, —souls crushed and ruined, evil triumphant, and God silent. It was weeks and months that Tom wrestled, in his own soul, in darkness and sorrow. He thought of Miss Ophelia's letter to his Kentucky friends, and would pray earnestly that God would send him deliverance. And then he would watch, day after day, in the vague hope of seeing somebody sent to redeem him; and, when nobody came, he would crush back to his soul bitter thoughts, —that it was vain to serve God, that God had forgotten him. He sometimes saw Cassy; and sometimes, when summoned to the house, caught a glimpse of the dejected form of Emmeline, but held very little communion with either; in fact, there was no time for him to commune with anybody.

One evening, he was sitting, in utter dejection and prostration, by a few decaying brands, where his coarse supper was baking. He put a few bits of brushwood on the fire, and strove to raise the light, and then drew his worn Bible from his pocket. There were all the marked passages, which had thrilled his soul so often, —words of patriarchs and seers, potets and sages, who from early time had spoken courage to man, —voices from the great cloud of witnesses who ever surround us in the race of life. Had the word lost its power, or could the failing eye and weary sense no longer answer to the touch of that mighty inspiration? Heavily sighing, he put it in his pocket. A coarse laugh roused him; he looked up, —Legree was standing opposite to him.

"Well, old boy," he said, "you find your religion don't work, it seems! I though I should get that through your wool, at last!"

The cruel taunt was more than hunger and cold and nakedness. Tom was silent.

"You were a fool," said Legree; "for I meant to do well by you, when I bought you. You might have been better off than Sambo, or Quimbo either, and had easy times; and, instead of getting cut up and thrashed every day or two, ye might have had liberty to lord it round, and cut up the other niggers; and ye might have had, now and then, a good warming of whiskey punch. Come, Tom, don't you think you'd better be reasonable? —heave that ar old pack of trash in the fire, and join my church!"

"The Lord forbid!" said Tom, fervently.

"You see the Lord an't going to help you; if he had been, he wouldn't have let *me* get you! This yer religion is all a mess of lying trumpery, Tom. I know all about it. Ye'd better hold to me; I'm somebody, and can do something!"

"No, Mas'r," said Tom; "I'll hold on. The Lord may help me, or not help; but I'll hold to him, and believe him to the last!"

"The more fool you!" said Legree, spitting scornfully at him, and spurning him with his foot. "Never mind; I'll chase you down, yet, and bring you under,—you'll see!" and Legree turned away.

When a heavy weight presses the soul to the lowest level at which endurance is possible, there is an instant and desperate effort of every physical and moral nerve to throw off the weight; and hence the heaviest anguish often precedes a return tide of joy and courage. So was it now with Tom. The atheistic taunts of his cruel master sank his before dejected soul to the lowest ebb; and, though the hand of faith still held to the eternal rock, it was with a numb, despairing grasp. Tom sat, like one stunned, at the fire. Suddenly everything around him seemed to fade, and a vision rose before him of one crowned with thorns, buffeted and bleeding. Tom gazed, in awe and wonder, at the majestic patience of the face; the deep, pathetic eyes thrilled him to his inmost heart; his soul woke, as, with floods of e-motion, he stretched out his hands and fell upon his kness, —when, gradually, the vision changed: the sharp thorns became rays of glo-ry; and, in splendor inconceivable, he saw that same face bending compassionately towards him, and a voice said, "He that overcometh shall sit down with me on my throne, even as I also overcame, and am set down with my Father on his throne."

第四篇　《汤姆叔叔的小屋》Uncle Tom's Cabin

How long Tom lay there, he knew not. When he came to himself, the fire was gone out, his clothes were wet with the chill and drenching dews; but the dread soul-crisis was past, and, in the joy that filled him, he no longer felt hunger, cold, degradation, disappointment, wretchedness. From his deepest soul, he that hour loosed and parted from every hope in the life that now is, and offered his own will an unquestioning sacrifice to the Infinite. Tom looked up to the silent, ever-living stars, —types of the angelic hosts who ever look down on man; and the solitude of the night rang with the truimphant words of a hymn, which he had sung often in happier days, but never with such feeling as now:

"The earth shall be dissolved like snow,
　　The sun shall cease to shine;
　But God, who called me here below,
　　Shall be forever mine.
"And when this mortal life shall fail,
　　And flesh and sense shall cease,
　I shall possess within the veil
　　A life of joy and peace.
"When we've been there ten thousand years,
　　Bright shining like the sun,
　We've no less days to sing God's praise
　　Than when we first begun."

Those who have been familiar with the religious histories of the slave population know that relations like what we have narrated are very common among them. We have heard some from their own lips of a very touching and affecting character. The psychologist tells us of a state, in which the affections and images of the mind become so dominant and overpowering, that they press into their service the outward senses, and make them give tangible shape to the inward imagining. Who shall measure what an all-pervading Spirit may do with these capabilities of our mortality, or the ways in which He may encourage the desponding souls of the desolate? If the poor forgotten slave believes that Jesus hath appeared and spoken to him, who shall contradict him? Did He not say that his mission, in all ages, was to bind up the broken-hearted, and set at liberty them that are bruised?

When the dim gray of dawn woke the slumberers to go forth to the field, there was among those tattered and shivering wretches one who walked with an exultant tread; for firmer than the ground he trod on was his strong faith in Almighty, eternal love. Ah, Legree, try all your forces now! Utmost agony, woe, degradation, want, and loss of all things, shall only hasten on the process by which he shall be made a king and a priest unto God!

From this time, an inviolable sphere of peace encompassed the lowly heart of the oppressed one, —an everpresent Saviour hallowed it as a temple. Past now the bleeding of earthly regrets; past its fluctuations of hope, and fear, and desire; the human will, bent, and bleeding, and struggling long, was now entirely merged in the Divine. So short now seemed the remaining voyage of life, —so near, so vivid, seemed eternal blessedness, —that life's uttermost woes fell from him unharming.

All noticed the change in his appearance. Cheerfulness and alertness seemed to return to him, and a quietness which no insult or injury could ruffle seemed to possess him.

"What the devil's got into Tom?" Legree said to Sambo. "A while ago he was all down in the mouth, and now he's peart as a cricket."

"Dunno, Mas'r; gwine to run off, mebbe."

"Like to see him try that," said Legree, with a savage grin, "wouldn't we, Sambo?"

第四篇 《汤姆叔叔的小屋》Uncle Tom's Cabin

"Guess we would! Haw! haw! ho!" said the sooty gnome, laughing obsequiously. "Lord, de fun! To see him stickin' in de mud,—chasin' and tarin' through de bushes, dogs a holdin' on to him! Lord, I laughed fit to split, dat ar time we cotched Molly. I thought they'd a had her all stripped up afore I could get 'em off. She car's de marks o' dat ar spree yet."

"I reckon she will, to her grave," said Legree. "But now, Sambo, you look sharp. If the nigger's got anything of this sort going, trip him up."

"Mas'r, let me lone for dat," said Sambo. "I'll tree de coon. Ho, ho, ho!"

This was spoken as Legree was getting on to his horse, to go to the neighboring town. That night, as he was returning, he thought he would turn his horse and ride round the quarters, and see if all was safe.

It was a superb moonlight night, and the shadows of the graceful china-trees lay minutely pencilled on the turf below, and there was that transparent stillness in the air which it seems almost unholy to disturb. Legree was at a little distance from the quarters, when he heard the voice of some one singing. It was not a usual sound there, and he paused to listen. A musical tenor voice sang,

"When I can read my title clear
　To mansions in the skies,
　I'll bid farewell to every fear,
　And wipe my weeping eyes.
"Should earth against my soul engage,
　And hellish darts be hurled,
　Then I can smile at Satan's rage,
　And face a frowning world.
"Let cares like a wild deluge come,

第四篇 《汤姆叔叔的小屋》Uncle Tom's Cabin

And storms of sorrow fall,
May I but safely reach my home,
My God, my Heaven, my All."

"So ho!" said Legree to himself, "he thinks so, does he? How I hate these cursed Methodist hymns! Here, you nigger," said he, coming suddenly out upon Tom, and raising his ridingwhip, "how dare you be gettin' up this yer row, when you ought to be in bed? Shut yer old black gash, and get along in with you!"

"Yes, Mas'r," said Tom, with ready cheerfulness, as he rose to go in.

Legree was provoked beyond measure by Tom's evident happiness; and, riding up to him, belabored him over his head and shoulders.

"There, you dog," he said, "see if you'll feel so comfortable, after that!"

But the blows fell now only on the outer man, and not, as before, on the heart. Tom stood perfectly submissive; and yet Legree could not hide from himself that his power over his bond thrall was somehow gone. And, as Tom disappeared in his cabin, and he wheeled his horse suddenly round, there passed through his mind one of those vivid flashes that often send the lightning of conscience across the dark and wicked soul. He understood full well that it was God who was standing between him and his victim, and he blasphemed him. That submissive and silent man, whom taunts, nor threats, nor stripes, nor cruelties, could disturb, roused a voice within him, such as of old his Master roused in the demoniac soul, saying, "What have we to do with thee, thou Jesus of Nazareth? — art thou come to torment us before the time?"

Tom's whole soul overflowed with compassion and sympathy for the poor wretches by whom he was surrounded. To him it seemed as

第四篇 《汤姆叔叔的小屋》Uncle Tom's Cabin

if his life-sorrows were now over, and as if, out of that strange treasury of peace and joy, with which he had been endowed from above, he longed to pour out something for the relief of their woes. It is true, opportunities were scanty; but, on the way to the fields, and back again, and during the hours of labor, chances fell in his way of extending a helping-hand to the weary, the disheartened and discouraged. The poor, worn-down, brutalized creatures, at first, could scarce comprehend this; but, when it was continued week after week, and month after month, it began to awaken long-silent chords in their benumbed hearts. Gradually and imperceptibly the strange, silent, patient man, who was ready to bear every one's burden, and sought help from none, —who stood aside for all, and came last, and took least, yet was foremost to share his little all with any who needed,—the man who, in cold nights, would give up his tattered blanket to add to the comfort of some woman who shivered with sickness, and who filled the baskets of the weaker ones in the field, at the terrible risk of coming short in his own measure,—and who, though pursued with unrelenting cruelty by their common tyrant, never joined in uttering a word of reviling or cursing,—this man, at last began to have a strange power over them; and, when the more pressing season was past, and they were allowed again their Sundays for their own use, many would gather together to hear from him of Jesus. They would gladly have met to hear, and pray, and sing, in some place, together; but Legree would not permit it, and more than once broke up such attempts, with oaths and brutal execrations,—so that the blessed news had to circulate from individual to individual. Yet who can speak the simple joy with which some of those poor outcasts, to whom life was a joyless journey to a dark unknown, heard of a compassionate Redeemer and a heavenly home? It is the statement of missionaires, that, of all races of the earth, none have received the Gospel with such eager docility as the African. The principle of reliance and unquestioning faith, which is its foundation, is more a native element in this race than any other; and it has often been found among them, that a stray seed of truth, borne on some breeze of accident into hearts the most ignorant, has sprung up into fruit, whose abundance has shamed that of higher and more skilful culture.

The poor mulatto woman, whose simple faith had been wellnigh crushed and overwhelmed, by the avalanche of cruelty and wrong which had fallen upon her, felt her soul raised up by the hymns and passages of Holy Writ, which this lowly missionary breathed into her ear in intervals, as they were going to and returning from work; and even the half-crazed and wandering mind of Cassy was soothed and calmed by his simple and unobtrusive influences.

Stung to madness and despair by the crushing agonies of a life, Cassy had often resolved in her soul an hour of retribution, when her hand should avenge on her oppressor all the injustice and cruelty to which she had been witness, or which *she* had in her own person suffered.

One night, after all in Tom's cabin were sunk in sleep, he was suddenly aroused by seeing her face at the hole between the logs, that served for a window. She made a silent gesture for him to come out.

Tom came out the door. It was between one and two o'clock at night, —broad, calm, still moonlight. Tom remarked, as the light of the moon fell upon Cassy's large, black eyes, that there was a wild and peculiar glare in them, unlike their wonted fixed despair.

"Come here, Father Tom," she said, laying her small hand on his wrist, and drawing him forward with a force as if the hand were of steel; "come here, —I've news for you."

"What, Misse Cassy?" said Tom, anxiously.

第四篇 《汤姆叔叔的小屋》Uncle Tom's Cabin

"Tom, wouldn't you like your liberty?"

"I shall have it, Misse, in God's time," said Tom.

"Ay, but you may have it to-night," said Cassy, with a flash of sudden energy. "Come on."

Tom hesitated.

"Come!" said she, in a whisper, fixing her black eyes on him. "Come along! He's asleep—sound. I put enough into his brandy to keep him so. I wish I'd had more, —I shouldn't have wanted you. But come, the back door is unlocked; there's an axe there, I put it there, —his room door is open; I'll show you the way. I'd done it myself, only my arms are so weak. Come along!"

"Not for ten thousand worlds, Misse!" said Tom, firmly, stopping and holding her back, as she was pressing forward.

"But think of all these poor creatures," said Cassy. "We might set them all free, and go somewhere in the swamps, and find an island, and live by ourselves; I've heard of its being done. Any life is better than this."

"No!" said Tom, firmly. "No! good never comes of wickedness. I'd sooner chop my right hand off!"

"Then *I* shall do it," said Cassy, turning.

"O, Misse Cassy!" said Tom, throwing himself before her, "for the dear Lord's sake that died for ye, don't sell your precious soul to the devil, that way! Nothing but evil will come of it. The Lord hasn't called us to wrath. We must suffer, and wait his time."

"Wait!" said Cassy. "Haven't I waited?"—waited till my head is dizzy and my heart sick? What has he made me suffer? What has he made hundreds of poor creatures suffer? Isn't he wringing the life-blood out of you? I'm called on; they call me! His time's come, and I'll have his heart's blood!"

"No, no, no!" said Tom, holding her small hands, which were

clenched with spasmodic violence. "No, ye poor, lost soul, that ye musn't do. The dear, blessed Lord never shed no blood but his own, and that he poured out for us when we was enemies. Lord, help us to follow his steps, and love our enemies."

"Love!" said Cassy, with a fierce glare; "love *such* enemies! It isn't in flesh and blood."

"No, Misse, it isn't," said Tom, looking up; "but *He* gives it to us, and that's the *victory*. When we can love and pray over all and through all, the battle's past, and the victory's come, —glory be to God!" And, with streaming eyes and choking vocie, the black man looked up to heaven.

And this, oh Africa! latest called of nations, —called to the crown of thorns, the scourge, the bloody sweat, the cross of agony, —this is to be *the* victory; by this shalt thou reign with Christ when his kingdom shall come on earth.

The deep fervor of Tom's feelings, the softness of his voice, his tears, fell like dew on the wild, unsettled spirt of the poor woman. A softness gathered over the lurid fires of her eye; she looked down, and Tom could feel the relaxing muscles of her hands, as she said,

"Didn't I tell you that evil spirits followed me? O! Father Tom, I can't pray, —I wish I could. I never have prayed since my children were sold! What you say must be right, I know it must; but when I try to pray, I can only hate and curse. I can't pray!"

"Poor soul!" said Tom, compassionately. "Satan desires to have ye, and sift ye as wheat. I pray the Lord for ye. O! Misse Cassy, turn to the dear Lord Jesus. He came to bind up the broken-hearted, and comfort all that mourn."

Cassy stood silent, while large, heavy tears dropped from her downcast eyes.

"Misse Cassy," said Tom, in a hesitating tone, after surveying her a moment in silence, "if ye only could get away from here, —if the thing was possible, —I'd 'vise ye and Emmeline to do it; that is, if ye could go without blood-guiltness, —not otherwise."

"Would you try it with us, Father Tom?"

"No," said Tom; "time was when I would; but the Lord's given me a work among these yer poor souls, and I'll stay with 'em and bear my cross with 'em till the end. It's different with you; it's a snare to you, —it's more'n you can stand, —and you'd better go, if you can."

"I know no way but through the grave," said Cassy. "There's no beast or bird but can find a home somewhere; even the snakes and alligators have their places to lie down and be quiet; but there's no place for us. Down in the darkest swamps, their dogs will hunt us out, and find us. Everybody and everything is against us; even the very beasts side against us, —and where shall we go?"

Tom stood silent; at length he said,

"Him that saved Daniel in the den of lions, —that saved the children in the fiery furnace, —Him that walked on the sea, and bade the winds be still, —He's alive yet; and I've faith to believe he can deliver you. Try it, and I'll pray, with all my might, for you."

But what strange law of mind is it that an idea long overlooked, and trodden under foot as a useless stone, suddenly sparkles out in new light, as a discovered diamond?

Cassy had often revolved, for hours, all possible or probable schemes of escape, and dismissed them all, as hopeless and impracticable; but at this moment there flashed through her mind a plan, so simple and feasible in all its details, as to awaken an instant hope.

"Father Tom, I'll try it!" she said, suddenly.

"Amen!" said Tom; "the Lord help ye!"

《汤姆大伯的小屋或贱民生涯》（节选）

黄继忠　译

第三十八章　胜利

感谢上帝，使我们得胜。①

我们有许多人在令人厌倦的人生旅程中，不是有时感到生不如死吗？一个殉道者即使在面临死亡这种可怕的肉体痛苦时，也能从他恐怖的厄运中找到莫大的鼓舞与安慰。他内心会感到激情昂扬、热血沸腾，经得起生死关头的痛苦，因为那就是天国的荣耀和永恒的安息诞生的时刻。

可是要活下去，在卑微、痛苦、下贱、恼人的奴役下，一天一天消沉、颓唐、麻木不仁地捱下去，这种精神上的长期损耗和折磨，这种内在生命一点一滴、一个时辰一个时辰、一天一天的消蚀，这才是对人的本质最彻底的考验呢。

汤姆站在他的迫害者对面，听着他威吓的话，心想自己的时刻已经到来。这时，他反而觉得勇气百倍，觉得赴汤蹈火，在所不辞了，因为只要再跨一步，就可以见到耶稣和天堂了。然而等他一走开，当时那种慷慨激昂的气概一过去，肉体的创痛和疲惫感又回来了，对自己处境的极端屈辱、绝望和走投无路的感觉又回来了，一天的时间就显得腻烦得不得了。

---

① 见《新约圣经·哥林多前书》第十五章第五十七节。

第四篇　《汤姆叔叔的小屋》Uncle Tom's Cabin

汤姆的伤还远远没有复原时,雷格里就逼他照常下地去干活。紧接着又是日复一日的痛楚和劳累,再加上一颗卑鄙、恶毒的心所能想得出来的各种残暴不仁的坏主意,他的苦罪自然就更加深重了。我们这些人中,凡是经过一番患难的(尽管我们在患难中还有各种附带的安慰),一定都知道:一个人在这种环境中,脾气总是很暴躁。汤姆对伙伴们乖戾的脾气已经不以为奇了;不但如此,他发现连自己往常那种温和、乐观的脾气,在苦难的不断侵袭下,也被打乱了阵脚,已经成了强弩之末,难以维持下去了。他以前满以为可能有点闲工夫看看《圣经》,但是这地方根本没有闲暇这么回事。在农忙高潮时,雷格里索性逼着黑奴们连轴转,连礼拜天也不例外。他何乐而不为呢?这样既可以多收棉花,跟别人打的赌,又可以打赢。如果多累死了几个农奴,他可以再买几个体格更结实的。早先,汤姆干完活回来还经常在微弱的柴火旁看上一节《圣经》;可是自从他受了那顿毒打之后,回去时往往已经疲惫不堪,一看书就觉得头晕眼花,因而在精疲力尽之余,也想跟别人一样躺下来睡觉。

迄今为止,一直支持他的宗教信仰和心灵的平安,如今被颠簸不安和灰心失望的情绪取而代之了。难道这有什么稀罕吗?在神秘莫测的人生道路上,他经常面临这个最令人沮丧的问题:人性遭到摧残和糟蹋,恶人耀武扬威,而上帝则沉默不语。在黑暗和痛苦中,汤姆内心进行了好几个星期、好几个月的搏斗。他想起了奥菲丽亚小姐写给坎特基老主人家的那封信,殷切地祈求上帝派人来营救他。接着他便天天盼望着!暗自指望能看到一个奉命来救赎他的人。当他看不见有人来时,往往压抑不住内心的怨恨,觉得信奉上帝毫无用处,上帝已经抛弃了他。他常常看见凯茜;有时被召到大宅子去,也偶尔瞥见闷闷不乐的爱弥琳;但是很少跟她们说话。事实上,他也没有时间和任何人谈话。

有一天晚上,他坐在一堆快要熄灭的柴火旁边烤着粗饼子当晚饭,心情万分沮丧和忧郁。他往火里添了几根柴,以便把火烧得旺一些。接着,便从口袋里掏出那本又破又旧的《圣经》。那些他划过线、以往经常使他感动的段落都在那里,都是自古以来始祖、先知、诗人和圣贤们激励人心的话,无数为上帝作见证的人的声音。在人生的旅程中,他们永远活在我们中间。难道他们的话丧失了力量吗?还是他自己日益衰退的目力和迟钝的感觉不能再响应那伟大的启示了呢？汤姆深深叹了一口气,把《圣经》塞回口袋里去。一阵粗野的笑声惊动了他。他抬头一看,面前站的是雷格里。他说:"哼,伙计,看起来,你大概也发现你的宗教不灵了吧？我早就知道终归会叫你这个脑袋瓜子明白过来的。"

这种恶毒的辱骂比饥饿、寒冷和叫你赤身裸体更令人难堪。汤姆没有作声。

"你真是个蠢货,"雷格里说。"我把你买回来的时候本来打算好好对待你的。你的日子本来可以过得比山宝和昆宝还舒服、还轻松。不但不会每天或隔一天挨一次打,而且满可以在庄园上大摇大摆,揍别的黑奴；还可以时常痛痛快快地喝一顿威士忌喷趣酒。得啦,汤姆,我看你还是放聪明点儿！把那本破书扔进火里去,改信我的教吧!"

汤姆坚决回答说,"这种事上帝不允许!"

"你明明知道上帝不会保佑你。要是他会的话,那他就不会让你落到我手里来！宗教这玩意儿全是骗人的鬼话,汤姆。我全知道。你还是依仗我的好；我有势力,又有办法!"

"不,老爷,"汤姆说,"我一定要坚持我的信仰。不管上帝保佑不保佑我,我要依靠他、相信他到底。"

"那就更蠢了!"雷格里说着,一面轻蔑地朝汤姆吐了口唾沫,又踢了他一脚。"没关系,我早晚要叫你认输,叫你屈服。你等着瞧吧!"接着,雷格里回头就走了。

当一种强大的压力把一个人压得忍无可忍时,他就会立刻调动他全部体力和意志力进行垂死挣扎,企图掀翻这个重压。由于这个道理,痛苦达到最高潮之后,退潮时往往会给人带来喜悦和勇气。汤姆现在的心境正是如此。他的恶东家那些目无神明的辱骂,使他本来就很消沉的心情降到了最低潮；虽然他那坚定有力的手依旧牢牢抓住那永恒的岩石不放,然而手腕却已麻木,握力已经不济事了。汤姆正坐在柴火旁边出神,陡然之间,周围的一切似乎都消失了。一个头戴荆棘之冠、被人打得鲜血淋淋的人显现在他眼前。汤姆怀着敬畏和惊奇的心情,凝视着那张庄严而坚忍的面孔。那双深邃和悲天悯人的眼睛深深打动了他的心。他的灵魂觉醒了,他不由得热情奔放地伸出双手跪下去。这时那幻景渐

第四篇 《汤姆叔叔的小屋》Uncle Tom's Cabin

渐变了,犀利的荆棘变成了一道道辉煌的金光。他看见那张面孔在灿烂无比的金光中慈祥地俯视着他,还有一个声音在说,"得胜的,我要赐他在我宝座上与我同坐,就如我得了胜,在我父的宝座上与他同坐一般。"①

  汤姆自己也不知道在那里躺了多久。他醒来时火已熄灭,他的衣服已经被寒气袭人的露水浸透了。然而可怕的灵魂危机却已安然渡过。现在,他心里充溢着喜悦,不再感到饥饿、寒冷、屈辱、失望和痛苦了。从那时起他心底深处已经放弃了尘世的一切希望,把自己的意志毫不犹豫地奉献给永恒的上帝了。汤姆抬起头望着那缄默和永恒的星星:它们好象是带着微笑永远俯视着人间的众天使。这时,黑夜的沉寂忽然被一首歌颂胜利的赞美诗所划破;那是他在往日欢乐的日子里时常唱的一首,却从来没有唱得象现在这样感情充沛过:

   地球将如白雪一样溶化无遗,
    太阳将不再照耀;
   但那俯视人间召唤我的上帝,
    却永远不会把我弃抛。

   当生命消亡的时候,
    肉体和知觉将不再留存;
   我在天国却将享受
    欢乐和宁静的新生。

   当我们在天国度过了万年时光,
    有如旭日一样光明灿烂;
   但赞美上帝的日子却依旧悠久漫长,
    就如我们刚入天堂时一般。

---

  ① 见《新约圣经·启示录》第三章第二十一节。

第四篇 《汤姆叔叔的小屋》Uncle Tom's Cabin

凡熟悉我国黑奴宗教故事的人都会知道,作者所写的情况在他们中间很普遍。我听见他们亲口讲过一些动人肺腑的故事。心理学家谈到过这种现象:当一个人的感情和幻想激动得难以控制时,它们会强制外部的感官为它们服务,迫使它们将内心的幻象转变为具体形象。有谁能估计得出无所不在的圣灵会怎样利用凡人的这些潜在能力,会用什么方式来鼓舞苦命人的沮丧灵魂呢?如果一个孤苦伶仃的黑奴相信耶稣曾对他现身说法,谁又能驳斥他呢?难道耶稣不是说过,他的使命就是要在千秋万代中使伤心者得到安慰,受害者得到解放吗?

当朦胧的曙光唤醒人们下地的时候,在那群衣不蔽体、冷得发抖的苦命人中间,有一个人踏着轻快的步子,因为他对万能、永恒的上帝之爱的深切信仰比他脚下踩的土地还要坚实。啊,雷格里,现在,把你浑身的解数都使出来吧!极度的痛苦、灾难、屈辱、贫困和一无所有都只能促使他早日成为上帝名下的祭司!

从此以后,这个被压迫者的谦卑的心灵就形成了一个不可侵犯的平安区,无所不在的救主使它变成了一座圣殿。现在,他不再为尘世的恩怨而伤心了;不再为尘世的希望、恐惧和情欲波动了。那受尽屈辱和创痛、久经考验的凡人的意志,已经和神的意旨合而为一了。如今,生命的旅程已经那么短了,天国的幸福已经那么近、那么清楚了;因此,人世间最可怕的灾难,也已经伤害不了他了。

人人都发现他的转变。他好象又恢复了过去那种愉快和灵活的样子,态度变得镇定自若,似乎任何凌辱和损伤都无法搅乱他的平静了。

"真见鬼,汤姆是怎么了?"雷格里问山宝道。"前两天还是垂头丧气的,现在却这么精神勃勃。"

"我也说不上,老爷,恐怕是打算逃跑吧。"

雷格里狞笑道:"那就让他试试看吧,对不对,山宝?"

"可不是吗!哈!哈!哈!"那黑小子谄媚地笑道。"天哪,那才有趣呢!看着他陷在泥坑里,在树林中被追得到处乱窜,被猎狗死死咬住不放!天哪,那次我们追摩莉的时候,我肚子都快笑炸啦。我真害怕来不及把狗赶开,那些狗会把她一身咬得稀烂。那一次可真热闹,她身上现在还有疤呢!"

"她恐怕得带着这些疤进棺材罗,"雷格里说。"不过,山宝,你留心点,要是那个黑家伙真打这种主意,你可得把他打听出来。"

"老爷,这事包在我身上。"山宝说。"我有办法对付这只老狐狸!"

说这番话时,雷格里正要上马进城去。当他晚上回来时,决定掉转马头,到黑奴村子里去巡查一番,看看是否平安无事。

那天夜晚月色皎洁,两行亭亭玉立的楝树清晰如绘地倒映在草地上。夜空晶莹而宁静,简直是神圣不可侵犯。雷格里来到离村子不远的地方,听见有人在唱歌。这在那地方是罕有的事,因此他就停下来听听。一个悦耳的男高音唱道:

> 当我在九天的宫殿里
> 　　清清楚楚看到我的名字,
> 我将擦干我的眼泪,
> 　　不再有丝毫畏惧。
>
> 假如全世界向我的灵魂合力进攻,
> 　　朝我发射毒箭阵阵,
> 我将笑对撒旦的怒容,
> 　　面对那来势汹汹的众生。
>
> 任凭忧患象洪水滚滚而来,
> 　　痛苦象雷雨般倾泻,
> 我只求平安回到我的家宅、
> 　　我的上帝、我的天堂、我的万有世界。

"噢,"雷格里自言自语道,"他原来有这种想法!这些倒霉的美以美会赞美诗真可恨!嗨,你这个黑混蛋!"他出其不意地闯到汤姆面前,扬起马鞭来喝道。"该睡觉的时候,你怎么敢在这里大吵大嚷?闭上你的黑嘴,给我滚进去!"

"是,老爷。"汤姆欣然从命,站起身来就往里走。

第四篇 《汤姆叔叔的小屋》Uncle Tom's Cabin

汤姆那种明显的快活劲儿使雷格里气得无名火三丈高。因此他打马上前,挥起鞭子就朝汤姆的脑袋和肩膀抽去。

"哼!你这狗东西,"雷格里骂道,"看你这下子还痛快不痛快!"

然而,如今鞭子只是打在汤姆的肉体上,不象以前那样,打在他的心灵上了。汤姆俯首贴耳地站在一旁。但雷格里心里明白,不知怎么,他对这个奴隶的慑服力已经完全丧失了。当汤姆进屋之后,他在掉转马头的那一瞬间,心里陡然象闪电一样豁然开朗起来(恶人阴暗的灵魂往往也有被良知照亮的时候)。他心里完全明白,是上帝在庇护那个受难的人。因此他就破口咒骂起上帝来。这个俯首贴耳、一声不响、任你怎么辱骂、威胁、鞭挞和虐待也无动于中的黑人,使他内心发出了怨言,就象昔日他的救主使魔鬼的灵魂发出怨言一样:"拿撒勒人耶稣,我们与你有什么相干?——时候还没有到,你就上这里来叫我们受苦吗?"①

汤姆心中对他周围那些苦命人充满了怜悯和同情。他觉得他这辈子的痛苦已经结束,如今渴望把自己灵魂中的平安和喜悦(这是上帝赏赐给他的奇异的宝藏)倾注一些给他们,以便减轻一点他们的痛苦。这种机会的确很少,可是在下地和回家的途中,在干活的时候,他还是碰得到机会,给那些疲惫不堪、悲观失望的人们一点帮助。那些精疲力尽、麻木不仁的苦命人,起先简直不能理解他这种举动;然而一个星期又一个星期、一个月又一个月地继续下去,它终于触动了他们那麻不仁的心灵中沉寂已久的心弦。渐渐地、不知不觉地,这个沉默寡言、富于耐性的奇人,乐于分担别人的重担,对别人却毫无所求;对谁都那么谦让,自己却甘居末位,有所得时,取得最少;然而只要有人需要,他总是抢先把自己的那一点点与人分享;在寒冷的夜晚,他常常把自己的破毯子让给有病、冷得发抖的妇人,给她增添一点温暖;在地里,他时常冒着极大的危险,不顾自己分量不足,把棉花塞进别人的篮子里。尽管他受到东家残暴的迫害,却从来不跟别人一起咒骂他一句。这个人终于对他们产生了一种不可思议的力量。农忙季节过去之后,利用礼拜天的时间,他们又可以做点自己的私事了。许多人常常聚在汤姆身边听他讲耶稣的故事。

---

① 见《新约圣经·马太福音》第八章第二十九节。

他们都愿意聚集在一个地方一起祷告、唱赞美诗、听他讲道;可是雷格里不准他们这样做,屡次哄散这种聚会,一面咒骂不休。因此,这类好消息只好个别传递。对于这些被社会遗弃的苦命人来说,人生只是一个毫无乐趣的旅程,不知导向什么样的黑暗世界。当他们之中有些人听说有一位慈悲的救主和天堂时,谁能说出他们那种淳朴的喜悦呢?传教士们都说,在全世界所有的民族中,没有一个民族接受福音象非洲人那样迫切和驯良。它的基础是推心置腹的信仰和依赖这一基本道理。非洲人的这一天性,其他民族是望尘莫及的。黑人中时常见到这种情况:一颗随风飘扬的真理种子,偶尔落在一些最愚昧的心田中,后来开花结果,茂盛无比,往往使一些具有高尚修养的文明人羞愧无地。

那苦命的混血女人,在山崩地裂般的残酷迫害下,她淳朴的信仰几乎被彻底摧毁。可是,由于在下地和回家途中,常常听到那谦卑的传道者低声唱赞美诗或吟诵《圣经》,渐渐又觉得精神振奋起来;就连神经多少有点错乱的凯茜,也在他那淳朴而谦虚的态度面前受到感化,因而觉得自己的痛苦减轻了些,心情也平静了些。

一生的苦难刺激得凯茜如疯如狂,走投无路。她心里时常盘算找个好机会报仇雪恨,亲手向她的仇人讨还她亲眼看见的以及亲身遭受的全部冤债。

有一天夜里,汤姆那间小屋里的人都已入睡,他忽然在圆木头板壁中间当做窗户用的洞孔里瞥见凯茜的面孔,不由大吃一惊。她默默招手叫他出去。

汤姆立即走出门去。那时正是午夜一点钟,外面皓月当空,万籁俱寂。月光照在凯茜乌黑的大眼睛上,汤姆发现里面放射出一种狂乱而异样的光芒,不象平日那种凝滞而绝望的神情。

"过来,汤姆老爹,"凯茜说,一面用小手抓住汤姆的手腕,使劲拽着他往前走,仿佛她的手是钢盘铁骨铸成的。"过来,我跟你说一件事。"

"什么事啊,凯茜小姐?"汤姆连忙问道。

"汤姆,你想不想得到自由?"

"小姐,当上帝的时刻来临时,我就自由了,"汤姆说。

"哎,可是今天夜里你就可以得到自由了,"凯茜陡然劲头十足地说。"走。"

汤姆犹豫了一下。

"走啊,"她那双黑眼睛盯着汤姆,一面低声说。"走吧!他睡着了,睡得死极了。我在他的白兰地酒里放了麻醉药,所以他才睡得这么死。麻醉药再多一点就好了,那就用不着你啦。走吧!"

"那可千万使不得啊,小姐!"汤姆坚决地说,一面站住了脚,拦住匆匆往前走的凯茜。

"可是你得替所有这些苦命人想一想啊,"凯茜说。"我们可以让他们全部得到自由,到沼地里去找个小岛住在一起。听说从前有人这样做过。无论什么样的生活也比这儿强啊!"

"不!"汤姆坚定地说,"不!坏事决不会有好结果的,我宁愿砍断我的右手也不干这种事。"

"那我来干吧!"凯茜说着转身就走。

"哦,凯茜小姐!"汤姆跪在她面前央求道,"看在为你舍命的、亲爱的救主面上,切不要把你宝贵的灵魂出卖给魔鬼吧!这样做不会有什么好结果的。上帝没有叫我们报复啊。我们必须耐心等待他的安排。"

"等待!"凯茜说,"难道我没有等待吗?——我不是等得头昏眼花、心烦意乱了吗?我受的是什么罪啊!这几百个苦命人受的又是什么罪啊?他不是把你都快折磨死了吗?这是我义不容辞的事;他们在召唤我!他的末日已经到来,我该要他的狗命了!"

"不,不,不!"汤姆拉住那双捏得铁紧、由于激动而一阵阵抽搐着的小手说;"不,你这迷途的羔羊啊!千万不能这样做。慈悲、亲爱的救主从来不让别人流血,只是他自己流血,而那是当我们与他为敌时他为我们流的。上帝啊,帮助我们以他为榜样,爱我们的敌人吧!"

"爱!"凯茜眼睛里冒出凶恶的光焰说。"爱这样的敌人!血肉做成的人是绝对办不到的。"

"是的,小姐,你说得不错,"汤姆扬起头来说。"可是上帝赐给了我们这种爱心,那就是胜利。当我们能在任何环境中不顾一切地爱和祷告时,战斗就结束了,胜利就到来了。荣耀归于上帝!"说到这里,那黑人哽哽咽咽、泪眼汪汪地抬起头来,仰望着苍天。

而这将是(哦,非洲啊,你最后受召唤的民族!上帝召唤你去戴荆棘之冠,受鞭挞,流血汗,背起苦难的十字架)——这将是你的胜利。当上帝的国降临人间时,你将因此和基督一同为王。

汤姆那深切而炽热的感情、柔和的声音和他的泪珠,有如甘露一般落在那苦命女子狂乱而不平静的心灵上。她眼睛里那可怕的光焰渐渐和缓下来了。她垂下了双目。当她说话的时候,汤姆觉得她手上的肌肉也渐渐放松了。

"我不是对你说过,我有恶鬼附身吗?啊,汤姆老爹,我不能做祷告——我要是能做就好了。自从我的儿女被卖掉以后,我就再也不做祷告了。你的话很对,我知道。可是当我祷告的时候,我却只能恨和咒诅。我没有办法祷告啊!"

"苦命的女人!"汤姆怜悯地说。"撒旦想要得到你,象筛麦子一样挑选了你。我来替你向上帝祷告吧。哦,凯茜小姐,向亲爱的救主耶稣祈求吧。他到世上来就是使伤心人得到治疗,使苦命人得到安慰啊!"

凯茜默默无言地站在那里,豆大一点的泪珠从她低垂的眼睛里落下来。

"凯茜小姐,"汤姆默默注视了她半晌之后,吞吞吐吐地说,"要是你能从这里逃出去——要是有这种可能的话——我倒劝告你和爱弥琳这样做。那就是说,不要伤人命,否则可不行。"

"你愿不愿跟我们一起跑呢,汤姆老爹?"

"不!"汤姆说,"以前我倒想,可是上帝给了我一个使命,要我留在这些苦命人中间。我要跟他们在一起,把我的十字架背到底。你们却不一样。这地方对你们来说是个陷阱。你们受不了。要是有办法的话,你们最好还是走。"

"我看没有办法,只有死路一条,"凯茜说。"飞禽走兽都能找到个栖身之所,连蟒蛇和穿山甲都有个安息的地方;只有我们没有。即使逃到最阴森的沼地里,他们的猎狗也会追踪而来,找到我们的。谁都和我们作对,什么东西都跟我们作对,连狗都和我们过不去。我们往哪里逃呢?"

第四篇 《汤姆叔叔的小屋》Uncle Tom's Cabin

汤姆沉默了半晌,最后说:"他在狮子洞里拯救过但以理①;他在烈火的窑中拯救过他的儿女②;他在海上行走,喝退了海风③。他依旧活着,我完全相信他会拯救你们。试试看吧,我一定使劲替你们祈祷。"

这是多么奇怪的一种思想规律啊!一个长期被人忽略的想法,象一块毫无用处的石头一般,被人踩在脚下;突然之间,它又象一颗新发现的宝石,放射出新的光芒。

凯茜考虑过各种逃走的办法(往往一想就是好几个小时),但都因为毫无希望或难以实现而放弃了。可是,这时她忽然想起了另一个主意。具体步骤非常简单,而且切实可行,因此立即使她产生了希望。

"汤姆老爹,我试试看吧!"她忽然说道。

"阿门!"汤姆说,"上帝保佑你们!"

---

① 见《旧约圣经·但以理书》第六章。
② 见《旧约圣经·但以理书》第三章。
③ 见《新约圣经·马太福音》第十四章。

第四篇 《汤姆叔叔的小屋》Uncle Tom's Cabin

《黑奴吁天录》(节选)

张培均 译

胜 利

"感谢上帝,他给了我们胜利。"

我们中间有许多人,在人生厌倦的道路上,不是有时候会感觉到,一死了之远比生活下去容易得多吗?

一个殉道者面对死亡,甚至有肉体上的痛苦与恐怖,可他就在这死亡的恐怖中,找到强有力的刺激品和滋补剂。激动、热情、生气横溢的振奋,会使他在苦难的最后关头慷慨就义,而不朽的光荣与永久的安息就在此刻诞生。

但是,活下去吧,——一天一天的时间挨过去,在卑贱、辛苦、低微、折磨的奴役之中,每一根神经都感到挫折与抑郁,每一种感觉的能力都被遏制,——这长期损耗在心上的痛苦牺牲,这缓慢的、一天天血在流去的内心生活,一滴复一滴,一小时又一小时,——这是对于男男女女的彻底考验,看他们到底是何等样人。

托姆和他的迫害者面对面站着,听着迫害者的威吓,自己心灵在思索,时候快要到了。他的心勇敢地在里面胀大,他以为能够忍受拷打与火烧,怀着憧憬,耶稣和天堂只有跬步之远,任何痛苦都能忍受。但是,迫害者走了,当时的奋激过去以后,他伤痕累累的疲软四肢又痛起来了,——极度受人贱视、被人遗弃、绝无希望的观念,又回复了;这日子过得真是够厌倦的。

第四篇 《汤姆叔叔的小屋》Uncle Tom's Cabin

远在他的创伤治愈之前,雷格利就坚持安排他做正常的田间工作;于是疼痛与疲困一天天袭来了,并且由于那卑鄙恶毒的心肠中满是恶念,想出些带侮辱性的不道德行为,使托姆的疼痛困疲更为加剧。无论什么人,在我们这里的环境下,经受了疼痛的折磨,即使有常常伴随着我们而来的慰藉,也一定知道,疼痛要带来烦躁愤怒的。托姆对于伙伴们经常脾气恶劣,再不觉得奇怪;而他要保持一生习惯的温和愉快,也很是勉强,他也被同样的坏脾气闯进来了。他妄想空闲的时候读读《圣经》;可是,这里就没有所谓"空闲"这件事。在这大忙紧张季节,雷格利毫不犹豫,胁迫全体工人工作,礼拜天和非礼拜天一样。他何乐而不为呢?——这样可以多收棉花,又可以赢得赌注;若是再有几个工人做死了,就再买几个好的。起初,托姆每天做完苦役回来以后,常常借摇曳的火光,读一两节《圣经》;可是遭受残酷的虐待之后,回得家来,筋疲力尽,想读书也只觉得头晕目眩,不得不和其他工人一同躺下。

宗教上的安宁与信赖,一直支持着托姆,现在变成了灵魂的簸荡和失望的黑暗,这岂不奇怪吗?神秘的生命中最最令人沮丧的问题,经常出现在他眼前,——灵魂已经被压碎而毁灭,邪恶获得了胜利,而上帝却沉默不语。多少个星期,多少个月,托姆在心灵里、在黑暗之中、在悲哀之中,苦苦奋斗。他想到奥菲里亚小姐写给肯塔基朋友们的信,并诚挚地祷告上帝派人来拯救他。他抱着渺茫的希望,指望会得到什么人的解救;他日复一日地守候着,不见有人来,悲痛的思想涌进他的心灵;事奉上帝没有用处,上帝已经把他遗忘了。他有时候看见卡舍,有时候被叫到房子里去,瞥见一下埃米琳垂头丧气的样子,但是很少和她们交往;事实上他也没有时间跟任何人交往。

有一天晚上,他极度沮丧困倦,坐在几段燃着的枯木旁边,火上烤着他的粗糙晚餐。他添加一点木柴,尽量把火烧大些,然后从袋里扯出那本旧《圣经》来。这里全是常常激动他心灵的有名章节,——大主教的语言、先知、诗人以及圣人的语言,在古代就告诉大家要有勇气,——还有大群证人所讲的话,证人在人生的历程中一直是在我们周围的。这种话语已经失去力量了吗?或者,衰弱的眼睛和迟钝的感觉,对于强大的灵感的刺激,不能作出反应了吗?托姆沉重地叹了一口气,将《圣经》收入袋里。一个粗鲁的笑声惊醒了他;他抬头一看,——雷格利站在他对面。

"怎么!老伙计,"他说道,"好象你发现你的宗教不灵了吧!我认为我最后还是能叫你明白过来的!"

听到这恶毒的咒骂,比饥寒与赤身露体还要难受。托姆不吱声。

"你是个蠢家伙,"雷格利说,"我买你的时候,就打算给你优待的。你本可以比桑波和坤波随便哪一个都好得多,把日子过得很舒服;你本可以到处去逞逞威风、骂骂别的黑人,而不用自己每一两天就得受伤害挨鞭抽;你本可以常常喝杯威士忌混合酒,好好暖和暖和。来,托姆,你不觉得明白道理比较好些吗?——把这本尽是废话的老书丢在火里,来参加我的教会!"

"主不许!"托姆热烈地说。

"你看,这个主不来援助你呀;要是来援助你的话,你早就不会落到我手里来了!你这个宗教,全是乱七八糟的骗人的胡说,托姆。这东西我全知道。你还是来跟着我吧。我是个重要人物,能做出了不起的事业来的!"

"不,主人,"托姆道,"我要坚持。主可能援助我,也可能不援助;但是我要跟着他,相信他,直到终了。"

"你越来越蠢了!"雷格利说着,轻蔑地向他吐一口唾沫,又踢他一脚。"不要紧,我要逼到你走投无路,把你毁掉,你等着瞧吧!"雷格利转身就走。

一个很沉的重压,压在心灵上,到了最低的仅能耐得住的程度,每一根肉体上和精神上的神经,就有猝然而来、奋不顾身的一股劲,将重压摔开;所以在极大的痛苦之后,接踵而来的往往是愉快和胆略,如潮水的回复一般。现在的托姆就是如此。他残暴的主人的无神论者的冷嘲热讽,使他早已低沉的心灵更加下沉,达于极点,如退潮干涸;虽然他那信仰的手依旧抓住这块永久的基石①,那是用一只冻僵了的、失望了的手来抓住的。托姆坐在火跟前象个发呆的人。忽然之间,他周围的一

---

① 指信仰基督有"万世基石"("Rock of Ages")之称。

第四篇 《汤姆叔叔的小屋》Uncle Tom's Cabin

切象消失了,面前出现一片幻景:一个戴了荆棘冠冕的人,被人打伤了,流着血。托姆既害怕又奇怪,凝视着这脸上严肃忍耐的表情、这深陷而令人怜悯的眼睛,直感动到他的内心深处;他的灵魂警醒了,热情有如潮涌,伸出双手,跪在地下,——这幻景渐渐起了变化:锐利的荆棘变为荣耀的光;并且在不可想象的华丽光辉中,他看见那同一个脸,低下来怜悯地向着他,发出声音,说道:"凡是能克服的,就和我一起坐在我的宝座上,犹如我已克服了,被安排和父在一起,坐在父的宝座上。"

在那里呆了多少时候,托姆自己也不知道。当他清醒过来的时候,已经树柴烧完,火光熄灭,露湿沾衣,寒气袭人;而这可怕的灵魂危机既经过去以后,心里就充满了欢乐,不觉得饥饿、寒冷、落魄、失望、困苦。这时候他的灵魂深处,失掉了、离开了当时人生的一切希望,他把自己的意愿奉献给上帝,作为绝对的牺牲。托姆抬头望着寂静的、千秋万代的星星——这天使大军的象征永远看着下界的人类;在这万籁俱寂的夜里,响起了那凯旋的赞美诗的歌声。

"地球象雪一样融化,
　　太阳不放光华;
　上帝永远是我的啊,
　　我在这下界,他在向我召唤。

"这尘世的生命将结束,
　　停止了,这肌肉与知觉,
　我将在天国的光荣中,
　　获得生命,平安而快乐。

"我已经在这里一万年,
　　发出的万丈光芒象太阳,
　我们有这么多歌颂上帝的日子,
　　和我们开始的时候一样。"

第四篇 《汤姆叔叔的小屋》Uncle Tom's Cabin

对于全体奴隶的宗教历史熟悉的人，就知道类似我们上面所叙述的那种情况，在他们中间甚为普遍。我们听见几个人亲口说过令人非常感动的情形。心理学家告诉我们，在这种情况下，心之所钟与心上的形象，变得占据优势而压倒一切，以致迫使外面的官能为其服务，为内在的想象赋予捉摸得到的形状。谁能估计出，无所不在的上帝，会借凡人的能力做什么事情呢？会以什么方法来鼓励那些凄凉孤寂的伤心人呢？若是这可怜的、被遗忘的奴隶，相信耶稣在他面前出现，而且跟他说了话，谁会来反驳他呢？主不是说过吗？古今往来，他的使命，就是把破碎的心包扎好，使受了创伤的人获得自由。

灰蒙蒙的晨光，唤醒了沉睡的奴隶，他们又下地工作了。在那些衣衫破烂、颤颤抖抖的人中间，有个人举步欢跃，因为他对万能的上帝——这个永久的爱——的坚强信仰，比他走的这块土地还要硬实。啊，雷格利，现在你来试试你的一切力量吧！极端的苦恼、悲痛、落魄、匮乏、丢失一切，只会催促他的进程，使他在上帝的眼里成为一个国王、一个教士！

从这时候起，有个不可侵犯的和平区域围绕着这个被压迫者的谦恭的心，——永存的救世主基督称之为一所庙。现在，世俗的悔恨过去了，希望、恐惧、捉摸不定的欲望过去了；人类的意志、爱好、悲痛以及长期的奋斗等等，完全消融于神圣的上帝里面。现在人生所剩的航程象是如此短促，——永久的幸福象是如此近在眼前，如此生动逼真，——以致极端的祸患纷纷离去，无所侵害了。

大家注意到他容貌的变化。他好象恢复了兴致勃勃和机敏谨慎，可是他完全沉浸在沉默之中，没有什么侮辱或伤害会叫他情绪发生波动。

"到底有什么东西钻进托姆的肚子里去了呢？"雷格利问桑波。"一会儿以前他还是愁容满面，而现在却象蟋蟀一样愉快活泼。"

"我不知道，主人；可能是预备逃走吧。"

"倒喜欢看他去尝试一下，"雷格利说道，来一个凶悍的狞笑，"我们就这样好吗，桑波？"

"我想让他试试也好！哈哈！哈哈！嘀嘀！"这个黑矮子胁肩谄笑。"天哪，真有趣！看他陷在泥里，——追逐、飞跑，冲过丛林，狗一直钉着

第四篇 《汤姆叔叔的小屋》Uncle Tom's Cabin

不放!天哪,那一次我们捉住莫莉,我肚子都笑痛了。我想起了,在我叫它们散开之前,它们已经把她的衣服都撕得精光了。弄得她周身伤痕。"

"我断定她要这样地走向坟墓里去,"雷格利说。"但是现在,桑波,你留神。如果这黑鬼想逃跑,就抓住他。"

"主人,让我一个人干就是了,"桑波道,"我叫这只狐狸精弄得上不得上,下不得下。哈!哈!哈!"

雷格利说话的时候,正骑马要到邻近的镇上去。那天晚上回来时,他心想还是回转马头到工人住宅那里去兜一转,看看是否平安无事。

这是一个美丽的月夜,优雅的楝树的树影,密致地洒落在下面的草坪上,如铅笔画的一般;那边的空气透明清静,如若加以骚扰,几乎好象亵渎了神圣。雷格利离工人住宅还有一点儿路,就听见一个人的歌声。这不是那里常有的声音,于是他停下来倾听。一个美妙的男高音唱道:

"我能向天上的邸宅殿宇
　　把我的称号宣读清楚,
我就拭干哭泣的泪眼,
　　告别一切畏惧。

"要是地球对我的灵魂进行反对,
　　地狱的短剑投掷过来,
那我就能嘲笑魔王的忿怒,
　　面对世界的蹙额颦眉。

"让忧虑象洪水般涌来,
　　悲伤如风暴般袭来,
我还是会安全抵家,
　　我的上帝,我的天堂,我的万有之神。"

"原来如此,嘿!"雷格利自言自语道,"他是如此想的,是吗?这些美以美会的赞美诗歌我恨透啦!现在你这个黑鬼,"他说着话,突然过来攻击托姆,举起手里的鞭子,"你应该睡觉,怎么你还敢发出这样的吵闹？闭住你的老黑嘴,滚你的蛋,进去!"

"是,主人,"托姆起身进屋去的时候欢欢喜喜地回答,他随时随地都是这种欢喜劲儿。雷格利被托姆得意的欢欣惹恼了,火冒万丈,于是将马骑到他跟前,照准头上肩上痛打。

"喏,你这只狗,"他道,"这下,看你是不是这么舒服!"

但是现在这个打击,只打在人的外部,不象从前那样打在人的心上了。托姆绝对恭顺地站着,而雷格利对自己也无法隐瞒,不知怎么的,他对这个受束缚的奴隶没有威力了。托姆进入小屋,人影消失,雷格利忽然催马转身,一道闪耀的光,通过他的心头,这闪光往往把良心上的闪电,送入黑暗而邪恶的灵魂。他完全明白,这是上帝插在他与这个受害者之间,而他是在污辱这个受害者。那位恭顺而沉默的人,辱骂、恐吓、鞭挞、以及一切残暴行为,都不能动摇他；他在内心里激起一个声音,就象古时候救主在魔鬼的灵魂里激起的声音一样,说道:"我与你有什么关系呢,你这个拿撒勒地方的基督？你这么早就来叫我们吃苦头了？"

托姆的整个灵魂里,充溢着对周围这些可怜虫的怜悯和同情。以他自己来说,他生命的悲痛象是已经过去了,而且,似乎希望在上帝所赐给他的宁静与快乐的奇异宝库中,拿些出来救助那些可怜人的灾难。的确,机会并不多,但是,在下田工作来回的路上、在工作的期间,机会就来了,他去对那些疲倦无力的、心灰意懒的、受挫沮丧的人们,伸出援助之手。这些可怜的、劳苦得半死不活的、被当作禽兽看待的家伙,起初几乎不懂得这一点。可是继续了一周复一周,一月复一月,他们麻痹之心久久沉睡的心弦,开始觉醒了。这个奇怪、静默、忍耐的人,看见任何人有负担,就帮助人家负担起来,却从来不找别人来帮助自己。——他站在一旁便于人家先走,自己却落在最后；有东西,他取得最少,但是将自己少量的东西全部送给困乏、需要的人,这种事情他却走在最前面。——这个人在寒冷的夜里,取下自己破旧的毛毯,去盖在发抖的病妇的被子上；在田间,把棉花装入弱者的篮子里,甘于自己的篮子斤两不足而冒天大的危险。——他虽然也承受了他们共同的暴君的残酷虐待,当大家诅咒时,他却不插一言。——这个人终于在他们中间,逐步

第四篇 《汤姆叔叔的小屋》Uncle Tom's Cabin

逐步、不知不觉地树立起意想不到的威望。较忙的季节过去以后,他们恢复了礼拜天,可以各自做点事情,许多人便想集拢来,听托姆讲耶稣的事情。他们喜欢聚集一起,在某个地方一同祷告和唱歌;但是雷格利不许,他恶毒咒骂,几次破坏这样的企图,——所以神圣的消息只能在个人与个人之间传递。那些可怜的被遗弃的人们,把人生看作是毫无乐趣的旅程,走向不可名状的黑暗,其中有些人听到有慈悲的救世主,还有一个天国做归宿,谁能说得出这样纯真的快乐呢?据传教士的报告,地球上的全体民族,没有一个民族能接受"福音",象非洲民族那么热情而易教。信赖的真谛,和赖以为基础的盲目信仰,在这个种族里,和其它种族比较起来,更是本地原有土生的成分;在他们中间往往发现这样的事情:真理的一粒飘荡的种子,乘着某一事件的微风,吹进最愚蠢的心里就发芽、成长,其果实之丰盛,叫文化较高较精深的地方的收获,感到惭愧。

这个可怜的混血儿妇人,残暴和冤屈象山石崩裂那样落到她的身上,她的纯朴的信仰几乎已被毁掉、已被压倒,现在由于这位低级的传教士在出工收工往返的时候,时常将赞美诗与《圣经》的章节吹进她的耳朵里,她的灵魂又抬头升高了;甚至于那个半疯癫的、心猿意马的卡舍,也受了托姆的诚朴而谦恭的影响,得到慰藉而平和了。

一生中毁灭性的苦楚,将卡舍刺激得发疯而失望,她心灵上时常下着决心,总有一个时候要叫他得到报应;对这个压迫者所施加于人的一切冤屈与残暴,凡是亲眼看见的或是亲身遭受的,全都要加以报复。

有一天夜里,托姆小屋子里的人都睡熟了。两根圆木中间有个孔洞作窗子用;托姆忽然醒来,从孔洞里看见卡舍的面孔,她悄悄地对他做个手势,叫他出去。

托姆走出户外。那是深夜,约莫一点到两点光景,——月明如洗,辽阔、安宁、万籁岑寂。月光照在卡舍睁大的眼睛上,托姆看见她眼睛里有狂暴的特殊强烈的闪光,不同于平时那种呆板凝滞的失望神情。

"到这里来,托姆爸爸,"她说,把小手抓住托姆的手腕,拉他前去,她的手腕象钢铁一般有力。"这里来,——我有消息告诉你。"

"什么,卡舍姑娘?"托姆急切地说。

第四篇 《汤姆叔叔的小屋》Uncle Tom's Cabin

"托姆,你喜欢自由吗?"

"在上帝那里的时候,姑娘,我将获得自由,"托姆说。

"嘿!你今天晚上就能获得自由,"卡舍说道,突然有一股劲。"跟我来。"

托姆犹豫不决。

"来嘛!"她以悄悄的声音说,一对黑眼睛直钉着托姆。"跟着来!他在睡觉呢——睡得很死。我在他的白兰地里放足了东西叫他这么睡的。我倒该多放些进去,——我本来没有打算找你。可是,来吧,后门没有上锁;有一把斧头是我放在那里的,——他房门开着;我来给你指点路径。我原预备自己干的。但我膀子没有力。跟我来吧!"

"万万不可,姑娘!"托姆坚定地阻止她,揪住她的背部,当她硬要前去的时候。

"但是,想想所有这些可怜的人吧,"卡舍道,"我们可以将他们全部释放,到沼泽地里的什么地方去找一个岛屿,自己谋生;我已经听到过有人这样干的。任何生活总比这里的生活好些。"

"不行!"托姆坚决说道,"不行! 邪恶不能产生善良,我情愿砍掉自己的右手!"

"那么我去干,"卡舍说着,转身就走。

"啊,卡舍姑娘!"托姆道,一个箭步跑到她前面去挡住,"看在亲爱的主的分上,主耶稣是为你们而死的,不要这样子把你的灵魂卖给魔鬼! 别无其它,只有灾祸来临。主并没有叫我们发怒,我们必须忍受,等待他的日子的到来。"

"等待!"卡舍道,"我不是已经等待过了吗? ——一直等待到我头昏眼花、痛心疾首吗?他给我吃了什么苦头?他叫几百个穷苦可怜的人吃了什么苦头?他不是正在把你的生命的血绞出来吗?我是被召唤来干的;是他们召唤我的啊! 他的日子来到了,我要他心里的血!"

"不行,不行,不行!"托姆边说,边抓住她的小手,这小手捏紧拳头,猛烈痉挛。"不行,你这个可怜的,失魂落魄的家伙,决不可以这样做。这位亲爱的、天国里神圣的主,从来不叫人家流血,只流自己的血,并且当我们是敌人的时候,他就为我们流血了。主啊! 帮助我们追随你,亦步亦趋,爱我们的敌人。"

"爱!"卡舍说,射出凶猛的愤怒目光,"爱这样的敌人!这个东西,不是血和肉做成的。"

"是的,姑娘,这不是血肉做成的,"托姆道,抬头望着上方。"但是,主把这东西给我们,那就是胜利。当我们能够爱一切人,替一切人祷告,遍及全体,战斗就过去了,胜利就来到了,——荣耀归于上帝!"于是这位黑人,眼睛里泪流如注,声音窒息难言,仰望着苍天。

啊!非洲!这个最近才称之为民族的,——召唤到耶稣的荆棘冠冕面前来,这灾难、这血汗、这苦痛磨难,——这就是你们将来的胜利;就是为此,你们将和基督一同统治国家,当基督的国来到地上的时候。

托姆柔和的声音里,含着深度的热情。他的眼泪象露水一样,落在这个可怜女子的狂野而动荡不安的心灵上。柔和的表情遮盖了她眼睛里的红色火光;她两目下视,托姆觉得她手上的肌肉松弛了;当时她说道:

"我不是告诉你,邪恶的幽灵跟着我吗? 啊!托姆爸爸,我不会祷告,——要是我能祷告就好了。从孩童时候卖出来以后,我从来没有祷告过!你所说的一定是正确的,我知道一定正确;可是当我试着祷告的时候,我只会憎恨和咒骂,我不会祷告!"

"可怜的人哪!"托姆说体恤的话,"魔王撒旦正要你去呢,象麦子一样把你筛出来。我替你向主祷告。啊!卡舍姑娘,回过来求亲爱的主耶稣吧。他会给心碎的人以治疗,给所有悲哀的人以安慰。"

卡舍站定,不吱一声,眼睛看着下面,大点的泪珠直往下落。

托姆悄悄把她打量一番,以迟疑的口气说:

"卡舍姑娘,只要你能离开此地,——如果事情是可能的话,——我劝你和埃米琳一同去做;这是说,如果你们能够不去犯杀人罪的话,而并不是别的。"

"你和我们一起去试试看好不好,托姆爸爸?"

"不行,"托姆道,"我要做的话,那是在过去的时候。现在主已经在这里这些可怜人中间,叫我做一桩工作,我要和他们呆在一起,和他们一道,背起我的十字架,直到终了。你可不同;这对于你是个陷阱,——

第四篇 《汤姆叔叔的小屋》Uncle Tom's Cabin

你忍受不了,——要是能够走的话,你最好还是走吧。"

"我知道,每条路都通向坟墓,"卡舍道,"没有一只禽兽不能在什么地方找到一个家的;甚至蛇和鳄鱼也有个地方躺下来安静休息,可是我们就没有地方。在下面沼泽地里,他们的狗将侦察出来,找到我们。每一个人,每一样东西,都是反对我们的;就是那几只畜生也是站在他的一边反对我们的,我们到什么地方去呢?"

托姆默默站着,最后他说道:

"在狮子坑里救但以理的主①,——救火窑里的三个孩子的主②,——在海上走路的主③,以及叫风浪平息的主④,——这个主还是活着的;并且我有信心,相信他能够救你们。试试看,我将尽我所能,为你们祷告。"

一种意见,久已丢在一边,踩在脚下,当做一块无用的石头一般,会突然发出新的光辉,如同新发现的一颗钻石,这是思想上的多么奇怪的规律啊!

卡舍往往费了多少小时作出一切可能逃脱的计划,然后又把全部计划推翻,认为没有希望,不切实际;然而,就在这个当儿,她心头闪现出一个计划,如此简单,而且所有细节都可付诸实施,好象立即唤起了希望。

"托姆爸爸,我去试试看!"她忽然说。

"阿门!"托姆道,"愿主帮助你!"

---

① 大利乌王下令将但以理投入狮子坑中,说道,"你常事奉的上帝,必能救你。"王用印封闭那坑。次日黎明,急往视之,说,"但以理啊,你所事奉的上帝能救你脱离狮子吗?"但以理说,"愿王万岁,上帝差遣使者封住狮子的嘴,使狮子不能伤我,因我在上帝面前无辜。"——见《圣经》"但以理书"第六章,第十六到二十一节。

② 尼布甲尼撒王下令将沙得拉、米煞、亚伯尼歌三人投入窑中,热度增加七培,王看见四个人在火中游行,其中一个人的相貌象是神子。

③ 见"马可福音"第六章,第四十七到五十节。

④ 见"马可福音"第八章,第二十三到二十七节。

第五篇 理解的困惑与作者的意图
——《论语》两种译文的对比分析

崔永禄

《论语》成书于春秋战国时代,是一部记载孔子及其弟子言论的著作。孔子一生坎坷,曾在鲁国做过小官,鲁定公时做过司寇等职。后去职周游各国,希望能实现其政治主张,但皆不为所用。晚期聚徒讲学,据传贤人七十,弟子三千。曾修订《诗》、《书》、《春秋》等古代文献。与弟子问答,弟子各有所记。孔子死后,"弟子相与辑而论纂,故谓之《论语》"。(班固:汉书)

孔子的思想,时代久远,博大精深,曾为历代统治阶级所用,对中国古代思想和文化产生了巨大的影响,就是在现代中国人的思想中也可以看到儒学的影子,因此《论语》已被译成各国文字。较早而且影响较大的要算 James Legge 的翻译。较新的译文我所见有二:一是 Analects of Confucius 由亚瑟·威利(Arthur Waley)翻译,纽约出版;另一是 Essential Confucius,由托玛斯·柯立瑞(Thomas Cleary)所译,Harper San Fransisco 出版。因这两个版本有较大的差异,进行比较可以使我们发现不少问题,得到很多启迪,因此选了《论语》的一些段落,附以相应的译文,以便进行比较,以学习他们的经验,摸索翻译的某些规律。

一、化隐为显,保留风格

威利和柯立瑞都对孔子的思想做了大量的研究工作,对译文的表达也精益求精,力求忠实通顺,并尽力保留原文的风格,译文许多地方都值得我们学习借鉴。

由于《论语》言简意赅,所以两位译者在许多地方都采用了增补的翻译手法,以显喻隐,使译文贴切易懂,可属上乘翻译。

1. 孰谓鄹人之子知礼乎?

第五篇 《论语》Analects of Confucius

　　这里的"鄹人之子"指孔子,暗含不敬之意。柯立瑞译为 Who says that old man knows the classical rites? 用 old man 译"鄹人之子"表示原文中不尊重的口气,在表示"礼"的 rites 之前加上一个 classical,也十分得体。

　　威利译为 Don't tell me that this son of a villgae from Zou is expert in matters of ritual. 译者没有用原文的反问形式,而用 Don't tell me 这一地道的英语口语表达方式,非常成功。"鄹人之子"的译法,开始加一个 this,中间又加一个 village,可说把原来不尊重的口气表达得维妙维肖。"礼"的译法,也在 ritual 前加了一个 matters of,"知"用 expert 表达出来,这些方法均很有匠心。

　　2. 不患无位,患所以立。

　　这句中的"立",意思虽很明显,但却比较抽象,译好也不十分容易。柯立瑞用 that whereby you may effectively become established 这样一个从句来翻译,明显采用了加词法。Established 选词也很确切,前面再加一个 effectively,则更使译文明晰有力。威利则用了 qualities that entitle him to office,和前面的"位"相呼应,译文也很理想。

　　3. 大哉,尧之为君也！巍巍乎,唯天为大,唯尧则之。荡荡乎,民无能名焉。巍巍乎,其有成功也。焕乎,其有文章。

　　这段的译文尤其值得学习研究。为了歌颂尧,文中用了五个形容词,"大哉"、"巍巍乎"、"荡荡乎"、"巍巍乎"和"焕乎",放在句首,采用倒装形式,使强调作用鲜明突出,一气呵成,气势磅礴。

　　柯立瑞用了"great indeed was…","such was…","magnificent was…"和"brilliant was…","Sublime was…"四个倒装句子,第二句虽未采用倒装形式,但也用了 with magnificent gradeur,把它放在句首,起到了倒装的作用。威利用了"greatest was…","So boundless was…","Sublime was…"和"danzzling(was)…"四个倒装句子,均保存了原文的形式和气魄,忠实地传达出原文的风格。

　　值得研究的是,中国古汉语中经常采用形容词加感叹词放在句首,句子倒装的形式来组成感叹句,这在现代汉语中反倒不多见。可在英语中,把形容词和副词放在句首倒是感叹句的基本表达方式。不知为什么现代汉语放弃了这一有力的表达手段。回过头来看,也许正因为古汉语和现代英语在感叹句组成方面的相似,使得上述句子的翻译变得容易起来。

应该指出,柯立瑞和威利并未都采用现代英语感叹句的形式,即没有全部用 what, how 和 so 等,有几个句子只是采用了倒装的形式,用形容词开头,这也许就是为了传达原文的风格吧。

二、理解的困惑

让我们先看一看这一段译文:

原文:

曾子曰:"吾日三省吾身:为人谋而不忠乎?与朋友交而不信乎?传不习乎?"

柯译:Master zeng, one of the pupils of Confucius, said, "I examine myself three times a day: Have I been unfaiathful in planning for others? Have I been unreliable in conversation with friends? Am I preaching what I haven't preached myself?"

威译:Master Zeng said, Every day I examine myself on three points: In acting on behalf of others, have I always been loyal to their interests? In intercourse with my friends, have I always been ture to my word? Have I failed to repeat the precepts that have been handed down to me?

这一段译文的主要区别在于如何理解"三省"和如何理解"传不习乎"。柯立瑞译为每日自省三次,威利则译为每天在三个方面进行反省。现在汉语的理解为,"三"在"省"前,应表示次数。但"三"强调非只一次,就像平时说的"再三再四"一样,并不是指具体三次。"传不习乎",柯立瑞译为 Am I preaching what I haven't preached myself, 把"传"理解为"去传给别人","传播孔子的学说",而不是"孔子传给的东西"。威利译为 repeat the precepts that have been handed down to me,即"传给我的东西是否温习了"。这种译法比较符合原意。

柯立瑞的理解也有一定道理。从句子的结构来看,前两个句子的前半部分"为人谋""和"与朋友交"均为动词短语,其主语为"吾"。第三个句子为平行句,也应为相似结构。所以柯立瑞的理解也不足为奇。

应该指出,柯立瑞在这里用了 conversation 一词来翻译"交往"。Conversation 现在英语中一般作"谈话"讲,"交往"是这个词很古的一个用法。柯立瑞显然是在用词的古意来表示"论语"古汉语的表达方式,以尽力体现汉语原文的风格。

所以产生理解上的问题我考虑有如下原因:一是孔子的思想内涵深刻,用以表达的语言又十分简练,往往一个概念就表达了非常复杂的内容。如孔子的思想的核心是"仁",这个概念可表达多层次的意思,如"仁者爱人","己所不欲,勿施于人";"仁"的最高境界是"博施于民,而能济众";而要施仁,则必须以"礼"为规范,即"克己复礼为仁"。这些不同层次的意思往往引起翻译的困惑。

第二次是语言的原因。孔子时代的古汉语,距现在久远,就是当代中国人理解起来都有困难。况且在这个两千多年的时间里,曾出现过不同本子的"论语",后人又做过不少的注解诠释工作,如三国魏何晏的《论语集解》,宋朱熹的《论语集注》等,注解在一些地方也有歧见。这就增加了理解的难度。例如:

1. 不义而富且贵,于我如浮云。

柯译:Riches and status unjustly obtained are to me like floating clouds.

威译:Any thought of accepting wealth and rank by means I know to be wrong is remote from me as the clouds that float above.

显然,对于:如浮云"的理解,两位译者是有较大差别的。

2. 有德必有言,有言者不必有德。

柯译:Those who have virtue have something to say, but those who have something to say do not necessarily have virtue.

威译:One who has accumulated moral power will certainly possess eloquence; but he who has eloquence does not necessarily possess moral power.

"Have something to say"和"possess eloquence"都未能很好地表达出原文的意思。对"有言"比较好的理解应该是"说出有道理的话"。

3. 加我数年,五十以学《易》,可以无大过矣。

柯译:Give me a few more years, so that I will have studied the Book of Change for fifty years, and I may eliminate major errors.

威译:Give me a few more years, so that I may have spent a whole fifty in study, and I believe that after all I should be fairly free from error.

汉语中原来的意思是,我再多活几年,到五十岁再学习《易经》。柯立瑞译为"过几年我就学了五十年的《易经》",威利译为"再过几年,我就学习了整五十年",都与原文大相径庭。

4. 吾党之小子狂简,斐然成章,不知所以裁之。

柯译:The youth of my neighbourhood are free-spirited and splendidly cultured. I don't know how their fine tuning will be accomplished.

威译:The little ones at home are headstrong and careless. They are perfecting themselves in all the showy insignia without any idea how to use them.

"小子"在《论语》中是孔子用来指自己学生的用语。柯立瑞译成"青年人",不如威利的little ones。"狂"指"有志向",并无多少贬义,威利用的headstrong 常指"刚愎自用,桀傲不逊"的意思,因此贬义过多。这里一个重要的词是"裁之",其行为主使者是孔子。汉语中,尤其是古汉语中,主语经常省略。威利忽视了这一点。柯立瑞虽主语搞对,但"裁之"的理解又不对。"裁之"这里的意思是"裁割以正"的意思,整句话说的是孔子不知道如何指导他们。

总之,由于理解的原因,或理解不同,或理解不准确,造成了译文的差别。甚至有的不能传达原文深刻的意图,出现误解,这是值得认真思考的。为了避免因理解造成的译文的损失,译者加深对译文的研究自然十分重要。但像译《论语》这样的古典文献,中外学者加强交流,互相切磋,在翻译过程中进行合作,也是保证翻译成功的一条重要途径。

三、译者的意图

翻译的过程是一个译者在原作和译作读者之间进行斡旋的过程。一方面,译者要深刻了解原作的意图,忠实地把它传达出来;另一方面则要考虑到读者能否接受的因素,对语言、文化的诸方面进行调整。在这一过程中,译者常常有所侧重。玄奘虽提出"既须求真,又须喻俗"的原则,名为照顾两面,但他又提出"五不译",实际上是要尽量保持原文的特征。鲁迅提出只能改变外国人的服装,而不能削低他们的鼻子,改变他们眼睛的颜色,也是同一个意思。严复呢,他提出了"信达雅"三原则,但心目中是"雅"压倒一切,读者占了绝对的位置。钱钟书先生的"化境"要译文是原文脱胎换骨的新生,但他赞扬林琴南的译文,重心似乎也在读者一边。

从《论语》的两种译文来看,有不少地方可以为我们提供线索,借以窥探译者在翻译过程中所遵循的原则。例如对"子曰"这一句子的译法,柯立瑞译为 Confucius said,威利则译为 The master said.

直呼孔子为 Confucius 是符合西方的传统的。西方对作者一般都直呼其名而不加表示职称、身份等的词语。柯立瑞这样作显然是为了方便西方读者。称孔子为"子"而讳其名,是一种尊敬的表示。威利为了传达中文的含义,用了 the master 一词,表示"先师"之意,这就尽可能地保留了原文中的人际关系和中文的文化特征。这样做虽然会使西方读者感到不太习惯,但有利于他们了解中国文化,有利于他们了解原文的内容、风格及原作者的意图。

两位译者所以采用不同的方法,在很大程度上取决于他们不同的翻译意图。柯立瑞在他所译《论语》的前言中写道:

> The aim of this presentation of the teachings of Confucius has been to produce a streamlined version in a convenient format, centered on a translation that reads easily and yields meanings directly without distracting the reader unnecessarily by the interjection of Sinological complications. (Clearly P. ix)

第五篇 《论语》Analects of Confucius

这段话说得十分清楚,他就是要搞一个易懂的英文版本,使读者不为中文的文化特征所困惑,而且他采用了《易经》64 卦的形式,把《论语》各段落重新进行编排,认为这有助于克服若干世纪中因文化变革和孔学研究的分歧所引起的直接了解孔子思想的困难(... helps to surmount yet another problem, which is the difficulty of access to the basic sayings of Confucius that has been caused by centuries of shifting conventions and controversies in later Confucian scholarship.) (Cleary P. ix)至于目的是否达到,我们这里暂且不论,但译者的意图是清楚的。

威利则有自己的想法。他认为以往的《论语》翻译完全依赖朱熹对《论语》的解释。然而,在威利看来,朱熹不是一个真正的学者,他只是一个神职人员似的人物,是一个福音派传教士。他用程朱理学来解释孔子。如孔子多次说自己缺乏知识,有缺点,朱熹则马上解释说,这是一种为礼貌而讲的谦虚,"一个圣人怎么能真正犯错误呢,一个圣人怎么能真正不知道呢"。所以威利要译出自己的版本,意在让欧洲读者了解《论语》作者们的初衷。(... there is room for a version such as mine, which attempts to tell the European readers what it meant to those who compiled it.)(Waley p76)

由于翻译时意图的不同,他们在翻译过程中就采用了不同的方法。例如:

1. 不有博弈者乎?

柯译:Are there no games to play?

威译:Are there no games such as draughts?

柯立瑞只用了 games 一词,可泛指各种游戏,在英语中没有对应表达方式的情况下,这种做法也是可取的,应该说它基本上传达出了原文的意思。柯立瑞的意图是尽量避免中国文化的特殊事物给外国读者带来的不必要的理解方面的困难。

威利则采用了不同的做法,他特别用 draughts 来指棋类,因为汉语的"弈"为棋类之一种,这种译法就体现了威利尽量多地传达孔子的原意,尽量保留原文特征的意图。

然而由于文化的原因,威利的译文也有一些问题。英文的 draughts 是指国际跳棋,而孔子所说的"弈",应该是指中国古代的围棋。围棋在中国有古老的历史,据传它为尧所发明,春秋战国时期已比较流行了,所以用 draughts 来译也有不妥之处。

我们再看下面的例子:

2. 子曰:"善人,吾不得而见之矣;得见有恒者,斯可矣。亡而为有,虚而为盈,约而为泰,难乎有恒矣。"

柯译:I haven't gotten to meet a good person, but if I get to meet someone who is constant, that will do. Those who pretend to have what they lack, who pretend to fullness when they are empty, can hardly be constant.

威译:A faultless man I cannot hope ever to meet, the most I can hope for is to meet a man of fixed principles. Yet where all around I see Nothing pretending to be Something, Emptiness pretending to be Fullness, Penury pretending to be Affluence, even a man of fixed principles will be none too easy to find.

如果我们仔细比较,就会发现这段话的两种译文很值得研究。柯立瑞的译文通顺易懂,但却略去了"约而为泰",少了一层意思。威利则比较更多地注重传达原文的内容和风格。首先,他把"亡""有","虚""盈","约""泰"以拟人方式处理,英文字用大写字头,以代表一类人,这就再现了原文的特殊表达方式和深刻的内涵。进而译文着重译出这种情况下,"有恒"的人就很难找到,意思是"有恒"不仅仅做到是困难的,这样的人也是不多的。这就与前面的"得见有恒者,斯可矣"相呼应,传达出了孔子的原意。应该说,这种译法是成功的。而且为了使译文读者容易接受,威利在译文组织上下了一番功夫,加了 where all around 和 none too easy 之类的用语,使译文流畅易懂,而且用 fixed priciple 来译"有恒"比 constant 也更注重思想方面,含义更为深刻。

四、结论

《论语》的英译本,国外已有数种,这里只比较了柯立瑞和威利的两种译本。柯立瑞的译本通顺易懂,删减了许多因文化因素可能会给西方读者带来困难的地方,因而为西方读者,特别是一般的非学者型读者了解孔子带来了极大的方便;威利的译本则尽量保留原文的文化风貌,注意细节的传译,尤其宜于学者进行研究使用。两位译者均苦心孤诣,尽量以明了的英语传达孔子艰深的思想,许多地方译文均表现出译者高超的翻译能力和技巧,值得我们学习研究。

但两译文均有不少令人难以满意之处。特别是在中国孔子为代表的儒家思想被越来越多的西方人认识到其对社会进步以及经济发展的价值的时候,更为完美的译本就变得非常必要。中外译者应该联合起来,总结前人的经验,克服不足,把中国古代灿烂的文化介绍给世界各国人民。

参考文献:
1. 刘俊田等:《四书全译》,贵州人民出版社,1994 年。
2. Hatim, B. & Mason, I. *Discourse and the Translator*. Longman, London and New York, 1990.
3. Cleary, Thomas. *The Essential Confucius*. Harper san fransisco, 1992.
4. Waley, Arthur. *The Analects of Confucius*. Quality Paperback Book Club, New York, 1992.

《论语》(节选)
Analects of Confucius(Excerpt)

(每段两种译文,第一种为 Thomas Cleary 译;第二种为 Arthur Waley 译)

1. 曾子曰:"吾日三省吾身:为人谋而不忠乎?与朋友交而不信乎?传不习乎?"

Master Zeng, one of the pupils of Confucius, said,"I examine myself three times a day: Have I been unfaithful in plannig for others? Have I been unreliable in conversation with friends? Am I preaching what I haven't preached myself?"(1:4)

Master Tseng said, Every day I examine myself on there points: In acting on behalf of others, have I alway been loyal to their interests? In intercourse with my friends, have I always been true to my word? Have I failed to repeat the precepts that have been handed down to me?

2. 子游问孝,子曰:"今之孝者,是谓能养。至于犬马,皆能有养。不敬,何以别乎?"

A discipie asked Confucius about filial piety.

Confucius said,"People who practice filiality today say they are providing a living, but even dogs and horses are taken care of; without respect, what is the difference?"(2:7)

Tzu-yu asked about the treatment of parents. The Master said, 'Filial sons are people who see to it that their parents get enough to eat. But even dogs and horses are cared for to that extent. If there is

第五篇 《论语》Analects of Confucius

no feeling of respect, wherein lies the difference?

3. 子入太庙,每事问。或曰:"孰谓鄹人之子知礼乎？入太庙,每事问。"子闻之,曰:"是礼也。"

Confucius went into the great national shrine and asked about everything, someone remarked, "Who says that old man knows the classical rites? When he goes to the great shrine he asks about everything."

Hearing of this, Confucius said, "This is part of the ritual."(3:15)

When the Master entered the Grand Temple he asked questions about everything there, someone said, Do not tell me that this son of a village from Tsou is expert in matters of ritual. When he went to the Grand Temple, he had to ask about everything. The Master hearing of this said, Just so! Such is the ritual.

4. 子曰:"不患无位,患所以立。不患莫己知,求为可知也。"

Confucius said, "Don't worry about having no position; worry about that whereby you may effectively become established. Don't worry that no one recognizes you; seek to be worthy of recognition." (4:14)

The Master said, He does not mind not being in office; all he minds about is whether he has qualities that entitle him to office. He does not mind failing to get recognition; he is too busy doing the things that entitle him to recognition.

5. 子曰:"吾未见刚者。"或对曰:"申枨。"子曰:"枨也欲,焉得刚？"

Confucius said, "I have never seen anyone who was firm." Someone named a certain disciple. Confucius said, "He is covertous—how can he be firm?"(5:11)

The Master said, I have never yet seen a man who was truly steadfast. Someone answered daying, 'Shen Cheng.' The Master said, Cheng! He is at the mercy of his desires. How can he be called steadfast?

6. 子在陈,曰:"归与!归与!吾党之小子狂简,斐然成章,不知所以裁之。"

When Confucius was in the state of Chu, he said, "Shall I go home? Shall I go home? The youth of my neighbourhood are free-spirited and splendidly cultured; I don't know how their fine tuning will be accomplished."(5:22)

When the Master was in Chen he said, Let us go back, let us go back! The little ones at home are headstrong and careless. They are perfecting themselves in all the showy insignia of culture without any idea how to use them.

7. 冉求曰:"非不说子之道,力不足也。"子曰:"力不足者,中道而废,汝今画。"

A student said, "It is not that I do not like the teacher's way, but my strength is insufficient."

Confucius said, "Those whose strength is insufficient give up along the way; now you are drawing the line."(6:12)

Jan Chiu said, It is not that your Way does not command itself to me, but that it demands powers I do not possess. The Master said, He whose strength gives out collapses during the course of the journey (the Way); but you deliberately draw the line.

8. 子曰:"饭疏食,饮水,曲肱而枕之,乐亦在其中矣。不义而富且贵,于我如浮云。"

Confucius said, "Even if my fare is plain and my lifestyle austere, I still find pleasure in them. Riches and status unjustly attained are to me like floating clouds."(7:15)

The Master said, He who seeks only coarse food to eat, water to drink and a bent arm for pillow, will without looking for it find happiness to boot. Any thought of accepting wealth and rank by means that I know to be wrong is as remote from me as the clouds that float above.

9. 子曰:"加我数年,五十以学《易》,可以无大过矣。"

Confucius said, "Give me a few more years, so that I will have studied the Book of Change for fifty years, and I may eliminate major errors."(7:16)

The Master said, Give me a few more years, so that I may have spent a whole fifty in study, and I believe that after all I should be fairly free from error.

10. 子曰:"圣人,吾不得而见之矣;得见君子者,斯可矣。"子曰:"善人,吾不得而见之矣;得见有恒者,斯可矣。亡而为有,虚而为盈,约而为泰,难呼有恒矣。"

Confucius said, "I haven't gotten to meet a sage, but if I get to meet an exemplary person, that will do. I haven't gotten to meet a good person, but if I get to meet someone who is constant, that will do. Those who pretend to have what they lack, who pretend to fullness when they are empty, can hardly be constant."(7:25)

The Master said, A Divine Sage I cannot hope ever to meet; the most I can hope for is to meet a true gentleman. The Master said, A faultless man I cannot hope ever to meet; the most I can hope for is to meet a man of fixed principles. Yet where all around I see Nothing pretending to be Something, Emptiness pretending to be Fullness; Penury pretending to be Affluence, even a man of fixed principles will be none too easy to find.

11. 子曰:"笃信好学,守死善道,危邦不入,乱邦不居。天下有道则见,无道则隐。邦有道,贫且贱焉,耻也;邦无道,富且贵焉,耻也。"

Confucius said, "Study eagerly with earnest faith; keep to the good way even onto death. Do not enter a dangerous state; do not stay in a chaotic state. When the Way prevails in the world, appear in public life; when the Way does not prevail, disappear. When a country has the Way, it is a disgrace to be poor and lowly there. When a country lacks the Way, it is a disgrace to be rich and noble there."(8:13)

The Master said, Be of unwavering good faith, love learning, if attacked be ready to die for the good Way. Do not enter a State that pursues dangerous courses, nor stay in one where the people have rebelled. When the Way prevails under Heaven, then show yourself; when it does not prevail, then hide. When the Way prevails in your own land, count it a disgrace to be needy and obscure; when the Way does not prevail in your land, then count it a disgrace to be rich and honoured.

12. 子曰:"大哉,尧之为君也!巍巍乎,唯天为大,唯尧则之。荡荡乎,民无能名焉。巍巍乎,其有成功也。焕乎,其有文章。"

Confucius said, "Great indeed was the leadership of (the ancient sage-king) Yao! With magnificent grandeur, only Heaven is great, and only Yao emulated it. Such was their freedom that the people had no name for it. Magnificent was his achievement of works; brilliant was his establishment of culture."(8:19)

The Master said, Greatest, as lord and ruler, was Yao. Sublime, indeed was he. 'There is no greatness like the greatness of Heaven', yet Yao could copy it. So boundless was it that people could find no name for it; yet sublime were his achievements, dazzling the insignia of his culture!

13. 子曰:"衣敝缊袍,与衣狐貉者立,而不耻者,其由也与?'不忮不求,何用不臧?'"子路终身诵之。子曰:"是道也,何足以臧?"

One of the disciples always used to say: "Neither harming nor importuning—how can this not be good?"

第五篇 《论语》Analects of Confucius

Confucius said, "How can this way be enough to be considered good?"(9:28)

The Master said, 'Wearing a shabby hemp-quilted gown, yet capable of standing unabashed with those who wore fox and badge.' That would apply quite well to Yu, would it not?

Who harmed none, was foe to none,

Did nothing that was not right.

Afterwards Tzulu(Yu) kept on continually chanting those lines to himself. The Master said, Come now, the wisdom contained in them is not worth treasuring to that extent.

14. 季路问事鬼神,子曰:"未能事人,焉能事鬼?"曰:"敢问死。"曰:"未知生,焉知死?"

Some one asked Confucius how to serve ghosts and spirits.

Confucius said, "As long as you are unable to serve people, how can you serve ghosts?"

The inquirer also asked about death.

Confucius said, "As song as you do not know life, how can you know death?"(11:12)

Tzulu asked how one should serve ghosts and spirits. The Master said, Till you have learnt to serve men, how can you serve ghosts? Tzulu then ventured upon a question about the dead. The Master said, Till you know about the living, how are you to know about the dead?

15. 齐景公问政于孔子,孔子对曰:"君君,臣臣,父父,子子。"公曰:"善哉!信如君不君,臣不臣,父不父,子不子,虽有粟,吾得而食诸?"

The ruler of a certain state asked about government.

Confucius replied, "Have leaders be leaders, have administrators as administrators, have fathers be fathers, have sons be sons."

The ruler said, "Good! Of a truth, if leaders do not lead, administrators do not administer, fathers do not behave as fathers, and sons do not behave as sons, then even if there were grain, how can I eat of it?"(12:11)

Duke Ching of Chi asked Master K'ung about government. Master K'ung replied saying, Let the prince be a prince, the minister a minister, the father a father and the son a son. The Duke said, How true! For indeed when the prince is not a prince, the minister not a minister, the father not a father, the son not a son, one may have a dish of millet in front of one and yet not know if one will live to eat it.

16. 子夏为莒父宰,问政,子曰:"无欲速,无见小利。欲速则不达,见小利则大事不成。"

One of the disciples of Confucius who had become the administrator of a city asked the teacher about government.

Confucius said, "Don't wish for speed; don't see small advantages. If you wish for speed, you won't succeed; if you see small advantages, great things will not be accomplished."(13:17)

When Tzu-hsiz was Warden of Chu-fu, he asked for advice about government.

The Master said, Do not try to hurry things. Ignore minor considerations. If you hurry things, your personality will not come into play. If you let yourself be distracted by minor considerations, nothing important will ever get finished.

17. 子曰:"有德者必有言,有言者不必有德。仁者必有勇,勇者不必有仁。"

Confucius said, "Those who have virtue have something to say, but those who have something to say do not necessarily have virtue. Humanitarians are courageous, but the courageous are not necessarily humane."(14:5)

第五篇 《论语》Analects of Confucius

The Master said, One who has accumulated moral power will certainly also possess eloquence; but he who has eloquence does not necessarily possess moral power. A Good Man will certainly also possess courage; but a brave man is not necessarily Good.

18. 子曰:"君子道有三,我无能焉;仁者不忧,知者不惑,勇者不惧。"子贡曰:"夫子自道也。"

Confucius said, "There are three things in the path of cultivated people of which I am incapable: the humane do not worry; the knowing are not confused; the brave are unafraid."(14∶30)

The Master said, the Ways of the true gentleman are three. I myself have met with success in none of them. For he that is really Good is never unhappy; he that is really wise is never perplexed, he that is really brave is never afraid. Tzu-kung said, That, Master, is your own Way!

19. 子曰:"人无远虑,必有近忧。"

Confucius said, "People who do not think far enough ahead inevitably have worries near at hand."(15∶12)

The Master said, He who will not worry about what is far off will soon find something worse than worry close at hand.

20. 子曰:"饱食终日,无所用心,难矣哉!不有博弈者乎?为之,犹贤乎已。"

Confucius said, "To eat your fill but not apply your mind to anything all day is a problem. Are there no games to play? Even that would be smarter than doing nothing."(17∶22)

The Master said, Those who do nothing all day but cram themselves with food and never use their minds are difficult, are there not games such as draughts? To play them would surely be better than doing nothing at all.

第六篇 《红楼梦》两种译文之比较赏析

王 雪

《红楼梦》是中国古典文学中最优秀的作品之一。一般学者认为,前八十回为曹雪芹所作,后四十回为高鹗所续。全书通过一个贵族官僚家庭的盛衰历史的描叙,塑造了一系列优秀的典型人物,并对腐朽的封建社会作了深刻的解剖和强烈的批判,堪称中国古代小说中最伟大的现实主义的长篇叙事作品。《红楼梦》不仅有深刻的思想价值,而且具有卓越的艺术成就,被视为中国封建社会的"百科全书"。书中从世态言情、国体家风、典章故实、官制礼俗、宗教哲理,到服饰器用、建筑园林、琴棋书画、诗词戏文、饮馔医药等等,无不熔铸汇通。尽管全书布局庞大,但结构完整,书中大大小小的生活画面浑然天成,摇曳多姿,丰富多彩。此外,《红楼梦》的语言也达到了中国古典小说的高峰,乃至中国古代文学的高峰,不仅对中国文学产生了深远的影响,而且对世界文学也有着深远的影响。它是中国文学史上的一个奇迹,是中国传统文化孕育出来的一株阆苑仙葩。

《红楼梦》从成书到现在已有二百余年的历史,其间曾数次被译成外国文字,以飨外国读者。目前已有十余种外文译本和节译本,其中有两种译本影响较大:一种是 *The Dream of Red Mansion*,由杨宪益,戴乃迭夫妇(Gladys Yang)翻译(以下简称杨译);另一种是 *The Story of the Stone*,由戴卫·霍克斯(David Hawkes)和约翰·敏福德(John Minford)合译(以下简称霍译)。

The Dream of Red Mansion 的主要译者杨宪益是中国当代成就卓著的翻译家、外国文学研究家。杨氏的翻译思想视忠实为第一要义,认为"翻译作品可以多一点异国情调,因为翻译毕竟是翻译"。*The Story*

第六篇 《红楼梦》 The Story of the Stone

of the Stone 的主要译者戴卫·霍克斯,系当代英国汉学家。霍克斯虽非第一个把《红楼梦》译介到西方之人,但是 1973 年他英译的《石头记》(第一卷,第 1—26 回)问世后,从此开始了《红楼梦》在西方的全译期。霍氏坚持"一切皆译,哪怕是双关语"的原则,并强调"译者有三责",即尽责于作者,尽责于读者并尽责于文本。但也承认"此三责决非同一之物,每每难于取得和谐"。因此其译作主要倾向于一种"交际翻译","旨在使译文读者能够尽可能感受到和原文读者所感受到的一样效果"。

下面笔者从《红楼梦》原作中选出第三回"金陵城起复贾雨村,荣国府收养林黛玉",作为范例,分析评述两家译本在传递不同背景的文化信息和再现原作审美体验两方面所采取的处理原则和方法,以供翻译同行们借鉴。

一、文化信息的传递

"文化"是社会学术语。按照社会学家和人类学家的定义,"文化"一词的涵义较广。从翻译角度来讲,我们所说的"文化"是指一个社会的整个生活方式或一个民族的全部活动方式。它包括一个民族的思想体系、伦理道德、官僚制度、风俗习惯、文学艺术、语言等。不同的民族文化渊源不同,因此各民族之间彼此的性格气质和生活主式也不同。中国文化博大精深,源远流长,自成一体。而西方文化的主源则是希腊神话及圣经,英国文化自然也不例外。因此要把《红楼梦》这样一部代表中国文化背景的鸿篇巨著翻译成代表西方文化的英语所遇到的困难是多方面的,尤其是在文化方面。正如美国语言学家、翻译理论家尤金·奈达(Eugene Nida)在翻译科学探索中指出的:"如果两种文化有亲缘关系,而两种语言迥异,译者就应该在译文中进行大量的形式转换。在这种情况下,相似的文化通常可以提供一系列内容方面的对应语,比起语言和文化都迥异的情况,翻译上的困难相应地会少得多。事实上文化差异比语言差异给译者带来复杂得多的问题"。(Nida,1964)见于文化方面给翻译带来的困难,中西方翻译理论家们都尝试着提出了一些理论性的指导原则。在中国,翻译实践家们历来以严复的"信达雅"为翻译标准;在西方,主要以奈达的"等值翻译理论"或英国著名的翻译理论家彼得纽马克的"交际翻译"和"语义翻译"理论为指导原则。事实上,这三种理论"殊途同归"(劳陇,1990),具有理论上的一致性。都认为"信"作为翻译第一标准是对的。因为这是翻译的本质所决定的。"不信"就不成其为翻译。信是基点,其次译文还要"达意",就是要使译文发挥与原文同样的功能,也就是说要使译文读者得到与原文读者所得到的同样的意义。最后在信、达的基础上,要充分考虑译文读者的接受性,用纽马克的话说,就是"交际翻译";用严复的话说,就是"雅"。

下面笔者将提到的中西方翻译理论融会在一起,对两家译本就不同背景文化信息传递方面所采取的处理原则作逐一比较评析。

《红楼梦》的第三回描写了林黛玉初进荣国府被贾母收养的情景,以及贾雨村如何走贾府这一后门重登仕途的过程。篇幅虽不长,但所涉及的文化内容却很广泛,其中涉及到了称谓、宗教、礼俗、建筑、器用、服饰、美术、诗词等。而这些内容往往带有浓厚的"民族色彩"。因此,"信"在这里就显得至关重要。即译者应在译文中"尽可能地传达原文的准确涵义";(纽马克,1988)力图再现原作的风姿;表现出原文的民族文化特征。例如:

1.…"况且这通身的气派,竟不像老祖宗的外孙女,竟是个嫡亲的孙女,怨不得老祖宗天天口头心头一时不忘"…

  杨译:"Her whole air is so distinguished! She doesn't take after her father, son-in-law of our Old Ancestress, but looks more like a Chia. No wonder our Old Ancestress couldn't put you out of her mind and was for ever talking or thinking about you."

  霍译:"And everything about her so distingue! She doesn't take after your side of the family, Grannie. She's more like Jia."

通常在小说中某些特定的词语如称谓往往具有丰富的内涵意义和一定的民族文化特性。要把它们用非常贴切的英语尽可能完全移植过来,确非一件易事。这里霍译本将"老祖宗"译成"Grannie",从所指层面来看,其信息在原文和译文中是等值。而在语用层面上,即从内涵意义来看,这个信息与原文的差距则较大。从原文中我们知道,王熙凤称贾

第六篇 《红楼梦》 The Story of the Stone

母"老祖宗"一来是讨好贾母,二来是表明贾母在贾家的身份地位。因此,"老祖宗"一词在原文中并非一般意义下的"老祖宗"或"奶奶",而是有着特定的涵义的。这样看来,霍译"老祖宗"为"Grannie"对原文来讲显然不够忠实。而杨译将"老祖宗"直译为"Old Ancestress",这样既表明了贾母在贾家受尊敬、有权威的意思,又保存了原文的文化意义,可以说是"信"的典范。

2.…"因贱荆去世,都中家岳母念及小女无人倚傍教育,前已遣了男女船只来接,因小女未曾大痊,故未及行"…

杨译:"Since my wife's death my mother-in-law in the capital has been worried because my daughter has no one to bring her up. She has sent two boats with male and female attendants to fetch the child, but I delayed her departure while she was unwell."

霍译:"Since my poor wife passed on, my mother-in-law in the capital has been worried about the little girl having no one to look after her, and has already sent some of her folk here by barge to fetch her away. The only reason she has so far not gone is that she has not been quite recovered from her illness."

中国封建社会男尊女卑、男女有别的思想是中国封建社会思想体系的一个特点。如《家塾蒙求》说:"男子居外,女子居内;男不入,女不出;男不言内,女不言外;男女之有别,人道之大者也。"这一点在《红楼梦》有所体现。如在本例句中林如海说:"贾府遣来男女船只来接黛玉",从语言上反映了当时的社会习俗,男女之间接受不亲。贾府是贵族门第,在大庭广众之中,这规矩是必须遵守的。因此杨译"遣了男女船只"译为"has sent two boats with male and female attendants"忠实地传达了原文的意义,反映了当时中国封建社会的文化背景。至于霍译,它在某种程度上倾向于一种"交际翻译",把重点放在译文读者和目的语(也就是译入语)上。将"遣了男女船只"译为"has already sent some of her folk here by barge"显而易见,译者发挥创造的成分似乎多了一些,

第六篇 《红楼梦》The Story of the Stone

对原文来讲也不够忠实,译文没有如实反映原文的文化背景。

  3. 王夫人因说到:"你舅舅今日斋戒去了,再见罢。……"

  杨译:"Your uncle's observing a fast today," said Lady Wang. "You will see him some other time."

  霍译:'Your uncle is in retreat today,' said Lady Wang. 'He will see you another time.'

  在东方的文化里,人们通常出于宗教信仰的缘故,在祭祀、礼佛或举行隆重大典之前,进行"斋戒"——即吃素忌酒,独处静养,整洁身心,屏除杂念,以示虔诚。而在西方的宗教信仰里却没有"斋戒"的习俗。所以霍译从译文读者的角度出发,将"斋戒"译为"is in retreat"而"retreat"实际上是指"retirement for a time for religious meditation (Chamber,925)"只表示独处静思,整洁身心之意,没有传达出原文的准确涵义。因此导致了原文民族文化意义的亏损。与之相反,杨译则采用了"observing a fast",这样处理不仅将东方人的宗教习俗传达给译文读者,而且准确地再现原文的意义。

  由上述的几个例子的比较,不难看出,在保留原文的民族色彩上,杨译较霍译忠实于原文,忠实于原文的意义。诚然,忠实故然重要,但还必须搞清"内容的信"和"形式的信",以求得"功能对等"。严复说:"顾信矣不达,虽译犹不译也。"这用奈达的话说,就是:"如果翻译的形式对等而不能传达原作的意思,那就等于不译"。(因为它没有发挥翻译的功能)所以译文必须信而且达,才能达到"功能对等"的效果。《红楼梦》是中国古典文学中的经典巨著,文学色彩浓厚,求其信是本,但还要通顺地的词句,正确地传达原文的意思。例如:

  4. 贾母正面榻上独坐,两边四张空椅,熙凤忙拉了黛玉在左边第一张椅子上坐了,黛玉十分推让。

  杨译:The Lady Dowager was seated alone on a couch at the head of the table with two empty chairs on each side. Hsi-feng took Tai-yu by the hand to make her sit in the first place on the left, but she persistently declined the honour.

第六篇 《红楼梦》 The Story of the Stone

霍译：The table at which Gradmother Jia presided, seated alone on a coach, had two empty chairs on either side. Xi-feng tried to seat Dan-yu in the one on the left nearer to her grandmother——an honour which she strenuously resisted…

两种译文都可以说传达了原文的信息，仔细比较，杨译可以说是试图做到绝对地忠实于原著，以至达到逐字逐句形式对等的翻译，虽忠实，但却给人一种英语不地道的感觉。"信"故然是翻译的基础，很重要，但如果译者囿于语义翻译的范畴，过分拘泥于原文，强调绝对的信，就是"信矣不达，译犹不译也。"至于霍译，不仅在用词上随手拈来，不事雕琢，而且巧妙地让译文读者了解中国封建社会的礼俗。是信而达的翻译。

5. 心较比干多一窍，病如西子胜三分。

杨译：She looked more sensitive than Pikan[1], more delicate than Hsi Shih[2].

  1. A prince noted for his great intelligence at the end of the Shang Dynasty.

  2. A famous beauty of the ancient kingdom of Yueh.

霍译：She had more chambers in her heart than the martyred Bi Gan; And suffered a tithe more pain in it than the beautiful Xi shi.

"比干"、"西施"作为中国历史上的著名人物，在普通汉语读者中一个是智慧的象征，一人是美的象征。但英语读者却不见得知道他们是何许人，又与黛玉有什么关系。杨译本为了让英语读者领会其深层的文化蕴意，先采用意译来表达"心较比干多一窍，病如西子胜三分"是言黛玉聪明无比，且病弱娇美胜过西施。然后加了脚注(1. A prince noted for his great intelligence at the end of the Shang Dynasty. 2. A famous beauty of the ancient kingdom of Yueh.)以此介绍有关的文化背景，让英语读者充分了解"比干"、"西施"人物传说的深刻内涵，从而达到文化信息移植。这种变通的手法使译文既忠于原文又达意。而霍译采用直译的手法并且没有加注补义,这样原语文化信息便难免遗失,读者也会如堕云雾,更谈不上达意。

从例(4)、(5)分析比较看,杨译及霍译在达意上各有千秋,难分伯仲。那么两家译文在考虑译文读者的接受性上,也就是严复所说的"雅"字标准上又如何呢?请看例句:

6. 雨村先整了衣冠,带了小童,拿着"宗侄"的名帖至荣府的门前投了。

杨译:Yu-tsun spruced himself up and went with his pages to the gate of the Jung Mansion, where he handed in his visiting-card on which he had styled himself Chia Cheng's "nephew".

霍译:Yu-cun, dressed in his best and with the two servant-boys at his heels, betook himself to the gate of the Rong Mansion and handed in his visiting-card, on which he had been careful to prefix the word 'kinsman' to his own name.

"宗侄"在中国文化里指同宗中同辈亲友的儿子。而在西方文化里的确没有一个对等的词来表达此意。因为不同的称谓在中国的文化里,反映在语言上就是有关的词汇发达,概念切分很细,需根据不同的概念使用不同的词汇。而在英语国家里有关的概念切分与之不对应。所以原文中的某些所指对象无等值物。在这种情况下,霍译借助相近的所指对象以取得等值效果。因此将"宗侄"译为"kinsman";将"宗侄的名帖"译为"his visiting-card, on which he had been careful to prefix the word 'kinsman' to his own name."很好地发挥了译文的优势。既合乎严复所说的"言之有文,行之弥远"的标准,也容易为读者所接受和理解。而杨译则将"宗侄"译为"Chia Cheng's nephew",试图忠实于原文,保留原文的文化信息,而实际上"宗侄"一词与前面提到的"老祖宗"一词相比较,其民族文化特性显得十分浅淡,并且英语读者也有类似的文化背景知识,只不过英语词的概念切分不如汉语细致。鉴于这种情况,

第六篇 《红楼梦》 The Story of the Stone

译者应多考虑到译文读者的接受性,使译文更倾向于译入语的语言形式,达到使译文读者更容易理解和接受的效果。

7. 近入堂屋中,抬头迎面先看见一个赤金九龙青地大匾,匾上写着斗大的三个字,是"荣禧堂",后有一行小字"某年月日,书赐荣国公贾源",又有"'万几宸翰'之宝"。

杨译：Once inside the hall she looked up and her eye was caught by a great blue table with nine gold dragons on it, on which was written in characters large as peck measures:

Hall of Glorious Felicity.

Small characters at the end recorded the date on which the Emperor had confered this table upon Chia Yuan, the Duke of Jungkuo, and it bore the Imperial seal.

霍译：High overhead on the wall facing her as she entered the hall was a great blue board framed in gilded dragons, on which was written in large gold characters.

THE HALL OF EXALTED FELICITY

with a column of small characters at the side giving a date and the words '...written for Our beloved Subject, Jia Yuan, Duke of Rong-guo, followed by the Emperor's private seal, a device containing the words kingly cares' and royal brush' in archaic seal-script.'

在中国的文化里"万几宸翰之宝",是用于皇帝墨迹之印玺上的文字。万几,亦作"万机"。形容皇帝政务繁忙,日理万机。宸翰就是皇帝的墨迹。宝是皇帝所用印章的专称。而在英国的文化里,译文读者也具备相同的文化背景知识。因此霍译以交际为主旨将"万几宸翰之宝"译为"the Emperor's private seal, a device containing the words 'kingly cares' and 'royal brush' in archaic seal-script.'"这样译,说是一种妥协不容否定,因为它导致了"万几宸翰之宝"这一具体文化意象的亏损,但从功能和接受的角度看,无疑又是恰当的译笔。英国人的"'kingly cares' and royal brush' in archaic seal-script."与中国的"万几宸翰之宝"实质上相差无几,宏观上讲也属于一种文化重合现象。所以霍译置换了原文文化背景,让译文读者通过英国的文化产生中国式的联想与情感体验。这种"交际翻译"法合乎严复所说的"雅"字标准。至于杨译,前面笔者提到,它主要倾向于一种"语义翻译"强调忠实于原文。如果译文过分忠实于原文,忽略译文读者的接受性,就很难达到"言之有文,行之弥远"的标准。因此杨译"万几宸翰之宝"为"the Imperial seal."是否欠妥,还需斟酌。

综上只是对两种译本在传递文化信息方面所采取的处理原则进行的肤浅评述。从达意上看,二者难分上下,但从表达上看,杨译多注重保留民族文化特性。读起来有"异国情调"。但过多地考虑原文的形式,有时手脚放不开,造成很多句子太表面化。而霍译主要以交际为主,很多地方译得十分传神。译文流畅通顺,是地道的英语,但是原文的民族文化色彩在译文中显得浅淡。

二、审美体验的再现

翻译还不单是语言转换。它是审美主体(译者)通过审美中介(译者的审美意识)将审美客体(原文)转换为另一审美客体(译文)的一种审美活动。同时也是思维方式的转变。这种思维方式的转变不是指搞文字上的对号入座,而是如何用本民族的思维方式来表达原文的意蕴,如何在风格上尽量与原文保持一致,最终如何正确地再现原文的审美体验。《红楼梦》堪称一部典型的美学体验小说。它的文学语言高度成熟,高度完善,表现了中国古代小说艺术上的最高成就。从翻译角度来讲,保证这种语言的风格是非常困难的,然而在保持风格等值这一点上,两种译本的翻译家们都显示了深厚的艺术修养。下面试从两种译文如何再现原文的模糊美和节奏美来进行比较分析。

1. 模糊美

模糊性是人类语言的客观属性,但由于民族文化、社会生活和习俗的不同,各种语言的模糊性也存在着一定的差异,但这并不妨碍不同语

第六篇 《红楼梦》 The Story of the Stone

言之间的翻译。"只要译者能捕捉着在模糊、朦胧意境和美感中的形象化意念,就可用译文化语言将这种模糊性勾画出来"。请看例句:

1. 两弯似蹙非蹙罥烟眉,一双似喜非喜含情目。态生两靥之愁,娇袭一身之病。泪光点点,娇喘微微。闲静时如娇花照水,行动处似弱柳扶风。心较比干多一窍,病如西子胜三分。

杨译:Her dusky arched eyebrows were knitted and yet not frowning, her speaking eyes held both merriment and sorrow; her very frailty had charm. Her eyes sparkled with tears, her breath was soft and faint. In repose she was like a lovely flower mirrored in the water; in motion, a pliant willow swaying in the wind. She looked more sensitive than Pikan[1], more delicate than Hsi Shih[2].

1. A prince noted for his great intelligence at the end of the Shang Dynasty.
2. A famous beauty of the ancient kindom of Yueh.

霍译:Her mist-wreathed brows at first seemed to frown, yet were not frowning; Her passionate eyes at first seemed to smile, yet were not merry; Habit had given a melancholy cast to her tender face;

Nature had bestowed a sickly constitution on her delicate frame.

Often the eyes swam with glistening tears;

Often the breath came in gentle gasps.

In stillness she made one think of a graceful flower reflected in the water;

In motion she called to mind tender willow shoots caressed by the wind.

She had more chambers in her heart than the mar-

第六篇 《红楼梦》The Story of the Stone

tyred Bi Gan;
And suffered a tithe more pain in it than the beautiful Xi shi.

这段赞文见于宝黛初会时，它描写了林黛玉弱不禁风的病态美和多愁善感的性格。林黛玉的这种"稀世"之美在曹雪芹的笔下写活了。他首先用了大量的模糊语。如"罥烟眉"、"含情目"、"两靥之愁"、"一身之病"、"泪光点点"、"娇喘微微"、"娇花照水"、"弱柳扶风"，并且在这些词的前面加了模糊限制语。如，"似"，"非"，"如"等使其变得更加模糊。霍译正是挖掘了原文的深层含义，用译文语言将这种模糊勾画出来。它将"似蹙非蹙"译为"at first seemed to frown, yet were not frowning"；"似喜非喜"译为"at first seemed to smile, yet were not merry"，把由远而近，由乍看到仔细看这种模糊的意念表现得十分传神。"罥烟眉"对"her mist-wreathed brows"；"含情目"对"her passionate eyes"；"两靥之愁"对"a melancholy cast to her tender face"；"一身之病"对"a sickly constitution on her delicate frame"；"泪光点点"对"Often the eyes swam with glistening tears"；"娇喘微微"对"Often the breath came in gentle gasps"，以译文的古雅对原文的古雅，给人一种古香古色之感，而且语体与原文风格相对应。接着"闲静时如娇花照水，行动处似弱柳扶风"，这两句原文用了"如"和"似"来限制"娇花照水"和"弱柳扶风"，来增强其模糊的概念。因此霍译将笔锋一转，采取迂回表达方式"she made one think of a graceful flower reflected in the water; she called to mind tender willow shoots caressed by the wind."来引发译文读者对黛玉之美的想象，既传神又富有诗意。这段原文的最后两句语义更为模糊，用"心较比干多一窍，病如西子胜三分"来言黛玉聪明无比，美貌绝顶。霍译为了求得与原文的对应采取了直译的手法。但是应该加上脚注。因为以英语为母语的英国人并不知道比干、西子是何许人。这是本段译文唯一的欠缺。倒是杨译弥补了霍译本最后两句译文的不足，采用了意译加注的办法。但是从整段译文看，杨译有许多地方需要斟酌。首先语言与原文不是十分对应，语言较通俗、大众化、不古

第六篇 《红楼梦》 The Story of the Stone

雅,形象比较鲜明。如,"罥烟眉"、"含情目"分别被译成"her dusky arched eyebrows";"her speaking eyes"、"态生两靥之愁,娇袭一身之病"合译为"her very frailty had charm"用词太白话,语体与原文的风格不协调,失去了诗意和视觉美。另外,"似蹙非蹙"与"似喜非喜"的语意模糊结构也未译出。

2. 第一个肌肤微丰,合中身材,腮凝新荔,鼻腻鹅脂,温柔沉默,观之可亲。

  杨译:The first was somewhat plump and of medium height. Her cheeks were the texture of newly ripened lichees, her nose as sleek as goose fat. Gentle and demure, she looked very approachable.

  霍译:The first girl was of medium height and slightly plumpish, with cheeks as white and firm as a fresh lychee and a nose as white and shiny as soap made from the whitest goose-fat. She had a gentle, sweet, reserved manner. To look at her was to love her.

原文采用了四字结构来描述迎春的外表及性格。这段文字虽不像上一个例子用了一些模糊限定词,但隐含在文中。如:"微丰"、"合中"、"新荔"、"鹅脂",这些词实际上语义都很模糊。杨译采用"somewhat plump and of medium height"霍译采用"of medium height and slightly pumpish"来对原文的"肌肤微丰,合中身材",既达意又传神。在译"腮凝新荔,鼻腻鹅脂"这两句时,两种译本都采用了译语的模糊限定词"as...as"来表达原文的模糊概念,可谓抓住了语言模糊这一功能,灵活而优美地用译文形式尽善尽美地表现出来了。

2. 节奏美

任何文学作品都离不开节奏,好的文学作品通常借助于语句的长短、语气的轻重缓疾来表现人物的思想情感的变化和发展。从生理角度讲,人的呼吸有一定的长度、一定的起伏。人不可能一口气把要说的话都说完,当中就需要有停顿。而停顿的长短也不一样。如果长短轻重合适,就会产生节奏。有了节奏就像有了音乐,有了美妙的旋律一样好听。

第六篇 《红楼梦》The Story of the Stone

《红楼梦》这部小说在这方面表现得尤为突出。无论是小说中的诗歌还是人物对话乃至某个艺术细节的描写所用语言都富有节奏感。《红楼梦》两种译本的翻译家们正是理解和体会到原文的节奏美感,因此在译文中将其发挥得淋漓尽致,使人感到译文与原文"异质同构,共感共鸣"。

1. 无故寻愁觅恨,有时似傻如狂。纵然生得好皮囊,腹内原来草莽。潦倒不通世务,愚顽怕读文章。行为偏僻性乖张,那管世人诽谤!

富贵不知乐业,贫穷难耐凄凉。可怜辜负好韶光,于国于家无望。天下无能第一,古今不肖无双。寄言纨绔与膏粱,莫效此儿形状!

杨译:Absurdly he courts care and melancholy
And raves like any madman in his folly;
For though endowed with handsome looks is he,
His heart is lawless and refractory.
Too dense by far to understand his duty,
Too stubborn to apply himself to study,
Foolhardy in his eccentricity,
He's deaf to all reproach and obloquy.
Left cold by riches and nobility,
Unfit to bear the stings of poverty,
He wastes his time and his ability,
Failing his country and his family.
First in this world for uselessness is he,
Second to none in his deficiency.
Young fops and lordings all, be warned by me:
Don't imitate this youth's perversity!

霍译: 1
Oft-times he sought out what would make him sad;
Sometimes an idiot seemed and sometimes mad.

第六篇 《红楼梦》 The Story of the Stone

  Though outwardly a handsome sausage-skin,
  He proved to have but sorry meat within.
  A harum-scarum, to all duty blind,
  A doltish mule, to study disinclined;
  His acts outlandish and his nature queer;
  Yet not a whit cared he how folk might jeer!

2

  Prosperous, he could not play his part with grace,
  Nor, poor, bear hardship with a smiling face.
  So shamefully the precious hours he'd waste
  That both indoors and out he was disgraced.
  For uselessness the world's prize he might bear;
  His gracelessness in history has no peer.
  Let gilded youths who every dainty sample
  Not imitate this rascal's dire example!

  这两首《西江月》用寓褒于贬的手法，把贾宝玉那叛逆者的思想、性格，概括地揭示出来。《西江月二首》有的句子是七言，有的句子是六言。二、三、四行的韵脚是标准的，且从头到尾押的一律是响亮的 ang 韵，因此音乐效果很强。全首词读起来抑扬顿挫，富有节奏感。要想把这种效果完美地再现出来是很不容易的。霍译本在押韵上采用的一律是 aabbccdd 韵式，两行押一个韵。并且还巧妙地运用了译文的扬抑格调，每行基本为十个音节，五个音步，读起来铿锵有力，产生的音乐效果足可与原诗媲美。杨译本采用了抑扬格调，每行十一个音节，五个音步，全文押一个韵。读起来朗朗上口，颇能传达出原诗的气势。两种译本虽各自使用的韵式不同，但其达到的音乐效果却是金声玉振，难分轩轾。

  2. 宝玉听了，登时发作起狂病，摘下那玉，就狠命摔去，骂道："什么罕物，连人之高低不择，还说'通灵'不'通灵'呢！我也不要这劳什子了！"

  杨译：This instantly threw Pao-yu into one of his frenzies. Tearing off the jade he flung it on the ground.

第六篇 《红楼梦》The Story of the Stone

"What's rare about it?" he stormed. "It can't even tell good people from bad. What spiritual understanding has it got? I don't want this nuisance either."

霍译：This sent Bao-yu off instantly into one of his fits. Snatching the jade from his neck he hurled it violently on the floor as if to smash it and began abusing it passionately. 'Rare object! Rare object! What's so lucky about a stone that can't even tell which people are better than others? Beastly thing! I don't want it!'

《红楼梦》里宝玉的这一段发作，在曹雪芹的笔下，不做作，不拖沓，长短相间，起伏顿挫，节奏感很强。原文使用了对比、反衬、连续继承来衬托宝玉的情绪波动。而两种译文也相应地采用了连续继承、对比和反衬。达到了与原文同等的效果。

模糊美和节奏美是再现原文审美体验必不可少的手段。两译文在此方面虽各有所长，但霍译可以说是形神并备，产生的效果基本与原文接近。

概括言之，通过对《红楼梦》第三回的两译文在以上两方面的比较，可以看出两种译文都传达出了原文的基本思想，而且都称得上是不可多得的"上乘佳作"。只是两种译文所遵循的原则有所不同。所以给读者的感受也不同，杨译是忠实于原作，笔译流畅，含有"异国情调"读起来新鲜有趣，不失其艺术的感染力。霍译是"文从字顺，极为流利顺畅，读起来非常爽快，像是用英文写就的原著"。（张培基，1980年第1期）

参考文献

1. 劳陇："殊途同归"《外国语》，1990年，第5期。
2. 林天煌：《中国翻译词典》，湖北教育出版社，1997年。
3. Newmark, Peter. Approaches to Translation, UK: Pucamon. 1982.
4. Nida, E. A. Toward a Science of Translating, The Netherlands: E. J. Brill. 1964.

第六篇 《红楼梦》 The Story of the Stone

5. 文旭:"语义模糊与翻译"《中国翻译》,1996年,第2期。
6. 夏力力:"文学翻译与节奏美学",《中国翻译》,1996年,第6期。
7. 袁锦翔:《名家翻译研究与赏析》,湖北教育出版社,1990年。
8. 杨为珍、郭荣先:《红楼梦词典》,山东文艺出版社,1986年。
9. 喻云根:《英美名著翻译比较》,湖北教育出版社,1986年。
10. 张成柱:"模糊学在文学翻译中的应用",《中国翻译》,1989年,第2期。
11. 张培基:"略论《红楼梦》新英译的习语处理",《外国语》,1980年,第1期。
12. 周方珠:"文学翻译中民族色彩的处理"《中国翻译》,1995年,第3期。

附：

《红楼梦》(节选)

曹雪芹

第三回　金陵城起复贾雨村
　　　　荣国府收养林黛玉

却说雨村忙回头看时，不是别人，乃是当日同僚一案参革的号张如圭者。他本系此地人，革后家居，今打听得都中奏准起复旧员之信，他便四下里寻情找门路，忽遇见雨村，故忙道喜。二人见了礼，张如圭便将此信告诉雨村，雨村自是欢喜，忙忙的叙了两句，遂作别各自回家。冷子兴听得此言，便忙献计，令雨村央烦林如海，转向都中去央烦贾政。雨村领其意，作别回至馆中，忙寻邸报看真确了。次日，面谋之如海。如海道："天缘凑巧，因贱荆去世，都中家岳母念及小女无人依傍教育，前已遣了男女船只来接，因小女未曾大痊，故未及行。此刻正思向蒙训教之恩未经酬报，遇此机会，岂有不尽心图报之理。但请放心。弟已预为筹画至此，已修下荐书一封，转托内兄务为周全协佐，方可稍尽弟之鄙诚，即有所费用之例，弟于内兄信中已注明白，亦不劳尊兄多虑矣。"雨村一面打恭，谢不释口，一面又问："不知令亲大人现居何职？只怕晚生草率，不敢骤然入都干渎。"如海笑道："若论舍亲，与尊兄犹系同谱，乃荣公之孙：大内兄现袭一等将军，名赦，字恩侯；二内兄名政，字存周，现任工部员外郎，其为人谦恭厚道，大有祖父遗风，非膏粱轻薄仕宦之流，故弟方致书烦托。否则不但有污尊兄之清操，即弟亦不屑为矣。"雨村听了，心下方信了昨日子兴之言，于是又谢了林如海。如海乃说："已择了出月初

第六篇 《红楼梦》 The Story of the Stone

二日小女入都,尊兄即同路而往,岂不两便?"雨村唯唯听命,心中十分得意。如海遂打点礼物并饯行之事,雨村一一领了。

那女学生黛玉,身体方愈,原不忍弃父而往;无奈他外祖母致意务在必去,且兼如海说:"汝父年将半百,再无续室之意;且汝多病,年又极小,上无亲母教养,下无姊妹兄弟扶持,今依傍外祖母及舅氏姊妹去,正好减我顾盼之忧,何反云不往?"黛玉听了,方洒泪拜别,随了奶娘及荣府几个老妇人,登舟而去。雨村另有一只船,带两个小童,依附黛玉而行。

有日到了都中,进入神京,雨村先整了衣冠,带了小童,拿着宗侄的名帖,至荣府的门前投了。彼时贾政已看了妹丈之书,即忙请入相会。见雨村相貌魁伟,言语不俗,且这贾政最喜读书人,礼贤下士,济弱扶危,大有祖风;况又系妹丈致意,因此优待雨村,更又不同:便竭力内中协助,题奏之日,轻轻谋了一个复职候缺。不上两个月,金陵应天府缺出,便谋补了此缺,拜辞了贾政,择日上任去了,不在话下。

且说黛玉自那日弃舟登岸时,便有荣国府打发了轿子并拉行李的车辆久候了。这林黛玉常听得母亲说过,他外祖母家与别家不同。他近日所见的这几个三等仆妇,吃穿用度,已是不凡了,何况今至其家。因此步步留心,时时在意,不肯轻易多说一句话,多行一步路,惟恐被人耻笑了去。自上了轿,进入城中,从纱窗向外瞧了一瞧,其街市之繁华,人烟之阜盛,自与别处不同。又行了半日,忽见街北蹲着两个大石狮子,三间兽头大门,门前列坐着十来个华冠丽服之人。正门却不开,只有东西两角门有人出入。正门之上有一匾,匾上大书"敕造宁国府"五个大字。黛玉想道:这必是外祖之长房了。想着,又往西行,不多远,照样也是三间大门,方是荣国府了。却不进正门,只进了西边角门。那轿夫抬进去,走了一射之地,将转弯时,便歇下退出去了。后面的婆子们已都下了轿,赶上前来。另换了三四个衣帽周全十七八岁的小厮上来,复抬起轿子。众婆子步下围随至一垂花门前落下。众小厮退出,众婆子上来打起轿帘,扶黛玉下轿。林黛玉扶着婆子的手,进了垂花门,两边是抄手游廊,当中是穿堂,当地放着一个紫檀架子大理石的大插屏。转过插屏,小小的三间厅,厅后就是后面的正房大院。正面五间上房,皆雕梁画栋,两边穿山游廊厢房,挂着各色鹦鹉、画眉等鸟雀。台矶之上,坐着几个穿红着绿的丫头,一见他们来了,便忙都笑迎上来,说:"刚才老太太还念呢,可巧就来了。"于是三四人争着打起帘笼,一面听得人回话:"林姑娘到了。"

黛玉方进入房时,只见两个人搀着一位鬓发如银的老母迎上来,黛玉便知是他外祖母。方欲拜见时,早被他外祖母一把搂入怀中,"心肝儿肉"叫着大哭起来。当下地下侍立之人,无不掩面涕泣,黛玉也哭个不住。一时众人慢慢解劝住了,黛玉方拜见了外祖母。此即冷子兴所云之史氏太君,贾赦贾政之母也。当下贾母一一指与黛玉:"这是你大舅母,这是你二舅母,这是你先珠大哥的媳妇珠大嫂子。"黛玉一一拜见过。贾母又说:"请姑娘们来。今日远客才来,可以不必上学去了。"众人答应了一声,便去了两个。

不一时,只见三个奶嬷嬷并五六个丫鬟,簇拥着三个姊妹来了。第一个肌肤微丰,合中身材,腮凝新荔,鼻腻鹅脂,温柔沉默,观之可亲。第二个削肩细腰,长挑身材,鸭蛋脸面,俊眼修眉,顾盼神飞,文彩精华,见之忘俗。第三个身量未足,形容尚小。其钗环裙袄,三人皆是一样的妆饰。黛玉忙起身迎上来见礼,互相厮认过,大家归了坐。丫鬟们斟上茶来。不过说些黛玉之母如何得病,如何得医服药,如何送死发丧。不免贾母又伤感起来,因说:"我这些儿女,所疼者独有你母,今日一旦先舍我而去,连面也不能一见,今见了你,我怎不伤心!"说着,搂了黛玉在怀,又呜咽起来。众人忙都宽慰解释,方略略止住。

众人见黛玉年貌虽小,其举止言谈不俗,身体面庞虽怯弱不胜,却有一段自然的风流态度,便知他有不足之症。因问:"常服何药,如何不急为疗治?"黛玉道:"我自来是如此,从会吃饮食时便吃药,到今日未断,请了多少名医修方配药,皆不见效。那一年我三岁时,听得说来了一个癞头和尚,说要化我去出家,我父母固是不从。他又说:'既舍不得他,只怕他的病一生也不能好的了。若要好时,除非从此以后总不许见哭声;除父母之外,凡有外姓亲友之人,一概不见,方可平安了此一世。'疯疯癫癫,说了这些不经之谈,也没人理他。如今还是吃人参养荣丸。"贾母道:"正好,我这里正配丸药呢。叫他们多配一料就是了。"

一语未了,只听后院中有人笑声,说:"我来迟了,不曾迎接远客!"

第六篇 《红楼梦》 The Story of the Stone

黛玉纳罕道:"这些人个个皆敛声屏气,恭肃严整如此,这来者系谁,这样放诞无礼?"心下想时,只见一群媳妇丫鬟围拥着一个人从后房门进来。这个人打扮与众姑娘不同,彩绣辉煌,恍若神妃仙子:头上戴着金丝八宝攒珠髻,绾着朝阳五凤挂珠钗;项上带着赤金盘螭璎珞圈;裙边系着豆绿宫绦、双鱼比目玫瑰佩;身上穿着缕金百蝶穿花大红洋缎窄褃袄,外罩五彩刻丝石青银鼠褂;下着翡翠撒花洋绉裙。一对丹凤三角眼,两弯柳叶吊梢眉,身量苗条,体格风骚,粉面含春威不露,丹唇未启笑先闻。黛玉连忙起身接见。贾母笑道:"你不认得他,他是我们这里有名的一个泼皮破落户儿,南省俗谓作'辣子',你只叫他'凤辣子'就是了。"黛玉正不知以何称呼,只见众姊妹都忙告诉他道:"这是琏嫂子。"黛玉虽不识,也曾听见母亲说过,大舅贾赦之子贾琏,娶的就是二舅母王氏之内侄女,自幼假充男儿教养的,学名王熙凤。黛玉忙陪笑见礼,以"嫂"呼之。这熙凤携着黛玉的手,上下细细打谅了一回,仍送至贾母身边坐下,因笑道:"天下真有这样标致的人物,我今儿才算见了!况且这通身的气派,竟不象老祖宗的外孙女儿,竟是个嫡亲的孙女,怨不得老祖宗天天口头心头一时不忘。只可怜我这妹妹这样命苦,怎么姑妈偏就去世了!"说着,便用帕拭泪。贾母笑道:"我才好了,你倒来招我。你妹妹远路才来,身子又弱,也才劝住了,快再休提前话。"这熙凤听了,忙转悲为喜道:"正是呢!我一见了妹妹,一心都在他身上了,又是喜欢,又是伤心,竟忘记了老祖宗。该打,该打!"又忙携黛玉之手,问:"妹妹几岁了? 可也上过学? 现吃什么药? 在这里不要想家,想要什么吃的、什么玩的,只管告诉我。丫头老婆们不好了,也只管告诉我。"一面又问婆子们:"林姑娘的行李东西可搬进来了? 带了几个人来? 你们赶早打扫两间下房,让他们去歇歇。"

说话时,已摆了茶果上来。熙凤亲为捧茶捧果。又见二舅母问他:"月钱放过了不曾?"熙凤道:"月钱已放完了。才刚带着人到后楼上找缎子,找了这半日,也并没有见昨日太太说的那样的,想是太太记错了?"王夫人道:"有没有,什么要紧。"因又说道:"该随手拿出两个来给你这妹妹去裁衣裳的,等晚上想着叫人再去拿罢,可别忘了。"熙凤道:"这倒是我先料着了,知道妹妹不过这两日到的,我已预备下了,等太太回去过了目好送来。"王夫人一笑,点头不语。

　　当下茶果已撤,贾母命两个老嬷嬷带了黛玉去见两个母舅。时贾赦之妻邢氏忙亦起身,笑回道:"我带了外甥女过去,倒也便宜。"贾母笑道:"正是呢,你也去罢,不必过来了。"邢夫人答应了一声"是"字,遂带了黛玉与王夫人作辞,大家送至穿堂前。出了垂花门,早有众小厮们拉过一辆翠幄青䌷车,邢夫人携了黛玉,坐在上面,众婆子们放下车帘,方命小厮们抬起,拉至宽处,方驾上驯骡,亦出了西角门,往东过荣府正门,便入一黑油大门中,至仪门前方下来。众小厮退出,方打起车帘,邢夫人搀着黛玉的手,进入院中。黛玉度其房屋院宇,必是荣府中花园隔断过来的。进入三层仪门,果见正房厢庑游廊,悉皆小巧别致,不似方才那边轩峻壮丽;且院中随处之树木山石皆在。一时进入正室,早有许多盛妆丽服之姬妾丫鬟迎着,邢夫人让黛玉坐了,一面命人到外面书房去请贾赦。一时人来回话说:"老爷说了:'连日身上不好,见了姑娘彼此倒伤心,暂时不忍相见。劝姑娘不要伤心想家,跟着老太太和舅母,即同家里一样。姊妹们虽拙,大家一处伴着,亦可以解些烦闷。或有委屈之处,只管说得,不要外道才是。'"黛玉忙站起来,一一听了。再坐一刻,便告辞。邢夫人苦留吃过晚饭去,黛玉笑回道:"舅母爱惜赐饭,原不应辞,只是还要过去拜见二舅舅,恐领了赐去不恭,异日再领,未为不可。望舅母容谅。"邢夫人听说,笑道:"这倒是了。"遂令两三个嬷嬷用方才的车好生送了姑娘过去。于是黛玉告辞。邢夫人送至仪门前,又嘱咐了众人几句,眼看着车去了方回来。

　　一时黛玉进了荣府,下了车。众嬷嬷引着,便往东转弯,穿过一个东西的穿堂,向南大厅之后,仪门内大院落,上面五间大正房,两边厢房鹿顶耳房钻山,四通八达,轩昂壮丽,比贾母处不同。黛玉便知这方是正经正内室,一条大甬路,直接出大门的。进入堂屋中,抬头迎面先看见一个赤金九龙青地大匾,匾上写着斗大的三个大字,是"荣禧堂",后有一行小字"某年月日,书赐荣国公贾源",又有"万几宸翰之宝"。大紫檀雕螭案上,设着三尺来高青绿古铜鼎,悬着待漏随朝墨龙大画,一边是金蜼彝,一边是玻璃盉。地下两溜十六张楠木交椅,又有一副对联,乃乌木联牌,镶着錾银的字迹,道是:

第六篇 《红楼梦》 The Story of the Stone

座上珠玑昭日月,堂前黼黻焕烟霞。
下面一行小字,道是:"同乡世教弟勋袭东安郡王穆莳拜手书。"

原来王夫人时常居坐宴息,亦不在这正室,只在这正室东边的三间耳房内。于是老嬷嬷引黛玉进东房门来。临窗大炕上铺着猩红洋罽,正面设着大红金钱蟒靠背,石青金钱蟒引枕,秋香色金钱蟒大条褥。两边设一对梅花式洋漆小几。左边几上文王鼎匙箸香盒;右边几上汝窑美人觚——觚内插着时鲜花卉,并茗碗痰盒等物。地下面西一溜四张椅上,都搭着银红撒花椅搭,底下四副脚踏。椅之两边,也有一对高几,几上茗碗瓶花俱备。其余陈设,自不必细说。老嬷嬷们让黛玉炕上坐,炕沿上却有两个锦褥对设,黛玉度其位次,便不上炕,只向东边椅子上坐了。本房内的丫鬟忙捧上茶来。黛玉一面吃茶,一面打谅这些丫鬟们,妆饰衣裙,举止行动,果亦与别家不同。

茶未吃了,只见一个穿红绫袄青缎掐牙背心的丫鬟走来笑说道:"太太说,请林姑娘到那边坐罢。"老嬷嬷听了,于是又引黛玉出来,到了东廊三间小正房内。正房炕上横设一张炕桌,桌上磊着书籍茶具,靠东壁面西设着半旧的青缎靠背引枕。王夫人却坐在西边下首,亦是半旧的青缎靠背坐褥。见黛玉来了,便往东让。黛玉心中料定这是贾政之位。因见挨炕一溜三张椅子上,也搭着半旧的弹墨椅袱,黛玉便向椅上坐了。王夫人再四携他上炕,他方挨王夫人坐了。王夫人因说:"你舅舅今日斋戒去了,再见罢。只是有一句话嘱咐你:你三个姊妹倒都极好,以后一处念书认字学针线,或是偶一顽笑,都有尽让的。但我不放心的最是一件:我有一个孽根祸胎,是家里的'混世魔王',今日因庙里还愿去了,尚未回来,晚间你看见便知了。你只以后不要睬他,你这些姊妹都不敢沾惹他的。"

黛玉亦常听得母亲说过,二舅母生的有个表兄,乃衔玉而诞,顽劣异常,极恶读书,最喜在内帏厮混;外祖母又极溺爱,无人敢管。今见王夫人如此说,便知说的是这表兄了。因陪笑道:"舅母说的,可是衔玉所生的这位哥哥?在家时亦曾听见母亲常说,这位哥哥比我大一岁,小名就唤宝玉,虽极憨顽,说在姊妹情中极好的。况我来了,自然只和姊妹同处,兄弟们自是别院另室的,岂得去沾惹之理?"王夫人笑道:"你不知道原故:他与别人不同,自幼因老太太疼爱,原系同姊妹们一处娇养惯了的。若姊妹们有日不理他,他倒还安静些,纵然他没趣,不过出了二门,背地里拿着他两个小幺儿出气,咕唧一会子就完了。若这一日姊妹们和他多说一句话,他心里一乐,便生出多少事来。所以嘱咐你别睬他。他嘴里一时甜言蜜语,一时有天无日,一时又疯疯傻傻,只休信他。"

黛玉一一的都答应着。只见一个丫鬟来回:"老太太那里传晚饭了。"王夫人忙携黛玉从后房门由后廊往西,出了角门,是一条南北宽夹道。南边是倒座三间小小的抱厦厅,北边立着一个粉油大影壁,后有一半大门,小小一所房室。王夫人笑指向黛玉道:"这是你凤姐姐的屋子,回来你好往这里找他来,少什么东西,你只管和他说就是了。"这院门上也有四五个才总角的小厮,都垂手侍立。王夫人遂携黛玉穿过一个东西穿堂,便是贾母的后院了。于是,进入后房门,已有多人在此伺候,见王夫人来了,方安设桌椅。贾珠之妻李氏捧饭,熙凤安箸,王夫人进羹。贾母正面榻上独坐,两边四张空椅,熙凤忙拉了黛玉在左边第一张椅子上坐了,黛玉十分推让。贾母笑道:"你舅母你嫂子们不在这里吃饭。你是客,原应如此坐的。"黛玉方告了座,坐了。贾母命王夫人也坐了。迎春姊妹三个告了座方上来。迎春便坐右手第一,探春左第二,惜春右第二。旁边丫鬟执着拂尘、漱盂、巾帕。李、凤二人立于案旁布让。外间伺候之媳妇丫鬟虽多,却连一声咳嗽不闻。寂然饭毕,各有丫鬟用小茶盘捧上茶来。当日林如海教女以惜福养身,云饭后务待饭粒咽尽,过一时再吃茶,方不伤脾胃。今黛玉见了这里许多事情不合家中之式,不得不随的,少不得一一改过来,因而接了茶。早见人又捧过漱盂来。黛玉也照样漱了口。盥手毕,又捧上茶来,这方是吃的茶。贾母便说:"你们去罢,让我们自在说话儿。"王夫人听了,忙起身,又说了两句闲话,方引凤、李二人去了。贾母因问黛玉念何书。黛玉道:"只刚念了《四书》。"黛玉又问姊妹们读何书。贾母道:"读的是什么书,不过是认得两个字,不是睁眼的瞎子罢了!"

一语未了,只听外面一阵脚步响,丫鬟进来笑道:"宝玉来了!"黛玉心中正疑惑着:"这个宝玉,不知是怎生个惫懒人物,懵懂顽童?倒不见那蠢物也罢了。"心中想着,忽见丫鬟话未报完,已进来了一位年轻的公

第六篇 《红楼梦》 The Story of the Stone

子:头上戴着束发嵌宝紫金冠,齐眉勒着二龙抢珠金抹额;穿一件二色金百蝶穿花大红箭袖,束着五彩丝攒花结长穗宫绦,外罩石青起花八团倭缎排穗褂;登着青缎粉底小朝靴。面若中秋之月,色如春晓之花,鬓若刀裁,眉如墨画,面如桃瓣,目若秋波。虽怒时而若笑,即瞋视而有情。项上金螭璎珞,又有一根五色丝绦,系着一块美玉。黛玉一见,便吃一大惊,心下想道:"好生奇怪,倒象在那里见过一般,何等眼熟到如此!"只见这宝玉向贾母请了安,贾母便命:"去见你娘来。"宝玉即转身去了。一时回来,再看,已换了冠带:头上周围一转的短发,都结成小辫,红丝结束,共攒至顶中胎发,总编一根大辫,黑亮如漆,从顶至梢,一串四颗大珠,用金八宝坠脚;身上穿着银红撒花半旧大袄,仍旧带有项圈、宝玉、寄名锁、护身符等物;下面半露松花撒花绫裤腿,锦边弹墨袜,厚底大红鞋。越显得面如敷粉,唇若施脂,转盼多情,语言常笑。天然一段风骚,全在眉梢;平生万种情思,悉堆眼角。看其外貌最是极好,却难知其底细。后人有《西江月》二词,批宝玉极恰,其词曰:

　　无故寻愁觅恨,有时似傻如狂。纵然生得好皮囊,腹内原来草莽。潦倒不通世务,愚顽怕读文章。行为偏僻性乖张,那管世人诽谤!

　　富贵不知乐业,贫穷难耐凄凉。可怜辜负好韶光,于国于家无望。天下无能第一,古今不肖无双。寄言纨绔与膏粱:莫效此儿形状!

贾母因笑道:"外客未见,就脱了衣裳,还不去见你妹妹!"宝玉早已看见多了一个姊妹,便料定是林姑妈之女,忙来作揖。厮见毕,归坐。细看形容,与众各别:两弯似蹙非蹙罥烟眉,一双似喜非喜含情目。态生两靥之愁,娇袭一身之病。泪光点点,娇喘微微。闲静时如姣花照水,行动处似弱柳扶风。心较比干多一窍,病如西子胜三分。宝玉看罢,因笑道:"这个妹妹我曾见过的。"贾母笑道:"可又是胡说,你又何曾见过他?"宝玉笑道:"虽然未曾见过他,然我看着面善,心里就算是旧相识,今日只作远别重逢,亦未为不可。"贾母笑道:"更好,更好,若如此,更相和睦了。"宝玉便走近黛玉身边坐下,又细细打量一番,因问:"妹妹可曾读书?"黛玉道:"不曾读,只上了一年学,些须认得几个字。"宝玉又道:"妹妹尊名是那两个字?"黛玉便说了名。宝玉又问表字。黛玉道:"无字。"宝玉笑道:"我送妹妹一个妙字,莫若'颦颦'二字极妙。"探春便问何出。宝玉道:"《古今人物通考》上说:'西方有石名黛,可代画眉之墨。'况这林妹妹眉尖若蹙,用取这两个字,岂不两妙!"探春笑道:"只恐又是你的杜撰。"宝玉笑道:"除《四书》外,杜撰的太多,偏只我是杜撰不成?"又问黛玉:"可也有玉没有?"众人不解其语,黛玉便忖度着因他有玉,故问我有也无,因答道:"我没有那个。想来那玉是一件罕物,岂能人人有的。"宝玉听了,登时发作起痴狂病来,摘下那玉,就狠命摔去,骂道:"什么罕物,连人之高低不择,还说'通灵'不'通灵'呢!我也不要这劳什子了!"吓的众人一拥争去拾玉。贾母急的搂了宝玉道:"孽障!你生气,要打骂人容易,何苦摔那命根子!"宝玉满面泪痕泣道:"家里姐姐妹妹都没有,单我有,我说没趣;如今来了这们一个神仙似的妹妹也没有,可知这不是个好东西。"贾母忙哄他道:"你这妹妹原有这个来的,因你姑妈去世时,舍不得你妹妹,无法处,遂将他的玉带了去了:一则全殉葬之礼,尽你妹妹之孝心;二则你姑妈之灵,亦可权作见了女儿之意。因此他只说没有这个,不便自己夸张之意。你如今怎比得他?还不好生慎重带上,仔细你娘知道了。"说着,便向丫鬟手中接来,亲与他带上,宝玉听如此说,想一想大有情理,也就不生别论了。

当下,奶娘来请问黛玉之房舍。贾母说:"今将宝玉挪出来,同我在套间暖阁儿里,把你林姑娘暂安置碧纱厨里。等过了残冬,春天再与他们收拾房屋,另作一番安置罢。"宝玉道:"好祖宗,我就在碧纱厨外的床上很妥当,何必又出来闹的老祖宗不得安静。"贾母了想了一想说:"也罢了。"每人一个奶娘并一个丫头照管,余者在外间上夜听唤。一面早有熙凤命人送了一顶藕合色花帐,并几件锦被缎褥之类。

黛玉只带了两个人来:一个是自幼奶娘王嬷嬷,一个是十岁的小丫头,亦是自幼随身的,名唤作雪雁。贾母见雪雁甚小,一团孩气,王嬷嬷又极老,料黛玉皆不遂心省力的,便将自己身边的一个二等丫头,名唤鹦哥者与了黛玉。外亦如迎春等例,每人除自己乳母外,另有四个教引嬷嬷,除贴身掌管钗钏盥沐两个丫鬟外,另有五六个洒扫房屋来往使役的小丫鬟。当下,王嬷嬷与鹦哥陪侍黛玉在碧纱厨内。宝玉之乳母李嬷

第六篇 《红楼梦》 The Story of the Stone

嬷,并大丫鬟名唤袭人者,陪侍在外面大床上。

原来这袭人亦是贾母之婢,本名珍珠。贾母因溺爱宝玉,生恐宝玉之婢无竭力尽忠之人,素喜袭人心地纯良,克尽职任,遂与了宝玉。宝玉因知他本姓花,又曾见旧人诗句上有"花气袭人"之句,遂回明贾母,更名袭人。这袭人亦有些痴处:伏侍贾母时,心中眼中只有一个贾母;如今服侍宝玉,心中眼中又只有一个宝玉。只因宝玉性情乖僻,每每规谏宝玉,心中着实忧郁。

是晚,宝玉李嬷嬷已睡了,他见里面黛玉和鹦哥犹未安息,他自卸了妆,悄悄进来,笑问:"姑娘怎么还不安息?"黛玉忙让:"姐姐请坐。"袭人在床沿上坐了。鹦哥笑道:"林姑娘正在这里伤心,自己淌眼抹泪的说:'今儿才来,就惹出你家哥儿的狂病,倘若摔坏了那玉,岂不是因我之过!'因此便伤心,我好容易劝好了。"袭人道:"姑娘快休如此,将来只怕比这个更奇怪的笑话儿还有呢! 若为他这种行止,你多心伤感,只怕你伤感不了呢。快别多心!"黛玉道:"姐姐们说的,我记着就是了。究竟那玉不知是怎么个来历? 上面还有字迹?"袭人道:"连一家子也不知来历,上头还有现成的眼儿,听得说,落草时是从他口里掏出来的。等我拿来你看便知。"黛玉忙止道:"罢了,此刻夜深,明日再看也不迟。"大家又叙了一回,方才安歇。

次日起来,省过贾母,因往王夫人处来,正值王夫人与熙凤在一处拆金陵来的书信看,又有王夫人之兄嫂处遣了两个媳妇来说话。黛玉虽不知原委,探春等却都晓得是议论金陵城中所居的薛家姨母之子姨表兄薛蟠,倚财仗势,打死人命,现在应天府案下审理。如今母舅王子腾得了信息,故遣他家内的人来告诉这边,意欲唤取进京之意。

附：

The Story of the Stone (Excerpt)

Translated by David Hawkes

CHAPTER 3

Lin Ru-hai recommends a private tutor
to his brother-in-law
And old Lady Jia extends a compassionate welcome
to the motherless child

When Yu-cun turned to look, he was surprised to see that it was Zhang Ru-gui, a former colleague who had been cashiered at the same time and for the same reason as himself. Zhang Ru-gui was a native of these parts, and had been living at home since his dismissal. Having just wormed out the information that a motion put forward in the capital for the reinstatement of ex-officials had been approved, he had been dashing about ever since, pulling strings and soliciting help from potential backers, and was engaged in this activity when he unexpectedly ran into Yu-cun. Hence the tone of his greeting.

As soon as they had finished bowing to each other, Zhang Ru-gui told Yu-cun the good news, and after further hurried conversation they went their separate ways.

Leng Zi-xing, who had overheard the news, proposed a plan. Why should not Yu-cun ask his employer Lin Ru-hai to write to his

第六篇 《红楼梦》 The Story of the Stone

brother-in-law Jia Zheng in the capital and enlist this support on his, Yu-cun's, behalf? Yu-cun agreed to follow this suggestion, and presently the two friends separated.

Back in his quarters, Yu-cun quickly hunted out a copy of the *Gazette*, and having satisfied himself that the news was authentic, broached the matter next day with Lin Ru-hai.

'It so happens that an opportunity of helping you has just presented itself,' said Ru-hai, 'Since my poor wife passed on, my mother-in-law in the capital has been worried about the little girl having no one to look after her, and has already sent some of her folk here by barge to fetch her away. The only reason she has so far not gone is that she has not been quite recovered from her illness. I was, however, only just now thinking that the moment to send her had arrived. And as I have still done nothing to repay you for your kindness in tutoring her for me, you may be sure that now this opportunity has presented itself I shall do my very best to help you.'

'As a matter of fact, I have already made a few arrangements. I have written this letter here entrusting my brother-in-law with your affair, explaining my indebtedness to you and urging him to see it properly settled. I have also made it quite clear in my letter that any expenses which may be involved are to be taken care of; so you have nothing to worry about on that account.'

Yu-cun made an elaborate bow to his patron and thanked him profusely. He then ventured a question.

'I am afraid I do not know what your relation's position is at the capital. Might it not be a little embarrassing for a person in my situation to thrust himself upon him?'

Ru-hai laughed. 'You need have no anxiety on that score. My brothers-in-law in the capital are your own kinsmen. They are grandsons of the former Duke of Rong-guo. The elder one, Jia She, is a

第六篇 《红楼梦》The Story of the Stone

hereditary official of the First Rank and an honorary colonel; the younger one, Jia Zheng, is an Under Secretary in the Ministry of Works. He takes very much after his late grandfather: a modest, generous man, quite without the arrogance of the pampered aristocrat. That is why I have addressed this letter to him. If I did not have complete confidence in his willingness to help you, I should not have put your honour at risk by soliciting him; nor, for that matter, should I have taken the trouble to write the letter.'

Yu-cun now knew that what Zi-xing had told him was the truth and he thanked Lin Ru-hai once again.

'I have fixed the second day of next month for my little girl's journey to the capital,' said Ru-hai. 'If you cared to travel with her, it would be convenient for both of us.'

Yu-cun accepted the suggestion with eager deference. Everything, he thought to himself, was turning out very satisfactorily. Ru-hai for his part set about preparing presents for his wife's family and parting gifts for Yu-cun, all of which Yu-cun in due course took charge of.

At first his little pupil could not be persuaded to part from her father; but her grandmother was insistent that she should go, and Ru-hai added his own reasons.

'I'm half a century old now, my dear, and I have no intention of taking a second wife; so there will be no one here to act as a mother to you. It isn't either, as if you had sisters who could help to take care of you. You know how often you are poorly. And you are still very young. It would be a great weight off my mind to know that you had your Grandmother Jia and your uncles' girls to fall back on. I really think you ought to go.'

After this Dai-yu could only take a tearful leave of her father and go down to the boat with her nurse and the old women from the Rong

第六篇 《红楼梦》 The Story of the Stone

mansion who had been sent to fetch her. There was a separate boat for Yu-cun and a couple of servant-boys to wait on him, and he too now embarked in the capacity of Dai-yu's escort.

In due course they arrived in the capital, and Yu-cun, dressed in his best and with the two servant-boys at his heels, betook himself to the gate of the Rong mansion and handed in his visiting-card, on which he had been careful to prefix the word 'kinsman' to his own name. By this time Jia Zheng had already seen his brother-in-law's letter, and accorded him an interview without delay.

Yu-cun's imposing looks and cultivated speech made an excellent impression on Jia Zheng, who was in any case always well-disposed towards scholars, and preserved much of his grandfather's affability with men of letters and readiness to help them in any sort of trouble or distress. And since his own inclinations were in this case reinforced by his brother-in-law's strong recommendation, the treatment he extended to Yu-cun was exceptionally favourable. He exerted himself on his behalf to such good effect that on the very day his petition was presented Yu-cun's reinstatement was approved, and before two months were out he was appointed to the magistracy of Ying-tian-fu in Nanking. Thither, having chosen a suitable day on which to commence his journey, and having first taken his leave of Jia Zheng, he now repaired to take up his duties.

But of him, for the time being, no more.

On the day of her arrival in the capital, Dai-yu stepped ashore to find covered chairs from the Rong mansion for her and her women and a cart for the luggage ready waiting on the quay.

She had often heard her mother say that her Grandmother Jia's home was not like other people's houses. The servants she had been in contact with during the past few days were comparatively low-ranking ones in the domestic hierarchy, yet the food they ate, the clothes they wore, and everything about them was quite out of the ordinary. Dai-yu tried to imagine what the people who employed these superior beings must be like. When she arrived at their house she would have to watch every step she took and weigh every word she said, for if she put a foot wrong they would surely laugh her to scorn.

Dai-yu got into her chair and was soon carried through the city walls. Peeping through the gauze panel which served as a window, she could see streets and buildings more rich and elegant and throngs of people more lively and numerous than she had ever seen in her life before. After being carried for what seemed a very great length of time, she saw, on the north front of the east-west street through which they were passing, two great stone lions crouched one on each side of a triple gateway whose doors were embellished with animal-heads. In front of the gateway ten or so splendidly dressed flunkeys sat in a row. The centre of the three gates was closed, but people were going in and out of the two side ones. There was a board above the centre gate on which were written in large characters the words:

NING-GUO HOUSE

Founded and Constructed by

Imperial Command

Dai-yu realized that this must be where the elder branch of her grandmother's family lived. The chair proceeded some distance more down the street and presently there was another triple gate, this time with the legend

RONG-GUO HOUSE

above it.

Ignoring the central gate, her bearers went in by the western entrance and after traversing the distance of a bowshot inside, half turned a corner and set the chair down. The chairs of her female at-

第六篇 《红楼梦》 The Story of the Stone

tendants which were following behind were set down simultaneously and the old women got out. The places of Dai-yu's bearers were taken by four handsome, fresh-faced pages of seventeen or eighteen. They shouldered her chair and, with the old women now following on foot, carried it as far as an ornamental inner gate. There they set it down again and then retired in respectful silence. The old women came forward to the front of the chair, held up the curtain, and helped Dai-yu to get out.

Each hand resting on the outstretched hand of an elderly attendant, Dai-yu passed through the ornamental gate into a courtyard which had balustraded loggias running along its sides and a covered passage-way through the centre. The foreground of the courtyard beyond was partially hidden by a screen of polished marble set in an elaborate red sandalwood frame. Passing round the screen and through a small reception hall beyond it, they entered the large courtyard of the mansion's principal apartments. These were housed in an imposing five-frame building resplendent with carved and painted beams and rafters which faced them across the courtyard. Running along either side of the courtyard were galleries hung with cages containing a variety of different-coloured parrots, cockatoos, white-eyes, and other birds. Some gaily-dressed maids were sitting on the steps of the main building opposite. At the appearance of the visitors they rose to their feet and came forward with smiling faces to welcome them.

'You've come just at the right time! Lady Jia was only this moment asking about you.'

Three or four of them ran to lift up the door-curtain, while another of them announced in loud tones,

'Miss Lin is here!'

As Dai-yu entered the room she saw a silver-haired old lady advancing to meet her, supported on either side by a servant. She knew that this must be her Grandmother Jia and would have fallen on her knees and made her kotow, but before she could do so her grandmother had caught her in her arms and pressing her to her bosom with cries of 'My pet!' and 'My poor lamb!' burst into loud sobs, while all those present wept in sympathy, and Dai-yu felt herself crying as though she would never stop. It was some time before those present succeeded in calming them both down and Dai-yu was at last able to make her kotow.

Grandmother Jia now introduced those present.

'This is your elder uncle's wife, Aunt Xing. This is your Uncle Zheng's wife, Aunt Wang. This is Li Wan, the wife of your Cousin Zhu, who died.'

Dai-yu kotowed to each of them in turn.

'Call the girls!' said Grandmother Jia. 'Tell them that we have a very special vistor and that they need not do their lessons today.'

There was a cry of 'Yes ma'am' from the assembled maids, and two of them went off to do her bidding.

Presently three girls arrived, attended by three nurses and five or six maids.

The first girl was of medium height and slightly plumpish, with cheeks as white and firm as a fresh lychee and a nose as white and shiny as soap made from the whitest goose-fat. She had a gentle, sweet, reserved manner. To look at her was to love her.

The second girl was rather tall, with sloping shoulders and a slender waist. She had an oval face under whose well-formed brows large, expressive eyes shot out glances that sparkled with animation. To look at her was to forget all that was mean or vulgar.

The third girl was undersized and her looks were still somewhat babyish and unformed.

All three were dressed in identical skirts and dresses and wore i-

第六篇 《红楼梦》 The Story of the Stone

dentical sets of bracelets and hair ornaments.

Dai-yu rose to meet them and exchanged curtseys and introductions. When she was seated once more, a maid served tea, and a conversation began on the subject of her mother: how her illness had started, what doctors had been called in, what medicines prescribed, what arrangements had been made for the funeral, and how the mourning had been observed. This conversation had the foreseeable effect of upsetting the old lady all over again.

'Of all my girls your mother was the one I loved the best,' she said, 'and now she's been the first to go, and without my even being able to see her again before the end. I can't help being upset!' And holding fast to Dai-yu's hand, she once more burst into tears. The rest of the company did their best to comfort her, until at last she had more or less recovered.

Everyone's attention now centred on Dai-yu. They observed that although she was still young, her speech and manner already showed unusual refinement. They also noticed the frail body which seemed scarcely strong enough to bear the weight of its clothes, but which yet had an inexpressible grace about it, and realizing that she must be suffering from some deficiency, asked her what medicine she took for it and why it was still not better.

'I have always been like this,' said Dai-yu. 'I have been taking medicine ever since I could eat and been looked at by ever so many well-known doctors, but it has never done me any good. Once, when I was only three, I can remember a scabby-headed old monk came and said he wanted to take me away and have me brought up as a nun; but of course, Mother and Father wouldn't hear of it. So he said, "Since you are not prepared to give her up, I am afraid her illness will never get better as long as she lives. The only way it might get better would be if she were never to hear the sound of weeping from this day onwards and never to see any relations other than her own mother and father. Only in those conditions could she get through her life without trouble." Of course, he was quite crazy, and no one took any notice of the things he said. I'm still taking Ginseng Tonic Pills.'

'Well, that's handy,' said Grandmother Jia. 'I take the Pills myself. We can easily tell them to make up a few more each time.'

She had scarcely finished speaking when someone could be heard talking and laughing in a very loud voice in the inner courtyard behind them.

'Oh dear! I'm late,' said the voice. 'I've missed the arrival of our guest.'

'Everyone else around here seems to go about with bated breath,' thought Dai-yu. 'Who can this new arrival be who is so brash and unmannerly?'

Even as she wondered, a beautiful young woman entered from the room behind the one they were sitting in, surrounded by a bevy of serving women and maids. She was dressed quite differently from the others present, gleaming like some fairy princess with sparkling jewels and gay embroideries.

Her chignon was enclosed in a circlet of gold filigree and clustered pearls. It was fastened with a pin embellished with flying phoenixes, from whose beaks pearls were suspended on tiny chains.

Her necklet was of red gold in the form of a coiling dragon.

Her dress had a fitted bodice and was made of dark red silk damask with a pattern of flowers and butterflies in raised gold thread.

Her jacket was lined with ermine. It was of a slate-blue stuff with woven insets in coloured silks.

Her under-skirt was of a turquoise-coloured imported silk crêpe embroidered with flowers.

第六篇 《红楼梦》 The Story of the Stone

She had, moreover,
> eyes like a painted phoenix,
> eyebrows like willow-leaves,
> a slender form,
> seductive grace;
> the ever-smiling summer face
> of hidden thunders showed no trace;
> the ever-bubbling laughter started
> almost before the lips were parted.

'You don't know her,' said Grandmother Jia merrily. 'She's a holy terror this one. What we used to call in Nanking a "peppercorn". You just call her "Peppercorn Feng". She'll know who you mean!'

Dai-yu was at a loss to know how she was to address this Peppercorn Feng until one of the cousins whispered that it was 'Cousin Lian's wife', and she remembered having heard her mother say that her elder uncle, Uncle She, had a son called Jia Lian who was married to the niece of her Uncle Zheng's wife, Lady Wang. She had been brought up from earliest childhood just like a boy, and had acquired in the schoolroom the somewhat boyish-sounding name of Wang Xi-feng. Dai-yu accordingly smiled and curtseyed, greeting her by her correct name as she did so.

Xi-feng took Dai-yu by the hand and for a few moments scrutinized her carefully from top to toe before conducting her back to her seat beside Grandmother Jia.

'She's a beauty, Grannie dear! If I hadn't set eyes on her today, I shouldn't have believed that such a beautiful creature could exist! And everything about her so *distingué*! She doesn't take after your side of the family, Grannie. She's more like a Jia. I don't blame you for having gone on so about her during the past few days—but poor little thing! What a cruel fate to have lost Auntie like that!' and she dabbed at her eyes with a handkerchief.

'I've only just recovered,' laughed Grandmother Jia. 'Don't you go trying to start me off again! Besides, your little cousin is not very strong, and we've only just managed to get her cheered up. So let's have no more of this!'

In obedience to the command Xi-feng at once exchanged her grief for merriment.

'Yes, of course. It was just that seeing my little cousin here put everything else out of my mind. It made me want to laugh and cry all at the same time. I'm afraid I quite forgot about you, Grannie dear. I deserve to be spanked, don't I?'

She grabbed Dai-yu by the hand.

'How old are you dear? Have you begun school yet? You mustn't feel homesick here. If there's anything you want to eat or anything you want to play with, just come and tell me. And you must tell me if any of the maids or the old nannies are nasty to you.'

Dai-yu made appropriate responses to all of these questions and injunctions.

Xi-feng turned to the servants.

'Have Miss Lin's things been brought in yet? How many people did she bring with her? You'd better hurry up and get a couple of rooms swept out for them to rest in.'

While Xi-feng was speaking, the servants brought in tea and various plates of food, the distribution of which she proceeded to supervise in person.

Dai-yu noticed her Aunt Wang questioning Xi-feng on the side:

'Have this month's allowances been paid out yet?'

'Yes. By the way, just now I went with some of the women to the upstairs storeroom at the back to look for that satin. We looked and looked, but we couldn't find any like the one you described yesterday. Perhaps you misremembered.'

'Oh well, if you can't find it, it doesn't really matter,' said Lady Wang. Then, after a moment's reflection, 'You'd better pick out a couple of lengths presently to have made up into clothes for your little cousin here. If you think of it, send someone round in the evening to fetch them!'

'It's already been seen to. I knew she was going to arrive within a day or two, so I had some brought out in readiness. They are waiting back at your place for your approval. If you think they are all right, they can be sent over straight away.'

Lady Wang merely smiled and nodded her head without saying anything.

The tea things and dishes were now cleared away, and Grandmother Jia ordered two old nurses to take Dai-yu round to see her uncles; but Uncle She's wife, Lady Xing, hurriedly rose to her feet and suggested that it would be more convenient if she were to take her niece round herself.

'Very well,' said Grandmother Jia. 'You go now, then. There is no need for you to come back afterwards.'

So having together with Lady Wang, who was also returning to her quarters, taken leave of the old lady, Lady Xing went off with Dai-yu, attended across the courtyard as far as the covered way by the rest of the company.

A carriage painted dark blue and hung with kingfisher-blue curtains had been drawn up in front of the ornamental gateway by some pages. Into his Aunt Xing ascended hand in hand with Dai-yu. The old women pulled down the carriage blind and ordered the pages to take up the shafts, the pages drew the carriage into an open space and harnessed mules to it, and Dai-yu and her aunt were driven out of the west gate, eastwards past the main gate of the Rong mansion, in again through a big black-lacquered gate, and up to an inner gate, where they were set down again.

Holding Dai-yu by the hand, Aunt Xing led her into a courtyard in the middle of what she imagined must once have been part of the mansion's gardens. This impression was strengthened when they passed through a third gateway into the quarters occupied by her uncle and aunt; for here the smaller scale and quiet elegance of the halls, galleries and loggias were quite unlike the heavy magnificence and imposing grandeur they had just come from, and ornamental trees and artificial rock formations, all in exquisite taste, were to be seen on every hand.

As they entered the main reception hall, a number of heavily made-up and expensively dressed maids and concubines, who had been waiting in readiness, came forward to greet them.

Aunt Xing asked Dai-yu to be seated while she sent a servant to call Uncle She. After a considerable wait the servant returned with the following message:

'The Master says he hasn't been well these last few days, and as it would only upset them both if he were to see Miss Lin now, he doesn't feel up to it for the time being. He says, tell Miss Lin not to grieve and not to feel homesick. She must think of her grandmother and her aunts as her own family now. He says that her cousins may not be very clever girls, but at least they should be company for her and help to take her mind off things. If she finds anything at all here to distress her, she is to speak up at once. She mustn't feel like an outsider. She is to make herself completely at home.'

Dai-yu stood up throughout this recital and murmured polite assent whenever assent seemed indicated. She then sat for about another quarter of an hour before rising to take her leave. Her Aunt Xing was very pressing that she should have a meal with her before she went, but Dai-yu smilingly replied that though it was very kind of her aunt to offer, and though she ought really not to refuse, nevertheless she still had to pay her respects to her Uncle Zheng, and feared that it would be disrespectful if she were to arrive late. She hoped that she might accept on another occasion and begged her aunt to excuse her.

'In that case, never mind,' said Lady Xing, and instructed the old nurses to see her to her Uncle Zheng's in the same carriage she had come by. Dai-yu formally took her leave, and Lady Xing saw her as far as the innner gate, where she issued a few more instructions to the servants and watched her niece's carriage out of sight before returning to her rooms.

Presently they re-entered the Rong mansion proper and Dai-yu got down from the carriage. There was a raised stone walk running all the way up to the main gate, along which the old nurses now conducted her. Turning right, they led her down a roofed passage-way along the back of a south-facing hall, then through an inner gate into a large courtyard.

The big building at the head of the courtyard was connected at each end to galleries running through the length of the side buildings by means of 'stag's head' roofing over the corners. The whole formed an architectural unit of greater sumptuousness and magnificence than anything Dai-yu had yet seen that day, from which she concluded that this must be the main inner hall of the whole mansion.

High overhead on the wall facing her as she entered the hall was a great blue board framed in gilded dragons, on which was written in large gold characters

THE HALL OF EXALTED FELICITY

with a column of smaller characters at the side giving a date and the words '... written for Our beloved Subject, Jia Yuan, Duke of Rong-

第六篇 《红楼梦》The Story of the Stone

guo', followed by the Emperor's private seal, a device containing the words 'kingly cares' and 'royal brush' in archaic seal-script.

    A long, high table of carved red sandalwood, ornamented with dragons, stood against the wall underneath. In the centre of this was a huge antique bronze *ding*, fully a yard high, covered with a green patina. On the wall above the *ding* hung a long vertical scroll with an ink-painting of a dragon emerging from clouds and waves, of the kind often presented to high court officials in token of their office. The *ding* was flanked on one side by a smaller antique bronze vessel with a pattern of gold inlay and on the other by a crystal bowl. At each side of the table stood a row of eight yellow cedar-wood armchairs with their backs to the wall; and above the chairs hung, one on each side, a pair of vertical ebony boards inlaid with a couplet in characters of gold:

    (on the right-hand one)
May the jewel of learning shine in this house more effulgently than the sun and moon.

    (on the left-hand one)
May the insignia of honour glitter in these halls more brilliantly than the starry sky.
This was followed by a colophon in small characters:
    With the Respectful Compliments of your Fellow-
    Student, Mu Shi, Hereditary Pince of Dong-an.
    Lady Wang did not, however, normally spend her leisure hours in this main reception hall, but in a smaller room on the east side of the same building. Accordingly the nurses conducted Dai-yu through the door into this side apartment.

    Here there was a large kang underneath the window, covered with a scarlet Kashmir rug. In the middle of the kang was a dark-red bolster with a pattern of medallions in the form of tiny dragons, and a long russet-green seating strip in the same pattern. A low rose-shaped table of coloured lacquer-work stood at each side. On the left-hand one was a small, square, four-legged *ding*, together with a bronze ladle, metal chopsticks, and an incense container. On the right-hand one was a narrow-waisted Ru-ware imiation *gu* with a spray of freshly cut flowers in it.

In the part of the room below the kang there was a row of four big chairs against the east wall. All had footstools in front of them and chair-backs and seat-covers in old rose brocade sprigged with flowers. There were also narrow side-tables on which tea things and vases of flowers were arranged, besides other furnishings which it would be superfluous to enumerate.

The old nurses invited Dai-yu to get up on the kang; but guessing that the brocade cushions arranged one on each side near the edge of it must be her uncle's and aunt's places, she deemed it more proper to sit on one of the chairs against the wall below. The maids in charge of the apartment served tea, and as she sipped it Dai-yu observed that their clothing, makeup, and deportment were quite different from those of the maids she had seen so far in other parts of the mansion.

Before she had time to finish her tea, a smiling maid came in wearing a dress of red damask and a black silk sleeveless jacket which had scalloped borders of some coloured material.

'The Mistress says will Miss Lin come over to the other side, please.'

The old nurses now led Dai-yu down the east gallery to a reception room at the side of the courtyard. This too had a kang. It was bisected by a long, low table piled with books and tea things. A much-used black satin back-rest was pushed up against the east wall. Lady Wang was seated on a black satin cushion and leaning against another comfortable-looking back-rest of black satin somewhat farther forward on the opposite side.

Seeing her niece enter, she motioned her to sit opposite her on the kang, but Dai-yu felt sure that this must be her Uncle Zheng's place. So, having observed a row of three chairs near the kang with covers of flower-sprigged brocade which looked as though they were in fairly constant use, she sat upon one of those instead. Only after much further pressing from her aunt would she get up on the kang, and even then she would only sit beside her and not in the position of honour opposite.

'Your uncle is in retreat today,' said Lady Wang. 'He will see you another time. There is, however, something I have got to talk to you about. The three girls are very well-behaved children, and in future, when you are studying or sewing together, even if once in a while they may grow a bit high-spirited, I can depend on them not to go too far. There is only one thing that worries me. I have a little monster of a son who tyrannizes over all the rest of this household. He has gone off to the temple today in fulfilment of a vow and is not yet back; but you will see what I mean this evening. The thing to do is never to take any notice of him. None of your cousins dare provoke him.'

Dai-yu had long ago been told by her mother that she had a boy cousin who was born with a piece of jade in his mouth and who was exceptionally wild and naughty. He hated study and liked to spend all his time in the women's apartments with the girls; but because Grandmother Jia doted on him so much, no one ever dared to correct him. She realized that it must be this cousin her aunt was now referring to.

'Do you mean the boy born with the jade, Aunt?' she asked. 'Mother often told me about him at home. She told me that he was

第六篇 《红楼梦》 The Story of the Stone

one year older than me and that his name was Bao-yu. But she said that though he was very wilful, he always behaved very nicely to girls. Now that I am here, I suppose I shall be spending all my time with my girl cousins and not in the same part of the house as the boys. Surely there will be no danger of *my* provoking him.'

Lady Wang gave a rueful smile. 'You little know how things are here! Bao-yu is a law unto himself. Because your grandmother is so fond of him she has thoroughly spoiled him. When he was little he lived with the girls, so with the girls he remains now. As long as they take no notice of him, things run quietly enough. But if they give him the least encouragement, he at once becomes excitable, and then there is no end to the mischief he may get up to. That is why I counsel you to ignore him. He can be all honey-sweet words one minute and ranting and raving like a lunatic the next. So don't believe anything he says.'

Dai-yu promised to follow her aunt's advice.

Just then a maid came in with a message that 'Lady Jia said it was time for dinner', whereupon Lady Wang took Dai-yu by the hand and hurried her out through a back door. Passing along a verandah which ran beneath the rear eaves of the hall they came to a corner gate through which they passed into an alley-way running north and south. At the south end it was traversed by a narrow little building with a short passage-way running through its middle. At the north end was a white-painted screen wall masking a medium-sized gateway leading to a small courtyard in which stood a very little house.

'That,' said Lady Wang, pointing to the little house, 'is where your cousin Lian's wife, Wang Xi-feng, lives, in case you want to see her later on. She is the person to talk to if there is anything you need.'

There were a few young pages at the gate of the courtyard who, when they saw Lady Wang coming, all stood to attention with their hands at their sides.

Lady Wang now led Dai-yu along a gallery, running from east to west, which brought them out into the courtyard behind Grandmother Jia's apartments. Entering these by a back entrance, they found a number of servants waiting these who, as soon as they saw Lady Wang, began to arrange the table and chairs for dinner. The ladies of the house themselves took part in the service. Li Wan brought in the cups, Xi-feng laid out the chopsticks, and Lady Wang brought in the soup.

The table at which Grandmother Jia presided, seated alone on a couch, had two empty chairs on either side. Xi-feng tried to seat Dai-yu in the one on the left nearer to her grandmother—an honour which she strenuously resisted until her grandmother explained that her aunt and her elder cousins' wives would not be eating with them, so that, since she was a guest, the place was properly hers. Only then did she ask permission to sit, as etiquette prescribed. Grandmother Jia then ordered Lady Wang to be seated. This was the cue for the three girls to ask permission to sit. Ying-chun sat in the first place on the right opposite Dai-yu, Tan-chun sat second on the left, and Xi-chun sat second on the right.

While Li Wan and Xi-feng stood by the table helping to distribute food from the dishes, maids holding fly-whisks, spittoons, and napkins ranged themselves on either side. In addition to these, there were numerous other maids and serving-women in attendance in the outer room, yet not so much as a cough was heard throughout the whole of the meal.

When they had finished eating, a maid served each diner with tea on a little tray. Dai-yu's parents had brought their daughter up to believe that good health was founded on careful habits, and in pur-

第六篇 《红楼梦》 The Story of the Stone

suance of this principle, had always insisted that after a meal one should allow a certain interval to elapse before taking tea in order to avoid indigestion. However, she could see that many of the rules in this household were different from the ones she had been used to at home; so, being anxious to conform as much as possible, she accepted the tea. But as she did so, another maid proferred a spittoon, from which she inferred that the tea was for rinsing her mouth with. And it was not, in fact, until they had all rinsed out their mouths and washed their hands that another lot of tea was served, this time for drinking.

Grandmother Jia now dismissed her lady servers, observing that she wished to enjoy a little chat with her young grandchildren without the restraint of their grown-up presence.

Lady Wang obediently rose to her feet and, after exchanging a few pleasantries, went out, taking Li Wan and Wang Xi-feng with her.

Grandmother Jia asked Dai-yu what books she was studying.

'*The Four Books*,' said Dai-yu, and inquired in turn what books her cousins were currently engaged on.

'Gracious, child, they don't study books,' said her grandmother; 'they can barely read and write!'

While they were speaking, a flurry of footsteps could be heard outside and a maid came in to say that Bao-yu was back.

'I wonder,' thought Dai-yu, 'just what sort of graceless creature this Bao-yu is going to be!'

The young gentleman who entered in answer to her unspoken question had a small jewel-encrusted gold coronet on the top of his head and a golden headband low down over his brow in the form of two dragons playing with a large pearl.

He was wearing a narrow-sleeved, full-skirted robe of dark red material with a pattern of flowers and butterflies in two shades of gold. It was confined at the waist with a court girdle of coloured silks braided at regular intervals into elaborate clusters of knotwork and terminating in long tassels.

Over the upper part of his robe he wore a jacket of slate-blue Japanese silk damask with a raised pattern of eight large medallions on the front and with tasselled borders.

On his feet he had half-length dress boots of black satin with thick white soles.

As to his person, he had:

a face like the moon of Mid-Autumn,

a complexion like flowers at dawn,

a hairline straight as a knife-cut,

eyebrows that might have been painted by an artist's brush,

a shapely nose, and

eyes clear as limpid pools,

that even in anger seemed to smile,

and, as they glared, beamed tenderness the while.

Around his neck he wore a golden torque in the likeness of a dragon and a woven cord of coloured silks to which the famous jade was attached.

Dai-yu looked at him with astonishment. How strange! How very strange! It was as though she had seen him somewhere before, he was so extraodinarily familiar. Bao-yu went straight past her and saluted his grandmother, who told him to come after he had seen his mother, whereupon he turned round and walked straight out again.

Quite soon he was back once more, this time dressed in a completely different outfit.

The crown and circlet had gone. She could now see that his side hair was dressed in a number of small braids plaited with red silk,

第六篇 《红楼梦》 The Story of the Stone

which were drawn round to join the long hair at the back in a single large queue of glistening jet black, fastened at intervals from the nape downwards with four enormous pearls and ending in a jewelled gold clasp. He had changed his robe and jacket for a rather more worn-looking rose-cloured gown, sprigged with flowers. He wore the gold torque and his jade as before, and she observed that the collection of objects round his neck had been further augmented by a padlock-shaped amulet and a lucky charm. A pair of ivy-coloured embroidered silk trousers were partially visible beneath his gown, thrust into black and white socks trimmed with brocade. In place of the formal boots he was wearing thicksoled crimson slippers.

She was even more struck than before by his fresh complexion. The cheeks might have been brushed with powder and the lips touched with rouge, so bright was their natural colour.

His glance was soulful,
 yet from his lips the laughter often leaped;
  a world of charm upon that brow was heaped;
  a world of feeling from those dark eyes peeped.

In short, his outward appearance was very fine. But appearances can be misleading. A perceptive poet has supplied two sets of verses, to be sung to the tune of *Moon On West River*, which contain a more accurate appraisal of our hero than the foregoing descriptions.

1

Oft-times he sought out what would make him sad;
Sometimes an idiot seemed and sometimes mad.
Though outwardly a handsome sausange-skin,
He proved to have but sorry meat within.
A harum-scarum, to all duty blind,
A doltish mule, to study disinclined;
His acts outlandish and his nature queer;

第六篇 《红楼梦》The Story of the Stone

Yet not a whit cared be how folk might jeer!

2

Prosperous, he could not play his part with grace,
Nor, poor, bear hardship with a smiling face.
So shamefully the precious hours he'd waste
That both indoors and out he was disgraced.
For uselessness the world's prize he might bear;
His gracelessness in history has no peer.
Let gilded youths who every dainty sample
Not imitate this rascal's dire example!

'Fancy changing your clothes before you have welcomed the visitor!' Grandmother Jia chided indulgently on seeing Bao-yu back again. 'Aren't you going to pay your respects to your cousin?'

Bao-yu had already caught sight of a slender, delicate girl whom he surmised to be his Aunt Lin's daughter and quickly went over to greet her. Then, returning to his place and taking a seat, he studied her attentively. How different she seemed from the other girls he knew!

Her mist-wreathed brows at first seemed to frown, yet were not frowing;

Her passionate eyes at first seemed to smile, yet were not merry.

Habit had given a melancholy cast to her tender face;

Nature had bestowed a sickly constitution on her delicate frame.

Often the eyes swam with glistening tears;

Often the breath came in gentle gasps.

In stillness she made one think of a graceful flower reflected in the water;

In motion she called to mind tender willow shoots caressed by the wind.

She had more chambers in her heart than the martyred Bi Gan;

第六篇 《红楼梦》 The Story of the Stone

And suffered a tithe more pain in it than the beautiful Xi Shi.

Having completed his survey, Bao-yu gave a laugh.

'I have seen this cousin before.'

'Nonsense!' said Grandomother Jia. 'How could you possibly have done?'

'Well, perhaps not,' said Bao-yu, 'but her face seems so familiar that I have the impression of meeting her again after a long separation.'

'All the better,' said Grandmother Jia. 'That means that you should get on well together.'

Bao-yu, moved over again and, drawing a chair up beside Dai-yu, recommenced his scrutiny.

Presently: 'Do you study books yet, cousin?'

'No,' said Dai-yu. 'I have only been taking lessons for a year or so. I can barely read and write.'

'What's your name?'

Dai-yu told him.

'What's your school-name?'

'I haven't got one.'

Bao-yu laughed. 'I'll give you one, cousin. I think "Frowner" would suit you perfectly.'

'Where's your reference?' said Tan-chun.

'In the *Encyclopedia of Men and Objects Ancient and Modern* it says that somewhere in the West there is a mineral called "dai" which can be used instead of eye-black for paintig the eyebrows with. She has this "dai" in her name and she knits her brows together in a little frown. I think it's a splendid name for her!'

'I expect you made it up,' said Tan-chun scornfully.

'What if I did?' said Bao-yu. 'There are lots of made-up things in books—apart from the *Four books*, of course.'

He returned to his interrogation of Dai-yu.

'Have you got a jade?'

The rest of the company were puzzled, but Dai-yu at once divined that he was asking her if she too had a jade like the one he was born with.

'No,' said Dai-yu. 'That jade of yours is a very rare object. You can't expect everybody to have one.'

This sent Bao-yu off instantly into one of his mad fits. Snatching the jade from his neck he hurled it violently on the floor as if to smash it and began abusing it passionately.

'Rare object! Rare object! What's so lucky about a stone that can't even tell which people are better than others? Beastly thing! I don't want it!'

The maids all seemed terrified and rushed forward to pick it up, while Grandmother Jia clung to Bao-yu in alarm.

'Naughty, naughty boy! Shout at someone or strike them if you like when you are in a nasty temper, but why go smashing that precious thing that your very life depends on?'

'None of the girls has got one,' said Bao-yu, his face streaming with tears and sobbing hysterically. 'Only I have got one. It always upsets me. And now this new cousin comes here who is as beautiful as an angel and she hasn't got one either, so I *know* it can't be any good.'

'Your cousin did have a jade once,' said Grandmother Jia, coaxing him like a little child, 'but because when Auntie died she couldn't bear to leave her little girl behind, they had to let her take the jade with her instead. In that way your cousin could show her mamma how much she loved her by letting the jade be buried with her; and at the same time, whenever Auntie's spirit looked at the jade, it would be just like looking at her own little girl again.'

第六篇 《红楼梦》 The Story of the Stone

'So when your cousin said she hadn't got one, it was only because she didn't want to boast about the good, kind thing she did when she gave it to her mamma. Now you put yours on again like a good boy, and mind your mother doesn't find out how naughty you have been.'

So saying, she took the jade from the hands of one of the maids and hung it round his neck for him. And Bao-yu, after reflecting for a moment or two on what she had said, offered no further resistance.

At this point some of the older woment came to inquire what room Dai-yu was to sleep in.

'Move Bao-yu into the closet-bed with me,' said Grandmother Jia, 'and put Miss Lin for the time being in the green muslin summer-bed. We had better wait until spring when the last of the cold weather is over before seeing about the rooms for them and getting them settled permanently.'

'Dearest Grannie,' said Bao-yu pleadingly, 'I should be perfectly all right next to the summer-bed. There's no need to move me into your room. I should only keep you awake.'

Grandmother Jia, after a moment's reflection, gave her consent. She further gave instructions that Dai-yu and Bao-yu were each to have one nurse and one maid to sleep with them. The rest of their servants were to do night duty by rota in the adjoining room. Xi-feng had already sent across some lilaccoloured hangings, brocade quilts, satin coverlets and the like for Dai-yu's bedding.

Dai-yu had brought only two of her own people with her from home. One was her old wet-nurse Nannie Wang, the other was a little ten-year-old maid called Snowgoose. Considering Snowgoose too young and irresponsible and Nannie Wang too old and decrepit to be of much real service, Grandmother Jia gave Dai-yu one of her own maids, a body-servant of the second grade called Nightingale. She also gave orders that Dai-yu and Bao-yu were to be attended in other respects exactly like the three girls: that is to say, apart from the one wet-nurse, each was to have four other nurses to act as chaperones, two maids as body-servants to attend to their washing, dressing, and so forth, and four or five maids for dusting and cleaning, running errands and general duties.

These arrangements completed, Nannie Wang and Nightingale accompanied Dai-yu to bed inside the tent-like summer-bed, while Bao-yu's wet-nurse Nannie Li and his chief maid Aroma settled him down for the night in a big bed on the other side of the canopy.

Like Nightingale, Aroma had previously been one of Grandmother Jia's own maids. Her real name was Pearl. Bao-yu's grandmother, fearful that the maids who already waited on her darling boy could not be trusted to look after him properly, had picked out Pearl as a girl of tried and conpicuous fidelity and put her in charge over them. It was Bao-yu who was responsible for the curious name 'Aroma'. Discovering that Pearl's surname was Hua, which means 'Flowers', and having recently come across the line

The flowers' aroma breathes of hotter days

in a book of poems, he told his grandmother that he wanted to call his new maid 'Aroma', so 'Aroma' her name thenceforth became.

Aroma had a certain dogged streak in her nature which had made her utterly devoted to Grandmother Jia as long as she was Grandmother Jia's servant, but which caused her to become just as exclusively and single-mindedly devoted to Bao-yu when her services were transferred to him. Since she found his character strange and incomprehensible, her simple devotion frequently impelled her to remonstrate with him, and when, as invariably happened, he took not the least notice of what she said, she was worried and hurt.

That night, when Bao-yu and Nannie Li were already asleep,

《红楼梦》 The Story of the Stone

Aroma could hear that Dai-yu and Nightingale on their side of the canopy had still not settled down, so, when she had finished taking down her hair and making herself ready for bed, she tiptoed through the muslin curtains and in a friendly way inquired what was the matter. Dai-yu invited her to sit down, and when she had seated herself on the edge of the bed, Nightingale proceeded to tell her what was troubling her new mistress.

'Miss Lin is all upset. She has just been crying her eyes out because she says she only just arrived here today, and yet already she has started young hopeful off on one of his turns. She says if that jade had been really smashed, it would have been all her fault. That's what she's so upset about. I've had no end of a job trying to comfort her.'

'You musn't take on so, Miss,' said Aroma. 'You'll see him do much stranger things than that before he's finished. If you allow yourself to feel hurt every time he carries on like that, he will always be hurting you. Try not to be so sensitive, Miss!'

Dai-yu thanked her and promised to bear in mind what she had said, and after talking a little longer, they all settled down and went to sleep.

*

Rising early next day, they visited Grandmother Jia to wish her a good morning and then went over to Lady Wang's. They found her closeted with Wang Xi-feng, deep in discussion of a letter which had just arrived from Nanking, and attended by two women who had come with a message from Lady Wang's elder brother and sister-in-law. Tan-chun and the girls told Dai-yu, who knew nothing of the matter under discussion, that they were talking about Xue Pan, the son of their Aunt Xue who lived in Nanking.

It seemed that Xue Pan, relying on wealth and family pull to protect him from the consequences, had taken another man's life. The case was at present under investigation by the Yingtian-fu yamen. Their uncle Wang Zi-teng had been informed of it, and had sent these messengers to the members of the family in the Rong mansion to suggest that they should invite Xue Pan to the capital.

But the outcome of this discussion will be dealt with in the following chapter.

第六篇 《红楼梦》 The Story of the Stone

The Dream of Red Mansion(Excerpt)

Translated by Yang Xianyi and Gladys Yang

CHAPTER 3

Lin Ju-hai Recommends a Tutor to His
Brother-in-Law
The Lady Dowager Sends for Her Motherless
Grand-Daughter

To continue. Yu-tsun turned and saw that it was Chang Ju-kuei, a native of this place and his former colleague who had also been dismissed from his post for the same reason as himself, and had returned home to Yangchow. Now there was word from the capital that a request for the reinstatement of former officials had been sanctioned, and he was busily pulling strings to find some opening. He congratulated Yu-tsun the instant he saw him and lost no time, once greetings had been exchanged, in telling him the good news. Yu-tsun was naturally overjoyed, but after some hurried remarks each went his own way.

Leng Tzu-hsing, who had heard everything, at once proposed asking Lin Ju-hai to enlist the support of Chia Cheng in the capital. Accepting his advice, Yu-tsun went back alone to verify the report from the *Court Gazette*.

The next day he laid his case before Lin Ju-hai.

"What a lucky coincidence!" exclaimed Ju-hai. "Since my wife's death my mother-in-law in the capital has been worried because my daughter has no one to bring her up. She has sent two boats with male and female attendants to fetch the child, but I delayed her departure while she was unwell. I was wondering how to repay you for your goodness in teaching her; now this gives me a chance to show my appreciation. Set your mind at rest. I foresaw this possibility and have written a letter to my brother-in-law urging him to do all he can for you as a small return for what I owe you. You mustn't worry either about any expenses that may be incurred—I've made that point clear to my brother-in-law."

Yu-tsun bowed with profuse thanks and asked: "May I know your respected brother-in-law's position? I fear I am too uncouth to intrude on him."

Ju-hai smiled. "My humble kinsmen belong to your honourable clan. They're the grandsons of the Duke of Jungkuo. My elder brother-in-law Chia Sheh, whose courtesy name is En-hou, is a hereditary general of the first rank. My second, Chia Cheng, whose courtesy name is Tusn-chou, is an undersecretary in the Board of Works. He is an unassuming, generous man who takes after his grandfather. That is why I am writing to him on your behalf. If he were some purse-proud, frivolous official, I'd be dishonouring your high principles, brother, and I myself would disdain to do such a thing."

This confirmed what Tzu-hsing had said the previous day, and once more Yu-tsun expressed his thanks.

"I've chosen the second day of next month for my daughter's departure for the capital," continued Ju-hai. "It would suit both parties, surely, if you were to travel together?"

Yu-tsun promptly agreed with the greatest satisfaction, and took the gifts and travelling expenses which Ju-hai had prepared.

第六篇 《红楼梦》 The Story of the Stone

His pupil Tai-ju, who had just got over illness, could hardly bear to leave her father, but she had to comply with the wishes of her grandmother.

"I am nearly fifty and don't intend to marry again," Ju-hai told her. "You're young and delicate, with no mother to take care of you, no sisters or brothers to look after you. If you go to stay with your grandmother and uncles' girls, that will take a great load off my mind. How can you refuse?"

So parting from him in a flood of tears, she embarked with her nurse and some elderly maid-servants from the Jung Mansion, followed by Yu-tsun and two pages in another junk.

In due course they reached the capital and entered the city. Yu-tsun spruced himself up and went with his pages to the gate of the Jung Mansion, where he handed in his visiting-card on which he had styled himself Chia Chen's "nephew."

Chia Cheng, who had received his brother-in-law's letter, lost no time in asking him in. Yu-tsun cut an impressive figure and was by no means vulgar in his conversation. Since Chia Cheng was well-disposed to scholars and, like his grandfather before him, delighted in honouring worthy men of letters and helping those in distress, and since moreover his brother-in-law had recommended Yu-tsun, he treated him uncommonly well and did all in his power to help him. The same day that he presented a petition to the throne Yu-tsun was rehabilitated and ordered to await an appointmtent. In less than two months he was sent to Chinling to fill the vacated post of prefect of Yingtien①. Taking leave of Chia Cheng he chose a day to proceed to his new post. But no more of this.

To return to Tai-yu. When she disembarked, a sedan-chair from

---

① Another name for Nanking.

the Jung Mansion and carts for her luggage were waiting in readiness. She had heard a great deal from her mother about the magnificence of her grandmother's home; and during the last few days she had been impressed by the food, costumes and behaviour of the relatively low-ranking attendants escorting her. She must watch her step in her new home, she decided, be on guard every moment and weigh every word, so as not to be laughed at for any foolish blunder. As she was carried into the city she peeped out through the gauze window of the chair at the bustle in the streets and the crowds of people, the like of which she had never seen before.

After what seemed a long time they came to a street with two huge stone lions crouching on the north side, flanking a great triple gate with beast-head knockers, in front of which ten or more men in smart livery were sitting. The central gate was shut, but people were passing in and out of the smaller side gates. On a board above the main gate was written in large characters: Ningkuo Mansion Built at Imperial Command.

Tai-yu realized that this must be where the elder branch of her grandmother's family lived.

A little further to the west they came to another imposing triple gate. This was the Jung Mansion. Instead of going through the main gate, they entered by the smaller one on the west. The bearers carried the chair a bow-shot further, then set it down at a turning and withdrew. The maid-servants behind Tai-yu had now alighted and were proceeding on foot. Three or four smartly dressed lads of seventeen or eighteen picked up the chair and, followed by the maids, carried it to a gate decorated with overhanging flowery patterns carved in wood. There the bearers withdrew, the maids raised the curtain of the chair, helped Tai-yu out and supported her through the gate.

Inside, verandahs on both sides led to a three-roomed entrance

第六篇 《红楼梦》 The Story of the Stone

hall in the middle of which stood a screen of marble in a red sandalwood frame. The hall gave access to the large court of the main building. In front were five rooms with carved beams and painted pillars, and on either side were rooms with covered passageways. Cages of brilliantly coloured parrots, thrushes and other birds hung under the eaves of the verandahs.

Several maids dressed in red and green rose from the terrace and hurried to greet them with smiles.

"The old lady was just talking about you," they cried. "And here you are."

Three or four of them ran to raise the door curtain, and a voice could be heard announcing, "Miss Lin is here."

As Tai-yu entered, a silver-haired old lady supported by two maids advanced to meet her. She knew that this must be her grandmother, but before she could kowtow the old lady threw both arms around her.

"Dear heart! Flesh of my child!" she cried, and burst out sobbing.

All the attendants covered their faces and wept, and Tai-yu herself could not keep back her tears. When at last the others prevailed on her to stop, Tai-yu made her kowtow to her grandmother. This was the Lady Dowager from the Shih family mentioned by Leng Tzu-hsing, the mother of Chia Sheh and Chia Cheng, who now introduced the family one by one.

"This," she said, "is your elder uncle's wife. This is your second uncle's wife. This is the wife of your late Cousin Chu."

Tai-yu greeted each in turn.

"Fetch the girls," her grandmother said. "They can be excused their lessons today in honour of our guest from far away."

Two maids went to carry out her orders. And presently the three young ladies appeared, escorted by three nurses and five or six maids.

The first was somewhat plump and of medium height. Her cheeks were the texture of newly ripened lichees, her nose as sleek as goose fat. Gentle and demure, she looked very approachable.

The second had sloping shoulders and a slender waist. She was tall and slim, with an oval face, well-defined eyebrows and lovely dancing eyes. She seemed elegant and quick-witted with an air of distinction. To look at her was to forget everything vulgar.

The third was not yet fully grown and still had the face of a child.

All three were dressed in similar tunics and skirts with the same bracelets and head ornaments.

Tai-yu hastily rose to greet these cousins, and after the introductions they took seats while the maids served tea. All the talk now was of Tai-yu's mother. How had she fallen ill? What medicine had the doctors prescribed? How had the funeral and mourning ceremonies been conducted? Inevitably, the Lady Dowager was most painfully affected.

"Of all my children I loved your mother best," she told Tai-yu. "Now she has gone before me, and I didn't even have one last glimpse of her face. The sight of you makes me feel my heart will break!" Again she took Tai-yu in her arms and wept. The others were hard put to it to comfort her.

All present had been struck by Tai-yu's good breeding. For in spite of her tender years and evident delicate health, she had an air of natural distinction. Observing how frail she looked, they asked what medicine or treatment she had been having.

"I've always been like this," Tai-yu said with a smile. "I've been taking medicine ever since I was weaned. Many wellknown doctors

第六篇 《红楼梦》 The Story of the Stone

have examined me, but none of their prescriptions was any use. The year I was three, I remember being told, a scabby monk came to our house and wanted to take me away to be a nun. My parents wouldn't hear of it. The monk said, 'If you can't bear to part with her she'll probably never get well. The only other remedy is to keep her from hearing weeping and from seeing any relatives apart from her father and mother. That's her only hope of having a quiet life.' No one paid any attention, of course, to such crazy talk. Now I'm still taking ginseng pills."

"That's good," approved the Lady Dowager. "We're having pills made, and I'll see they make some for you."

Just then they heard peals of laughter from the back courtyard and a voice cried:

"I'm late in greeting our guest from afar!"

Tai-yu thought with surprise, "The people here are so respectful and solemn, they all seem to be holding their breath. Who can this be, so boisterous and pert?"

While she was still wondering, through the back door trooped some matrons and maids surrounding a young woman. Unlike the girls, she was richly dressed and resplendent as a fairy.

Her gold-filigree tiara was set with jewels and pearls. Her hair-clasps, in the form of five phoenixes facing the sun, had pendants of pearls. Her necklet, of red gold, was in the form of a coiled dragon studded with gems. She had double red jade pendants with pea-green tassels attached to her skirt.

Her close-fitting red satin jacket was embroidered with gold butterflies and flowers. Her turquoise cape, lined with white squirrel, was inset with designs in coloured silk. Her skirt of kingfisher-blue crepe was patterned with flowers.

She had the almond-shaped eyes of a phoenix, slanting eyebrows as long and drooping as willow leaves. Her figure was slender and her manner vivacious. The springtime charm of her powdered face gave no hint of her latent formidability. And before her crimson lips parted, her laughter rang out.

Tai-yu rose quickly to greet her.

"You don't know her yet." The Lady Dowager chuckled. "She's the terror of this house. In the south they'd call her Hot Pepper. Just call her Fiery Phoenix."

Tai-yu was at a loss how to address her when her cousins came to her rescue. "This is Cousin Lien's wife," they told her.

Though Tai-yu had never met her, she knew from her mother that Chia Lien, the son of her first uncle Chia Sheh, had married the niece of Lady Wang, her second uncle's wife. She had been educated like a boy and given the school-room name Hsi-feng. ① Tai-yu lost no time in greeting her with a smile as "cousin."

Hsi-feng took her hand and carefully inspected her from head to foot, then led her back to her seat by the Lady Dowager.

"Well," she cried with a laugh, "this is the first time I've set eyes on such a ravishing beauty. Her whole air is so distinguished! She doesn't take after her father, son-in-law of our Old Ancestress, but looks more like a Chia. No wonder our Old Ancestress couldn't put you out of her mind and was for ever talking or thinking about you. But poor ill-fated little cousin, losing your mother so young!" With that she dabbed her eyes with a handkerchief.

"I've only just dried my tears. Do you want to start me off again?" said the old lady playfully. "Your young cousin's had a long journey and she's delicate. We've just got her to stop crying. So don't reopen that subject."

---

① Splendid Phoenix.

第六篇 《红楼梦》 The Story of the Stone

Hsi-feng switched at once from grief to merriment. "Of course," she cried. "I was so carried away by joy and sorrow at sight of my little cousin, I forgot our Old Ancestress. I deserve to be caned." Taking Tai-yu's hand again, she asked, "How old are you, cousin? Have you started your schooling yet? What medicine are you taking? You mustn't be home sick here. If you fancy anything special to eat or play with, don't hesitate to tell me. If the maids or old nurses aren't good to you, just let me know."

She turned then to the servants. "Have Miss Lin's luggage and things been brought in? How many attendants did she bring? Hurry up and clear out a couple of rooms where they can rest."

Meanwhile refreshments had been served. And as Hsi-feng handed round the tea and sweetmeats, Lady Wang asked whether she had distributed the monthly allowance.

"It's finished," was Hsi-feng's answer. "Just now I took some people to the upstairs storeroom at the back to look for some brocade. But though we searched for a long time we couldn't find any of the sort you described to us yesterday, madam. Could your memory have played you a trick?"

"It doesn't matter if there's none of that sort," said Lady Wang. "Just choose two lengths to make your little cousin some clothes. This evening don't forget to send for them."

"I've already done that," replied Hsi-feng. "Knowing my cousin would be here any day, I got everything ready. The material's waiting in your place for your inspection. If you pass it, madam, it can be sent over."

Lady Wang smiled and nodded her approval.

Now the refreshments were cleared away and the Lady Dowager ordered two nurses to take Tai-yu to see her two uncles.

At once Chia Sheh's wife, Lady Hsing, rose to her feet and suggested, "Won't it be simpler if I take my niece?"

"Very well," agreed the Lady Dowager. "And there's no need for you to come back afterwards."

Lady Hsing assented and then told Tai-yu take her leave of Lady Wang, after which the rest saw them to the entrance hall. Outside the ornamental gate pages were waiting beside a blue lacquered carriage with kingfisher-blue curtains, into which Lady Hsing and her niece entered. Maids let down the curtains and told the bearers to start. They bore the carriage to an open space and harnessed a docile mule to it. They left by the west side gate, proceeded east past the main entrance of the Jung Mansion, entered a large black-lacquered gate and drew up in front of a ceremonial gate.

When the pages had withdrawn, the curtains were raised, and Lady Hsing led Tai-yu into the courtyard. It seemed to her that these buildings and grounds must be part of the Jung Mansion garden; for when they had passed three ceremonial gates she saw that the halls, side chambers and covered corridors although on a smaller scale were finely constructed. They had not the stately splendour of the other mansion, yet nothing was lacking in the way of trees, plants or artificial rockeries.

As they entered the central hall they were greeted by a crowd of heavily made-up and richly dressed concubines and maids. Lady Hsing invited Tai-yu to be seated while she sent a servant to the library to ask her husband to join them.

After a while the servant came back to report, "The master says he hasn't been feeling too well the last few days, and meeting the young lady would only upset them both. He isn't up to it for the time being. Miss Lin mustn't mope or be homesick here but feel at home with the old lady and her aunts. Her cousins may be silly creatures, but they'll be company for her and help to amuse her. If anyone is unkind to her, she must say so and not treat us as strangers."

Tai-yu had risen to her feet to listen to this message. Shortly after this she rose again to take her leave. Lady Hsing insisted that she stay for the evening meal.

"Thank you very much, aunt, you're too kind," said Tai-yu. "Really I shouldn't decline. But it might look rude if I delayed in calling on my second uncle. Please excuse me and let me stay another time."

"You're quite right," said Lady Hsing. She told a few elderly maids to escort her niece back in the same carriage, whereupon Tai-yu took her leave. Her aunt saw her to the ceremonial gate and after giving the maids some further instructions waited to see them off.

Back in the Jung Mansion, Tai-yu alighted again. The nurse led her eastwards, round a corner, through an entrance hall into a hall facing south, then passed through a ceremonial gate into a large courtyard. The northern building had five large apartments and wings on either side. This was the hub of the whole estate, more imposing by far than the Lady Dowager's quarters.

Tai-yu realized that this was the main inner suite, for a broad raised avenue led straight to its gate. Once inside the hall she looked up and her eye was caught by a great blue tablet with nine gold dragons on it, on which was written in characters large as peck measures:

Hall of Glorious Felicity.

Smaller characters at the end recorded the date on which the Emperor had conferred this tablet upon Chia Yuan, the Duke of Jungkuo, and it bore the Imperial seal.

On the large red sandalwood table carved with dragons an old bronze tripod, green with patina, stood about three feet high. On the wall hung a large scroll-picture of black dragons riding the waves. This was flanked by a bronze wine vessel inlaid with gold and a crystal bowl. By the walls were a row of sixteen cedar-wood armchairs; and above these hung two panels of ebony with the following couplet inset in silver:

> Pearls on the dais outshine the sun and moon;
> Insignia of honour in the hall blaze like
> iridescent clouds.

Small characters below recorded that this had been written by the Prince of Tungan, who signed his name Mu Shih and styled himself a fellow provincial and old family friend.

Since Lady Wang seldom sat in this main hall but used three rooms on the east side for relaxation, the nurses led Tai-yu there.

The large *kang* by the window was covered with a scarlet foreign rug. In the middle were red back-rests and turquoise bolsters, both with dragon-design medallions, and a long greenish yellow mattress also with dragon medallions. At each side stood a low table of foreign lacquer in the shape of plumblossom. On the left-hand table were a tripod, spoons, chopsticks and an incense container; on the right one, a slenderwaisted porcelain vase from the Juchow Kiln containing flowers then in season, as well as tea-bowls and a spittoon. Below the *kang* facing the west wall were four armchairs, their covers of bright red dotted with pink flowers, and with four footstools beneath them. On either side were two tables set out with teacups and vases of flowers. The rest of the room need not be described in detail.

The nurses urged Tai-yu to sit on the *kang*, on the edge of which were two brocade cushions. But feeling that this would be presumptuous, she sat instead on one of the chairs on the east side. The maids in attendance served tea, and as she sipped it she studied them, observing that their make-up, clothes and deportment were quite different from those in other families. Before she had finished her tea in came a maid wearing a red silk coat and a blue satin sleeveless jacket

第六篇 《红楼梦》 The Story of the Stone

with silk borders. With a smile this girl announced:

"Her Ladyship asks Miss Lin to go in and take a seat over there."

At once the nurses conducted Tai-yu along the eastern corridor to a small three-roomed suite facing south. On the *kang* under the window was a low table laden with books and a tea-sevice. Against the east wall were a none too new blue satin back-rest and a bolster.

Lady Wang was sitting in the lower place by the west wall on a none too new blue satin cover with a back-rest and a bolster. She invited her niece to take the seat on the east. But guessing that this was Chia Cheng's place, Tai-yu chose one of the three chair next to the kang, which had blackdotted antimacassars, looking none too new. Not until she had been pressed several times did she take a seat by her aunt.

"Your uncle's observing a fast today," said Lady Wang. "You'll see him some other time. But there's one thing I want to tell you. Your three cousins are excellent girls, and I'm sure you'll find them easy to get on with during lessons, or when you're learning embroidery or playing together. Just one thing worries me: that's my dreadful son, the bane of my life, who torments us all in this house like a real devil. He's gone to a temple today in fulfilment of a vow, but you'll see what he's like when he comes back this evening. Just pay no attention to him. None of your cousins dare to provoke him."

Tai-yu's mother had often spoken of this nephew born with a piece of jade in his mouth, his wild ways, aversion to study and delight in playing about in the women's apartments. Apparently he was so spoiled by his grandmother that no one could control him. She knew Lady Wang must be referring to him.

"Does aunt mean my elder cousin with the jade in his mouth?" she asked with a smile. "Mother often spoke of him. I know he's a

第六篇 《红楼梦》The Story of the Stone

year older than me, his name is Pao-yu, and for all his pranks he's very good to his girl cousins. But how can I provoke him? I'll be spending all my time with the other girls in a different part of the house while our boy cousins are in the outer courtyards."

"You don't understand," replied Lady Wang with a laugh. "He's not like other boys. Because the old lady's always doted on him, he's used to being spoilt with the girls. If they ignore him he keeps fairly quiet though he feels bored. He can always work off his temper by scolding some of his pages. But if the girls give him the least encouragement, he's so elated he gets up to all kinds of mischief. That's why you mustn't pay any attention to him. One moment he's all honey-sweet; the next, he's rude and recalcitrant; and in another minute he's raving like a lunatic. You can't take him seriously."

As Tai-yu promised to remember this, a maid announced that dinner was to be served in the Lady Dowager's apartments. Lady Wang at once led her niece out of the back door, going west along a corridor and through a side gate to a broad road running from north to south. On the south side was a dainty three-roomed annex facing north; on the north a big screen wall painted white, behind which was a small door leading to an apartment.

"That's where your cousin Hsi-feng lives." Lady Wang pointed out the place. "So next time you know where to find her. If you want anything just let her know."

By the gate several young pages, their hair in tufts, stood at attention. Lady Wang led Tai-yu through an entrance hall running from east to west into the Lady Dowager's back courtyard. Stepping through the back door, they found quite a crowd assembled who, as soon as they saw Lady Wang, set tables and chairs ready. Chia Chu's widow, Li Wan, served the rice while Hsi-feng put out the chopsticks

第六篇 《红楼梦》 The Story of the Stone

and Lady Wang served the soup.

The Lady Dowager was seated alone on a couch at the head of the table with two empty chairs on each side. Hsi-feng took Tai-yu by the hand to make her sit in the first place on the left, but she persistently declined the honour.

"Your aunt and sisters-in-law don't dine here," said her grandmother with a smile. "Besides, you're a guest today. So do take that seat."

With a murmured apology, Tai-yu obeyed. The Lady Dowager told Lady Wang to sit down; then Ying-chun and the two other girls asked leave to be seated. Ying-chun first on the right, Tan-chun second on the left, and Hsi-chun second on the right. Maids held ready dusters, bowls for rinsing the mouth and napkins, while Li Wan and Hsi-feng standing behind the diners plied them with food.

Although the outer room swarmed with nurses and maids, not so much as a cough was heard. The meal was eaten in silence. And immediately after, tea was brought in on small trays. Now Lin Ju-hai had taught his daughter the virtue of moderation and the harm caused to the digestive system by drinking tea directly after a meal. But many customs here were different from those in her home. She would have to adapt herself to these new ways. As she took the tea, however, the rinse-bowls were proffered again, and seeing the others rinse their mouths she followed suit. After they had washed their hands tea was served once more, this time for drinking.

"You others may go," said the Lady Dowager now. "I want to have a chat with my grand-daughter."

Lady Wang promptly rose and after a few remarks led the way out, followed by Li Wan and Hsi-feng. Then her grandmother asked Tai-yu what books she had studied.

'I've just finished the *Four Books*,' said Tai-yu. "But I'm very ignorant." Then she inquired what the other girls were reading.

"They only know a very few characters, not enough to read any books."

The words were hardly out of her mouth when they heard footsteps in the courtyard and a maid came in to announce, "Pao-yu is here."

Tai-yu was wondering what sort of graceless scamp or little dunce Pao-yu was and feeling reluctant to meet such a stupid creature when, even as the maid announced him, in he walked.

He had on a golden coronet studded with jewels and a golden chaplet in the form of two dragons fighting for a pearl. His red archer's jacket, embroidered with golden buttterflies and flowers, was tied with a coloured tasselled palace sash. Over this he wore a turquoise fringed coat of Japanese satin with a raised pattern of flowers in eight bunches. His court boots were of black satin with white soles.

His face was as radiant as the mid-autumn moon, his complexion fresh as spring flowers at dawn. The hair above his temples was as sharply outlined as if cut with a knife. His eyebrows were as black as if painted with ink, his cheeks as red as peach-blossom, his eyes bright as autumn ripples. Even when angry he seemed to smile, and there was warmth in his glance even when he frowned.

Round his neck he had a golden torque in the likeness of a dragon, and a silk cord of five colours, on which hung a beautiful piece of jade.

His appearance took Tai-yu by surprise. "How very strange!" she thought. "It's as if I'd seen him somewhere before. He looks so familiar."

Pao-yu paid his respects to the Lady Dowager and upon her instructions went to see his mother.

第六篇 《红楼梦》 The Story of the Stone

He returned before long, having changed his clothes. His short hair in small plaits tied with red silk was drawn up on the crown of his head and braided into one thick queue as black and glossy as lacquer, sporting four large pearls attached to golden pendants in the form of the eight precious things. His coat of a flower pattern on a bright red ground was not new, and he still wore the torque, the precious jade, a lockshaped amulet containing his Buddhistic name, and a lucky charm. Below could be glimpsed light green flowered satin trousers, black-dotted stockings with brocade borders, and thick-soled scarlet shoes.

His face looked as fair as if powdered, his lips red as rouge. His glance was full of affection, his speech interspersed with smiles. But his natural charm appeared most in his brows, for his eyes sparkled with a world of feeling. However, winning as his appearance was, it was difficult to tell what lay beneath.

Someone subsequently gave an admirable picture of Pao-yu in these two verses written to the melody of *The Moon over the West River*:

> Absurdly he courts care and melancholy
> And raves like any madman in his folly;
> For though endowed with handsome looks is he,
> His heart is lawless and refractory.
> Too dense by far to understand his duty,
> Too stubborn to apply himself to study,
> Foolhardy in his eccentricity,
> He's deaf to all reproach and obloquy.
> Left cold by riches and nobility,
> Unfit to bear the stings of poverty,
> He wastes his time and his ability,
> Failing his country and his family.

第六篇 《红楼梦》The Story of the Stone

> First in this world for uselessness is he,
> Second to none in his deficiency.
> Young fops and lordlings all, be warned by me:
> Don't imitate this youth's perversity!

With a smile at Pao-yu, the Lady Dowager scolded, "Fancy changing your clothes before greeting our visitor. Hurry up now and pay your respects to your cousin."

Of course, Pao-yu had seen this new cousin earlier on and guessed that she was the daughter of his Aunt Lin. He made haste to bow and, having greated her, took a seat. Looking at Tai-yu closely, he found her different from other girls.

Her dusky arched eyebrows were knitted and yet not frowning, her speaking eyes held both merriment and sorrow; her very frailty had charm. Her eyes sparkled with tears, her very frailty had charm. Her eyes sparkled with tears, her breath was soft and faint. In repose she was like a lovely flower mirrored in the water; in motion, a pliant willow swaying in the wind. She looked more sensitive than Pi Kan①, more delicate than Hsi Shih②.

"I've met this cousin before," he declared at the end of his scrutiny.

"You're talking nonsense again," said his grandmother, laughing. "How could you possibly have met her?"

"Well, even if I haven't, her face looks familiar. I feel we're old friends meeting again after a long separation."

"So much the better." The Lady Dowager laughed. "That means you're bound to be good friends."

Pao-yu went over to sit beside Tai-yu and once more gazed fixed-

---

① A prince noted for his great intelligence at the end of the Shang Dynasty.
② A famous beauty of the ancient Kingdom of Yueh.

第六篇 《红楼梦》 The Story of the Stone

ly at her.

"Have you done much reading, cousin?" he asked.

"No," said Tai-yu, "I've only studied for a couple of years and learned a few characters."

"What's your name?"

She told him.

"And your courtesy name?"

"I have none."

"I'll give you one then," he proposed with a chuckle. "What could be better than Pin-pin?"①

"Where's that from?" put in Tan-chun.

"*The Compendium of Men and Object Old and New* says that in the west is a stone called *tai* which can be used instead of graphite for painting eyebrows. As Cousin Lin's eyebrows look half knit, what could be more apt than these two characters?"

"You're making that up, I'm afraid," teased Tan-chun.

"Most works, apart from the *Four Books*, are made up; am I the only one who makes things up?" he retorted with a grin. Then, to the mystification of them all, he asked Tai-yu if she had any jade.

Imagining that he had his own jade in mind, she answered, "No, I haven't. I suppose it's too rare for everybody to have."

This instantly threw Pao-yu into one of his frenzies. Tearing off the jade he flung it on the ground.

"What's rare about it?" he stormed. "It can't even tell good people from bad. What spiritual understanding has it got? I don't want this nuisance either."

In consternation all the maids rushed forward to pick up the jade while the Lady Dowager in desperation took Pao-yu in her arms.

---

① Knitted Brows.

"You wicked monster!" she scolded. "Storm at people if you're in a passion. But why should you throw away that precious thing your life depends on?"

His face stained with tears, Pao-yu sobbed, "None of the girls here has one, only me. What's the fun of that? Even this newly arrived cousin who's lovely as a fairy hasn't got one either. That shows it's no good."

"She did have one once," said the old lady to soothe him. "But when your aunt was dying and was unwilling to leave her, the best she could do was to take the jade with her instead. That was like burying the living with the dead and showed your cousin's filial piety. It meant, too, that now your aunt's spirit can still see your cousin. That's why she said she had none, not wanting to boast about it. How can you compare with her? Now put it carefully on again lest your mother hears about this."

She took the jade from one of the maids and put it on him herself. And Pao-yu, convinced by her tale, let the matter drop.

Just then a nurse came in to ask about Tai-yu's quarters.

"Move Pao-yu into the inner apartment of my suite," said his grandmother. "Miss Lin can stay for the time being in his Green Gauze Lodge. Once spring comes, we'll make different arrangements."

"Dear Ancestress!" coaxed Pao-yu. "Let me stay outside Green Gauze Lodge. I'll do very well on that bed in the outer room. Why should I move over and disturb you?"

After a moment's reflection the Lady Dowager agreed to this. Each would be attended by a nurse and a maid, while other attendants were on night duty outside. Hsi-feng had already sent round a flowered lavender curtain, satin quilts and embroidered mattresses.

Tai-yu had brought with her only Nanny Wang, her old wet-

第六篇 《红楼梦》 The Story of the Stone

nurse, and ten-year-old Hsueh-yen, who had also attended her since she was a child. Since the Lady Dowager considered Hsueh-yen too young and childish and Nanny Wang too old to be of much service, she gave Tai-yu one of her own personal attendants, a maid of the second grade called Ying-ko. Like Ying-chun and the other young ladies, in addition to her own wet-nurse Tai-yu was given four other nurses as chaperones, two personal maids to attend to her toilet and five or six girls to sweep the rooms and run errands.

Nanny Wang and Ying-ko accompanied Tai-yu now to Green Gauze Lodge, while Pao-yu's wet-nurse, Nanny Li, and his chief maid Hsi-jen made ready the big bed for him in its outer room.

Hsi-jen, whose original name was Chen-chu, had been one of the Lady Dowager's maids. The old Lady so doted on her grandson that she wanted to make sure he was well looked after and for this reason she gave him her favourite, Hsi-jen, a good, conscientious girl. Pao-yu knew that the her surname was Hua① and remembered a line of poetry which ran, "the fragrance of flowers assails men," So he asked his grandmother's permission to change her name to Hsi-jen②.

Hsi-jen's strong point was devotion. Looking after the Lady Dowager she thought of no one but the Lady Dowager, and after being assigned to Pao-yu she thought only of Pao-yu. What worried her, though, was that he was too headstrong to listen to her advice.

That night after Pao-yu and Nanny Li were asleep, Hsi-jen noticed that Tai-yu and Ying-ko were still up in the inner room. She tiptoed in there in her night clothes and asked:

"Why aren't you sleeping yet, miss?"

"Please sit down, sister," invited Tai-yu with a smile.

---

① Flower.
② Literally "assails men."

Hsi-jen sat on the edge of the bed.

"Miss Lin has been in tears all this time, she's so upset," said Ying-ko. "The very day of her arrival, she says, she's made our young master fly into a tantrum. If he'd smashed his jade she would have felt to blame. I've been trying to comfort her."

"Don't take it to heart," said Hsi-jen. "I'm afraid you'll see him carrying on even more absurdly later. If you let yourself be upset by his behaviour you'll never have a moment's peace. Don't be so sensitive."

"I'll remember what you've said," promised Tai yu. "But can you tell me where that jade of his came from, and what the inscription on it is?"

Hsi-jen told her, "Not a soul in the whole family knows where it comes from. It was found in his mouth, so we hear, when he was born, with a hole for a cord already made in it. Let me fetch it here to show you."

But Tai-yu would not hear of this as it was now late. "I can look at it tomorrow," she said.

After a little more chat they went to bed.

The next morning, after paying her respects to the Lady Dowager, Tai-yu went to Lady Wang's apartments. She found her and Hsi-feng discussing a letter from Chinling. With them were two maid-servants who had brought a message from the house of Lady Wang's brother.

Tai-yu did not understand what was going on, but Tan-chun and the others knew that they were discussing Hsueh Pan, the son of Aunt Hsueh in Chinling. Presuming on his powerful connections, he had had a man beaten to death and was now to be tried in the Yingtien prefectural court. Lady Wang's brother Wang Tzu-teng, having

第六篇 《红楼梦》 The Story of the Stone

been informed of this, had sent these messengers to the Jung Mansion to urge them to invite the Hsueh family to the capital. But more of this in the next chapter.

第七篇 《水浒传》三种英译本之比较鉴赏

张 怡

《水浒传》是中国古典小说"四大奇书"之一,作者施耐庵是元末明初小说家。这一鸿篇巨制流传至今已有四五百年的历史了,其间它曾数次被译成外国文字,以飨外国读者,并受到广泛好评。现今笔者从中选出三种影响较大的英译本,试对它们进行比较,以帮助读者鉴赏这一古典名著的翻译。这三种译本分别是:*All Men Are Brothers*,由赛珍珠(Pearl S. Buck)翻译(以下简称赛译);*Water Margin*,由杰克逊(J. H. Jackson)翻译(以下简称杰译);Outlaws Of The Marsh,译者是沙博理(Sidney Shapiro)(以下简称沙译)。

第一位译者赛珍珠(1892—1973)是大家都比较熟悉的一位美国女作家,1935年诺贝尔文学奖获得者。她出生于西弗吉尼亚州的一个传教士家庭。小时候随父母到中国,身受中国古老文化的熏陶,被人誉为"中国通"。可是她了解中国并不深刻,仅能描写中国旧社会的个别现象,不能触及社会问题的实质。鲁迅评价她时说,她只了解"一点浮面的情况,只有我们做起来,方够留下一个真相。"对于她翻译的《水浒传》,鲁迅也有非议,认为她把书名意译为《皆兄弟也》,"便不确,因为梁山泊中人,是并不将一切人都作兄弟看的。"第二位译者杰克逊把书名直接译为"Water Margin(水泮)",可以说是字对字的直译了。《现代汉语大词典》(王同亿编)将"浒"释义为"水边,水岸",杰克逊用"Margin"来译"浒",可能是要作到绝对地忠实于原文吧!但是译文读者则必须在读过译本全书后,才会真正明白"Water Margin"原来是用地方代指一群集结于此地的"不法之徒"。第三位译者沙博理的译本可以说是迄今为止流传最广的一种。他将书名《水浒传》译作"Outlaws of The Marsh",采用了一种直译和意译相结合的处理方法。这一译文既交待了小说中故事发生的主要地点"Marsh",也点明了小说中的主要人物"Outlaws"。然而"Marsh"一词仅作"沼,泽"讲,用在此处来译"浒",是事有欠妥当,还需斟酌。

《水浒传》为中国文学史上一部以北宋末年农民起义为题材,描写农民起义全过程的长篇小说。它以章回体的形式广泛而深刻地反映了宋朝封建统治黑暗的社会现实,是具有划时代意义的文学巨著。通过一部《水浒传》,作者以其生花妙笔,写尽了轰轰烈烈的一百单八将,只见"人有其性情,人有其气质,人有其形状,人有其声口"(见金圣叹《〈水浒传〉序言》)。长久以来,《水浒传》之所以演成家喻户晓、妇孺皆知、历久不衰的盛况,恰恰在于小说内容上的博大精深,以及作者艺术上的独具匠心。作者的一腔热血,满腹情怀,凝于笔端,力透纸背,确实是功力非凡。《水浒传》在我国小说史上占有十分重要的地位,不仅因为它有深刻的思想价值,还因为它取得了卓越的艺术成就。这种成就主要体现在写人艺术的重大突破上。据有关专家统计,小说中有名有姓的人物约有八百多个,这些人物五光十色,应有尽有,社会各个阶级与阶层的人物几乎囊括殆尽。其中许多人物写得栩栩如生,给人留下了十分深刻的印象。诸如宋江、李逵、武松、鲁智深、林冲、石秀等一二十个个性鲜明的典型形象至今还为老百姓们津津乐道。《水浒传》的语言也颇有艺术表现力,令人一听说话,就知道说话人是谁。

对于这样一部具有极高思想价值与艺术成就的作品,三位译者皆是殚精竭虑、煞费苦心地想要把它成功地翻译出来,以让译文读者能够在最大程度上享受到和原文读者所能享受到的一样的乐趣。通过比较三种译文,读者不难发现赛译倾向于一种"语义翻译"(Semantic Translation),杰译倾向一种"交际翻译"(Communicative Translation),而沙译则介乎两者之间。我们都知道,翻译历来有"直译"和"意译"两种主要方向之争,这主要是"取决于译者的重点是作者还是读者,是原语还是目的语"(奈达,1964)。① 这种区别一直是问题的中心所在。而翻译

---

① 此处引文为笔者自己翻译。

中直译和意译的对立也由于各种语言结构的不同、文化的差异以及一些显著的文学特征变得越来越尖锐。因此,英国当代著名翻译理论家彼得·纽马克提出了"交际翻译"与"语义翻译",作为其翻译理论的核心。前者"试图使译文读者能够尽可能感受和原文读者所感受到的一样的效果";而后者则"旨在目的语的语义与句法结构允许的范围内,尽可能地传达原文的准确涵义"(纽马克,1988)。

下面笔者从《水浒传》原作中选出第四十七回"扑天雕双修生死书,宋公明一打祝家庄"作为范例,试将它的三个译本逐一进行比较(赛译中的第四十六回,杰译中的第四十六回,沙译中的第四十七回)。

第四十七回的主要内容是:杨雄与石秀离开祝家庄后,巧遇杜兴。杜兴介绍祝家庄、扈家庄、李家庄三家盟誓,共拒梁山的情况及李家庄主扑天雕李应。李应修书去祝家庄取时迁,被祝氏三杰臭骂一顿,扯了书札。李应与祝彪在独龙冈前交锋,被祝彪射中臂膀。杨雄、石秀回梁山泊搬兵。宋江带两路人马,到独龙山前安寨,派石秀和杨林去看路径,石秀在酒店遇到钟离老人,问了盘陀路,方知遇见白杨树便转弯才是活路,否则都是死路。杨林因不知盘陀路而被捉。宋江不见石秀、杨林,急于救人,杀奔祝家庄来,中计被围。

小说作为最常见的一种文学形式,有其自身的特点,所以译者在翻译时一般应该遵循"四化"的原则,即形象化、通俗化、个性化和风格化。所谓形象化,也就是我们常说的翻译中的形似问题。在翻译中,译者应尽量把原文的意象完好无损地移植过来,以使译文在最大限度上收到与原文相类似的效果,所以忠实于原作是译者所要遵循的第一信条。所谓通俗化,就是要求译者时刻牢记所有小说语言的共性,要做到通俗易懂,简洁明了;切忌咬文嚼字,随意堆砌辞藻,哗众取宠。因此译者在翻译时就必须充分考虑到这一点,一定要使自己的译文读起来行文流畅,简洁自然,像一部小说。个性化是小说的生命所在。《水浒传》人物描写的杰出成就之一,就是人物语言的个性化。金圣叹点评《水浒传》说:"一样人,便还他一样说话,真是绝奇本事。"三言两语就能呼出一个人物来,没有对人物的深刻了解和仔细观察是办不到的。在翻译时,译者就应当尽量突出人物描写的个性化,使译文在最大限度上收到与原文类

第七篇《水浒传》Outlaws of the Marsh

似的效果,做到一人一面,不可雷同。翻译的风格化是由原著的风格或作者本人的风格所决定的。译者只要做到充分地理解原文,忠实地再现原文,就可以传神地体现出原文的风格。正如我国著名翻译家王佐良先生所说的那样:"一切照原作,雅俗如之,深浅如之,口气如之,文体如之。"以上的后"三化"便可以归结为我们常说的翻译中的神似问题。形似是翻译的基本要求,而神似则是翻译的最终目标。刘重德先生在《翻译原则刍议》一文中,参考严复和泰特勒中外两家之见,取其精华,并结合个人翻译的体会,把翻译原则修订为既一目了然,又比较全面的"信、达、切"三字。如果把这一三字标准和小说翻译中的"四化"原则结合起来,我们可以说,遵循形象化原则,就是要求"信"——保全原文意义;遵循通俗化和个性化原则,就是要求"达"——译文明白通顺;至于遵循风格化原则,则是要求"切"——切合原文风格。

首先来比较一下三种译文在"信",也就是遵循小说翻译的形象化原则上有何不同。"信"是翻译的基本要求,因此它在这里也就显得至关重要。小说开头有一句杨雄向石秀介绍杜兴的话。

"杨雄道:'这个兄弟,姓杜,名兴,祖贯是中山府人氏。因为他面颜生得粗莽,以此人都叫他做鬼脸儿。'"

赛译:"Yang Hsiung answered, 'This brother is surnamed Tu and his name is Hsing, and his ancestors were men of Chung Shan Fu. Because his face is so coarse and wild men all call him The Devil Faced.'"

杰译:"Yang Hsiung raised the man and then introduced him to Shih Hsiu as Tu Hsing of Chung Shan Fu. He had a fierce face, and therefore people called him the Devil Faced Man."

沙译:"'Du Xing is his name. He's from the prefecture of Zhongshan. Because of his crude features everyone calls him Demon Face.'"

原文中这种介绍人物的方式在小说之中是很常见的。通常当有新人物登场亮相之际,便会由他自己或是别人介绍他的姓名、籍贯和一些显著特征。其实这些介绍用语都是最平常不过的话,可是要把它们用非常贴切的英语尽可能地完全移植过来,确也非一件易事。赛译可以说是试图要做到绝对地忠实于原著,以至到了字对字直接翻译的程度。"姓杜,名兴"是我们汉语,尤其是古汉语中所特有的一种说法,它相当于英语中的"His name is Tu Hsing"或是"He's Tu Hsing"。西方人不像我们中国人那样在名字上大做文章,他们只把名字当成一个人的代号而已。赛译在这里直接将"姓杜,名兴"译作"is surnamed Tu and his name is Hsing",可能是想让译文读者更加深刻地领会到中国人名字的学问,以便忠实地再现原文,但却给人一种呆板生涩的感觉。赛珍珠本人很了解中国,而且被誉为"中国通"。她的译文在某种程序上又有语义翻译的倾向,所以她更注重的是原著以及作者本身。至于"祖贯是中山府人氏",赛译还专门处理成"and his ancestors were men of Chung Shan Fu",这不能不说是一种忠实过头的死译了。我们知道汉语里"祖贯"其实就是"祖籍"或"籍贯",和"ancestors"的意思相差比较远。另外,赛译用"his face is so coarse and wild"来译"他面颜生得粗莽",笔者也不敢苟同。读过原著之后,我们知道"面颜生得粗莽",是指杜兴生得貌丑形粗,阔脸方腮,眼突耳大,"一似酆都焦面王"而言的。用"coarse and wild"来形容"his face",似乎也有不妥。"信"固然是翻译的基础,很重要,但如果译者囿于语义翻译的范畴,过分拘泥于原文,强调绝对的"信",那他的译文也要变成"原译"了。至于杰译,笔者在前面也已经指出,它在某种程度上倾向于一种交际翻译。因为汉语,尤其是古汉语对译者来说毕竟是一种外语,所以他把重点放在了译文读者和目的语(也就是译入语)上,试图使译文读者能够尽可能感受到和原文读者所感受到的一样的效果。显而易见,杰译在这里把杨雄的直接陈述转化为第三人称的间接转述,这样译者发挥创造的成分似乎多了些,对原文来讲也不够忠实。译文将这句话转化成平铺直叙的间接引语,使译文无法通过对话来展示小说人物的个性特点,其表现力是明显地差了大截。尽管杰译也几乎全部传递出原文中的信息,却是却让人感到力度不够。沙译可以说是三种译文中比较令人满意的一种。译者把持"信"的标准,在不存在文学和文化冲突的前提下,尽量做到把原文的意象完好无损地移植过来,以使译文读者获得和原文读者一样的感受。但是其中仍有两处译法叫人置疑,

第七篇《水浒传》Outlaws of the Marsh

需作进一步商榷。第一处为"中山府"的译法,沙译是"the prefecture of Zhong-shan"。笔者在《牛津现代高级英汉双解词典》中查到:"prefecture"一词是指"府"的概念内涵与"prefecture"并不对等,这种译法只会使译文读者更加迷惑。倒不如赛译和杰(法、日等国之)省、郡、州等最大的地方行政区划。"很显然,在我国宋朝时,"府"的概念内涵与"prefcture"并不对等,这种译法只会使译文读者更加迷惑。倒不如赛译和杰译直接用汉语拼音"Fu"来对等翻译"府",使译文读者一目了然,原来"Chung Shan Fu"即是中国古代的一个行政区划而已。第二处是沙译对于"面颜生得粗莽"的处理——"his crude features"。"Crude"含有"粗糙的、粗鲁的、粗制滥造的"等意思,用在这里似乎不足以表达杜兴容貌"ugly"之内涵,所以叫译文读者难以把"his crude features"和"鬼脸儿"联系在一起。

本章中有一处描写宋江下令进兵,一打祝家庄时的场面,原文如下:

"摇旗呐喊,擂鼓鸣锣,大刀阔斧,杀奔祝家庄来。"

这里作者只用了十八个字,但结构工整、节奏紧凑,读后使人感到一种宋江及其人马威风凛凛、锐不可挡的气势。尽管原文很短,但是因为涉及到一些中国古代军事用语,所以在翻译时还是有一定难度的。下面我们就看一看这三位译者是如何来译这句话的。

赛译:"Then waving their flags and shouting their war cries, beating their drums and gongs with their great knives and their broadaxes, they went charging toward the village, killing as they went until they might reach the Ridge Of The Lonely Dragon."

杰译:"There was at once a great hubbub, waving their flags, beating of drums and gongs, and a great display of swords and axes."

沙译:"Amid waving flags, pounding drums and braying gongs, the raiders, shouting and brandishing swords and axes, marched rapidly on the Zhu Family Manor."

原文中作者使用了三个成语和一个六字动词短语来描写人物当时的动作,而译文若要将这三个成语和一个短语排列起来的话,似乎有些冗长累赘,所以我们可以看到三种译文在不同程度上都做了一些转化。赛译把原文的成语与短语的组合转化成了一个主从复合句,并且用两个含有动词现在分词的独立结构成分和一个介词短语来对等翻译原文中的三个四字成语。尽管原文的意思全都包含在内,但是却让人感到译文过于拖沓冗长,节奏感不强,破坏了原文的行文之美。杰译将原文的动作描写转化成为一种静态描写,用一个"there be"句型将原文中的三个四字成语铺展开来,而且还分割成几个名词片语,使原文的节奏感在某种程度上得到再现,笔者认为这也不失为一种好译法。沙译则巧妙地将原文转化为一个主从复合句。前面一部分是一个由介词"amid"引导的状语,后一部分则是一个包含动词现在分词短语的主从复合句。这样,译者就将原文中只有十八个字的短句,转换成了既有静态描写(waving flags, pounding drums and braying gongs),又有动态描写(shouting and brandishing swords and axes, marched rapidly)的一个长句。在这里译者想要"尽可能地传达原文准确涵义"的苦心便也可以窥斑见豹了。

前观已经提到过,杰译在某种程度上倾向于一种交际翻译,而交际翻译可能会"更加顺畅,更加简洁,更加清晰,更加直接,更加归化,符合一种特定的语域,有欠译的趋向"(纽马克,1988)。[①] 但是,这并不说明通过交际翻译可以对原文进行任意地删改,甚至是整句意思的删除。原文中有这样一句话:"听得背后法环响得渐近,石秀看时,却见杨林带一个破笠子,身穿一领旧法衣,手里擎着法环,于路摇将过来。……"而在杰译中却根本找不到与之对等的译文。在小说创作中,作家为了刻画一个人物,往往从多方面入手,如人物的音容笑貌,衣着服饰,行为举止等等。这里作者通过石秀的观察,对杨林的衣着服饰和行为举止作了描述,以进一步刻画杨林这一人物。而杰译却忽略了这一句,以致于译文读者在读过译文之后,可能还搞不清楚杨林进入祝家庄所装扮的"解魇

---

① 此处引文为笔者自己翻译。

第七篇《水浒传》Outlaws of the Marsh

的法师，"(priest)到底是一副什么打扮，这不能不说是杰译中的一大失误。

其次，我们再来比较一下三种译本在"达"，也就是遵循小说翻译的通俗化与个性化的原则上有何不同。我们知道，小说拥有和其它任何文学体裁所不同的语言特点，它更加接近生活，也更适合反映生活。而《水浒传》在语言运用上的通俗化特色历来为人所称道。那么，三位译者在对待原作语言运用方面的突出特点是怎样处理的呢？请看原作中的这样一个范例：

"李应纵马赶将去，祝彪把枪横担在马上，左手拈弓，右手取箭，搭上箭，拽满弓，觑得较亲，背翻身一箭。"

原文不长，但却用几个动词"纵、赶、横担、拈、取、搭、拽、觑、翻"等生动地描写出了祝彪佯败箭射李应时的场面。用如此简洁易懂的语言真实地再现出这一系列复杂的动作，恐怕是原作中为人所称道的语言特色吧！

赛译："But Li Yün urged his horse on in pursuit. The Tiger Cub held his weapon upright on his horse. With his left hand he reached for his bow, with his right he took at the same time his arrow and he fitted the arrow to the bow, and he stretched full his bow, he took true aim and turning, he let fly the arrow."

杰译："Placing his spear on the horse he took his bow and arrow, and turning his body shot at Li Ying who was following close behind."

沙译："Li Ying gave chase. Tiger Cub rested his lance athwart his animal's neck, fitted an arrow to his bow and drew it to the full. Twisting in the saddle, he aimed and let fly."

我们可以看到，作为一种语义翻译，赛译倾向于"过于复杂，过于呆板，过于具体，过于集中，追求的是译者的思想过程而非其目的。它有超译的趋向,也就是比原文更加具体"(纽马克,1988)。① 的确,赛译在此处试图无一遗漏地传递出原文的信息,甚至有超译的趋向。它用"urged, held, reached, took, fitted, stretched, took aim, turning"等动词或动词短语形式来对等表现原文中的动词,可以说译者在遣词造句上是下了一番功夫的。不过译文当中反复出现多次的"he"和"his"则给人一种重复松散之感,似乎无法体现出原作中祝彪偷射李应时那种惊心动魄的紧张气氛。笔者个人认为这是赛译过于拘泥于原作的原因。杰译尽管没有逐字逐句依照原文去翻译,也没有逐一找到和原作对等的动词形式,但是却能给人一种简洁明快、一目了然的感觉。杰译用两个动词现在分词短语表达原作中的"横担"与"翻身",并用另两个短句来表现"拈弓搭箭"和(射)一箭"。译者甚至还把原作中"李应纵马赶过去"这样一个主谓句转化为英语中的定语从句,以便巧妙地把译文组织成一句话,使译文读者能够领略到这一系列动作不过是在转瞬之间发生的。沙译可以说是介于以上两种译文之间的,它既无赛译的松散累赘,也不似杰译的紧凑干练。它把原文意思分成三句话来表达,基本上用顺畅易懂的语言再现出了原文,符合刘重德先生所提出的翻译时的"达"的原则。原作中还有一例描写杜兴凭借李应的亲笔书札去祝家庄索要时迁,反遭侮辱,忿忿而归的场面。原文如下:

"(杜兴)入得庄门,见他模样,气得紫涨了面皮,龇牙露嘴,半晌说不得话。"

赛译:"He was so angered the skin of his face was empurpled and his teeth were bared. For a time he could not speak..."

杰译:"His face was red with passion, and as he raised his lips he showed the tightly set teeth. For some time he could not speak."

沙译:"His face was tight with rage and his teeth were bared. For several minutes he was unable to speak."

在汉语中,"紫涨了面皮"和"龇牙露嘴"都是用来形容人在盛怒之

---

① 此处引文为笔者自己翻译。

第七篇《水浒传》Outlaws of the Marsh

下的样子,但并不一定就指"紫色的脸皮"和"露出的牙齿"。三位译者在翻译时都尽力想要表现出杜兴当时那种怒气冲天的样子。但是赛译直截了当用"the skin of his face was empurpled and his teeth were bared"来表现"紫涨了面皮,龇牙露嘴",未免有些牵强。这一译文确实符合"信"的标准,忠实于原文,但是译文读者在读过这一句后,是否会把"empurpled face"、"bared teeth"与"so angered"联系在一起呢?他们也许还会认为这是中国古人生气时所特有的反应吧!因此,笔者认为这一句赛译只信不达,是死译。而杰译用"red with passion"和"the tightly set teeth"则棋高一着,因为此处将"紫"转化为"红",将"龇牙"转化为"咬紧牙关",更加符合译人语的表达方式,也就更加易于被译文读者所接受。沙译则另辟蹊径,用"tight with rage"来再现"紫涨了面皮",尽管也表现出了杜兴当时怒气冲天的样子,但是力度似乎不如杰译的"red with passion"。另外,沙译也用了"his teeth were bared"来表现"龇牙露嘴",给人一种突兀的感觉,是否还可以做进一步改进呢?

在"达"的标准上,笔者还想就三种译本对于原作语言运用的个性特点的翻译情况进行比较。《水浒传》中,作者施耐庵淋漓尽致地表现出了小说中人物的典型性格特征。提起《水浒传》中的人物形象,个个性格鲜明,形神皆备,光彩耀人。在小说创作中,人物的语言以及人物之间的对话是塑造人物性格的最佳方式,所谓"闻其声如见其人"。所以小说翻译也是如此,译者应当在忠实于原作的基础上,尽量保存原作的丰姿,传神地再现出原作语言运用的个性特点。原作中有这样一段李逵和宋江之间的对话:

　　李逵笑道:'量这个乌庄,何须哥哥费力,只兄弟自带二三百个孩儿杀将去,把这乌庄上的人都砍了,何须要人去先打听。'宋江喝道:'你这厮休胡说!且一壁厢去,叫你便来。'

赛译:"Li K'uei laughed and said, 'But for such an accursed village as this why should you trouble yourself so much, my elder brother? Let me just take two or three hundred of your children and we will kill our way in! We will slaughter every person in this accursed village. Why should we want men to first and spy out?' But Sung Jiang shouted out, saying, 'Do not speak as a fool! Go aside, you! When I call you then only are you to come!'"

杰译:"Li K'wei laughed at this. 'There is no need to send spies. If you let me have two hundred men I could enter the village, and settle this matter quite easily.' 'Don't talk nonsense!' shouted Sung Ch'iang 'You can wait outside until I call for you.'"

沙译:"Li Kui laughed. 'That friggin manor. Why trouble yourself? I'll take two or three hundred of the lads, and we'll carve our way in and cut all the wretches done. What do you need scouts for?' 'You're talking rot. Get out of here and don't come till I call you!'"

读过这段原文之后,李逵的粗莽与率直,宋江的稳重与缜密已是跃然纸上。我们知道,李逵在归顺梁山之前,一直混迹于市井之间,没有读过什么书,因此说话不免粗俗无礼;而宋江凡事都思虑周全,工于心计。相比之下,他讲话则更注意方式方法,使人信服。所以,译者在翻译时就要考虑到二人性格的不同,注意人物语言运用的个性化特点,尽量忠实地再现原作中人物的不同性格。赛译基本上做到了忠实于原文,用"an accursed village"来对应"鸟庄",并用一个感叹句与一个反诘句来突出强调李逵的卤莽与急不可耐,欲与祝家庄一决雌雄的迫切心情。然而,由于译者太过注重原作本身,因此译文过于呆板,读起来口语化程度不够。至于宋江所喝道的"你这厮休胡说!",赛译为"Do you speak as a fool?",笔者也认为这一表达不切,似乎没有再现出宋江当时对李逵那种嗔怪的态度。在《水浒词典》(胡竹安编)中,"一壁厢"被解释为"即一旁,一方之意"。故赛译中宋江所说的"Go aside, you!"更贴近原文,也更符合宋江说话的口吻。在杰译中,李逵的话被用两个结构工整的句子译出,少了几分粗野气,却平添了几分书卷味。另外,原作中李逵所使用的一些鄙俗语,如"鸟庄"等也未得到体现,就小说翻译的个性化原则而言,这不能不说是杰译的一个失误。但是对于宋江所说的"你这厮休胡说!",杰译把它处理为"Don't talk nonsense!",则更加贴近原文。沙译是这三种译文中最符合"达"字标准的译文。译者用"that friggin manor"来与"这鸟庄"对等,表现出李逵的粗鲁。与前面两位译者不同,沙译没有用"Let me..."或是"If you let me..."这样的句型,而是用了"I'll take"来充分体现李逵做事不顾后果,大包大揽的"英雄气概"。再者,沙泽在翻译宋江的话时,也较有分寸地表现出宋江作为梁山头领对手下兄弟讲话的那种权威性,使原著作者通过语言运用来再现人物性格的匠心得以成功的再现。

最后,笔者想从"切",也就是遵循小说翻译的风格化原则的角度对三种译本进行比较。译文的风格,可以分为两个方面,一是原文的风格能否体现于译文中;二是译文本身的风格是否既有译者的个性,同时又具有较强的可读性,或大众接受性。前者在于原文的修辞特点是否传达出来了,而后者则是译文本身的修辞问题。下面笔者将从原作和译文中各选取范例加以比较。例如,原作中有一段杜兴向杨、石二人介绍独龙冈情况,当介绍到祝家庄时,其中有这样一句话

"又有一个教师,唤作铁棒栾廷玉,此人有万夫不挡之勇。"

"万夫不挡之勇"是汉语中的一个成语,在《现代汉语巨典》(大连出版社,毛学河,倪文杰主编)当中,它的释义是这样的:"一万个人也抵挡不住的勇猛,形容极其勇猛,无人匹敌。"但是"万夫"并非确指一万个人,只是言其人数多而已。因此这条成语用在原作当中,多少有些夸张的作用。我们就来比较一下三种译本对于这种夸张用法的不同处理。

赛译:"They have a teacher who is called Luan T'ing Yu, The Iron Stuff. Among ten thousand there is not one to match him."

杰译:"They had a drill instructor named Luan Ting-yu, nicknamed Iron Stuff, who was invincible."

沙译:"They have an arms instructor, Luan Tingyu, who's known as the Iron Stuff. Ten thousand men are no match for him."

以上三种译文在栾廷玉的诨号"铁棒"上取得了一致,都译为"the Iron Stuff",但是在"教师"一词的翻译上却有分歧。这里"教师"应该是祝家庄的武术教练,所以赛译中的"teacher"显然是不正确的。杰译中的

"drill instructor"和沙泽中的"arms instructor"都能表达"武术教练"的意思,但"drill instructor"似乎更加符合中国古代请武师做本庄院武术教练的事实。对于原作中的关键地方"此人有万夫不挡之勇",三位译者的处理方式也各不相同。赛译中"Among ten thousand there is not one to match him.",似乎是把"万夫"当成一个确指数目,背离了原文的意图,没有充分传递出原作中那种夸张修辞的效果。杰译中用"who was invincible"确实传递出了原文的内涵,形容栾廷玉勇猛异常,无人匹敌。但是这种意译的方法却难以让译文读者也同样感受到原作中所使用修辞手法的妙处,因而也不能算是成功的译文。而沙泽中的"Ten thousand men are no match for him",可以说是形神兼备,既忠实于原文,表达顺畅,又传达了原作作者想要通过夸张这种修辞手段所产生的效果,因而这一译文更易于被读者接受。原作中语言简洁自然,层次清晰明了,句子短小精干,用词浅显易懂,但是简洁并不等于简单,用词浅显也不等于索然无味,所以要译出原作的风格也并非易事。

一部《水浒传》中,出现了众多梁山英雄好汉的诨名。这些名号形意并茂,以栩栩如生的形象展现出人物的典型性格特征。翻译时应尽可能地保留其形象。有的诨号只需直译便可形意兼得,例如"黑旋风"李逵,三种译文都译作"The Black Whirlwind"(本文所引用的杰译的第四十六回中有一处译为"The Small Whirlwind",可能是译者一时的疏忽或失误)。"Black"点明其容貌特征,"Whirlwind"又显示其英勇威武,故而这个"黑旋风"的形象与性格特征便尽现读者眼前了。又如"鬼脸儿"杜兴,赛、杰、沙三位译者分别把它直译为"The Devil Faced"、"the Devil Faced Man"和"Demon Face",这样从字面上都表现出了杜兴的特点——貌丑形粗。但由于文化因素的介入,有些诨号在译入语中找不到对应的形象,因此译者只好巧做变形处理,求得"神似"。例如:"一丈青"扈三娘,在《水浒语词词典》(李法白、刘镜芙编)中释义:"青:春色,言容貌美好;一丈:言身材修长。扈三娘容颜娇好,武艺不凡,善于骑在马上使日月双刀。"对于这一诨号,赛译是"The Ten Foot Green Snake",杰译是"Pure One"沙译是"Ten Feet of Steel."赛译中将"青"转化为"Green Snake",使扈三娘在译文读者的心目中平添了一股狠毒,而少了几分妩媚,没有表达出她容貌娇好的内涵。杰译则完全是脱离原文的"胡译"了,根本未能传达出原文中的意象。沙译把"青"转化为"Steel",这似乎与扈三娘手中的一对日月双刀相照应,力求与原文神似。只是这一译文也未能体现出她美好的容貌,所以这是沙译中的一个小小的遗憾。

综观以上数例,这三种译本各有得失,都有深得原作"丰姿"的佳译,也有译走样的败笔。就方法而言,赛译偏重形式,多采用语义翻译,尽量做到忠实原作内容,却又往往貌合神离。杰译以交际翻译为主,不拘泥于原作形式,笔法灵活多变,不乏神似之笔。但由于其过于追求译文效果,对原作内容删减太过自由,故多有失真之处。沙译则介于两者之间,语义翻译和交际翻译兼而有之,遣词造句较为得当,相对更加接近原作的艺术特色。就语言风格而言,赛译行文通畅,但略显滞重平淡,不如原作简洁明快。杰译洗练地道,富于文采,但欧化的味道太浓,是译者自己的风格,而非原作的风格。而沙译则浓淡相宜,较之赛译简洁自然,又比杰译忠于原文。经过对三种译文进行比较,沙译的译风最为严谨,漏译与误译的现象较少,基本做到完好无损地移植原作内容。赛译和杰译在某种程度上都有误译与漏译现象,尤其是杰译,犯了译家之大忌,数处出现删除原文内容的现象,并对原文段落进行任意地组合,大有编译之嫌。而赛译在有些地方则出现了误译现象,例如:将"江湖上"译为"by river and lake";将"早膳"译为"an early meal";将"好汉"译为"the good fellows"等等。就译本来说,沙译的可读性最大。不过,我们应当注意这样一个事实,即赛译早在本世纪 30 年代就已经出版。当时的语言,无论书面语还是口语,都与今天有很大差别。所以赛译的遣词造句,不可避免地带有那个时期翻译文学的特点。但是,从介绍中国文学的角度衡量,赛珍珠确实是将这一名著介绍给西方读者的功不可没之人。

参考文献

1. 关永礼等:《中国古典小说鉴赏词典》,中国展望出版社,1989 年。
2. 侯　健:《中国小说大词典》,作家出版社,1991 年。
3. 胡竹安:《水浒词典》,汉语大词典出版社,1989 年。

4. 霍松林:《中国古典小说六大名著鉴赏词典》,华岳文艺出版社,1988年。
5. 李法白、刘镜芙:《水浒语词词典》,上海辞书出版社,1989年。
6. 刘重德:《翻译原则刍议》,《翻译通讯》,1983年第4期。
7. 施耐庵、罗贯中:《水浒全传》,兵麓书社,1988年。
8. 张国光:《〈水浒〉与金圣汉研究》,中州书画社,1981年。
9. Buck, Pearl S. (trans.) *All Men Are Brothers*. New York, The John Day Company, 1933.
10. Jackson, J. H. (trans.) *Water Margin*. Hongkong, Commercial Press Ltd, 1963.
11. Jin Di & Nida, Eugene A. *On Translation*. Beijing, China Foreign Translation Publishing Company, 1984.
12. Newmark, Peter, *Approaches to Translation*. London, Oxford, 1981.
13. Nida, Eugene A. *Toward a Science Of Translating*. Leiden, E. J. Brill, 1964.
14. Shapiro, Sidney. (trans.) *Outlaws Of The Marsh*. Beijing, Foreign Language Press, 1980.

第七篇《水浒传》Outlaws of the Marsh

附：

《水浒传》（节选）

施耐庵　罗贯中

第四十七回　扑天雕双修生死书
　　　　　宋公明一打祝家庄

　　话说当时杨雄扶起那人来，叫与石秀相见。石秀便问道："这位兄长是谁？"杨雄道："这个兄弟，姓杜，名兴，祖贯是中山府人氏，因为他面颜生得粗莽，以此人都叫他做鬼脸儿。上年间做买卖，来到蓟州，因一口气上打死了同伙的客人，吃官司监在蓟州府里。杨雄见他说起拳棒都省得，一力维持救了他。不想今日在此相会。"杜兴便问道："恩人，为何公事来到这里？"杨雄附耳低言道："我在蓟州杀了人命，欲要投梁山泊去入伙。昨晚在祝家店投宿，因同一个来的火伴时迁，偷了他店里报晓鸡吃，一时与店小二闹将起来，性起把他店屋放火都烧了。我三个连夜逃走，不提防背后赶来。我弟兄两个搠翻了他几个，不想乱草中间，舒出两把挠钩，把时迁搭了去。这两个乱撞到此，正要问路，不想遇到贤弟。"杜兴道："恩人，要慌，我叫放时迁还你。"杨雄道："贤弟少坐，同饮一杯。"

　　三人坐下，当下饮酒，杜兴便："小弟自从离了蓟州，多得恩人的恩惠，来到这里，感承此间一个大官人见爱，收录小弟在家中做个主管。每日拨万论千，尽托付与杜兴身上，甚是信任，以此不想回乡去。"杨雄道："此间大官人是谁？"杜兴道："此间独龙冈前面，有三座山冈，列着三个村坊。中间是祝家庄，西边是扈家庄，东边是李家庄。这三处庄上，三村里算来，总有一二万军马人家。惟有祝家庄最豪杰，为头家长唤做祝朝奉,有三个儿子,名为祝氏三杰,长子祝龙,次子祝虎,三子祝彪。又有一个教师,唤做铁棒栾廷玉,此人有万夫不当之勇。庄上自有一二千了得的庄客。西边那个扈家庄,庄主扈太公,有个儿子,唤做飞天虎扈成,也十分了得;惟有一个女儿最英雄,名唤一丈青扈三娘,使两口日月双刀,马上如法了得。这里东村庄上,却是杜兴的主人,姓李,名应,能使一条浑铁点钢枪,背藏飞刀五口,百步取人,神出鬼没。这三村结下生死誓愿,同心共意,但有吉凶,递相救应。惟恐梁山泊好汉过来借粮,因此三村准备下抵敌他。如今小弟引二位到庄上,见了李大官人,求书去搭救时迁。"杨雄又问道:"你那李大官人,莫不是江湖上唤扑天雕的李应?"杜兴道:"正是他。"石秀道:"江湖上只听得说独龙冈有个扑天雕李应是好汉,却原来在这里。多闻他真个了得,是好男子,我们去走一遭。"杨雄便唤酒保计算酒钱。杜兴那里肯要他还,便自招了酒钱。

　　三个离了村店,便引杨雄、石秀来到李家庄。杨雄看时,真是好大庄院,外面周回一遭阔港,粉墙傍岸,有数百株合抱不交的大柳树,门外一座吊桥,接着庄门。入得门来,到厅前,两边有二十余座枪架,明晃晃的都插满军器。杜兴道:"两位哥哥在此少等,待小弟人去报知,请大官人出来相见。"杜兴入去,不多时,只见李应从里面出来,杨雄、石秀看时,果然好表人物,有临江仙词为证:鹘眼鹰睛头似虎,燕颔猿臂狼腰,疏财仗义结英豪。爱骑雪白马,喜著绛红袍。背上飞刀藏五把,点钢枪斜嵌银条,性刚谁敢犯分毫。李应真壮士,名号扑天雕。

　　当时李应出到厅前,杜兴引杨雄、石秀上厅拜见。李应连忙答礼,便教上厅请坐,杨雄、石秀再三谦让,方才坐了。李应便教取酒来且相待。杨雄、石秀两个再拜道:"望乞大官人致书与祝家庄,来救时迁性命,生死不敢有忘。"李应教请门馆先生来商议,修了一封书缄,填写名讳,使个图书印记,便差一个副主管赍了,备一匹快马,星火去祝家庄取这个人来。

　　那副主管领了东人书札,上马去了,杨雄、石秀拜谢罢。李应道:"二位壮士放心,小人书去,便当放来。"杨雄、石秀又谢了。李应道:"且请去后堂,少叙三杯等待。"两个随进里面,就具早膳相待。饭罢,吃了茶,李应问些枪法,见杨雄、石秀说的有理,心中甚喜。

第七篇《水浒传》Outlaws of the Marsh

　　巳牌时分，那个副主管回来，李应唤到后堂问道："去取的这人在那里？"主管答道："小人亲见朝奉，下了书，倒有放还之心。后来走出祝氏三杰，反焦躁起来，书也不回，人也不放，定要解上州去。"李应失惊道："他和我三家村里结生死之交，书到便当依允，如何恁地起来？必是你说得不好，以致如此。杜主管，你须自去走一遭，亲见祝朝奉，说个仔细缘由。"杜兴道："小人愿去，只求东人亲笔书缄，到那里方才肯放。"李应道："说得是。"急取一幅花笺纸来，李应亲自写了书札，封皮面上使一个讳字图书，把与杜兴接了。后槽牵过一匹快马，备上鞍辔，拿了鞭子，便出庄门，上马加鞭，奔祝家庄去了。李应道："二位放心，我这封亲笔书去，少刻定当放还。"杨雄、石秀深谢了，留在后堂饮酒等待。

　　看看天色待晚，不见杜兴回来，李应心中疑惑。再教人去接，只见庄客报道："杜主管回来了。"李应问道："几个人回来？"庄客道："只是主管独自一个跑马回来。"李应摇着头道："却又作怪。往常这厮不是这等兜搭，今日缘何恁地？"杨雄、石秀都跟出前厅来看时，只见杜兴下了马，入得庄门，见他模样，气得紫涨了面皮，龇牙露嘴，半晌说不的话。有诗为证：面貌天生本异常，怒时古怪更难当。三分不象人模样，一似郓都焦面王。

　　李应出到厅前，连忙问道："你且言备细缘故，怎么地来。"杜兴气定了，方才道："小人赍了东人书札，到他那里第三重门下，却好遇见祝龙、祝虎、祝彪弟兄三个坐在那里。小人声了三个喏，祝彪喝道：'你又来做甚么？'小人躬身禀道：'东人有书在此拜上。'祝彪那厮变了脸，骂道：'你那主人恁地不晓人事！早晌使个泼男女来这里下书，要讨那个梁山泊贼人时迁，如今我正要解上州里去，又来怎地？'小人说道：'这个时迁不是梁山泊伙内人数，他自是蓟州来的客人。今投见敝庄东人，不想误烧了官人店屋，明日东人自当依旧盖还，万望俯看薄面，高抬贵手，宽恕宽恕。'祝家三个都叫道：'不还，不还！'小人又道：'官人请看东人亲笔书札在此。'祝彪那厮接过书去，不也不拆开来看，就手扯的粉碎，喝叫把小人直叉出庄门。祝彪、祝虎发话道：'休要惹老爷性发，把你那李应捉来，也做梁山泊强寇解了去。'小人本不敢尽言，实被那三个畜生无礼，把东人百般秽骂，便喝叫庄客来拿小人，被小人飞马走了。于路上气死小人，叵耐那厮枉与他许多年结生死之交，今日全无些仁义。"诗曰：徒闻似漆与如胶，利害场中忍便抛。平日若无真义气，临时休说死生交。

李应听罢，心头那把无明业火高举三千丈，按纳不下，大呼："庄客，快备我那马来！"杨雄、石秀谏道："大官人息怒，休为小人们坏了贵处义气。"李应那里肯听，便去房中披上一副黄金锁子甲，前后兽面掩心，穿一领大红袍，背胯边插着飞刀五把，拿了点钢枪，戴上凤翅盔，出到庄前，点起三百悍勇庄客。杜兴也披一副甲，持把枪上马，带领二十余骑马军。杨雄、石秀也抓扎起，挺着朴刀，跟着李应的马，径奔祝家庄来。

日渐衔山时分，早到独龙冈前，便将人马排开。原来祝家庄又盖得好，占着这座独龙山冈，四下一遭阔港。那庄正造在冈上，有三层城墙，都是顽石垒砌的，约高二丈。前后两座庄门，两条吊桥。墙里四边，都盖窝铺，四下里遍插着枪刀军器，门楼上排着战鼓铜锣。李应勒马，在庄前大叫："祝家三子，怎敢毁谤老爷！"只见庄门开处，拥出五六十骑马来，当先一骑似火炭赤的马上，坐着祝朝奉第三子祝彪。怎生装束？头戴缕金荷叶盔，身穿锁子梅花甲。腰悬锦袋弓和箭，手执纯钢刀与枪。马额下垂照地红缨，人面上生撞天杀气。

李应见了祝彪，指着大骂道："你这厮口边奶腥未退，头上胎发犹存，你爷与我结生死之交，誓愿同心共意，保护村坊。你家但有事情，要取人时，早来早放，要取物件，无有不奉。我今一个平人，二次修书来讨，你如何扯了我的书札，耻辱我名，是何道理？"祝彪道："俺家虽和你结生死之交，誓愿同心协意，共捉梁山泊反贼，扫清山寨，你如何却结连反贼，意在谋叛？"李应喝道："你说他是梁山泊甚人？你这厮却冤平人做贼，当得何罪？"祝彪道："贼人时迁已自招了，你休要在这里胡说乱道，遮掩不过。你去便去，不去时，连你捉了，也做贼人解送！"

李应大怒，拍坐下马，挺手中枪，便奔祝彪。祝彪纵马去战李应。两个就独龙冈前，一来一往，一上一下，斗了十七八合，祝彪战李应不过，拨回马便走。李应纵马赶将去，祝彪把枪横担在马上，左手拈弓，右手取箭，搭上箭，拽满弓，觑得较亲，背翻身一箭。李应急躲时，臂上早着。李应翻筋斗，坠下马来。祝彪便勒转马来抢人。杨雄、石秀见了，大喝一声，拈两条朴刀，直奔祝彪马前杀将来。祝彪抵当不住，急勒回马便走，早被

第七篇《水浒传》Outlaws of the Marsh

杨雄一朴刀,戳在马后股上。那马负疼,壁直立起来,险些儿把祝彪掀在马下,却得随从马上的人,都搭上箭射将来。杨雄、石秀见了,自思又无衣甲遮身,只得退回不赶。杜兴也自把李应救起上马,先去了。杨雄、石秀跟了众庄客也走了。祝家庄人马赶了二三里路,见天色晚来,也自回去了。

杜兴扶着李应,回到庄前,下了马,同入后堂坐。众宅眷都出来看视,拔了箭矢,伏侍卸了衣甲,便把金疮药敷了疮口,连夜在后堂商议。杨雄、石秀与杜兴说道:"既是大官人被那厮无礼,又中了箭,时迁亦不能够出来,都是我等连累大官人了。我弟兄两个,只得上梁山泊去,恳告晁、宋二公并众头领,来与大官人报仇,就救时迁。"因辞谢了李应。李应道:"非是我不用心,实出无奈。两位壮士,只得休怪。"叫杜兴取些金银相赠,杨雄、石秀那里肯受。李应道:"江湖之上,二位不必推却。"两个方才收受,拜辞了李应。杜兴送出村口,指与大路。杜兴作别了,自回李家庄,不在话下。

且说杨雄、石秀取路投梁山泊来,早望见远远一处新造的酒店,那酒旗儿直挑出来。两个入到店里,买些酒吃,就问路程。这酒店却是梁山泊新添设做眼的酒店,正是石勇掌管。两个一面吃酒,一头动问酒保上梁山泊路程。石勇见他两个非常,便来答应道:"你两位客人从那里来?要问上山去怎地?"杨雄道:"我们从蓟州来。"石勇猛可想起道:"莫非足下是石秀么?"杨雄道:"我乃是杨雄,这个兄弟是石秀。大哥如何得知石秀名?"石勇慌忙道:"小子不认得。前者戴宗哥哥到蓟州回来,多曾称说兄长。闻名久矣,今得上山,且喜,且喜。"三个叙礼罢,杨雄、石秀把上件事都对石勇说了。石勇随即叫酒保置办分例酒来相待。推开后面水亭上窗子,拽起弓,放了一枝响箭。只见对港芦苇丛中,早有小喽罗摇过船来。石勇便邀二位上船,直送到鸭嘴滩上岸。石勇已自先使人上山去报知。早见戴宗、杨林下山来迎接。俱各叙礼罢,一同上至大寨里。

众头领知道有好汉上山,都来聚会,大寨坐下。戴宗、杨林引杨雄、石秀上厅参见晁盖、宋江并众头领。相见已罢,晁盖细问两个踪迹,杨雄、石秀把本身武艺,投托入伙先说了,众人大喜,让位而坐。杨雄渐渐说到有个来投托大寨同入伙的时迁,不合偷了祝家店里报晓鸡,一时争闹起来，石秀放火烧了他店屋，时迁被捉；李应二次修书去讨，怎当祝家三子坚执不放，誓愿要捉山寨里好汉，且又千般辱骂，叵耐那厮十分无礼。不说万事皆休，才然说罢，晁盖大怒，喝叫："孩儿们将这两个与我斩讫报来！"正是：杨雄、石秀少商量，引带时迁行不臧。豪杰心肠虽似火，绿林法度却如霜。

宋江慌忙劝道："哥哥息怒，两个壮士不远千里而来，同心协助，如何却要斩他？"晁盖道："俺梁山泊好汉，自从火并王伦之后，便以忠义为主，全施仁德于民。一个个兄弟下山去，不曾折了锐气。新旧上山的兄弟们，各各都有豪杰的光彩。这厮两个，把梁山泊好汉的名目去偷鸡吃，因此连累我等受辱。今日先斩了这两个，将这厮首级去那里号令，便起军马去，就洗荡了那个村坊，不要输了锐气。孩儿们快斩了报来。"宋江劝住道："不然。哥哥不听这两位贤弟却才所说，那个鼓上蚤时迁，他原是此等人，以致惹起祝家那厮来，岂是这二位贤弟要玷辱山寨？我也每每听得有人说，祝家庄那厮要和俺山寨敌对。即目山寨人马数多，钱粮缺少，非是我等要去寻他，那厮倒来吹毛求疵，因此正好乘势去拿那厮。若打得此庄，倒有三五年粮食。非是我们生事害他，其实那厮无礼。哥哥权且息怒，小可不才，亲领一支军马，启请几位贤弟们下山去打祝家庄。若不洗荡得那个村坊，誓不还山。一是与山寨报仇，不折了锐气；二乃免此小辈被他耻辱；三则是许多粮食，以供山寨之用；四者就请李应上山入伙。"吴学究道："公明哥哥之言最好，岂可山寨自斩手足之人？"戴宗便道"宁乃斩了小弟，不可绝了贤路。"众头领力劝，晁盖方才免了二人。杨雄、石秀也自谢罪。宋江抚谕道："贤弟休生异心，此是山寨号令，不得不如此。便是宋江，倘有过失，也须斩首，不敢容情。如今新近又立了铁面孔目裴宣做军政司，赏功罚罪，已有定例。贤弟只得恕罪恕罪。"杨雄、石秀拜罢，谢罪已了，晁盖叫去坐在杨林之下。山寨里都唤小喽罗来参贺新头领已毕，一面杀牛宰马，且做庆喜筵席。拨定两所房屋，教杨雄、石秀安歇，每人拨十个小喽罗伏侍。

当晚席散。次日再备筵席，会众商量议事。

宋江教唤铁面孔目裴宣，计较下山人数，启请诸位头领，同宋江去打祝家庄，定要洗荡了那个村坊。商量已定，除晁盖头领镇守山寨不动外,留下吴学究、刘唐并阮家三弟兄、吕方、郭盛,护持大寨。原拨定守滩、守关、守店有职事人员,俱各不动。又拨新到头领孟康管造般只,顶替马麟监督战船。写下告示,将下山打祝家庄头领分作两起:头一拨,宋江、花荣、李俊、穆弘、李逵、杨雄、石秀、黄信、欧鹏、杨林,带领三千小喽罗,三百马军,披挂已了,下山前进;第二拨便是林冲、秦明、戴宗、张横、张顺、马麟、邓飞、王矮虎、白胜,也带三千小喽罗,三百马军,随后接应。再着金沙滩、鸭嘴滩二处小寨,只教宋万、郑天寿守把,就行接应粮草。晁盖送路已了,自回山寨。

且说宋江并众头领径奔祝家庄来,于路无话。早来到独龙山前,尚有一里多路,前军下了寨栅。宋江在中军帐里坐下,便和花荣商议道:"我听得说祝家庄里路径甚杂,未可进兵,且先使两个人去探听路途曲折,知得顺逆路程,却才进去与他敌对。"李逵便道:"哥哥,兄弟闲了多时,不曾杀得一人,我便先去走一遭。"宋江道:"兄弟,你去不得。若是破阵冲敌,用着你先去。这是做细作的勾当,用你不着。"李逵笑道:"量这个鸟庄,何须哥哥费力,只兄弟自带三二百个孩儿杀将去,把这个鸟庄上人都砍了,何须要人先去打听。"宋江喝道:"你这厮休胡说!且一壁厢去,叫你便来。"李逵走开去了,自说道:"打死几个苍蝇,也何须大惊小怪。"宋江便唤石秀来说道:"兄弟曾到彼处,可和杨林走一遭。"石秀便道:"如今哥哥许多人马到这里,他庄上如何不提备,我们扮作甚么人入去好?"杨林便道:"我自打扮了解魇的法师去,身边藏了短刀,手里擎着法环,于路摇将入去。你只听我法环响,不要离了我前后。"石秀道:"我在蓟州原曾卖柴,我只是挑一担柴进去卖便了。身边藏了暗器,有些缓急,匾担也用得着。"杨林道:"好,好。我和你计较了,今夜打点,五更起来便行。"正是只为一鸡小忿,致令众虎相争。所以古人有篇西江月道得好:软弱安身之本,刚强惹祸之胎。无争无竞是贤才,亏我些儿何碍!钝斧锤砖易碎,快刀劈水难开。但看发白齿牙衰,惟有舌根不坏。

且说石秀挑着柴担先入去,行不到二十来里,只见路径曲折多杂,四下里弯环相似,树木丛密,难认路头,石秀便歇下柴担不走。听得背后法环响得渐近,石秀看时,却见杨林头带一个破笠子,身穿一领旧法衣,手里擎着法环,于路摇将进来。石秀见没人,叫住杨林说道:"看见路径弯杂难认,不知那里是我前日跟随李应来时的路。天色已晚,他们众人都是熟路,正看不仔细。"杨林道:"不要管他路径曲直,只顾拣大路走便了。"石秀又挑了柴,只顾望大路先走,见前面一村人家,数处酒店肉店。石秀挑着柴,便望酒店门前歇了,只见各店内都把刀枪插在门前,每人身上穿一领黄背心,写个大"祝"字,往来的人,亦各如此。石秀见了,便看着一个年老的人,唱个喏,拜揖道:"丈人,请问此间是何风俗?为甚都把刀枪插在当门?"那老人道:"你是那里来的客人?原来不知,只可快走。"石秀道:"小人是山东贩枣子的客人,消折了本钱,回乡不得,因此担柴来这里卖,不知此间乡俗地理。"老人道:"只可快走别处躲避,这里早晚要大厮杀也。"石秀道:"此间这等好村坊去处,怎地了大厮杀?"老人道:"客人,你敢真个不知,我说与你。俺这里唤做祝家村,冈上便是祝朝奉衙里。如今恶了梁山泊好汉,现今引领军马在村口,要来厮杀。却怕我这村里路杂,未敢入来,现今驻扎在外面。如今祝家庄上行号令下来,每户人家,要我们精壮后生准备着,但有令传来,便去策应。"石秀道:"丈人村中,总有多少人家?"老人道:"只我这祝家村,也有一二万人家,东西还有两村人接应。东村唤做扑天雕李应李大官人,西村唤扈太公庄,有个女儿,唤做扈三娘,绰号一丈青,十分了得。"石秀道:"似此,如何却怕梁山泊做甚么?"那老人道:"若是我们初来时,不知路的,也要吃捉了。"石秀道:"丈人,怎地初来时要吃捉了?"老人道:"我这村里的路,有首诗说道:'好个祝家庄,尽是盘陀路。容易入得来,只是出不去。'"石秀听罢,便哭起来,扑翻身便拜,向那老人道:"小人是个江湖上折了本钱,归乡不得的人,倘或卖了柴出去,撞见厮杀,走不脱,却不是苦?爷爷,怎地可怜见小人,情愿把这担柴相送爷爷,只指小人出去的路罢。"那老人道:"我如何白要你的柴?我就买你的。你且入来,请你吃些酒饭。"

石秀便谢了,挑着柴,跟那老人入到屋里。那老人筛下两碗白酒,盛一碗糕糜,叫石秀吃了。石秀再拜谢道:"爷爷指教出去的路径。"那老人道:"你便从村里走去,只看有白杨树,便可转弯,不问路道阔狭。但有白杨树的转弯,便是活路,没那树时,都是死路,如有别的树木转弯,也不是活路。若还走差了,左来右去,只走不出去。更兼死路里地下埋藏着竹签铁蒺藜,若是走差了,踏着飞签,准定吃捉了,待走那里去。"石秀拜谢了,便问:"爷爷高姓?"那老人道:"这村里姓祝的最多,惟有我复姓钟离,土居在此。"石秀道:"酒饭小人都吃够了,改日当厚报。"

正说之间,只听得外国闹吵。石秀听得道拿了一个细作。石秀吃了一惊,跟那老人出来看时,只见七八十个军人背绑着一个人过来。石秀看时却是杨林,剥得赤条条的,索子绑着。石秀看了,只暗暗地叫苦,悄悄假问老人道:"这个拿了的是甚么人?为甚事绑了他?"那老人道:"你不见说他是宋江那里来的细作?"石秀又问道:"怎地吃他拿了?"那老人道:"说这厮也好大胆,独自一个来做细作,打扮做个解魇法师,闪入村里来。却又不认这路,只拣大路走了,左来右去,只走了死路,又不晓的白杨树转弯抹角的消息。人见他走得差了,来路跷蹊,报与庄上官人们来捉他,这厮方才掣出刀来,手起伤了四五个人。当不住这里人多,一发上,因此吃拿了。有人认得他从来是贼,叫做锦豹子杨林。"

说言未了,只听得前面喝道,说是庄上三官人巡绰过来。石秀在壁缝里张时,看见前面摆着二十对缨枪,后面四五个人骑战马,都弯弓插箭;又有三五对青白哨马,中间拥着一个年少的壮士,坐在一匹雪白马上,全副披挂了弓箭,手执一条银枪。石秀自认得他,特地问老人道:"过去相公是谁?"那老人道:"这个正是祝朝奉第三子,唤做祝彪,定着西村扈家庄一丈青为妻。弟兄三个,只有他第一了得。"石秀拜谢道:"老爷爷指点寻路出去。"那老人道:"今日晚了,前面倘或厮杀,枉送了你性命。"石秀道:"爷爷,可救一命则个。"那老人道:"你且在我家歇一夜,明日打听得没事,便可出去。"石秀拜谢了,坐在他家,只听得门前四五替报马报将来,排门分付道:"你那百姓,今夜只看红灯为号,齐心并力,捉梁山泊贼人,解官请赏。"叫过去了,石秀问道:"这个人是谁?"那老人道:"这个官人是本处捕盗巡检,今夜约会要捉宋江。"石秀见说,心中自忖了一回,讨个火把,叫了安置,自去屋后草窝里睡了。

却说宋江军马在村口屯驻,不见杨林、石秀出来回报,随后又使欧鹏去到村口,出来回报道:"听得那里讲动,说道捉了一个细作,小弟见路径又杂难认,不敢深入重地。"宋江听罢,忿怒道:"如何等得回报了进兵?又吃拿了一个细作,必然陷了两个兄弟。我们今夜只顾进兵,杀将入去,也要救他两个兄弟。未知你众头领意下如何?"只见李逵便道:"我先杀入去,看是如何?"宋江听得,随即便传将令,教军士都披挂了。李逵、杨雄前一队做先锋,使李俊等引军做合后,穆弘居左,黄信在右,宋江、花荣、欧鹏等中军头领,摇旗呐喊,擂鼓鸣锣,大刀阔斧,杀奔祝家庄来。比及杀到独龙冈上,是黄昏时分。

宋江催趱前军打庄。先锋李逵脱得赤条条的,挥两把夹钢板斧,火剌剌地杀向前来。到得庄前看时,已把吊桥高高地拽起了,庄门里不见一点火。李逵便要下水过去,杨雄扯住道:"使不得。关闭庄门,必有计策。待哥哥来,别有商议。"李逵那里忍得住,拍着双斧,隔岸大骂道:"那鸟祝太公老贼,你出来,黑旋风爷爷在这里!"庄上只是不应。宋江中军人马到来,杨雄接着,报说庄上并不见人马,亦无动静。宋江勒马看时,庄上不见刀枪人马,心中疑惑,猛省道:"我的不是了。天书上明明戒说,临敌休急暴。是我一时见不到,只要救两个兄弟,以此连夜进兵,不期深入重地。直到了他庄前,不见敌军,他必有计策,快教三军且退。"李逵叫道:"哥哥,军马到这里了,休要退兵,我与你先杀过去,你们都跟我来。"

说犹未了,庄上早知,只听得祝家庄里一个号炮,直飞起半天里去。那独龙冈上千百把火把,一齐点着,那门楼上弩箭如雨点般射将来。宋江急取旧路回军,只见后军头领李俊人马先发起喊来,说道:"来的旧路都阻塞了,必有埋伏。"宋江教军马四下里寻路走。李逵挥起双斧,往来寻人厮杀,不见一个敌军。只见独龙冈上山顶又放一个炮来,响声未绝,四下里喊声震地,惊的宋公明目睁口呆,罔知所措。

你便有文韬武略。怎逃出地网天罗?正是安排缚虎擒龙计,要捉惊天动地人。毕竟宋公明并众头领怎地脱身,且听下回分解。

第七篇《水浒传》Outlaws of the Marsh

Outlaws of the Marsh (Excerpt)

Translated by Sidney Shapiro

FORTY-SEVEN

Heaven Soaring Eagle Writes Two Letters
Requesting Reprieve;
Song Jiang's First Attack on
the Zhu Family Manor

Yang Xiong raised the man to his feet and called Shi Xiu over.

"Who is this brother?" asked Shi Xiu.

"Du Xing is his name. He's from the prefecture of Zhongshan. Because of his crude features everyone calls him Demon Face. Last year he came to Qizhou as a trader. He killed one of the other merchants in his company in a fight, and was brought before the prefect and committed to my prison. I talked with him and found him very knowledgeable about hand-to-hand fighting and jousting with staves. So I used my influence and got him off. I never expected to meet him in this place."

"Are you here on official business, benefactor?" asked Du Xing.

Yang leaned close to his ear. "I killed a man in Qizhou and want to join the band in Liangshan Marsh. We spent last night at the Zhu Family Inn. Shi Qian, who's travelling with us, stole their rooster and we ate it, and the waiter raised a fuss. We got angry and set fire to the inn and ran away in the night. Pursuers caught up with us and we two knocked down several, but a couple of hooked poles reached out of the thicket and dragged Shi Qian away. We barged around until we came here. We were just about to ask for directions when you unexpectedly arrived, brother."

"Don't let it worry you, benefactor. I'll get them to return Shi Qian to you."

"Sit down and have a drink with us."

The three men sat and drank. Du Xing said: "Since leaving Qizhou I benefited greatly from your kindness. Here, a big official took a liking to me and appointed me his steward. Every day all the thousand and one things in his household are in my hands. He trusts me completely. That's why I have no thought of going home."

"Who is this big official?"

"Before Lone Dragon Mountain are three cliffs, and on each of these is a village. Zhu Family Village is in the center, Hu Family Village is to the west, Li Family Village is to the east. These three villages and their manors have a total of nearly twenty thousand fighting men. Zhu Family Manor is the strongest. It is headed by Lord Zhu, who has three sons, known as the Three Warriors. The eldest is called Dragon, the second is called Tiger, the third is called Tiger Cub. They have an arms instructor, Luan Tingyu, who's known as the Iron Staff. Ten thousand men are no match for him. The manor has nearly two thousand fearless vassals.

"Hu Family Manor, to the west, is headed by Squire Hu. He has a son named Hu Cheng, the Flying Tiger, who is a powerful fighter. He also has a daughter, an extremely courageous girl, known as Ten Feet of Steel because of the two long gleaming swords she wields. She's an excellent horsewoman.

"My master heads the eastern manor. His name is Li Ying, and he's skilled with a steel-flecked iron lance. On his back he carries five concealed throwing knives. He can hit a man at a hundred paces, quicker than you can blink.

"The three villages have a solemn pact. If one is attacked by evil-doers, the others must go to its rescue. They're worried that bold fellows from Liangshan Marsh will raid them for grain, so they've prepared to defend themselves, together. I will take you to meet my master, and we'll request him to write a letter asking for Shi Qian's release."

"Your master Li Ying, isn't he the one known in the gallant fraternity as Heaven Soaring Eagle?" queried Yang Xiong.

"The very same."

Shi Xiu said: "I've heard that Li Ying of Lone Dragon Mountain is a chivalrous fellow. So this is where he's from. They say he's remarkable fighter, a real man. We'll go to him."

Yang asked the waiter for the bill, but Du Xing insisted on paying. The three left the tavern. Du led them to the Li Family Manor. It was a huge affair. Fronting on a river cove, it was surrrounded by whitewashed walls beside which grew hundreds of willows each thicker than two arms could embrace. They crossed a lowered drawbridge to the manor gates and entered. Twenty racks on either side of the outer chamber of the main hall were filled with gleaming weapons.

"Please wait here a moment, brothers," said Du. "I will inform the master that you've come."

Du Xing went inside. Shortly afterwards he emerged with Li Ying. Du brought Yang and Shi into the reception chamber, where they kowtowed. Li Ying returned the courtesy and invited them to be seated. The two visitors and their host politely argued over who should sit where, but finally took their places. Li called for wine.

Again the two visitors kowtowed. They said: "We beseech you, sir, to send a letter to the Zhu Family Manor, asking them to spare the life of Shi Qian. We shall never forget your kindness, now or in the hereafter."

Li Ying summoned the family tutor, dictated a letter, and affixed his seal. He directed his assistant steward to deliver it at once on a fast horse and return with the captive. The man took the missive, mounted, and left. Yang and Shi expressed their thanks.

"You needn't worry," said Li Ying. "When they get my letter, they'll release him."

The two thanked him again. "Please come with me to the rear chamber," said their host. "We can have a few drinks while we're waiting."

They went with him and found that breakfast had been prepared. When they finished eating, tea was served. Li asked them some questions about jousting with spears. Their replies showed they knew what they were talking about, and Li was very pleased.

At mid-morning the assistant steward returned. Li Ying, in the rear chamber, asked: "Where is the man you were sent to fetch?"

"I sent the letter in," said the messenger, "confident they would let him go. Instead, the three sons came out and were quite unpleasant. They wouldn't answer your letter, and they wouldn't release the man. They're determined to turn him over to the prefectural authorities."

Li Ying was surprised. "Our three villages have a life-and-death alliance. They ought to respect my letter. How can they behave like that? You must have spoken rudely, to provoke such a response." He turned to Du Xing. "Steward, you'd better go yourself. See Lord Zhu personally, and explain the circumstances."

"I will, sir. But I suggest you write a missive in your own hand. Then, they'll have to let him go."

"Very well," said Li Ying. On a flowery sheet of paper he wrote a letter, added his personal seal to the envelope and handed it to Du Xing.

第七篇《水浒传》Outlaws of the Marsh

A fast horse was led out from the stable, already saddled and bridled. Whip in hand, Du walked through the manor gates, mounted, struck the animal a sharp blow, and galloped off towards the Zhu Family Manor.

"Don't worry," Li Ying said to his two callers. "When they receive this personal letter, they're sure to let him go quickly."

Yang Xiong and Shi Xiu profusely thanked the squire. He drank wine with them, while waiting in the rear chamber.

Daylight was beginning to fade, and still Du Xing hadn't returned. Li Ying became concerned, and he sent men down the road to meet him. A vassal soon came in and reported:

"Steward Du is approaching."

"Who else is with him?"

"He's galloping back alone."

Li Ying shook his head in wonderment. "Very strange. He isn't usually so dilatory. Why is he slow today?"

He left the hall, followed by Yang and Shi. Du had dismounted and was just entering the manor gates. His face was tight with rage and his teeth were bared. For several minutes he was unable to speak.

"Tell us in detail," said Li Ying. "What happened?"

Du Xing controlled himself with an effort. "I carried your letter to their third big gate, and found, by coincidence, the three sons sitting there. I hailed them courteously. 'What do you want?' Tiger Cub snarled. I bowed and said: 'My master has sent me with this letter. I respectfully submit it.' His face darkened, and he replied: 'How can your master be so ignorant? The wretch he sent this morning brought a letter asking us for that Liangshan Marsh bandit Shi Qian. We're going to take him before the prefect. Why have you come again?' I said: 'Shi Qian isn't a member of the Liangshan Marsh band. He's a merchant from Qizhou who's come to see my master. There was a misunderstanding and he burned down your inn. My master undertakes to rebuild it. As a courtesy to us, please be lenient and forgive him.' The three brothers shouted: 'We're not going to let him go.' I said: 'Please, sirs, at least read the letter my master has written.' Tiger Cub took it and, without opening it, tore it to shreds. He yelled for his men to throw me out of the manor. He and Tiger said: 'Don't make your betters angry, or we'll'—I wasn't going to tell you this, but those animals really were too crude— 'we'll nab that Li Ying and take him up before the court as a Liangshan Marsh bandit as well!' They yelled for their vassals to lay hands on me, but I jumped on my horse and raced away. I was burning with rage all the way home. What scoundrels! After all these years of close alliance, to behave so churlishly!"

When Li Ying heard this, his fury burst out of control and spurted sky-high. "Vassals," he roared, "bring me my horse!"

"Calm yourself, sir," Yang and Shi pleaded. "Don't spoil the local harmony for our sakes."

But Li would not listen. He put on golden armor with animal-faced discs, chest and back, and over that a voluminous red cape. Behind him, he affixed five throwing knives. He took his steel-flecked spear, donned his phoenix-winged helmet, strode out of the manor gates, and selected three hundred of his toughest vassals. Du Xing also put on armor, got a lance, and mounted. With him were twenty other horsemen. Yang and Shi girded up their robes. Halberds at the ready, they followed Li Ying's horse as the company advanced rapidly on the Zhu Family Manor.

The sun was sinking in the western hills when they reached Lone Dragon Cliff. They spread out in battle formation. The manor was strategically well situated upon a cliff and surrounded by a broad stream. It was enclosed by three sets of walls, one within the other, each twenty feet high and built of sturdy rock. The front and rear gates of the manor were equipped with drawbridges. Within the walls were huts bristling with weapons. In the gate-house atop the wall were war drums and gongs.

Li Ying reined in his horse in front of the manor. "Three sons of the Zhu Family," he shouted. "How dare you slander me!"

The manor gates opened and out rode fifty or sixty horsemen. In the lead, astride a charcoal roan steed, was Tiger Cub, third son of Lord Zhu. Li Ying shook his finger at the youth.

"The smell of milk hasn't gone from your lips. You've still got baby hair on your head. Your father has a life-and-death alliance with me. We've sworn to defend our villages jointly. When your family is in difficulty and needs men, we give them at once. When it needs materials, we never stint. Today, in good faith, I sent you two letters. Why did you tear them up? Insult me? Why have you committed this outrage?"

"Yes, we have a pact with you to defend our mutual interests," Tiger Cub retorted, "and to grab any bandits from Liangshan Marsh and destroy their mountain lair. How is it you're colluding with them? Are you planning to become a rebel too?"

"Who says Shi Qian is from Liangshan Marsh? You're slandering an innocent man. That's criminal."

"He's already confessed. Your lies aren't any use. They can't conceal the facts. Now, get out of here. If you don't, we'll grab you for a bandit and turn you in as well."

Furious, Li Ying whipped up his horse and charged at Tiger Cub with levelled lance. The youth spurred his own mount forward, and the two fought before Lone Dragon Cliff. To and fro, up and down, nearly eighty rounds they battled. Tiger Cub realized he couldn't vanquish his adversary. He turned his horse and ran. Li Ying gave chase. Tiger Cub rested his lance athwart his animal's neck, fitted an arrow to his bow and drew it to the full. Twisting in the saddle, he aimed and let fly. Li Ying dodged, but the arrow struck him in the shoulder, and he tumbled to the ground. Tiger Cub wheeled his mount and started back, intending to seize him.

Yang Xiong and Shi Xiu uttered a great shout and dashed in the path of the youth's horse with raised halberds. Tiger Cub knew he was no match for them, and again he hurriedly turned his mount. Yang jabbed the horse in the withers, and it reared in pain, nearly unseating its rider. Zhu Family archers, who had followed after the horsemen, began whizzing arrows at Yang and Shi. They had no armor, and had to withdraw. By then, Du Xing had lifted Li Ying to his steed and ridden away. Yang and Shi followed in the wake of the retreating Li Family vassals. The Zhu Family forces pursued them for two or three *li*. But daylight was fading, and they returned to their manor.

Holding Li Ying, Du Xing rode home. At the gate he dismounted and helped his master into the rear chamber. The women of the household came in to attend him. They extracted the arrow, removed his armor, and applied a poultice to the wound.

That night, the men conferred. Yang and Shi said to Du Xing: "That rogue has insulted Li Ying. He's wounded him with an arrow and we haven't rescued Shi Qian. It's all our fault for having involved your master. We two will go to Mount Liangshan and entreat Chao and Song and the other leaders to come and avenge him and rescue Shi Qian." They thanked Li Ying and requested leave to depart.

"It's not that I didn't try, but the odds were too great," said Li Ying. "Please forgive me." He directed Du Xing to present Yang and Shi with gold and silver. They didn't want to accept, but Li Ying said: "We're all in the gallant fraternity. No need for courtesy."

Only then did they take his gifts. They kowtowed and bid him farewell. Du Xing saw them to the edge of the village and pointed out the main road, then returned to the Li Family Manor. Of that we'll say no more.

Yang and Shi pushed on towards Liangshan Marsh. They saw in the distance a newly built tavern, its wine pennant fluttering in the breeze. On arrival, they ordered drinks and asked directions. Actually, this tavern was a lookout place recently added by the men on Mount Liangshan. Shi Yong was in charge. He overheard them asking the waiter how to get to the fortress, and could see that they were no ordinary men. He walked over to their table.

"Where are you two gentlemen from? Why do you want to go up the mountain?" he queried.

"We're from Qizhou," Yang Xiong replied.

Shi Yong suddenly remembered. "Then you must be Shi Xiu."

"No, I'm Yang Xiong. This is Shi Xiu. How do you know his name, brother?"

"We haven't met. But not long ago brother Dai Zong stopped here on his way back from Qizhou and told me a lot about him. Today, you two want to go up the mountain. That's very good news."

The three exchanged courtesies, and Yang and Shi told Shi Yong of their encounter with the Zhu Family. Shi Yong directed the waiter to serve them the best wine. He opened the window of the pavilion overlooking the water, bent his bow, and shot a whistling arrow. Instantly, a bandit rowed a boat over from the reeds in the cove opposite. Shi Yong escorted the two on board and delivered them to Duck's Bill Shore. He had sent a man ahead to report, and now Dai Zong and Yang Lin came down the mountain to welcome them. After courtesies were exchanged, they went together to the stronghold.

When the leaders were informed that more bold fellows had arrived, they convened a meeting in the hall and sat in their chairs of rank. Dai Zong and Yang Lin led in Yang Xiong and Shi Xiu and presented them to Chao and Song and the other leaders. Chao questioned them carefully on their backgrounds. The two told of their skill with arms and of their desire to join the band. The leaders were very pleased, and offered them seats.

After a time Yang Xiong said: "There is a man named Shi Qian who also wants to join. But unfortunately he stole a rooster that heralded the dawn at the Zhu Family Inn and we got into a row. Shi Xiu burned the place down and Shi Qian was captured. Li Ying sent two letters requesting his release, but the three sons of the Zhu Family have refused to let him go. They've vowed to take all the gallants in this stronghold, and they've cursed and reviled you in every way. Those varlets have no sense of fitness whatsoever."

If he hadn't told this, nothing would have happened. But he did, and Chao Gai flew into a rage.

"Children," he shouted to the assembled bandits, "take these two out, cut off their heads, and report back."

Song Jiang hastily intervened. "Calm yourself, brother. These two warriors have come a long distance, and with one thought in mind—to help us. Why do you want them executed?"

"Ever since our bold fellows took over here from Wang Lun, we've always placed chivalry and virtuous behavior towards the people first. Brother after brother has gone down the mountain, but none of them has injured our prestige. All our brothers, new or old, are honorable and chivalrous. These rogues, in the name of the gallants of Liangshan Marsh, stole a rooster and ate it, shaming us by association. They must be decapitated, and their heads displayed at the scene of the crime as a warning. I will personally lead our forces down and purge the Zhu Family Village so that our reputation for valor will not be lost. Children, off with their heads!"

"Wait," said Song Jiang. "Didn't you hear what these two brothers just said? Shi Qian the Flea on a Drum has always been light-fingered. It was his behavior that provoked the Zhu Family. In what way have these two brothers shamed our stronghold? I've heard many people say that the Zhu Family Manor is hostile to us. Cool down, brother. We have many men and horses, but we're short of money and grain. Although we're not looking for trouble with the Zhu's, since they've started the provocations, this is a good chance to go down and nab them. When we defeat the manor, we'll capture enough grain to last us four or five years. We're not seeking an excuse to harm them, but those oafs are really much too rude. You are the highest leader here, brother. Why sally forth on minor matters? I have no talent, but with a contingent of men and horses, and the help of some of our brothers, I'd like to attack the Zhu Family Manor. If we don't wipe it out, we won't return. For one thing, only vengeance will restore our prestige. Secondly, We must pay those pipsqueaks for their insults. Thirdly, we'll get a lot of grain for the use of our fortress. And fourthly, we can ask Li Ying to come up and join our band."

"A very good idea," said Wu Yong. "We in the fortress shouldn't destroy men who are like our own hands."

"I'd rather you decapitated me than hurt one of our brothers," said Dai Zong.

At the urging of all the leaders, Chao Gai finally pardoned Yang Xiong and Shi Xiu. They thanked him and kowtowed.

"Don't be angry," Song Jiang said to them soothingly. "It's a rule of our stronghold, and we must obey. Even I could be decapitated if I violated it. I could expect no forgiveness. Pei Xuan, the Ironclad Virtue, has recently been made provost marshal, and rules regarding rewards and punishments have been promulgated. Don't hold it against us, please."

Chao asked Yang Xiong and Shi Xiu to take seats after Yang Lin, and all the rank and file bandits were summoned to join in congratulating the new chieftains. Cows and horses were slaughtered and a celebration feast was laid. Living quarters were allocated to Yang and Shi, and ten bandits were appointed to each as attendants.

The banquet ended that evening, and the next day they feasted again. Then the leaders conferred. Song Jiang directed Ironclad Virtue to compile a list of men to go down the mountain, and he invited the other leaders to accompany him in a raid on the Zhu Family Manor. He was determined to demolish it. It was agreed that Wu Yong, Liu Tang, the three Ruan brothers, Lü Fang and Guo Sheng would remain to hold the fortress, in addition to Chao Gai. Those guarding the shore, the gates and the taverns would also remain at their posts. Newly arrived Meng Kang, who had been appointed boat builder, would replace Ma Lin as the supervisor of war vessels. A written announcement was drawn stating that the leaders participating in the raid on the Zhu Family Manor were divided into two units. The first included Song Jiang, and would head a body of three thousand foot soldiers and three hundred cavalry. When armored and equipped, this would go first, as the van.

The second unit would include Lin Chong, and would also head three thousand foot soldiers and three hundred cavalry. This body would follow, as reinforcements.

Song Wan and Zheng Tianshou would continue holding the small forts at the Shore of Golden Sands and Duck's Bill Shore, respectively, and be responsible for supplying the attackers with grain and fodder.

Chao Gai saw the raiders off and returned to the stronghold.

Song Jiang's party made straight for the Zhu Family Manor. Nothing untoward happened on the way, and they soon were approaching Lone Dragon Mountain. When they were about a *li* or so away, they pitched camp. Song Jiang's tent was in the middle, and he sat there conferring with Hua Rong.

"I hear the roads to the manor are very tricky," he said, "and that it's difficult to move up on them with soldiers. I'll send a couple of men to scout out which paths are best. Then we can advance and engage the foe."

"I've been idle for a long time, brother," said Li Kui. "I haven't killed a single person. Let me go in first."

"Not you, brother," said Song Jiang. "If we needed a shock assault, I'd send you. But this is careful, delicate work. You're not suitable."

Li Kui laughed. "That friggin manor. Why trouble yourself? I'll take two or three hundred of the lads, and we'll carve our way in and cut all the wretches down. What do you need scouts for?"

"You're talking rot. Get out of here, and don't come till I call you."

Li Kui left, muttering to himself: "All that fuss about swatting a few flies."

Song Jiang summoned Shi Xiu and said: "You've been here before. I'd like you and Yang Lin to scout around."

"Since you've come with a large force, they're of course on their guard at the manor. How should we disguise ourselves?"

"I'll dress up as an exorcist," said Yang Lin, "and conceal a knife in my clothes. I'll carry a prayer wheel as I walk along. The moment you hear the sound of it, come up to me and stay close."

"I sold fuel in Qizhou," said Shi Xiu. "I'll tote a load as if I was selling again. I also will have a concealed weapon. In an emergency I can use the carrying-pole as well."

"Good. We'll work out the details, and prepare tonight. We'll get up at the fifth watch and go."

The next morning, Shi Xiu left first with his load of fuel. Before he had twenty *li*, he encountered a complicated maze of paths which seemed to go round in circles through thick groves of trees. He couldn't figure them out. Shi Xiu set down his load. Behind, he heard the hum of an approaching prayer wheel. Yang Lin, a broken straw hat on his head, wearing an old priest's robe and twirling prayer wheel, was coming towards him with stately tread. No one else was in sight, so Shi Xiu spoke to him:

"These paths all twist and turn. I can't remember which was the one I took with Li Ying the other day. It was nearly dark and they knew the way and travelled fast. I wasn't able to get a good look."

"Stay off the paths, then, and stick to the main road."

Shi Xiu shouldered his load again and continued on. He saw a village ahead, and several taverns and butcher shops. He walked up to the gate of one of the taverns. He noticed that racks of weapons stood in front of every shop, and that all the men in them wore golden vests with the word "Zhu" emblazoned on the backs. People on the streets were similarly dressed. Shi Xiu respectfully hailed an old man who was passing by and bowed.

"May I ask you about a local custom, grandpa? Why are there weapons at every door?"

"Where are you from, stranger? If you don't know, you'd better leave quickly."

"I'm a date-seller from Shandong. I've lost my capital and can't go home. Now I sell fuel. I'm not familiar with your local ways."

"Go quickly. Get out of sight. There's going to be a big battle here soon."

"How can that be, a nice place like this?"

"You really don't know? Well, I'll tell you. This is called Zhu Family Village. It's ruled by Lord Zhu, whose manor is up on that cliff. He's offended the bold fellows in Liangshan Marsh, and they've come with men and horses to kill us all. But the paths to our village are too complicated, and they're camped outside. The manor has directed every able-bodied young man to get ready. The moment the order comes, they're to rush to the aid of our fighters."

"How many people have you here in this village, grandpa?"

"Nearly twnty thousand. And we can count on help from the villages to our east and west. The eastern one is ruled by Heaven Soaring Eagle Li Ying. The western one belongs to Squire Hu. He has a daughter called Ten Feet of Steel who's a terror with weapons."

"In that case, you've nothing to fear from Liangshan Marsh!"

"That's right. If we ourselves had just arrived, we too could be easily captured."

"What do you mean, grandpa?"

"We have a jingle that goes:

A fine Zhu Family Village,
Its paths twist round about,
Getting in is easy,
But just try getting out!"

Shi Xiu began to weep. He flopped to the ground and kowtowed. "I'm a poor trader who lost his capital on the road and can't go home, and now I'm selling fuel," he cried. "This is awful. I've landed in the middle of a battle and can't escape. Pity me, grandpa. I'll give you this load of fuel, only show me the way out!"

"I don't want your fuel for nothing. I'll buy it from you. Come with me. I'll treat you to some food and wine."

Shi Xiu thanked him, shouldered his load, and went with the old man to his house. His host poured out two bowls of white wine, filled another with rice gruel, and set them before him. Again Shi Xiu expressed his thanks.

"Grandpa," he begged, "tell me how to get out of here."

"You just turn whenever you reach a white poplar. Take the path that starts from there, whether it be narrow or broad. Any other path leads to a dead end. No other tree will do. If you take a wrong path, you'll never get out, whether you go left or right. The dead-end trails are strewn with hidden bamboo spikes and iron prongs. You're liable to step on them, and you're sure to be captured. You wouldn't have a chance of getting away."

The young man kowtowed and thanked him. "What is your name, grandpa?"

"Most people in this village have the surname of Zhu. Only my family is named Zhongli. We've always been here."

"I've had enough food and wine. Some day I'll repay you well."

While they were talking, they heard a clamor outside. A voice shouted: "We've caught a spy." Startled, Shi Xiu and the old man hurrid into the courtyard. They saw seventy or eighty soldiers escorting a man with his hands tied behind his back. Shi Xiu recognized Yang Lin. He had been stripped naked. Shi Xiu groaned inwardly.

"Who is that?" he made a pretense of asking the old man.

"Why is he bound?"

"Didn't you hear them say he's spy sent by Song Jiang?"

"How was he caught?"

"He's a bold rascal. He came alone, disguised as an exorcist priest, barging into the village. Since he didn't know the way, he could only follow the main road. Left or right would have taken him into dead ends. He's never heard the secret of the white poplars. Someone saw him wandering off on a wrong turning, and thought he looked suspicious. So he reported to the manor, and they sent men to nab him. The rogue pulled a knife and wounded four or five of them. But they were too many, and he was overpowered. Now he's been recognized as a robber. They say he's called Yang Lin the Elegant Panther."

Down the road a voice exclaimed: "The Third Son of the manor has come of patrol."

Through a crack in the courtyard wall Shi Xiu saw twenty foot soldiers with red-tasseled spears, followed by five mounted men, all with bows and arrows. Behind, another four or five riders on white horses were gathered protectively around a young warrior on a snow-white steed. In full armor, he carried a bow and arrows, and gripped a lance. Shi Xiu recognized him, but feigned ignorance.

"Who is that young gentleman passing by?"

"Lord Zhu's third son, Tiger Cub. He's engaged to Ten Feet of Steel of the Hu Family Manor, west of here. Of the three sons, he's the most terrific fighter."

Shi Xiu again thanked the old man and said: "Please point out which road I should take."

"It's late already, and a battle may be raging ahead. You'll be throwing your life away."

"Save me, grandpa, I beg you."

"Spend the night here. Tomorrow, if things are quiet, you can leave."

Shi Xiu thanked him, and remained. Four or five mounted men were going from door to door and exhorting the populace: "If you see a red signal lantern tonight, use might and main to catch the Mount Liangshan bandits and claim the reward."

When they had gone, Shi Xiu asked: "Who was that official with them?"

"He's our local sheriff. Tonight they're planning to capture Song Jiang."

Shi Xiu gave this some thought. Then he borrowed a torch, said good night, and retired to sleep in a thatched hut in the rear.

Song Jiang and his forces were encamped outside the village. Neither Shi Xiu nor Yang Lin had returned. Ou Peng was sent to the village entrance to check. After a while he reported back.

"People are saying they've caught a spy. Those paths are very complicated. I didn't dare to go further in."

Song Jiang grew angry. "I can't wait for a report any longer. Now the word is they've caught a spy. That means our two brothers have been trapped. We'll attack tonight, regardless. We'll fight our way in and rescue them. How do the rest of you feel about it?" he asked the other leaders.

"I'll go first," said Li Kui. "Just to see what it's like."

Song Jiang ordered all men to arm themselves and put on their gear. Li Kui and Yang Xiong would be the vanguard. Li Jun would command the rear. Mu Hong would take the left flank, Huang Xin the right. Song Jiang, Hua Rong and Ou Peng would lead the central contingent.

Amid waving flags, pounding drums and braying gongs, the raiders, shouting and brandishing swords and axes, marched rapidly on the Zhu Family Manor.

It was dusk when they reached Lone Dragon Cliff. Song Jiang urged the forward contingent to attack the manor. Li Kui, stripped to the buff and brandishing two steel battle-axes, rushed ahead like a streak of fire. But at the manor, he found the drawbridge raised and not a light showing anywhere. Li Kui was going to jump into the moat and swim across, but Yang Xiong stopped him.

"No, don't. If they've closed the manor gates, they must have some scheme. Wait till brother Song Jiang arrives, then we'll decide what to do."

To Li Kui this was unbearable. He smote his battle-axes and shouted up the cliff: "Lord Zhu, you friggin crook, come out! Your master Black Whirlwind is here, waiting!"

There was no response from the manor.

Song Jiang, followed by Yang, arrived with his men. The manor was quiet. He reined in his horse and looked. Not a weapon or a soldier was in sight. Warily, he thought: "I'm wrong. The Heavenly Books say clearly: 'Avoid rashness in the face of the enemy.' I didn't foresee this. I thought only of rescuing our two brothers, and moved my troops up through the night. I didn't expect that when I got in deep, right up to their manor, that the foe's army wouldn't show. They must be up to something."

He ordered his three contingents to withdraw at once. Li Kui objected.

"We've come this far. You mustn't retreat," he cried. "You and I will fight our way in. All of you, follow me!"

Before the words were out of his mouth, the manor knew about it. A signal rocket arched through the sky. On the cliff thousands of torches suddenly flared. Arrows showered down from the gate-house above the wall. Song Jiang hastily withdrew his forces along the road on which it had come. The rear guard under Li Jun set up a shout.

"We're cut off! They've laid an ambush!"

Song Jiang directed his men to seek other roads. Li Kui, flourishing his axes, dashed about, looking for adversaries, but he couldn'nt find a single enemy soldier. Another signal rocket soared from the cliff. Before the sound of it had died away, thunderous shouts rang from all sides. Pop-eyed and slackmouthed with astonishment, Song Jiang was completely at a loss. In spite of his civil and military skills, he had fallen into the net.

Truly, a plan for snaring tigers and dragons was being used to catch a heaven-startling, earth-shaking man.

How did Song Jiang and the other leaders escape? Read our next chapter if you would know.

Water Margin (Excerpt)

Translated by J. H. Jackson

CHAPTER 46

*THE STRIKING HAWK TWICE WRITES
A LETTER; SUNG CHIANG FIRST
ATTACKS THE CHU VILLAGE*

Yang Hsiung raised the man and then introduced him to Shih Hsiu as Tu Hsing of Chung Shan Fu. He had a fierce face, and therefore people called him the Devil Faced Man. Previously he had come to Chi Chow Fu, and had entered into business with some other men. During a quarrel with his partner he had lost his temper and killed him. He had been arrested and tried, but Yang Hsiung, knowing that he was very skillful with the cudgel and lance, had saved his life by getting a light sentence passed.

The man asked, "On what official business do you come here, my benefactor?"

Yang Hsiung whispered in his ear, "I committed murder at Chi Chow Fu, and am now escaping to Liang Shan Po, where I shall join the brigands." He then told him about all the trouble at the inn and how Shih Ch'ien had been captured.

"You need not worry about that matter," said Tu Hsing, "because I can arrange for Shih Ch'ien to be released."

第七篇《水浒传》Outlaws of the Marsh

They asked him to join them at the wine. Tu Hsing then explained that at that village he was entrusted by the headman with important matters, and he had great influence there. There were three villages in close alliance, and altogether they supported an armed force of about 20,000 men. The most influential headman was Chu Chao-feng who had three valiant sons named Dragon, Tiger, and Tiger's Cub. They had a drill instructor named Luan Ting-yu, nicknamed Iron Staff, who was invincible. In the western village was a headman who had a son called Hu Cheng, nicknamed Flying Tiger, who was very courageous. His sister, Hu San-niang, nicknamed Pure One, was a skilled rider, and could fight with a sword in each hand. At the village on the east side was a man Li Ying, nicknamed Striking Hawk, who was his master who always carried five swords on his back, and could throw these a hundred paces, and kill men at that distance. These villages supported each other whatever the risk or danger, and were prepared to fight against the brigands of Liang Shan Po when they came to command the grain. He (Tu Hsing) offered to take them to Li Ying and get him to release Shih Ch'ien.

They accepted this offer, and settled their accounts with the innkeeper. They then followed Tu Hsing to the village. Yang Hsiung noticed that it was a big village, with a moat all round. The banks of the moat were very high, and on the top were many hundreds of large willows. They crossed a drawbridge and passed through a gate in a wall. They came to the principal hall in front of which were over twenty racks filled with spears, swords, etc., all of which were polished bright and in good order.

Tu Hsing asked the other two to wait outside while he went inside to announce their arrival. It was not long before Li Ying came out, and after being introduced invited Yang Hsiung and Shih Hsiu to come inside. When they had had some wine Yang Hsiung explained the object of their visit, and as a result Li Ying told his scribe to write a letter asking for the release of Shih Ch'ien, and sent a mounted messenger with it to the neighboring village. It was not long before the messenger returned and reported that the headman had at first been willing to release Shih Ch'ien. But when his three sons heard of it they objected, and insisted upon Shih Ch'ien being sent to the magistrate for trial.

Li Ying was surprised at this, and wondered what was the use of the alliance when even his urgent letter had been ignored. He asked Tu Hsing to go there himself, and try to secure the release.

Tu Hsing agreed to go, but asked Li Ying to write a letter by his own hand which he would take with him. This was done, and mounting a horse Tu Hsing galloped off.

It was almost night time before Tu Hsing returned. As he dismounted they saw that he was in a towering rage. His face was red with passion, and as he raised his lips he showed the tightly set teeth. For some time he could not speak.

"Take your time and tell us all about it." said Li Ying at last.

Tu Hsing slowly repressed his anger, and then spoke, "I took your letter to the village and dismounted at the third gate where the three sons of Chu Chao-feng were seated. I saluted them separately and then Tiger's Cub called out, 'Well, what do you come here for?'

"I replied in a respectful manner, 'I have here a letter from my master.' I presented it. Tiger's Cub showed annoyance as he replied, 'Why does your master not understand human affairs? Early this afternoon he sent some fellow here with a letter asking for that brigand Shih Ch'ien to be released. Just now we are going to send him to the magistrate so why have you come here?'

"I replied that Shih Ch'ien was not a bandit, but was a guest on his way to visit my master. He made a mistake in setting fire to his inn. That you would go tomorrow and make full compensation for the damage done, and hoped that they would overlook the offense and accept a full apology."

"Then all replied, 'That cannot be done.' So I requested them to kindly read your letter, but Tiger's Cub simply took it from me, and tore it into bits without reading it. He then ordered me to get out of their village at once. They also warned me not to incite them to anger any further or they would... I would not dare to speak the whole truth—but they said they would arrest you, sir, also as a bandit of the Liang Shan Po, and send you to the yamen. They told their servants to seize me but I jumped on the horse and galloped off. It is evident that the sworn alliance between our villages is no longer of any value, as those fellows are quite unreasonable."

While Li Ying listened to this he became more and more annoyed, and at last called out, "You men! Quickly get my horse ready."

Yang Hsiung and Shih Hsiu asked him to keep cool as they did not wish to see the peaceful relations between the villages disturbed by what they had done. But Li Ying took no notice of this, went indoors, put on his metal mail, with a large silk gown over it, put his five swords on his back, and took a spear in his hand; put on his iron helmet; and summoned three hundred men to accompany him. Tu Hsing also put on his mail armor, and got twenty horsemen to follow him. Yang Hsiung and Shih Hsiu took their swords, and also followed.

It was late in the afternoon when they reached the other village, and there the men stood in ranks. The village was situated on raised ground and had three proteecting walls, one inside the other. The walls were built of stone, and were about twenty feet high. The village was surrounded by a moat, over which were two drawbridges in front of the north and south gates. In the towers at the gates were drums, gongs, etc. for summoning the men to fight.

Li Ying reined in his horse before the bridge, and shouted, "Why have you three sons of Mr. Chu, defamed me?" At once the gate of the village was opened, and a body of about fifty horsemen galloped out. In front rode the third son, Tiger's Cub, on a roan-colored horse.

Li Ying pointing at him shouted, "You fellow still have your milk teeth and childhood's tufts of hair. Your father entered into a sworn alliance with me to defend these villages. If your family had trouble we would render unlimited assistance, or if short of something we would supply it. Today I sent a letter which you tore up. Why did you insult my messenger in that way? Have you no decency?"

Tiger's Cub replied, "Our family entered into an alliance with you so that we could together resist the encroachments of the bandits at Liang Shan Po. But now you have become intimate with them and intended open rebellion."

"Why do you say that I am intimate with bandits? Why have you arrested an ordinary man, and falsely accused him?"

"The prisoner has already confessed that he is a thief so why do you talk in this wild disorderly manner? You cannot hide his crime. You clear off at once, or I will arrest you also."

Li Ying was now very angry, and whipping his horse he galloped forward. Tiger's Cub crossed the bridge, and did the same. They met in combat, and charged each other about eighteen times. As the Tiger's Cub could not overcome Li Ying he at last turned his horse round and retreated. Placing his spear on the horse he took his bow and arrow, and turning his body shot at Li Ying who was following close behind. Li Ying tried to avoid the arrow, but it struck him in the shoulder, and he fell off his horse. Tiger's Cub pulled his horse round, and rushed forward to seize Li Ying.

Yang Hsiung and Shih Hsiu seeing the danger of Li Ying shouted, seized their swords, and rushed towards Tiger's Cub, who seeing that the odds were against him retreated. As the horse turned, however,

第七篇《水浒传》Outlaws of the Marsh

Yang Hsiung struck it, and the animal reared with the pain. Tiger's Cub was almost thrown off, but kept his seat. The villagers now rushed forward, and as Yang Hsiung and Shih Hsiu were not wearing their mail they now retreated along with Tu Hsing, Li Ying, and their followers. They were pursued for about a mile when the villagers returned to the village as it was getting dark.

Upon reaching their village Li Ying had his wound dressed, and then the four men discussed the position. Yang Hsiung expressed regret that all this trouble had arisen through their affairs, and considered that there was no way of obtaining the release of Shih Ch'ien. They thought that the best thing was for them to proceed to Liang Shan Po, where they would petition Ch'ao Kai to send an expedition to avenge the insult to Li Ying.

Li Ying agreed to this, and pressed the two men to accept some silver to cover their expenses. At last they accepted the money and left at once for Liang Shan Po. Li Ying and Tu Hsing remained behind.

Yang Hsiung and Shih Hsiu soon reached the neighborhood of Liang Shan Po, and stayed at the inn kept by Shih Yung as an outpost. When they inquired about the road to Liang Shan Po, Shih Yung asked where they came from, and what business they had at the stronghold. When Yang Hsiung said they came from Chi Chou, Shih Yung immediately asked if his name was Shih Hsiu, and when they had all been introduced Shih Yung explained that he had heard all about Shih Hsiu from Tai Tsung who had just returned, and was staying at the stronghold. Shih Yung then shot a whistling arrow across the lake, and soon a party of bandits appeared in boats. They crossed the lake, and were taken up to the stronghold where they were duly introduced to all the leaders. They explained fully all that had occurred at the Chu village, and how Li Ying had been grossly insulted.

When Ch'ao Kai had heard all the details he was angry, and said,

"We have gathered here many loyal and brave men, and have bestowed much benefit on the people in the surrounding country. When we go on any expedition we are never deficient in valor. All our brothers here are great heroes. But these two men have been implicated in a petty theft of a chicken, and if we associate with them we shall lose our great reputation. So we must kill these two men, and send their heads to the village to show the people that we have nothing to do with robbers. Then as the people in the village have reviled us we must go there and destroy their village. Thus we shall preserve our reputation for valor."

Sung Chiang however spoke, "That will not do. These two men did not take part in the theft as that was the affair of Shih Ch'ien who was traveling with them. What they have done was not disgraceful. We have heard several times that that village has been unfriendly to us. Elder brother, restrain your anger. We have not got a big stock of grain or money, but let us not make too much of that. As they however have insulted us we can go and punish them for that. If we defeat them we shall have food supplies for at least five years. You cannot go yourself because you are our leader, but I will go and command the punitive expedition. If I fail then I will not return. I finally propose that Li Ying be admitted to our numbers."

"What you say is extremely proper," said Wu Yung. "It would not do to kill our brothers who are willing to join us."

"It would be better if you kill me instead of these men," said Tai Tsung.

All the other leaders expressed their support of these views, and Ch'ao Kai agreed. Yang Hsiung and Shih Hsiu expressed their apologies.

The following day Sung Chiang took three thousand bandits, three hundred mounted men, and nine other leaders. He also placed a similar number of men in charge of Lin Ch'ung and nine other leaders, and

第七篇《水浒传》Outlaws of the Marsh

these were to be his reserves. They soon reached the neighborhood of the Chu village and encamped. A tent was erected for Sung Chiang, and there he discussed matters with Hwa Jung. "I have heard that round this village there are numerous small roads so that it would not be advisable to send our men there at present. We must first send two spies to find out all about the roads, and then we can advance with greater security."

Li K'wei offered to go as a spy, as he said he had not killed a man for a long time.

"You must not go now," said Sung Chiang, "because we shall want you when the fighting commences."

Li K'wei laughed at this. "There is no need to send spies. If you let me have two hundred men I could enter the village, and settle this matter quite easily."

"Don't talk nonsense!" shouted Sung Chiang. "You can wait outside until I call for you."

As he went out however Li K'wei called out, "Those villagers are only like flies. Why are you so nervous?"

Sung Chiang summoned Shih Hsiu, and instructed him to go into the village with Yang Lin.

"The people will already be on the qui vive as your men are here," said Shih Hsiu. "How can we enter the village without being seen?"

"I can get into the village disguised as a priest," said Yang Lin. "I will carry the prayer rings, and shake them as I go along. You (Shih Hsiu) can follow me some distance behind."

"At Chi Chou I sold firewood," said Shih Hsiu, "and I think that I may get in the village with a load of firewood."

Yang Lin thought this a good idea, and they both agreed to start off that evening. They started off about 5 p.m. and had about three miles to go. They noticed the numerous paths and roads on all sides, and that the country was well covered with dense trees. Shih Hsiu put down his load, and spoke to Yang Lin as there was no one about. "There are so many footpaths about that I have not yet recognized the road I was on with Li Ying. As it is now getting dark we cannot make out our way very clearly."

"We need not worry about that," replied Yang Lin. "Let us follow what appears to be the main road."

They continued their way, and soon came to a place where there were shops and inns, and Shih Hsiu stopped in front of an inn. There were many men there with uniforms bearing the character Chu. He spoke to an old man, "Sir, what is the reason for these swords being staked at every door?"

"Where do you come from?" asked the old man. "As you do not know you had better go on your way."

"I am from Shantung, and having no money I brought this firewood into the village to sell it. I do not know the customs of this place."

"You had better get away at once and seek refuge," said the old man. "It will not be long before there is big fighting here."

"What will the fighting be about?"

"You evidently do not know, but I will tell you. This village hates the bandits of Liang Shan Po, but they are now encamped just outside the village. Our chief has summoned all the men to assemble here."

"And how many men are there in this village?"

"In this village there are about ten thousand men, but the other village would also join us in any fighting."

"Why are you afraid of Liang Shan Po brigands when you have so many men?"

"Even I myself was nearly seized when I first came here. There is an old saying that the roads round this place are so well arranged that men might enter the village, but they could not get out."

第七篇《水浒传》Outlaws of the Marsh

Shih Hsiu burst into tears, and bowing said, "What hard lines for me! I cannot go back even if I sell my firewood. So I will give you this firewood if you will tell me how I can get away."

"I cannot accept your offer, but I do not mind buying the firewood from you. Please come inside my house, and take a meal before returning."

Shih Hsiu thanked him for this, and followed the old man into the house. After partaking of the congee offered, Shih Hsiu again asked to be shown the way out.

"You just go your way in the village until you come to a poplar tree where you can turn. You must not turn if there is no poplar tree, or there would be death. No other trees will do—take no notice of them. If you make one mistake your position will be hopeless, as on the other roads there are hidden pointed stakes and hooks."

Shih Hsiu thanked him for the information, and asked for his name. The man's name was Chungli. Shih Hsiu then departed promising to reward him for the food and wine some other day. Just then there was a great uproar outside, and voices were calling out, "A spy is seized!" Looking out Shih Hsiu saw about eighty armed men with a prisoner whom he recognized as Yang Lin. Shih Hsiu was much surprised, and turning to the old man asked, "Who is the man? Why have they bound him?"

"Have you not heard them say that he is a spy? He has evidently got in the village in the disguise of a priest, and not knowing the roads he has taken the wrong road and has been captured. Somebody has recognized him as the bandit, Yang Lin." Just then a patrol of about fifty men came up in charge of a young man on a white horse. Shih Hsiu recognized him, but asked the old man who he was.

"That is the third son of Mr. Chu, our headman, and is named Tiger's Cub. The Pure One is betrothed to him."

Shih Hsiu again thanked him, and asked to be shown the road. The man urged him not to go that day, as there was great danger and it was getting dark. After further pressing, Shih Hsiu again went indoors. Shortly afterwards there was knocking at the street door, and a voice called out, "The red lamp will be the signal tonight, and when you people see it, you must join the attack on the brigands." When the man had gone Shih Hsiu asked who he was, and was informed that he was the official thief-catcher and that that night he hoped to arrest Sung Chiang. Shih Hsiu thought matters over, and then taking a fire, he bade the old man good night and went to the room at the back, and slept there.

Sung Chiang was waiting in his tent for a long time, and at last as Shih Hsiu and Yang Lin had not returned he sent out O Peng to see whether he could get any news. When he returned he reported that he had heard cries in the village about a spy. The paths were so numerous and complicated that he dared not go any farther.

Upon hearing this Sung Chiang was very angry. "Evidently they have captured our two brothers so why should we wait here any longer as we cannot get any inside information. We must attack at once, and try to save the lives of our brothers. What do you think of that?" he asked the other leaders.

"I will fall on slaughtering." offered Li K'wei.

Sung Chiang issued orders that all the men should prepare for an immediate advance. Li K'wei and Yang Hsiung were to be in charge of the vanguard; Li Chun in charge of the rear guard; Mu Heng on the left wing; Huang Hsin on the right wing, while Sung Chiang, Hwa Jung, and O Peng took charge of the main body. There was at once a great hubbub, waving of flags, beating of drums and gongs, and a great display of swords and axes. It was evening. Upon reaching the village Li K'wei found that the bridge had been drawn up, and as there were no lights showing in the village he thought of going through the water. But Yang Hsiung held him back, and said, "As the village gates are closed it may be only a plot or trap for us. We will wait until the other leaders arrive, and then we will discuss matters."

Li K'wei could not endure any delay so lifting aloft his two axes he yelled, "That fellow Mr. Chu! You come out! The Small Whirlwind is waiting here for you."

No reply came from the village to this challenge. Just then Sung Chiang and the other leaders came up, and were told of the position. Sung Chiang was surprised not to see even a single man on the other side, and also became suspicious. Suddenly he remarked, "I have made a mistake. In the three Divine Books I received it was stated quite clearly, 'In warfare make no undue haste.' I forgot about this in my haste to save the lives of our comrade and have brought troops here without proper plans for entering the village. Now that I am here the enemy hides. There is evidently a plot, and I must at once give orders for a retreat."

Li K'wei said, "But as we have come so far we cannot retreat without doing someting. I will go forward, and you can follow me."

While he was speaking a skyrocket went up from the village, and instantly on all the hills surrounding the village there were numerous lights from torches. From the tower above the village gate came a shower of arrows. Sung Chiang gave the orders for retreat, but Li Chun, leader of the rear guard, came and said, "The road we arrived by is now all obstructed, and there is probably an ambush." Sung Chiang gave an order for a number of horsemen to try and find some other road. Just then another skyrocket went up on one of the surrounding hills, followed by loud shouts from all sides. Sung Chiang was quite perplexed.

Even the strategist with the most elaborate plans could not avoid

getting into a tight corner?
> Plans to catch a tiger,
> Or a dragon in its den,
> Are ready to capture,
> The extraordinary men.

All Men Are Brothers (Excerpt)

Translated by Pearl S. Buck

CHAPTER XLVI

The Eagle Who Smites The Heavens twice writes a letter of brotherhood. Sung Chiang goes for the first time to attack the village of the Chu family.

IT IS SAID:

At the time when Yang Hsiung lifted up that man and Shih Hsiu saw him then Shih Hsiu asked, saying, "Who is this brother?"

Yang Hsiung answered, "This brother is surnamed Tu and his name is Hsing, and his ancestors were men of Chung Shan Fu. Because his face is so coarse and wild men all call him The Devil Faced. Last year he came to Chi Chou to do business and in a fit of anger he killed his fellow traveler and so he was taken to court and put into the gaol at Chi Chou. I, seeing that he understood boxing and the use of all weapons, made every effort to save him, and I did not think to meet him again here today."

Tu Hsing then asked, saying, "Most Gracious, what official matter brings you hither?"

Yang Hsiung put his mouth to his ear and said, "I killed a person in Chi Chou and now we are turning to the mountain lair to join them there. Last night we sought shelter in the inn of the Chu family, and because a fellow traveler of ours, Shih Ch'ien, stole a fowl of the inn and ate it, in a moment of time a quarrel arose with the keeper of the inn. His temper rose and in the end we burned the inn. We three then escaped by night nor did we trouble ourselves that behind us would come pursuers. We two brothers stabbed several of them, but we did not think that out of the wild grass there should be thrust forth two barbed spears and that they would hook Shih Ch'ien away. We two ran hither, then, and were about to ask the way, and we did not think to meet you, Good Brother!"

Then Tu Hsing said, "Most Gracious, do not be in such haste. I will bid them free Shih Ch'ien for you."

And Yang Hsiung said, "Good Brother, stay a little and drink a cup with us."

The three then sat down and they drank wine, and Tu Hsing said, "Ever since I left Chi Chou I have received greatly of your kindness and I came hither and thanks to a certain great lord here he let me stay as a bailiff in his house. Every day I send out money or I bargain with this one and that and all such matters he places upon me and greatly does he trust me. Because of this I do not now wish to return to my home."

And Yang Hsiung asked, "Who is this great lord?"

Then Tu Hsing answered, "Before The Ridge Of The Lonely Dragon are three ridges and upon each ridge is a village. The one in the middle is the village of the Chu family, the one on the west is the village of the Hu family, the one on the east is the village of the Li family. The three villages and these three farmilies have altogether some ten thousand or so of men and horses. But the village of the Chu family is the best. The head of this village is named Chu Ch'ao Feng. He has three sons, who are the braves of the Chu family. The eldest is called Chu The Dragon, the next is called Chu The Tiger, and the third son is called

第七篇《水浒传》Outlaws of the Marsh

Chu The Tiger Cub. They have a teacher who is called Luan T'ing Yü, The Iron Staff. Among ten thousand there is not one to match him. In the village there are 5 to 7 hundred of fierce, able tenants. In the village to the west belonging to the Hu family the head is the old lord Hu. He has a son called Hu Ch'en, and he is also exceedingly fearsome. He has besides a daughter most heroic of all, and her name is The Ten Foot Green Snake The Goodwife Hu. She uses double knives that are like sun and moon in her hands. On horseback in battle she is a terror to see. In the village to the east is my lord. His surname is Li and his name is Yün and he can wield a staff of pure iron. On his shoulders he wears five flying knives, and even at a hundred paces away these knives are dreadful. Now the people of these three villages have made a vow that they will live and die together and that they will have one heart and one mind. Whichever village has a calamity the others will help it. Fearing lest the good fellows of the mountain lair will come to ask them for goods, they are prepared to withstand them. Now I will take you two honnored ones to the village and when you have seen the lord Li, I will ask for a letter to be sent to save Shih Ch'ien."

Again Yang Hsiung asked, "That lord Li of yours—is he not the one who far and wide is called The Eagle Who Smites The Heavens?"

And Tu Hsing answered, "It is indeed he."

Then Shih Hsiu said, "By river and lake I have heard it said there is upon The Ridge Of The Lonely Dragon a Li called The Eagle Who Smites The Heavens who is indeed a good fellow. And so he is here then! I have long heard that indeed he is an astounding and very fine fellow. Let us go therefore the once."

Then Yang Hsiung bade the serving man to bring the wine account. But how could Tu Hsing be willing to let him pay for the wine? He would do this himself.

The three then left the village wine shop and Yang Hsiung and Shih

Hsiu were led to the village. Now when Yang Hsiung looked about he saw it was a very fine large village. All around the outside flowed a stream and beside it was a whitewashed wall, and there were many great elms so large that two men could not reach around them. Outside the village gate was a drawbridge. They crossed over this and entering the village gate went into the great hall. On both sides of the hall were more than twenty racks for weapons and they were filled with glittering weapons. And Tu Hsing said, "Wait here for a little while, my two Honorable Brothers, and wait until I go and announce your coming and ask my lord to come out and meet you."

Tu Hsing was not long gone before he returned and they saw Li Yün the lord come from inside, and Tu Hsing led Yang Hsiung and Shih Hsiu in to make obeisance. In great haste the lord Li made response and he invited them to come in and sit down. But Yang Hsiung and Shih Hsiu were thrice courteous before they would sit down. Then Li Yün commanded that wine should be brought out to entertain them. Again did Yang Hsiung and Shih Hsiu make obeisance and say, "We do pray the great lord will send a letter to the village of the Chu family and save the life of Shih Ch'ien. Then living or dead we will not dare to forget your mercy."

So Li Yün commanded that the tutor should be sent for who wrote a letter and he worte the lord's own name to it and he set his seal upon it also. Then the lord commanded that one be sent with the letter and a swift horse prepared that he might go to the village of Chu to seek for the man. So the messenger took his lord's letter and mounted the horse and was gone. Then Yang Hsiung and Shih Hsiu made obeisance in thanks and the lord Li replid, "Let the hearts of the two braves be at rest. As soon as my letter reaches there he will be released."

Again Yang Hsiung and Shih Hsiu thanked him and the lord Li said, "Pray come into the inner hall and we will drink some wine and wait."

The three then went with him within, and an early meal was prepared for them to eat, and when they had eaten and while they were drinking their tea, the lord Li asked concerning some methods of using weapons. Seeing that Yang Hsiung and Shih Hsiu answered very well he was pleased in his heart.

About mid-morning the messenger returned and the lord Li called him into the inner hall and asked him, saying, "Where is the man you went to seek?"

The messenger answered, "I saw Chu Ch'ao Feng myself and I gave him the letter and he had the heart to let him go free. But the three Chu braves came out and they grew angry and they would not write an answering letter nor would they let the man go free and they are determined to send him into the city to court."

The lord Li gave a start of fear at this and he said, "They are under a covenant with me and our vow is made with each other already. If my letter reached him, he ought to have answered it. How has it come about thus? Surely it is that you have spoken wrongly that it has come about thus. Tu Hsing, do you go and see Chu Ch'ao Feng yourself and tell him in detail how all this came about."

Then Tu Hsing said, "This lowly one is willing to go. Only I do ask my lord to write a letter himself. Only thus will they be willing to free him when I reach there."

And the lord Li said, "You have spoken well."

Then he brought out a sheet of flowered letter paper and the lord Li himself wrote a letter. Upon the envelope he set a seal of his name and rank and this he gave to Tu Hsing and Tu Hsing went to the back and chose a swift horse and he put on it saddle and bridle. Then he took a whip and going out of the gate he mounted the horse and whipped him several times and so hastened to the village of the Chu family.

And lord Li said to Yang Hsiung and Shih Hsiu again, "Let your hearts be at rest, Honored Sirs. This letter written with my own pen will surely free him in a very short time."

Then deeply did Yang Hsiung and Shih Hsiu bow their thanks and there in the inner hall they drank wine and waited. Seeing that the sky darkend with night and they did not see Tu Hsing return doubt arose in lord Li's heart and he sent men out to meet him. Then these villagers made report, saying, "The bailiff Tu Hsing has returned."

Then Li Yün asked, saying, "How many men have come back?"

The villagers said, "Only the bailiff himself has come running back alone."

Then Li Yün shook his head and said, "Here is a strange thing. Usually they do not treat me so meanly as this. Why is it they are thus today?" And he came out of the outer hall and Yang Hsiung and Shih Hsiu came with him. There they saw Tu Hsing come down from his horse and he came to the gate of the village. When they saw his appearance he was so angered the skin of his face was empurpled and his teeth were bared. For a time he could not speak and at last Li Yün asked him, saying, "Pray speak out all the cause for this. How has this come about?"

But Tu Hsing had to let his anger go down before he could speak, and he said, "This lowly one took my lord's letter and I went to the third gate and there I met the three brothers, Chu The Dragon, Chu The Tiger, and Chu The Tiger Cub. There they sat. I made three greetings. But Chu The Tiger Cub shouted out, 'For what have you come hither again?' Then I bowed and said humbly, 'My lord has a letter here.' Then that Chu The Tiger Cub changed the look of his face and he began to curse, saying, 'That lord of yours—how is it he knows so little of propriety? This morning a worthless evil fellow came hither bringing a letter and he sought for that robber from the robbers' lair,

Shih Ch'ien. Now even as I am about to send him into the city court how is it you are come again?' This lowly one then replied, 'This Shih Ch'ien is not one of the horde at the robbers' lair. He is only a traveler from Chi Chou and he was coming to see the lord of our humble village. In carelessness he burned your inn, but our lord will have it built again as it was before. Ten thousand times do I hope you will consider our poor pride and raise your hand high in mercy and let him go free. Forgive—forgive!' Then the three Chus all began to cry out, 'We will not give him back—we will not give him back,—Again did I say,' My lord, pray look for yourselves at this letter that my lord has written with his own pen for you.' But those three Chus, although they took the letter, they did not open it to read it; they tore it into many pieces and they shouted to a villager to thrust me out of the gate by my neck. And Chu The Tiger and Chu The Tiger Cub said too, 'Do not rouse the anger of your superiors! Or we will—'I do not dare to tell you plainly what they said for those three beasts are without any sense of propriety, and they said, 'And we will take that Li of yours, that Li Yün of yours, and we will treat him like a robber of the robbers' lair and send him to court, too!' Then they shouted to the villagers to seize me but I made my horse fly and so I came away. But on the road I was like to die of my anger—those accursed—for naught have we sworn all these years of brotherhood—to be so without any righteousness or mercy today—"

Li Yün heard to the end and the uncontrollable anger of his heart rose as it were thirty thousand feet into the air nor could he smother it down and in a great voice he called to the villagers, "Saddle me my horse immediately!"

Then Yang Hsiung and Shih Hsiu exhorted him, saying, "Great lord, cease your anger. Do not because of ones so lowly as we are spoil the harmony of this place."

But how could Li Yün be willing to hear them? He went into his room and he put on a yellow robe of war and girdled it with a clasp and he put on his front and back shield with the faces of beasts upon them. Over this he wore a full robe of red and on his back he hung his bow and his flying arrows. He took his staff of iron and steel and wore his helmet winged like a phoenix, and he went outside the village. There he counted out three hundred fierce brave villagers and they also put on their garments of war. With his weapon in his hand he mounted his horse, and with him also he took some twenty horsemen. And Yang Hsiung and Shih Hsiu also tied up their garments securely and grasping their swords they went with Li Yün beside his horse and they all hastened to the village of Chu, and as the sun was about to sink behind the mountains they had already come to the front of The Ridge of The Lonely Dragon and there they lined up their men and horses.

Now this village of Chu was better built than the village of Li and they claimed the whole ridge as their land. Around it was a broad stream and the village was set on the very top of the ridge. It was encircled by three walls about twenty feet high and all made of great piled rocks. There were two gates, one back, one front, and a drawbridge to each. Within the walls were built small houses and in all of them were swords, spears, and weapons of all sorts. On the towers of the walls were placed drums and brass gongs of war.

And Li Yün sat upon his horse at the front of the village and he shouted in a mighty voice and he said, "You three of the house of Chu! How dare you curse me and speak evil of me?"

Then was the gate of the village seen to open and out charged some fifty or sixty horses. The front horse was as red as coals and upon it sat the third son of Chu, The Tiger Cub! But Li Yün pointed at him and cursed mightily, saying, "Such as you! There is still the smell of milk on your lips—you have your newborn hair still on your head—your father swore the vow of brotherhood with me to live and die together so that

第七篇《水浒传》Outlaws of the Marsh

whatever we did we would be of the same mind and heart and protect our villages. If there were trouble in your house and he came to ask me for men in the morning I would send men that same morning. If you wanted anything I would not once deny you. Now I have but a common fellow for whom I have written twice to ask him of you and why did you tear up my letter and spoil my name? What sort of reason is this?"

Then Chu The Tiger Cub answered, "My house did swear such a vow that we would stay together in heart and mind to fight against the robbers of the great lair and we swore that we would sweep the lair clean. How is it you have joined with these rebels? Is it your wish to be a rebel?"

Li Yün shouted out, "And whom do you say is in the great lair? Such as you—you take a common man for a robber and what crime is this!"

The Tiger Cub replied, "This robber Shih Ch'ien has already confessed what he is. Do not talk here so foolishly and wildly. You cannot cover it up! If you are going, then go—or we will seize you also and we will send you as a robber as well!"

Then indeed was Li Yün mightily angry and he beat his horse and with his weapons in his hands he charged upon The Tiger Cub. The Tiger Cub gave his horse free rein also that he might go and fight against Li Yün and there before The Ridge Of The Lonely Dragon these two fought back and forth and from side to side for some seventeen or eighteen rounds. But the Tiger Cub could not overcome Li Yün. He turned his horse and was about to retreat. But Li Yün urged his horse on in pursuit. The Tiger Cub held his weapon upright on his horse. With his left hand he reached for his bow, with his right he took at the same time his arrow and he fitted the arrow to the bow, and he stretched full his bow, he took true aim and turning, he let fly the arrow. In great haste Li Yün dodged to one side, but the arrow was already in the arm.

He fell off his horse upon the ground. Then Chu The Tiger Cub turned his horse again to seize Li Yün. Yang Hsiung and Shih Hsiu, seeing this, gave a great shout and they took their two swords and they dashed forward toward The Tiger Cub's horse to kill him. The Tiger Cub could not withstand them and in great haste he turned his horse to go. But Yang Hsiung had already thrust his sword in the horse's thigh and in great pain the horse reared itself upright and nearly threw its rider upon the ground.

Then those men who had come out with The Tiger Cub all rushed forward, their arrows fixed to aim. Seeing this Yang Hsiung and Shih Hsiu thought to themselves, "We have no armor nor shields and there is naught for us to do but to retreat and pursue no more."

Now Tu Hsing had long ago lifted Li Yün up from the ground and mounting their horses they had already gone away. So Yang Hsiung and Shih Hsiu went with the villagers and so departed also. The soldiers and horsemen and villagers of the village of the Chu family pursued them for a mile or so and then seeing that it grew dark with night, they went home also.

Tu Hsing supported Li Yün and they went back to the front of the village and there dismounted and they went back into the inner hall and sat down. Then the women of the house came out to see him and when the arrow had been pulled out they tended him and they took off his garments of war and they spread ointment upon the wound.

That same night they all took counsel together in the inner hall. And Yang Hsiung and Shih Hsiu said to the bailiff Tu Hsing, "This great lord has been cursed by those lawless fellows and even struck with an arrow and Shih Ch'ien still cannot come forth free. It is all because of us that the great lord has become so entangled. We two brothers can but go on to the mountain lair and there see Ch'ao Kai and Sung Chiang and implore their aid, and so also implore all the chieftains that they may come and take revenge for the great lord, and at the same time save Shih Ch'ien."

Thus saying they went to take their farewell of Li Yün and to thank him and Li Yün said, "It was not that I did not use my heart in it, but truly it was that I could not help it. I pray you, Sir Braves, that you will not blame me therefore."

Then he bade Tu Hsing to take out gold and silver and give it to them. But how could Yang Hsiung and Shih Hsiu be willing to receive it? Yet Li Yün said, "Nevertheless, pray accept it, Sirs."

Only then were the two willing to receive the gift. Then they bade Li Yün farewell and Tu Hsing escorted them outside the village gate and pointed out the highway and then he bade them farewell and went back to the village alone. Of this no more need be told.

Let it be told further. Yang Hsiung and Shih Hsiu followed the road toward the robbers' lair and soon they saw in the far distance a newly erected wine shop and the flag hung high before it. The two went into the inn and bought some wine to drink and then they asked the direction of the road. Now this wine shop was one newly built by the robbers for the purpose of spying out the land, and Shih Yung was the keeper of it. As the two drank therefore they asked the serving man what road to take to the mountain lair. Shih Yung, seeing that these two were no common fellows, then came forward himself to talk with them and he said, "From whence have two such honored guests come? And why is it you ask the road up the mountrin?"

Yang Hsiung replied, "We have come from Chi Chou."

Then Shih Yung suddenly bethought himself and he asked, "It must be this honorable one is Shih Hsiu?"

Yang Hsiung replied, "I am only Yang Hsiung. This brother is Shih Hsiu. But how is it that you, Elder Brother, know the name of Shih Hsiu?"

In great haste Shih Yung replied, "This lowly one does not know him. But when our brother Tai Chung went to Chi Chou and returned he said he had known the brother Shih Hsiu. Long have I heard your name and we are rejoiced to have you come up the mountain."

When these three had all made obeisance, Yang Hsiung and Shih Hsiu told Shih Yung all that had happened. Immediately Shih Yung commanded the serving man to bring wine that they might all drink, and he opened the windows of the pavilion in the water and let fly a singing arrow. Then out of the reeds opposite there came soon robbers rowing a boat. Shih Yung then invited the other two to get into the boat and he escorted them to The Duck's Bill Beach. Now Shih Yung had already sent men up the mountain to annouce who was coming and they soon saw Tai Chung and Yang Ling coming down the mountain to meet them. When each one of them had made obeisance and had performed the rites of courtesy, they went together into the great lair.

All the chiefs now knew it that this day there were good fellows coming up the mountain and they all came to meet togeher, and they sat down in the hall of the great lair. And Tai Chung and Yang Ling led Yang Hsiung and Shih Hsiu into the hall to make obeisance before Ch'ao Kan and Sung Chiang and all the chieftains. When they had met each other Ch'ao Kai asked closely into the history of these two. Then Yang Hsiung and Shih Hsiu told what skill they had in weapons, and all were very pleased and gave them seats in their ranks. Then Yang Hsiung slowly said, "There was one who came with us to join this great lair who is called Shih Ch'ien, who did what he should not and in the inn he stole the fowl that crew for the dawn and in a moment there was a quarrel sprung up. Shih Hsiu set fire to the place and burned up the inn and its goods and Shih Ch'ien was captured by them. Li Yün twice wrote a letter to free him but unluckily the three sons of the house of Chu would not let the man go. They swore they would seize all the good fellows in the mountain lair and in every sort of way they insulted and cursed us. Truly indeed those hateful things are without any propriety whatever."

Now if he had not spoken these words to Ch'ao Kan ten thousand things would never have happened, for he had scarce finished speaking when Ch'ao Kai fell into a great rage and he shouted, "Children, kill me these two men and show me their heads when you have done it!"

In great haste Sung Chiang said, "Elder Brother, cease your anger. These two braves, not fearing the distance, came from far away and they came hither to help us. Why then would you kill them?"

Ch'ao Kai said, "We good fellows of the mountain, ever since we killed Wang Lün, have always held first loyalty and propriety. We have always treated the common people with mercy and with righteousness. Whenever we go down the mountain we have never once lost our pure passion. All our brothers here on the mountain, whether newly come or here of old, have the demeanor of noblemen. But these two things have taken our fair name to go and steal fowls to eat and they have made us share their shame! Today then we will first kill these twain and we will hang their heads there by the burned inn for a sign to all men. I will myself take fighting men and horses and lay waste that village, so that our pure passion may not be lost. Children, quickly kill these and bring their heads to me!"

But Sung Chiang exhorted him, saying, "It is not so. Elder Brother, have you not heard what these two good brothers have just now said? That Flea On A Drum Shih Ch'ien has ever been a thief like this, and so because of this he roused the anger of the Chu family. How then is it that these two good brothers have put us to shame? I have often heard men say also that those men in the village of the Chu family would fain war against us here in the lair. Elder Brother, cease your wrath at once therefore. Now our men and horses in the lair are countless in number, but we lack money and food. If we do not go and seek them out for a battle, then those things will come and seek trouble with us, as though one blew aside the hair on a beast's skin to seek for hidden disease. For thus well enough it is for us to seize this chance to go and fight them. If we can capture this village we will have food enough for three or five years. It is not that we have made a quarrel to injure them, but indeed they are without any law at all. But you are chief of the lair and you cannot go hither and thither on these small frays. But I, lowly and unskilled as I am, will myself take men and horses and I will ask some of my good brothers to go down the mountain with me to attack the village of the Chu family. If we do not lay waste that village I will never come up the mountain again. In the first place, I do this so that we will not lose our pure passion of purpose. In the second place, only thus can we wipe away the shame of being cursed by such small men as these. In the third place, we shall gain a great deal of food to give to the lair to use. In the fourth place, we must invite Li Yün to come up the mountain and join us."

Then Counsellor Wu Yung said, "Our brother Sung Chiang speaks very fitly. How can we brothers in the lair kill those of our own number, as though hand should kill foot?"

Then Tai Chung said, "I would cut off my own head rather than have these two brothers beheaded, for then would the brave men of all other places fear to come hither any more."

Thus did all the chiefs exhort, and only then did Ch'ao Kai consent to change his command, and Yang Hsiung and Shih Hsiu then made their apologies. But Sung Chiang comforted them, saying, "Good Brothers, do not think amiss. This is the rule of our lair, and we cannot but act thus. If even I committed some fault even I also would lose my head, and I would not dare beg repeal because of my place. Now the command has been made that The Iron Faced, P'ei Hsüan shall be chief of police among the fighting men, and there are laws fixed for reward

第七篇《水浒传》Outlaws of the Marsh

and for punishment. Good Brothers, you can but pardon us, therefore. "

Then Yang Hsiung and Shih Hsiu having made obeisances and given apologies, Ch'ao Kai called out, "Go and sit below Yang Ling!"

Then all the lesser robbers were bade to come and make their congratulations to the new chiefs. Cows and horses were butchered and a feast of welcome made. Two houses were set apart and there Yang Hsiung and Shih Hsiu were told to settle themselves, and each person was given two lesser robbers as serving men.

That night after they had feasted and scattered they met again to feast on the second day. When they were all gathered together they took counsel together and Sung Chiang told The Iron Faced P'ei Hsüan to count off certain men to go down the mountain, and he invited other chieftains also to go with him to attack the village of Chu, for he was determined to lay waste that whole village. When they had decided about the affair, besides Ch'ao Kai who stayed always to guard the lair, there stayed behind Wu Yung, Liu T'ang and the three Juan brothers, Lü Fang and Kao Shen to protect the great lair. All those who had certain tasks assigned to their care such as guarding the shores and guarding the gates, tending the wine shops, and all such as these did not go forth. Moreover, the newly appointed boat master Meng K'an was changed for the old master Ma Ling, and a proclamation was written that all chieftains who went down the mountain to attack the village of Chu were to be divided into two companies. The first company was to be Sung Chiang, Hua Yung, Li Chün, Mu Hung, Li K'uei, Yang Hsiung, Shih Hsiu, Huang Hsin, Ou P'eng and Yang Ling, and they led with them three thousand robbers and three hundred horsemen and they put on their armor and took their weapons and went down the mountain and on their way.

The second company was Ling Ch'ung, Ch'ing Ming, Tai Chung, Chang Heng, Chang Shun, Ma Ling, Teng Fei, Wang The Dwarf

Tiger and Pei Sheng, and they also led forth three thousand robbers and three hundred horsemen and they followed behind the others. Then were appointed to the two lesser lairs of The Golden Sands and The Duck's Bill Beach Sung Wan and Chen T'ien Shou. They were to remain there and bring food for men and feed for the horses. And Ch'ao Kai escorted the warriors for a distance and then he returned alone to the lair.

Let it be told now how Sung Chiang and the other chieftains all hastened as fast as they could to the village of the Chu family. Of the journey there is nothing to be told for they soon came to the front of The Lonely Dragon Ridge and there was about a third of a mile and a little more to go. The fighting men in front set their ten tents in the from of a square and Sung Chiang's tent stood in the middle. There he took counsel with Hua Yung and he said, "I have heard it said that the small paths into the village of the Chu family are many and confused and it is not possible to take fighting men thither. Let us therefore first send two men in to spy out and hear how the paths wind themselves for we must know clearly what road goes to and what road goes from the village before we can send fighting men in to do battle with them there."

Then Li K'uei said, "Elder Brother, I have been idle for how long and I have not killed a single man all that time. I will go first for once."

But Sung Chiang replied, "Brother, you may not go. When we break the ranks of the enemy and charge in, then will we use you at the front. But this is an affair of spying and we cannot use you."

Li K'uei laughed and said, "But for such an accursed village as this why should you trouble yourself so much, my Elder Brother? Let me just take two or three hundred of our children and we will kill our way in! We will slaughter every person in this accursed village. Why should we want men to go first and spy out?"

But Sung Chiang shouted out, saying, "Do not speak as a fool! Go

第七篇《水浒传》 Outlaws of the Marsh

aside, you! When I call you then only are you to come!"

Li K'uei went away then and to himself he muttered, "What is the use of making such an ado over killing a few files!"

Then Sung Chiang called Shih Hsiu to come and he said, "Brother, you have already been there. Do you set out early in the morning therefore with Yang Ling."

Shih Hsiu said then, "Now has my elder brother come hither with many men and horses, and will not the village be well prepared for it? How shall we best disguise ourselves to go in?"

Then Yang Ling said, "I will disguise myself as an exorcist priest and in my robes I will hide a dagger and in my hands I will take my sounding wheel and as I go I will trun it around and around. When you hear the sound of it then do not leave my side."

And Shih Hsiu said, "I was once a seller of fuel in Chi Chou. I will therefore but carry in a load of fuel to sell and it will be well enough. I will hide a weapon at my side also, and if something unforeseen comes suddenly to pass I can use my carrying pole as weapon also."

Yang Ling replied, "Good, good. Now we have planned this together and tonight we will make all ready and we will rise at the fifth watch and set forth."

When the next morning was come Shih Hsiu went first carrying his load of fuel and he had gone scarcely seven miles when he saw the paths were many and crossed each other often and on all four sides there were circling, intersecting paths. There were many trees also and it was hard to know what direction to take. Then he put down his load and did not go forward, for he heard beside him begin slowly the sound of the exorcist's wheel. When Shih Hsiu looked he saw Yang Ling, on his head a large broken hat, on his person an old robe of a Taoist priest and in his hand he whirled the sounding wheel. Thus he came all the way whirling it. Shih Hsiu, seeing there was not a person near, called out to

Yang Ling, "These roads are very tangled, and I do not know which road it was that I came the other day with Li Yün. The night was dark then, too, and they all knew the way and came and went quickly and I could not see how they went."

Yang Ling said, "But let us pay no heed to whether the paths go straight or crooked. Let us but follow the big road."

Again Shih Hsiu took up his load and he went ahead on the big road. At last ahead of him he saw a village full of people and there were many meat shops and wine shops. Shih Hsiu, bearing the fuel, went to the door of a wine shop and there put down his load. Then he saw that every shop had knives and weapons thrust into the earth before the door. Every man wore also a yellow sleevelesss jacket, and on the jackets were printed a large character Chu and every man who came and went was so garbed. Shih Hsiu saw this and he looked at an old man and called greeting and made obeisance and said, "Elder One, pray tell me what the customs of this place are and why do they thrust all their knives and weapons before their doors?"

That old man replied, "And from whither are you a traveler that you do not know that you can but go quickly on your way?"

Shih Hsiu said, "I am a traveler from Shantung come out to sell dates and I have lost my capital and I cannot return to my native place. For this I have carried fuel hither to sell. But I do not know the customs here nor do I know how the land lies."

Then the old man said, "You can but go speedily on your way and hide somewhere else. There is soon to be a great war here."

But Shih Hsiu asked, "But in such a good and pleasant village as this how can they wish to war such a great war?"

The old man replied, "Sir Guest, I do not know whether you be true or not but I will tell you this. We here are called the village of the Chu family and on the ridge there is the house of our chieftain Chu Ch'ao

Feng. Now we have offended the good fellows of the robbers' lair and they have brought soldiers and horsemen to the mouth of the village and they have come to attack and to kill us. But they do fear the entangled paths to our village and so they dare not to come on. They all wait outside and we have already sent out a command from the village that every man of every house who is young and strong shall be prepared for battle. When the command comes they are to rush to our aid."

Shih Hsiu asked, "But how many men have you here in this village, Elder One?"

The old man said, "Only in this one village we have some ten or twenty thousand men. To the east and west are two more villages who will support us. The east village belongs to the lord Li Yün and the west belongs to the lord Hu. He has a daughter who is third daughter of the house of Hu and her nickname is The Ten Foot Green Snake and she is altogether terrible."

Again Shih Hsiu asked, "Then why should such parts as these fear the robbers' lair?"

Again that old man replied, "But even if we ourselves came for the first time and did not know the road they would take us too."

And Shih Hsiu asked, "Eleder One, how do you mean when you first came you would be taken?"

The old man replied, "Of these paths in our village men of old have said, 'How good a village is this of the Chu family, to which all the roads circle and entwine! It is easy to go in but one cannot escape from it.'"

When Shih Hsiu heard this he began to weep, and he fell down and made obeisance and he cried to the old man, "I am but one who travels far and wide and who have lost my capital and I can never return to my home. If I sell my load and go out and I come upon the war and cannot escape will it not be bitter for me then? My Father, have pity on me and

I will give you this load of fuel! My Father, only point me out the path!"

Then that old man said, "And why should I take your fuel for nothing? I will buy it of you. Come in, then. Pray drink some wine and eat some rice."

Then Shih Hsiu thanked him and taking up his load he went with that old man and so into the house, and the old man poured out two bowls of white wine and he filled a bowl with gruel made from the polishings of rice and he bade Shih Hsiu eat it. Then again Shih Hsiu made obeisance and he thanked him, saying, "Father, do you but tell me now the path out."

And the old man said, "Go out from the village and you will see a white poplar tree. There you may turn. Pay no heed to whether the road be narrow or wide, but wherever the road turns by a white poplar that is the way. If there is not such a tree, then the road is dead. If there is any other tree, it is not the road either. If you go astray, however you turn you cannot get out. Moreover in the earth of these paths there are hidden pointed bamboos and pointed iron prongs. If you go astray you may also fall into a trap and a barb will fly at you and you will be caught. Whither do you think to go?"

And Shih Hsiu made obeisance and he gave thanks and he asked then, "Father, what is your noble surname?"

That old man siad, "Of those surnamed Chu the village has the most. There is only I have a double surname and it is Chung Li and I have lived here long."

Ang Shih Hsiu said, "I have eaten enough of both food and wine and on another day I will repay you richly."

Now in the midst of this talk they heard a confusion and a quarreling outside and Shih Hsiu heard them say, "We have caught a spy!"

第七篇《水浒传》Outlaws of the Marsh

At this Shih Hsiu gave a start of fear and when he went out with the old man to see what was amiss, there he saw some seventy or eighty fighting men leading a man with his hands bound behind him. When Shih Hsiu lookd at this man it was no other than Yang Ling, stripped naked and with thongs binding him. When Shih Hsiu had seen this he could but cry bitterness to himself secretly and in a low voice he asked the old man falsely, saying, "Who is this man they have seized? And why is he thus bound?"

The old man replied, "Did you not hear them say he is a spy from Sung Chiang's side?"

Again Shih Hsiu asked, saying, "How is it he was taken?"

And the old man replied, "Then said this thing had the greatest sort of daring. He came here alone as a spy and he wore as disguise the robe of a Taoist exorcist and so he came into the village. But he did not know the paths and so he came only by the big road and he came winding right and left and so he fell into the blind paths. Nor did he know the trick of the white poplar trees that they are signs. Men seeing that he had gone astray began to suspect him as to where he had come from, and they sent report to the guards of the head of the village that they should come and seize him. Then this thing took out his dagger and whenever he moved his hand he wounded some four or five men. But he could not withstand so many men as are here and when they all charged upon him they captured him. There were some who knew him as a robber before and he was called The Five Hued Leopard Yang Ling—"

But before he finished speaking they heard a shout in front, "The third lord of the Chu family comes to examine the people in the streets!"

Now Shih Hsiu was standing and he was peeping out of a crack in the corner of the wall and he saw twenty pair of pointed staves on which waved tassels of horsehair dyed red, and there were four or five men who followed behind on horseback, and they all carried bows and quivers full of arrows. There were three or five pairs of pure white horses and they encircled a young warrior in their midst. He rode upon a snow-white horse, and he wore armor from head to foot, and his bow and his quiver of arrows hung upon his person. In his hand was a silver weapon.

Now Shi Hsiu knew him very well but he asked the old man falsely, saying, "Who is this lord who passes by?"

And that old man replied, "This man is no other than the third son of the head of the village, who is Chu Ch'ao Feng, and his name is Chu The Tiger Cub. He is already betrothed to the maid in the western village of Hu, she who is called The Ten Foot Green Snake. There are three brothers but he is the most terrible of all."

Then Shih Hsiu made obeisance and he gave thanks, saying, "Father, pray point me out the path by which I must go out."

That old man said, "Today it is late and if there is a battle ahead you will have lost your life for nothing."

Then Shih Hsiu said, "My father, save this life of mine!"

And that old man said, "Pray rest a night here in my home. Tomorrow we will listen and if there is no trouble then you shall go out."

So Shih Hsiu made obeisance of thanks again and he stayed at the old man's house. Then he saw suddenly four or five horsemen coming to make report and they went to every house, and they gave the command, saying, "Oh you people, tonight you are to see the red lamps as signals. With united heart and united strength go forth to seize the robbers of the robbers' lair! Then will we take them to the magistrate and ask for our reward!" Thus shouting they went past and on their way. Then Shih Hsiu asked, saying, "Who are these men?"

That old man replied, "The offcial is the police of this village, and tonight they have all covenanted together that they will seize Sung Chiang."

Shih Hsiu, hearing what was said, pondered for a time in his heart and then he asked the old man for a torch and bade him a good and peaceful night. Then he went into his own thatched room and lay down.

Let it then be told of Sung Chiang and his men and horsemen who waited encamped about the village. They did not see Yang Ling and Shih Hsiu come back to make report, and therefore again they sent Ou P'eng to go to the mouth of the village. He came back and made report, saying, "I hear the people inside stirring and talking together and they say they have caught a spy. But seeing how tangled the road paths were and how hard to tell one from the other, I did not dare to go deeply in."

Sung Chiang listened to the end of his speech and his anger rose in him and he said, "How can we wait until they come back and make report before our fighting men can go in? We have already lost a spy to them and surely our two brothers are held there. This night our fighting men can but press in, killing as we go for we must save our two brothers. But I do not know that all the chieftains think of this."

Then Li K'uei was seen to say, "I will kill my way in first and see how things are."

Sung Chiang heard this and at once he sent forth a command to tell the fighting men to put on armor and weapons and Li K'uei and Yang Hsiung were to go in first as vanguard. Li Chün and others were to bring up the rear. Mu Hung at he left and Huang Hsin at the right, and Sung Chiang, Hua Yung, Ou P'eng and others were chiefs in the midst of the ranks.

Then waving their flags and shouting their war cries, beating their drums and gongs with their great knives and their broadaxes they went charging toward the village, killing as they went until they might reach The Ridge Of The Lonely Dragon.

Now this was the time of twilight and Sung Chiang urged the front men on to attack the village. The vanguard Li K'uei stripped stark naked and grasping two long-handled battle axes, went leaping ahead like a flame. When he came to the village and looked about the drawbridge was already high drawn and there was not a flicker of light to be seen at the gate of the village. Li K'uei then was about to go down into the water of the moat and so cross over, but Yang Hsiung laid hold on him and said, "This you may not do. They have close the village gate and assuredly there is a plot here. Wait until our Elder Brother comes and we will plan a way."

But how could Li K'uei be patient? Clapping his broadaxes together he roared curses at the other shore and he said, "That cursed old thief of a lord Chu! Come out, you! Your elder The Black Whirlwind is here!"

But there came no answer from the village. Then Sung Chiang and all the chiefs and horsemen and fighting men arrived, and Yang Hsiung went to meet them and he said, "We see neither men nor horses at the village nor is there a sound of anyone stirring."

Then Sung Chiang reined in his horse and he looked about him. There could be seen no weapon nor blade, neither man nor horse about the village. He began to have doubts in his heart and suddenly he bethought himself, "This is my mistake! Those heavenly books commanded me very clearly forbidding me, saying, 'Do not be impatient before battle.' But I did not at that time foresee this. I thought only to save my two brothers, and for this have I led my men out even in the night. I did not dream I would have already come so deeply into danger. If we go straight to the front of the village and see no enemy there, then assuredly there is a plot."

Then quickly he shouted out, "Retreat, all!"

But Li K'uei cried out, saying, "Elder Brothers, the fighting men and the horses have already come to this point, do not retreat! I will go with you two and we will first kill our way across. All of you come after me."

第七篇《水浒传》Outlaws of the Marsh

But before he had finished speaking it was already known in the village. There was heard the sound of a single signal rocket that flew across the heavens. Straightway upon The Ridge Of The Lonely Dragon there flamed a hundred thousand torches and they were all flaring. Beneath the gate house on the village wall the arrows came out like a shower of rain. In great haste Sung Chiang went back by the road they had come. Then the chieftains and the men bringing up the rear, Li Chün and his horses and men, first set up a shout, saying, "The road by which we came is all close and assuredly there are men in ambush!"

Then Sung Chiang sent out men and horsemen to seek in all four directions for a road by which to go. Li K'uei, brandishing his two axes, ran hither and thither seeking for someone to kill. But there was not an enemy to be seen. Only upon the crest of The Ridge Of The Lonely Dragon a rocket again was set free. Before the report of it was ended there rose a roar of voices from all four sides that made the very earth shake and it so frightened Sung Chiang that his eyes were fixed and his mouth ajar. He did not know what to do.

Though one had all the books that tell of the feints of war, how still could he escape the nets spread upon earth and sky?

Truly,

They have trapped the tiger and they hold the dragon fast,

The greatest hero under heaven is captured at last.

How then did Sung Chiang and the chieftains escape? Pray hear it told in the next chapter.

第八篇 《聊斋志异》三个英译本的比较

柳绪燕

《聊斋志异》是我国文学史上一部重要著作。它成书于 17 世纪初文言小说衰败之际。随着《水浒传》、《金瓶梅》、《三国演义》等作品的问世，白话小说、章回小说日渐风行，文言小说以其生涩、难懂日渐衰败。而《聊斋志异》的出现，无异于给文言小说注入了新的活力，并标示着文言小说颠峰的到来。《聊斋志异》一书具有极高的文学价值，被誉为文言小说之集大成者。

鲁迅先生曾经指出,《聊斋志异》是"用传奇法，而以志怪"。它继承并发展了六朝志怪、唐传奇等文学形式。蒲松龄通过对"花鬼妖狐"等虚幻世界的描写，来表现他长期郁积于心底的"孤愤"之情，也是对当时"花面逢迎，世人如鬼"的社会的抨击与揭露。通过创造的各种艺术形象，针砭时弊，劝人警醒。

《聊斋志异》之所以被誉为文言小说的颠峰之作，并在中国文学史上占有重要的一席之地，除其深刻的社会意义及鲜明、生动的艺术形象外，另一重要原因，则应归功于《聊斋志异》的语言。《聊斋志异》虽被划归为文言小说之列，但其语言与以往的文言文不同。不少评论家，包括许多国外评论界，都将其部分篇章视为语言凝练、优美，抒情气息浓郁的散文精品。单就其语言来说，蒲松龄剔除了文言文的僵硬、刻板，又克服了口语体的粗糙、随意，并将二者完美地结合起来，使《聊斋志异》的语言既有文言文的高贵、典雅，又生动、准确地反映了人物的性格，塑造了典型形象，具有浓郁的生活气息。甚至有人认为，蒲松龄的语言，是表现《聊斋志异》特定内容的最好文字。这也许就是无论怎样的白话文翻译，也未必可得原作之丰姿的缘故吧。

第八篇《聊斋志异》Strange Stories from A Chinese Studio

《聊斋志异》的艺术魅力,不仅吸引了广大中国读者,而且也深深吸引并影响着外国读者。对蒲松龄所描绘的花狐鬼怪的奇怪,对中国文化的渴求,也呼唤着《聊斋志异》的外文译本。到目前为止,已发行的主要有三种译本。最早的要算 1906 年 Kelly, Walsh Limited 出版发行的 *Strange Tales from a Chinese Studio*,译者为 Herbert. A. Giles. Giles,为著名汉学家、翻译家,吕淑湘先生曾称他为"一代汉学权威,卓越的翻译大师"。其译作颇丰,除《聊斋志异》外,他还翻译了大量诗作,对中国文化的传播作出了贡献;另一译本除个别篇目外,均为我国著名翻译家杨宪益、戴乃迭夫妇所译,名为 *Selected Tales from Liao Zhai*;第三个译本为两位英国学者 Denis. C 及 Victor H. Mair 所译的 *Strange Tales from Make-do Studio*。

《聊斋志异》一书内容丰富,共有故事 600 多篇,其艺术价值也各不相同。以上提到的三个译本,都不是《聊斋志异》的全译本,而是选取书中一部分篇目进行翻译。其中,*Strange Tales From a Chinese Studio*(以下简称 G 译)发行最早,也是目前涵盖内容最多的译本,共有译文 160 多篇。*Selected Tales From Liao Zhai*(以下简称 Y 译)仅包括 19 个名篇,而 *Strange Tales From Make—do Studio*(以下简称 D 译)共包括 51 篇。总的说来,三个译本各具特色,各自语言风格于丝丝入微处有着具体的差别。粗略划分,译作可分为两类:一类为最早的 G 译,译文变动较大,不太忠实于原文,是以译文读者为中心的,可以归入 Peter Newmark 所说的 *communicative translation* 一类。彼得·纽马克在《翻译的方法》中指出:"交际型翻译试图使译文对译语者产生与原文对原语读者相同的效果。理论上,交际型翻译只针对译语读者,而译语读者并不希望在阅读中遇到任何晦涩难懂的地方,相反地,他们期待着译者将国外的东西大胆地移入本族文化"[1] 仅在标题翻译中,译者就作了较大改动。如《婴宁》一文,Giles 根据本人对原作故事的理解,将其译为 Ying Ning, or the Langhing Girl。当然,这样的翻译对原文内容并无改变,也不会影响读者对译文的理解,但终归是加上了译者自己的理解,

---

[1] 为笔者自译。

属于随意改动原文了。在《太原狱》的翻译中,译者采用归化(adaptation)法,将其译为 Another Solomon. 所谓归化,即"用与原词语有相同使用频度,但一般都带有某些译语文化色彩的词语来翻译原语词语"。其功能"在于能使译文读来比较地道和生动"(柯平,1984)。其他题目,如 A Chinese Solomon 等种种改译现象屡见不鲜。更为有趣的是,在《贾奉雉》的翻译中,译者因小说内容与美国著名小说家华盛顿·欧文(Washington Irving)的《瑞普·安·温可》(Rip Van Winkle)有异曲同工之妙而将其改译为 A Rip Van Winkle. 固然,Rip Van Winkle 在西方影响很大,欧文也被誉为"美国文学之父",但是,如果译文读者读到此,恐怕会以为蒲松龄老先生是因袭,起码是受到了欧文先生的启发,才写出了《贾奉雉》这篇文字。但稍加考证,我们就会发现欧文生于1783 年,而《聊斋志异》成书于清初 17 世纪,至少要比 Rip Van Winkle 的发表早近一个世纪。如果让译文读者有这样的错觉,岂不是大大委屈了蒲老先生?如果依照 Giles 先生的原则,我看倒是 Rip Van Winkle 的汉译本该叫《贾奉雉》才对。在论及归化法时,柯平在其《释义、归化和回译》中指出,使用归化手段时,"从原作者的角度来看,要避免归化后的成份使译语读者对原文信息或原语文化产生不正确的理解"。而 Giles 的译文恰恰使我们有了类似错觉。看来,还是避免使用为妙。鲁迅先生也是反对归化的,他很早就指出:"动笔之前,就先得解决一个问题,竭力使它归化,还是尽量保存洋气呢?……只求易懂,不如创作,或者改作,将事改为中国事,人也化为中国人,如果还是翻译,那么,首先的目的,就在博览外国的作品,不但移情,也要益智。至少是知道何时何地,有这等事,和旅行国外,是很相像的:它必须有异国情调,就是所谓洋气。……凡是翻译,必须兼顾着两面,一当然力求其易解,一则保存着原作的丰姿。"

显而易见,译者的用心是为了译文读者一目了然,为更好理解原文扫除"障碍"。但这样的译文,完全脱离中国文化,又怎能实现文化传播的功能呢?

第二类译文,可以将 Y 译与 D 译归为同组。这两种译本,在译者所采取的翻译态度,或所遵循的翻译理论方面,有很多共同之处。这两个译本可以视为 Newmark 在 Approaches to Translation 中所谈到的语义型翻译(Semantic translation)。纽马克指出:"语义型翻译试图在译语、语义、句法结构所允许的范围内,争取最大限度地与原文对等。语义型翻译仅限于原语文化自身,只帮助读者理解构成文本信息的主要部分的外延意义。"① 这两个译本,都紧紧依靠原文,争取最大限度地"信",忠实于原文作者及原语读者。但我们将这两个译本归为同类,并不意味着两个译本存在着很大的差别。也许是由于 Denis C 和 Victor. H. Mair 是以英语为母语,并兼取 G 译及 Y 译之所长的缘故,他们的译作在遣词造句、语言准确、贴切、流利程度上更符合译语习惯,更能体现原作的语言魅力。

　　在这两类、三个译文的比较中,另一显著特点就是,第一类 G 译随意增删现象普遍存在。如在原作中占重要地位的"异史氏曰"一部分,在 G 译中全部被删去。我们知道,《聊斋志异》的魅力之一,就在于它不同于以往的志怪、传奇小说"发明神道之不诬"(《搜神记》序),而是通过取法《史记》之"太史公曰",于篇末阐发议论,抒发一已一见。据统计,全书的"异史氏曰"共一百九十四则。这些文字或短短十几字,或长至数百言,或痛陈所感,或专写一事一物,无不散发着艺术魅力。"异史氏曰"一段,不仅深为研究《聊斋志异》的学者所喜爱,也深受广大普通读者所欢迎,已成为《聊斋志异》不可分割的一部分。正像是画龙点睛之笔,如果全部舍弃不译,未免损失太大,其文学价值、艺术魅力也将丢失殆尽了。除"异史氏曰"一部分外,G 译中随译者喜好而增删的现象同样存在。例如在上文提到的《贾奉雉》中 Giles 省略了大部分与 Rip Van Winkle 内容不同的部分,只保留了他如何寻仙、遇仙、返尘的部分。至于贾回乡之后的生活情况,译者则以其"冗长乏味"(注释语)而全部略去不译。这样一来,读者的误会岂不是更深? 蒲老先生恐怕难逃"抄袭"的罪名了。与 G 译不同,Y 译与 D 译均保留了"异史氏曰",虽然在文学处理上各有千秋,但总的说来,还是基本保留了原作的丰姿。

　　下面,我们将摘取几段原文与译文进行比较、分析,以便对三个译

---

① 为笔者自译。

本有更进一步的认识。

《罗刹海市》讲述了马骥海上遇难、漂流到一个以世人之丑反以为美的岛国,并巧入龙宫,入赘为婿,而后重返人间、夫妻分离的故事。马骥返回人间三年后,接回了自己的孩子,并得龙女书信一封,其中一段的原文、译文分别为:

忽忽三年,红尘永隔;盈盈一水,青鸟难通。结想为梦,引领为劳。茫茫蓝蔚,有恨如何也! 顾念弃月嫦娥,且虚桂府;投梭织女,犹怅银河。我何人斯,而能永好?

G 译:Three years have passed away and destiny still keeps us apart. I have been with you in my dreams until I am quite worn out. Does the blue sky look down upon any grief like mine? Yet change-ngo lives solitary in the moon, and Chih Nu laments that she cannot cross the Silver River. Who am I that I should expect happiness to be mine?

Y 译:Three years have slipped quickly away while we have been seperated by the ocean, with no blue bird to carry our massages. I long for you in my dreams, gazing in grief at the azure sky. Yet even the goddess of the moon pines in loneliness under the cassia tree, and the Weaving Maid grieves as she watches the Milky Way which seperates her from her love. Why should I alone enjoy wedded happiness?

D 译:Three years have gone by in a flash; the world of red dust is forever out of reach. The messager is hard put to cross this great expanse water. Longing has taken shape as dreams; my neck is weary with gazing into the boundless blue. What good are my regrets? My thoughts now trun to Chang'e, who ran away to the moon only to spend a lone life of loneliness in Cassia Mansion, and Weaving Maid, who once threw down her shuttle but to this day ruefully watches her lover from across the Milky Way. Who am I, that I should have everlasting love?

第八篇《聊斋志异》Strange Stories from A Chinese Studio

读过原文，我们会发现其文字优美、长于用典。以对称的句式来体现三年来龙女对马骥的思念以及尘仙异路，人鬼殊途，怅然若失的情感。

综观三段译文，我们会发现，三段文字在篇幅上逐级递增，而似乎在准确性上以及译文质量上也存在着这样的趋势。从结构上说，G 译与 Y 译均未能再现出原文句式对称，使用字数相同的四字句的特点。只有 D 译，通过使用 the world... the messager 及 Chang'e, who... Weaving Maid, who... 等句型，基本上做到对称，虽然在用字字数上不如原文用四字句那样简洁、明快，但由于英汉文的巨大差别，也不失为好的译文。而且，原文中"有恨如何也"及"我何斯人，而能永好"两句，前后呼应，对于表现龙女企盼相聚，但又无可奈何，无限思恋，却又无限伤悲，满怀希望又深知尘仙永隔的强烈感情表现得淋漓尽致。而在译文中，Giles 将"茫茫蓝蔚，有恨如何也"译作"Does the blue sky look down upon any grief like mine?"，这对于表现龙女的无奈，甚至是责备的口气似乎有些意犹未尽之感。杨氏夫妇将其译为"gazing in grief at the azure sky"，则失去了龙女的那份哀怨之情，而后面的"Why should I alone enjoy wedded happiness"似乎暗示着龙女对婚姻幸福的怨恨，而她与马骥的夫妻分离，骨肉离散，又是天经地义，无可厚非。读起来语气与原文真的是大相径庭了。D 译中，用了两个问句"What good are my regrets?"，"Who am I, that I should have everlastin love?"。第一句对表现龙女由于尘仙殊途而难以平息心中的思念，却又无计可施、无法可想内心矛盾完全表现了出来。第二句，以及 G 译的"Who am I should expect happiness to be mine?"同样表现了龙女对嫦娥、织女的同情，以及通过她们类似的遭遇、思念来反衬自己，暗示自己也同她们一样，毫无办法，只能孤独、清苦地生活。同时也反应出龙女与马骥无力改变命运，对这种有缘无分的爱情生活的无奈与慨叹。

原文这段文字的另外一个特点，就是善于用典。短短几句，共有四处用典。或者表现天各一方，音信皆无的无奈，或者表现常相思念，无限惆怅的爱恋之情。用典也是中国文言写作，尤其是骈文、散文写作的一大特点，这样可以使文字简洁，形象生动。这些典故或来源于中国古代的民间传说,或来源于书籍、典章。总之,都是中国文化中不可分割的精髓。也只有深谙中国文化,尤其是古代文化的读者才能深刻体会其中包含的深刻的内容。比较这三个译文,其中用注最多的是 Giles 的译文,该译文就"青鸟"、"嫦娥"、"织女"给了三个注释,简要介绍了三个典故的含义。其次,杨氏夫妇及 Denis 均在文内进行解释性说明,使读者在阅读中即明了典故的含义。但笔者认为,青鸟、嫦娥、织女等都是中国文学中经常引用的典故,很具典型意义。试想,青鸟又岂是一个 letter-bird 或 messager 所能涵盖的? 青鸟语出《山海经·西山经》"又西二百二十里,曰三危之山,三青鸟居之"。晋郭璞注:"三青鸟为西王母取食者,别自栖息于此山也"。因此,"青鸟"不仅喻指信使,同时也指仙使,故李商隐有"蓬山此去无归路,青鸟殷勤为探看"(《无题》)之句,刘禹锡作"青鸟去时云渐断,恒娥归处月宫深"(《怀妓》其四)。如果我们翻译工作者不老老实实,原原本本地将这个典故的来源、寓意告诉译文读者,想来,他们,甚至是作为原文读者的我们也无法透彻理解其中深义。对于这些中华文化的结晶,翻译工作者有责任、有义务将它们介绍给外国读者。语言是文化的载体,语言的交流不仅仅是为了传达信息,更多的是为了获取新知识,扩大文化占有量。尤其是中国文化,其博大精深并没有引起足够多人的重视。难怪许多著名学者大声疾呼:外国人对中国的知识知道得不是太多了,而是太少了。我国著名翻译家许渊冲先生曾痛心地说:"试问,中国的大学生有几个不了解美国文化? 又有几个美国大学生了解中国文化?"的确,在中美、中西文化交流中,存在着极大的差距。而作为翻译工作者,作为文化交流媒介的我们,则应该多从译文读者的角度想一想。试想:如果我是外国人,我会不会知道何为 letter-bird,我会不会想知道为什么嫦娥要抛家别夫逃往天宫去过冷清的日子,为什么织女每年要渡过银河。如果我们真的能设身处地地为译文读者想一想,并把传播中国文化为已任深深地印在脑子里,就会不怕麻烦,为中译外的作品多加几个脚注。

关于对这段原文的文字处理,我们可以举"忽忽三年,红尘永隔;盈盈一水,青鸟难通"的译文为例,稍加说明。Giles 用了 destiny 一词来译"红尘"。我们通常用"红尘"指代世俗世界或与仙界形成对照。此处龙

第八篇《聊斋志异》Strange Stories from A Chinese Studio

女与马骥一个人间,一个仙宫,尘仙异路,无法相聚。而并非命运弄人,所以 destiny 显然不是最佳选择。杨译用"We have been separated by the ocean",将抽象概念具体化了。二人不是被仙界凡尘所阻隔,而是被茫茫无尽的大海所分离。表达虽比较清楚,但对于传达原文的意义,二人的无奈稍显不足。就这两个译本的句式而言,也给人以直陈事实之感。而我们知道,经过三年的离别,龙女今日得以托寄锦书,该是何等激动与兴奋!因此她所使用的语气也该充分体现她的这种感情。相形之下,只有 D 译,虽采取了完全直译的办法,反倒将龙女的语气表达了出来。"the world of red dust is forever out of reach."读过上文的读者肯定会知道,龙宫、龙女都是凡世所无的,这样 the world of red dust 不会造成生晦、难懂的影响。我们知道,在西方有谚:Men are from dust and will return to dust. 所以,the world of red dust 形象、生动地写出了喧嚣、纷乱的尘世,恰巧与仙家形成对比。而且,Denis 二人用"out of reach"来体现龙女对马骥深深的向往与爱恋。她不是不想到红尘中去,但却被囿于仙境,骨肉、亲人无法团聚。所以说,在此句炼字方面,D 译略胜一筹。

但另外一点,原文仅有 59 字,而三种译文在长度上是呈上升趋势的,Giles 将原文秩序打乱,揉在一起进行意译,对原文改变太大,算不得妙译。就杨译与 D 译而言,杨译明显用字少于 D 译,而且,基本采用直译法将原文表达清楚、明晰。因此,在简洁程度上,D 译似乎又稍逊杨译。

下面,我们再就同一书信中另外一段文字进行一下比较、分析。在信的后半部分,龙女重温了她与马骥许下的誓言并云:"君似征人,妾作荡妇,即置而不御,亦何得谓非琴瑟哉?"这里,"征人"是指常年在外,不能返乡的游子,而"荡妇"为荡子之妇的省略,不可作现今或通常意义上的荡妇解。这段文字的三种译文分别为:

    G 译:"You are my Ulysses, I am your Penelope; though not actually leading a married life, how can it be said that we are not husband and wife."

    Y 译:"You are the wanderer and I the longing wife at home; but even though we cannot be together, we remain husband and wife."

D 译:"You are like a wayfarer, and I am the wayfarer's wife, but yet though the lute and harp are left long unplayed, no one can say they do not harmonize."

原文用琴、瑟比喻夫妻,用"置而不御"喻夫妻分离,无法相聚。不难看出,G译完全采用意译的方法,以便读者能够毫不费力地理解原文。Giles 主动将译文适应译语文化,用 Ulysses, Penelope 这两个希腊、罗马神话中的著名人物来代替与之有相似特征的"征人"及"荡妇"。对于译文读者来说,当然带来了理解上的方便,但对于原文读者的我们,看到如此译文,未免会有些气愤了。译者虽然加注,说明这仅仅是中文名称的对等名,我们仍旧担心粗心的读者会略去不读,而以为中西文化是相同的。或堂而皇之地以为西方文化已"一统天下"了。杨译采用了直译加意译的办法,将原文前半部分较好理解的部分直译,而后半部分的比喻则用意译将其比喻意义译出。这样,一方面方便了读者理解,又避免了译文读者对中国文化可能产生的不必要的误解。笔者以为,杨先生的译文要优于吉尔斯先生的译文。但遗憾的是,原文用喻被省,似乎使译文缺少了韵味。与前两个译文不同,D 译完全采用直译法。这里,一句"though the lute and harp are left long unplayed, no one can say they do not harmonize."比意译更能传达龙女与马骥之间虽不能相聚,但仍相爱,并有着和谐、甜美生活的深情,正像琴瑟弹奏出的优美、和谐的音符,比较容易理解。况且,上文已经提到"you are like a wayfarer, and I am the wayfather's wife.",所以夫妻关系已经为读者所共知,接下来的比喻,是用来喻指夫妻二人这一事实,是不会引起歧意或误解的。只有译出了比喻,才能说是真正再现了原作的意境。

在论及直译与意译时,彼得·纽马克说:"直译不仅仅是翻译中的最好方法,也是唯一可行的方法。"所以,在文字处理上,我们应尽已所能,争取最大限度的信。尽量采取直译方法,并注意发挥译文优势,以保存原作的丰姿。

《促织》是《聊斋志异》中的名篇,以其新颖的立意,其中所蕴含的深

第八篇《聊斋志异》Strange Stories from A Chinese Studio

刻社会意义及现实意义吸引了大批读者。因此,无论是中学课本,还是美术片、连环画,《促织》都成了人们首选的篇目,被越来越多的读者所喜爱。《促织》中,写到成名被打,其妻求占问卜之后,有这样一段话描写成名忍痛执图去寻蟋蟀:

(成)乃强起扶杖,执图诣寺后,有古陵蔚起。循陵而走,见蹲石鳞鳞,俨然类画。遂于蒿莱中侧听徐行,似寻针芥,而心、耳、目力俱穷,绝无踪响。冥搜未已,一癞头蟆猝然跃去。成益愕,急逐之。蟆入草间。蹑迹披求,只有虫伏棘根,遽扑之,入石穴中。

G 译:So he forced himself to get up, and leaning on a stick, went out to seek crickets behind the temple. Rounding an old grave, he came upon a place where stones were lying scattered about as in the picture, and then he set himself to watch attentively. He might as well have been looking for a needle or a grain of mustard-seed; and by degrees he became quite exhausted, without finding anything, when suddenly an old frog jumped out. Cheng was a little startled, but immediately pursued the frog, which retreated into the bushes. He then saw one of the insects he wanted sitting at the root of a bramble; but on making a grab at it, the cricket ran into a hole.

Y 译:So taking the paper with him, he struggled along, with the help of a stick to the back of the monastery. There he found an old grave overgrown with brambles. Skirting this, he saw that the stones lying scattered around were exactly like the painting. He pricked up his ears and limped slowly through the brambles, but he might just as have been looking for a needle or a grain of mustard-seed. Though he strained every nerve he found nothing. As he was groping around, a toad hopped into sight. Cheng gave a start and hurried after it. The toad slipped into the undergrowth and, following it, he saw a cricket at the root of a bramble. He snatched at it, but the cricket leaped into a crevice in a rock...

第八篇《聊斋志异》Strange Stories from A Chinese Studio

D 译:Cheng dragged himself out bed, propped himsef up with a cane and proceeded, drawing in hand, to the rear of the monastery. The overgrown ruins of an ancient tomb stood before him. Following the edge of the tomb, he saw boulders squatting one on top of the other like fish scales, precisely as in the drawing. He walked slowly through a jungle of weeds, cocking his head to catch the slightest sound and looking for all the world as if he were searching for a mustard-seed. He could no longer maintain the intentness of eyes, ears and mind, but he had not yet seen or heard a cricket. He was still groping about, when suddenly to his great amazement a wart-headed toad leapt from underfoot. He stayed close behind it as it ducked into a dense growth of grass. He stepped gingerly into the grass, spreading the blades spart with his hands to get a better look. There, crouching at the base of a bramble-bush was an insect. He hurriedly grabbed for it, but it ducked into a hole in the stones.

不难发现,G 译中合并、省略成份很多。如 Giles 将"古陵蔚起,循陵而走"译为"Rounding an old grave",读起来似乎有些突然,怎么到了庙后却又绕着古陵走？下面的"侧听徐行"仅用了"watch attentively"来译,而原文不仅描绘成名寻找时的用心,而且是动静结合,既"听"又"行",这四个字,可以使读者真切地体会到成名小心翼翼、边走边听、边寻找,同时,又迫于伤痛而无法快走的情景。杨译与 D 译在此句处理上都优于 G 译。杨氏夫妇用"He pricked up his ears and limped slowly through the brambles",Denis 二人"Walked slowly...cocking his head to catch the slightest sound and looking for all the world."杨译与 D 译相比,我们会发现,杨氏夫妇显然要比 D 译译得准确、简练。D 译虽然将"侧听徐行"中的每一个字都明白无误地译出,但译文稍显冗长,不如杨氏夫妇用"picked up...limped"两词更能生动、形象地将原文所包含的意思全部译出。我们可以认为,在这句的翻译上,杨氏夫妇确实做到传达作品之精神,找到了体现原作韵味的完美译语,并将原文、译文发挥得淋漓尽致。接下来"而心、目、耳力俱穷"一句。Giles 直译将其译为"He became quite exhausted, without findng anything."只解释了原文大意,没有传达出原文所表现出的成名经过长时间的找寻,心力交瘁而导致的疲惫,这种译文法(paraphrase)可以说完全没有传达出原文之美,也忽视了作者写作意图。而杨译"he strained every nerve"虽然译出了精神上的疲乏,却没有像原文一样突出心、目、耳力的穷尽,而且失去了与上文"侧听徐行"的呼应。只有 D 译,没有忽略这一细节描写。"He could no longer maintain the intentness of eyes, ears and mind"才将成名心力交瘁及失望、甚至是绝望的情形体现出来。应该看到,蒲松龄之所以强调"而心、目、耳力俱穷"这一细节描写,而不以其繁琐,实在是独具匠心,对于突出形象生动性绝对不是可有可无的。将原文逐字译出,有利于抓住读者的心,对于烘托扣人心弦的气氛是不可或缺的。

紧随其后的另一细节描写:"蹑迹披求",只有 D 译才予以了足够的重视。我们知道,"蹑"为轻手轻脚,唯恐惊动某人某事之意;而"披"者为用手拨开杂草,以求看得清楚之意。G 译中没有一定体现了这四个字所表现的内容,而杨译,只用了"following it"是不足以表现当时的情景的。只有 D 译,才将原文直接译出,对于表现当时的紧张心情有很大裨益。完全直译,虽然所用字数较多,不及原文简约,但鉴于英汉,尤其是古代汉语与现代英语之间的巨大差别,也不失为一种补救方法。起码要优于舍弃不译。关于古文的翻译问题,也是翻译界长期争论而无定论的课题,有待有一进探索研究。

就《聊斋志异》全书而言,其文字之精简,准确,优美,不亚于许多精美散文,所以力求译文文字的优美、典雅、凝炼也就成了译者不可推卸的责任。

从上述的几个译例中,我们看到,三个译本各有特色。在炼字方面,当推 Denis 及 Mair 先生译本为上,译者基本遵循直译的原则,在语言运用上略胜一筹,但仍在细微之处稍有不足。杨氏夫妇所译作品基本也采用直译法,在简洁程度、文化因素处理方面占有优势。而 G 译,也许是由于中译英的较早尝试吧,与原文出入较大。同时,由于译者遵循的是以意译为主的翻译原则,以译语读者、文化为中心,则在其生动程度、准确性上显得不足。起码在原文读者看来,是无法令人满意的。

对于一篇文章,一本书的翻译,没有绝对"标准"的译本,而只能说尺有所短,寸有所长。我们只是想通过对不同译本的比较,来提高自己的欣赏水平,并从好的译例中汲取营养,吸收经验及处理方法,以期提高自己的译文水平。同时,通过对译文里存在问题的分析、研究,思考解决问题的方法。

参考文献

Newmark, Peter. *Approches to Translation*.
蒲松龄:《聊斋志异》,岳麓书社,1997年。
Herbert. A. Giles. (Trans.)*Strange Stories from a Chinese Studio*. Shanghai. Kelly and Walsh, Limited, 1908.
Yang Xianyi and GladysYang. (Trans.) *Selected Tales of Liao Zhai*. Beijing. Chinese Literature Publishing House, 1981.
Denis C and Victor H. Mair. (Trans.) *Strange Tales from MaKe-do Studio*. Beijing. Froeign Language Press, 1989.
吴组湘:《聊斋志异欣赏》,北京大学出版社,1986年。

附：

《聊斋志异》(节选)

蒲松龄

罗刹海市

马骥,字龙媒,贾人子。美丰姿。少倜傥,喜歌舞。辄从梨园子弟①,以锦帕缠头,美如好女,因复有"俊人"之号。十四岁,入郡庠,即知名。父衰老,罢贾而居。谓生曰:"数卷书,饥不可煮,寒不可衣。吾儿可仍继父贾。"马由是稍稍权子母②。

从人浮海③,为飓风引去,数昼夜至一都会。其人皆奇丑;见马至,以为妖,群哗而走。马初见其状,大惧;迨知国中之骇己也,遂反以此欺国人。遇饮食者,则奔而往;人惊遁,则啜其余。久之,入山村。其间形貌亦有似人者,然褴褛如丐。马息树下,村人不敢前,但遥望之。久之,觉马非噬人者,始稍稍近就之。马笑与语。其言虽异,亦半可解。马遂

---

① 梨园子弟:戏曲艺人。《新唐书·礼乐志》,谓唐玄宗曾选乐工及宫女数百人,亲授乐曲于梨园。后因称演戏的场所为"梨园",称戏曲艺人为"梨园子弟"。

② 权子母:指经商。权,权衡。子母,原指货币的大小、轻重,后来指利息和本钱。

③ 浮海:泛海;航海。此指到海外经商。

第八篇《聊斋志异》Strange Stories from A Chinese Studio

自陈所自①。村人喜,遍告邻里,客非能搏噬者。然奇丑者望望然而去②,终不敢前;其来者,口鼻位置,尚皆与中国同。共罗浆酒奉马。马问其相骇之故,答曰:"尝闻祖父言:西去二万六千里,有中国,其人民形象率诡异③。但耳食之④,今始信。"问其何贫。曰:"我国所重,不在文意,而在形貌。其美之极者,为上卿⑤;次任民社⑥;下焉者,亦邀贵人宠⑦,故得鼎烹以养妻子⑧。若我辈初生时,父母皆以为不祥,往往置弃之;其不忍遽弃者,皆为宗嗣耳。"问:"此名何国?"。曰:"大罗刹国⑨。都城在北去三十里。"马请导往一观。于是鸡鸣而兴⑩,引与俱去。天明,始达都。都以黑石为墙,色如墨,楼阁近百尺。然少瓦,覆以红石;拾其残块磨甲上,无异丹砂。时值朝退,朝中有冠盖出,村人指曰:"此相国也⑪。"视之,双耳皆背生,鼻三孔,睫毛覆目如帘。又数骑出,曰:"此大夫也⑫。"以次各指其

---

① 自陈所自:自己陈述来历。所自,从哪里来。
② 望望然而去:掉头不顾而去。《孟子·公孙丑》上:"望望然去之,若将浼焉。"
③ 率:全,都。诡异:怪异。
④ 耳食:指不加审察,轻信传闻。《史记·六国年表序》:"学者牵于所闻,见秦在帝位日浅,不察终始,举而笑之,不敢道。此与以耳食无异。"《索隐》:"言俗以浅识,举而笑秦,此犹耳食,不能知味也。"
⑤ 上卿:周官制,最尊贵的诸侯臣称上卿。《公羊传·襄公十一年》:"古者上卿下卿,上士下士。"
⑥ 任民社:古称直接理民的地方官为"职任民社"。民社,人民和社稷。
⑦ 邀:获取。
⑧ 鼎烹:美食,贵人所享。此指贵人赐与的"残杯冷炙"。鼎,古代炊器,三足两耳。
⑨ 罗刹:梵语音译,意思是恶鬼。这里作为国名。《文献通考》谓罗刹国朱发黑面,兽牙鹰爪,作市以夜,昼则掩面。
⑩ 兴:起床。
⑪ 相国:宰相。
⑫ 大夫:古诸侯国中,国君之下有卿、大夫、士三级。这里指位次于相国的高级官员。

第八篇《聊斋志异》Strange Stories from A Chinese Studio

官职,率挈挈怪异①;然位渐卑,丑亦渐杀②。无何,马归,街衢人望见之,噪奔跌蹶,如逢怪物。村人百口解说③,市人始敢遥立。既归,国中咸知村有异人,于是搢绅大夫,争欲一广见闻,遂令村人要马。然每至一家,阍人辄阖户,丈夫女子窃窃自门隙中窥语;终一日,无敢延见者。村人曰:"此间一执戟郎④,曾为先王出使异国,所阅人多,或不以子为惧。"造郎门。郎果喜,揖为上客⑤。视其貌,如八九十岁人。目睛突出,须卷如猬⑥。曰:"仆少奉王命,出使最多;独未尝至中华。今一百二十余岁,又得睹上国人物,此不可不上闻于天子。然臣卧林下,十余年不践朝阶,早旦,为君一行。"乃具饮馔,修主客礼。酒数行,出女乐十余人,更番歌舞。貌类夜叉⑦,皆以白锦缠头,拖朱衣及地。扮唱不知何词,腔拍恢诡⑧。主人顾而乐之,问:"中国亦有此乐乎?"曰:"有。"主人请拟其声,遂击桌为度一曲。主人喜曰:"异哉!声如凤鸣龙啸,从未曾闻。"翼日,趋朝,荐诸国王。王忻然下诏。有二三大夫,言其怪状,恐惊圣体。王乃止。郎出告马,深为扼腕⑨。居久之,与主人饮而醉,把剑起舞,以煤涂面作张飞。主人以为美,曰:"请君以张飞见宰相,宰相必乐用之,厚禄不难致。"马曰:"嘻!游戏犹可,何能易面目图荣显⑩?"主人固强之,马乃诺。

---

① 挈挈(zhěng—níng 争宁):毛发散乱貌。
② 杀:煞;减。
③ 百口解说:极力解说。百,多。口,代指语言。
④ 执戟郎:古代警卫宫门的官员。《史记·淮阴侯列传》:"臣事项王,官不过郎中,位不过执戟。"秦汉郎官中有中郎、侍郎、郎中等,负责执戟宿卫殿门,故称执戟郎。
⑤ 揖:拱手为礼。这里是尊奉的意思。
⑥ 须卷(quán 拳)如猬:胡须密集象刺猬。卷,弯曲。
⑦ 貌类夜叉:此据铸雪斋抄本,原作"貌类如夜叉"。
⑧ 腔拍恢诡:腔调和节奏都很特别。恢诡,离奇。
⑨ 扼腕:紧握己腕,表示愧惜。
⑩ 易面目图荣显:改换面貌来谋取荣华显贵;指迎合世俗所好,换取功名利禄。易,改变。

主人设筵,邀当路者饮①,令马绘面以待。未几,客至,呼马出见客。客讶曰:"异哉!何前嬉而今妍也!"遂与共饮,甚欢。马婆娑歌"弋阳曲"②,一座无不倾倒③。明日,交章荐马④。王喜,召以旌节⑤。既见,问中国治安之道⑥,马委曲上陈⑦,大蒙嘉叹,赐宴离宫⑧。酒酣,王曰:"闻卿善雅乐,可使寡人得而闻之乎?"马即起舞,亦效白锦缠头,作靡靡之音⑨。王大悦,即日拜下大夫⑩。时与私宴⑪,恩宠殊异。久而官僚百执事颇觉其面目之假⑫;所至,辄见人耳语,不甚与款洽。马至是孤立,惘然不自安⑬。

① 当路者:居于要职的人,指掌握政权的官员。《孟子·公孙丑》:"夫子当路于齐。"
② 婆娑:形容舞姿;此指起舞。弋阳曲:南曲腔调的一种,明清时代流行于江西弋阳,故名。《顾曲麈淡》谓弋阳腔是"俗腔",昆山腔是"雅乐"。马骥唱俗腔,罗刹国王却认为是"雅乐";这说明罗刹国雅俗颠倒。
③ 倾倒:佩服。
④ 交章:纷纷上奏章。
⑤ 召以旌节:派人持旌节去召唤他。古礼,君有所命,召唤大夫用旌、旄。旌节,以竹为竿,上级以牦牛尾和五彩鸟羽,古代出使者持之,以为凭证。
⑥ 治安之道:治国安邦的法则。
⑦ 委曲:原原本本地。
⑧ 离宫:别宫。古时帝王于正式宫殿之外,别筑宫室,供随时游处,称"离宫"。
⑨ 靡靡之音:淫靡的乐曲;本指俗腔,而罗刹国好之,视为雅乐。
⑩ 拜:授官。下大夫:古官名,周王室及诸侯各国,卿以下有大夫,大夫分上中下三等。
⑪ 时与私宴:经常参加皇帝的家宴。与,参与。
⑫ 百执事:犹言百官。《书·盘庚》:"邦伯师长,百执事之人,尚皆隐哉。"执事,指各部门专职人员。
⑬ 惘然:不安的样子。

第八篇《聊斋志异》Strange Stories from A Chinese Studio

遂上疏乞休致①,不许;又告休沐②,乃给三月假。于是乘传载金宝③,复归山村。村人膝行以迎。马以金资分给旧所与交好者,欢声雷动。村人曰:"吾侪小人受大夫赐,明日赴海市,当求珍玩,用报大夫。"问:"海市何地?"曰:"海中市,四海鲛人④,集货珠宝;四方十二国,均来贸易。中多神人游戏。云霞障天,波涛间作。贵人自重,不敢犯险阻,皆以金帛付我辈,代购异珍。今其期不远矣。"问所自知,曰:"每见海上朱鸟来往,七日,即市。"马问行期,欲同游瞩。村人劝使自贵。马曰:"我顾沧海客,何畏风涛?"

未几,果有踵门寄资者,遂与装资入船。船容数十人,平底高栏。十人摇橹,激水如箭。凡三日,遥见水云幌漾之中,楼阁层叠;贸迁之舟⑤,纷集如蚁。少时,抵城下。视墙上砖,皆长与人等。敌楼高接云汉⑥。维舟而入,见市上所陈,奇珍异宝,光明射目,多人世所无。一少年乘骏马来,市人尽奔避,云是"东洋三世子"⑦。世子过,目生曰:"此非异域人?"即有前马者来诘乡籍⑧。生揖道左,具展邦族⑨。世子喜曰:"既蒙辱临,缘分不浅!"于是授生骑,请与连辔。乃出西城。方至岛岸,所骑嘶跃入水。生大骇失声。则见海水中分,屹如壁立。俄睹宫殿,玳瑁为梁⑩,鲂鳞作瓦;四壁晶明,鉴影炫目。下马揖入。仰视龙君在上,世子启奏:"臣

① 乞休致:请求辞官退居。清制,自陈衰老而批准休致的,称"自请休致";非自己所请,谕旨令其休致的,称"勒令休致"。
② 休沐:休息沐浴;指短期休假。汉制,吏五日一休沐;唐代十日一休沐。
③ 乘传(zhuàn 撰):乘驿站的传车。传,传车,古代驿站的公用车辆。马骥休沐,得用传乘,可见深得国王恩宠。
④ 鲛人:神话传说,谓南海有鲛人,善纺织,所织薄纱叫"鲛绡";鲛人常哭泣,其泪则凝为珠,见《博物志》和《述异记》。
⑤ 贸迁:贸易。
⑥ 敌楼:城楼。云汉:天河;这里指高空。
⑦ 世子:帝王或诸侯的嫡妻所生之子。
⑧ 前马者:在马前开路的人。
⑨ 具展:一一陈述。邦族:籍贯与姓氏。
⑩ 玳瑁为梁:以玳瑁为饰的屋梁。玳瑁,龟类动物,背甲光亮,可作装饰。

游市廛,得中华贤士,引见大王。"生前拜舞①。龙君乃言:"先生文学士,必能衙官屈、宋②。欲烦椽笔赋'海市'③,幸无吝珠玉④。"生稽首受命。授以水精之砚⑤,龙鬣之毫⑥,纸光似雪,墨气如兰。生立成千余言。献殿上。龙君击节曰⑦:"先生雄才,有光水国矣!"遂集诸龙族,宴集采霞宫,酒炙数行,龙君执爵而向客曰:"寡人所怜女,未有良匹,愿累先生。先生倘有意乎?"生离席愧荷⑧,唯唯而已。龙君顾左右语。无何,宫人数辈,扶女郎出。珮环声动⑨,鼓吹暴作。拜竟,睨之,实仙人也。女拜已而去。少时酒罢,双鬟挑画灯⑩,导生入副宫⑪。女浓妆坐伺。珊瑚之床,饰以八宝⑫;帐外流苏⑬,缀明珠如斗大;衾褥皆香耎。天方曙,则雏女妖鬟,奔入满侧。生起,趋出朝谢。拜为驸马都尉⑭。以其赋驰传诸海。诸海龙

① 拜舞:跪拜舞蹈。舞蹈,古朝仪之一。
② 衙官屈宋:意思是超过屈原、宋玉。《续世说》谓杜审言曾自夸:"吾之文章合得屈、宋作衙官,吾之书迹合得王羲之北面。"衙官,唐代刺史的属官。以屈原、宋玉为其衙官,是说自己的作品压倒屈、宋。
③ 椽笔:如椽之笔,比喻能写文章的大手笔。赋海市:第一篇描写海市的赋。赋,文体名,这里指作赋。
④ 珠玉:比喻美好的文章。
⑤ 水精:即水晶。
⑥ 龙鬣(liè 列)之毫:用龙的鬣毛制成的笔。
⑦ 击节:抚手或拍板以调节乐曲,表示激赏。这里指赞赏。
⑧ 离席:离座站起,表示恭敬。愧荷:以自愧的心情表示感激。
⑨ 珮环:珮和环都是古时佩在身上的玉饰。
⑩ 双鬟:指幼婢。古时幼女结双鬟。
⑪ 副宫:旁宫。
⑫ 八宝:指金银、珍珠、玛瑙等各种珠宝。
⑬ 流苏:用彩丝或鸟羽做成的垂缨。
⑭ 驸马都尉:官名,汉武帝时置,掌副车之马,秩二千石,多以宗室及外戚诸公子孙担任。魏晋以后,帝婿例加驸马都尉称号,简称驸马,皆非实职。

第八篇《聊斋志异》Strange Stories from A Chinese Studio

君,皆崙员来贺①;争折简招驸马饮。生衣锈裳,驾青虬②,呵殿而出③。武士数十骑,背雕弧④,荷白棓⑤,晃耀填拥。马上弹筝⑥,车中奏玉⑦。三日间,遍历诸海。由是"龙媒"之名,噪于四海。宫有玉树一株,围可合抱;本莹澈,如白琉璃,中有心,淡黄色,稍细于臂;叶类碧玉,厚一钱许,细碎有浓阴。常与女啸咏其下。花开满树,状类蔷蔔⑧。每一瓣落,锵然作响。拾视之,如赤瑙雕镂⑨,光明可爱。时有异鸟来鸣,毛金碧色,尾长于身,声等哀玉⑩,恻人肺腑。生闻之,辄念乡土。因谓女曰:"亡出三年,恩慈间阻⑪,每一念及,涕膺汗背⑫。卿能从我归乎?"女曰:"仙尘路隔⑬,不能相依。妾亦不忍以鱼水之爱⑭,夺膝下之欢⑮。容徐谋之。"生闻之,涕不自禁。女亦叹曰:"此势之不能两全者也!"明日,生自外归。龙君曰:"闻都尉有故土之思,诘旦趣装,可乎?"生谢曰:"逆旅孤臣,过蒙优宠,

---

① 崙员:派专人。
② 驾青虬(qiú 求):驾驭青虬拉的车子。《离骚》:"驷玉虬以乘鹥兮,溘埃风余上征。"王逸注:"有角曰龙,无角曰虬。"
③ 呵殿:古时贵官出行的威仪。呵,在前喝道。殿,在后随从。
④ 背:据铸雪斋抄本,原作"皆"。雕弧:雕有纹彩的弓。
⑤ 棓:同"棒"。
⑥ 筝:古代弦乐的一种。
⑦ 玉:指玉笛之类的管乐。
⑧ 蔷(zhān 沾)蔔:栀子花。
⑨ 赤瑙:红色玛瑙。
⑩ 声等哀玉:声音如同玉制乐器所奏的哀婉曲调。
⑪ 恩慈间阻:指与父母隔离。父母慈爱有恩,故以"恩慈"代称。
⑫ 涕膺汗背:涕泪沾胸,汗流浃背;形容悲伤与惶恐。
⑬ 仙尘:仙境与尘世。
⑭ 鱼水之爱:喻夫妇之爱。
⑮ 膝下之欢:指父子之情。

啣报之诚①,结于肺肝。容暂归省,当图复聚耳。"入暮,女置酒话别。生订后会。女曰:"情缘尽矣。"生大悲,女曰:"归养双亲,见君之孝。人生聚散,百年犹旦暮耳,何用作儿女哀泣?此后妾为君贞②,君为妾义③,两地同心,即伉俪也,何必旦夕相守,乃谓之偕老乎?若渝此盟,婚姻不吉。倘虑中馈乏人④,纳婢可耳⑤。更有一事相嘱:自奉裳衣⑥,似有佳朕⑦,烦君命名。"生曰:"其女耶,可名龙宫;男耶,可名福海。"女乞一物为信⑧。生在罗刹国所得赤玉莲花一对,出以授女。女曰:"三年后四月八日,君当泛舟南岛,还君体胤⑨。"女以鱼革为囊,实以珠宝,授生曰:"珍藏之,数世吃著不尽也。"天微明,王设祖帐⑩,馈遗甚丰。生拜别出宫。女乘白羊车,送诸海涘⑪。生上岸下马。女致声珍重,回车便去,少顷便远。海出复合,不可复见。

　　生乃归。自浮海去,咸谓其已死;及至家,家人无不诧异。幸翁媪无恙,独妻已他适。乃悟龙女"守义"之言,盖已先知也。父欲为生再婚;生

---

① 啣报之诚:感恩图报的心情。啣报,指啣环报恩。《后汉书·杨震传》注引《续齐谐记》:东汉杨宝救了一只黄雀,夜间梦见一个黄衣童子衔四枚白环相报,谓当使其子孙洁白,位登三公。后杨宝子孙四世,果都显贵。
② 贞:封建时代妻不改嫁叫"贞"。
③ 义:此指封建时代丈夫因妻守贞,己亦不重婚另娶。
④ 中馈乏人:无人主持家务。古代妇女在家料理饮食、祭品等事务,叫做"主中馈"。
⑤ 纳婢:娶婢女为妾。封建时代纳妾不算娶妻,这样仍然算作对前妻"守义"。
⑥ 自奉裳衣:意为自结婚以来。奉裳衣,指妻子侍奉丈夫衣着。古时上曰衣,下曰裳。《诗·齐风·东方未明》:"东方未明,颠倒衣裳。"
⑦ 佳朕:佳兆,指怀孕。朕,征兆。
⑧ 信:信物;凭证。
⑨ 体胤:亲生儿女。胤,后嗣。
⑩ 设祖帐:意为设宴饯别。古时出行,为行者祭奠路神,祝福饯别,叫"祖祭"。祖祭时设置的帷帐叫"祖帐"。
⑪ 海涘(sì 四):海边。涘,水边。

第八篇《聊斋志异》Strange Stories from A Chinese Studio

不可,纳婢焉。谨志三年之期,泛舟岛中。见两儿坐浮水面,拍流嬉笑,不动亦不沉。近引之,儿哑然捉生臂①,跃入怀中。其一大啼,似嗔生之不援己者。亦引上之。细审之,一男一女,貌皆婉秀。额上花冠缀玉,则赤莲在焉。背有锦囊,拆视,得书云:"翁姑计各无恙。忽忽三年,红尘永隔;盈盈一水,青鸟难通②。结想为梦,引领成劳③,茫茫蓝蔚,有恨如何也!顾念奔月姮娥,且虚桂府④;投梭织女,犹怅银河⑤。我何人斯⑥,而能永好?兴思及此,辄复破涕为笑。别后两月,竟得孪生。今已啁啾怀抱⑦,颇解言笑⑧;觅枣抓梨,不母可活。敬以还君。所贻赤玉莲花,饰冠作信。膝头抱儿时,犹妾在左右也。闻君克践旧盟⑨,意愿斯慰。妾此生不二,之死靡他⑩。奁中珍物,不蓄兰膏;镜里新妆,久辞粉黛。君似征

---

① 哑(è厄)然:发出笑声的样子。哑,笑声。
② "盈盈一水"二句:意谓虽然一水之隔,但却音信难通。《古诗十九首》:"盈盈一水间,脉脉不得语。"盈盈,水清浅的样子。青鸟,借指使者。《汉武故事》:七月七日,日正中,汉武帝见青鸟从西方来。东方朔说,西王母即将到来。不久,果然到来。后因以青鸟称传信的使者。
③ 引领:形容殷切盼望。领,颈。
④ "奔月姮娥"二句:意谓象嫦娥这样仙女尚且在月宫孤身独处。姮娥,即嫦娥,传说是后羿的妻子,因偷吃不死药,飞升月宫。见《淮南子·览冥训》。桂府,相传月宫有桂树,高五百丈,后因称月宫为"桂府"。见《酉阳杂俎》。
⑤ "投梭织女"二句:意谓天上的织女,尚且因天河阻隔,不能同牛郎团聚,而感到惆怅。织女,神话人物,为天帝孙女,长年织造云锦,嫁与河西牛郎以后,织造中断,天帝怒,责令她与牛郎分离,只准每年七夕渡河与牛郎相会。故事初见于《古诗十九首》。怅,恨。银河,天河。
⑥ 斯:兮,语气词。
⑦ 啁啾(zhōu jiū 周究):小鸟鸣声。这里形容幼儿学话的声音。
⑧ 言笑:"据铸雪斋抄本,原作"笑言"。
⑨ 克践旧盟:能够履行旧时的盟誓;指守义不娶。克,能。
⑩ 之死靡他:到老死也无他心;指誓不改嫁。

第八篇《聊斋志异》Strange Stories from A Chinese Studio

人,妾作荡妇①,即置而不御②,亦何得谓非琴瑟哉③?独计翁姑亦既抱孙,曾未一觌新妇,揆之情理,亦属缺然。岁后阿姑窀穸④,当往临穴⑤,一尽妇职。过此以往,则'龙宫'无恙,不少把握之期⑥;'福海'长生,或有往还之路。伏惟珍重⑦,不尽欲言。"生反覆省书揽涕⑧。两儿抱颈曰:"归休乎⑨!"生益恸,抚之曰:"儿知家在何许?"儿啼,呕哑言归。生视海水茫茫,极天无际;雾鬟人渺⑩,烟波路穷⑪。抱儿返棹,怅然遂归。生知母寿不永⑫,周身物悉为预具⑬,墓中植松楸百余⑭。逾岁,媪果亡。灵舆至殡宫⑮,有女子缞绖临穴⑯。众方惊顾,忽而风激雷轰,继以急雨,转瞬已失所在。松柏新植多枯,至是皆活。福海稍长,辄思其母,忽自投入海,

① 荡妇:荡子妇;出游不归者的妻子。《古诗十九首》:"昔为倡家女,今为荡子妇。荡子行不归,空床难独守。"
② 置而不御:意谓两地远隔,仍保持夫妇名义。御,用;因喻夫妇为琴瑟之设词。
③ 琴瑟:喻夫妇。《诗·周南·关雎》:"窈窕淑女,琴瑟友之。"以琴瑟谐合喻夫妇和合。
④ 窀穸(zhūn—xī 谆细):墓穴。这里指下葬。
⑤ 临穴:亲临墓穴。
⑥ 把握:携手,握手;指见面。
⑦ 伏惟:恭敬地希望。惟,希望。
⑧ 揽涕:挥泪。
⑨ 归休乎:回家吧?休,语词。
⑩ 雾鬟人渺:意谓已看不到龙女。雾鬟,借指想望中的龙女。杜甫《月夜》:"今夜鄜州月,闺中只独看。……香雾云鬟湿,清辉玉臂寒。"渺,渺茫。
⑪ 烟波路穷:烟波之上,漫无道路。穷,尽。
⑫ 不永:不长。
⑬ 周身物:指死者的服饰、棺椁等物。
⑭ 楸:楸树。
⑮ 灵舆:灵车。殡宫:停放灵柩的墓穴。
⑯ 缞绖(cuī—dié 崔喋):封建丧礼规定的子女所穿的孝服。缞,披在胸前的麻布。绖,系在额部和腰上的麻带。

第八篇《聊斋志异》Strange Stories from A Chinese Studio

数目始还。龙宫以女子不得往,时掩户泣。一日,昼瞑,龙女忽入,止之曰:"儿自成家,哭泣何为?"乃赐八尺珊瑚一树,龙脑香一帖①,明珠百颗,八宝嵌金合一双,为嫁资。生闻之突入,执手啜泣。俄顷,疾雷破屋,女已无矣。

异史氏曰:"花面逢迎,世情如鬼②。嗜痂之癖,举世一辙③。'小惭小好,大惭大好'④。若公然带须眉以游都市⑤,其不骇而走者盖几希矣。彼陵阳痴子,将抱连城玉向何处哭也⑥?呜呼!显荣富贵,当于蜃楼海市中求之耳⑦!"

---

① 龙脑香:由龙脑树所提炼的香料,即冰片。一贴:一包。
② "花面逢迎"二句:意谓装出一副假面目,迎合世俗所好;如此世态与鬼域无异。花面,本指女子饰面,这里指装扮一副假面孔。
③ "嗜痂之癖"二句:谓怪僻的嗜好,天下都有。《南史·刘穆之传》,谓南朝宋人刘邕嗜食疮痂,以为味似鳆鱼。后世因称乖僻的嗜好为"嗜痂"。这里用以比喻颠倒美丑、屈意逢迎的怪癖。举,全,一辙,一样。
④ 小惭小好,大惭大好:唐代韩愈《与冯宿论文书》:"时时应事作俗下文字,下笔令人惭,及示人,则人以为好矣。小惭者亦蒙谓之小好,大惭者即必以为大好矣。"意谓世人喜欢虚假的迎合。惭,指曲意取悦别人,违背自己的本心。
⑤ "公然带须眉"句:意谓保持男子汉的本色立身行事,耻于媚俗诌世。须眉,胡须、眉毛,代指男子。
⑥ "彼陵阳痴子"二句:意谓真正才德之士,不被赏识,将无处倾诉他的委曲和悲痛。陵阳痴子,指春秋时楚人卞和,曾受封陵阳侯。卞和在楚山发现一璞玉,曾献给楚厉王和楚武王,都被视为石头。卞和被诬欺诳,先后被刖双脚。楚文王即位,卞和抱璞哭于荆山之下。楚文王使人问之。卞和曰:"臣非悲刖。宝玉而题之以石,贞士而名之为诳,所以悲也。"楚文王使人剖璞,果得宝玉,称为"和氏璧"。见《韩非子·和氏》。连城玉,价值连城的宝玉,指和氏璧。
⑦ 蜃(shèn 慎)楼海市:喻虚幻世界。蜃,蛟类。旧说蜃能吐气为楼台,称为"蜃楼",也称"海市"。实为一种因光线折射作用而出现的虚影,多现于海上或沙漠。此句以幻域否定现实。

促 织

　　宣德间①,宫中尚促织之戏②,岁征民间③。此物故非西产④;有华阴令欲媚上官⑤,以一头进⑥,试使斗而才,因责常供。令以责之里正⑦。市中游侠儿⑧,得佳者笼养之,昂其直,居为奇货⑨。里胥猾黠⑩,假此科敛丁口⑪,每责一头,辄倾数家之产。邑有成名者,操童子业⑫,久不售⑬。为人迂讷⑭,遂为猾胥报充里正役,百计营谋不能脱。不终岁,薄产累

---

① 宣德间:宣德年间。宣德,明宣宗朱瞻基的年号(1426－1435)。
② 促织:蟋蟀的别名。《帝京景物略》卷三《胡家村》条,谓蟋蟀"斗则矜鸣,其声如织,故幽州谓之促织也。"
③ 征:征收,勒令交纳。
④ 西:西部地区,这里指陕西。
⑤ 华阴:县名,在今陕西省。
⑥ 进:进奉。
⑦ 里正:古时有"里正",明代称"里长"。明代役法规定,各地以邻近的一百一十户为"一里",从中推丁多粮多的十户,轮流充当里长,故又称"富户役"。里长负责催征粮税及分派徭役。后来赋役日渐繁苛,富户贿赂官府,避免承当,而使中、下户担任。任里长的中下户,不敢向豪绅富户征派,往往被迫自己赔垫,有的甚至倾家荡产。
⑧ 游侠儿:古称抑强扶弱、具有侠义精神的人为"游侠"。这里指游手好闲、不务正业的青年。
⑨ 居为奇货:囤积起来当作珍贵的财货。居,居积、囤积。
⑩ 里胥:乡里中的公差。胥,官府中的小吏。猾黠:狡猾奸诈。
⑪ 科敛丁口:按人口摊派费用。科敛,摊派、征收。丁口,泛指人口;男人称"丁",女子称"口"。
⑫ 操童子业:意谓读书欲考秀才。操,从事,童子业,指"童生"。科举时代凡没有考中秀才的人统称"童生"。
⑬ 不售:志愿未遂,指没有考中。售,达到、实现。
⑭ 迂讷:迂阔而拙于言辞。

第八篇《聊斋志异》Strange Stories from A Chinese Studio

尽。会征促织,成不敢敛户口,而又无所赔偿,忧闷欲死。妻曰:"死何裨益①?不如自行搜觅,冀有万一之得。"成然之。早出暮归,提竹筒铜丝笼,于败堵丛草处探石发穴,靡计不施,迄无济;即捕得三两头,又劣弱不中于款②。宰严限追比③;旬余,杖至百,两股间脓血流离,并虫亦不能行捉矣。转侧床头,惟思自尽。

时村中来一驼背巫,能以神卜。成妻具资诣问。见红女白婆④,填塞门户。入其舍,则密室垂帘,帘外设香几。问者爇香于鼎⑤,再拜。巫从旁望空代祝,唇吻翕辟⑥不知何词。各各竦立以听。少间,帘内掷一纸出,即道人意中事,无毫发爽⑦。成妻纳钱案上,焚拜如前人。食顷,帘动,片纸抛落。拾视之,非字而画:中绘殿阁,类兰若⑧;后小山下,怪石乱卧,针针丛棘,青麻头伏焉⑨;旁一蟆⑩,若将跳舞。展玩不可晓⑪。然睹促织,隐中胸怀。摺藏之,归以示成。成反复自念,得无教我猎虫所耶?细瞻景状,与村东大佛阁真逼似。乃强起扶杖,执图诣寺后。有古陵蔚

---

① 裨益:补益。
② 不中(zhòng 重)于款:不合规格。中,符合。款,款式、规格。
③ 严限追比:严定期限,按期查验催逼。旧时地方官府规定限期要求差役或百姓完成任务或交清赋欠,并按期查验完成情况。逾期不能完成则施杖责。查验有一定期限,每误一期责打一次,叫"追比"。
④ 红女白婆:红妆少女和白发老妇。
⑤ 爇香:烧香。鼎:三足香炉。
⑥ 翕(xī 西)辟:一合一开
⑦ 无毫发爽:没有丝毫差错。爽,差错。
⑧ 兰若:梵文"阿兰若"的音译,即佛寺。
⑨ 青麻头:一种上等品种蟋蟀的名称。《帝京景物略》卷三,谓"凡促织,青为上,黄次之,赤次之,黑又次之,白为下。"后文"蝴蝶"、"螳螂"、"油利挞"、"青丝额"等都是蟋蟀品种名。
⑩ 蟆:虾蟆。跳舞:跳跃。
⑪ 展玩:展视玩味。玩,玩味、思索。

起①；循陵而走，见蹲石鳞鳞②，俨然类画。遂于蒿莱中，侧听徐行，似寻针芥③；而心目耳力俱穷，绝无踪响。冥搜未已④，一癞头蟆猝然跃去⑤。成益愕，急逐趁之⑥。蟆入草间。蹑迹披求⑦，见有虫伏棘根；遽扑之，入石穴中。掭以尖草⑧，不出；以筒水灌之，始出。状极俊健，逐而得之。审视，巨身修尾，青项金翅。大喜笼归，举家庆贺，虽连城拱璧不啻也⑨。土于盆而养之⑩，蟹白栗黄⑪，备极护爱，留待限期，以塞官责。

　　成有子九岁，窥父不在，窃发盆，虫跃掷径出，迅不可捉，及扑入手，已股落腹裂，斯须就毙。儿惧，啼告母。母闻之，面色灰死，大骂曰："业根⑫！死期至矣！而翁归⑬，自与汝复算耳！"儿涕而出。未几成归，闻妻言，如被冰雪。怒索儿，儿渺然不知所往。既得其尸于井，因而化怒为悲，

---

①　古陵蔚起：茂密丛草中古墓隆起。蔚，草木茂盛的样子。
②　蹲石鳞鳞：乱石蹲踞，密集象鱼鳞。
③　针芥：针和芥子，喻非常细小的东西。
④　冥搜：到处搜索。冥，幽远。
⑤　癞头蟆：癞虾蟆。猝然：突然。
⑥　逐趁：追赶。
⑦　蹑迹披求：拨开丛草，跟踪寻求。蹑，追随。披，分开。
⑧　掭(tiǎn)：轻轻拨动。
⑨　虽连城拱璧不啻(chì 赤)也：即便是价值连城的大璧玉，也比不上它。《史记·廉颇、蔺相如列传》：战国时，赵国得和氏璧，秦国愿以十五城交换。故称和氏璧为"连城璧"，谓其价值连城。拱璧，大璧。《左传·襄公二十八年》："与我共拱璧。"《疏》："此璧两手拱抱之，故为拱璧。"不啻，不止。
⑩　土于盆而养之：《帝京景物略》卷三《胡家村》，谓都人繁殖蟋蟀，"其法土于盆而养之，虫生子土中。"此指用装有泥土的盆蓄养促织。
⑪　蟹白栗黄：蟹肉和栗实，喂养蟋蟀的饲料。
⑫　业根：犹言祸根。业，佛教名词，指过去所作。业有善有恶，此指恶业。
⑬　而翁：你父亲。而，你。

第八篇《聊斋志异》Strange Stories from A Chinese Studio

抢呼欲绝①。夫妻向隅②,茅舍无烟,相对默然,不复聊赖③。日将暮,取儿藁葬。近扶之,气息惙然④。喜置榻上,半夜复苏。夫妻心稍慰。但蟋蟀笼虚,顾之则气断声吞,亦不敢复究儿。自昏达曙,目不交睫。

东曦既驾⑤,僵卧长愁。忽闻门外虫鸣,惊起觇视,虫宛然尚在。喜而捕之。一鸣辄跃去,行且速。覆之以掌,虚若无物;手裁举,则又超忽而跃⑥。急趁之。折过墙隅,迷其所往。徘徊四顾,见虫伏壁上。审谛之,短小,黑赤色,顿非前物。成以其小,劣之。惟傍徨瞻顾,寻所逐者。壁上小虫,忽跃落衿袖间⑦,视之,形若土狗,梅花翅,方首长胫,意似良。喜而收之。将献公堂,惴惴恐不当意,思试之斗以觇之。村中少年好事者;驯养一虫,自名"蟹壳青",日与子弟角,无不胜。欲居之以为利,而高其直,亦无售者⑧。径造庐访成。视成所蓄,掩口胡卢而笑⑨。因出己虫,纳比笼中。成视之,庞然修伟,自增渐怍,不敢与较。少年固强之。顾念蓄劣物终无所用,不如拼博一笑。因合纳斗盆。小虫伏不动,蠢若木鸡⑩。少年又大笑。试以猪鬣毛,撩拨虫须,仍不动。少年又笑。屡撩之,

---

① 抢呼:头碰地,口喊天,形容悲痛已极。抢,碰、撞。
② 向隅:失意悲伤。《说苑·贵德》:"今有满堂饮酒者,有一人独索然向隅而泣。则一堂之人皆不乐矣。"
③ 不复聊赖:不再有所指望。聊赖,依赖,指生活或感情上的凭借。
④ 惙(chuò 绌)然:形容呼吸微弱。
⑤ 东曦(xī 析)既驾:东方太阳已经升起。曦,阳光。驾,指羲和为日御。《初学记》引《淮南子·天文训》:"爰止羲和,爰息六螭。"许慎注:"日乘车,驾以六龙,羲和御之。"
⑥ 超忽:远远地。
⑦ 衿:同"襟"。
⑧ 售:这里作"买"讲。
⑨ 掩口胡卢而笑:笑不可忍,自掩其口。胡卢,也作"卢胡",强自忍笑的样子。
⑩ 蠢若木鸡:形容外形呆蠢无有生气。木鸡,木雕的鸡,喻呆板无生气。古时善斗鸡的,要求把鸡训练得不虚骄,不恃气,安闲镇定,"望之似木鸡",才能战胜敌鸡。见《庄子·达生》。

第八篇《聊斋志异》Strange Stories from A Chinese Studio

虫暴怒，直奔，遂相腾击，振奋作声。俄见小虫跃起，张尾伸须，直龁敌领。少年大骇，解令休止。虫翘然矜鸣①，似报主知。成大喜。方共瞻玩，一鸡瞥来②，径进以啄。成骇立愕呼。幸啄不中，虫跃去尺有咫③；鸡健进，逐逼之，虫已在爪下矣。成仓猝莫知所救，顿足失色。旋见鸡伸颈摆扑；临视，则虫集冠上，力叮不释。成益惊喜，掇置笼中。

翼日进宰。宰见其小，怒诃成。成述其异，宰不信。试与他虫斗，虫尽靡④；又试之鸡，果如成言。乃赏成。献诸抚军⑤。抚军大悦，以金笼进上，细疏其能⑥。既入宫中，举天下所贡蝴蝶、螳螂、油利挞、青丝额……一切异状，遍试之，无出其右者⑦。每闻琴瑟之声，则应节而舞。益奇之。上大嘉悦⑧，诏赐抚臣名马衣缎。抚军不忘所自；无何，宰以"卓异"闻⑨。宰悦，免成役⑩。又嘱学使，俾入邑庠⑪。由此以善养虫名，屡得抚军殊宠。不数岁，田百顷，楼阁万椽⑫，牛羊蹄躈各千计⑬。一出门，裘马过世

---

① 翘然：谓两翅振起。矜鸣：骄傲地鸣叫。
② 瞥来：突然而来。瞥，眼光一掠，形容迅疾。
③ 尺有咫（zhǐ 止）：一二尺远。咫，周制八寸为咫。
④ 靡：披靡，被打败。
⑤ 抚军：明清时巡抚的别称。
⑥ 细疏其能：在表章上详细陈述蟋蟀的本领。疏，向皇帝陈述政事的奏章。
⑦ 右：上，古时以右为上。
⑧ 嘉悦：赞美、喜悦。
⑨ 以"卓异"闻：以"卓异"的考绩上报。明清时每三年对官员举行一次考绩，外官的考绩叫"大计"，由州、县官上至府、道、司层层考察属员，再汇送督、抚作最后考核，然后报呈吏部。"大计"最好的考语为"卓异"，意思是才能卓越优异。闻，上报。
⑩ 免成役：指免去成名担任里正的差役。
⑪ 俾：使。入邑庠：入县学，即取得生员资格。
⑫ 万椽（chuán 船）：犹言万间。
⑬ 牛羊蹄躈（qiào 叫）各千计：意思是牛羊各二百头。躈，语出《语史·货殖列传》。躈，尻窍，肛门。又作"噭"。噭，嘴。牛羊每头四蹄一躈，合以"千计"，则为二百头。

家焉①。

异史氏曰："天子偶用一物，未必不过此已忘；而奉行者即为定例。加之官贪吏虐，民日贴妇卖儿②，更无休止。故天子一跬步③，皆关民命，不可忽也。独是成氏子以蠹贫④，以促织富，裘马扬扬。当其为里正、受扑责时，岂意其至此哉！天将以酬长厚者⑤，遂使抚臣、令尹，并受促织恩荫⑥。闻之：一人飞升，仙及鸡犬⑦。信夫！"

据《聊斋志异》手稿本

---

① 裘马过世家：衣着排场超过世族之家。裘马，车马衣裘，指豪华生活。
② 贴妇卖儿：典妻鬻子。贴，典质。南朝宋明帝曾用"百姓卖儿贴妇钱"，兴建湘宫寺。
③ 跬（kuǐ 傀）步：指一举一动。举一足叫"跬"，举两足叫"步"。
④ 蠹：蛀虫，这里指里胥。
⑤ 长（zhǎng 掌）厚者：忠厚老实的人。
⑥ 并受促织恩荫：封建时代，子孙可以因父、祖的功劳而得到朝廷恩赐的功名或官爵，叫作"恩荫"。这里说"受促织恩荫"是讽刺、嘲骂。
⑦ 一人飞升，仙及鸡犬：《列仙传》谓汉淮南王刘安学道，服仙药飞升，"余药器存庭中，鸡犬舐之皆飞升。"这里以之讽刺促织受宠，众官得益。

Strange Stories from A Chinese Studio (Excerpt)

Translated by Herbert A. Giles

LXIII. THE LO-CH'A COUNTRY AND THE

SEA-MARKET①

Once upon a time there was a young man, named Ma Chün, who was also known as Lung-mei. He was the son of a trader, and a youth of surpassing beauty. His manners were courteous, and he loved nothing better than singing and playing. He used to associate with actors, and with an embroidered handkerchief round his head the effect was that of a beautiful woman. Hence he acquired the sobriquet of the Beauty. At fourteen years of age he graduated and began to make a name for himself; but his father, who was growing old and wished to retire from business, said to him, "My boy, book-learning will never fill your belly or put a coat on your back; you had much better stick to the old thing." Accordingly, Ma from that time occupied himself with scales and weights, with principal and interest, and such matters.

He made a voyage across the sea, and was carried away by a

---

① The term "sea-market" is generally understood in the sense of *mirage*, or some similar phenomenon.

第八篇《聊斋志异》Strange Stories from A Chinese Studio

typhoon. After being tossed about for many days and nights he arrived at a country where the people were hideously ugly. When these people saw Ma they thought he was a devil, and all ran screeching away. Ma was somewhat alarmed at this, but finding that it was they who were frightened at him, he quickly turned their fear to his own advantage. If he came across people eating and drinking he would rush upon them, and when they fled away for fear, he would regale himself upon what they had left. By-and-by he went to a village among the hills, and there the people had at any rate some facial resemblance to ordinary men. But they were all in rags and tatters like beggars. So Ma sat down to rest under a tree, and the villagers, not daring to come near him, contented themselves with looking at him from a distance. They soon found, however, that he did not want to eat them, and by degrees approached little closer to him. Ma, smiling, began to talk; and although their language was different, yet he was able to make himself tolerably intelligible, and told them whence he had come. The villagers were much pleased, and spread the news that the stranger was not a man-eater. Nevertheless, the very ugliest of all would only take a look and be off again; they would not come near him. Those who did go up to him were not very much unlike his own countrymen, the Chinese. They brought him plenty of food and wine. Ma asked them what they were afraid of. They replied, "We had heard from our forefathers that 26,000 *li* to the west there is a country called China. We had heard that the people of that land were the most extraordinary in appearance you can possibly imagine. Hitherto it has been hearsay; we can now believe it." He then asked them how it was they were so poor. They answered, "You see, in our country everything depends, not on literary talent, but on beauty. The most beautiful are made ministers of state; the next handsomest are made judges and magistrates; and the third class in looks are empolyed in the palace of the king. Thus these are enabled out of their pay to provide for their wives and families. But we, from our very birth, are regarded by our parents as inauspicious, and are left to perish, some of us being occasionally preserved by more humane parents to prevent the extinction of the family." Ma asked the name of their country, and they told him it was Lo-ch'a. Also that the capital city was some 30 *li* to the north. He begged them to take him there, and next day at cock-crow he started thitherwards in their company, arriving just about dawn. The walls of the city were made of black stone, as black as ink, and the city gate-houses were about 100 feet high. Red stones were used for tiles, and picking up a broken piece Ma found that it marked his finger-nail like vermilion. They arrived just when the Court was rising, and saw all the equipages of the officials. The village people pointed out one who they said was Prime Minister. His ears drooped forward in flaps; he had three nostrils, and his eye-lashes were just like bamboo screens hanging in front of his eyes. Then several came out on horseback, and they said these were the privy councillors. So they went on, telling him the rank of all the ugly uncouth fellows he saw. The lower they got down in the official scale the less hideous the officials were. By-and-by Ma went back, the people in the streets marvelling very much to see him, and tumbling helter-skelter one over another as if they had met a goblin. The villagers shouted out to reassure them, and then they stood at a distance to look at him. When he got back, there was not a man, woman, or child in the whole nation but knew that there was a strange man at the village; and the gentry and officials became very desirous of seeing him. However, if he went to any of their houses the porter always slammed the door in his face, and the master, mistress, and family, in general, would only peep at, and speak to him through the cracks. Not a single one dared receive him face to face; but, finally, the village people, at a loss what to do, bethought themselves of a man who had been sent by a former king on official

第八篇《聊斋志异》Strange Stories from A Chinese Studio

business among strange nations. "He," said they, "having seen many kinds of men, will not be afraid of you." So they went to his house, where they were received in a very friendly way. He seemed to be about eighty or ninety years of age; his eyeballs protruded, and his beard curled up like a hedgehog. He said, "In my youth I was sent by the king among many nations, but I never went to China. I am now one hundred and twenty years of age, and that I should be permitted to see a native of your country is a fact which it will be my duty to report to the Throne. For ten years and more I have not been to Court, but have remained here in seclusion; yet I will now make an effort on your behalf." Then followed a banquet, and when the wine had already circulated pretty freely, some dozen singing girls came in and sang and danced before them. The girls all wore white embroidered trubans, and long scarlet robes which trailed on the ground. The words they uttered were unintelligible, and the tunes they played perfectly hideous. The host, however, seemed to enjoy it very much, and said to Ma, "Have you music in China?" He replied that they had, and the old man asked for a specimen. Ma hummed him a tune, beating time on the table, with which he was very much pleased, declaring that his guest had the voice of a phoenix and the notes of a dragon, such as he had never heard before. The next day he presented a memorial to the Throne, and the king at once commanded Ma to appear before him. Several of the ministers, however, represented that his appearance was so hideous it might frighten His Majesty, and the king accordingly desisted from his intention. The old man returned and told Ma, being quite upset about it. They remained together some time until they had drunk themselves tipsy. Then Ma, seizing a sword, began to attitudinise, smearing his face all over with coal-dust. He acted the part of Chang Fei,① at which his host was so delighted that he begged him to appear before the Prime Minister in the character of Chang Fei. Ma replied, "I don't mind a little amateur acting, but how can I play the hypocrite② for my own personal advantage?" On being pressed he consented, and the old man prepared a great feast, and asked some of the high officials to be present, telling Ma to paint himself as before. When the guests had arrived, Ma was brought out to see them; whereupon they all exclaimed, "Ai-yah! how is it he was so ugly before and is now so beautiful!?" By-and-by, when they were all taking wine together, Ma began to sing them a most bewitching song, and they got so excited over it that next day they recommended him to the king. The king sent a special summons for him to appear, and asked him many questions about the government of China, to all of which Ma replied in detail, eliciting sighs of admiration from His Majesty. He was honoured with a banquet in the royal guest-pavilion, and when the king had made himself tipsy he said to him, "I hear you are a very skillful musician. Will you be good enough to let me hear you?" Ma then got up and began to attitudinise, singing a plaintive air like the girls with the turbans. The king was charmed, and at once made him a privy councillor, giving him a private banquet, and bestowing other marks of royal favour. As time went on his fellow officials found out the secret of his painted face,③ and whenever he was among them they were always whispering together, besides which they avoided being near him as much as possible. Thus Ma was left to himself, and found his position anything but pleasant in

① A famous General who played a leading part in the wars of the Three Kingdoms. See No. ⅩCⅢ., note 8.
② A hit at the hypocrisy of the age.
③ Showing that hypocrisy is bad policy in the long run.

consequence. So he memorialised the Throne, asking to be allowed to retire from office, but his request was refused. He then said his health was bad, and got three months' sick leave, during which he packed up his valuables and went back to the village. The villagers on his arrival went down on their knees to him, and he distributed gold and jewels amongst his old friends. They were very glad to see him, and said, "You kindness shall be repaid when we go to the sea-market; we will bring you some pearls and things." Ma asked them where that was. They said it was at the bottom of the sea, where the mermaids[①] kept their treasures, and that as many as twelve nations were accustomed to go thither to trade. Also that it was frequented by spirits, and that to get there it was necessary to pass through red vapours and great waves. "Dear Sir," they said, "do not yourself risk this great danger, but let us take your money and purchase these rare pearls for you. The season is now at hand." Ma asked them how they knew this. They said, "Whenever we see red birds flying backwards and forwards over the sea, we know that within seven days the market will open." He asked when they were going to start, that he might accompany them; but they begged him not to think of doing so. He replied. "I am a sailor; how can I be afraid of wind and waves?" Very soon after this people came with merchandise to forward, and so Ma packed up and went on board the vessel that was going.

This vessel held some tens of people, was flat-bottomed, with a railing all round, and, rowed by ten men, it cut through the water like an arrow. After a voyage of three days they saw afar off faint outlines of towers and minarets, and crowds of trading vessels. They soon arrived at the city, the walls of which were made of bricks as long as a man's

---

① The tears of Chinese mermaids are said to be pearls.

body, the tops of its buildings being lost in the Miky Way.① Having made fast their boat, they went in, and saw laid out in the market rare pearls and wondrous precious stones of dazzling beauty, such as are quite unknown amongst men. Then they saw a young man come forth riding upon a beautiful steed. The people of the market stood back to let him pass, saying he was the third son of the king; but when the prince saw Ma, he exclaimed, "This is no foreigner," and immediately an attendant drew near and asked his name and country. Ma made a bow, and standing at one side told his name and family. The prince smiled, and said, "For you to have honoured our country thus is no small piece of good luck." He then gave him a horse and begged him to follow. They went out of the city gate and down to the sea-shore, whereupon their horses plunged into the water. Ma was terribly frightened and screamed out; but the sea opened dry before them and formed a wall of water on either side. In a little time they reached the king's palace, the beams of which were made of tortoise-shell and the tiles of fishes' scales. The four walls were of crystal, and dazzled the eye like mirrors. They got down off their horses and went in, and Ma was introduced to the king. The young prince said, "Sir, I have been to the market, and have got a gentleman from China." Whereupon Ma made obeisance before the king, who addressed him as follows:—"Sir, from a talented scholar like yourself I venture to ask for a few stanzas upon our sea-market. Pray do not refuse." Ma thereupon made a *k' o-t 'ou*, and undertook the king's command. Using an ink-slab of crystal, a brush of dragon's beard, paper as white as snow, and ink scented like the larkspur,② Ma

---

① See No. XIX., note I.

② Good ink of the kind miscalled "Indian" is usually very highly scented; and from a habit the Chinese have of sucking their writing-brushes to a fine point, the phrase "to eat ink" has become a synonym of "to study."

immediately threw off some thousand odd verses, which he laid at the feet of the king. When His Majesty saw them, he said, "Sir, your genius does honour to these marine nations of ours." Then, summoning the members of the royal family, the king gave a great feast in the Coloured Cloud pavilion; and, when the wine had circulated freely, seizing a great goblet in his hand, the king rose and said before all the guests, "It is a thousand pities, Sir, that you are not married. What say you to entering the bonds of wedlock?" Ma rose blushing and stammered out his thanks; upon which the king, looking round, spoke a few words to the attendants, and in a few moments in came a bevy of Court ladies supporting the king's daughter, whose ornaments went tinkle, tinkle, as she walked along. Immediately the nuptial drums and trumpets began to sound forth, and bride and bridegroom worshipped Heaven and Earth together.① Stealing a glance, Ma saw that the princess was endowed with a fairy-like loveliness. When the ceremony was over she retired, and by-and-by the wine party broke up. Then came several beautifully dressed waiting-maids, who with painted candles escorted Ma within. The bridal couch was made of coral adorned with eight kinds of precious stones, and the curtains were thickly hung with pearls as big as acorns. Next day at dawn a crowd of young slave-girls trooped into the room to offer their services; whereupon Ma got up and went off to Court to pay his respects to the king. He was then duly received as royal son-in-law and made an officer of state. The fame of his poetical talents spread far and wide, and the kings of the various seas sent officers to congratulate him, vieing with each other in their invitations to him. Ma dressed himself in gorgeous clothes, and went forth riding on a superb steed, with a mounted body-guard all splendidly armed. There were musicians

---

① This all-important point in a Chinese marriage ceremony is the equivalent of our own "signing in the vestry."

on horseback and musicians in chariots, and in three days he had visited every one of the marine kingdoms, making his name known in all directions. In the palace there was a jade tree, about as big round as a man could clasp. Its roots were as clear as glass, and up the middle ran, as it were, a stick of pale yellow. The branches were the size of one's arm; the leaves like white jade, as thick as a copper cash. The foliage was dense, and beneath its shade the ladies of the palace were wont to sit and sing. The flowers which covered the tree resembled grapes, and if a single petal fell to the earth it made a ringing sound. Taking one up, it would be found to be exactly like carved cornelian, very bright and pretty to look at. Form time to time a wonderful bird came and sang there. Its feathers were of a golden hue, and its tail as long as its body. Its notes were like the tinkling of jade, very plaintive and touching to listen to. When Ma heard this bird sing, it called up in him recollections of his old home, and accordingly he said to the princess, "I have now been away from my own country for three years, separated from my father and mother. Thinking of them my tears flow and the perspiration runs down my back. Can you return with me?" His wife replied, "The way of immortals is not that of men. I am unable to do what you ask, but I cannot allow the feelings of husband and wife to break the tie of parent and child. Let us devise some plan." When Ma heard this he wept bitterly, and the princess sighed and said, "We cannot both stay or both go." The next day the king said to him, "I hear that you are pining after your old home. Will tomorrow suit you for taking leave?" Ma thanked the king for his great kindness, which he declared he could never forget, and promised to return very shortly. That evening the princess and Ma talked over their wine of their approaching separation. Ma said they would soon meet again; but his wife averred that their married life was at an end. Then he wept afresh, but the princess said, "Like a filial son you are going home to your parents. In the meetings

第八篇《聊斋志异》Strange Stories from A Chinese Studio

and separations of this life, a hundred years seem but a single day; why, then, should we give way to tears like children? I will be true to you; do you be faithful to me; and then, though separated, we shall be united in spirit, a happy pair. Is it necessary to live side by side in order to grow old together? If you break our contract your next marriage will not be a propitious one; but if loneliness① overtakes you then choose a concubine. There is one point more of which I would speak, with reference to our married life. I am about to become a mother, and I pray you give me a name for your child." To this Ma replied, "If a girl I would have her called Lung-kung; if a boy, then name him Fu-hai."② The princess asked for some token of remembrance, and Ma gave her a pair of jade lilies that he had got during his stay in the marine kingdom. She added, "On the 8th of the 4th moon, three years hence, when you once more steer your course for this country, I will give you up your child." She next packed a leather bag full of jewels and handed it to Ma, saying, "Take care of this; it will be a provision for many generations." When the day began to break a splendid farewell feast was given him by the king, and Ma bade them all adieu. The princess, in a car drawn by snow-white sheep, escorted him to the boundary of the marine kingdom, where he dismounted and stepped ashore. "Farewell!" cried the princess, as her returning car bore her rapidly away, and the sea, closing over her, snatched her from her husband's sight. Ma returned to his home across the ocean. Some had thought him long since dead and gone; all marvelled at his story. Happily his father and mother were yet alive, though his former wife had married another man; and so he understood why the princess had pledged him to constancy, for she already knew that this had taken place. His father wished him to take

---

① Literally, "if you have no one to cook your food."
② "Dragon Palace" and "Happy Sea," respectively.

another wife, but he would not. He only took a concubine. Then, after the three years had passed away, he started across the sea on his return journey, when lo! he beheld, riding on the wave-crests and splashing about the water in playing, two young children. On going near, one of them seized hold of him and sprang into his arms; upon which the elder cried until he, too, was taken up. They were a boy and girl, both very lovely, and wearing embroidered caps adorned with jade lilies. On the back of one of them was a worked case, in which Ma found the following letter:—

"I presume my father and mother-in-law are well. Three years have passed away and destiny still keeps us apart. Across the great ocean, the letter-bird would find no path.① I have been with you in my dreams until I am quite worn out. Does the blue sky look down upon any grief like mine? Yet Ch'ang-ngo② lives solitary in the moon, and Chih Nü③ laments that she cannot cross the Silver River. Who am I that I should expect happiness to be mine? Truly this thought turns my tears into joy. Two months after your departure I had twins, who can already prattle away in the language of childhood, at one moment snatching a date, at another a pear. Had they no mother they would still live. These I now send to you, with the jade lilies you gave me in their hats, in token of the sender. When you take them upon your knee, think that I am standing by your side. I know that you have kept your promise to me, and I am happy. I shall take no second husband, even unto death. All thoughts of dress and finery are gone from me; my looking-glass sees no new fashions; my face has long been unpowdered, my eyebrows

---

① Alluding to an old legend of a letter conveyed by a bird.
② See No. V., note 2.
③ The "Spinning Damsel," or name of a star in Lyra, connected with which there is a celebrated legend of its annual transit across the Milky Way.

第八篇《聊斋志异》Strange Stories from A Chinese Studio

unblacked. You are my Ulysses, I am your Penelope;① though not actually leading a married life, how can it be said that we are not husband and wife. Your father and mother will take their grandchildren upon their knees, though they have never set eyes upon the bride. Alas! there is something wrong in this. Next year your mother will enter upon the long night. I shall be there by the side of the grave, as is becoming in her daughter-in-law. From this time forth our daughter will be well; later on she will be able to grasp her mother's hand. Our boy, when he grows up, may possibly be able to come to and fro. Adieu, dear husband, adieu, though I am leaving much unsaid." Ma read the letter over and over again, his tears flowing all the time. His two children clung round his neck, and begged him to take them home. "Ah, my children," said he, "where is your home?" Then they all wept bitterly, and Ma, looking at the great ocean stretching away to meet the sky, lovely and pathless, embraced his children, and proceeded sorrowfully to return. Knowing, too, that his mother could not last long, he prepared everything necessary for the ceremony of interment, and planted a hundered young pinetrees at her grave. ② The following year the old lady did die, and her coffin was borne to its last resting-place, when lo! there was the princess standing by the side of the grave. The lookers-on were much alarmed, but in a moment there was a flash of lightning, followed by a clap of thunder and a squall of rain, and she was gone. It was then noticed that many of the young pine-trees which had died were one and all brought to life. Subsequently, Fu-hai went in search of the mother for whom he pined so much, and after some days' absence returned. Lung-kung, being a girl, could not accompany him, but she mourned

---

① These are of course only the equivalents of the Chinese names in the text.
② To keep off the much-dreaded wind, which distrubs the rest of the departed.

much in secret. One dark day her mother entered and bade her dry her eyes, saying, "My child, you must get married. Why these tears?" She then gave her a tree of coral eight feet in height, some Baroos camphor,① one hundred valuable pearls, and two boxes inlaid with gold and precious stones, as her dowry. Ma having found out she was there, rushed in, and, seizing her hand, began to weep for joy, when suddenly a violent peal of thunder rent the building, and the princess had vanished.②

LXIV. THE FIGHTING CRICKET

During the reign of Hsüan Tê,③ cricket fighting was very much in vogue at court, levies of crickets being exacted from the people as a tax. On one occasion the magistrate of Huayin, wishing to make friends with the Governor, presented him with a cricket which, on being set to fight, displayed very remarkable powers; so much so that the Governor commanded the magistrate to supply him regularly with these insects. The latter, in his turn, ordered the beadles of his district to provide him with crickets; and then it became a practice for people who had nothing else to do to catch and rear them for this purpose. Thus the price of

---

① For which a very high price is obtained in China.
② Episodes which appear in this story and in "The Princess of the Tung-t'ing Lake" have been woven together to form the socalled Japanese "tale of Urashima, the fisher-lad who was beloved of the Sea King's daughter." See the *Fortnightly Review*, July 1906, p. 99, and Aston's *Japanese Literature*, p. 39.
③ Of the Ming dynasty; reigned A.D. 1426—1436.

crickets rose very high; and when the beadle's ① runners came to exact even a single one, it was enough to ruin several families.

Now in the village of which we are speaking there lived a man named Ch'êng, a student who had often failed for his bachelor's degree; and, being a stupid sort of fellow, his name was sent in for the post of beadle. He did all he could to get out of it, but without success; and by the end of the year his small patrimony was gone. Just then came a call for crickets, and Ch'êng, not daring to make a like call upon his neighbours. was at his wit's end, and in his distress determined to commit suicide. "What's the use of that?" cried his wife. "You'd do better to go out and try to find some." So off went Ch'êng in the early morning, with a bamboo tube and a silk net, not returning till late at night; and he searched about in tumble-down walls, in bushes, under stones, and in holes, but without catching more than two or three, do what he would. Even those he did catch were weak creatures, and of no use at all, which made the magistrate fix a limit of time, the result of which was that in a few days Ch'êng got one hundred blows with the bamboo. This made him so sore that he was quite unable to go after the crickets any more, and, as he lay tossing and turning on the bed, he

---

① These beadles are chosen by the officials from among the respectable and substantial of the people to preside over a small area and be responsible for the general good behaviour of its inhabitants. The post is one of honour and occasional emolument, since all petitions presented to the authorities, all mortgages, transfers of land, &. c., should bear the beadle's seal or signature in evidence of their *bonâ-fide* character. On the other hand, the beadle is punished by fine, and sometimes bambooed, if robberies are too frequent within his jurisdiction, or if he fails to secure the person of any malefactor particularly wanted by his superior officers. And other causes may combine to make the post a dangerous one; but no one is allowed to refuse acceptance of it point-blank.

determined once again to put an end to his life.

About that time a hump-backed fortune-teller of great skill arrived at the village, and Ch'êng's wife, putting together a trifle of money, went off to seek his assistance. The door was literally blocked up—fair young girls and white-headed dames crowding in from all quarters. A room was darkened, and a bamboo screen hung at the door, an altar being arranged outside at which the fortune-seekers burnt incense in a brazier, and prostrated themselves twice, while the soothsayer stood by the side, and, looking up into vacancy, prayed for a response. His lips opened and shut, but nobody heard what he said, all standing there in awe waiting for the answer. In a few moments a piece of paper was thrown from behind the screen, and the soothsayer said that the petitioner's desire would be accomplished in the way he wished. Ch'êng's wife now advanced, and, placing some money on the altar, burnt her incense and prostrated herself in a similar manner. In a few moments the screen began to move, and a piece of paper was thrown down, on which there were no words, but only a picture. In the middle was a building like a temple, and behind this a small hill, at the foot of which were a number of curious stones, with the long, spiky feelers of innumerable crickets appearing from behind. Hard by was a frog, which seemed to be engaged in putting itself into various kinds of attitudes. The good woman had no idea what it all meant; but she noticed the crickets, and accordingly went off home to tell her husband. "Ah," said he, "this is to show me where to hunt for crickets;" and, on looking closely at the picture, he saw that the building very much resembled a temple to the east of their village. So he forced himself to get up, and, leaning on a stick, went out to seek crickets behind the temple. Rounding an old grave, he came upon a place where stones were lying scattered about as in the picture, and then he set himself to watch attentively. He might as well have been looking for a needle or a grain of mustard-seed; and by degrees he became quite exhausted, without finding anything, when suddenly an old frog jumped out. Ch'êng was a little startled, but immediately pursued the frog, which retreated into the bushes. He then saw one of the insects he wanted sitting at the root of a bramble; but on making a grab at it, the cricket ran into a hole, from which he was unalbe to move it until he poured in some water, when out the little creature came. It was a magnificent specimen, strong and handsome, with a fine tail, green neck, and golden wings; and, putting it in his basket, he returned home in high glee to receive the congratulations of his family. He would not have taken anything for this cricket. He put it into a bowl, and fed it with white crab's flesh and with the yellow kernel of the sweet chestnut, tending it most lovingly, and waiting for the time when the magistrate should call upon him for a cricket.

Meanwhile, a son of Ch'êng's, aged nine, one day took the opportunity of his father being out to open the bowl. Instantaneously the cricket made a spring forward and was gone; and all efforts to catch it again were unavailing. At length the boy made a grab at it with his hand, but only succeeded in seizing one of its legs, which thereupon broke, and the little creature soon afterwards died. Ch'êng's wife turned deadly pale when her son, with tears in his eyes, told her what had happened. "Oh, you young rascal! won't you catch it when your father comes home," said she; at which the boy ran away, crying bitterly. Soon after Ch'êng arrived, and when he heard his wife's story he felt as if he had been turned to ice, and went in search of his son, who, however, was nowhere to be found, until at length they discovered his body lying at the bottom of a well. Their anger was thus turned to grief, and death seemed as though it would be a pleasant relief to them as they sat facing each other in silence in their thatched and

第八篇《聊斋志异》Strange Stories from A Chinese Studio

smokeless① hut. At evening they prepared to bury the boy; but, on touching the body, lo! he was still breathing. Overjoyed, they placed him upon the bed, and towards the middle of the night he came round; but they found that his mind was weak, and he wanted to go to sleep. His father, however, caught sight of the empty bowl in which he had kept the cricket, and ceased to think any more about his son, never once closing his eyes all night; and as day gradually broke, there he lay stiff and stark, until suddenly he heard the chirping of a cricket outside the house door. Jumping up in a great hurry to see, there was his lost insect; but, on trying to catch it, away it hopped directly. At last he got it under his hand, though when he came to close his fingers on it, there was nothing in them. So he went on, chasing it up and down, until finally it hopped into a corner of the wall; and then, looking carefully about, he espied it once more, no longer the same in appearance, but small, and of a dark red colour. Ch'eng stood looking at it, without trying to catch such a worthless specimen, when all of a sudden the little creature hopped into his sleeve; and, on examining it more nearly, he saw that it really was a handsome insect, with wellformed head and neck, and forthwith took it indoors. He was now anxious to try its prowess; and it so happened that a young fellow of the village, who had a fine cricket which used to win every bout it fought, and was so valuable to him that he wanted a high price for it, called on Ch'eng that very day. He laughed heartily at Ch'eng's champion, and, producing his own, placed it side by side, to the great disadvantage of the former. Ch'eng's countenance fell, and he no longer wished to back his cricket; however, the young fellow urged him, and he thought that there was no use in rearing a feeble insect, and that he had better sacrifice it for a laugh; so they put them together in a bowl. The little cricket lay quite

---

① A favourite Chinese expression, signifying the absence of food.

still like a piece of wood, at which the young fellow roared again, and louder than ever when it did not move even though tickled with a pig's bristle. By dint of tickling it was roused at last, and then it fell upon its adversary with such fury, that in a moment the young fellow's cricket would have been killed outright had not its master interfered and stopped the fight. The little cricket then stood up and chirped to Ch'êng as a sign of victory; and Ch'êng, overjoyed, was just talking over the battle with the young fellow, when a cock caught sight of the insect, and ran up to eat it. Ch'êng was in a great state of alarm; but the cock luckily missed its aim, and the cricket hopped away, its enemy pursuing at full speed. In another moment it would have been snapped up, when, lo! to his great astonishment, Ch'êng saw his cricket seated on the cock's head, holding firmly on to its comb. He then put it into a cage, and by-and-by sent it to the magistrate, who, seeing what a small one he had provided, was very angry indeed. Ch'êng told the story of the cock, which the magistrate refused to believe, and set it to fight with other crickets, all of which it vanquished without exception. He then tried it with a cock, and as all turned out as Ch'êng had said, he gave him a present, and sent the cricket in to the Governor. The Governor put it into a golden cage, and forwarded it to the palace, accompanied by some remarks on its performances; and when there, it was found that of all the splendid collection of His Imperial Majesty, not one was worthy to be placed alongside of this one. It would dance in time to music, and thus became a great favourite, the Emperor in return bestowing magnificent gifts of horses and silks upon the Governor. The Governor did not forget whence he had obtained the cricket, and the magistrate also well rewarded Ch'êng by excusing him from the duties of beadle, and by instructing the Literary Chancellor to pass him for the first degree. A few months afterwards Ch'êng's son recovered his intellect, and said that he had been a cricket, and had proved himself a very skilful fighter. The Governor, too, rewarded Ch'êng handsomely, and in a few years he was a rich man, with flocks, and herds, and houses, and acres, quite one of the wealthiest of mankind.

第八篇《聊斋志异》Strange Stories from A Chinese Studio

Selected Tales of Liao Zhai(Excerpt)

Translated by Yang Hsienyi and Gladys Yang

The Rakshas and the Sea Market

Ma Ji, whose other name was Longmei, was the son of a merchant. A handsome, unconventional lad, he loved singing and dancing; and his habit of mixing with actors and wearing a silk handkerchief on his head made him look as beautiful as a girl and won him the nickname Handsome. At the age of fourteen he entered the prefectural school, where he was winning quite a name for himself when his father, growing old, decided to retire.

"Son," said the old man, "books cannot fill your belly or put a coat on your back. You had better follow your father's trade."

Ma, accordingly, turned his hand to business.

While on a sea voyage with other traders, Ma was carried off by a typhoon. After several days and nights he reached a city where all the inhabitants were appallingly ugly; yet at the sight of him they exclaimed in horror and fled as if he were a monster. At first Ma was alarmed by their hideous looks; but as soon as he discovered that they were even more afraid of him, he made the most of their fear. Wherever he found them eating or drinking he would rush upon them, and when they scattered in alarm he would regale himself upon all they left.

Later, Ma made his way to a mountain village where the people showed more resemblance to human beings. But they were a ragged, beggarly lot. As he rested under a tree, the villagers gazed at him from a distance, not daring to approach; but realizing after some time that he would not eat them, they began to draw nearer, and Ma addressed them with a smile. Although they spoke different tongues, each side could understand something of what the other said. And when Ma told them that he came from China, the villagers were pleased and spread the news that this stranger was not a cannibal after all. The ugliest of them, however, would turn away after one look at Ma, not daring to draw near. Those who did go up to him had features not entirely different from the Chinese; and as they brought him food and wine Ma asked why they were so afraid of him.

"We were told by our forefathers," they answered, "that nearly nine thousand miles to our west is a country called China inhabited by the most extraordinarylooking race. We knew this by hearsay only before; but you have provided proof of it."

Asked the reason for their poverty, they replied: "In our country we value beauty, not literary accomplishments. Our most handsome men are appointed ministers, those coming next are made governors and magistrates, while the third class have noble patrons and receive handsome pensions for the support of their families. But we are considered as freaks at birth, and our parents nearly always abandon us, only keeping us in order to continue the family line."

When Ma inquired the name of their country, they told him that it was The Great Kingdom of Rakshas, and that their capital lay about ten miles to the north. And upon Ma's expressing a desire to be conducted there, they set off with him the next day at cock-crow and reached the city at dawn. The city walls were made of stone as black as ink, with towers and pavilions a hundred feet high. Red stones were used for tiles, and picking up a fragment of one Ma found that it marked his finger-nail just like vermilion. They arrived as the court was rising, in time to see the official equipages. The villagers pointed out the prime minister, and

Ma saw that his ears drooped forward in flaps, he had three nostrils, and his eyelashes covered his eyes like a screen. He was followed by some riders whom the villagers said were privy councillors. They informed Ma of each man's rank; and, although all the officials were ugly, the lower their rank the less hideous they were.

When Ma turned to leave, the citizens of the capital exclaimed in terror and started flying in all directions as if he were an ogre. Only when the villgers assured them that there was nothing to be afraid of did these city people dare stand at a distance to watch. By the time he got back, however, there was not a man, woman or child in the country but knew that a manmonster was there; so all the gentry and officials were curious to see him and asked the villagers to fetch him. But whatever house he went to, the gate-keeper would slam the door in his face while men and women alike dared only peep at him through cracks and comment on him in whispers. Not a single one had the courage to invite him in.

Then the villagers told him: "There is a captain of the imperial guard here who was sent abroad on a number of missions by our late king. He has seen so much that he may not be afraid of you."

So they called on the captain, and he was genuinely pleased to meet Ma, treating him as an honuoured guest. Ma saw that his host who looked like a man of ninety, had protruding eyes and a beard like a hedgehog's.

"In my youth," said the captain, "His Majesty sent me to many countries, but never to China. Now at the age of one hundred and twenty, I have been fortunate enough to meet one from your honourable country! I must report this to the king. Living in retirement, I have not been to the court for more than ten years; but I will go there for your sake early tomorrow morning."

He plied Ma with food and drink, showing him every courtesy.

第八篇《聊斋志异》Strange Stories from A Chinese Studio

After they had drunk a few cups of wine, a dozen girls came in to dance and sing in turn. They looked like devils, but wore white silk turbans and long red dresses which trailed on the ground; and Ma, who could not understand the performance or the songs, found the music weird in the extreme. His host, however, listened appreciatively and asked eventually whether China could boast equally fine music. Receiving an affirmative answer, the old man begged him to sing a few bars. So, beating time on the table, Ma obliged with a tune.

"How strange!" exclaimed the captain, delighted. "It is like the cries of phoenixes or dragons. I have never heard anything resembling this before."

The following day the old man went to the court to recommend Ma to the king, who decided to summon him for an audience. But when two ministers declared that Ma's revolting appearance might shock His Majesty, the king changed his mind. The captain, quite upset, returned to tell Ma of the failure of his mission.

One day, after Ma had stayed with the captain for some time, under the influence of wine he smeared his face with coal dust to perform a sword dance in the role of Zhang Fei.①

"You must appear before the prime minister with your face painted like that," urged the captain, who admired this disguise immensely. "He is sure to patronize you, and will certainly procure you a big salary."

"It is all very well to disguise oneself in fun," protested Ma with a laugh. "But how can I play the hypocrite for the sake of personal gain?"

He gave in, however, when his host insisted.

---

① A famous general in the period of the Three Kingdoms(AD 220—280). He is represented on the traditional stage as a man with a dark face and long whiskers.

第八篇《聊斋志异》Strange Stories from A Chinese Studio

Then the captain invited a number of high officials to a banquet, and bade Ma paint his face in readiness. When the guests arrived and Mar was called out to meet them, they were all amazed.

"How strange!" they cried. "He used to be so ugly; but now he is quite handsome."

Drinking together, they were soon on the best of terms; and when Ma danced and sang country tunes, they were delighted. The very next day they recommended him to the king, who summoned him to court to question him about the government of China. And his diplomatic answers pleased the king so much that a feast was held in Ma's honour in the pleasure palace.

"I hear that you are skilled in music," said the king as they were drinking. "Will you perform for me?"

Ma immediately rose to dance and sing vulgar tunes, wearing a white turban in imitation of the girls; and the king was so amused the he promptly appointed him a privy councillor, thereafter dining with him frequently and showing him extraordinary favour.

As time went on, however, the other officials realized that Ma's face was painted. Wherever he went, people would whisper behind his back or treat him coldly; and such isolation made him uneasy. He addressed a memorial to the throne, requesting permission to retire; but the king refused, granting him only three months' leave. Ma then went back in a carriage loaded with gold and jewels to the mountain village, where the villagers welcomed him on their knees; and, amid thunderous applause, he distributed his wealth among his old friends.

"We are humble people," they said, "yet Your Grace has treated us so kindly! When we go to the Sea Market, we shall look for some precious objects to repay you."

Ma asked where this market was.

"It is a market in the middle of the ocean," they told him, "where mermaids from all the seas bring their jewels and merchants from all the twelve countries around come to trade. Deities frolic there among the coloured clouds and tossing waves; but rich men and high officials will not risk the journey, commissioning us to buy treasures for them instead. The time for the market is at hand."

"How do you know the date?" demanded Ma.

They explained that red birds flew over the ocean seven days before the market; but when Ma asked them when they were going to start, and whether he might go with them, the villagers begged him not to take such a risk.

"I am a sailor," protested Ma. "The wind and waves hold no fears for me."

Soon after this, people came with money to buy goods, then the villagers loaded their wares and boarded a vessel capable of carrying several dozen men. This was a flat-bottomed boat surrounded by a high railing; and with ten men at the oars it cut through the water like an arrow. After a voyage of three days they could make out in the distance, between the moving clouds and water, pavilions rising one behind the other and busy traffic of trading junks. By and by they came to a city, which had walls made of bricks as long as a man's body, and a citadel towering to the sky. Here they moored their boat and went ashore to inspect the treasure displayed in the market—precious stones which dazzled the eye, seldom seen in the world of men.

Then a young man rode up, and all the market people hastened to make way for him, crying that this was the Third Prince of Dongyang. The prince's eye fell on Ma as he passed, and he exclaimed:

"This stranger is not from these parts!"

Some of his outriders came to ask Ma where he hailed from; and Ma, bowing at the roadside, told them.

"A kind fate has favoured us with your visit!" cried the prince with a smile. He gave Ma a horse and bade him ride with them out of the West Gate. Upon reaching the shore, their steeds neighed and leapt into the waves; but as Ma cried out in dread the sea parted to form a wall of water on either side; and presently a palace came into sight. It had rafters of tortoise-shell and tiles of fish scales, while its dazzling walls of bright crystal reflected all around. Here they dismounted, and Ma was led into the presence of the dragon king who was seated on his throne.

"In the market I came across a talented man from China," the prince reported. "I have brought him here to Your Majesty."

Ma stepped forward to bow to the ground.

"You are a great scholar, sir," said the dragon king, "not inferior to Qu Yuan, Song Yu and other poets of old. May I ask you to compose a poem on our Sea Market? Pray do not refuse."

Having bowed his agreement, Ma was given a crystal inkstone, dragon's beard brush, paper as white as snow, and ink as fragrant as orchids. Without hesitation he dashed off over one thousand characters which he presented to the dragon king, who marked the rhythm with one hand as he read the poem.

"Your genius sheds glory on our watery kingdom, sir," said the king.

He then summoned all his dragon kinsmen to feast at the Palace of Rosy Clouds, and, when the wine had circulated freely, raising a goblet in one hand he said to Ma: "My beloved daughter is still unmarried. I would like to entrust her to you, if you have no objection."

Ma rose, blushing, and stammered out his thanks. At once the dragon king gave an order to his attendants, and presently palace maids led in the princess whose jade pendants tinkled as she walked. Trumpets and drums sounded for the wedding ceremony, and Ma, stealing a look at his bride, found her divinely beautiful. After the ceremony the princess left the hall; and, the feast at an end, two maids holding painted candles led Ma into the inner palace. There the princess was sitting, magnificently arrayed. The bridal bed was of coral, studded with jewels, the curtains were adorned with coloured feathers and decked with huge pearls, and the bedding was soft and scented.

The next morning at dawn, when girl attendants entered to offer their services, Ma got up and went to thank the king. He was duly installed as the royal son-in-law and appointed an official; copies of his poem were despatched to all the seas, and the dragon rulers of the different oceans sent special envoys to convey their congratulations to the king and invite Ma to feast with them. Then, in embroidered robes and riding on a green-horned dragon, he sallied forth with a magnificent equipage, accompanied by dozens of knights on horseback who carried carved bows and white staffs. They formed a glittering cavalcade, with musicians on horseback and in chariots playing harps and jade flutes. Thus in three days Ma passed through the different seas, and his fame spread throughout the marine world.

In the palace grew a jade tree, so large that a man could barely encircle it with his arms. The trunk was as transparent as glass and pale yellow in the centre; the branches were slighter than a human arm; and the jasper leaves, little thicker than a coin, cast a fine checkered shade. Ma and his bride often recited poems under this tree, which bore a profusion of blossoms like gardenias. Whenever a petal fell it made a tinkling sound, and picked up proved to be as lovely and bright as carved red agate. Often a strange bird would come to sing here. Its feathers were gold and green, its tail longer than its entire body, and its flutelike voice so clear and plaintive that none who heard it could fail to be moved. Whenever Ma listened to its song, he was carried back in spirit to his native land.

"I have been away from my home and my beloved parents for three years," he told the princess. "The thought of this makes tears well to my eyes and perspiration start out on my back. Will you accompany me home?"

"An immortal must not live like a mortal," she replied. "I cannot go with you, but neither would I let the love of husband and wife stand in the way of your love for your parents. Let us consider this again later."

Hearing this, Ma could not refrain from tears, and the princess sighed.

"It is clear that you cannot have both wife and parents," she said.

Next day, when Ma returned to the palace from an outing, the dragon king addressed him.

"I hear that you are longing for your home," he said. "Would you like to leave tomorrow?"

Ma thanked the king earnestly.

"Your servant came here as a stranger," he said, "yet you have conferred such honours upon me that I am overwhelmed with gratitude. I shall go to pay my family a short visit, but I hope to return again."

That evening when the princess prepared a parting feast, Ma spoke once more of his proposed return.

"Ah, no," said she. "We can never meet again."

Ma, hearing this, was overcome with grief.

"To go back to your parents shows true filial piety," the princess assured him. "Fate holds endless encounters and separations, and a hundred years pass like a single day; then why should we give way to tears like children? I mean to remain true to you, and I am sure you will be faithful to me. Loving each other in far distant places, we can still be one in spirit; there is no need to remain together morning and night. If you break this pledge, your next marriage will be unlucky; but if you need someone to look after you, you can take a maid as your concubine. I have something to ask you, too. I am now with child, and I would like you to choose a name for it."

"If it is a girl," said Ma, "call her Dragon Palace. If a boy, Happy Sea."

Then the princess asked him for a token, and he gave her a pair of red cornelian lilies he had obtained in the land of the Rakshas.

"Three years from now, on the eighth day of the fourth moon," she charged him, "sail into the south sea and I shall give you your child." Then she handed him a fish-scale bag filled with jewels, saying: "Keep this well. It will support your family for generations."

At dawn the dragon king held a farewell feast for Ma and bestowed many other gifts on him, after which Ma bid them all adieu and left the palace, escorted by the princess in a carriage drawn by white rams. But as soon as he reached the ocean's shore and dismounted the princess said farewell and turned swiftly away, the salt waves closing over her as she disappeared. Then Ma returned home.

Everybody believed that Ma had been lost at sea, so his family was amazed at his return. His parents were well, but his wife had married again; and Ma realized that when the dragon princess had spoken of keeping faith, she must have known this. His father urged him to marry another wife, but he refused, taking only a concubine. He kept in mind the date, and three years later sailed south again until he saw two children on the ocean's bosom, gambolling and frolicking upon the waves. As he drew near and leant over them, one chold seized his arm with a laugh and leapt on to his knee, while the other cried out as if to reproach him for neglecting it. When he had pulled the second child aboard too, he saw that one was a boy and the other a girl. They were beautiful children. Fastened to their coloured hats were his red cornelian lilies, and on the boy's back he found an embroidered bag containing the following letter:

I know that your parents are well. Three years have slipped quickly away while we have been separated by the ocean, with no bluebird to carry our messages. I long for you in my dreams, gazing in grief at the azure sky. Yet even the goddess of the moon pines in loneliness under the cassia tree, and the Weaving Maid grieves as she watches the Milky Way which separates her from her love. Why should I alone enjoy wedded happiness? This thought makes me smile at my tears. Two months after you left I gave birth to twins, who can now prattle and laugh in my lap, and hunt for dates and pears. Since they can manage without a mother now, I am sending them to you; and you will know them by the red cornelian lilies which you gave me. When you take them on your knee, you may imagine that I am beside you. It comforts me to know that you have kept faith; and I too shall remain true to you until death. I no longer rouge or powder my face or darken my eyebrows before the mirror. You are the wanderer and I the loving wife at home; but even though we cannot be together, we remain husband and wife. I feel it is wrong, though, that your parents should have their grandchildren without meeting their daughter-in-law; so next year when your mother leaves the world, I shall come to the burial and pay my respects. After that, if all goes well with Dragon Palace it may be possible to meet again; and if Happy Sea remains well, a path may be found for a visit. Please take good care of yourself. This letter cannot express all that I want to say.

Ma read and reread this letter, weeping, until the two children put their arms around his neck and said: "Father! Can we go home?"

Pierced to the heart, he fondled them, asking: "Where is our home?"

The children whimpered, and cried for their mother. And Ma gazed at the wild expanse of ocean stretching boundless to the horizon; but no princess appeared, nor any road through the misty waves. There was nothing for it but to take the children home.

第八篇《聊斋志异》Strange Stories from A Chinese Studio

Knowing now that his mother's death was near, Ma made everything ready for her funeral, and planted a hundred pine trees in the ancestral graveyard. The next year, when his mother died and the interment took place, a woman appeared beside the grave in deep mourning. As they gazed at her in wonder, a wind sprang up, thunder crashed and rain poured down, and the woman disappeared. But many of the pine trees planted by Ma, which had withered, revived after this rain.

When Happy Sea grew bigger, he still missed his mother; and once he disappeared suddenly into the sea, returning only several days later. But Dragon Palace, being a girl, could not leave home; and she often wept in her room. One day the sky grew dark, and the dragon princess entered Ma's house to comfort her daughter.

"You will have your own home soon," she said. "Don't cry, child."

She gave the girl as her dowry a tree of coral eight feet high, a packet of Baroos camphor, a hundred pearls and two gold boxes set with precious stones. When Ma heard of her coming, he rushed in and took her hands, weeping. But with a clap of thunder the princess vanished.

The recorder of these marvels comments: Men must put on false, ugly faces to please their superiors—such is the hypocritical way of the world. The foul and hideous are prized the world over. Something of which you feel a little ashamed may win praise; while something of which you feel exceedingly ashamed may win much higher praise. But any man who dares to reveal his true self in public is almost certain to shock the multitude and make them shun him. Where, indeed, can that fool of Lingyang① take his priceless jade to weep? Alas! I shall seek my fortune in castles in the clouds and mirages of the sea.

---

① A man of Lingyang presented a piece of uncut jade to the King of Chu in the Spring and Autumn period (722 — 481 BC); but the king, not recognizing its value, chopped off the donor's feet in anger.

The Cricket

During the reign of Xuan De, cricket fights were popular at court and a levy of crickets was exacted every year. Now these insects were scarce in the province of Shaanxi, but the magistrate of Huayin—to get into the good books of the governor—presented a cricket which proved a remarkable fighter. So much so that his county was commanded to present crickets regularly and the magistrate ordered his bailiffs to produce them. Then young fellows in town began to keep good crickets and demand high prices for them, while the crafty bailiffs seized this chance to make money. Thus each cricket they collected was the ruin of several households.

Now in this town lived a scholar named Cheng Ming, who had failed repeatedly in the district examination. This slow-witted pedant was appointed beadle on the recommedation of the crooked bailiff and could not evade this service hard as he tried. In less than a year his small patrimony was exhausted. Then came another levy of crickets. Cheng dared not extort money from the country folk but neither could he pay the sum himself. At his wit's end, he longed to die.

"What good would dying do?" demanded his wife. "You had better go out and look for a cricket yourself. There is just one chance in ten thousand that you may catch one."

Cheng agreed. With a bamboo tube and wire cage he searched from dawn till dusk among ruins and waste land, peering under rocks and exporing crevices, leaving no stone unturned—but all in vain. The two or three crickets he caught were poor specimens which did not come up to standard. The magistrate set him a time limit and beat him when he failed, till in little more than ten days he had received some hundred strokes and his legs were so covered with sores that he could not continue his search. Tossing painfully on his bed, his one thought was to die.

Then to their village came a hump-backed diviner who could tell fortunes by consulting spirits. Cheng's wife, taking money, went to ask his advice. She found his gate thronged with pink, blooming girls and whitehaired old women. Entering, she saw a curtain before the inner room, with incense on a table in front of it. Those come to ask their fortune burned incense in a tripod and kowtowed. The diviner prayed beside them, staring into space, but though his lips moved no one knew what it was he said and all listened respectfully. Finally a slip of paper was tossed from the inner room with the answer to the question asked— an answer which invariably proved correct.

Cheng's wife put her money on the table, burned incense and kowtowed like the other women. Presently the curtain moved and a piece of paper fluttered to the ground. Instead of writing it had a painting of a building like a temple with a small hill behind covered with rocks of every shape and overgrown with thorns. A cricket was crouching there while beside it a toad was making ready to spring. She had no idea what this meant, but the cricket at least had some connection with their problem. Accordingly she folded the paper and took it home to her husband.

Cheng wondered. "Is this supposed to show me where I should look for a cricket?"

On examining the picture closely, he recognized Great Buddha Monastery east of the village. So taking the paper with him, he struggled along with the help of a stick to the back of the monastery. There he found an old grave overgrown with brambles. Skirting this, he saw that the stones lying scattered around were exactly like the painting. He pricked up his ears and limped slowly through the brambles, but he might just as well have been looking for a needle or a grain of mustardseed. Though he strained every nerve he found nothing. As he was groping around, a toad hopped into sight. Cheng gave a start and hurried after it. The toad slipped into the undergrowth and, following it, he saw a cricket at the root of a bramble. He snatched at it but the cricket leapt into a crevice in a rock and would not come out though he prodded it with a straw. Not till he poured water on it, did it emerge. It seemed a fine specimen and he picked it up. Seen close to, it had a large body and long tail, dark neck and golden wings, and he was a happy man as he carried it home in the cage to delight his household, who considered it more precious than the rarest jade. The cricket was kept in a pot and fed upon white crab's flesh and the yellow kernel of chestnuts, tended with loving care till such time as the magistrate should ask for it.

Now Chen had a son of nine, who uncovered this pot on the sly while his father was out. At once the cricket jumped out and sprang about so nimbly that he could not catch it. Finally the boy grabbed it, but in doing so tore off a leg and crushed it so that the next moment it died. The frightened child ran crying to his mother. When she heard what had happened she turned as pale as death.

"You wicked boy!" she cried. "You'll catch it when your father comes home!"

Her son went off in tears. Soon Cheng came back and when he heard his wife's story he felt as if he had been turned to ice. In a passion he searched for his son, who was nowhere to be found until at last they discovered his body in the well. Then anger turned to sorrow. Cheng cried out in anguish and longed to kill himself. Husband and wife sat with their faces to the wall in their thatched and smokeless cottage in silent despair. As the sun began to set he prepared to bury the boy, but upon touching the child found there was still breath in him. Overjoyed, he laid the small body on the couch, and towards the middle of the night the child came round. Cheng and his wife began to breathe again, but their son remained in a trance with drooping eyelids. The sight of the empty cricket cage brought back Cheng's grief, but he dared not scold the child now. He did not close his eyes all night, and as the sun rose in the east he was still lying in stark despair when a cricket chirped outside the door. He rose in amazement to look, and sure enough there was a cricket. He clutched at it, but it chirped and hopped away. He put his hands over it but to no avail; when he turned up his palms the cricket escaped again. So he chased it up and down till it disappeared round the corner of the wall, and while searching for it he discovered another cricket on the wall. But this was a little, dark red insect, not to be compared with the first. Deciding that it was too small to be worth catching, Cheng looked round again for the one he had lost. At once the small cricket hopped from the wall to his sleeve, and he saw it resembled a mole-cricket with speckled wings, a square head and long legs—it might be a good one. So he was glad to keep it.

Cheng meant to present this cricket to the yamen, but fearing that it might not do he decided first to give it a trial fight. Now a young fellow in that village had a cricket called Crab Blue which had beaten every other insect it fought, and its owner wanted such an exorbitant price for it that it had remained on his hands. This man called on Cheng and laughed to see his cricket, producing his own for comparison. At the sight of this large, handsome insect, Cheng felt even more diffident and dared not offer a fight. The young man, however, insisted on a match; and since his poor cricket was useless in any case Cheng thought he might as well sacrifice it for a laugh. So the two combatans were put in one basin, where the small one crouched motionless as a stick of wood. The young man laughed heartily and prodded it with a pig's bristle, but still it made no move. At that he laughed louder and louder until at last the cricket was roused to fury. It hurled itself at its opponent, attacking savagely. In an instant it had leapt forward with bristling tail and seized the other by the neck. The horrified young man made haste to separate

第八篇《聊斋志异》Strange Stories from A Chinese Studio

the two contestants, while the little cricket chirped proudly as if to announce its victory to its master. Cheng was glorying in this sight when a cock bore down on the cricket and pecked at it. Cheng gave a cry, rooted to the ground in horror; but luckily the cock missed the small cricket which leapt a foot or more away. The cock gave chase, the cricket was under its claws. Cheng, unable to intervene, stamped his foot and turned pale. But the next thing he knew the cock was flapping its wings and craning its neck—his cricket had fastened its teeth in the cock's comb. Amzaed and exultant, he put the criket back in its cage.

Later Cheng presented this a cricket to the magistrate, who abused him angrily for producing one so small. Refusing to believe Cheng's account of the little creature's exploits, the magistrate pitted it against some others crickets and it defeated them all. He tried it with a cock, and again it turned out exactly as Cheng had said. Then the magistrate rewarded Cheng and presented this cricket to the governor, who put it in a golden cage and sent it joyfully to the emperor with a detailed report of its prowess.

In his palace the emperor tried the cricket with Butterfly, Praying Mantis, Yolita, Green Forehead and many other champions, but none was a match for it. And he prized it even more highly when he found that it would dance in time to music. In high good humour, he rewarded the governor with fine steeds and silk garments. And the governor, not forgetting where the cricket came from, within a short time commended the magistrate for outstanding merit. The magistrate, pleased in his turn, exempted Cheng from his duties and ordered the local examiner to see that he passed the next examination.

A year later Cheng's son was restored to his senses. He said, "I dreamed I was a cricket, a quick, good fighter. Now I have woken up."

The governor also rewarded Cheng so handsomely that within a few years he owned vast estates, whole streets of houses and countless flocks and herds. When he went abroad, his furs and carriage were more splendid than a noble's.

The recorder of these marvels comments: The emperor may do a thing once and forget it afterwards, but those who carry out his orders make this general rule. Then when officials are greedy for profit and their underlings are bullies, men are driven to sell their wives and children. This shows that since each step an emperor takes is fraught with consequence for his subjects it behoves him to be very careful. This man Cheng, first impoverished by rapacious officials, grew so rich thanks to a cricket that he went about in magnificent carriages and furs. He can never have dreamed of such good fortune when he was a beadle and was being beaten! Because Heaven wished to reward an honest man, the governor and magistrate also benefited from the cricket. It is true, as the ancients said: "When a man becomes immortal and soars to heaven, his chickens and dog attain immortality too."

Strange Tales from Make-Do Studio

Translated by Denis C. and Victor H. Mair

18. The Ráksasas and the Ocean Bazaar

Ma Jun, also known as Dragon Messenger, was a merchant's son. He had striking good looks and in his untrammeled youth gave himself up to the pleasures of singing and dancing. He frequented the Pear Garden, where he amused himself in the company of the actors. Wrapping his head in a brocade turban he had all the charm of an attractive woman, and hence was given the nickname "Stunner." He also made a name for himself by being admitted to the prefectural acadamy at fourteen.

When age and declining health made the young scholar's father give up business and go into retirement, he said these words to his son: "Those books you have read cannot feed you when you are hungry and cannot keep you warm when you are cold. You sholuld take over my business, son." From then on Ma devoted part of his attention to matters of investment and profit.

Ma embarked on an ocean voyage with a party of other passengers, but it happened that they were blown off course by a typhoon. After several days the ship came to a city in which all the inhabitants were freakishly ugly. They ran off in an uproar as Ma approached, taking him for a monster. When Ma first saw this he was greatly frightened, but once he realized they were afraid of him, he used their fear to gain the upper hand. Finding a group of them sitting at table, he rushed toward them and, after they dashed away in fright, gulped down the food they left. After a time he went into a mountain village, where some of the inhabitants looked almost human, though they wore the tattered rags of beggars. Ma sat down to rest beneath a tree. The villagers watch him from a distance, not daring to approach. After a while, when they realized that Ma was not a man-eating monster, they finally edged toward him. Ma smiled and talked with them. Although their speech was strange, it was halfway comprehensible. Without being asked, Ma told where he had come from. The delighted villagers told everyone in the neighborhood that the stranger was not violent. Still the freakishly ugly ones stole furtive looks at him and ran off, never daring to come near. Those who did come close had mouths and noses in just about the same places as we do here in China. Together they hunted up wine and served it to Ma.

Ma asked why they had been afraid of him. "I once heard my grandfather say," one of them replied, "that 8,500 miles to the west lies a land called the Middle Kingdom, and the people there are all grotesque in appearance. I knew it only by hearsay, but now I believe it."

Ma asked why they were so poor. Someone answered, "In our country what is valued is appearance rather than literary ability. The most handsome among us become high ministers at court; the fairly handsome are given posts in local administrative offices; and the somewhat handsome can support their wives and children in style by winning the favor of some nobleman. As for people like us, we are thought to be bearers of evil fortune, and our parents often abandon us at birth. All the people who cannot bear to abandon their offspring straightaway are thinking about the continuity of their family line."

"What is the name of this kingdom?" ask Ma.

"The Great Kingdom of the Rákṣasas," was the answer. "The capital is ten miles north of here." Ma asked them to lead him there for

第八篇《聊斋志异》Strange Stories from A Chinese Studio

a look. And so they arose at cock's crow the next day and took him there. They reached the capital after daybreak. The walls of the city were built of stone as black as ink, and the storied buildings were nearly a hundred feet high. There were few rooftiles to be seen. Instead, the buildings were covered with shingles of red stone. Ma picked up a loose piece and rubbed it against his armor; it was exactly like cinnabar.

Just then came the time for dismissal of the morning court session at the palace. The villagers pointed to one of the dignitaries who were coming out of the palace gate: "That is the prime minister." Ma saw that his ears were attached to the back of his head, his nose had three nostrils and his eyelashes covered his eyes like curtains. Then several men came out on horseback. "Those are privy counselors," said the villagers. As the officials came out in succession, the villagers pointed out their ranks. All of them had grotesque, monstrous faces, but as the lower ranks came out the degree of ugliness gardually abated. Before long Ma started back toward the village. People in the streets who saw him screamed and fell over one another trying to run away, as if they had met with a monster. Only when the villagers had gone to great lengths to reassure them did the city dwellers dare to stand and watch from a distance.

After they returned to the village, everyone in the kingdom, regardless of rank, knew there was an unusul person there. Members of the gentry and court officials, eager to broaden their horizons, told the villagers to invite Ma to visit them, but whenever he showed up at someone's house, the gatekeeper would close the door, and the men and women alike would only venture to peer at him and speak with him through cracks in the door. This would go on all day without anyone asking him in for a visit.

One villager said, "There in an officer of the guard living in this district who was sent abroad as emissary by our former king. He has had experience with many sorts of people, so he may not be frightened of you."

They went to the officer's house and, as the villager had foreseen, he was delighted at their visit and received Ma as an honored guest. Apparently between eighty and ninety years of age, he had goggle eyes and hair that stood out like a hedgehog's.

"In my youth I went on more diplomtic missions for the king than anyone else, but the Middle Kingdom of China is the one place I have never been. Now I am over a hundred and twenty years old, and at last I have the chance to see someone from your esteemed country. The king simply must be informed of this. Though I have been leading a life of retirement and have not set foot upon the palace steps these past ten years or more, I will make the trip for your sake in the morning."

Observing all the formalities of a host to his guest, he then had wine and victuals set out. After they had drunk several rounds, he brought out ten or so female entertainers with faces like *yaksa* monsters, who took turns singing and dancing. All of them wore white brocade turbans on their heads and flowing red robes that dragged on the ground. Ma could not make out the lyrics, but he found the tune and rhythm oddly fascinating. The host watched them with immense enjoyment.

"Do you have entertainment like this in the Middle Kingdom?" he asked.

"Oh, yes," answered Mr.

The host asked him to imitate the music for them, so Ma drummed on the table and performed a song.

"Well if that isn't most extraordinary!" exclaimed the delighted host. "The melody makes me think of phoenixes calling and dragons roaring. It is unlike anything I have ever heard." The next day he went to court and recommended Ma to the king. The king gladly commanded that Ma be brought before him, but when a few high counselors claimed

第八篇《聊斋志异》Strange Stories from A Chinese Studio

that Ma's monstrous appearance might result in a shock injurious to His Majesty's health, the order was rescinded. The old officer of the guard came out and gave Ma the news of this crushing disappointment.

　　Ma stayed with the officer for a long while. One day, when he and his host were in their cups, he smeared his face with soot to look like Zhang Fei① and began to dance with sword in hand. The host thought he was attractive and said, "Why don't you make yourself up as Zhang Fei and go to see the prime minister. I am sure he will be delighted to find a place for you. An ample salary is within your grasp."

　　"Hah! It is one thing to play games, but why should I put on a new face to chase after honor and fame?" But when the host insisted, Ma gave in. The host invited the ranking officials to a feast and told Ma to wait on them with his face painted. Before long the guests arrived, and Ma was called out to meet them.

　　"Isn't that strange!" said the guests in surprise. "How could someone who was once so ugly turn into such a good looking fellow?" Whereupon they all drank together with exceeding joy. Ma swayed with the rhythm as he sang the Yiyang Melody,② and every person at the table was positively bowled over. The next day a number of petitions recommending Ma were sent to the throne. The king was so delighted he summoned Ma with a big fanfare. During their first audience the king asked how law and order were maintained in the Middle Kingdom. Ma gave a detailed explanation which met with sighs of admiring approval. The king granted him the favor of dining with him in the royal hostel. When both were mellow with wine, the king said, "I have heard that

---

① A famous general of The Three Kingdoms period (220—265). In popular lore he is always protrayed with a very dark face.

② A loud, sonorous style of singing that originated in the country of the same name (Jiangxi province) during the Yuan and Ming dynasties.

you are skilled in fine music. Might I be so fortunate as to hear you perform?" So Ma got up to dance. He sang softly and languidly, in the style of the white-turbaned entertainers. The king was overjoyed. On that very day he gave Ma the title of deputy minister. He often dined privately with Ma and showered him with exceptional generosity and favor. After a time the other officials and administrators were fairly certain of the falseness of Ma's countenance. Wherever he went, he would see people whispering to one another instead of greeting him cordially. Being thus ostracized made Ma ill at ease, so he submitted a request for retirement, but this was not granted. Again he requested official leave, and was given a vacation of three months.

Ma lost no time loading his gold and jewels onto a stage coach and returning to the mountain village. The villagers came out to greet him on their knees. Joyful cries rang through the air when Ma divided gold coins among his old friends.

The villagers said, "Since we lowly folk have been honored by your gifts, we will set out for the ocean bazaar tomorrow and seek precious gems to repay you."

"Where is the ocean bazaar?" asked Ma.

"Mermen from the four seas gather at the ocean bazaar to trade in pearls and jewels. People from four directions and twelve kingdoms all come to trade with them. Many deities are engaged in pleasurable pastimes there. The sky is filled with clouds, and great waves roll ashore from time to time. People of rank are too concerned for their personal safety to expose themselves to these dangers, so they entrust us with their gold and silk in order to purchase rare treasures for them. Now the date of the bazaar is not distant."

Ma asked how they knew it.

"When red birds are seen flying back and forth over the sea, the opening of the bazaar is seven days away."

Ma asked their time of departure and expressed a desire to make the trip with them and do some sightseeing. The villagers begged him to consider his personal safety.

"But I am a seafarer. Do you suppose I fear rough weather?" Before long there were people at the gate bringing valuables to invest in the voyage. Ma helped the crew stow the valuables on board the ship. It was a flat-bottomed craft with high gunwales and room for several dozen men. With ten men at the oars it churned up a seething wake and skimmed along like an arrow. After three days they glimpsed buildings and towers one behind the other through the shifting clouds that hung over the water. Trading ships converged on the place like ants. In no time they drew up beneath the city wall, which was made of bricks as long as a man's body. The battlements towered into the clouds above. Having moored their ship and entered the city, they saw displayed in the bazaar strange treasures and rare gems of dazzling brilliance, many never seen in the world of men.

Just then a young man, mounted on a splendid stallion rode up to them. The shopkeepers and buyers scattered before him, saying that he was the "third crown prince of the Eastern Ocean." As the crown prince rode by he eyed the scholar and said, "Isn't this man from a faraway country?" A runner came over to Ma and wanted to know his native land. Ma greeted him from the side of the road and made known the land and people of his birth.

"Since you've honored us by coming here, it is plain that there is a deep bond of fate between us!" exclaimed the prince happily. He gave the scholar a mount and invited him to ride alongside. Riding beyond the western wall, they came to the shore of the island, where their mounts neighed and plunged into the water. The scholar was struck dumb with terror, but he soon saw that they were in an open space, with walls of seawater arching above them. Suddenly a palace appeared ahead, its beams made of tortoise shell and its roof tiled with scales of bream. The crystalline walls mirrored the shapes around them with blinding brilliance. Dismounting, the prince motioned Ma inside. At the head of the hall before them was the Dragon Lord. The crown prince informed the throne: "While riding through the bazaar I found this worthy scholar from the Middle Kingdom whom I have brought for an audience with Your Highness." The scholar stepped forward and made an elaborate bow.

"I see sir, that you are a man of literary accomplishment," said the Dragon Lord. "I am sure you are good enough to lord it over famous poets of antiquity like Qu Yuan and Song Yu. Might I trouble you to brandish your rafter-sized inkbrush to write a rhapsody on the ocean bazaar? Please do not grudge us your precious words."

The scholar touched his forehead to the floor in acknowledgement. He was given a crystal inkstone, a dragonbristle inkbrush, paper with the bright smoothness of snow and an inkstick exuding the fragrance of orchids. Without stopping to think, he completed a piece of over a thousand words and offered it to the throne. The dragon lord beat time while reciting the rhymed prose.

"Sir, your great talent has brought much glory to my acquatic kingdom!" he said.

So it was that the hosts of dragondom were assembled for a feast in Glowing-Cloud Palace. After several rounds of wine and several courses of roast meat, the dragon lord raised his cup and said to his guest: "I have not yet found a good match for my beloved daughter. Sir, I would like to inflict her upon you. Would this be in accordance with your wishes?"

The scholar rose to his knees from the mat, so overcome with gratitude that he could only stammer, "Yes, yes." The Dragon Lord turned and spoke to his attendants. Before long a group of court maids

第八篇《聊斋志异》Strange Stories from A Chinese Studio

led forth a young woman, jade rings tinkling at her waist as she moved. A sudden fanfare rang out. When he had finished bowing the scholar gave her an appraising glance: She was a veritable fairy maiden. She bowed and withdrew.

Soon the drinking ceased. Maids with hair done up in double buns bearing painted candles led the scholar into a side palace. The girl sat there waiting in her finest adornments. The coral bed was studded with a galaxy of gems, and shining pearls the size of spoons were knotted into the tassels that hung outside the canopy. The quilts were fragrant and yielding.

At the crack of dawn, budding young girls and bewitching maids ran in and stood in a row around the bed. The scholar rose, hurried to court and thanked the king. He was given the title of royal son-in-law. Because his rhapsody was rapidly disseminated throughout the four seas, the dragon lords from all quarters sent special envoys to congratulate him and deliver invitations to banquets. The scholar dressed in brocades and rode about on a green, horned dragon. He set forth from the palace with warning shouts to clear his way. An entourage of several dozen mounted knights bearing carved bows and white staffs clustered about him, their armor flashing. There were mounted musicians strumming zithers and others in a carriage playing jade flutes. Within three days the scholar had journeyed to all the oceans. From then on the name Dragon Messenger resounded throughout the four seas.

A jade tree as big in girth as a man's embrace grew in the palace. The trunk was shimmeringly transparent, like clear glass, with a pale yellow center slightly thinner than an arm. The leaves resembled green jade and were a bit thicker than copper coins. This profuse foliage cast dense shade, in which the scholar and his bride often sang and chanted poetry. Thy whole tree was blooming with flowers that looked like gardenias. Each time a petal fell a distinct tinkle could be heard. Upon close inspection each gleaming, delicate petal seemed to be sculpted of red agate.

Rare birds with feathers of iridescent blue and tails longer than their bodies often alighted on the tree and sang strains every bit as heart-rending as notes from a plaintive jade flute. Everytime the scholar heard them, he thought of his homeland. One day he spoke of this to his wife: "Three years have passed since I lost touch with my family. Everytime I think of separation from my parents, snivel drips onto my chest and sweat drenches my back. Would you go back with me?"

"Faerie and earth have separate roads," she said. "They cannot remain together. I cannot bear, for the sake of our marital love, to deny you the happiness of being at your parents' side. Give me time to think of a way." The scholar, could not help but cry to hear her. His wife, too, heaved a sigh and said, "You cannot have it both ways!"

The next day when the scholar came back to the palace the dragon lord said to him: "I am told that you are homesick. How will it be if we have your baggage ready the first thing tomorrow morning?"

The scholar thanked him: "I was solitary wanderer far from home until you made me your subject and lavished your favor and concern upon me. From the depths of my heart I feel a sincere wish to repay you. Let me go home to visit for a time: I will try to meet with you again."

When evening came, the girl had set out wine for a farwell. The scholar wanted to set a time to meet again, but she said, "The affinity that bound us together has run out." The scholar was deeply grieved.

"Go back and care for your parents," she said. "Show them what a filial son you are. The hundred years of a human life, with its meetings and parting, is like a single day. What is the good of whining like a child? From this day on I shall remain chaste for your sake, and you will be true to me in your thoughts. Though we will be in different places, our hearts will be as one, so we will still be husband and wife. We can grow old together without having to remain side by side day and night. If either of us transgresses this vow, heaven will not bless our marriage. If you worry that there is no one to do the housekeeping, you can take a maid. I have one more thing to tell you. After serving you all this time, I have noticed signs of a joyous event to come. Would you please give this child a name?"

"If the baby is a girl, name her Dragon-Palace; if it is a boy, name him Blessing-Sea," said the scholar.

His wife begged for a token of their vow. The scholar brought out a pair of red jade lotuses he had gotten in the Kingdom of Ráksasas and gave them to her.

"Three years from now on the eighth day of the fourth month make sure to sail around South Island," she said. "I will return your flesh and blood to you." She filled a fish-skin pouch with pearls and gems, gave it to him and said, "Keep this well. Your family can live off it for generations."

At the first faint light of dawn the king had a farewell party set up for the departure, and there bounteous gifts were heaped before the scholar. With a parting bow the scholar left the palace. The girl, riding in a cart drawn by white rams, saw him to the shore. He rode onto the beach and dismounted. She bid him farewell, then turned the cart around and left. In a few short moments, she was far away. The waters of the sea closed back togerther, hiding her from view.

Then the scholar started homeward. His voyage had lasted so long that everyone assumed him dead, but now, to his family's amazement, he turned up to home. Fortunately his parents were in good health, but his wife had married again. The meaning of the dragon girl's words "be true to me" finally became clear to him. She must have known of this already. The father wanted to arrange another marrige, but the scholar would not allow it and took a maid instead.

第八篇《聊斋志异》 Strange Stories from A Chinese Studio

With the appointed time engraved in his mind, the scholar sailed to the island three years later. There he saw two children sitting afloat on the surface of the water. They were amusing themselves by splashing with their hands, yet this neither caused them to move nor to sink. He drew up to them and held out his hands. One child grabbed his wrist and jumped giggling into his arms. The other wailed as if vexed at the scholar for not lending a helping hand. This one too was lifted aboard. A closer look showed that one was a girl and the other a boy. Both had fair, appealing features. On their heads were coronets studded with jade; in the middle of each was one of the red lotuses. One of them bore a brocade pouch. The scholar opened it and found a letter which read:

"I trust that father and mother are in good health. Three years have gone by in a flash: the world of red dust is forever out of reach. The messenger is hard put to cross this great expanse water. Longing has taken shape as dreams: my neck is weary with gazing into the boundless blue. What good are my regrets? My thoughts now turn to Chang'e, who ran away to the moon only to spend a lone life of loneness in Cassia Mansion, and Weaving Maid, who once threw down her shuttle but to this day ruefully watches her lover from across the Milky Way. Who am I, that I should have everlasting love? Once this thought arises, tears give way to laughter. Two months after we parted, I was blessed, to my amazement, with twins. Now they are babbling in arms, and understand something of speech and laughter. They grab whatever fruits they see and can live without their mother's milk. Now I worshipfully return them to you. I have decorated their coronets with the red jade lotus flowers you gave me, as a token of the fulfillment of my vow. When you lift the children to your knees and embrace them, it will be like having me at your side. I felt comforted to hear that you are conscientiously observing your vow of yesteryear. I will be faithful to you all my life: unto dearth there will be no change. I no longer keep perfumed unguents within my trousseau, and the reflection in my mirror has long ago said farewell to powder and mascara. You are like a wayfarer, and I am the wayfarer's wife. But yet, though the lute and harp are left long unplayed, no one can say they do not harmonize. Now, I trust, my in-laws can be with their grandchildren, though they have never met their daughter-in-law. Thinking of my duty to them, I cannot help feeling much regret. When the time comes for mother's interment, I will perform my duty by going to mourn at her tomb. Here's hoping that Dragon-Palace will henceforth remain in good health, and that I will not miss the chance to hold her in my arms. May Blessing-Sea live long and travel back and forth between us. Not having finished all that I wished to say, I entreat you to take good care of yourself." The scholar pored repeatedly over the letter, wiping tears from his eyes. His two children threw their arms around his neck, saying: "Oh, please, let's go back!"

This only added to the scholar's misery. He caressed them and asked, "Do you children know how to find your home?" Their only answer was to burst into sobs and wail that they wanted to go home.

The scholar looked out over the boundless sea; as far as the eye could see stretched a ravelling mist devoid of human presence, a road leading nowhere through the foggy waves. He held his children close as he made for the ship, and returned in discouragement.

The scholar, knowing that his mother's days were numbered, made ready her burial accoutrements beforehand and planted over a hundred pine and catalpa trees in the enclosure around her tomb. Sure enough, after a year passed, the old woman died. When the hearse reached the final resting place, a woman in hempen mourning clothes stood before the tomb. Suddenly, as the mourners stared in surprise, a fierce wind began to blow and thunder rumbled. This was followed by heavy rain. In the blink of an eye she was gone. Many of the pines and catalpas had died from being transplanted, but after this they all came to life.

As Blessing-Sea grew a little older he thought often of his mother. One day he was seen to throw himself into the sea, and he did not return till several days later. Dragon-Palace, being a girl, could not go, and so she cried in her room day after day. One day the light of the sun dimmed; in an instant the dragon lord's daughter appeared and calmed her: "Someday you will have a family of your own. What good will crying do?" She gave her daughter a dowry consisting of an eight-foot tree of coral, a packet of broneol camphor, one hundred gleaming pearls and a pair of small gold boxes set with eight sorts of gems. Hearing her voice, the scholar burst into the room and took her by the hand, sobbing. In a moment a sharp clap of thunder shook the room, and she was gone.

The Chronicler of the Tales comments: "The ways of the world are no different from the ways of goblins; both would have us paint our faces to curry favor. When it comes to proclivities for eating scabs and such, the whole world is in the same rut. Moderately embarrassing actions receive moderate praise; greatly embarrassing actions receive great praise. ① If a person were to amble through a city with his true face exposed for all to see, few must be the ones who would not take to their

---

① From a letter by the famous Tang dynasty poet and prose stylist Han Yu (768－824), in which he confesses his shame at having written some perfunctory pieces because of social obligations.

heels in fright. Whose shoulder can the Fool of Lingyang① cry on with his fabled jade worth fifteen cities? Alas! Glory and wealth can only be found in castles in the air and ocean bazaars."

---

① An allusion to Bian He of the state of Chu during the Spring and Autumn period (722—484 B. C.), who presented two kings successively with a jade enclosed in an uncut stone, and each time was accused of trying to pass off sham jade as genuine and punished by the loss of one of his feet. When the third king came to the throne, he summoned Bian He, had the stone carved up and found the jade inside. The jade was later claimed by a king to be worth the price of fifteen cities.

19. The Cricket

During the Xuande reign period (1462—1435) of the Ming dynasty cricket keeping was a popular amusement in the palace. The insects were levied annually from the populace. Live crickets were not originally a Shaanxi product until a magistrate in Huayin county who was anxious to win favor with his superiors presented one, which was tried in the ring and found to be an outstanding fighter. From then on Huayin County was charged with providing crickets to the court regularly. The magistrate delegated the responsibility to the headman in each ward. Young idlers in the marketplace kept the best of them in cages, forcing prices up by cornering the market. Cunning ward administrators used this as an excuse to impose a head tax on the peasants. For every cricket that was requisitioned, several families were driven into bankruptcy.

In the district there was a man named Cheng Ming, a long unsuccessful candidate for the Bachelor of Letters degree. The crafty ward administrator, seeing that Cheng was impractical and slow of speech, recommended him for the position of headman. Cheng made numerous futile attempts to free himself from the obligations of this office. Before a year had passed his meager resources were used up. Then came the cricket levy. Cheng did not dare collect money from the households, nor could he fulfil the duty out of his own funds. He was so despondent he wanted to kill himself.

"What good would killing yourself do?" said his wife. "It would be better to look for a cricket yourself. There is a slight chance you might find one."

This made sense to Cheng. He went out in the mornings and returned at nightfall, bamboo pail and wire cage in hand, poking under stones and opening burrows amid crumbling walls and thick growths of grass. There was nothing he did not try, but it was no use. The few that he did manage to catch were too puny to fit the regulations. The magistrate's deadline was rigorously enforced, and he was given a total of a hundred strokes with a cane over a period of ten days. Blood and puss oozed from his buttocks and, what was worse, he was unable to go looking for the insects at all. He tossed and turned on his bed, his mind filled with thoughts of suicide.

 It was then that a hunchbacked shamaness who performed divinations with the help of a spirit-familiar came to the village. Cheng's wife scraped up a sum of money and went to call on her. Smartly dressed young women and white-haired old ladies were milling around the door. Inside the house was a curtained-off sanctum, with an altar standing outside the curtain. Petitioners lit incense in the censer and kowtowed twice, while the shamaness stood to one side looking off into space and pronouncing an invocation for them, her lips contorted with unintelligible mutterings. Everyone stood stiffly listening until shortly a piece of paper, bearing a message that dealt with the petitioner's troubles, was thrown out from within the curtain. The messages were never off by a hair.

 Cheng's wife placed her money on the table, lit incense, and kowtowed like those before. After the time it takes to eat a meal passed by, the curtain moved and a slip of paper was tossed out onto the ground. Picking it up, she saw not words but a drawing depicting a group of buildings, apparently those of a monastery. Behind it at the foot of a hill was a jumble of odd-looking boulders. There, at the edge of a dense bramble thicket, crouched a shiny black cricket. Beside it was a toad that seemed to be on the point of leaping. She spread the drawing out and pored over it, unable to make out its meaning. Still the cricket was just what she had been looking for. She folded the paper up, tucked it away and took it back to show Cheng who, after much reflection, wondered if the picture were not telling him where to hunt for a cricket. Careful scrutiny of the scene in the drawing revealed a close resemblance to the Great Buddha Abbey east of the village.

  Cheng dragged himself out of bed, propped himself up with a cane and proceeded, drawing in hand, to the rear of the monastery. The overgrown ruins of an ancient tomb stood before him. Following the edge of the tomb, he saw boulders squatting one on top of the other like fish scales, precisely as in the drawing. He walked slowly through a jungle of weeds, cocking his head to catch the slightest sound and looking for all the world as if he were searching for a needle or a mustard seed. He could no longer maintain the intentness of eyes, ears and mind, but he had not yet seen or heard a cricket. He was still groping about, when suddenly to his great amazement a wart-headed toad leapt from underfoot. He stayed close behind it as it ducked into a dense growth of grass. He stepped gingerly into the grass, spreading the blades apart with his hands to get a better look. There, crouching at the base of a bramble-bush was an insect. He hurriedly grabbed for it, but it ducked into a hole in the stones. He poked at it with a sharp blade of grass, but it would not come out. Finally, by pouring water from his bucket into the hole, he was able to flush the robust-looking cricket out. He gave chase and caught it. A closer look showed it to have a thick torso, a long tail, a blue-green neck and metallic wings. Great was Cheng's joy as he put it in the cage and returned home.

  The whole family rejoiced as if he had found a treasure more precious than the legendary piece of jade to the worth of fifteen cities. ① They put it in a basin and nourished it on crab meat and chestnuts, going to every extreme to give it the best of care. They planned to keep it until the deadline, when Cheng would use it to discharge his official

---

 ① See "The Raksasas and the Ocean Bazaar," Note 4.

第八篇《聊斋志异》Strange Stories from A Chinese Studio

duty.

　　But one day Cheng's nine-year-old son, seeing that his father was out, furtively lifted the lid off the basin. The cricket hopped straight out, so quickly that the boy could not grab it. He jumped and caught it in his hand, breaking off a leg and cracking its abdomen. In a few short moments it was dead. The terrified boy ran crying to tell his mother. Her face paled to the hue of ashes at what she heard.

　　"A bad seed, that's what you are!" she cursed him loudly, "Your day of doom will not be long now! When your father comes home he'll settle accounts with you." The boy ran out sniveling. Cheng soon returned. When his wife told him what had happened, it was as if a heap of freezing snow had been dumped on his head. He called angrily for his son but the boy was nowhere to be seen. Soon afterwards, they found his body in a well. Cheng's rage turned to sorrow. Stricken half-dead with grief, he struck his head on the ground and cried out to heaven. Husband and wife went inside and each turned their sobbing faces toward separate corners. No cooking fire was lit in their thatched hut that night. They had come to their wit's end and could only stare dumbly at one another. As the day drew to an end, they prepared to wrap their son in a grass mat for burial. Touching him, they found that he was now breathing haltingly. Joyfully they placed him on the bed. In the middle of the night he regained consciousness, which relived his parents somewhat, but his breath came in gasps and he had the vacant look of a sleepwalker. Looking at the empty cricket cage was enough to rob them of breath and make their voices die in their throats, but they dared not question their son again. Their eyes did not close for the whole night. When the sun in the east began its course through the heavens they lay down stiffly, brooding sleeplessly.

　　Suddenly there was a chirping outside their door. They got up in amazement to observe: there was the cricket looking as sound as ever.

Jumping for joy, they ran to catch it, but it gave a chirp and hopped rapidly away. Cheng covered it with a cupped hand, but he seemed to have grasped nothing but thin air. As soon as he lifted his hand the cricket leapt swiftly out from under it. He followed it closely, but lost it when it rounded the corner of a wall. As he walked about distractedly, looking all around him, he saw a cricket crouching on the wall. A careful look showed that it was short, small and reddish-black in color— certainly not the one he had been chasing. It was worthless to him because of its small size. He went on walking aimlessly and staring in all directions for the one he had been chasing. All of a sudden the little cricket jumped off the wall and landed on the side of his robe. It was built like a mole cricket, with finely veined wings, a square head and long neck. It impressed him as a good specimen, so he was glad to keep it. His plan was to present it at the yamen, but the thought that it might not meet the magistrate's expectations made him shudder, so he decided to observe how it would perform in a fight.

A young man known as a busybody in the village was keeping a cricket which he had named Crabshell Blue. He matched it daily with the crickets of other young men, and it was always emerged victorious. He was holding onto it until he could turn a nice profit, but nobody would pay the high price he asked. One day this young man went to Cheng's house for a visit. Seeing the cricket Cheng was keeping, he had to stifle a laugh with his hand. He took out his cricket and put it into the cage. Cheng was discomfited at the sight of its huge build. He dared not pick up the gauntlet, but the young man insisted. It occurred to Cheng that keeping an inferior specimen would be useless anyway, and that he might as well set his cricket against the other for a laugh. Both insects were placed in a fighting basin. The small one crouched motionless, looking as foolish as a wooden chicken. ① The young man guffawed once more as he used a boar bristle to poke at the cricket's antennae. Still it did not move, provoking the young man into another burst of laughter. He prodded it repeatedly. The insect exploded with rage and ran at its opponent. They attacked one another with flying leaps, rousing themselves to battle with defiant chirps. In an instant the small cricket jumped up, its antennae and tail stiffly erect, and bit down on its opponent's neck. The frightened young man pulled them apart and put an end to the fight. The small crickt drew itself up and chirped proudly, as if it were reporting victory to its master.

Cheng was overjoyed. As he and his guests were admiring the winner, a chicken caught sight of it, ran over and delivered a peck at the small cricket. Cheng stood there numb with dread and cried out in alarm. Luckily the chicken's beak had missed its mark; the cricket leaped a foot and some inches away. The chicken lunged forward and bore down upon it. Before Cheng could come to its rescue, the insect was under the chicken's claws; he turned pale and stamped his feet helplessly. But in the next moment he saw the chicken stretching its neck and fluttering about. Much to his amazed delight upon closer inspection, he found the cricket hanging tenaciously onto the fowl's comb. He picked it up, put it in its cage and presented it to the magistrate the next day.

The magistrate berated Cheng angrily for bringing such a puny cricket, nor was he convinced by Cheng's account of the cricket's extraordinary prowess. The cricket was tried in the ring against others of its kind; all were vanquished. When it was tried against a chicken the

---

① A fable in *Zhuang-zi*, a work of the Warring States period (475—221 B. C.), describes a superb gamecock as having such a placid exterior that it seemed to be made of wood.

outcome confirmed Cheng's story. The magistrate thereupon rewarded him and presented the cricket to the provincial governor. The governor, greatly delighted, presented it to the emperor in a golden cage along with a memorial detailing its abilities.

After the champion was taken into the palace, all sorts of unusual crickets, such as "butterflies," "mantises," "oily beaters" and "silky green foreheads" were tried against it, but none could get the better of it. When it heard the music of lutes and zithers it hopped to the beat, which made people marvel at it all the more. The emperor was so pleased that he called for the provincial governor and gave him thoroughbred horses and satins for clothing. The governor did not forget the source of his good fortune; before long word was going around that the magistrate was an "outstanding" official. The delighted magistrate released Cheng from his duties as headman and instructed the civil examiner to grant him admission to the district academy.

A little more than a year later Cheng's son regained his faculties, claiming that he had been transformed into an agile, combative cricket and that today his soul had finally re-entered his body. The provincial governor rewarded Cheng generously. Within a few years Cheng possessed 1,500 acres of fields; pavilions and storied buildings in such number that thousands of rafters had been used to roof them over; and sheep and horses numbering in the hundreds. The furs he wore and the horses he rode when he went out could not have been equalled by an aristocratic family.

The Chronicler of the Tales comments: "The emperor may use something once on a whim and give it no more thought, but for the people who carry out his wishes it becomes a fixed article of tribute. With the greed of officials and the cruelty of administrators on top of this, there is no end to hardships which make peasants give up their wives and sell their children. Thus every time the emperor takes a step the lives of the people are affected. There is no room for carelessness. Cheng's case was unique: after being reduced to poverty by the depradations of corrupt officials, a cricket brought him wealth enough to go about flaunting furs and fine horses. Back in the days when he was beaten for failing to fulfill his duties as headman, how could he have foreseen that such a fortune was in store for him? Heaven made the provincial governor and magistrate enjoy the benefits of the cricket's favor as a means of rewarding one man's honesty. When the Taoist master in the old story perfected the elixir and rose to heaven, immortality redounded even to his dogs and chickens. There is much truth in this!"

第九篇　诗歌翻译别是一家
——《枫桥夜泊》等唐诗的两种译文比较

陆　林

　　诗歌翻译别是一家。提"别"字在于诗歌翻译离不开创造性的思维活动和高超的艺术手段。诗歌是语言高度浓缩、形神兼备的艺术品。诗歌中的词汇容量大，文化内涵丰富，艺术风格独特。因此，"忠实"与"达意"在译诗中虽难做到，但它是翻译最基本的要求，而在这一基础上力求形神兼备，才是理想的追求。

　　下面我们以三首广为流传的唐诗的两种英译为例加以比较说明。

　　《望庐山瀑布》、《黄鹤楼送孟浩然之广陵》和《枫桥夜泊》均为盛唐七绝，是中国诗这座高峰的顶点。"诗之难于绝句"。（张炎《词源》卷下）李白是五七言绝句的圣手。（《唐诗选》上）这里所选的前两首绝句为李白艺术风格的代表作。沈德潜说："七言绝句，以语近情遥，含吐不露为贵；只眼前景，口头语，而弦外有音，使人神远，太白有焉"。（《唐诗别裁集》）第一首"瀑布"诗极富浪漫主义想象，情怀豪迈，诗句奔放，瀑布形象雄奇瑰丽。第二首虽写"离别"，但诗意却随着江水荡漾，表达的友情既真率又含蓄深厚。两首诗均有"语近情遥"、"含吐不露"、"弦外有音，使人神远"的艺术效果。后一首"夜泊图"为张继之作，是一首情思缠绵，意境悠远的佳篇。张继的艺术风格有"清丽自然"，（王启兴　毛治中《唐诗三百首评注》）不事雕饰之美誉。要把这三首思想内容丰富、艺术形式完美、艺术风格独特的中国古诗之精品译成英文，逾越两种文字的障碍，把这每首中的二十八字所表达的"意美"、"音美"、"形美"全部再

第九篇　唐诗 Poems of Tang Dynasty

现出来,译者必备对两种语言精深的造诣、披荆斩棘的独创精神和高超的翻译艺术;否则是难以做到的。

我们选取的两种译文分别出自许渊冲先生的《唐宋诗词三百首》和王守义与约翰·诺弗尔合作的《唐宋诗词英译》。许渊冲先生是北京大学教授,著名翻译家。许先生在中国古诗词英译方面自成一派,译著颇丰。其译作有《诗经》、《唐诗三百首》、《宋词三百首》等。王守义先生是黑龙江大学教授。约翰·诺弗尔是美国著名诗人。他们共同合译了《唐诗》、《宋诗》。就这里选取的三首诗的英译而言,两家译作展示了当代译界中在译诗方面迥异的风格,可谓"各领风骚"。赏析"奇文"与"佳译",可以从中体会诗歌翻译的独特性与高难之处。

我们先看《望庐山瀑布》的译文。

许译此诗的特点是准确把握原作的意旨,译法灵活;注重"神似",兼顾"形似"并能传达"音美"。许译的"神似"主要体现在炼词与表达的功夫上。他能准确把握原诗的精华,以灵活多变的艺术手段再现原作的意境与气势,实有过人之处。如诗中跌宕的气势出于"七言诗第五字要响"。(魏庆之《诗人玉屑》)作者巧妙地用"生"、"挂"、"落"的致力之处,给瀑布图以动态、以气势,使其变幻在动与静、虚与实之中。译者紧逼原作,巧妙地运用译语优势:英语动词的时态、语态、情态表达,生动地再现了原诗的意境。

诗的第一句写瀑布的背景。在诗人的笔下,香庐峰顶天立地,周围云海弥漫,缥缈于青山蓝天之间,在红日的照耀下生出紫色的烟雾。此句中的生字把本是静止的庐山峰写活了。许译用英文动词"exhales"("散发出"或"呼出")将物(庐山峰)拟人,这里的"一般现在时"使读者感到景象就在眼前;以"a wreath of cloud"传译"紫烟",其中"wreath"("花环")虽是名词,却有"缭绕"及"色彩绚丽"的生动意象。这一行字字用得精当,富有想象的空间,诗味甚浓。从译诗中我们也同样看到了一幅山间烟云冉冉上升,袅袅浮游,极富浪漫主义色彩的背景。

诗的第二句中前四字"遥看瀑布"点题,后三字"挂前川"是诗人望中所见。瀑布本直流而下,诗人偏用一"挂"字,化动为静,与上句相对成文,使白浪翻滚、汇流成河的瀑布从高耸入云的峰顶直挂到水面。译者与作者心灵契合,创造性地发挥了作者的奇特想象,以英语动词"upended"("被倒覆")这一被动态形式,来形容远望中的瀑布像"倒挂"的飞流,使人感到大自然有神奇的伟力,竟能把这巨物高挂于山川之间。这一字译出了弦外之音。无疑,此处译语优势的发挥使译诗的文采与原诗具有同等的艺术魅力。这里既体现了译者对原文的独特理解,又显示着译者对译文的驾驭能力。

在诗的第三句中,瀑布显得更有气势。"飞"字把瀑布凌空而出,飞散而降的气派描绘得极为生动。"直下"写出山高峻,水流急,势不可挡的瀑布奇观。译文中以"dashes down"作谓语,既顺应主语"倒挂的飞流"的走向(飞下),又表达出瀑布凌空而落的磅礴气势。

最后一句,诗人以化实为虚的手法,从现实生活出发,把喷珠溅玉的瀑布从高空而下想象成自九天落下的银河。诗人驰骋的想象,犹如"视通万里"(刘勰:《文心雕龙·神思》),但夸张中见自然,新奇中见真切。译者发挥主体创造精神,用英语动词"fall"的虚拟式"fell",把现实中的瀑布和想象中的银河自然地联系在一起,不见翻译的痕迹,切近真实地传达了"落"字所活画出的高空突兀,巨流倾泻的跌宕气势。

兼顾"形似"并能传达"音美"是许渊冲汉诗英译的见长之处。绝句是四行诗。英诗的四行诗格尤以狭义的四行诗(quatrain)最符合绝句形式,即一首完整的四行诗。四行诗的韵脚比较多,译者按原诗的诗思节奏,择用 aabb 尾韵。为了押好韵脚,译者在诗句的语序方面做了必要的调整。例如第二行采用介词短词前置的句式("Like an upended stream the cataract sounds loud"),就是为了使这一句末的"loud"和前句末的"cloud"押上韵脚。除此之外,诗句中多处用头韵及带有辅音[s]或[θ]的单词,虽不整齐化一,也增添了与意境相和谐的韵调。例如第一行中的"sunlit","censer","exhales"和"wreath"。第三行中的"dashes"和"down","three"和"thousand","feet"和"from"。

音律方面,译诗采用了抑扬格(iambic),且音步数目能做到每行相同,含六个音步(hexameter)。以第一行为例:

The sun | lit Cen | ser peak | exhales | a wreath | of cloud

由此可见,译者为保留原作的"形美"和"音美"颇费了一番苦功,使

第九篇 唐诗 Poems of Tang Dynasty

译诗大体上遵循了原诗的基本形态和自然节奏。

和许译相比,王守义与约翰·诺弗尔合译此诗的特点在形式上也是以诗译诗;所不同的是,许译用格律体,王诺(简称)合译用自由体。如这首译诗的音节、分行、押韵等都没有一定的限制,长短句交错。全诗尽管无韵,读起来也朗朗上口,原因是译者以意群为音组,每组一顿,有抑抑扬扬之音;另外,诗句虽不以行限定,却按原诗的语言节奏自然流转,较好地再现了李白"天然去雕饰"的艺术标准。在语言形式上则有顺应其诗体的特点,表达清楚地道,自然流畅,富有内在的韵律。这种译法的选择是与他们的翻译主张分不开的,即用以格律韵律的方法译中国古诗词"只能得到相似的效果,并未真实地反映出原诗的诗歌形式和语言形式"。(王守义《论中国古诗词英译》)从客观上讲,诗歌的形式是为其内容服务的。无论采用哪种形式,只要译诗译出了原诗的意境、神韵、美感,就是一首好的译诗。

王诺合译的《望庐山瀑布》,以自然流畅的诗句贴近原作飘逸潇洒的风格,但由于文字只突出传译原文的表层含义,在创造瀑布形象和描写瀑布气势方面比许译"略输文采"。例如,王诺两位先生在译原作中的画龙点睛之笔"生"、"挂"、"落"之处,用的是"rises"、"hangs"、"spilling",给人的感觉是意象生动不足,气势不足,弦外知之音难觅。还有,以"purple smoke rises"译"生紫烟"使人有顾此失彼之感,因为"烟"译活了,"香炉"仍是静物,与原诗形象不符。"hangs"一词如实地描绘了瀑布的静态景观,但该词与下句的"dropping"相对成文后,效果与原意相悖:似乎"挂在青山与蓝天之间的巨物""落"下之后便不在那里了。此外"spilling"一词虽能较好地再现瀑布"喷珠溅玉"的美丽景观,但不如"fall"的气势足。由此可见,诗歌是一件艺术品,其中充满了想象的空间。在诗歌翻译中,英汉两种语言的表层形式不同使意象的创造更具挑战性。把握好一词一语的翻译要考虑整体的意境,使局部美与整体美和谐统一。尽可能忠实完美地再现原诗的内容与美感。

下面我们来看第二道《黄鹤楼送孟浩然之广陵》译文。

李白的七绝被称谓"妙绝古今"。这首诗是写李白送友人去广陵的情景,表现了对友人的深厚情谊。友人是在春光明媚的繁华季节扬帆东去的,去的是江南名城扬州,那是诗人向往的地方。因此诗中既有依依难舍的情味又有愉快畅想的气氛。全诗以景见情,寓情于景,思想感情的表达含蓄深厚,充分体现了李白七言绝句的艺术特色。

两家译作对原诗意旨的把握都比较准确。译出了原作的诗情画意,但在总体构思,表现形式及细节的处理上风格迥异。这说明了译者在再现原作的同时,往往免不了打上个人理解与认识的烙印。

例如,许译在总体构思上采用"译气不译字"(傅勇林)的手法,能挥洒自如地增减词语,变换句式,词语的诗情画意就比较浓厚。王诺合译则在把握住原作的意旨、风格后,敢于摆脱原作形式的束缚,充分发挥合译中用母语表达的优势,词语上多采用英语读者喜闻乐见的表达方式,给人的感觉是,随手拈来,一看就懂。

在表现形式上,许译显示出了娴熟的翻译技巧,做到了格律谨严而不失自然,句式整齐而富于变化,从而使译诗中文字的表层意义有灵活转化的余地,较好地再现了原诗"语近情遥","使人神远"的艺术效果。王诺合译在表现形式上也构思奇巧,诗句双行排列有致,共分四片,大体上贴近原诗的结构。这一手法会使读者自然地联想到诗中所描述的两位诗人缠绵离别,恋恋不舍的情景,同时也象征着诗人的诗思似江水在胸中荡漾。

在细节的处理上,两家各有长短。如许译用"the west where the Yellow Crane towers"译"黄鹤楼",不惜以繁出之,但这样一来既交代了友人是自西向东而行,又讲述了有关黄鹤楼的古老传说(即黄鹤楼是仙人飞上天空去的地方),传出了文化内涵,动人遐想,还达到了押韵的目的。可见"繁"之有理。相形之下,王诺合译的这一楼阁之名为"yellow crane pavilion"就显得组合方式有些生硬,缺乏想象力,诗味欠浓了。第二句"烟花三月下扬州"意境优美,文字绮丽,被誉为"千古丽句"。许译想诗人之所想,创造性地运用对称整齐的句式,使"and"一边是"green with willows",一边是"red with flowers",译出了满目春色,传出了生机勃勃的节奏。许译没有直译"烟花"可能有两个原因:一是语言的障碍,直译效果恐怕不佳;二是"烟花"的含义为"繁花似锦",是指看不尽,看不透的大片阳春烟景。此句难译,但译者运思奇巧。王诺合译的这一句是"sailing to yangzhou in march while blossoms curl like smoke on the river",有遗憾之处,即其中"on the river"举义过窄,宽阔的画面缩小了,没有一路上到处是繁花似锦的意象,也没有描述出整个春光。三四两句的意境是"眼看帆去远,心逐江水流"。(李白《江夏行》)许译对表达方式进行了调整,把"尽"字前移,使之更符合英语表达习惯,同时还增加了几个不影响深层意义的词语,如"his"、"where I see",大概主要是为了增加音节,照顾韵律并使意义更为清楚,字句虽不如原诗凝炼,但也勾画出了诗人目送行舟,江边怅惘的形象。另外,许译的"孤帆远影碧空尽"一句中没有直译"孤帆",以"His lessening sail is lost in the boudless blue sky"来表现小船渐渐消失在远方,诗人心中若有所失的生动画面。但笔者认为,只照顾"孤"字的深层意义还不够,这里"孤"字的表层意义也很重要,因为它对景物的勾画起重要作用。原诗中辽阔的江面上,碧水连天,只见一叶白帆顺流而去。这本是夸张,诗人借以表达自己心系友人,情有独钟的真实感情。和许译相比,王诺合译的这两句也有独到之处。他们先是以感叹句"how for away the lone sail fading into the clear blue sky"抒发诗人在送别好友时那种依依难舍的心情,其中的"the lone sail"忠实地再现了"孤帆"的表层及深层含义;然后,以"only"位于句首,勾画出帆影已经消失了,诗人还在翘首凝望,此时才注意到只有浩荡的长江如在天边流动。

可以这样讲,诗歌翻译是难中之难:一方面,诗歌翻译不同于诗歌创作,译诗必须忠实于原诗。另一方面,译者在再现原诗的内容和美感的同时,又要尽可能达其意,传其神,存其境,况且"诗无达诂"。以上所举的两家之译就说明了这一点。

最后让我们来看第三首《枫桥夜泊》的译文。

《枫桥夜泊》是一首意境清远,情景交融的作品。诗中描写了苏州城外江边的夜景:在逐渐西沉的残月下,天空像布满了秋霜,耳边偶尔传来一两声乌鹊的啼鸣;在朦胧的夜色中,江边上的枫树只见黑黝黝的树影,江中的渔火在雾气茫茫中闪烁,这两种景色的对峙勾起了诗人的羁旅之愁;附近寒山寺传来低沉而悠长的夜半钟声使诗人的乡愁更加深沉。全诗以"愁眠"为主线,使其中的景物、色彩、音响、环境与夜泊江边客子的心绪、情怀十分协调统一,表现了诗人高超的艺术技巧。

　　细观此诗的两篇译作,可以看出译家在研究如何再现原作的思想内容和艺术风格上是颇费了一番思量的。从总体上讲,两首译作的成功之处在于抓住了原文的主线,用字的情调上处处与原作合拍;但由于语言的差异,未能再现张继所创造出的典型化的艺术的风格。就再现原诗的思想内容而言,两译互见高低,达意时近时远。就方法而论,许译的方法是以艺术语言译艺术语言;王诺合译则使用明白晓畅的英语,为原诗注入了时代的气息。下面以各自的译文为例:

　　许译的艺术性首先体现在译诗音乐结构的设计上。译诗格律整齐自不用说,突出的是每行中间留有一顿,一三行用"逗号",二四行用"字符",似乐谱中"渐缓"、"渐轻"的标示,使诗句读起来意味深长。其次,译诗中有些词用得很有特色,如第一句的"streaking"在句中为现在分词,做"cry"的伴随状况,生动地描绘出乌鹊啼叫着掠过霜天弥漫的夜空的景象,凄寒的意境译出来了,但原句中"月落"写所见,"乌啼"写所闻和"霜满天"写所感的鲜明层次,以及一个接一个先后承接的时间过程和感觉过程没有忠实地体现出来。第二句中用"dimly"对"sadly","lit"对"lie",且"fishing boats 'neath maples",这些词语的搭配组合颇见用心,巧妙地活画出"江枫"与"渔火"一动一静,一明一暗,一江上,一江边的景物,同时"sadly lie"在这里有双关意义,既指"孤子泊舟"又指怀着旅愁躺在舟上的诗人,情景交融,其运思细密与原作者不相上下。后面两句的处理采用了重新组合原诗句的方法,用"beyond"和"from"两个介词短语做状语,来传译钟声由远而近的感觉,主句中心词"bells break the dream and still"表达地道洒脱,音意相应合拍,不留翻译痕迹。这里"break"一词用得尤其传神,它摆脱了原诗中"到"字的表层意义,重在表现深夜寒山寺传来的袅袅钟声,震荡空际,打破了这深夜的寂静和诗人羁旅的思乡梦。可惜此句也有不当之处,如"姑苏城"译为"the city walls",译文读者会由此联想到庄严肃穆的古城楼呢,还是景色秀丽的江南水乡呢?可见,意象不是很准确。

　　王诺合译此诗不受原诗风格的约束,以第一人称陈述的形式把诗人的所见、所闻、所感予以描绘。译诗按原诗意分四片,脉络分明。在细节的处理上多处采用直译的方法,力求以最大限度贴近原文。如诗中"月落"指渐渐西沉的残月,"old moon"正好是英语的这一表达,其中"old"传译出了秋月感伤的意象。此处恰好再现了张继"自然清丽"的风格。"霜满天"是用习语表达方式传译的,真切自然,保留了原词语中夸张的口吻,完全切合诗人的感受,即深夜侵肌砭骨的寒意,从四面八方围向诗人夜泊的小舟,使他感到身外的茫茫夜气中正弥漫着满天霜华。此译显得轻松入理。下句江边和江上的景物是用"there are..."的套句引出来的,符合译语习惯,清楚易懂,但江面上星星点点的"渔火"译得略显冗长。另外,此句的舟中旅人与舟外景物的对峙状态译得太直了,没有那种无言交融的感觉。在诗的后两句里,"夜半钟声到客船"是《枫桥夜泊》这首诗的诗眼:枫桥的诗意美,有了寒山寺这所古刹的"夜半钟声",便带上了历史文化的色泽,而显得更加动人遐想,表现了诗人在枫桥夜泊所得到的最鲜明、最深刻、最具诗意美的感觉印象,就是这寒山寺的夜半钟声。王诺两位先生以"touches"译其中的关键字"到",只传译出了诗人卧听疏钟时的种种难以言传的感受,未能以醒豁的力度衬托出夜的静谧,深永和清寥。

通过以上三例唐诗的两种英译的赏析比较,我们不仅领略了译者敢攀高峰,逢山开路的精神,也从译作中得到了教益,开阔了我们的眼界。两译的高低优劣并不重要,重要的是通过赏析或评析推动翻译事业的发展。诗歌翻译要达到茅盾先生所提出的水准,即"用另一种语言,把原作的艺术意境传达出来,使读者在读译文的时候能像读原作一样得到启发、感受和美的感受",尚需不断地开拓进取,才能达到尽可能使译诗与原诗具有同样的魅力和生命力。

参考文献

1. 许渊冲:《翻译的艺术》,中国对外翻译出版公司,1984年。
2. 涂宗涛:《诗词曲格律纲要》,天津人民出版社,1982年。
3. 陈绍伟:《诗歌辞典》,花城出版社,1986年。
4. 萧涤非等:《唐诗鉴赏辞典》,上海辞书出版社,1983年。
5. 王启兴、毛治中:《唐诗三百首评注》,湖北人民出版社,1984年。

第九篇　唐诗 Poems of Tang Dynasty

6. 许渊冲:《唐宋诗词三百首》(*Golden Treasury of Tang and Song Poetry*),北京大学出版社,1996年。
7. 王守义、约翰·诺弗尔:《唐宋诗词英译》(*Poems from Tang and Song Dynasties*),黑龙江人民出版社,1989年。
8. 刘重德:《文学翻译十讲》,中国对外翻译出版公司,1995年。
9. 梁守涛:《英诗格律浅说》,商务印书馆,1979年。
10. 黄邦杰:《译艺谭》,中国对外翻译出版公司,三联书店香港分店,1995年。
11. 艾治平:《诗美思辨》,学林出版社,1996年。
12.《中译英技巧文集》:《中国翻译》编辑部,中国对外翻译出版公司,1997年。

第九篇　唐诗 Poems of Tang Dynasty

附：

望庐山瀑布

李　白

日照香炉生紫烟,
遥看瀑布挂前川,
飞流直下三千尺,
疑是银河落九天。

静夜思

李　白

床前明月光,
疑是地上霜,
举头望明月,
低头思故乡。

黄鹤楼送孟浩然之广陵

李　白

故人西辞黄鹤楼,
烟花三月下扬州,
孤帆远影碧空尽,
惟见长江天际流。

第九篇　唐诗 Poems of Tang Dynasty

枫桥夜泊

张　继

月落乌啼霜满天，
江枫渔火对愁眠，
姑苏城外寒山寺，
夜半钟声到客船。

回乡偶书

贺知章

（一）

少小离家老大回，
乡音无改鬓毛衰，
儿童相见不相识，
笑问客从何处来。

登鹳雀楼

王之涣

白日依山尽，
黄河入海流，
欲穷千里目，
更上一层楼。

第九篇　唐诗 Poems of Tang Dynasty

凉州词

王之涣

黄河远上白云间，
一片孤城万仞山，
羌笛何须怨杨柳，
春风不度玉门关。

春晓

孟浩然

春眠不觉晓，
处处闻啼鸟，
夜来风雨声，
花落知多少。

塞下曲

卢　纶

林暗草惊风，
将军夜引弓，
平明寻白羽，
没在石棱中。

伤秋

卢 纶

岁去人头白,
秋来树叶黄,
搔头向黄叶,
与尔共悲伤。

题菊花

黄 巢

飒飒西风满院栽,
蕊寒香冷蝶难来,
他年我若为青帝,
报与桃花一处开。

陇西行

陈 陶

誓扫匈奴不顾身,
五千貂锦丧胡尘,
可怜无定河边骨,
犹是春闺梦里人。

第九篇 唐诗 Poems of Tang Dynasty

许渊冲 译

Cataract on Mount Lu

Li Bo(701—762)

The sunlit Censer peak exhales a wreath of cloud;
Like an upended stream the cataract sounds loud.
It's torrent dashes down three thousand feet from high,
As if the Silver River① fell from azure sky.

A Tranquil Night

Before my bed a pool of light—
Can it be hoarfrost on the ground?
Looking up, I find the moon bright;
Bowing, in homesickness I'm drowned.

Seeing Meng Hao-ran off at Yellow Crane Tower

My friend has left the west where the Yellow Crane towers
For River Town green with willows and red with flowers.
His lessening sail is lost in the boundless blue sky,
Where I see but the endless River rolling by.

第九篇 唐诗 Poems of Tang Dynasty

Mooring by Maple Bridge at Night

Zhang Ji (fl. 753)

At moonset cry the crows, streaking the frosty sky;
Dimly lit fishing boats 'neath maples sadly lie.
Beyond the city walls, from Temple of Cold Hill
Bells break the ship-borne roamer's dream and midnight still.

Home-Coming

He Zhizhang (659—744)

Old, I return to the homeland I left while young,
Thinner has grown my hair, though I speak the same tongue.
My children, whom I meet, do not know who am I.
"Where are you form, dear sir?" they ask with beaming eye.

On the Stork Tower

Wang Zhihuan (688—742)

The sun beyond the mountain glows;
The Yellow River seawards flows.
You can enjoy a grander sight
By climbing to a greater height.

第九篇 唐诗 Poems of Tang Dynasty

Out of The Great Wall

The yellow sand uprises as high as white cloud;
The lonely town is lost amid the mountains proud.
Why should the Mongol flute complain no willows grow?
Beyond the Gate of Jade no vernal wind will blow.

Spring Morning

Meng Haoran (689—740)

This spring morning in bed I'm lying,
Not to awake till birds are crying.
After one night of wind and showers.
How many are the fallen flowers?

A Border Song

Lu Lun (748—800)

In gloomy woods grass shivers at wind's howl;
The general takes it for a tiger's growl.
He shoots and seeks his arrow-plume nex morn
Only to find a rock pierced'mid the thorn.

第九篇 唐诗 Poems of Tang Dynasty

Grief in Autumn

As years pass by, grey grows my hair;
When autumn's come, the trees stand bare.
Perplexed, I ask the yellow leaf,
"Do you like me feel gnawed by grief?"

To the Crhysanthemum

Huang Chao (?—884)

In soughing western wind you blossom far and nigh;
Your fragrance is too cold to invite butterfly.
Some day if I as Lord of Spring come into power,
I'll order you to bloom together with peach flower.

The Riverside Battleground

Chen Tao (812—885)

They would lay down their lives to wipe away the Huns;
They've bit the dust, five thousand sable-clad brave ones.
Alas! Their bones lie on riverside battleground,
But in dreams of their wives they still seem safe and sound.

第九篇 唐诗 Poems of Tang Dynasty

王守义　约翰·诺弗尔 译

Watching the Lu Mountain Falls

Li Bai

Purple smoke rises from the mountaintop
The peak looks like an incense burner in the sunlight
Far away I see the valley stretching before me
The whole waterfall hangs there
The torrent dropping three thousand feet
Straight down to the valley floor
I think it must be the milky way
Spilling to the earth from the heavens

Thoughts on a Quiet Evening

Li Bai

The floor is flooded with moonlight
Frost covered the old earth like that
I gaze at the moon
Shimmering in a dark court
Sad and homesick
I bow down my head

第九篇 唐诗 Poems of Tang Dynasty

Seeing Meng Haoran off

Li Bai

My old friend leaves yellow crane pavilion
He is going to the east
Sailing to yangzhou in march
While blossoms curl like smoke on the river
How far away the lone sail
Fading into the clear blue sky
Only the yangtze river remains
It is flowing at the edge of the world

Anchored at Night Near Maple Bridge

Zhang Ji

The old moon is going down
And the crows make a ruckus
The world is covered with frost
There are maples on the riverbank
And the lights of fishing boats
Drift with the current
I fall into a sad sleep
The monastary on cold mountain
It is outside the town of gusu
The sound of its bell
Touches the guestboat at midnight

第九篇 唐诗 Poems of Tang Dynasty

A Few Lines after Returning to My Hometown

He Zhizhang

Left home a child and came back an old old man
My hair has turned gray but my accent is the same
Kids in the village did not know me when we met
Said where did the guest come from with the funny
Smile

Climbing the Stork Kiosk

Wang Zhihuan

The pale sun is sinking behind the mountain
And the yellow river is running toward the sea
Since I want to look at the end of the earth
Which is hundreds of miles away
Well I have to climb these steps to do that

Liangzhou Song

Wang Zhihuan

The yellow river rises in the tall white clouds
A town is isolated here
It is locked in mountains thousands of feet high
No need for the qiang flute
Playing "poplar and willow" so sad a song
The spring wind never comes to this place
Outside the yumen pass

第九篇 唐诗 Poems of Tang Dynasty

At Dawn in Spring

Meng Haoran

Slept so well I didn't know it was dawn
Birds singing in every courtyard woke me up
The wind and rain troubled my dream last night
I think of all those petals swept to the ground

Reply to Zhang Puye's Border Song

Lu Lun

It is getting dark and the woods darker
And the uneasy wind
Disturbs the meadow
The commander drew his bowstring
Taut in the night
We looked for his feathered shaft
When dawn came again
We found it where he drove it
Deep in the pinnacle
That jutted from the rock

Sentiments in Fall

Lu Lun

So many years today
My hair sparse and white
And this is another autumn
Leaves yellow and dry
I scratch my head
And complain to these leaves
The deep sadness
They have fallen to share

On Chrysanthemums

Huang Chao

They are in color everywhere in the courtyard
Leaning against the chill of the west wind
No butterflies hang on the cold stamens
Or linger in the pungent fragrance
If in some year I become the god of flowers
I will set them glowing among the peach blossoms

第九篇　唐诗 Poems of Tang Dynasty

Trip to Long Xi

Chen Tao

They swore they would wipe out the hu invaders
They didn't care about their own safety
Five thousand lances were broken
When the hu horsemen struck them
It is so pitiful seeing the white bones
Scattered along the river
These relics are the husbands of dreams
Their wives are still waiting in their bedrooms